THE OFFICIAL®
PRICE GUIDE TO

Compact Discs

THE OFFICIAL® PRICE GUIDE TO

Compact Discs

FIRST EDITION

JERRY OSBORNE
and
PAUL BERGQUIST

HOUSE OF COLLECTIBLES • NEW YORK

Important Notice. All of the information, including valuations, in this book has been compiled from the most reliable sources, and every effort has been made to eliminate errors and questionable data. Nevertheless, the possibility of error, in a work of such immense scope, always exists. The publisher will not be held responsible for losses which may occur in the purchase, sale, or other transaction of items because of information contained herein. Readers who feel they have discovered errors are invited to *write* and inform us, so they may be corrected in subsequent editions. Those seeking further information on the topics covered in this book are advised to refer to the complete line of *Official Price Guides* published by the House of Collectibles.

Published by: House of Collectibles
201 East 50th Street
New York, New York 10022

Distributed by Ballantine Books, a division of Random House, Inc., New York, and simultaneously in Canada by Random House of Canada Limited, Toronto.

Manufactured in the United States of America

ISSN: 1073-2098

ISBN: 0-876-37923-4

Cover design by Kristine Mills
Cover photo by George Kerrigan

First Edition: March 1994

CONTENTS

Acknowledgments vii
Introduction xi
- Out-of-Print Discs xi
- Limited Edition Discs xi
- Promotional Issues xii
- How the Prices Are Determined xii
- How You Can Help xiii
- Wax Fax xiii
- Disc Grading xiii
- Value = Scarcity + Demand xiv
- Foreign Releases xiv
- Bootleg Discs xiv
- What to Expect When Selling Your Records to a Dealer xiv
- Concluding Thoughts xv

Sample Listing xvi
Compact Disc Listings, A – Z 1
Various Artists Compilations 237
Directory of Buyers and Sellers 281

ACKNOWLEDGMENTS

The most important element in the creation of this first edition CD price and reference guide has been the valuable input we received from dealers and other sellers of compact discs — especially those folks on our CD Team.

Over one year before press time, we assembled a team of some of the top CD dealers in the country, many of whom participated in the review of prices and reference information, as well as providing additional listings. To this dedicated group — and to a few folks who helped in other ways — we extend a special "thank you."

Alphabetically listed, here are the ladies and gentlemen on our first edition CD Team: Bob Alaniz, Marcia Bergquist, R.L. Bergquist, Harry Blaisure, Pat Brown, Gregory Cooper, Robin Dominguez, Steve Franz, Bruce Friedman, Jean-Marc Gargiulo, Chuck Gosson, Eddie Hammer, John Kopec, Howard Krumholtz, Al LeMieux, René Lucas, Charlie Neu, Fred Nurman, Dave Ocuma, Linda Ann Osborne, Craig W. Pattillo, Eduardo Ramos, Mark Silverberg, Adam Stanley, Dale A. Stirling, Gary Walsh, and Barbara Williams.

Since the compilation process for the second edition has already begun, we welcome suggestions, additions, and corrections from readers. Every single piece of data we acquire is carefully reviewed, with all the appropriate and usable data utilized in the next edition of this guide. See page xiii ("How You Can Help") for more information on how you can contribute to future editions.

As enthusiastically as we encourage your contribution, let us equally encourage that when you write or fax, you'll either type or print your name clearly on both the envelope and contents. It's as frustrating for us to receive a mailing of useful information, and not be able to credit the sender, as it probably is for the sender to not see his or her name in the Acknowledgments section.

Compact Discs

INTRODUCTION

In determining what should be included in *The Official Price Guide to Compact Discs,* we have considered many factors. Our goal is to make the guide helpful, convenient, and applicable; for avid music connoisseurs as well as for those who are simply curious about the value of their collection of compact discs.

As an author-publisher team, we have put together nearly 50 record guides and reference books over the past 20 years. Though compact disc collecting is a relatively recent hobby, the years of experience have taught us that it is the discs that have disappeared from the retail market that people most want to find listed in a price guide — the ones now deemed to be *collectible.*

For our purposes, however, merely being collectible does not guarantee a disc a spot in this guide. Each CD listed here must also, by the essence of its contents, fall within the scope of this publication.

The majority of the listings here are by pop, rock, and blues artists, with a sprinkling of country, jazz, and miscellaneous releases in the mix. You will not find, for example, classical and world music discs in this guide, regardless of how collectible they may be.

So just what is meant by the catch-all word, *collectible*? Well, in the world of compact discs, the term can apply to releases that fall into one or more of the following categories:

Out-of-Print Discs

Obviously anything that is no longer available from its manufacturer is an out-of-print item. Since the introduction in 1982 of CD technology, approximately a half-million discs have appeared worldwide, with perhaps 100,000 issued in the United States alone. Though the majority of these are still easily available — as a trip to any of the music superstores or a flip through some of the giant mail order catalogs will reveal — it's a certainty that many discs will eventually be deleted from manufacturer's catalogs. That's when we will want them listed here.

Not every music release remains in print for years and years, though the best-sellers usually do. At the other extreme, a few discs in this guide were either deleted before leaving the factory or recalled shortly after reaching distributors and retailers.

Limited Edition Discs

By design, limited editions go out of print much sooner than regular commercial issues. Since there is no specific quantity necessary for a release to qualify as a limited edition — ranging from a few dozen to 50,000 made — some are highly collectible and quite valuable while others are worth little, if anything, above their retail cost.

Among collectors, the most popular items in the limited edition category are those utilizing innovative or creative packaging. Our eight-page color section displays an attractive assortment of some of the more imaginative CD packages.

Another aspect of packaging is the increased interest in the cardboard longboxes of the '80s and early '90s. The late longbox — a term that didn't exist before compact discs — usually pictured the artist and displayed attractive graphics.

Unfortunately, most buyers — including astute collectors who should have known better — tossed the longboxes in the trash. It is now clear that a premium will continually be asked and paid for those CDs still accompanied by their longboxes.

Promotional Issues

As with a limited edition, the promotional edition of a CD title may be made in any quantity — from a handful to several thousand, depending on countless variables. Quantity notwithstanding, all promo discs are collectible to some extent and every one within the musical scope of this guide is worthy of inclusion. We welcome the details of any that we are missing.

Each promo title traditionally is made just one time and quickly distributed to the media. They can often be unobtainable from the company after only three or four weeks, since by then most have likely been shipped.

When intended for dee jay or club use, promo CDs may provide a seemingly endless array of mixes of the same song, or they may include bonus tracks — sometimes including otherwise unavailable material.

Rather than pass out free copies of multi-disc sets and elaborate boxed sets, the labels often prepare a *sampler* for the media. Since such samplers are commercially unavailable they are instantly desirable to collectors.

Most promotional issues are identified as such on the disc, box, accompanying printed materials — or on all of these — with pronouncements and or warnings like "Not for Sale," or "Loaned for Promotional Purposes Only," and "For Demonstration Use Only."

Two important sub-categories in the promotional arena are CD-singles and radio programs on compact disc. You will find numerous listings from both of these groups in this edition, especially CD-singles, which have recently become coveted by collectors.

As with their forerunner format — vinyl singles — CD-singles quickly go out of print when the window of opportunity for sales passes, thereby making *all* CD-singles collectible. Top sellers may be in stores for longer, but most CD-singles are available only for a few months.

Though not made for promotional purposes, there are a few test or experimental discs in this edition. These pilot or prototype CDs, produced during the manufacturing process, can rank among the most valuable since they rarely make it out of the factory.

How the Prices Are Determined

Values shown in the *Official Price Guide to Compact Discs* are averaged using information derived from a number of sources. Most influential in arriving at current prices is the input received from many of the nation's most active CD dealers and collectors.

Another extremely important source of pricing information is the ads in the magazines that serve the hobby, such as *DISCoveries*. We painstakingly review each of these publications, carefully comparing prices being asked to those shown in our most recent edition. If marketplace trading indicates prices in the guide need to be increased or decreased, the changes are made. With our frequent publishing schedule, it is never long before the corrected prices appear in print.

What makes this step in the pricing process so vital is that nothing more verifiably illustrates the collectible CD marketplace than everyday ads and sales catalogs.

CD prices, as with most collectibles, can vary drastically from one area of the country to another. Having reviewers and annotators scattered throughout North America, as well as overseas, enables us to present a realistic average of the highest and lowest current asking prices.

Although we believe the marketplace information in this edition to be accurate at press time, it is subject to market changes. At any time, any of a number of circumstances can either increase or decrease demand for certain material. Through diurnal research, keeping track of the day-to-day changes and discoveries taking place in the fascinating world of CD collecting is a relatively simple and ongoing procedure.

To ensure the greatest possible accuracy, prices in *The Official Price Guide to Compact Discs* are averaged from data culled from all of the aforementioned sources.

How You Can Help

We can never get too much input nor can we have too many reviewers. We wholeheartedly encourage you to submit whatever information you feel would be useful in building a better price guide. The quantity of data is not a factor.

When preparing additions for the guide, please try to list CDs in generally the same format we use: artist's name, label, selection number, title, year of release (if known), price range, whether a photo insert or booklet is used, and if the disc itself displays printed, silkscreen-like artwork. Since our data base is computer stored alphabetically by artist, there's no need to note the *Official Price Guide to Compact Discs* page number.

Wax Fax

One frequently used method of forwarding data to us is by fax. For your convenience, we now have two dedicated fax lines, one in Los Angeles and another in Washington. Both are shown below.

Use this service to quickly and easily transmit additions, corrections, price updates, and suggestions. Be sure to include your name, address, and phone number so we can acknowledge your contribution and contact you if necessary.

Please type or print your name clearly so we may accurately credit you in the next edition. Please submit all additions, corrections, and suggestions to either address:

Jerry Osborne
Box 255
Port Townsend, WA 98368

Paul Bergquist
6406 W. Olympic Blvd.
Los Angeles, CA 90048

Disc Grading

The prices in this edition are for NEAR-MINT condition copies. One of the beauties of compact disc technology is that, unlike vinyl recordings, they can withstand a seemingly unlimited number of plays and exhibit no noticeable wear. However, this doesn't mean that CDs are indestructible, as most readers have no doubt discovered. Even more susceptible to wear and tear are the sleeves, boxes, inserts, and all forms of paper products utilized in CD packaging.

To allow for items in something less than pristine mint, we have structured the following system of grading. The grading terms and definitions are very similar to that which is commonly used by vinyl record collectors.

MINT: A *mint* item must be absolutely perfect. Nothing less can be honestly described as mint. Even brand new purchases can easily be flawed in some manner and not qualify as mint, so to allow for tiny blemishes the grade priced in our series is *near-mint*. An absolutely pristine mint, or still sealed, disc may carry a slight premium above the near-mint range shown in the guide.

VERY GOOD: Records in *very good* condition should have a minimum of visual or audible imperfections, which should not detract much from your enjoyment of owning them. This grade is about halfway between good and near-mint.

For VERY GOOD condition, figure about 60% to 80% of the near-mint price range.

GOOD: Practically speaking, the grade of *good* means that the disc is good enough to fill a gap in your collection until a better copy becomes available. Good condition merchandise will show definite signs of wear, probably evidencing that no protective care was given the item. Even so, CDs in good condition must play all the way through without a snag.

For GOOD condition, figure about 20% to 40% of the near-mint price range.

It is very important to use the near-mint price range in this guide only as a starting point in appraising. Be honest about actual condition. Apply the same standards to discs you trade or sell as you would want one from whom you were buying to observe. Visual grading may be unreliable and accurate grading may require playing the disc (play-grading).

Value = Scarcity + Demand

All the price guides and reporting of previous sales in the world won't change the fundamental fact that true value is nothing more than what one person is willing to pay and what another is prepared to accept. Actual value is based on scarcity and demand. It's always been that way and always will. We include this observation in every one of our guides because it is so very important.

A recording — or anything for that matter — can be 50 or 100 years old, but if no one wants it, the actual value will certainly be minimal. Just because something is old does not necessarily make it valuable. Someone has to want it!

On the other hand, a recent CD release, perhaps just weeks old, can have exceptionally high value if it has already become scarce and is by an artist whose following has created a demand. A compact disc certainly does not have to be old to be valuable.

Foreign Releases

This guide lists only U.S. releases, or so we thought anyway. Not surprisingly, in dealing with thousands of CDs, a few overseas issues worked their way into the listings. In fact, two even got pictured in our color section (The Koo and Shonen Knife) and were not discovered until too late to omit them. Oh well.

This in no way indicates that the tens of thousands of overseas releases have no collector value. Just that the tremendous volume of material and the variances in pricing make it impossible for us to comprehensively document and price imports.

Bootleg Discs

Bootleg discs are not priced in this guide. For the record, a bootleg recording is one illegally manufactured, usually containing material not previously available in a legitimate form. With bootleg discs, the appropriate and deserving recipients of royalties are denied remuneration for their works.

When in doubt about the authenticity of an item, always consult with an expert. A knowledgeable dealer can usually spot a boot.

What to Expect When Selling to a Dealer

As nearly everyone in the hobby knows, there is a noteworthy difference between the prices reported in this guide and the prices that one can expect a dealer to pay when buying compact discs for resale. Unless a dealer is buying for a personal collection and without thoughts of resale, he or she is simply not in a position to pay full price. Dealers work on a percentage basis, largely determined by the total dollar investment, quality, and quantity of material offered as well as the general financial condition and inventory of the dealer at the time.

Another very important consideration is the length of time it will take the dealer to recover at least the amount of the original investment. The greater the demand for the stock and the better the condition, the quicker the return and therefore the greater the percentage that can be paid. Our experience has shown that, day-in and day-out, most dealers will pay from 25% to 50% of *guide* prices. And that's assuming they are planning to resell at guide prices. If they traditionally sell below guide, that will be reflected in what they can pay for stock.

If you have compact discs to sell, it would be wise to check with several dealers. In doing so you'll begin to get a good idea of the value of your collection to a dealer.

Also, consult the Directory of Buyers and Sellers in this guide for the names of many dealers who not only might be interested in buying, but from whom many collectible records and CDs are available for purchase.

Concluding Thoughts

The purpose of this guide is to report as accurately as possible the most recent prices asked and paid for records within the area of its coverage. There are two key words here that deserve emphasis: **Guide** and **Report.**

We cannot stress enough that this book is only a guide. There always have and always will be instances of CDs selling well above and below the prices shown within these pages. Though these extremes are recognized in the final averaging process, it's still important to understand that just because we show a CD as having a $25 near-mint value, doesn't mean that a collector should be hesitant to pay $35 for it. How badly he or she wants it and how often it's possible to purchase it *at any price* should be the prime factors considered, not the fact that we last reported it at a lower price. Of course, we'd like to know about sales of this sort so that the next edition can reflect the new pricing information.

Our objective is to report and reflect marketplace activity; not to *establish* prices. For that reason, and if given the choice, we'd prefer to be a bit behind the times rather than ahead. With this guide being regularly revised, it will never be long before the necessary changes are reported within these pages.

We encourage record companies, artist management organizations, talent agencies, publicists, and performers to make certain that we are on the active mailing list for new release information, press releases, bios, publicity photos, and anything pertaining to new recordings.

There is an avalanche of helpful information in this guide to aid the collector in determining what is valuable and what may not be worth fooling with, but the wise fan will also keep abreast of current trends and news through the pages of the fanzines and publications devoted to his/her favorite forms of music. ❑

SAMPLE LISTING

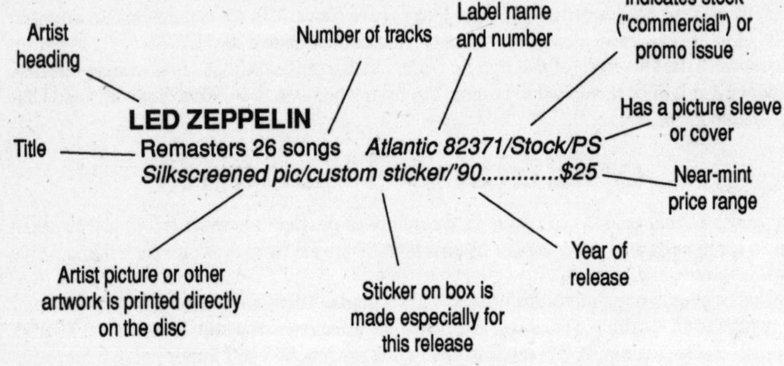

Artist heading
Number of tracks
Label name and number
Indicates stock ("commercial") or promo issue
Has a picture sleeve or cover
LED ZEPPELIN
Title
Remasters 26 songs Atlantic 82371/Stock/PS
Silkscreened pic/custom sticker/'90.............$25
Near-mint price range
Year of release
Artist picture or other artwork is printed directly on the disc
Sticker on box is made especially for this release

A HOUSE
Call Me Blue (3 versions) *Sire 3321/ promo/rear insert/silkscreened/'88* $4
Endless Art *Radioactive 2314/ promo/rear insert/'92* $4
I Don't Care *Radioactive 2199/promo/ps/'92* $4

A LIGHTER SHADE OF BROWN
Homies with guitar/without *Pump 19134/promo/silkscreened/'92* $4

A THOUSAND POINTS OF NIGHT
Read My Lips 2:51/5:54 *Polydor 767/promo/silkscreened/ps/'92* $5

A TRIBE CALLED QUEST
Hot Sex radio versions *Jive 42094/promo/ custom sticker/rear insert/'92* $5
Scenario 4 versions *Jive 42056/promo/ custom sticker/rear insert/'92* $6

A.L.T. & THE LOST CIVILIZATION
Tequila lp/club 7"/club 12" *Atco 4632/promo/rear insert* $4

A.T.E.E.M., THE
Yeah 5 versions *Select 014/promo/silkscreened/'92* $4

AARON, JAY
Misery's Edge *WB 4591/promo/'90* $4
Ronda *WB 4482/promo/rear insert/'90* $4

ABBOTT, GREGORY
Ill Prove It To You (edit) *Columbia 1085/promo/ps/'88* $4

ABC
Say It 5 versions *MCA 1431/promo/ps/'91* $8
Say It 5 versions *MCA 54055/stock/ps/'91* $7

ABDUL, PAULA
(It's Just) the Way That You Love Me edit & single mix *Virgin 2931/promo/silkscreened/'88* $7
(It's Just) The Way That You Love Me 7" edit/ 12" remix/7 dub/Houseafire remix *Virgin 2438/promo/ps/'88* $15
Blowing Kisses in the Wind edit & lp *Virgin 4245/promo/logo on orange/'91* $8
Cold Hearted lp & remix *Virgin 2776/promo/silkscreened/'88* $6
Forever Your Girl (remix) *Virgin 2647/promo/'89* $8
Knocked Out (3 vers) *Virgin 9329/promo/ps/'88* $10
Opposites Attract Derrick rap edit/radio edit *Virgin 3100/promo/silkscreened/'88* $8
Rush Rush 3 version *Virgin 3815/promo/rear insert/'91* $10
Straight Up *Virgin 2539/promo/'88* $12
The Promise of a New Day 5 versions *Virgin 4043/promo/silkscreened/'91* $10
Vibeology house 7"/house 12"/ underground sax dub/video edit *Virgin 4378/promo/logo on orange/'91* $10
Vibeology 6 versions *Virgin 4098/promo/logo on black/'91* $10
Will You Marry Me edit & lp *Virgin 4471/ promo/silkscreened/rear insert/'92* $6

ABDUL, PAULA/MC SKAT KAT
Skat Strut 5 versions *Virgin 3996/promo/ full color silkscreened pic/'91* $8

ABERCROMBIE, JOHN
While We're Young ep (Mirrors/Scomotion/ A Matter of Time) *ECM JA-2/promo/ silkscreened pic/gatefold hardcover ps/'92* $6

ABOVE THE LAW
4 the Funk of It 3 versions *Ruthless 73952/ promo/silkscreened/rear insert/'91* $6
Murder Rap/Another Execution *Ruthless 73230/ promo/silkscreened/ps/'90* $6
Untouchable/What Cha Can Prove (3 versions)/ Menace to Society *Epic 7336 promo/silkscreened logo/rear insert/'90* $6

ABSTRAC'
Right and Hype edit & lp *Reprise 3620/promo/'89* $3

AC/DC
Are You Ready *Atco 3746/promo/ silkscreened logo/ps/'90* $10
Big Gun *Columbia 5185/promo/ps/'93* $8
Dirty Deeds Done Dirt Cheap *Atco 4901/promo/rear insert* $10
Heatseeker *Atlantic 2208/promo/'88* $10
Highway to Hell edit/with Bonny intro *Atco 4755/promo/logo on black/ps/'92* $8
Mistress For Christmas *Atco 3639/promo/ red logo on white/ps/'90* $10
Moneytalks *Atco 3661/promo/ silkscreened logo/rear insert/'90* $8
Thunderstruck *Atco 3522/promo/ die cut gatefold hardcover ps/'90* $10

ACE OF BASE
All That She Wants *Arista 2614/ promo/ps/logo on red/'93* $5

ACETONE
Acetone (I'm Gone/For a Few Dollars More/ D.F.B./Cindy) *Yard CD2/stock/ gatefold hardcover ps* $5

ACKERMAN, WILLIAM
Imaginary Roads sampler w/artist introductions *Windham Hill 17639/promo/ps/'88* $8

ACOSTA RUSSEL
Deep in My Soul 5 versions
JRS 822/promo/ps/logo on white/'92 ....$5

ADAM ANT
Room at the Top 7" & lp *MCA 17903/promo/'89* .$6
Rough Stuff CHR mix/7" edit of 12"/12" remix ....
MCA 18375/promo/rear insert/'90 ....$7

ADAMS, BRYAN
(Everything I Do) I Do It For You
A&M 75021 7234 2/promo/logo on brown/gatefold "Robin Hood" ps/'91 ....$7
(Everything I Do) I Do It For You single & lp
A&M 75021 2380 2/stock/gatefold hardcover ps/sticker/logo on brown/'91 ....$7
All I Want Is You edit & lp
A&M 75021 5367/promo/logo on white $7
Can't Stop This Thing We Started 4:29 & 4:11
A&M 7276 2/promo/logo on pink/ps/'91 ....$7
Do I Have to Say the Words? edit & lp
A&M 75021 7384/promo/logo on white/ps/'91 ..$7
Reckless/In the Studio *#72/promo/aired 11/6/89* .$20
The Bryan Adams Story *Weekly Specials/promo/ Unistar/radio show 2/28-3/1/91* $20
There Will Never Be Another Tonight
A&M 75021 7315/promo/ps/'91 ....$6
Thought I'd Died and Gone to Heaven 4:56 & 5:48 ..
A&M 75021 7324/promo/logo on blue/ps ...$8
Touch the Hand *A&M 75021 7317/ promo/silkscreened/ps/'91* $7
Waking Up the Neighbors 15 tracks
A&M 75021 5367/promo silkscreened on stock/ps/'91 ....$12

ADAMS, OLETA
Circle of One *Fontana 314/promo/silkscreen/'90* .$4
Circle of One 4 versions *Fontana 445/promo/ logo on black/ps/'91* $7
Don't Let the Sun Go Down on Me (edit) ....
Polydor 608/promo/logo on white/'91 ....$4
Get Here *Fontana 315/promo/silkscreen/ps/'90* ..$6
Get Here (edit) *Fontana 376/promo/'90* $6
I Just Had to Hear Your .. *Fontana 945/promo/ gatefold hardcover ps/'93* $8
Rhythm of Life (3 versions) *Fontana 254/promo/ silkscreened/'90* $8

ADAMSKI
Born to Be Alive sampler (Born to Be Alive/ Never Goin' Down/Killer + 3)
MCA 2060/promo/ps/'91 ....$7
Killer 4:10/6:27/5:35 *MCA 18445/ promo/rear insert/'90* $6
The Space Jungle (3 versions) *MCA 53961/ stock/gatefold hardcover ps/'90* $7
Thank You (8 versions) *Capitol 79356/promo/ logo silkscreened/sticker/'89* $7
It Should Have Been Me 8 versions
Capitol 79746/ promo/logo on blue/rear insert/'91 ....$7
Warning (6 versions)/Love to See You Dancin'
Capitol 79981/promo/rear insert/'89 ....$7

ADORABLE
Sunshine Smile/Pilot/Obsessively Yours
SBK 19780/stock/ps/silkscreened/'93 ....$6

ADULT NET
Waking Up in the Sun
Fontana 116/promo/silkscreened/'89 ....$7

ADVENTURES
Broken Land (edit) *Elektra 2209/promo/ps/'88* $4
Broken Land/Dont Stand on Me
Elektra 000046/promo/3"/ps $5
Drowning in Sea of Love (edit)
Elektra 8012/promo $4
Your Greatest Shade of Blue
Elektra 8147/promo/silkscreened logo/'90 $3

AEROSMITH
Angel (2 versions) *Geffen 2895/promo/ps/'87* ...$12
Angel/Magic Touch *Geffen 2871/ promo/3"/custom card* $8
Cryin' lp & fade *Geffen 4528/promo/ps/'93* $8
Dude Looks Like a Lady *Geffen 2794/promo/ gatefold hardcover ps/'87* $12
F.I.N.E. (AOR mix) *Geffen 3806/promo/ps/'89* $8
Fever *Geffen 4552/promo/silkscreened//ps/'93* $8
Get a Grip 14 tracks *Geffen 24455/promo silkscreened on stock/ps/'93* $12
Get a Grip full cd special pak *Geffen 24520/ promo/gatefold "hide" cover/cust. sticker* ..$20
Janie's Got a Gun CHR edit remix/ CHR full intro remix/lp *Geffen 3794/ promo/ps/silkscreened logo/'89* $10
Livin' on the Edge 3 versions *Geffen 4498/ promo/silkscreened/ps/'93* $8
Livin' on the Edge 3 versions/Don't Stop/ Can't Stop Messin *Geffen 21821/ stock with promo stamp on disc/ps/'93* $6
Love in an Elevator(4 vers.)
Geffen 3645/promo/ps $12
Masters of Rock 2/12-2/25/90 *2 hour/2 CD/ promo/dj radio show/cue sheets* $50
Permanent Vacation show *In the Studio 121/ promo/cue sheet/hosted by S.Tyler* $30
Pump *Geffen 2-24269/promo/ leather bound (embossed) edition/'89* $30
Pump/In the Studio *#131/promo/aired 12/24/90* $30
Rag Doll (3 remix) *Geffen 3089/promo/ps/'88* ..$12
Rock This Way (lp length sampler)
Columbia 1365/promo/15 tracks $25
The Big Ten Inch Sampler (10 tracks)
Columbia 4236/promo/ps/'91 ....$20
The Other Side (3 versions)/ Theme From Waynes World/My Girl
Geffen 21458/stock/ps/'90 ....$8
The Other Side (4 vers.) *Geffen 3918/promo/ silkscreened/gatefold die cut hardcvr ps/'90* ..$12

The Other Side (lp & Matt Dike honky tonk vers.)
Geffen 4117/promo/silkscreened/ gatefold die cut hardcover ps/'90 ....$15
What It Takes CHR remix edit/lp *Geffen 3852/ promo/silkscreened logo on black/poster/ hardcover gatefold embossed ps/'90* $8

AEROSMITH/GUNS & ROSES
Rag Doll/Angel/Dude/Sweet Child/Welcome
Geffen 3132/promo/rear insert/'87 ....$15

AFRICAN UNITY
I Love the Way You Make Me Feel 5 vers.
Tabu 28965 1700/promo/logo silkscreen ps/'91 .$6

AFROS, THE
Feel It short, long, instrumental
Columbia 73403/promo/ps/'90 ....$5

AFTER 7
Baby I'm for Real 6 vers. *Virgin 12748/promo/'92* $6
Baby Im For Real 3 versions *Virgin 12727/ promo/silkscreened pic/rear insert/'92* $6
Can He Love U Like This edit & lp *Virgin 12759/ promo/rear insert/logo on red/'92*..............$6
Cant Stop (6 versions) *Virgin 3319/promo/'89* $6
Heat of the Moment (4 versions)
Virgin 3605/promo/'89.................................$6
Heat of the Moment 7" & 12"
Virgin GEMMA/promo/'89 ....$6
Heat of the Moment radio/percuss-a-pella/extend
Virgin 2753/promo/'89.................................$6
Kickin' It 4 versions *Virgin 12687/promo/ silkscreened/trifold hardcover ps/'92* $8
My Only Woman (5 versions)
Virgin 3479/promo/logo on red/'89............$6
Nights Like This *Virgin 3882/promo/ silkscreened red&black logo/'91* $6
Ready or Not edit/instrumental/lp
Virgin 3170/promo/'90................................$6
Truly Something Special edit & lp
Virgin 12787/promo/'92..............................$6

AFTERSHOCK
Always Thinking (5 versions) *Virgin 3226/promo/ silkscreened logo/'90* $5
Going Through the Motions (4 versions)
Virgin 3687/promo/silkscreened/'91..........$5
Slave to the Vibe 5 versions *Virgin 12754/ promo/rear insert/'93*..................................$5

AHA
Crying in the Rain *WB 4462/promo/'90*................$5

AIR SUPPLY
Without You edit & lp *Giant 4972/promo/'91* $5

AKIKO
How Could I Ask For More *Voss 5001/promo/ '89/silkscreened white/prod by R. Carpenter* ...$4

AL B SURE
Had Enuf 4:22 & 4:58 *WB 4809/promo/'90*.....$6
Had Enuf? *WB 4898/promo/'90* $5
If Im Not Your Lover lp/7"/12"/CHR mix
WB 3518/promo/'88 ....$6
Killing Me Softly (7 different versions)
WB 3388/promo/'88 ....$6
Missunderstanding 7 versions *WB 21744/stock/ gatefold hardcover ps/'90* $5
Missunderstanding (6 versions) *WB 4423/ promo/silkscreened/rear insert/'90*...........$6
Natalie 10 versions *WB 40712/stock/ custom sticker/'92* $6
Natalie edit & lp *WB 5785/promo/'92* $5
Private Times ... And the Whole 9! (15 tracks)
Uptown 26005/promo/silkscreened/pic/ gatefold diary container (with lock & key)/'90 ....$15
Right Now edit/lp/instrum. *WB 5593/promo/'92* ...$6

ALABAMA
Forever's As Far As I'll Go *RCA 2706/promo/'90* .$5
Then Again *RCA 62059/promo/logo on black/ rear insert/'91* $5

ALARM, THE
Change (14 tracks) *IRS 82018/ transparency cover/'89* $20
Curtain Call (12 song comp. w/live & extended)
IRS POPPY 1/promo/ps/'88...................$30
Happy Christmas (War is Over)
IRS 67040/promo/silkscreened/'90 ....$8
Love Don't Come Easy/Corridors of Power/ Working Class Hero *IRS IRSD 017/ promo/silkscreened/ps/'89* $8
Raw edit & lp *IRS 67056/promo/silkscreen/'91* ..$6
Sold Me Down the River 3:36/5:25 *IRS 0010/ promo/fold out die cut hard cover/'89* $12

ALEXANDER, DANIELE
She's There *Mercury 68/promo/ps/'89*..............$4
Where Did The Moon Go Wrong *Mercury 148/ promo/silkscreened/'89*............................$4
Who Can She Turn to *Mercury 442/promo/ silkscreened/rear insert/'91* $4

ALEXANDER, GREGG
In the Neighborhood lp & edit *A&M 17763/ promo/silkscreened/'89* $3

ALIAS
Haunted Heart lp & AOR mix *EMI 04538/ promo/silkscreened/rear insert/'90*............$5
More Than Words Can Say 3:53 & 3:35
EMI 04637/ promo/silkscreened/rear insert/'90............$4
Perfect World edit *Giant 4891/promo/'91* $4
Waiting For Love edit/aor/lp *EMI 4675/promo/ logo on black/rear insert/'90*......................$4
Waiting For Love (hot AC mix) *EMI 04707/promo/ silkscreen logo on white/rear insert/'90*.....$4

ALICE IN CHAINS
Angry Chair *Columbia 4840/promo/ps/'92* $8
Man in the Box edit& lp *Columbia 2257/ promo/ps/'90* $8
Rooster *Columbia 4946/promo/ps/'93* $7
Sea of Sorrow edit & lp *Columbia 4072/ promo/silkscreened/ps/'91* $8
Them Bones *Columbia 4769/promo/ps/'92* $7
We Die Young *Columbia 2163/promo/ps/'90* ... $8
What the Hell... *Columbia 5233/promo/ps/'93* $7
Would? *Columbia 4484/promo/ps/'92* $7

ALIEN
Tears Don't Put Out the Fire *Virgin 2842/ promo/silkscreened/'88* $4

ALL ABOUT EVE
Every Angel lp & extended + interview .... *Mercury 18/promo/ps/'88* $10
Road to Your Soul rock radio vers. & UK vers. *Merc.175/promo/silkscreened/'89* $5
Road to Your Soul edit & lp *Mercury 150/promo/silkscreened/'89* $6

ALLEN, PETER
Tonight You Made My Day *RCA 60703/promo/ps/'90* $4

ALLGOOD
It's Alright *A&M 31458 8132/ promo/silkscreened/ps/'93* $4

ALLIGATOR
Sea of Fire *IRS 009/promo/ps/'89* $6

ALLMAN BROTHERS
Bad Rain *Epic 4178/promo/rear insert/'91* $6
End of Line *Epic 4094/promo/silkscreened/ps/'91* . $6
Kind of Bird edit *Epic 4250/promo/ logo on blue & black/rear insert/'91* $6
Nobody Knows/Come On in My Kitchen (live) *Epic 4333/promo/rear insert/'91* $8

ALLMAN BROTHERS BAND
Dreams (7 track sampler) *Polydor 71/promo/ gatefold hardcover/'89* $25
Good Clean Fun *Epic 2075/promo/ps/'90* $6
It Ain't Over Yet *Epic 2258/promo/'90* $5
Melissa (live) *Epic 4609/promo/ps/'92* $6
Seven Turns edit & lp *Epic 2184/promo/ps/'90* ... $6

ALLMAN, GREGG
Ill Be Holding On (edit) *Virgin 3015/promo/'89* $5
Im No Angel (10 tracks) *Epic 40531/promo/ps/'87* $15
Just Before the Bullets Fly (full lengthwith bonus track) *Epic 1183/promo/ps/'88* $15

ALMIGHTY, THE
Devil's Toys/Loaded (live) *Polydor 624/promo/ logo on black/ps/'92* $6

ALMOND, MARC
Jacky 3 versions/Deep Night 12" mix/ A Love Outgrown *Sire 40234/ stock/gatefold hardcover ps/'91* $7
My Hand Over My .. 2 vers. *Sire 5332/promo/'91* . $6
My Hand Over My Heart single & grit+glitter mix/ Money For Love fiddle & ennio mix/ Night & No Morning/Deadly Serenade *Sire 40367/stock/gatefold hardcover ps* $7
The Desperate Hours (4 vers.) *Capitol 79173/ promo/silkscreened red/'90* $8

ALONSO, MARIA CONCHITA
Promesas *Sony Latin 10122/promo/ps/'92* $6

ALPERT, HERB
3 O'Clock Jump (3 versions) *A&M 17878/ promo/silkscreened logo/ps/'89* $6
Diamonds 8 vers. *A&M 17476/promo/JANET JACKSON/gatefold hardcover/silkscreened* .. $40
Jump Street (5 versions) *A&M 75021 7542 2/ promo/ps/'91* $6
Keep Your Eye on Me (extended) *A&M 17451/ promo/silkscreen/tri fold hardcover ps/'87* $12
North on South St. (7 vers.) *A&M 75021 7500 2/ promo/silkscreened/ps/'91* $8
Romance Dance *A&M 17977/promo/ silkscreened logo/'89* $6
Under a Spanish Moon 9 tracks *A&M 17593 promo/gatefold clothcvr (w/booklet)/'88* .. $15

ALPHAVILLE
Forever Young lp/new single mix/special extend. *Atlantic 2465/promo/rear insert/'88* $6
Romeos 7", lp & maxi versions *Atlantic 2681/ promo/silkscreened/prod by KLAUS SCHULZE/rear insert/'89* $6
The Mysteries of Love (3 versions) *Atlantic 3187/ promo/rear insert/'89* $6

ALSTON, GERALD
Hell of a Situation radio/lp/instrumental *Motown 3746310652/promo/ps/'92* $6
Send For Me radio/lp/instrumental *Motown 374631087/promo/ps/'92* $6

ALTERED STATE
Step Into My Groove 4 vers/Like Father/Drifting *WB 40155/stock/gatefold hardcover/'91* . $5
Step Into My Groove radio mix *WB 4876/promo/ die cut 2 part cover/'91* $5

ALTERN 8
Brutal 8 E 6 versions/One For John *Virgin 12642/stock/ps/'92* $5

ALTMAN, JEFF
I'll Flip You Like a Cheese Omelette ep (7 tracks) *Mercury 138/promo/silkscreened* $5

ALVIN & THE CHIPMUNKS
Achy Breaky Heart lp & edit/I Ain't No Dang ... *Epic 74776/promo/silkscreen/rear insert/'92* ... $5

ALVIN, DAVE
Every Night About This ..*Epic 2778/promo/ps/'87* . $8
Guilty Man *Hightone DAPRO 2/promo/ silkscreened Dave/'91* $7

AMBITIOUS LOVERS
Lust/It's Gonna Rain *Elektra 8306/promo/ silkscreened/rear insert/'90* $6

AMERICAN MUSIC CLUB
Over and Done sampler of early stuff & interview (20 tracks *Reprise 6066/ promo/ps/'93* $15
Over and Done/In My Role As the Most Hated Singer.../The Amyl Nitrate Dream of Pat Robertson *Reprise 6233/promo/ custom tour date sticker/'93* $8

AMG
I Wanna Be Yo Ho vocal remix & remixtramental/ Bitch Betta Have My Money vocal bitchmental *Select Street 015/ promo/silkscreened pic/'92* $5
Jiggable Pie radio/instru. *Select 009/ promo/silkscreened/'91* $6

AMINA
Belly Dance (5 vers.) *Mango 7845/promo/ps/'90* . $5

AMOS, TORI
Crucify (remix) *Atlantic 4598/promo/ps/ logo on black/'92* $8
Silent All These Years *Atlantic 4454/promo/ ps/silkscreened logo on white/'91* $8
Winter edit & lp *Atlantic 4800/promo/ silkscreened/rear insert/'91* $8
Winter/The Pool/Take to the Sky/Sweet Dreams/ Upside Down *Atlantic 87599/promo/ gatefold hardcover ps/stock/ silkscreened/lyric insert/'91* $8

AN EMOTIONAL FISH
Careless Child edit/lp *Atlantic 5230/promo* $5
Celebrate lp & ext. *Atlantic 3520/promo/ps/'90* .. $5
Celebrate/Anyway/Jonathon & Doodle Pip/ Brick It Up (live)/Celebrate (extended) *Atlantic 86136/stock/ gatefold hardcover ps/'90* $5
Grey Matter (3 vers.) *Atlantic 3769/promo/ps/'90* . $6
Live Bait (Celebrate/Grey Matter/Jonathan & Doodle Pip/All I Am/Rock and Roll/ Change - 1st five live) *Atlantic 3828/ promo/logo on black/ps/'91* $15
Rain 7" s.osborne mix/lp *Atlantic 5041/promo/ silkscreened/rear insert/'93* $6

ANA
Angel of Love *Epic 2124/promo/rear insert/'90* .. $4
Got to Tell Me Something lp/dance/dance edit *Epic 73317/promo/ps/'90* $5

AND WHY NOT?
The Face (7" mix) *Isl.6620/promo/rear insert/'90* . $4

ANDERSON BRUFORD WAKEMAN HOWE
Brother of Mine lp&edit *Arista 9842/promo/ps* .. $10
Order of the Universe edit/long edit/lp *Arista 9869/promo/ps/'89* $8
Quartet (I'm Alive) *Arista 9898/promo/ silkscreened logo on red/ps/'89* $8
selftitled (lp length) *Arista 90126/promo/ ps/silkscreened/'89* $20

ANDERSON, CARL
Once in a Lifetime Love/If Not For Love/ I Will Be There *GRP 9976/promo/ps/'92* .. $6

ANDERSON, JOHN
Money in the Bank *RCA 62443/ promo/ps/silkscreened/'93* $5

ANDERSON, JON
Far Far Cry edit remix *Enigma 254/promo/ silkscreened/ps/'89* $7
Hold On to Love *no label or #/promo/ps/'88* $7

ANDERSON, JON & KITARO
Island of Life short radio edit/long radio edit/lp *Geffen 4432/promo/ps/'92* $8

ANDERSON, LAURIE
Babydoll *WB 3900/promo/'89* $6
Beautiful Red Dress video & extended *WB 4390/promo/rear insert/'90* $7
Beautiful Red Dress video & extended/The Day the Devil *WB 9 21592/stock/ps/'90* $6
Strange Angels *WB 3826/promo/'89* $5

ANDERSON, MICHAEL
I Need You *A&M 17660/promo/silkscreened/'88* . $3
Sound Alarm 7"/lp *A&M 17568/promo/ps/'88* $4
True Love edit & lp *A&M 18016/promo/ silkscreened/'90* $4

ANDRESS, TUCK
Solo Guitar Tracks (Sweet P/Louie Louie/ Manonash edit/Man in the Mirror/Europa) *Windham Hill WD-90-02/promo/ps/'90* $6

ANGELA
Love Me For Being Me edit/vocal fade/extended fade *WB 3673/promo/'90* $5

ANGELFISH
Suffocate Me ep (Suffocate Me/You Can Love Her/Kimberly/Trash It) *Wasteland 9200/ stock/ps/silkscreened/'93* $5

ANGELICA
Next 2 U *Quality 15198/promo/silkscreened pic/ps/'92* $5

ANGELS, THE
Dogs Are Talking *Chrysalis 23470/promo/ trifold hardcover die cut ps/'89* $7
Let the Night Roll On edit & lp *Chrysalis 23495/promo/'89* $6

ANIMAL BAG
Everybody full length remix & intro short remix *Stardog 821/promo/silkscreened/ps/'92* ...$5
Hate St./Scum *Mercury 753/promo/ silkscreened/ps/'92* $5

ANIMAL LOGIC
As Soon As the Sun Goes Down (edit) *IRS 019/promo/ps/'90* $6
I Won't Be Sleeping Anymore *IRS 67066/ promo/silkscreened/rear insert/'91* $6
Rose Colored Glasses 2 vers./We Don't Need a Reason/Someone to Come Home to (live) ... *IRS 13827/stock/ps/'91* $6
Rose Colored Glasses 5 versions *IRS 67059/ promo/gatefold hardcover ps/'91* $8
Someday We'll Understand/Theres A Spy../ Someday We'll Understand/Firing Up the Sunset Gun + 1 (last 4 live) *IRS 018/promo/ps/'89* $20
Theres a Spy (In the House of Love) *IRS 012/ promo/gatefold textured cover/'89* $15

ANIMOTION
Calling It Love edit & lp *Polydor 55/promo/ps/'89* .$6
Room to Move 3:59/4:05/6:50 *Polydor 40/promo/ps/'89* $6

ANKA, PAUL
20 Original Masters (20 tracks) *Chrysalis 4737/promo/ps/'89* $18

ANKA, PAUL & OFRA HAZA
Freedom *Curb 073/promo/silkscreened/ rear insert/'91* $7

ANOTHER BAD CREATION
Iesha 4 versions *Motown 1058/promo/'90* $6
My World lp/instrum.l *Motown 1018/promo/'91* ...$6
Playground 2 vers. *Motown 1249/stock/ps/'91* .$6

ANTHRAX
Anti Social *Megaforce 2654/promo/ps/'89* $6
Belly of the Beast (live)/Madhouse (live)/H8 Red *Island 6654/promo/ps/'91* $12
Black Lodge edit/black strings mix *Elektra 8821/promo/silkscreen/rear insert* ...$7
Black Lodge tremelo mix/mellow to mad mix/ black strings mix/Love Her All I../Cowboy Song *Elektra 66277/stock/ gatefold hardcover ps/'93* $6
Bring the Noise/Milk *Island 6670/promo/ps/'91* ...$7
Got the Time edit & lp *Island 6632/promo/ps/'90* ..$6
I'm the Man 3 versions/Sabbath Bloody Sabbath/ Caught in Mosh/I Am the Law (last 2 live) *Megaforce 422 842 448/stock/ps/'87* $10
Only edit & lp *Elektra 8755/promo/ silkscreened/ps/'93* $6

ANTHRAX & VARIOUS
Q&A with Anthrax + songs by MEGADETH (Skin o My Teeth - live), BUTTHOLE SURFERS, KREATOR, NUCLEAR ASSAULT, *Foundation F4/promo/ die cut ps/March '91* $15

ANYTHING BOX
Jubilation (4 versions) *Epic 73356/promo/ps/'90* .$6
Living in Oblivion 4:40/4:22/5:55 *Epic 73231/ promo/silkscreened/rear insert/'90* $6
Soul on Fire/Our Dreams (2 versions)/ Living in Oblivion (slow mix) *Epic 2174/promo/ps/'90* $7

APACHE
Do Fa Self/Hey Girl 3 versions each *Tommy Boy 566/stock/ps/'93* $5
Gangsta Bitch 4 versions/Apache Ain't Shit.......... *Tommy Boy 541/stock/ps/'92* $5

APACHE INDIAN
Chok There 2 versions *Mango 857/promo/ rear insert/'93* $5

APFELBAUM, PETER
The World is Gifted (edit & lp)/Folksong *Antilles 6672/promo/ silkscreened/rear insert/'91* $6

APOLLO MILE
Dune Buggy 4 versions *Geffen 4286/promo/ ps/custom sticker/'91* $5

APOSTLES
I Could Be Anything *Victory 687/promo/ silkscreened/ps/'92* $5

APPOLONIA
Mismatch (4 versions) *WB 3394/promo/'88* $7
The Same Dream (5 vers.) *WB 3573/promo/'88* ..$7

AQUA VELVETS
Selftitled 10 tracks *Riptide 001/ps/'92* $8

AQUANETTAS
Beach Party (remix) *IRS 025/promo/ps/'90* $5

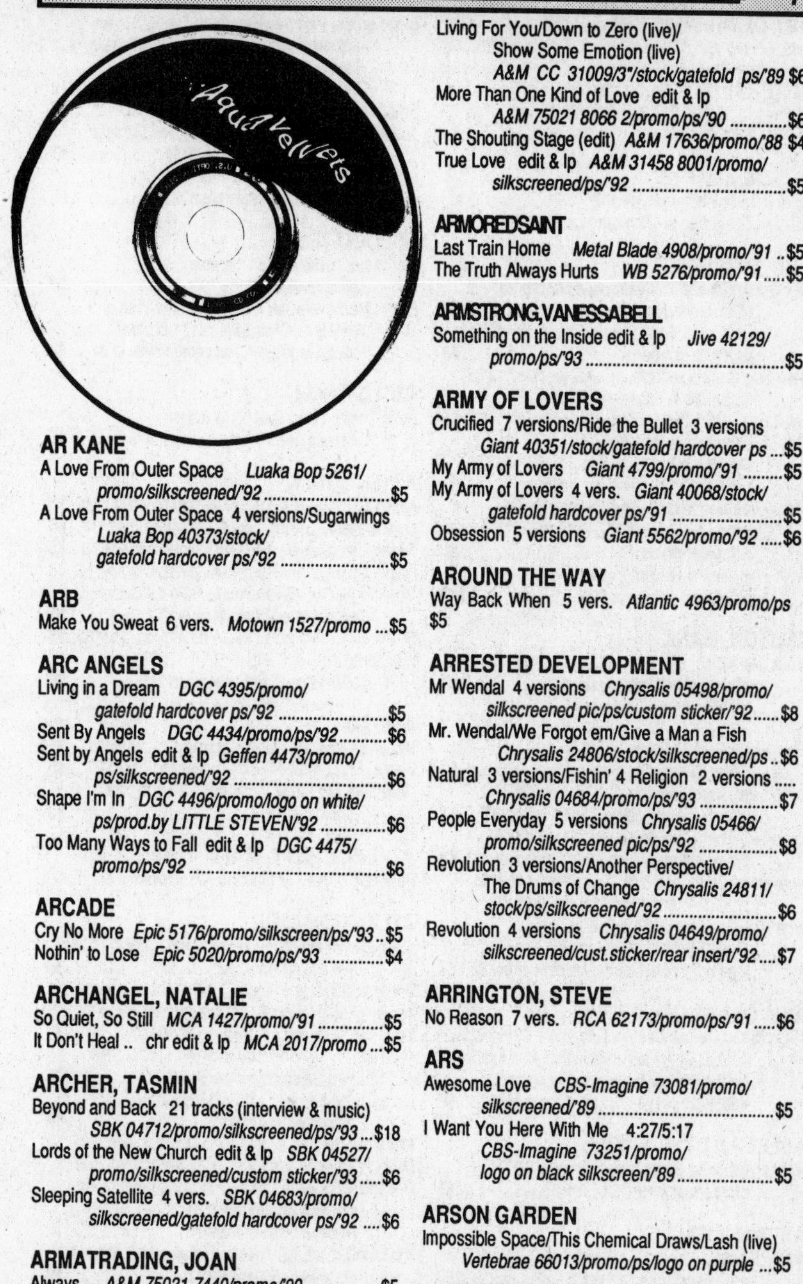

AR KANE
A Love From Outer Space *Luaka Bop 5261/ promo/silkscreened/'92* $5
A Love From Outer Space 4 versions/Sugarwings *Luaka Bop 40373/stock/ gatefold hardcover ps/'92* $5

ARB
Make You Sweat 6 vers. *Motown 1527/promo* ... $5

ARC ANGELS
Living in a Dream *DGC 4395/promo/ gatefold hardcover ps/'92* $5
Sent By Angels *DGC 4434/promo/ps/'92* $6
Sent by Angels edit & lp *Geffen 4473/promo/ ps/silkscreened/'92* $6
Shape I'm In *DGC 4496/promo/logo on white/ ps/prod.by LITTLE STEVEN/'92* $6
Too Many Ways to Fall edit & lp *DGC 4475/ promo/ps/'92* $6

ARCADE
Cry No More *Epic 5176/promo/silkscreen/ps/'93* .. $5
Nothin' to Lose *Epic 5020/promo/ps/'93* $4

ARCHANGEL, NATALIE
So Quiet, So Still *MCA 1427/promo/'91* $5
It Don't Heal .. chr edit & lp *MCA 2017/promo* ... $5

ARCHER, TASMIN
Beyond and Back 21 tracks (interview & music) *SBK 04712/promo/silkscreened/ps/'93* ... $18
Lords of the New Church edit & lp *SBK 04527/ promo/silkscreened/custom sticker/'93* $6
Sleeping Satellite 4 vers. *SBK 04683/promo/ silkscreened/gatefold hardcover ps/'92* $6

ARMATRADING, JOAN
Always *A&M 75021 7440/promo/'90* $5
Living For You *A&M 17594/promo/ps/'88* $5
Living For You/Down to Zero (live)/ Show Some Emotion (live) *A&M CC 31009/3"/stock/gatefold ps/'89* $6
More Than One Kind of Love edit & lp *A&M 75021 8066 2/promo/ps/'90* $6
The Shouting Stage (edit) *A&M 17636/promo/'88* $4
True Love edit & lp *A&M 31458 8001/promo/ silkscreened/ps/'92* $5

ARMOREDSAINT
Last Train Home *Metal Blade 4908/promo/'91* .. $5
The Truth Always Hurts *WB 5276/promo/'91* $5

ARMSTRONG,VANESSABELL
Something on the Inside edit & lp *Jive 42129/ promo/ps/'93* $5

ARMY OF LOVERS
Crucified 7 versions/Ride the Bullet 3 versions *Giant 40351/stock/gatefold hardcover ps* ... $5
My Army of Lovers *Giant 4799/promo/'91* $5
My Army of Lovers 4 vers. *Giant 40068/stock/ gatefold hardcover ps/'91* $5
Obsession 5 versions *Giant 5562/promo/'92* $6

AROUND THE WAY
Way Back When 5 vers. *Atlantic 4963/promo/ps* $5

ARRESTED DEVELOPMENT
Mr Wendal 4 versions *Chrysalis 05498/promo/ silkscreened pic/ps/custom sticker/'92* $8
Mr. Wendal/We Forgot em/Give a Man a Fish *Chrysalis 24806/stock/silkscreened/ps* .. $6
Natural 3 versions/Fishin' 4 Religion 2 versions ..... *Chrysalis 04684/promo/ps/'93* $7
People Everyday 5 versions *Chrysalis 05466/ promo/silkscreened pic/ps/'92* $8
Revolution 3 versions/Another Perspective/ The Drums of Change *Chrysalis 24811/ stock/ps/silkscreened/'92* $6
Revolution 4 versions *Chrysalis 04649/promo/ silkscreened/cust.sticker/rear insert/'92* $7

ARRINGTON, STEVE
No Reason 7 vers. *RCA 62173/promo/ps/'91* $6

ARS
Awesome Love *CBS-Imagine 73081/promo/ silkscreened/'89* $5
I Want You Here With Me 4:27/5:17 *CBS-Imagine 73251/promo/ logo on black silkscreen/'89* $5

ARSON GARDEN
Impossible Space/This Chemical Draws/Lash (live) *Vertebrae 66013/promo/ps/logo on purple* ... $5

ART OF NOISE
Moments in Love 2:59/3:39/6:59 *China 156/ promo/silkscreened logo on black/'89* $10

ART OF NOISE & TOM JONES
Kiss 3:30/8:16/8:09 *China 32/promo/ps/'88* $8

ARTERBERRY, BENITA
Changed 7" & alt.7" & lp/Thank You *SBK 05425/promo/ps/'91* $4

ARTZ & KRAFTZ
All of It radio/phat radio/all of 7" *Columbia 74721/promo/ps/'92* $5

ASH, DANIEL
Get Out of Control *Columbia 4872/promo/ silkscreened/ps/'92* $6
Get Out of Control 5 versions *Columbia 4825/ promo/silkscreened/ps/'92* $8
Here She Comes wobble mix edit/wobble mix/lp *Columbia 4956/promo/ps/'93* $6
This Love *RCA 2789/promo/silkscreened/ps/'91* .$6
This Love/Heaven is Waiting/ Coming Down (slow vers.) *RCA 2754/ promo/silkscreened/rear insert/'90* $8
This Love/Heaven is Waiting/Coming Down (slow vers.) *RCA 2764/stock/ silkscreened/ps* $6
Walk This Way 3 vers/interview (14:10) *RCA 2831/promo/ps/'91* $18

ASHTON, MARK
Black and White edit & lp *RCA 8806/promo/ silkscreened/rear insert/'88* $5

ASIA
(Bad Boys) Back in Town edit & lp *Great Pyramid 819/promo/logo on green* .$7
Days Like These *Geffen 4141/promo/ logo on blue/gatefold hardcover ps/'90* $7
Days Like These edit/lp/ac mix *Geffen 4144/ promo/silkscreen/gatefold hardcover/'90* ..$8
Heaven on Earth edit & lp *Great Pyramid 819/ promo/silkscreened logo on tan/ps/'92* $7
Who Will Stop the Rain? edit & lp *Great Pyramid 819/promo/ logo on green/gatefold hardcover ps/'92* ..$7

ASIA CLASSICS
Magic Shag Carpet deeelitefully edit & extended/ Aatavu Chanda/Tambala Masala/Mulatto/ Neeve Nanna n.o.w. mix *Luaka Bop 40636/stock/gatefold hardcover ps/'92* $6

ASLEEP AT THE WHEEL
Dance With Who Brung You *Arista 2178/ promo/rear insert/'91* $5

ASPHALT BALLET
Angry Youth *Virgin 12769/promo/ rear insert/silkscreened/'93* $5

Blood on the Highway/Hangman Swing/Suicide Saloon/Flesh and Bone/Unlucky Mr Lucky/ Taking a Walk (last 5 live) *Virgin 4408/promo/ps/'91* $12
Soul Survive *Virgin 4097/promo/'91* $5
Tuesday's Rain lp & edit *Virgin 4493/promo/ logo on green/rear insert/'91* $5
Unlucky Mr. Lucky *Virgin 4608/promo/ logo on black/rear insert/'92* $5

ASSOCIATES
Fire to Ice *Charisma 011/promo/ silkscreened logo/ps/'90* $6
Fire to Ice/Fever/Ever Since That Day/Wild and Lonely *Circa BILLYCD 1/promo/ silkscreened/lettered plastic sleeve/'91* $8

ASTLEY, JON
Been There, Done That 4:14 & 4:48 *Atlantic 2576/promo/rear insert/'88* $5

ASTLEY, RICK
Ain't Too Proud to Beg *RCA 9030/promo/ps/'89* .$6
Cry For Help (3 vers.) *RCA 2774/promo/ps/'91* ...$8
Giving Up on Love *RCA 8872/promo/ps/'89* $6
Giving Up on .. 5 vers. *RCA 8878/promo/ps/'88* .$8
Move Right Out (3 versions) *RCA 2839/promo/ silkscreened pic/rear insert/'91* $7
She Wants to Dance ... *RCA 8838/promo/ps/'88* ..$6
Wonderful You edit & lp *RCA 62068/promo/ silkscreened red/rear insert/'91* $6

ASWAD
Beautys Only Skin Deep *Island 125/promo/'89* ..$5
Best of My ... *Island 7850/promo/rear insert/'90* $5
Dont Turn Around (2 versions) *Mango 123/ promo/ps/'88* $8

ATKINS, CHET & MARK KNOPFLER
Poor Boy Blues *Columbia 73556/promo/'90* $6

ATLANTIC STARR
Always/All in the Name of Love (both edits) *WB 21946/stock/'92* $5
Bring It Back Home Again *WB 3733/promo/'89* ..$4
Family of Man *Epic 73532/promo/rear insert/'90* .$5
Love Crazy 5 vers. *Reprise 5190/promo/'91* $7
Love Crazy ac remix/soft remix/romantic remix *Reprise 5243/promo/'91* $6
Love Crazy edit & lp *WB 5036/promo/ silkscreened pic/'91* $6
Masterpiece 2 vers. *Reprise 5167/rear insert/'91* .$4
My First Love (3 versions) *WB 3461/promo/'89* ..$7
Unconditional Love all day versions/quiet storm edit/quiet storm mix 6:21 *Reprise 5514/promo/'91* $6
Unconditional Love edit with dialogue & without *Reprise 5156/promo/'91* $6

ATOM SEED
Get in Line/Castles in the Sky/What You Say/ Burn (last 2 live) *London 615/promo/ silkscreened logo on green/ps/'91* $6
Rebel 2:55 & 6:00 *London 541/promo/ logo on yellow/ps/'90* $5

ATOOZI
Calling Out Your Name (3 versions) *EMI 4705/ promo/silkscreened/rear insert/'90* $5

ATTAWAY, MURRAY
Fall So Far edit & lp *DGC 4539/promo/'93* $4
Under Jets *DGC 4500/promo/silkscreened/ps/'92* $4

AUSTIN, PATTI
Love is Gonna Getcha *GRP 9936/promo/ps/'90* .. $6
Smoke Gets in Your .. *Qwest 3271/promo/ps/'88* .. $6
Soldier Boy 3:32 & 5:59 *GRP 9950/promo/ps* $6
The Girl Who Used to.. *GRP 9920/promo/ps/'89* .. $6
Through the Test of Time radio edit & lp *GRP 9927/promo/ silkscreened pic/rear insert/'90* $6

AUTO & CHEROKEE
Taste 6 versions/Hook You Up *Morgan Creek 2959 26002/stock/ps/'92* ... $5

AVILA, BOBBY ROSS
La La Love 5 versions *Perspective 31458 8100/ promo/logo on red/ps/'93* $6
Merry Go Round (6 vers.) *RCA 9186/promo/ps* ... $6

AXTON, HOYT
Heartbreak Hotel *DPI 5001/promo/'90* $5

AZTEC CAMERA
Good Morning Britain *Sire 4453/promo/rear insert* $5
Good Morning Britain (8 versions) *Sire 21775/ stock/ps/'90* $5
Crying Scene *Sire 4328/promo/rear insert/'90* $5
The Crying Scene/True Colors/Salvation/I Threw I All Away (live) *Sire 21591/stock/ps/'90* ... $5

B.O.X.
Low Down vocal & percapella *PWL 537/promo/silkscreened/'91* $5
Rock 'Dat 3:30 & 5:03 *Mercury 617/promo/ silkscreened/'91* $6

B52S
Deadbeat Club remix edit/lp edit/lp *Reprise 3825/promo/'89* $7
Good Stuff 5 versions *Reprise 40561/stock/'92* .. $6
Good Stuff edit & lp *Reprise 5497/promo/ silkscreened logo/'92* $7
Love Shack lp & edit *Reprise 3679/promo/'89* .. $7
Love Shack (5 versions)/Channel Z (12" rock mix) *Reprise 21318/stock/ps/'89* $7
Revolution Earth 4 versions/Is That You Mo-Dean? 3 versions *Reprise 40642/stock/ gatefold hardcover ps/'92* $7
Revolution Earth edit/lp/co2 edit *Reprise 5677/promo/'92* $7
Roam edit & lp *Reprise 3856/promo/'89* $7
Roam 5 vers./Bushfire *Reprise 21441/stock/ps* . $7
Tell It Like It T-i-is edit & lp *Reprise 5663/promo/'92* $6

BABES IN TOYLAND
Bruise Violet edit & lp *Reprise 5612/promo/'92* . $6
Fontanelle (full length cd - all tracks) *Reprise 5609/promo/ps/'92* $12
He's My Thing ron saint germain mix/rave ogilvie overground mix *Reprise 6272/ promo/back tour date ps/'93* $6

BABY ANIMALS
Don't Tell Me What .. *Imago 28057/promo/ps/'93* .. $5
Early Warning *Imago 28005/promo/ps/'91* $5
One Word *Imago 28018/promo/ps/'91* $5
One Word lp/edit/top 40 edit *Imago 28023/ promo/ps/'92* $5
Painless *Imago 28012/promo/ps/'91* $5
selftitled 11 tracks *Imago 28004/promo/ gatefold diecut hardcover ps/'91* $12

BABY FORD
Fetish 6 versions *Sire 40449/stock/ gatefold hardcover ps/'92* $5
Let's Talk It Over 3 versions/Ooochy Koochy (live)/Change (3 versions)/Wigan (live) *Sire 21557/stock/ps/'90* $5

BABYFACE
Give U My Heart 4 versions *LaFace 4029/promo/logo on brown/ps* $6
Give U My Heart edit & soft mix *Laface 4031/promo/logo on brown/ps/'92* . $6
Give U My Heart edit/lp/instrumental *LaFace 4026/promo/logo on brown/ps* $6
Mary Mack 4 vers. *Solar 74543/promo/ps/'91* .. $6
My Kinda Girl (7 versions) *Epic 2086/promo/ silkscreened/'90* $6
My Kinda Girl (7 versions)/Whip Appeal *Solar 74510/stock/ps/'90* $6
Whip Appeal 4 versions *Epic 2014/promo/rear insert/'90* $6
Whip Appeal edit & lp *Solar 74007/promo/ silkscreened/ps/'90* $6

BABYLON A.D.
Bang Go the Bells friction mix/fat bottom mix/live .... *Arista 9935/promo/ps/'90* $5
Desperate edit & lp *Arista 3067/promo/ silkscreened/rear insert/'90* $5
The Kid Goes Wild (4 vers.) *Arista 2035/promo/ silkscreened logo/rear insert/'90* $5
Bad Blood *Arista 2421/promo/logo on red/ps/'92* . $5

So Savage the Heart 3 versions *Arista 2434/ promo/silkscreened/ps/'92* $5

BAD 4 GOOD

Nineteen *Atlantic 4720/promo/rear insert* $4

BAD BOYS BLUE

I Totally Miss You chr edit & lp *Coconut 17126/ promo/silkscreened pic/rear insert/'92* $4

BAD BRAINS

Rise/Unidentified *Epic 5292/promo/ silkscreened/rear insert/'93* $6

BAD COMPANY

Bad Company In the Studio *radio show/promo/ cue sheet 7/30/90* $25
Boys Cry Tough *Atco 3487/promo/silkscreened logo on black/rear insert/'90* $5
Holy Water *Atco 3316/promo/silkscreened/ ps/rear insert/'90* $7
How About That edit & lp *Atco 4699/promo/ silkscreened/ps/'92* $6
If You Needed Somebody *Atco 3488/promo/ logo on yellow/ps/'90* $6
Little Angel remix edit & lp *Atco 5032/promo/ silkscreened/ps/'93* $5
No Smoke Without a .. *Atlantic 2410/promo/'89* ...$5
No Smoke Without a Fire edit & lp/One Night *Atlantic 2515/promo/rear insert/'88* $5
Rock Stars radio show *2 CD set/ promo/interview & music (including rare b side)/extensive cue sheets* $40
Shake It Up *Atlantic 2626/promo/rear insert/'88* .$6
Stranger Stranger *Atco 3760/promo/ps/'90* $6
This Could Be the One *Atco 4836/promo/ silkscreened group pic/rear insert/'92* $7
Walk Through Fire *Atco 4053/promo/ps/'91* $6

BAD ENGLISH

Best of What I Got *Epic 1829/promo/ silkscreened logo/'89* $5
Forget Me Not lp & 7" edit *Epic 1633/promo/ silkscreened/'89* $5
Heaven is a 4 Letter Word *Epic 73307/promo/ silkscreened logo on blue/rear insert/'90* ..$5
Possession radio edit & lp *Epic 73398/promo/ silkscreened logo on white/rear insert/'90* .$5
Price of Love band remix edit *Epic 1945/ promo/logo on black silkscreen/'89* $5
Price of Love remix edit & remix *Epic 73094/ promo/silkscreened logo on bronze/'89* $5
Straight to Your Heart *Epic 73982/ promo/silkscreened/ps/'91* $5
The Time Alone With.. *Epic 74091/promo/ps/'91* ..$5
When I See You Smile *Epic 1828/promo/ silkscreened logo on purple/'89* $5

BAD MUTHA GOOSE & THE BROTHERS GRIMM

Be Somebody 3 versions/Pride/Time to Get/100% *Alpha International 73016/stock/ps/'91* $5

BAD RELIGION

Generator/Atomic Garden/Only Entertainment/ Anesthesia/I Want to Conquer the World (last 2 live) *Epitaph 86101/promo/ silkscreened/custom sticker/'92* $12

BAD ROMANCE

The House of My Father *Polydor 418/promo/ gatefold hardcover ps/silkscreened/'91* $5

BADLANDS

Dreams in the Dark *Atlantic 2734/ promo/rear insert/'89* $4
Joe's Blues-Soul ../Soul Stealer *Titanium 3992/ promo/silkscreened/rear insert/'91* $5
Whiskey Dust *Altantic 4145/promo/ps* $5
Winters Call edit & lp *Atlantic 2954/promo/ps/'89* $5

BAERWALD, DAVID

A Brand New Morning *A&M 31458 8049/ promo/silkscreened/ps/'92* $4
All For You edit & lp *A&M 18028/promo/ silkscreened pic/ps/'90* $5
Baerwald on Triage (20 tracks - interview & music).. *A&M 31454 8024/promo/ps/'93* $15
Dance remix & lp *A&M 75021 8104/promo/ logo on red/ps/'90* $6
The Got No Shotgun Hydrahead Octopus Blues edit & lp *A&M 31458 8041/promo/ logo on white/gatefold hardcover ps/'92* ...$6

BAIRD, DAN

I Love You Period *Def American 5661/promo/ps* ..$4
Look At What You Started chr edit *Def American 6142/promo/ps/'93* $4
Look At What You Started edit & lp *Def American 6136/promo/ps/'93* $4

BAKER, ANITA

Fairy Tales edit & lp *Elektra 8277/promo/ logo on blue/'90* $5
Giving You the Best .. *Elektra 8027/promo/'88* $4
Just Because edit & lp *Elektra 8046/promo/'88* $4
Lead Me Into Love *Elektra 8076/promo/'88* $4
Soul Inspiration (edit) *Elektra 8215/promo/'90* $5
Talk to Me edit & lp *Elektra 8172/promo/ps/'90* .$5

BAKER, ARTHUR

2X1 (4 versions) *A&M 17848/promo/'89* $7
Leave the Guns at Home edit/dissolving rap/ extended/churchapella + 1 *RCA 62120/ promo/silkscreened pic (of AL GREEN)/ rear insert/'91* $8

Leave the Guns at Home edit/extended/lp *RCA 62073/promo/silkscreened/ rear insert/AL GREEN/'91* $7

The Message is Love (4 vers.) *A&M 17938/promo* $7

BAKER, ARTHUR & NIKEETA

IOU 4 versions *RCA 62207/promo/ rear insert/logo on purple/'92* $7

BAKERS PINK

Watercolours *Epic 4944/promo/ps/'93* $4

BALAAM AND THE ANGEL

I Took a Little *Virgin 2963/promo/silkscreened/'89* $5

Little Bit of Love *Virgin 3264/promo/silkscreened* .$5

BALDWIN, BOB

On Our Own edit & lp *Atlantic 3501/ promo/rear insert/'90*.................................$4

BALLOON

Now That the Thrill's Gone/Paraffin Flat/ I Can't Leave Her *Balloon 001/promo/ gatefold hardcover ps/'92* $7

BALTIMORA

Tarzan Boy 5 versions *SBK 04681/promo/ logo on green/ps/'93* $12

BAMBAATAA, AFRIKA

Don't Stop... Planet Rock 7 versions *Tommy Boy 1052/ps/stock/'92*..................$6

Just Get Up & Dance 7 versions *EMI 56225/stock/ps/'91* $6

BANANARAMA

Love, Truth & Honesty 7" version & hot power edit .. *London 31/promo/ps/'88* $8

Nathan Jones 7" version & psycho mix (6:27) *London 46/promo/ps/silkscreened/'89* $8

Tripping on Your Love 3 versions *London 568/promo/silkscreened/ps/'91* $7

BAND OF SUSANS

Now ep (Pearls of Wisdom/Following My Heart/ Trash Train/Paint It Black 2 versions/ Now is Now remix) *Restless 72722/ stock/ps/'92*...$8

BAND, THE

The Band on CD (8 tracks) *Capitol 79379/ promo/rear insert/silkscreened logo/'90*..$15

BANDERAS

This is Your Life (2 versions) *London 419/promo/ silkscreened/gatefold hardcover ps/'91* $5

Why Aren't You In Love With Me? *London 542/promo/logo on brown/ps/'91* .$4

BANG

Holding My Heart (5 versions) *A&M 75021 8064/ promo/silkscreened/ps/'90* $5

BANG TANGO

Ain't No Jive ep (Dancin' on Coals/20th Century Boy/Someone Like You/Midnight Struck/ Attack of Life) *MCA 10531/stock/ps/'92* ...$5

Attack of Life *Mechanik 17848/promo/ silkscreened/rear insert/'89* $5

Breaking Up a Heart of Stone (remix edit) *MCA 18062/promo/silkscreened/'89* $5

Dancin' on Coals *Mechanic 1446/promo/ps/'91*...$5

Love Injection (remix edit) *Mechanik 18225/ promo/full band pic silkscreen/'90*.............$8

Midnight Struck edit *Mechanic 1652/ promo/silkscreened/ps/'91* $5

Someone Like You *MCA 18044/promo/'89*........$5

Someone Like You *Mechanic 17853/promo/ silkscreened/rear insert/'89* $5

Soul to Soul *Mechanic 1281/promo/ silkscreened/ps/'91* $5

Untied and True *Mechanic 1447/promo/ ps/silkscreened/'91* $5

BANGALORE CHOIR

Freight Train Rollin'/All or Nothin'/Doin' the Dance/ Angel in Black Giant 5004/promo/ custom sticker/rear insert/'92 ....$8

BANGLES

Be With You Columbia 1569/promo/ps/'89 ....$10

Eternal Flame Columbia 1417/promo/'88 ....$10

Everything limited tour CD picture CD with tour dates on back ps/promo/'89 ....$30

I'll Set You Free single & lp Columbia 1713/ promo/silkscreened/'88 ....$10

In Your Room Columbia 1313/promo/ps/'88 ....$10

In Your Room/Bell Jar/Hazy Shade of Winter CBS 653081/3"/ps/stock $7

BANKS, TONY

Angel Face edit & lp Giant 5308/promo/rear insert....................$5

I Wanna Change the .. edit Giant 5550/promo ...$6

BANKS, TONY/BANK STATEMENT

Raincloud Atlantic 3054/promo/rear insert/'89 ....$6

selftitled (lp) Atlantic 2-82007/promo/ custom sticker/special "bank statement" package/'89 ....$15

Throwback lp & edit Atlantic 2804/ promo/rear insert/'89...............................$6

BANTON, BURRO

Boom Wa Dis edit & 12"/Me No Fool (CAPTAIN REMO) 12" Stepsun/promo/'93 ......$6

BANTON, PATO

Bubbling Hot IRS 67102/promo/ silkscreened/rear insert/'92 ....$6

Wize Up/Pato & Roger Go ../Don't Sniff Coke + 1
IRS 67034/promo/rear insert/'90 .... $8

BAR KAYS
Tell Me Sumthin Good edit & instrumental
Tavdash JEA 01000/promo $6

BARBIE
Together We Can Do It Rincon 90062/promo/
logo on pink/'90 .... $6

BARBIE BONES
Submarine Soul edit & lp Restless 007/promo/
silkscreened/'91 .... $5

BARDENS, PETE
Gold Cinema 78360/promo $4

BARDENS, PETE & MICK FLEETWOOD
Whisper in Wind remix & lp Capitol 79418/promo $3

BARDEUX
Bleeding Heart edit & st james club mix
Enigma 109/promo/custom sticker/'88 ...... $8
I Love the Bass radio & dance mix Enigma 207/
promo/cust. sticker/silkscreened logo/'89 . $6
Thumbs Up (5 versions) Enigma 247/promo/
silkscreened/custom sticker/'89 .... $7
When We Kiss 2 vers./Sex Machine/Magic Carpet
Ride remix Enigma 75018/stock/3"/5" ps . $7

BARENAKED LADIES
Be My Yoko Ono Sire 5616/promo/'92 .... $5
Fight the Power Sire 6432/promo/
silkscreened/rear insert/'93 .... $5
If I Had $1000000 Sire 5825/promo/'92 .... $5

BARKMARKET
Grinder/Ten Convictions/Johnny Shiv/Clapdance
Def American 5343/promo/ps/'92 .... $5

BARNES, JIMMY
Im Still on Your Side Geffen 3285/promo/'88 ...... $5
Im Still on Your Side + 2 live Geffen 3244/
promo/ps/'88 .... $7
Lay Your Guns Down Atlantic 3673/
promo/rear insert/'90 .... $5
Let's Make it Last All Night Atlantic 3510/
promo/silkscreened/ps/'90 .... $5
Too Much Aint Enough Love (edit)
Geffen 3148/promo/'88 .... $5

BARONE, RICHARD
Cry Baby Cry/I Belong to Me Passport 6058/
promo/ps/silkscreened $4
I Only Took What I Needed MCA 18175/promo/
pic silkscreened/rear insert/'90 .... $8
River to River MCA 18240/promo/silkscreened/
rear insert/'90 .... $5
Where the Truth Lies MCA 18468/promo/ps/'90 . $6

BARR, ROSEANNE
I Enjoy Being a Girl 15 excerpts Hollywood 8261/
promo/rear insert/'90 .... $8

BARRY, JOHN
Dances With Wolves ep (The J.Dunbar Theme/
Dances With Wolves) Epic 2248/promo/
silkscreened/ps/'90 .... $8

BARSHA
Who's the Master? edit & instrumental
Virgin 3490/promo/'90 .... $5

BAS NOIR
Superficial Love 4 versions Atlantic 4418/
promo/rear insert/'92 .... $5

BASE, ROB
Turn It Out (3 versions) Profile 7275/promo/'89 . $5
Turn It Out (2 versions)/Get Up and Have a Good
Time (4 versions) Profile 7292/promo/
mistitled/insert with correct titles/
silkscreened/'90 .... $5

BASEHEAD
2000 BC 3 vers/Can It Be Imago 72787-25010/
stock/ps/'92 .... $6
Do You Wanna F**k (Or What)? 4 versions/
Hair smack remix Imago 72787 25027/
stock/ps/'92 .... $6
Not Over You 4 vers. Imago 28033/promo/ps $6
Split Personality 2 versions/Two Thousand
Brain Cells/Do You Wanna F**k
Or What live Imago 25044/stock/ps $6

BASH & POP
Loose Ends Sire 5941/promo/'93 .... $5
Never Aim to Please Sire 5976/promo/'93 .... $5

BASIA
5 live songs & 4 remix Epic 1276/promo/ps/'88 . $30
Baby You're Mine Epic 73405/promo/ps/'90 ... $6
Baby You're Mine/Ordinary People/Copernicus
Epic 1961/promo/ps/'90 .... $8
Brave New Hope 2 versions/Until You Come Back
to Me (6:35)/Cruising for Bruising (6:46)/
From Now On (band versions)/Masquerade/
Come to Heaven Epic 49K 73593/
stock/ps/'90 .... $7
Cruising For Bruising Epic 73239/promo/
silkscreened/ps/'90 .... $8
New Day For You edit & lp *Epic 1356/promo/*
silkscreened baby blue/'87 .... $8
Promises *Epic 1474/promo/logo on white/'87* .. $10
Promises/From Now On *Epic 2872/promo/*
custom sticker/'86 .... $12
Time and Tide *Epic 1137/promo/ps/'87* $10
Until You Come Back to Me 4 vers *Epic 2245*
promo/rear insert/logo silkscreened/'90 .. $10
Until You Come Back to Me (remix) *Epic 73485/*
promo/silkscreened/rear insert/'90 .... $7

BATHORY/TANKARD/RAGE
Father to Son/Chemical Invasion/ Flowers That Fade in my Hand *Noise International 4879/promo/ silkscreened/rear insert/'90* $7

BATON ROUGE
Walks Like a Woman *Atlantic 3198/promo/ps/'90* . $5

BATTLE, KATHLEEN & ITZHAK PERLMAN
The Bach Album sampler (4 tracks) *Deuts. Grammophon 737/promo/ps/'92* .. $12

BEACH BOYS
Crocodile Rock *Polydor 581/promo/ silkscreened/ps/'91* $8
Hot Fun in the Summertime *Brother 2/promo/ logo on white/rear insert/'92* $10
Kokomo *Elektra 8014/promo/'88* $10
Problem Child *RCA 2646/promo/ps/'90* $12
Problem Child (radio edit) *RCA 2674/promo/ rear insert/'90* $10
Somewhere Near Japan *Capitol 79823/promo/ silkscreened logo on red/'89* $8
Special 14 Track Sampler *Capitol 79168/promo/ silkscreened logo/ps/'90* $25
Still Cruisin' *Capitol 79735/promo/ silkscreened red/'89* $10

BEARS
Aches & Pains/Talking About Music Is Like.. *Primitive Man 17523/promo/ps/'88* $10

BEASLEY, WALTER
Just Kickin' It 12"/7"/lp *Mercury 186/promo/ silkscreened/'89* $6
You Are the One (3 versions)/Get Loose *Mercury 243/promo/silkscreened/'90* $6

BEASTIE BOYS
Frozen Metal Head (Gratitude/Time For Livin'/ Looking Down the ../So Whatcha Want/ Stand Together) *Capitol 79300/ promo/ps/logo on black/'92* $18
Gratitude/Stand Together live/Finger Lickin' Good cheese remix/Gratitude live/Honky Rink *Capitol 79558/promo/silkscreened/ custom sticker/'92* $15
Hey Ladies/Dis Yourself in '89 *Capitol 79699/promo/'89* $8
Jimmy James 3 versions/The Maestro/Boomin' Granny/Drinkin' Wine *Capitol 15836/ stock/ps/logo on black/'93* $8
Pass the Mic 3 versions/Drunken Praying Mantis Style/Netty's Girl *Capitol 15827/ promo/stock/ps/'92* $7
Pass the Mic lp & pt 2/Professor Booty/ Time For Livin' *Capitol 79178/promo/ silkscreened/ps/'92* $10
Shadrach *Capitol 79824/promo/silkscreened/'89* $8
So What'cha Want 4 versions/Skills to Pay the Bills/Groove Holmes 2 versions *Capitol 15847/stock/ps/'92* $7

BEAT FARMERS
Girl I Almost Married *MCA 17905/promo/custom sticker/'89* $7

THE BEATLES

1. LOVE ME DO
(Lennon/McCartney)
MPL Communications Ltd.

2. P.S. I LOVE YOU
(Lennon/McCartney)
MPL Communications Ltd.

3. LOVE ME DO (original single version)
(Lennon/McCartney)
MPL Communications Ltd.

℗ 1962 The copyright in this sound recording is owned by EMI Records Ltd.
© 1992 Apple Corps Ltd.

BEATLES
All Too Much - Beatles Rarities on Compact Disc. Vol. 14 (25 tracks) *On the Radio/ Westwood One/promo/ps/'93* $40
From Me To You/Thank You Girl *Capitol 44280/ 3"/stock/mono/plastic ps/'89* $7
I Want to Hold Your Hand/This Boy *Capitol 44304/ 3"/stock/plastic ps/'89* $7
Love Me Do lp& single/P.S. I Love You *Capitol 15940stock/ps/cust. sticker/'92* $8

BEATMASTERS, THE
Dunno What It Is (About You) 5 versions/ The Whisper *Rhythm King 40041/ stock/gatefold hardcover ps/'91* $5
Warm Love (6 versions)/Burn It Up (3 versions) *Sire 21739/stock/ps/'90* $5

BEATNUTS
Intoxicated Demons - the Radio Friendly ep (10 tracks) *Relativity 0185/promo/rear insert/'93* ... $7

BEATS INTERNATIONAL
Change Your Mind 3 versions *London 712/ promo/logo on blue/'92* $6
Dub Be Good to Me single edit & Norman Cooks vers. *Elektra 8164/promo/rear insert/'90* .. $6

Dub Be Good to Me (4 versions)/Invasion of the Freestyle/Invasion of Real Estate Agents *Elektra 66654/stock/ps/'90* $6
Wont Talk About It (7" mix/12" mix) *Elektra 8230/promo/'90* $6

BEAU NASTY
Paradise in the Sand radio edit & lp *WTG 1987/promo/silkscreened/rear insert/'89* $5
Shake It *WTG 1845/promo/ps/'89* $5

BEAUTIES, THE
Asses/Mothers Finest Gun/Battle Grounds/Something About the Pain *Gasoline Alley 54482/stock/ps/'92* $6
Something About the Pain ep (4 songs) .... *Gasoline Alley 54482/stock with dj outer box/bonus video/poster/bumper sticker* .. $15

BEAUTIFUL SOUTH
Old Red Eyes is Back *Elektra 8608/promo/'92* $5
A Little Time *Elektra 8256/promo/rear insert/'90* .. $5
I've Come For My Award *Elektra 8355/promo/rear insert/'90* $5
My Book (edit) *Elektra 8291/promo/silkscreened purple/rear insert/'90* $5
My Book/Big Beautiful South/Bigger Doesn't../Speak to Me *Elektra 66578/stock/gatefold hardcover ps/'91* $6
We Are Each Other *Elektra 8551/promo/ps/logo on green/'92* $5
You Keep It All In *Elektra 8154/promo/silkscreened green/'90* $5

BEAUTIFUL, THE
Highway *Giant 4399/promo/rear insert/'90* $4
John Doe/Back Inside/Storybook/The We in Me *Giant 5102/promo/rear insert/'92* $8
Storybook edit & lp *Giant 5587/promo/'92* $4

BECK, JEFF
Beckology: The Sampler 17 tracks *Epic 4275/promo/ps/'91* $20
Stand on It *Epic 1812/promo/ps/'89* $10
The Train Kept a Rollin'/The Stumble + 1 non BECK tune *WTG 1391/promo/'88* .. $12

BECK, ROBIN
First Time lp & ac *Mercury 197/promo/silkscreened pic/'89* $4
Save Up All Your Tears *Mercury 136/promo/silkscreened pic/'89* $4

BECKETT
Brother Louie edit & lp *Curb 068/promo/silkscreened logo/'91* $4
How Can the Girl Refuse *Curb 10532/promo/custom sticker/'89* $4

BEDLAM
Carnival Lights edit & lp *MCA 2115/promo/ps* $5

BEE GEES
Bodyguard edit & lp *WB 3905/promo/'89* $8
ESP (edit) *WB 2902/promo/ps/'87* $12
Happy Ever After edit *WB 5007/promo/'91* $8
One edit & lp *WB 3605/promo/'89* $8
When He's Gone (radio mix *WB 4737/promo/'91* . $8
You Win Again CD & intro edit *WB 3786/promo* .. $8
You Win Again (7" fade) *WB 2809/promo/gatefold hardcover ps* $8

BEE, ROBBY
Pow Wow Girls/We're the Boys *Warrior/promo* .. $5

BEGHE, FRANCESCO
Heaven Knows edit & lp/Lost in America *SBK 05369/promo/silkscreened/gatefold hardcover ps/'91* $6
Something About Your Touch *SBK 05408/promo/silkscreened/gatefold hardcover ps/'91* $6

BEL CANTO
Shimmering, Warm & Bright lp/remix/instrumental *Dali 8740/promo/silkscreened/rear insert* ... $6
Shoulder to the Wheel (3 versions)/Oyster *Nettwerk 026/promo/silkscreened logo/ps/'90* $6
Unicorn 6 versions *Dali 8663/promo/silkscreened/ps/'92* $7

BELEW, ADRIAN
Not Alone Anymore *Atlantic 3418/promo/ps/'90* .. $6
Oh Daddy *Atlantic 2704/promo/rear insert/'89* .. $6
Standing in the Shadow *Atlantic 4430/promo/silkscreened pic/rear insert/'92* $8

BELL BIV DEVOE
Above the Rim *MCA 2631/promo/ps/'93* $6
B.B.D. (I Thought It Was Me)? *MCA 1023/promo/rear insert/'90* $6
B.B.D. (I Thought It Was Me)? (4 versions) *MCA 1033/promo/rear insert/'90* $8
Do Me! (4 versions) *MCA 18382/promo/ps/silkscreened yellow/'90* $8
Gangsta lp/without rap/instrumental/suite *MCA 2491/promo/ps/'92* $8
Let Me Know Something?! 8 versions *MCA 1072/promo/'91* $8
Poison *MCA 18183/promo/'90* $6
Poison 4 versions *MCA 24056/stock/gatefold hardcover ps/'90* $6
Poison no ho version & 7" versions *MCA 18218/promo/'90* $7
She's Dope *MCA 1329/promo/ps/'90* $6
She's Dope (4 vers.) *MCA 1341/promo/ps/'91* $8
Something in Your Eyes edit & lp *MCA 2802/promo/rear insert/'93* $6
When Will I See You Smile Again 4:37 & 5:07 *MCA 1170/promo/rear insert/'90* $6
When Will I See You Smile Again? 3 versions *MCA 1318/promo/rear insert/'91* $8

BELLAMY, LISA
Work It 5 versions *Sire 40010/stock/ gatefold hardcover ps/'91* $5

BELLE, REGINA
Baby Come to 2 vers. *Columbia 1683/promo/ps* . $5
Dream in Color *Columbia 5156/promo/ps/'93* $5
How Could You Do It To Me remix & edit remix *Columbia 1052/promo/ps* $5
If I Could *Columbia 74864/promo/ps/'93* $5
Make It Like It Was edit/remix *Columbia 1946/promo/ps/'89* $6
Make It Like It Was 7"/lp *Columbia 73022/ promo/ps/'89* $6
So Many Tears (3 versions) *Columbia 2818/promo/ps/'87* $8
This is Love edit & lp *Columbia 73346/ promo/ps/silkscreened/'90* $5
What Goes Around 4:12/5:35 *Columbia 73201/ promo/gatefold hardcover ps/'90* $6

BELLTOWER, THE
Outshine the Sun *Eastwest 4740/promo/ silkscreened/rear insert/'91* $5

BELLY
Feed the Tree remix *Sire 5929/promo/'92* $6

BELOVED, THE
Celebrate Your Life 6 versions *Atlantic 4958/promo/ps/'93* $6
Hello single version/honky tonk versions/ edit of honky tonk *Atlantic 3163/promo/ps/'90* . $6
Hello 5 vers./Paradise *Atlantic 86235/stock/ps/'90* $6
Sweet Harmony 5 vers. *Atlantic 4991/promo/ps* ... $6
Time AfterTime 4:05/7:25 *Atlantic 3335/promo/ps* . $6
Time After Time (4 vers.)/Your Love Takes Me Higher/Pablo *Atlantic 86184/stock/ps/'90* $6

BEMSHI
Where's My Daddy/Maybe Heavens Better/123XI../ Color Me In/Golden Child *Capitol 79388/ promo/silkscreened/ps/'92* $5

BENATAR, PAT
One Love (edit)/Suffer the Little Childen- Hell is For Children (live)/Outlaw Blues *Chrysalis 23428/promo/rear insert/'89* $10
Payin' the Cost to Be the Boss *Chrysalis 23695/promo/ps/'91* $6
Please Come Home For Christmas *Chrysalis 23654promo/ps/'90* $8
So Long *Chrysalis 23753/promo/logo on black/ rear insert/'91* $8
True Love *Chrysalis 23696/promo/ps/'91* $6
True Love 11 tracks *Chrsysalis 21805/promo/ gatefold hardcover ps/transparency/ logo on blue/'91* $15

BENNETT, TONY
Rags to Riches *Atlantic 3643/promo/yellow silkscreened/rear insert/cust.sticker/'90* $6

BENOIT, DAVID
Moments edit *GRP 9966/promo/ps/'91* $5

BENOIT, DAVID & DAVID PACK
Every Corner of the World (edit) *GRP 9935/promo/ps/'90* $5

BENSON, GEORGE
Baby Workout *WB 4600/promo/'90* $5
Here There & Everywere vocal & instrumental *WB 3722/promo/'89* $5
Interview with George Benson/Words & Music *WB 3698/promo/rear insert/'89* $12
Lets Do It Again edit/lp *WB 3209/promo/ps/'88* .. $7
Twice the Love 7" remix & Guitar love mix *WB 3373/promo/'88* $6
Words & Music *WB 4561/promo only interview/ rear insert/'90* $15

BENSON, GEORGE & EARL KLUGH
Dreamin' edit & lp *WB 2798/promo/ custom sticker/'87* $6
Since You're Gone 2 versions *WB 2982/promo/ps/'88* $6

BENSON, GEORGE & PATTI AUSTIN
I'll Keep Your Dreams Alive *Great Pyramid 821/ promo/silkscreened/ps/'92* $7

BENSON, JODI
Voice in the Night *Sparrow 1284/promo/ silkscreened logo on aquamarine/ps/'91* .. $4

BERLIN
Take My Breath ..(remix) *DGC 4369/promo/'91* ... $8

BERNHARD, SANDRA
Without You I'm Nothing ep (Stevie Nicks + 2) *Enigma 185/promo/custom sticker* $8

BERRY, CHUCK
Maybellene/Together We Will Always Be/ Roll Over Beethoven/School Day *MCA 37280/stock/3"/ps/'88* $7

BERRYHILL, CINDY LEE
Indirectly Yours/Supernatural../She Had + 1 *Rhino 7979/Benelux/stock/ps/'88* $6
Supernatural Fact/Baby (Should I Have the Baby) *Rhino 90022/promo/silkscreen pic/ps/'89* $7

BESTKISSERSINTHEWORLD
Pickin' Flowers For *MCA 2561/promo/ silkscreened/ps/'93* $6
Puddin' ep (Pickin' Flowers For/60 Seconds/ Melanie/Smoke Rings/Laughable) *MCA 10694/stock/ps/silkscreened/'93* $7

Workin' on Donita/Goldfish Bowl/Slightly Used/ Vicodine/Hungover Together *Sub Pop 122/stock/ps/'91* $8

BETTIE SERVEERT

Tom Boy/Smile/Balentine/Maggot *Matador 032/stock/ps/'92* $6

BETTS, DICKEY

The Dickey Betts Band Live (Duane's Tune/Rock Bottom/Blue Sky/The Blues Aint Enought/ In Memory of Eliz.Reed/Duanes Tune) *Epic 1396/promo/'88* $22

BETTY BOO

Doin' the Do (4 versions) *Sire 4450/promo/ silkscreened pic/rear insert/'90* $6

Doin' the Do (7 versions)/Shame (2 versions) *Sire 21581/stock/ps/'90* $6

Hey DJ-I Cant Dance (5 versions) *Sire 4792/ promo/silkscreened pic/rear insert/'91* $6

Thing Goin' On lp/remix/hip hop *Sire 5877/ promo/silkscreened pic/'92* $6

Thing Goin' On 4 vers./I'm On My Way 3 vers. *Sire 40639/stock/gatefold hardcover ps* $6

Thing Goin' On lp & radio *Sire 5882/promo/'92* . $6

Where Are You Baby? 5 versions *Rhyth. King 40181/promo/gatefold hardcover ps/'91* ... $6

BEYOND, THE

Great Indifference/One Step Too Fire *Continuum 19204/promo/ps/'92* $6

BIANCA

My Emotions (3 versions) *WB 3906/promo/ rear insert/'90* $5

BIANCO, MATT

Dont Blame It On That Girl 2 versions *Atlantic 2620/promo/rear insert/'88* $7

BIG

Party & Bull 5 vers. *Uptown 2743/promo/ps/'93* .. $6

BIG AUDIO DYNAMITE

Contact 7" version/12" mix/club mix/lp *Columbia 73043/promo/silkscreen/ps/'89* $8

Free (Theme song from Flashback) film/lp/club *WTG 1957/promo/silkscreened logo/ rear insert/'90* $8

Just Play Music edit & lp & extended mix *Columbia 1232/promo/silkscreen pic/'88* .. $8

Other 99 *Columbia 1342/promo/'88* $6

Rush 3 versions/City Lights (7:18) *Columbia 44K 73844/stock/ps/'91* $6

Rush single & lp *Columbia 4018/promo/ logo on black/ps/'91* $6

BIG AUDIO DYNAMITE II

Ally Pally Paradiso dj live (Ritual Idea/Babe/Free/ Messiahs of the Milk Bar/City Lights/ Situation No Win + 3) *Columbia 4271/promo/ps/'91* $20

Innocent Child edit & lp *Columbia 4367/ promo/ps/'92* $6

The Globe 6 vers. *Columbia 74180/stock/ps/'91* . $6

The Globe edit & lp *Columbia 4191/promo/ logo on black/ps/'91* $7

BIG BIG SUN

Lilacs (Sarah) (remix) *Atlantic 2859/promo/ rear insert/'89* $4

BIG COUNTRY

King of Emotion *Reprise 3238/promo/ps/'88* $6

Peace in Our Time *Reprise 3338/promo/ps/'88* .. $8

The One I Love 2 versions/In a Big Country/ Look Away *Fox 62593/promo/ps/'93* ... $7

BIG DADDY KANE

Groove With It 2 vers. *Cold Chillin' 5092/promo* . $6

Hard Being the Kane 4:15 & 5:11 *Cold Chillin' 4897/promo/'90* $6

How U Get a Record Deal clean radio edit/instr. *Cold Chillin' 6116/promo/'93* $6

Ill Take You There edit, lp & remix *WB 3367/promo/'88* $7

Ooh, Aah, Nah-Nah-Nah master mix *Cold Chillin' 4974/promo/'91* $6

Smooth Operator fade/vocal/dub *Cold Chillin' 3805/promo/'89* $5

BIG DIPPER

Impossible Things/She Loves You/Rockin' in the Free World/Stranded in Jungle *Epic 2083/promo/ps/'90* $5

Love Barge/Start the Revolutions/Girl Who Lives ... *Epic 2009/promo/ps/'90* $5

BIG F, THE

Doctor Vine lp & edit *Elektra 8145/promo/ silkscreened/ps/'90* $4

Kill the Cowboy edit & lp *FFF 8179/promo/ silkscreened/rear insert/'89* $4

Patience Peregrine/Gone Ancient/Three Headed Boris/Towed *Chrys. 26019/stock/ps/'93* . $5

BIG HEAD TODD & THE MONSTERS

Broken Hearted Savior/It's Alright/Circle/ Bittersweet *Giant 5913/promo/ gatefold hardcover ps/'93* $5

BIG HOUSE

Dollar in My Pocket lp & single *RCA 62040/ promo/silkscreened/ps/'91* $4

BIG HUNK O CHEESE
You're Soaking In it ep (Lemmings/Art Show/ Honey/No Sympathy/Working ..) *Jack/stock/ps* $4

BIGOD 20
On the Run 3 versions/Like a Prayer/Tschirm Tschikwirk *Sire 40615/stock/ gatefold hardcover ps/'92* $5
The Bog (4 versions) *Sire 21755/stock/ps/'90* $5

BIGSTORM
Not Guilty *Sire 3536/promo/'89* $4

BILLY GOAT
Ali Rocka *Third Rail 10214/promo/silkscreen/'92* . $5
Chef *Third Rail 10158/promo/silkscreened/ rear insert/'92* $5

BIOHAZARD
Punishment (clean)/We're Only Gonna Die *Roadrunner 065/promo/logo on black/ custom sticker/'92* $6

BIRDLAND
Shoot You Down *Radioactive 1418/promo/ps* $5
Sleep With Me *Radioactive 1601/promo/ps/'91* .. $5

BISCUIT
Biscuit's in the House edit/lp/extended *Columbia 73585/promo/ps/'90* $5

BISHOP, STEPHEN
Mr. Heartbreak *Atlantic 3110/promo/ps/ silkscreened logo/'89* $6
Walking on Air *Atlantic 2899/promo/ silkscreened logo/rear insert/'89* $6
All I Want *Curb 086/promo/silkscreened/'91* $6

BIZ MARKIE
T.S.R. lp & instrumental/Busy Doing Nuthin' lp & remix & instrumental *Cold Chillin' 40264/stock/gatefold hardcover ps/'91* $5

BIZARRE INC.
I'm Gonna Get You top 40 edit *Vinyl Solution 74814/promo/ps/'92* $6
Took My Love 4 vers. *Vinyl Solution 44K 74862/ stock/ps/custom sticker/'93* $5
Took My Love edit/edit with rap/soul *Vinyl Solution 74969/promo/ps/'93* $5

BLACK
Comedy (12 tracks) *A&M/3 3" CDs/promo/ps/'88* $20
Everythings Coming Up Roses *A&M 17533/ promo/ps/'88* $6
Here It Comes Again radio & cd versions *A&M 75021 7274/promo/ps/'91* $6
Wonderful Life edit/lp/original *A&M 17754/promo/silkscreened/'89* $6
Wonderful Life re recording & old version *A&M 17742/promo/silkscreened/ps/'89* $6

BLACK & BLUE
Live it Up (prod by Gene Simmons) *Geffen 3034//promo/ps/'88* $5

BLACK & WHITE
Rainbow Bar & Girls orig rock mix/mix with rap *Atlantic 2636/promo/rear insert/'89* $5

BLACK 47
ep (Funky Ceili/James Connolly/Maria's Wedding/ Our Lady of the Bronx/Black 47) *SBK 0777 7 80971/stock/ps/'92* $6
Maria's Wedding edit & lp *SBK 04697/promo/ ps/logo on black/'93* $5

BLACK BOX
Everybody Everybody (5 versions) *RCA 2628/ promo/embossed can cover/'90* $20
Everybody Everybody (5 versions) *RCA 2628/ promo/ps/'90* $8
Fantasy 4 versions *RCA 62065/promo/ silkscreened/rear insert/'91* $10
Fantasy remix & lp *RCA 2788/promo/ps/'90* $7
I Don't Know Anybody Else (4 versions) *RCA 2738/promo/rear insert/'90* $8
I Don't Know Anybody Else (5 versions) *RCA 2735/promo/rear insert/'90* $8
Open Your Eyes 4 versions *RCA 62160/promo/ logo on orange/rear insert/'91* $8
Ride on Time 4 versions *RCA 62003/promo/ rear insert/'91* $8
Strike It Up 3 versions *RCA 2799/promo/ps/ custom sticker/'91* $8
Strike It Up 8 vers. *RCA 2785/promo/ps/'91* $10

BLACK CAT BONE
The Epic Continues *Chameleon 8549/promo/ silkscreened/rear insert/'92* $5

BLACK CROWES
Bad Luck Blue Eyes Goodbye edit/lp/live *Def American 6082/promo/ps/'93* $10
Hard to Handle lp & remix *Def American 4896/promo/'90* $8
Hard to Handle lp & remix *Def American 4162/promo/ps/'90* $8
Hotel Illness/Rainy Day Women *Def American 5778/promo/ps/'92* $7
Jealous Again *Def American 3869/promo/ps/'90* .. $8
Remedy *Def American 5406/promo/ps/'92* $8
Remedy edit *Def American 5474/promo/'92* $6
Seeing Things *Def American 4810/promo/ embossed ps/'90* $8
She Talks to Angels edit/live video edit/live video ... *Def American 4687/promo/gatefold ps* .. $12
Sometimes Salvation/Darling of Underground... *Def American 5916/promo/'92* $8

Southern Harmony & Musical Companion 10 tracks *Def American 26916/stock/ ltd edition multi-fold ps/'92* $15
Sting Me *Def American 5534/promo/ps/'92* $6
Thorn in My Pride (edit) *Def American 5633/ promo/ps/'92* $8
Thorn in My Pride/Sting Me (slow versions) *Def American 5610/promo/ps/'92* $10
Twice as Hard remix & lp/Jealous Again (acoustic) .. *Def American 4122/promo/ps/'90* $10

BLACK FLAMES, THE

Let Me Show You (3 versions) *Columbia 73588/ promo/ps/'90* $6
Watching You 3:54/6:59/5:05 *Columbia 73276/ promo/ps/'90* $6

BLACK SABBATH

Black Moon/Cloak and Dagger *IRS IRSD 002/ promo/silkscreened/ps/'89* $12
Feels Good to Me 2 vers./Paranoid (live - Nov.'89) *IRS 67032/promo/silkscreened/ rear insert/'90* $12
I *Reprise 5704/promo/'92* $7
The Gates of Hell/Headless Cross lp & edit *IRS 8202/promo/silkscreendesign/'89* $15
Time Machine *Reprise 5311/promo/'92* $7
TV Crimes *Reprise 5499/promo/'92* $7

BLACK SABBATH/BILL WARD

Snakes and Ladders *Chameleon 77/promo/ silkscreened pic/'92* $8

BLACK SHEEP

Flavor of the Month *Mercury 416/promo/ logo on red/ps/'91* $4
Strobelight Honey 3 versions *Mercury 674/ promo/gatefold ps/'92* $4

BLACK SORROWS, THE

The Chosen Ones US & Australian mix *Epic 1701/promo/'89* $5

BLACK UHURU & ICE T

Tip of Iceberg 6 vers./Take Heed *Mesa 76003/ stock/gatefold hardcover ps/'92* $6

BLACK VELVET BAND, THE

As You Go Down *Elektra 8129/promo/'89* $4
Lullaby *Elektra 8560/promo/ps/silkscreened/'92* ... $4
When Justice Came 2 vers. *Elektra 8098/promo* . $4

BLACK, CLINT

Put Yourself In My Shoes (10 tracks) *RCA 237/dj only package with full length cassette also/'90* $25
We Tell Ourselves 2 versions *RCA 62194/promo/rear insert/'92* $6

BLACK, CLINT & WYNONNA

A Bad Goodbye *RCA 62503/promo/'93* $6

BLACK, DAVID

Nobody But You edit/lp/instrumental *Bust It 79438/promo/ps/'92* $6

BLACK, FRANK

Conversation & Music with Frank Black *Elektra 8829/promo/custom sticker/silkscreened pic* $15
Hang on to Your Ego/Surf Epic/Ballad of J.Horton *Elektra 8762/promo/ps* $7
I Heard Ramona Sing *Elektra 8816/promo/ silkscreened/custom sticker/'93* $4
Los Angeles *Elektra 8731/promo/ps/silkscreen* $4

BLACK, MARY

Columbus *Gift Horse 79143/promo/ps/'89* $6

BLACKBIRD

Am I Killing You 3 versions *Scotti Bros 75342/ promo/silkscreened/'92* $7
Class War kmfdm remix/Am I Killing You remix/ Quicksand/I Need You *Scotti Bros 75340/ promo/silkscreened/ps/'92* $7
Take Me edit & lp *Scotti Bros 75320/promo/ silkscreened/ps/'92* $7

BLACKEYED SUSAN

None of It Matters lp & edit *Mercury 431/promo/ silkscreened/gatefold hardcover ps/'91* $5
Ride With Me *Mercury 554/promo/logo on black* .. $5
Satisfaction *Mercury 502/promo/logo on black/ps* $5

BLACKFOOT

Chilled to d'Bone *Nalli 1991/promo/rear insert/ silkscreened/'91* $6
Doin' My Job/Navarre/Soldier Blue *Nalli N 11347/promo/ps/'90* $6
Guitar Slingers Song & Dance *Nalli 1991/promo/ silkscreened/rear insert/'91* $6

BLACKSTREET

Baby Be Mine 6 versions *MCA 2505/promo/ rear insert/'92* $6
Baby Be Mine 9 versions *MCA 2697/promo/ rear insert/'93* $8

BLADES, RUBEN

Hopes on Hold (edit) *Elektra 2246/promo/'88* $4

BLAKE BABIES

Lament/Cesspool/Loose *Mammoth/stock/ silkscreened/ps/'89* $10

BLANDO, DEBORAH

Boy (Why You Wanna Make ..) with & without rap *Epic 73920/promo/ps/silkscreen/'91* .. $5

BLAZE

So Special (5 vers.) *Motown 1024/promo/'90* $6

BLEACH
Surround edit/remix/lp *Dali 8649/promo/silkscreened/rear insert/'92* $6
Trip & Slide radio remix *Dali 8697/promo/silkscreened/ps/'93* $5

BLESSING, THE
Denial *MCA 1545/promo/ps/'91* $4
Highway 5 edit & lp *MCA 1337/promo/silkscreened/ps/'91* $4
Hurricane Room edit & lp *MCA 1502/promo/ps* $4

BLIGE, MARY J.
I Don't Want to Do Anything unplugged edit/lp *Uptown 2776/promo/rear insert/'93* $7
Love No Limit 4 vers. *Uptown 2667/promo/ps/'93* $7
Real Love 4 versions *Uptown 2311/promo/rear insert/'92* $7
Real Love 5 versions *Uptown 54456/ps/stock* $6
Sweet Thing *Uptown 2548/promo/rear insert/'92* . $6
Sweet Thing live/lp/tv *Uptown 2581/promo/ps/'93* $10
You Remind Me 4 versions *Uptown 2098/promo/rear insert/'91* $7
You Remind Me 4 vers. *Uptown 54447/stock/ps* . $6

BLIND MELON
I Wonder edit & lp *Capitol 79586/promo/logo on purple/ps/'92* $6
No Rain lp & live/Drive/Soak the Sin last 2 live *Capitol 79693/promo/ps/cus. sticker/'92* .. $10
Tones of Home edit & lp *Capitol 79397/promo/logo on black/ps/'92* $6
Tones of Home/Dear Ol Dad/Deserted/Time *Capitol 79491/promo/logo on black/'92* $7
Tones of Home/Time/Wooh D.O.G. playground vers. *Capitol 15957/stock/ps/'92* $6

BLITZSPEER
Sonic Glory *Epic 4416/promo/logo on blue/ps/'92* $6

BLOC
Speak *A&M 75021 7509/promo/silkscreen/ps/'91* . $5

BLOCK, RORY
Faithless World edit/Silver Wings *Rounder 1011/promo/ps/'92* $5

BLONZ
Last Call (For Alcohol) *Imagine 2223/promo/rear insert/'90* $4

BLOOM, LUKA
I Need Love single ver. *Reprise 5306/promo/'92* .. $5
Rescue Mission/Delirious/This Is For Life/You Couldn't.../Dreams in America *Reprise 3990/promo/ps/'90* $8

BLU MAX
Strong Emotion 10 tracks *Nastymix 70210/promo/ps/'90* $8

BLUE AEROPLANES
.. And Stones (4 versions) *Chrysalis 23548/promo/ps/'90* $8
The Boy in the Bubble/Talkin' on the Otherphone/Disney Head *Chrysalis 23789/promo/silkscreened/rear insert/'91* $8

BLUE MAGIC
Romeo and Juliet vocal & instrumental *Def Jam 1439/promo/ps/'89* $6

BLUE MURDER
selftitled 9 tracks *Geffen 24212/dj silkscreened group pic/gatefold hardcover/'89* $15
Valley of the Kings radio edit & lp *Geffen 3407/promo/silkscreened pic/gatefold ps/'89* $8

BLUE NILE, THE
Hats (7 songs) *A&M 5284/promo/silkscreened/fold out & pop up cover/'89* $18
Headlights on the Parade edit & lp *A&M 18027/promo/silkscreened/ps/'89* $6
Headlights on the Parade remix & lp *A&M 75021 8079/promo/silkscreened/ps/'89* $6
The Downtown Lights edit & lp *A&M 17982/promo/silkscreened letters/ps/'89* $6
Downtown Lights 4:05/4:34/6:28 *A&M 18032/promo/silkscreened/ps/'90* $7
The Downtown Lights/Headlights On the Parade/Saturday Night (all edits) *A&M 18025/promo/silkscreened letters on blue/'90* $5

BLUE OYSTER CULT
Astronomy (4 versions) *Columbia 1218/promo/ps/silkscreened/'88* $15
In the Presence edit & lp *silkscreened/promo* $12

BLUE PEARL
(Can You) Feel the Passion 5 versions *SBK 19751/stock/ps/silkscreened/'92* $5

BLUE RODEO
Diamond Mine (2 edits & lp) *Atlantic 2702/ promo/silkscreened/rear insert/'89* $5
Lost Together *Atlantic 4727/promo/silkscreened/ rear insert/'92* $5

BLUE TEARS
Crush *MCA 1118/promo/rear insert/ logo on white/'90* $4
Rockin' With the Radio edit & lp *MCA 18277/ promo/ps/'90* $4

BLUE TRAIN
All I Need Is You 4:17 & 6:58 *Zoo 17024/promo/ps/'91* $5
All I Need Is You 9 versions *Zoo 17034/promo/ silkscreened/ps/'91* $6
The Hardest Thing 5 vers. *Zoo 17057/promo/ silkscreened pic/rear insert/'92* $6

BLUE ZONE UK
Jackie single & ext. *Arista 9725/promo/ps/'88* $5

BLUE, BUDDY
Guttersnipes n Zealots (interview/Bind Monkeys/ No Right to Die/Gun Sale../Something Inhuman) *RNA 90066/promo/ silkscreened/ps/'91* $12

BLUERUNNERS, THE
I Sho Do/Lame Pretender *Island 8691/promo/ logo silkscreened/custom sticker (with anti DAVID DUKE discussion)/'91* $6

BLUES BROTHERS BAND, THE
Never Found a Girl *Turnstyle 4630/promo/'92* .. $5

BLUES TRAVELER
All in the Groove edit & lp *A&M 75021 7282/ promo/logo on black/ps/'91* $5
But Anyway *A&M 75021 7405/promo/silkscreen* . $5
But Anyway edit & lp *A&M 75021 7508/promo/ps* $5
Conquer Me edit/video edit/lp *A&M 31458 8167/ promo/logo on black/ps/'93* $5
Conquer Me edit & lp *A&M 31458 8117/promo/ logo on black/ps/'93* $5
Mountain Cry edit & lp *A&M 75021 7329/promo/ logo on blue/ps/GREG ALLMAN/'91* $5
Sweet Pain edit & lp *A&M 75021 7314/promo/ logo on blue/ps/'91* $5

BLUR
Blur-ti-go ep (Bang now & trend mix/She's So High/Come Together/Fool/Popscene - last 4 live) *SBK 05455/promo/ps/ silkscreened/custom sticker/'92* $15
Focusing in With Blur interview & music *SBK 05424/promo/ps/'91* $15
There's No Other ..lp/move mix/aggress.move mix *SBK 05427/promo/logo on yellow/ps/'91* .. $8
There's No Other Way/Inertia/Mr Briggs/ I'm All Over *SBK 19747/stock/ps/'91* $6

BLVD
Never Give Up long/short *MCA 8804/promo/'88* . $3

BODEANS
AOR sampler 4 tracks *Slash 6545/promo/ custom sticker/'93* $6
Black, White and Blood Red lp & edit *Slash 4709/promo/'91* $5
Good Things *Slash 5139/promo/'91* $5
Good Work CD & live/Still the Night (live) *Slash 3757/promo/'89* $10
Jinga Bell Rock/Christmas Time *Slash 3863/promo/'89* $10
Only Love *Slash 2825/promo/ps* $5
Paradise *Slash 4895/promo/'91* $5
You Dont Get Much lp & edit *Slash 3575/promo* . $5

BODY & SOUL
Dance to the Drummer's Beat *Delicious 107/promo* $5

BODY COUNT
selftitled 18 tracks (with "Cop Killer") *Sire 26878/stock/ps/'92* $20
The Radio ep (There Goes the Neighborhood/ Voodoo/Bowels of the Devil/Mommas Gotta Die Tonight/Cop Killer) *Sire 5492/ promo/custom sticker/'92* $20
The Winner Loses *Sire 5647/promo/'92* $5
There Goes the Neighborhood clean & lp *Sire 5333/promo/'92* $5

BOFILL, ANGELA
Heavenly Love 4 versions *Jive 42132/promo/ custom sticker/rear insert/'93* $5
I Wanna Love Somebody edit/lp *Jive 42124/ promo/ps/'93* $5

BOGGUSS, SUZY
Heartache *Liberty 79636/promo/logo on blue/ rear insert/'93* $5
Mr Santa *Capitol 79902/promo/silkscreen/ps/'89* .. $5
Someday Soon *Capitol 79678/promo/'91* $5
Two Step Round the Christmas Tree/I Heard the Bells on Christmas Day *Liberty 79504/ promo/silkscreened/'92* $6

BOGOSIAN, ERIC
If They Ever Knew What I Was Thinking.. 18 track sampler from "Sex Drugs & Rock n Roll" *SBK 05351/promo/ps/'90* $10

BOLIN, TOMMY
A Retrospective (Teaser/People People/Gettin' Tighter + 2) *Geffen 3657/promo/ gatefold hard cover/silkscreened logo* $15

BOLLING, CLAUDE
3 Decades of ep (New York New York/Baroque & Blue/Blue Skies/Africaine/Slavonic Dance) *Milan Entertainment 002/promo/ silkscreened/custom sticker/'93* $7

BOLTON, MICHAEL
Georgia On my Mind single versions edit & single versions *Columbia 73490/promo/ hard cover "box like" ps/'90* $8
How Am I Supposed to Live Without You *Columbia 73017/promo/ps/'89* $7
How Can We Be Lovers single & AC mix *Columbia 73257/promo/silkscreen./ps* $8
Love is a Wonderful Thing *Columbia 73719/promo/ps/'91* $7
Love is a Wonderful Thing 4:43 & 5:29 *Columbia 4015/promo/ps/'91* $8
Missing You Now *Columbia 74184/promo/ps/'92* . $7
Soul Provider *Columbia 1630/promo/ps/'89* $7
Steel Bars *Columbia 74294/promo/ps/'92* $7
The Michael Bolton Story *The Weekly Specials/ Unistar/radio show/promo 12/6-8/91* $25
Time, Love and Tenderness edit & lp *Columbia 73889/promo/ps/'91* $7
To Love Somebody *Columbia 4806/promo/ps* ... $7
To Love Somebody/Now That I Found You *Columbia 38K 74733/stock/ps/'92* $6
Wait on Love *Columbia 1072/promo/ silkscreened purple/ps/'90* $6
When a Man Loves a Woman *Columbia 74020/ promo/ps/'91* $7
When Im Back on My Feet Again (remix) *Columbia 73342/promo/ps/'90* $8

BOMB THE BASS
Beat Dis (4 versions) *4th & Broadway 462/promo/ silkscreened pic/rear insert/'88* $8
Love So True 3 vers/You See me In 3D 2 vers./ Understand This *Rhythm King 40042/ stock/gatefold hardcover ps/'91* $6

BON JOVI
Bad Medicine *Mercury 27/promo/ps/'88* $12
Bad Medicine (edit)/99 in the Shade *Mercury 870 657/CD 3" stock w/ps* $10
Bed of Roses edit & lp *Mercury 838/promo/ silkscreened/ps/'92* $8
Born to Be My Baby/Love for Sale *Mercury 872 156/stock/3"/ps/'88* $15
I'll Sleep When I'm .. edit/lp/live *Jambco 939/ promo/silkscreened/ps/'93* $8
In These Arms edit/lp/live *Mercury 837/promo/ silkscreened/'93* $8
Keep the Faith edit & lp *Jambco 772/promo/ gatefold hardcover ps/silkscreen pic/'92* ... $8
Keep the Faith/I Wish Everyday Could Be Like Christmas/Living in Sin (live) *Mercury 864 433/stock/ps/'92* $6
Lay Your Hands on Me edit & lp *Mercury 87/ promo/silkscreened pic/ps/'89* $12
Living in Sin *Mercury 131/promo/silkscreen/'89* .. $8
Never Say Goodbye audio&video/Social Disease/ Edge of a Broken Heart/Raise Your Hands (last 3 audio only) *Mercury 870 702/ stock/ps/audio & video/'87* $25
Wanted Dead Or Alive short & long & live & acoustic *Mercury 01/promo/ps/'87* $25

BON JOVI, JON
Blaze of Glory edit & lp *Mercury 279/promo/ silkscreened/ps/'90* $8
Blaze of Glory/You Really Got Me Now *Mercury 875 896/stock/ps/'90* $6
Miracle edit & lp *Mercury 331/promo/ps/'90* ... $8

BONE CLUB
Beautiflu ep (Everything's on Fire/Arrive/It's Not Alright/Slomo/Slippin/Hubris) *Imago 72787 21013/stock/ps/'92* $5

BONEDADDYS, THE
Shoorah Shoorah *Chameleon 86/promo/ silkscreened logo/'90* $5

BONGIOVI, JODI
Keep the Light Burning remix *Alpha International 79838/promo/ silkscreened/ps/'89* $4
Somebody to Love *Alpha International 79731/ promo/ps/'89* $4

BONHAM
Bringing Me Down *WTG 2005/promo/logo silkscreened/rear insert/'89* $5
Change of a Season *WTG 4331/ promo/silkscreened/ps/'92* $5
Guilty *WTG 1912/promo/rear insert/'89* $5
Guilty edit & lp *WTG 1970/promo/rear insert/'89* . $5
Wait For You 3:54/5:01 *WTG 1859/promo/ rear insert/'89* $5
Wait For You (4 vers.) *WTG 1768/promo/ps/'89* $6

BONILLA, MARC
Slaughter on Memory Lane short/kinda short/ orig.artist intention *Reprise 5419/promo/'91* $6
White Noise *Reprise 5047/promo/'91* $5

BONNEY, SIMON
There Can Only Be One/Sun Don't Shine/ A Part of You/Caesar Needs a Brutus *Mute 8588/promo/silkscreened/ps/'92* $6

BOO RADLEYS
Boo! Forever ep (Does This Hurt?/Boo! Forever/ Buffalo Bill/Sunfly II) *Columbia 4801/promo/ps/'92* $6
Lazy Day/Vegas/Feels Like Tomorrow/Whiplashed .. *Columbia 4659/promo/ps/'92* $6

BOO YAA T.R.I.B.E.
Psyko Funk remix & lp *4th & B'way 510/ promo/rear insert/'90* $6
Rumors of a Dead Man edit *Hollywood Basic 10229/promo/silkscreened pic/'92* $6
Walk the Line edit & lp clean *4th Bway 518/ promo/ps/'90* $6

BOOGERMAN, THE
The Boogerman/Boogerman's Christmas Jam *Profile 7388/promo/silkscreened/ rear insert/'92* $6

BOOGIE DOWN PRODUCTIONS
13 and Good lp/remix/instrumental *Jive 42022/promo/rear insert/'92* $8
Duck Down 3 versions/We In There 2 versions/ Like a Throttle/Essays on BDP-ism *Jive 01241-42021/stock/ps/ silkscreened/'91* $6
Love's Gonna Getcha edit/extended soft/ext.hard *Jive 1367/promo/rear insert/'90* $8
We In There remix/lp/instrumental *Jive 42070/ promo/custom sticker/rear insert/'92* $8
Why Is That?/Jah Rulez/Who Protects Us From You?/You Must Learn/World Peace/ Self Destruction *Jive 1257/ promo/booklet ps/'89* $10

BOOK OF LOVE
Alice Everyday (4 versions) *Sire 4479/promo/'91* .$6
Alice Everyday (4 versions)/With a Little Love '90 versions/Candy Carol *Sire 21767/stock/ps/'90* $6
Counting the Rosaries 5 vers./Sunny Day 2 vers. ... *Sire 40240/gatefold hardcover ps/ stock/'91* $6
Hunny Hunny 3 versions *Sire 6332/promo/ silkscreened pic/'93* $6
Lullaby 7" versions/7" remix/pleasant dream mix/ insomnia mix *Sire 3355/promo/'88* $8
Pretty Boys & Pretty Girls (3 versions)/ Tubular Bells/interview *Sire 3197/ promo/rear insert/silkscreened/'88* $8
Sunny Day (remix) *Sire 4805/promo/ custom sticker/'91* $6

BOOKER T & THE MGS
Green Onions *Atco 3994/promo/ silkscreened logo/ps/'91* $7

BOOKER, CHUCKII
Games edit & lp *Atlantic 4766/promo/ silkscreened/ps/'92* $8
Touch 4 vers. *Atlantic 2857/promo/rear insert* $7
With All My Heart 4 versions *Atlantic 5140/ promo/rear insert* $7

BOOM CRASH OPERA
Her Charity *WB 2925/promo/ps* $4
Onion Skin lp & extended *WB 3967/promo/ ps/silkscreened logo on red/'90* $5
Talk About It/Dancing in the Storm *WB 4481/promo/'90* $5
These Here are Crazy Times (10 tracks) *WB 9 26160/promo/box ps/ bonus cassette/'90* $15

BOOM SHAKA
Jah Mek it Rock dance/radio/lp *Liberty 79444/ promo/silkscreened/rear insert/'92* $5

BOONE, LARRY
Everybody Wants to Hank Williams *Mercury 169/promo/silkscreened/'90* $5
Too Blue to Be True *Mercury 236/promo/ silkscreened/'90* $5

BOOTSAUCE
Love Monkey #9 edit & lp *Island 6716/promo/logo on yellow/ps/'92* ..$5
Reboot ep (Play With Me/Everyones a Winner 3 versions/Scratching the Whole 2 vers.) *Vertigo 510 118/stock/ps/ custom sticker/'92* $6
Rollercoaster's Child/Everyone's a Winner/Big, Bad & Groovy (last 2 live) *Island 6734/ promo/logo/custom sticker/'92* $6
Scratching the Whole (5 versions) *Next Plateau 50138/promo/'90* $6

BOSTON
Boston/In the Studio *dj radio show/promo/ hosted by TOM SHOLZ* $25
More Than a Feeling/Foreplay-Long Time *Epic 34K 02355/stock/3"* $6

BOUNCE THE OCEAN
Wasting My Time *Private 81001/ promo/silkscreened/rear insert/'91* $6

BOURGEOIS, BRENT

Can't Feel the Pain (edit) *Charisma 007/ promo/ps/'90* $5
Dare to Fall in Love single & lp *Charisma 001/ promo/box container/'90* $12
Funky Little Nothing *Charisma 14189/promo/ logo on orange/rear insert/'92* $5
I Dont Mind at All/Pencil & Paper *Island 2103/promo/ps/'87* $5
Time of the Season *Charisma 015/promo/ ps/silkscreened logo/'90* $5

This promotional CD contains two tracks from each of the first three releases in the SOUND+VISION series— including one bonus track from each album.

From **SPACE ODDITY** (RCD 10131/RALP/RACS)

1 Space Oddity 5:13
2 Conversation Piece 3:05 1970 B-side of "Prettiest Star"

From **THE MAN WHO SOLD THE WORLD** (RCD 10132/RALP/RACS)

3 All The Madmen 5:37
4 Holy Holy 2:20 Single A-side from 1970

From **HUNKY DORY** (RCD 10133/RALP/RACS)

5 Changes 3:33
6 Bombers 2:38 Previously unreleased track recorded 1971

RYKODISC
Promotion/Marketing
Pickering Wharf, Bldg. C-3G
Salem MA 01970
508 744 7678
508 741 4506 fax

RYKODISC
Sales/Distribution
200 N. 3rd Ave.
Minneapolis MN 55401
612 375 9162
612 375 0272 fax

BOWIE, DAVID

8 From Sound & Vision *Ryko S&V PRO 2/promo/ silkscreened disc & weird plastic insert cover/rear insert/'89* $20
Bang Bang live&studio/Modern Love/Loving the Alien *Manhattan 31593/promo/ps* $20
Black Tie White Noise chr mix 1/chr mix 2/ churban/urban/lp edit *Savage 50046/ promo/silkscreened/'93* $10
ChangesOneBowie 11 tracks *RCA 1732/stock/ps* $25
Fame 90 5 vers. *Ryko 1018/promo/insert/ps/'90* . $10
Fame 90 lp/queen latifahs rap/house mix *Ryko 04580/promo/ silkscreened/rear insert/'90* $10
Growin' Up *Ryko 9005/promo/silkscreened/ps* .. $12
High Tech Soul Sampl. (6 tracks) *Ryko 9016/ps* $15
Jump They Say 3 brothers mixes/leftfield remix/lp edit *no label or #/promo/'93* .. $12
Jump They Say 4 versions/I Feel Free *Savage 50036/promo/silkscreened/ps* ... $10
Jump They Say edit & single *Savage 50039/ promo/silkscreened/ps/'93* $8
Jump They Say rock mix/single edit *Savage 50044/promo/logo on green/'93* . $10
Miracle Goodnight *Savage 50048/promo/ silkscreened pic/'93* $10
Never Let Me Down edit/ext./lp/dub/acappella/ instrum. *EMI 31352/promo/ps/'87* $20
Real Cool World 6 versions *WB 40575/stock/ gatefold hardcover ps/'92* $6
Real Cool World edit & lp *WB 5600/promo/'92* .. $4
Round and Round/Sound & Vision: The CD Press Release (narrated by Kurt Loder) *Rykodisc 0120-21-22/promo/ silkscreened/ps/'89* $25
Space Oddity/Conversation Piece/All the Madmen/ Holy Holy/Changes/Bombers *Ryko 131-32-33/promo/ silkscreened pic/ps/'90* $20
World Premiere Weekend Interview *Savage 50043/ 2 cds/booklet ps/"Black Tie" album & interview &"Hist.Collage" (13:32 medl.)* .. $25

BOWIE, DAVID & 808 STATE

Sound and Vision 4 versions *Tommy Boy 510/ stock/ps/'91* $7

BOWIE, DAVID & ADRIAN BELEW

Pretty Pink Rose edit & lp *Atlantic 3294/promo/ gatefold hardcoverps/silkscreened/'90* ... $10

BOWIE, DAVID & ADRIAN BELEW

Pretty Pink Rose/Neptune Pool/ Shoe Salesman/Oh Daddy (Bowie only on 1st cut) *Atlantic 86200/stock/ps/'90* $7

BOWIE, DAVID & ENO

Bowie/Eno sampler 9 tracks (Sound & Vision/ Be My Wife/Some Are/Heroes/Joe the Lion/ Abdulmajid/D.J. +2) *Rykodisc 0142/ promo/ps/'91* $25

BOWIE, DAVID & PHILIP GLASS

Discussions on the "Low" Symphony *Point 662/ promo/silkscreened pic/4 minutes+ of interview/'93* $18

BOWIE, DAVID/TIN MACHINE

Baby Universal edit/extended/BBC live/Stateside BBC live *Victory 588/promo/ logo on blue/'91* $12
Heavens in Here edit & lp *EMI 4375/ promo/silkscreened logo/'89/rear insert* $8
One Shot *Victory 522/promo/trifold hardcover/ silkscreened/'91* $10
Prisoner of Love *EMI 04424/promo/silkscreened Bowie/'89/rear insert* $12
Under the God *EMI 4283/promo/ps/ silkscreened band silhouette/'89* $12

BOX, THE

Inside My Heart *Capitol 79652/promo/ silkscreened/rear insert/'89* $5
Temptation *Capitol 79353/promo/silkscreened/ rear insert/'89* $5

BOY GEORGE

Dont Take My Mind On a Trip 3:55/4:03/5:40/6:37 ... *Virgin 2468/promo/'89* $8

Dont Take My Mind On a Trip 4:02/5:07/3:55/5:2
Virgin 2648/promo/'89 ....$8
Live My Life (4 vers.) *Virgin 2139/promo/ps/'87* ..$10
The Crying Game *SBK 04708/promo/ silkscreened/custom sticker/'93* $8
The Crying Game hot mix *SBK 04732/promo/ logo on cream/'93* $7
Whisper edit & lp *Virgin BOY G/promo/ silkscreened logo/'89* $8
You Found Another Guy edit & 12" *Virgin 2758/ promo/silkscreened logo/'89* $8

BOY KRAZY

Good Times With Bad Boys radio & club
Next Plateau 906/promo/logo on red/ps ...$6
That's What Love Can Do radio & club & dub/ One Things Leads to Another
Next Plateau 857 025/stock/ps/'93 ....$5

BOY MEETS GIRL

Bring Down the Moon 4:15/5:00 *RCA 8807/ promo/gatefold ps w/lyrics/'88* $5

BOYS DONT CRY

We Got the Magic (2 versions)/Love Talk (remix)
Legacy no#/promo/ps $6

BOYS, THE

Doin' It With the B 6 vers. *Motown 3746310592/ promo/ps/'92* $7
I Had a Dream *Motown 1308/promo/ps/'91* $5
Thanx For the Funk 7 versions *Motown 1192/ promo/ps/'90* $7
The Saga Continues edit/lp/instrumental
Motown 3746310232/promo/ps/'92 ....$6

BOYZ II MEN

In the Still of Night *Motown 3746310822/promo* ...$7
It's So Hard to Say Goodbye to Yesterday
Motown 1641/promo/ps/'91 ....$6
Motownphilly 5 versions *Motown 4779/stock/ gatefold hardcover ps/'91* $8
Please Don't Go edit/lp/instrumental
Motown 3746310292/promo/ps/'92 ....$8
Sympin' (Ain't Easy) *Motown/promo/sticker/'92* ..$8
Uhh Ahh lp & instr. *Motown 1006/promo/ps/'91* ..$8
Uhh Ahh 7 versions *Motown 1019/promo/'91* .$10

BRADY, PAUL

Soul Child ac & chr *Fontana 425/promo/ silkscreened/rear insert/'91* $4
Soul Child edit & lp *Fontana 422/promo/ silkscreened/rear insert/'91* $4

BRAGG, BILLY

Accident Waiting to Happen red star versions/ Sulk/The Warmest Room/Revolution (last 2 live) *Elektra 8510/promo/ps/'92* .$10
Sexuality *Elektra 8413/promo/ps/logo on purple* ..$6
You Woke Up My Neighborhood *Elektra 8462/ promo/blue on black silkscreened/rear insert* ..$6
You Woke Up My Neighborhood/Ontario Quebec and Me/Bread and Circuses/ Heart Like a Wheel/Seven and Seven Is
Elektra 66483/stock/gatefold hardcvr ps ...$6

BRAITHWAITE, DARYL

As the Days Go By *CBS 1658/promo/ silkscreened/'89* $4

BRAND NEW HEAVIES

Bonafide Funk 7" edit & mainsource remix
Delicious Vinyl 4892/promo $6
Dream Come True 5 versions *Delicious 2002/ promo/rear insert/'92* $6
Heavy Rhyme Experience radio edit
Delic. Vinyl 4744/promo/rear insert/'92 .....$6
Never Stop *Delicious Vinyl 6673/promo/ logo on purple/rear insert/'91* $5
Stay This Way 8 vers. *Delicious Vinyl 868187/ stock/ps/'91* $6

BRAND NUBIAN

Love Me or Leave Me Alone clean versions
Elektra 8754/promo/silkscreened/'93 ....$5
Love Me or Leave Me Alone remix radio edit
Elektra 8713/promo/silkscreened/ps/'93 ...$5
Slow Down/To the Right (2 versions each)
Elektra 8313/promo/ps/'90 ....$5

BRANDON

Destiny (3 versions) *Alpha International 79527/ promo/ps/'91* $5

BRANIGAN, LAURA

Moonlight on Water 3:45/4:18/7:58
Atlantic 3303/promo/rear insert/'90 ....$7
Moonlight on Water edit & lp
Atlantic 3202/promo/ps/'90 ....$6
Never in a Million Years *Atlantic 3355/promo/ silkscreened on pink/rear insert/'90* $6

BRANNEN, JOHN

Desolation Angel (2 versions)
Apache 79253/promo/ps/'88 ....$4

BRAT PACK, THE

You're the Only Woman 4:02/4:03/7:41/5:09
A&M 17877/promo/silkscreened logo/'89 .$6

BRAXTON, TONI

Another Sad Love Song edit/lp/instrumental
LaFace 4047/promo/ps/silkscreened pic ..$6

BREATHE

All This I Should Have Known
A&M 17746/promo/ps/'88 ....$5
Does She Love That Man? *A&M 75021 7437/ promo/ps/'90* $5
Don't Tell Me Lies *A&M 17664/promo/ silkscreened/ps/'88* $5

How Can I Fall (fade) *A&M 17590/promo/ gatefold hardcover ps/'87* $5
Say a Prayer (6 versions) *A&M 75021 8108/ promo/ps/logo on black/'90* $6
Without Your Love *A&M 75021 7517/promo/ silkscreened logo on green/ps/'91* $5

BREAUX, ZACHARY
Groovin' 4 versions *NYC 4001/promo/ silkscreened/rear insert/'93* $5

BRECKER BROTHERS
Big Idea 3 vers/Give the Drummer Some/ On the Backside *GRP 9993/promo/ps* $5

BRECKER, MICHAEL
Suspone/Everything Happens When You're Gone/ Itsbynne Reel/Talking to Myself *Impulse 17730/promo/'88* $5

BREEDERS, THE
Do You Love Me Now? 2 versions/Safari/ So Sad About Us *Elektra 66432/stock/ silkscreened/gatefold hardcover ps/'92* $5

BRICKELL, EDIE
Black & Blue edit & lp *Geffen 4175/promo/ps* $5
A Hard Rain's Gonna Fall edit & lp *MCA 18117/promo/'89* $6
Circle *Geffen 3480/promo/'88* $6
Love Like We Do *Geffen 3543/promo/ps/'89* $6
Mama Help Me *Geffen 4175/promo/ gatefold hardcover ps/'90* $6
What I Am *Geffen 3221/promo/ps/'88* $10

BRIDGE 2 FAR
Heaven on Earth *WTG 1940/promo/ silkscreened pic/rear insert/'90* $5

BRIGHTMAN, SARAH
Captain Nemo edit & lp *A&M 31458 8114/ promo/gatefold hardcover ps/'93* $7
Love Changes Everything/Anything But Lonely *Polydor 255/promo/silkscreened pic/'90* ... $7
Mr Monotony *Polydor 62/promo/silkscreened/ps* .. $6

BRITNY FOX
Over and Out *Eastwest 4287/promo/ logo on red/rear insert/'91* $5

BRITTON
Hold On lp/remix *TRS/promo'88* $4

BROADCASTERS
Down in the Trenches *Enigma 053/promo/ps/'87* . $5

BROJOS, THE
Live Like a King edit & lp *WB 4081/promo/ rear insert/'90* $4
Slow Motion *WB 4510/promo/'90* $4

BROKEN GLASS
Worst of You Yet *Chrysalis 23500/promo/ps/'90* $5

BROKEN HOMES, THE
Lock & Key edit & lp *MCA 18505/promo/ rear insert/'90* $5

BROOKS & DUNN
Brand New Man/interview/3 radio psas *Arista 2232/promo/silkscreened/ps/'92* ... $15
Lost & Found *Arista 2460/promo/silkscreened/ps* $6
She Used to Be Mine/We'll Burn that Bridge *Arista 2602/promo/ps/logo on red/'93* $6

BROOKS, GARTH
Friends in Low Places/Thunder Rolls (both live) *Liberty 79365/promo/logo on purple/ custom sticker/'92* $15
God Rest Ye Merry Gentlemen/Silent Night *Capitol 79488/promo/silkscreened red & green/'90* $8
In Pieces radio interview *Liberty 79004/promo/ silkscreened/ps/'93* $20
Shameless 3:39 & 4:01 *Capitol 79008/ promo/logo on black/'91* $8
The Old Man's Back in Town *Liberty 79540/ promo/silkscreened/'92* $8
The Thunder Rolls 3:30 & 3:42 *Capitol 79722/ promo/logo on purple/'91* $8
Two of a Kind, Workin' on a Full House *Capitol 79538/promo/logo on green/'91* $8
Unanswered Prayers *Capitol 79382/promo/ silkscreened logo/'90* $8

BROOKS, KAREN & RANDY SHARP
Baby I'm the One 2 versions *Mercury 667/promo/rear insert/'92* $5
That's Another Story *Mercury 790/promo/ logo on blue/rear insert/'92* $5
That's Another Story ep (Baby Im the One/ All I Need/Last Call For Love/ If You Don't Really Love Her/ Thats Another Story) *Mercury 487/ promo/trifold hardcover ps/'92* $8

BROS
Too Much *Epic 73041/promo/silkscreen logo on metallic blue/'89* $5
When Will I Be Famous (3 versions) *Epic 1161/promo/ps/'88* $8

BROTHER BEYOND
Be My Twin (4 vers.) *Capitol 79826/promo/'89* ... $5
Just a Heartbeat Away 3:55/6:39 *EMI 04656/ promo/silkscreened/rear insert/'90* $5
The Girl I Used to Know single vers./power mix/ club mix *EMI 04521/promo/ silkscreened/rear insert/'90* $5

BROTHER CANE
That Don't Satisfy Me edit & lp/Got No Shame *Virgin 14092/promo/rear insert/'93* $5

BROTHERHOOD CREED
Helluva 4 versions *Gasoline Alley 2246/promo/rear insert/'92* $5
Hey Now 5 versions *Gasoline Alley 2254/promo/rear insert/'92* $5

BROTHERS FIGARO, THE
Selections From Gypsy Beat (My Gold Ring/Matinee/Cross Your Heart/My Gold Ring - last 3 live) *Geffen 4119/promo/gatefold hardcover ps/'90* $6

BROWN, BOBBY
Every Little Step (3 versions) *MCA 17768/promo/custom sticker/'89* $10
Get Away 12 vers. *MCA 2545/promo/ps/'93* $10
Good Enough 4 vers. *MCA 2439/promo/ps/'92* ...$8
Good Enough 7 vers. *MCA 2482/promo/ps/'92* $10
Humpin' Around 4 vers. *MCA 54343/stock/ps/'92* $6
Humpin' Around 9 vers. *MCA 2350/promo/ps* ..$10
Humpin' Around rap/non rap/humpstrumental *MCA 2135/promo/ps/'92* $8
On Our Own (3 versions) *MCA 17867/promo/custom sticker/'89* $10
Roni *MCA 17760/promo/custom sticker/'88* $6
That's the Way Love Is single vers.without rap/single/lp *MCA 2682/promo/rear insert* $6
That's the Way Love Is 8 versions *MCA 2660/promo/ps/'93* $8
That's the Way Love Is 9 versions *MCA 2623/promo/ps/'93* $10

BROWN, BOBBY/B. BROWN POSSE
Drop It On the One edit/lp/instrumental *MCA 2524/promo/ps/'93* $8

BROWN, GARY
Don't Make Me Beg Tonight 8 versions *Capitol 79092/promo/ps/'92* $6

BROWN, JAMES
(So Tired of Standing Still We Got To) Move On 5 versions *Scotti Bros 72392 75286/stock/ps/'91* $8
(So Tired of Standing Still ..) Move On edit & lp *Scotti Bros 75286/promo/silkscreened pic/'91* $8
How Long 5 versions *Scotti Brothers 75364/promo/silkscreened/ps/'93* $8
I'm Real 7" & 12" & FF Hyped Up Mix/Tribute *Scotti Brothers 1116/promo/'88* $10
It's Time to Love *Scott Bros 75295/promo/silkscreened James/rear insert/'91* $8
Papas Got a Brand New Bag pt 1 lp & live/Stay in School psa/Night Train/Get Up/drug abuse psa/Hot/1970 tour spot *Polydor 356/promo/silkscreened/'91* $15
Say it Loud - I'm Black I'm Proud B-Proud edit/sell out edit/extended *Polydor 454/promo/silkscreened/'91* $15

BROWN, JULIE
Girl Fight Tonight! (3 remixes) *Sire 3092/promo/ps/'88* $6

BROWN, MARTY
Every Now and Then *MCA 54118/promo/ps/'91* ..$5
Wildest Dreams *MCA 54252/promo/rear insert/'91* $5

BROWN, NORMAN
Love's Holiday edit & lp *Mojazz 374631079/promo/ps/'92* $6
Too High edit & lp & boyz ii men mix + 4 excerpts *Mojazz 374631035/promo/ps/'92* $6

BROWN, SAM
Stop (edit) *A&M 17642/promo/'88* $4

BROWN, SAWYER
Somewhere in the Night *Capitol 79110/promo/ps* $4

BROWN, SHIRLEY
Lets Make Love Tonight *Malaco 2179/promo/'92* $5

BROWNE, JACKSON
Anything Can Happen edit & lp *Elektra 8095/promo/'89* $7
Chasing You Into Light *Elektra 8117/promo/'89* ..$6
World in Motion *Elektra 8085/promo* $7

BROWNE, JACKSON & JENNIFER WARNES
Golden Slumbers *Hollywood 10037/promo/silkscreened/'92* $6

BRUBECK, DAVE/MISHA SEGAL
Quiet as the Moon/Zombooka 8 tracks *Musicmasters 01612-65070/promo/ps/'91* $6

BRUCE, JACK
No Surrender! *Epic 1874/promo/silkscreened red* .$7
Somethin Els (9 tracks) *CMP 6055/promo/ps/ERIC CLAPTON/'93* $18

BRYANT, SHARON
Body Talk (6 vers.) *Wing 187/promo/silkscreen* ..$6
Foolish Heart edit & lp *Wing 114/promo/silkscreened pic/'89* $6
Let Go (5 versions) *Wing 49/promo/ps/silkscreened/'89* $6
Can You Stop the Rain *Columbia 73745/promo/ps/'91* $5
Closer Than Close single & lp *Columbia 73925/promo/ps/'91* $5
Come on Over Tonight *Elektra 2252/promo/'88* ..$5
Lost in the Night remix *Columbia 73990/promo/logo on black/ps/'91* $5

Shower You With Love edit & lp
Columbia 74290/promo/ps/'91 .... $5

BRYSON, PEABO & REGINA BELLE
A Whole New World *Columbia 74751/promo/ "Aladdin" ps/'92* $5

BTO
Not Fragile/In the Studio *dj radio show/promo/ hosted by RANDY BACHMAN* $20

BUCK NAKED
Selftitled 12 tracks
Heyday 033/stock/ps/'92 .... $20

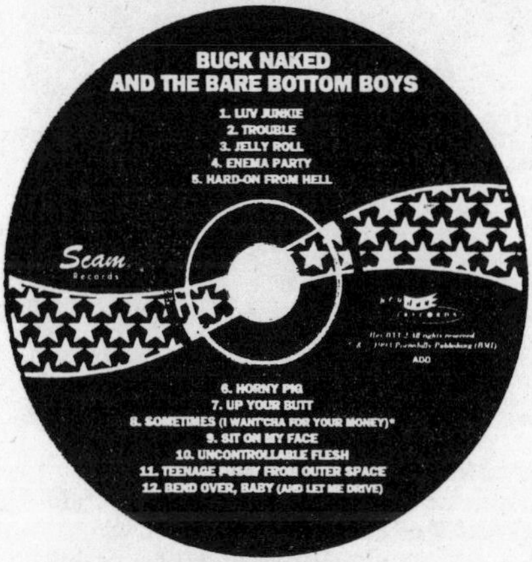

BUCK NAKED
AND THE BARE BOTTOM BOYS
1. LUV JUNKIE
2. TROUBLE
3. JELLY ROLL
4. ENEMA PARTY
5. HARD-ON FROM HELL
6. HORNY PIG
7. UP YOUR BUTT
8. SOMETIMES (I WANT'CHA FOR YOUR MONEY)*
9. SIT ON MY FACE
10. UNCONTROLLABLE FLESH
11. TEENAGE PUSSY FROM OUTER SPACE
12. BEND OVER, BABY (AND LET ME DRIVE)

BUCKINGHAM, LINDSEY
Countdown edit & lp *Reprise 5526/promo/'92* $4
Countdown soft mix *Reprise 5758/promo/'92* $5
Don't Look Down single versions
Reprise 6163/promo/'92 .... $4
Soul Drifter *Reprise 5828/promo/'92* $4
Words & Music (A Retrospective) 11 tracks + interspersed interview *Reprise 5482/ promo/ps/'92* $15
Wrong lp & edit *Reprise 5450/promo/ logo on brown/rear insert/'92* $4

BUCKWHEAT ZYDECO
My Lil Girl/On a Night Like.. *Island 2146/promo/ps* . $6

BUFFET, JIMMY
Carnival World *MCA 18045/promo/'89* $8
Another Saturday Night *MCA 54680/ promo/silkscreened/ps/'93* $6
Boats, Beaches, Bars &Ballads sampler (Volcano/ Livingston Satur. Night/Ragtop Day+13)
MCA 3031/promo/ps/'92 .... $15
Take Another Road *MCA 17897/promo/ custom sticker/'89* $8

BUGNON, ALEX
Piano in the Dark lp & 7"/Time is Running Out 7"
Orpheus 04220/promo/custom sticker/'88 $6

BULLENS, CINDY
Breakin' the Chain *MCA 17899/promo/ custom sticker/'89* $5

BULLET BOYS
12 Minute Warning ep (The Rising/When Pigs Fly/ The Show/Laughing With the Dead)
WB 6224/promo/rear insert/'93 .... $6
For the Love of Money edit & lp
WB 3393/promo/silkscreened/'89 .... $5
Hang on St. Christopher *WB 4779/ promo/silkscreened/'91* $5
Smooth Up *WB 3251/promo/rear insert/'88* $4
Smooth Up *WB 3251/promo/rear insert/ silkscreened/'88* $5
Talk to Your Daughter *WB 4937/promo/'91* $5
THC Groove *WB 4695/promo/silkscreened/'91* $5

BULLET LAVOLTA
My Protector/Over the Shoulder/Alright
RCA 62198/promo/ps/'92 .... $5

BURCH SISTERS, THE
Honey You Wont Break Me *Mercury 216/ promo/silkscreened/'90* $5

BURDON, ERIC
Run For Your Life Animal remix/extended mix/lp edit/instrumental *Striped Horse 615/ promo/silkscreened* $7
Run For Your Life extended/edit/instrumental
Striped Horse 1215/promo/ps/'88 .... $7
Sixteen Tons *Rhino 90041/promo/ps/'90* $7

BURKE, SOLOMON
Try a Little Tenderness *Bizarre Straight 90113/ promo/silkscreened/rear insert/'91* $6

BURNETT, T BONE
Criminals *Columbia 4631/promo/logo on red/ps* ... $6
The Killer Moon *Columbia 2908/promo/ps* $6
Wild Truth remix *Columbia 1122/promo/ps/'88* $6

BURNETTE, BILLY
Nothin' to Do *WB 5245/promo/'92* $5
Tangled Up in Texas *Capricorn 5931/promo/ps* ... $5
Tangled Up in Texas lp/dance *Capricorn 5702/ promo/ps/'92* $6
The Bigger the Love *Capricorn 6322/promo/ps* $5

BURNETTE, DORSEY
Very Very Best of Dorsey Burnette (27 tracks)
Chrys.21913/promo/ps/silkscreened/'91 . $15

BURNING TREE
Fly On *Epic 2035/promo/ silkscreened/rear insert/'90* $4

Live From Leeds (Burning Tree/Fly On/Mistreated Lover/Same Old Story) *Epic 2191/ promo/hardcover ps/'90* $7

BUSH, KATE

Cloudbusting lp & meterological mix/The Man With the Child in His Eyes/Sat In Your Lap .. *EMI 79002/promo/ps/'86* $25
Love and Anger *Columbia 1859/promo/ gatefold hardcover/silkscreened/'89* $20
Rocket Man *Polydor 589/promo/'91* $10
This Woman's Work *Columbia 2029/promo/ps* ... $10

BUTCHER, JON

Might As Well Be Free *Capitol 79525/promo/ silkscreened white w/logo/'89* $5
Send Me Somebody *Capitol 79510/promo/'89* .. $5

BUTLER, JERRY

Angel Flying Too Close../You're the Only One *Urgent 269/promo/logo on gold/'92* $6

BUTLER, JONATHAN

More Than Friends (single edit) *RCA 1174/promo/ps/'88* $4
Sarah, Sarah *RCA 1216/promo/ps/'89* $4

BUTTHOLE SURFERS

Independent Worm Saloon sampler (14 tracks - "except the ones with the swear words in them") *Capitol 79692/promo/cust.sticker* $12
The Hurdy Gurdy Man 2 versions/Barking Dogs *Rough Trade RUS 97/stock/ps/'90* $5
Who Was In My Room ..? edit *Capitol 79611/ promo/silkscreened/ps/'93* $6
Who Was In My Room Last Night? edit/ thompson-barbiero remix edit *Capitol 79740/promo/silkscreened/ custom sticker/'93* $6
You Don't Know Me *Capitol 79787/promo/ silkscreened/custom sticker/'93* $6

BUZZIN' COUSINS

Sweet Suzanne *Mercury 626/promo/ logo on blue/ps/'92* $5

BY ALL MEANS

Love Lies edit/extended/lp *Motown 3746310422/ promo/rear insert/'92* $5

BYRD, TRACY

Someone to Give My Love to *MCA 54497/promo/ gatefold hardcover ps/logo on black/'93* ... $6

BYRDS, THE

Early Byrds radio show *In the Studio 133/ promo/cue sheet/hosted by David Crosby, R.McGuinn and Chris Hillman* ... $25
Love That Never Dies *Columbia 2227/promo/ logo on red/ps/'90* $8

BYRNE, DAVID

Dirty Old Town *Sire 3929/promo/'89* $4
Forestry ep (Ava 3 vers./Ninevah industrial mix/ Machu Picchu) *WB 40177/stock/ gatefold hardcover ps/'91* $6
Girls on My Mind *Luaka Bop 5347/promo/'92* $4
Hanging Upside Down edit & lp *Luaka Bop 5530/promo/'92* $4
Interview w/BELEZA TROPICAL doing Brazil classics *Sire 3467/promo/rear insert/ custom sticker/'89* $12

She's Mad edit & lp *Luaka Bop 5290/ promo/silkscreened/ps/'92* $5
Words & Music from Luaka (54:04) *Sire 3820/ promo/silkscreened/rear insert/'89* $12

BYRNE, DAVID & JODY WATLEY

Don't Fence Me In/After You *Chrysalis 23626/ promo/ps/silkscreened/'90* $6

C & C MUSIC FACTORY

Gonna Make You Sweat 6:50/5:00/4:54 *Columbia 44K 73605/ps/stock/'90* $8
Gonna Make You Sweat (3 versions) *Columbia 73604/promo/ps/'90* $10
Here We Go (6 versions) *Columbia 73690/promo/ps/'91* $10
Just a Touch of Love radio mix/hot radio/ radio without rap *Columbia 74033/ promo/silkscreened/ps/'91* $8
Keep It Comin' 3:20/3:56/4:17 *Columbia 74432/promo/logo on red/'92* $7
Things That Make You Go Hmmm... 6 versions *Columbia 73687/promo/ps/'91* $12
Things That Make You Go Ummm.. 5 versions *Columbia 4123/promo/silkscreened/ps* $10
Things That Make You Go Ummmm 6 versions *Columbia 44K 73688/stock/ps/'91* $8

C'VELLO

Turn You On 5 versions *RCA 62148/promo/ silkscreen/rear insert/custom sticker/'91* $6

CAFFERTY, JOHN
Pride & Passion *Scotti Bros 1662/promo/ silkscreened pic/'89* $5
Runnin' Thru the Fire.. *Scotti Bros. 1858/promo/ silkscreened/'89* $5

CAGES, THE
Hometown *Capitol 79550/promo/logo on black/ps* $5
Too Tired *Capitol 79427/promo/silkscreened pic* .$5

CALDWELL, BOBBY
A Collection of Songs 10 tracks *Sin Drome/promo/ps/'91* $15
Don't Lead Me On/Stuck on You *Sin Drome SDC4/promo/rear insert/'91* $5
Even Now 4:22 & 5:05 *Sin Drome 3/promo/'89* ...$5
Janet radio/short urban/long urban *Sin Drome SD 8/promo/silkscreened/'91* ..$6
Real Thing *Sin Drome/promo/'90* $5

CALDWELL, TOY
Midnight Promises edit & lp *Cabin Fever 102/ promo/ps/GREGG ALLMAN, WILLIE NELSON, CHARLIE DANIELS, more/'92* .$7
Selftitled 12 tracks *Cabin Fever 100/promo/ die cut trifold cover/'92* $15

CALE, J.J.
Hold On Baby edit & lp *Silvertone 1319/promo/ps/'90* $6
No Time *Silvertone 1356/promo/ps/'90* ...$6

CALL, THE
Let the Day Begin *MCA 17851/promo/ custom sticker/'89* $5
Like You've Never Been Loved *MCA 1178/ promo/rear insert/'90* $5
What's Happened to.. *MCA 1008/promo/ps/'90* ...$5
When *MCA 18002/promo/'89* $5
You Run edit & lp *MCA 18012/promo/'89* $5

CALLOWAY
All the Way 4 versions *Solar 2110/promo/'90* $6
I Desire You 4 versions *Solar 74550/promo/ps* ..$6
I Wanna Be Rich 7" & extended *Epic 74005/ promo/ps/'89* $8
I Wanna Be Rich radio edit *Epic 2033/ promo/silkscreened/'89* $6
Let's Get Smooth 4 versions *Epic 74541/promo/ logo on blue/'92* $6
Sir Lancelot vocal & instrumental *Epic 74008/ promo/rear insert/'90* $6

CAMEO
Close Quarters edit & lp *Polygram 297/ promo/silkscreened/'90* $6
Emotion.Violenceedit & lp *Reprise 5224/promo* ..$6
I Want It Now 5 versions *Atlanta Artists 262/promo/'90* $7
Money 5 vers/Front Street *Reprise 40392/ stock/gatefold hardcover ps/'92* $6
Raw But Tasty 5 vers. *Reprise 5625/promo/'92* .$7
Real Men Wear Black 9 tracks *Atlanta Artists 846 297/promo/ gatefold velvety cover/'90* $15
That Kind of Guy edit & lp *Reprise 5431/promo* ..$5

CAMOUFLAGE
Heaven (I Want You) (4 versions) *Atlantic 3851/ promo/silkscreened green/ps/'91* $6
Love is a Shield 3:57/5:20/8:09 *Atlantic 2750/promo/rear insert/'88* $8
That Smiling Face (4 versions) *Atlantic 2664/promo/rear insert/'88* $6
The Great Commandment single version & 12" *Atlantic 2508/promo/rear insert/'88* $5

CAMPBELL, GLEN
Somebody Like That 10 tracks *Liberty 97962/ promo/silkscreened/'92* $15

CAMPBELL, JOHN
Ain't Afraid of Midnight edit/interview & excerpts from "Howlin' Mercy" *Elektra 8700/ promo/silkscreened/ps/'93* $10
Devil in My Closet edit & lp *Elektra 8595/ promo/ps/logo on black/'91* $5
When the Levee Breaks edit & lp *Elektra 8746/ promo/silkscreened/'93* $5
Wild Streak fade *Elektra 8417/ promo/silkscreened/ps/'91* $5

CAMPBELL, TEVIN
Alone With You edit & lp *Qwest 5484/promo/'91* .$5
Confused 7 versions *Qwest 40756/stock/ gatefold hardcover ps/'93* $6
Confused 7 versions *Qwest 5922/promo/'91* $7
Confused edit with rap/edit without/lp *Qwest 5743/promo/'91* $6
Goodbye edit without rap/lp *Qwest 5318/promo/'91* $5
Goodbye hakeem's remix & 12" dub *Qwest 5461/promo/'91* $6
Just Ask Me To *Qwest 4858/promo/'91* $5
One Song *Qwest 5623/promo/'91* $5
Round and Round *Paisley Park 4348/promo/ rear insert/'90* $5
Round and Round (4 vers.) *Paisley Park 21740/ stock/gatefold hardcover ps/'90* $6
Strawberry Letter 23 10 versions *Qwest 40569/stock/'91* $6
Strawberry Letter 23 4 versions *Qwest 5441/promo/'91* $7
Strawberry Letter 23 - 10 versions *Qwest 40569/ stock/gatefold hardcover ps/'91* $6
Tell Me What You Want Me to Do edit & lp *Qwest 5070/promo/silkscreened pic/'91* ...$6

CAMPBELL, TISHA
Love Me Down 4 versions *Capitol 79604/promo/ silkscreened/ps/'92* $6
Push 3 versions *Capitol 79516/promo/ps/'92* ...$7

CAMPER VAN BEETHOVEN
(I Was Born in a) Laundromat (edit)
Virgin 3118/promo/silkscreened/'89..........$6
Pictures of Matchstick Men (edit)
Virgin 2865/promo/silkscreened/'89..........$6
Pictures of Matchstick Men (remix)
Virgin 3024/promo/silkscreened logo/'89..$7
Turquoise Jewelry/Waka
Virgin 2471/promo/silkscreened/'88..........$7

CANDI
Saving all the Love (edit) *IRS 67049/promo/ logo on grey*..........$5
The World Just Keeps on Turning (5 versions)
IRS 67031/promo/silkscreened/ rear insert/'90..........$5

CANDLEBOX
Change edit & lp *Maverick 6250/promo/ custom sticker/'93*..........$6
Change lp & edit/Don't You/Mother's Dream
Maverick 6239/promo/rear insert/ custom sticker/'93..........$6
Change/Don't You/Mother's .. Maverick 6253/
promo/custom sticker/'93..........$6

CANDY SKINS, THE
Everybody Loves You *DGC 4526/promo/ps/'93* .$4
For What It's Worth chr remix & edit *DGC 4346/ promo/logo on blue/ps/'91*..........$5
Submarine Song *DGC 4235/promo/ps/'91*.......$4
Submarine Song/Freedom Bus/She Blew Me Away..
DGC 4241/promo/silkscreened/ gatefold hardcover ps/'91..........$6
Wembley *DGC 4471/promo/silkscreened/ps/'92*$4

CANDYFLIP
Redhills Road 3 vers. *Atlantic 3953/promo/ps/'90* $7
Strawberry Fields Forever 4:19 & 5:51
Atlantic 3412/promo/silkscreened/ps/'90..$5

CANDYLAND
Fountain o Youth edit & hands on mix
Eastwest 4066/promo/silkscreened/ rear insert/'91..........$6

CANDYMAN
Candyman Theme remix/lp/instrumental
Epic 4104/promo/silkscreened/ rear insert/'91..........$5
Knockin' Boots radio & 12"/Keep on Watcha Doin'
Epic 73450/promo/ps/'90..........$5
Nightgown 4 versions *Epic 73721/promo/ silkscreened/'91*..........$5
Oneighundredskytalkpinelevenotowo.. edit & lp/Everybody Wanna Be a Rappa
Epic 4220/promo/ps/silkscreened/'91.......$5

CAPALDI, JIM
Some Come Running(edit *Island 2675/promo/'88* .$5

CAPTAIN HOLLYWOOD PROJECT
More & More 4 vers. *a 72787-25028/ps/stock*....$5

CARA, IRENE & FREDDIE JACKSON
Love Survives *Curb 10570/promo/logo on blue/ "All Dogs Go to Heaven" ps/'89*..........$6

CARD, MICHAEL
We Will Find Him *Sparrow 1296/promo/ silkscreened/ps*..........$5

CAREY, MARIAH
Dreamlover *Columbia 5324/promo/ps/'93*.........$7
Emotions *Columbia 73977/promo/ps/'91*.......$8
I Don't Wanna Cry edit & lp *Columbia 73743/ promo/ps/'91*..........$8
I'll Be There MTV unplugged single
Columbia 74330promo/ps/'92..........$10
Love Takes Time *Columbia 73455/promo/ps/'90* .$8
Make it Happen 6 vers. *Columbia 44K 74189/ stock/ps/custom sticker/'92*..........$6
Make It Happen edit & lp *Columbia 74239/ promo/silkscreened pic/ps/'92*..........$8
Profile 33:50/Interview Responses 6:55
Columbia 3087/promo/ps with cues/'91..$22
Someday (4 vers.) *Columbia 73561/promo/ps/'90*.$8
The Weekly Specials/The Mariah Carey Story
Unistar/(1/24-26/92)/promo..........$25
Vision of Love *Columbia 73346/promo/ silkscreened pic/multi fold hardcover ps* $15
Vision of Love (10 songs) *Columbia 45202/ promo only tri fold hardcover/'90*..........$25

CARLISLE, BELINDA
(We Want) the Same.. (edit) *MCA 1053/promo/ silkscreened logo on green/rear insert/'89* $6
Do You Feel Like I Feel edit & lp
MCA 1570/promo/ps/'91..........$6
Leave a Light On *MCA 17984/promo/'89*..........$6
Live Your Life Be Free edit & lp
MCA 2087/promo/rear insert/'92..........$6
Summer Rain *MCA 18118/promo/'89*..........$6
Summer Rain 4:10/4:08/8:00
MCA 18171/promo/'90..........$8
Vision of You *MCA 18304/promo/rear insert/'89*..$6

CARLTON, LARRY
Josie lp&edit *MCA 17812/promo/gatefold ps/'89* .$6
Minute by Minute *MCA 53119/promo/ps/ '87/with MICHAEL MCDONALD*..........$6
On Solid Ground *MCA 17975/promo/'89*.......$5
Ringing the Bells of Christmas/Winter Wonderland ...
MCA 18057/promo/silkscreened/ rear insert/'89..........$6

CARLTON, LARRY & YELLOWJACKETS
Discovery & Four Corners sampler (4 tracks each) ..
MCA 17344/promo/ps/'87..........$15

CARMEN, ERIC
My Heart Stops *Arista 2264/promo/ps/'91*.......$6

CARMEN, ERIC & MERRY CLAYTON
Almost Paradise *RCA 8917/promo/'89* $6

CARNES, KIM
Crazy in Love *MCA 17670/promo/ps/'88* $6
Crazy in Love orig. & newly recorded
MCA 17683/promo/ps/'88 ....$7
Don't Cry Now single & lp *EMI 04736/promo/silkscreened/ps/'93* $5
Everybody Needs Someone
Ossum Possum/promo/ps/'90 ....$5
Gypsy Honeymoon *EMI 04655/promo/silkscreened/ps/'93* $5

CARPENTER, KAREN
If I Had You *A&M 17926/promo/silkscreen/'89* ..$12

CARPENTER, MARY CHAPIN
Going Out Tonight *Columbia 74038/promo/silkscreened pic/rear insert/'91* $5
Down at the Twist and Shout *Columbia 73838/promo/silkscreened/rear insert/'91* $5
Down at the Twist and Shout (extended)
Columbia 2263/promo/silkscreened/rear insert/'90 ....$7
Passionate Kisses *Columbia 4916/promo/ps/'92* .$5
State of the Heart (11 tracks)
Columbia 1741/promo/ps/'89 ....$12
The Hard Way *Columbia 74930/promo/rear insert/'92* $5
You Win Again *Columbia 73567/promo/rear insert/'90* $5

CARPENTERS
7 song sampler (Close to You/Still Crazy../Let Me Be the ../We've Only Just Begun/My Body Keeps Changing.. + 2)
A&M 75021 7246/promo/logo on brown silkscreened/'91 ....$15
Let Me Be the One *A&M 75021 7308/promo/silkscreened/ps/'91* $8

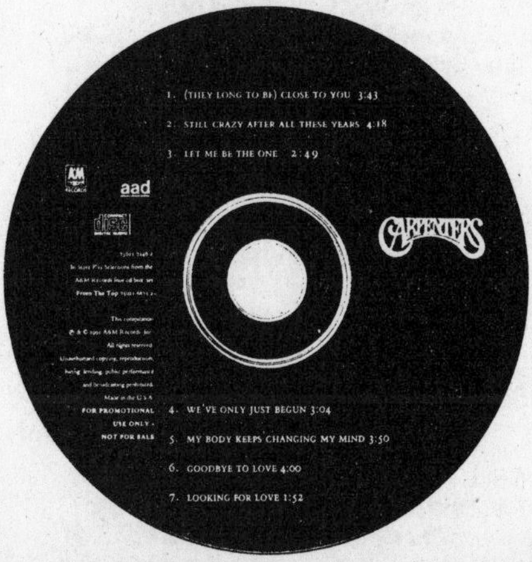

CARRACK, PAUL
Battlefield (4 versions) *Chrysalis 23484/promo/rear insert/'89* $6
I Live by the Groove (3 versions) *Chrysalis 23427/promo/custom sticker/'89* $6

CARRACK, PAUL & TERRI NUNN
Romance *Columbia 1514/promo/'89* $6

CARRADINE, KEITH
Look Around/Never Met a Man I Didn't Like
Columbia 4225/promo/ps/'91 ....$5

CARRERAS, JOSE & SARAH BRIGHTMAN
Amigos Para Siempre english & spanish/Opening Ceremony - Barcelona Games
Atlantic 4702/promo/logo on blue/ps/'92 ...$6

CARRERE, TIA
Why You Wanna Break .. *Reprise 5418/promo/'92*$5

CARRINGTON, TERRI LYNE
More Than Woman single & lp *Verve Forecast/promo/silkscreened pic/'89* $5
Real Life Story (special radio edition)
Verve Forecast TLC 2/promo/ps/'89/full length version with special edits $12

CARROLL, DINA
So Close 4 versions *A&M 31458 8098/promo/logo on red/gatefold hardcover ps/'92* $6
So Close edit & lp *A&M 31458 8085/promo/gatefold hardcover ps/logo on red/'93* $6
Special Kind of Love 4 ver. *A&M 31458 8147/promo/logo on brown/ps/'93* $6

CARS, THE
Coming Up You *Elektra 2171/promo/ps/'87* $7

CARTER
The Only Living Boy in New Cross/Panic
Chrysalis 19757/stock/ps/'92 ....$5

CARTER U.S.M.
Anytime, Anyplace, Anywhere *Chrysalis 23798/promo/rear insert/'91* $4

CARTER, BETTY
Droppin' Things/Memories of You *Verve BET 2/promo/silkscreened pic/'90* $7

CARTER, CARLENE
Come on Back *Reprise 4459/promo/'90* $5
I Fell in Love *Reprise 3932/promo/'90* $5
One Love *Reprise 4886/promo/'90* $5
The Sweetest Thing (edit)
Reprise 4701/promo/'90 ....$5

CARTWRIGHT, LIONEL
Be My Angel *MCA 54440/promo/logo silkscreened/ps/'92* $5
Standing on the Promises *MCA 54514/promo/ silkscreened pic/rear insert/'92* $5

CARWELL, SUE ANN
7 Days, 7 Nights 6 versions *MCA 2183/ promo/rear insert/'92* $6

CASE, PETER
Dream About You *Geffen 4379/promo/ gatefold hardcover ps/logo on green/'92* ..$6
Dream About You/Deja Blues/Why? *Geffen 4391/ promo/silkscreened/gatefold hardcover ps/'92* $8
Put Down the Gun *Geffen 3474/promo/ps/'89* ..$6

CASH, JOHNNY
Farmers Almanac *Mercury 170/promo/ silkscreened/'90* $6
Goin' by the Book *Mercury 320/promo/ silkscreened/'90* $6
The Greatest Cowboy Of Them All *Mercury 360/ promo/silkscreened/rear insert/'90* $6
The Mystery of Life *Mercury 397/promo/ logo on blue/rear insert/'91* $6
Wanted Man *Mercury 469/promo/logo on black/ rear insert/'91* $6

CASH, ROSANNE
Interiors (10 tracks) *Columbia 46079/ promo/silkscreened/rear insert/'90* $15
On the Surface *Columbia 2299/promo/ps/'91* ...$5
Real Woman *Columbia 4063/promo/ps/'91* $5
Seventh Avenue *Columbia 4953/promo/ps/'93*.$5

CASH, TOMMY & GEORGE JONES
Hank & George & Lefty & Me *Laurie L7CD 142/promo* $4

CASPER
War of Words video/radio/instrumental/ Adrenalin long/edit/instrumental *Capitol 79707/promo/logo on black/'91* $4

CASSIDY, DAVID
For All the Lonely edit & lp *Scotti Bros 75337/ promo/silkscreened/ps/'92* $6
Lyin' to Myself *Enigma 334/promo/ silkscreened pic/rear insert/'90* $6

CATHEDRAL
Ride *Columbia 5171/promo/ps/'93* $5
Soul Sacrifice/Autumn Twilight/Frozen Rapture/ Golden Blood *Columbia 53149/stock/ps*.$5

CATHERINE WHEEL
Black Metallic 7:19 & 4:09 & 5:30/Let Me Down *Fontana 693/promo/ps/'92* $7
Chrome 12 tracks *Mercury 314 518 039/ stock/ltd edition embossed gatefold cover/'93* $12
I Want to Touch .. remix *Fontana 735/promo/ps*..$5

CAUSE & EFFECT
Another Minute 7 versions/Unholy Day *Zoo 17065/promo/ps/'92* $8
Another Minute alt.edit & lp & 4:24/ Unholy Day 5:01/You Think You.. 8:00 *SRC 17064/promo/ps/silkscreened/'91* $8
What Do You .. 9 vers. *Exile 74001/stock/ps/'90* .$8
What Do You See radio/lp/extended *Zoo 17088/promo/silkscreened/'92* $6
You Think You Know Her 7 versions *Zoo 17043/ promo/silkscreened/rear insert/'91* $8

CAVE, NICK
I Had a Dream, Joe/The Good Son/The Carny/ The Mercy Seat (last 3 live) *Elektra 8622/promo/logo on black/ps* $10
Straight to You/Blue Bird *Mute 8566/promo/ ps/logo on black/'92* $6
Weeping Song single remix & lp *Elektra 8229/ promo/silkscreen red logo on black/'90* $7
Weeping Song remix/Train Song/B Side Song/ Helpless *Elektra 66605/stock/ps/'90* $5

CAVEDOGS, THE
Baba Ghanooj *Enigma 342/promo/silkscreened/ cust. sticker* $5
Bed of Nails *Enigma 337/promo/red logo on white/rear insert/'90* $5
Boy in a Plastic Bubble *Capitol 79153/promo/ logo on tan/ps/'92* $5
Leave Me Alone *Enigma 320/promo/silkscreened/ rear insert/'90* $5
Love Grenade *Capitol 79301/promo/logo on black/rear insert/'92* $5
Rock Takes a Holiday ep (Here Comes Rosie/ Sorrow/Part of This/Tarzan & His Arrow heads/Ghost Story) *Capitol 79096/ promo/silkscreened/ps/'92* $10
Tayter Country/Cherokee Fight Song/Heartland Jingo Polka/What's New Pussycat/Glass Eye/I Need .. (last 2 live) *Capitol 15706/ stock/ps/custom sticker/'91* $6
Tayter Country/Cherokee Fight Song/Heartland Jingo Polka/What's New Pussycat/Glass Eye/I Need You (last 2 live) *Capitol 79648/promo/'91* $8

CC DIVA
I'll Always Follow You 7 versions/I'm Gonna .. *Manhattan 04047/promo/ps/'88* $7
Grazing in the Grass (3 versions) *EMI 04236/promo/ps/'89* $7

CELL
Everything Turns/Free Money/So Cool/Hills demo ... *DGC 4531/promo/ps/logo on black/'93* $7

Fall *DGC 4492/promo/logo on black/ps/'93* $5

CELL MATES

Bottle of Sin *Scotti Bros 75335/promo/silkscreened/ps/'92* $5

CEREMONY

Could've Been Love edit & lp *DGC 4524/promo/silkscreened/gatefold hardcover ps/CHASTITY BONO (!)/'93* $5

CERVENKA, EXENE

Just Another Perfect Day edit & lp *RNA 90053/promo/silkscreened/rear insert/'90* $6

CETERA, PETER

Best of Times *WB 3280/promo/'88* $5
Best of Times/Livin' in the Limelight *WB 3325/promo/ps/'88* $5
Best of Times/Only Love Knows Why fade *WB 27712/stock/3"/3x6 ps/'88* $5
Holding Out (edit) *WB 3320/promo/'88* $5
One Good Woman edit/lp *WB 3152/promo/ps* $5
One Good Woman/One More Story *WB 27824/stock/3"/3x6 ps/'88* $5
Restless Heart *WB 5496/promo/cust.sticker/'92* .. $5

CETERA, PETER & CHAKA KHAN

Feels Like Heaven fade & lp *WB 5738/promo/'92* $6

CHAMPAIGN

My Fool *Malaco 2180/promo/silkscreened/'92* $5

CHANCE, JEFF

A Heartache on Her Hands *Mercury 798/promo/logo on white/rear insert/'92* $4
Thirty Days in Twenty Years *Mercury 443/promo/logo silkscreened/rear insert/'91* $4

CHANDLER, OMAR

Do You Really Want .. 4 vers. *MCA 1349/promo* . $5
This Must be Heaven lp/edit/instrumental *MCA 1400/promo/'91* $5

CHAPIN, HARRY

Remember When the Music/I Miss America *Dunhill 001/stock/3"/silkscreened pic/'87* ... $15

CHAPIN, TOM

Shovelling *A&M 17672/promo/silkscreened/ps* $5

CHAPMAN, BETH NIELSEN

All I Have (edit) *Reprise 4928/promo/'90* $5
I Keep Coming Back to.. *Reprise 5223/promo/'90* . $5
Life Holds On (remix) *Reprise 5218/promo/ps/'90* $5
Sampler (You Say You Will/I Don't Know/Dancer to the Drum) *Reprise 6390/promo/ps/logo on blue/'93* $10
The Moment You We're Mine *Reprise 6379/promo/logo on gold/ps/'93* $5
Walk My Way remix *Reprise 4637/promo/'90* $5
Walk My Way single mix *Reprise 4812/promo* $5
You Hold the Key ep (When I Feel This Way/Dance With Me Slow/The Moment You Were Mine) *Reprise 6371/promo/ps/'93* . $6

CHAPMAN, STEVEN CURTIS

Go There With You edit remix/remix *Sparrow 79725/promo/ps/'93* $5

CHAPMAN, TRACY

All That You Have is Your Soul edit & lp *Elektra 8132/promo/'89* $5
Baby Can I Hold You *Elektra 8037/promo/ps/'88* .. $6
Bang Bang Bang *Elektra 8555/promo/logo on white/ps/'92* $5
Born to Fight *Elektra 8151/promo/'90* $5
Crossroads *Elektra 8106/promo/ps/'89* $5
Dreaming on a World *Elektra 8525/promo/silkscreened pic/ps/'93* $5
Fast Car (edit) *Elektra 2217/promo/ps/'88* $8
Fast Car/For You *Elektra 000047/promo/3"/ps* ... $8
Talkin' Bout a Revolution *Elek. 8016/promo/'88* ... $5
Talkin' Bout a Revolution/Behind the Wall (live) *Elektra 69383/stock/3"/3x6 package/'87* . $10
This Time edit & lp *Elektra 8171/promo/silkscreened logo/rear insert/'89* $5

CHAPTERHOUSE

Falling Down/Feel the Same/Something More/Satin Safe *RCA 62019/promo/ps/'90* $5
Mesmerise/Precious One/Summer Chill/Then We'll Rise *RCA 62151/promo/logo on blue/custom sticker/rear insert/'91* $5

CHAQUICO, CRAIG

Acoustic Highway 9 tracks *Higher Octave 7050/booklet cover/'93* $12

CHARLATANS UK, THE

Can't Even Be Bothered/Tremelo Song (alt.take)/Happen to Die/Then/Chewing Gum .. (last 2 live) *RCA 62374/promo/ps/'92* $6
I Don't Want to See the Sights 3 versions/Me in Time/Occupation H. Monster *RCA 62274/promo/ps/'92* $6
Over Rising/Way Up There/Happen to Die/Opportunity3 *RCA 2882/stock/ps/'91* $6
Sproston Green remix edit & lp/Opportunity (extended) *RCA 2777/promo/ps/'91* $6
The Only One I Know (2 versions) *Beggars Banquet 2451/promo/ps/'90* $6
The Only One I Know/Everything Changed/Imperial 109/You Can Talk to Me *RCA 2690/promo/gatefold hardcover ps/'90* $6
Then (2versions)/Taurus Moaner (2 versions) *RCA 2452/promo/ps/'90* $6
Weirdo edit & lp *Beggars Banquet 62293/promo/rear insert/'92* $5
Weirdo lp & alt.take *RCA 62264/promo/ps/'92* ... $6

CHARLES & EDDIE

House is Not a Home 4 versions *Capitol 79576/ promo/silkscreened/ps/'92* $5

N.Y.C. (Can You Believe This City?) 5 versions *Capitol 79478/promo/silkscreened/ rear insert/'92* $6

Would I Lie to You 5 versions/Unconditional *Capitol 15879/stock/ps/'92* $5

Would I Lie to You? 5 versions *Capitol 79413/ promo/silkscreened/ps/'92* $6

CHARLES, RAY

Fresh Out of Tears *WB 4950/promo/'91* $4

I'll Take Care of You *WB 4425/promo/'90* $4

Living Without You edit & lp *WB 4696/promo/'90* $4

Still Crazy After All These Years edit/lp *WB 6215/promo/'93* $4

CHAVEZ, INGRID

Elephant Box 6 versions *Paisley Park 40170/ gatefold hardcover ps/stock/'91* $5

Elephant Box lp & hip hop 7" *Paisley Park 4929/promo/'91* $6

Hippy Blood 8 versions/Whispering Dandelions *Paisley Park 40270/stock/gatefold hardcover ps/'92* $5

Hippy Blood lp edit/free spirit edit/keep pumpin' it edit/latin light edit *Paisley Park 5155/ promo/ps/'91* $6

selftitled 11 tracks *Paisley Park 25879/ stock/ps/dj silkscreened/'91* $12

CHEAP TRICK

13 song dj only Greatest Hits comp. *Epic 1012/promo/silkscreened/'88* $22

Busted (11 tracks) *Epic 2129/promo/ps/'90* $15

Can't Stop Fallin' in Love radio mix & lp *Epic 73444/promo/silkscreened/ps/'90* $7

Dont Be Cruel (big new mix) *Epic 1216/promo/ps/'88* $8

Ghost Town *Epic 1326/promo/neat silkscreen/ rear insert/'88* $8

If You Need Me *Epic 73566/promo/silkscreen/ rear insert/'90* $7

Magical Mystery Tour 4:08/3:15 *Epic 4206/ promo/silkscreened logos/ps/'91* $7

Never Had a Lot to Lose *Epic 1458/promo/silkscreened blue/'88* $7

The Flame 4:30 & 5:37 *Epic 1050/promo/ silkscreened/rear insert/'88* $12

Wherever Would I Be *Epic 73580/ promo/silkscreened/rear insert/'90* $7

CHEAP TRICK/PETER GABRIEL

You Want It/In You Eyes (live 8:45) *WTG 1678/promo/'89* $12

CHEMICAL PEOPLE

Let It Go/Mid Air (edit) *Cruz 025/ps/stock/'92* $6

The Singles (24 songs - II live) *2" Pecker 1/ stock/ps/ltd edition of 1000* $15

CHER

Heart of Stone heartbeat versions fade & full *Geffen 4005/promo/'89* $8

Heart of Stone remix fade/remix/CHR/lp *Geffen 3989/promo/'89* $8

Heart of Stone (CHR version) *Geffen 3822/ promo/ps/logo silkscreen/'89* $7

Heart of Stone (lp length) *Geffen 24239/ silkscreened/dj only edition* $20

If I Could Turn Back Time (4 versions) *Geffen 3602/promo/'89* $8

Just Like Jesse James *Geffen 3664/promo/ps/'89* $6

Love & Understanding 5:25/4:40/5:45 *Geffen 4296/promo/custom sticker/'91* $6

Love & Understanding 3 versions *Geffen 4246/promo/ps/'91* $7

Love Hurts *Geffen 24421/box container/ lyric cards/dj only silkscreened/'91* $20

Love Hurts 11 tracks *Geffen 24369/stock with dj silkscreened/ps/'91* $15

Main Man *Geffen 3284/promo/'87* $8

Save Up All Your Tears 4 vers. *Geffen 4341/ promo/silkscreened/ps/cust. sticker/'91* $8

Save Up All Your Tears chr remix & lp *Geffen 4304/promo/ps/'91* $6

Skin Deep edit remix/extended dance mix *Geffen 3173/promo/ps/'88* $8

Shoop Shoop Song *Geffen 4176/promo/ps/'90* ... $6

We All Sleep Alone lp & remix *Geffen 2971/ promo/ps/'88* $8

When Lovers Become Strangers edit & lp *Geffen 4408/promo/ps/'92* $6

CHERRELLE

Affair 3:12 & 6:10 *Tabu 1456/promo/'88* $8

Never In My Life edit & lp *no label of #/promo/ custom sticker* $5

Never In My Life edit & lp *Tabu 28965 1703/ promo/silkscreened/ps/'91* $5

Still In Love With You 5 vers. *Tabu 28965 1817/ promo/logo on pink/ps/'91* $7

Tears of Joy 4 versions *Tabu 28965 1807/ promo/logo silkscreened/'91* $7
Tears of Joy lp/instrumental *Tabu 28965 1805/promo/ps/'91* $5

CHERRY, AVA
Gimme Gimme 3 versions *Critique 15505/promo/silkscreened pic* $5

CHERRY, NENEH
Buddy X *Virgin 12766/promo/silkscreened/ rear insert/'92* $5
Buddy X 5 versions *Virgin 12782/promo/ silkscreened/rear insert/'92* $7
Buffalo Stance (7" mix 4:08) *Virgin 2646/promo/silkscreened/'88* $8
Buffalo Stance edit & 7" *Virgin 2726/promo/silkscreened logo/'88* .. $8
Heart radio edit/edit/lp *Virgin 2989/promo/silkscreened/'88* $7
Kisses on Wind US edit & lp (minus intro) & remix *Virgin 2825/promo/'89* $7
Manchild edit & lp *Virgin 2988/promo/ silkscreened on purple/'88* $6
Manchild 3 versions *Virgin PLEN/promo/'89* $7
Money Love lp/extended/perfecto mix edit/ perfecto mix *Virgin 12709/promo/ rear insert/logo on green/'92* $6
Money Love 3 versions/I've Got You Under My Skin/Twisted *Virgin 12610/stock/ gatefold hardcover ps/'92* $5
Raw Like Sushi (full length) *Virgin/promo/ gatefold cover/silkscreened/'89* $15

CHIC
Chic Mystique 5 versions *WB 5069/promo/silkscreened pic/'90* $6
Chic Mystique 8 versions *WB 40225/stock/ gatefold hardcover ps/'92* $5
Chic-Ism 13 tracks *WB 9 26394/promo/ silkscreened/gatefold hardcover with psych finish/booklet/'91* $15
Your Love 4 versions *WB 5658/promo/'92* $7

CHICAGO
25 or 6 to 4/Make Me Smile *Columbia 38K-33193/3"/stock* $5
Chasin' the Wind *Reprise 4602/promo/silkscreened/'90* $5
Chasin' the Wind ac radio mix *Reprise 4699/promo/'91* $6
Chicago II/In the Studio *dj radio show/promo/ hosted by ROBERT LAMM/cue sheet* $25
Chicago V, VI, VII radio show *In the Studio 109/ promo/cue sheet/hosted by R.Lamm* $25
Explain it To My Heart edit & remix *Reprise 4636/promo/'91* $6
Hearts in Trouble edit & lp *DGC 4133/promo/ silkscreened/rear insert/'90* $4
I Dont Wanna Live Without Your Love *Reprise 3126/promo/ps/'88* $6
Look Away CHR mix/AC mix *Reprise 3219/promo/ps/'88* $6
Look Away remix/Come In From the Night *Reprise 27766/stock/3"/3x6 ps/'88* $6
We Can Last Forever (remix) *Reprise 3487/promo/'88* $5
What Kind of Man.... *Reprise 3777/promo/'89* $5
You Come to Senses *Reprise 4942/promo/'91* $5
You're Not Alone remix & lp *Reprise 27757/stock/3"/3x6 ps/'88* $6
You're Not Alone remix *Reprise 3233/promo/'88* . $5

CHICKASAW MUDD PUPPIES
McIntosh/Lookout *Wing 233/promo/silkscreened/ ps/MICHAEL STIPE/'91* $8
White Dirt (9 tracks) *Wing 843 217/ promo only gatefold burlap cover/'90* $15
Words & Knives/Cold Blue/Lodi/Nothin' *Mercury 433/promo/ps/silkscreened brown/MICHAEL STIPE/'91* $12

CHIEFS OF RELIEF
Freedom to Rock/Interview *Sire 3030/promo/ps* $5

CHIEFTAINS & RICKY SKAGGS
Cotton-Eyed Joe *RCA 61483/promo/'92* $6

CHIEFTAINS & ROGER DALTREY
Behind Blue Eyes *RCA 61039/promo/'92* $6

CHILD'S PLAY
Day After Night *Chrysalis 23572/promo/ps/'90* .. $4
Rat Race *Chrysalis 23586/promo/ps/'90* $4
Wind *Chrysalis 23673/promo/ps/'91* $4

CHILD, DESMOND
Legends - Volume 1 (w/BON JOVI, AEROSMITH, JOAN JETT, CHER, more) (15 tracks) *EMI 05379/promo/ps/'91* $15
Love on a Rooftop *Elektra 8350/promo/ silkscreened red/ps/'91* $4
Obsession edit & lp *Elektra 8505/promo/ silkscreened pic/rear insert/'91* $4
You're the Story of My Life edit *Elektra 8416/promo/ps/'91* $4

CHILD, JANE
Dont Wanna Fall in Love (7 versions)/World Lullabye *WB 21526/ps/stock/'90* $6
Dont Wanna Fall in Love 4:04/4:20/7:50 *WB 3867/promo/silkscreened/'89* $8
Here Not There radio *WB 6462/promo/silkscreened/'93* $5
Welcome to the Real World (4 versions) *WB 3724/promo/'89* $6
Welcome to Real World (6 vers.)/Hey Mr Jones *WB 21537/stock/ps/'90* $5

CHILDS, ANDY
Advance Music 10 tracks *RCA 66253/promo/ logo on brown/gatefold wallet like ps/booklet/'93* $10

CHILDS, TONI
Dont Walk Away (7" remix) *A&M 17605/promo/ps/'88* $6
I Want to Walk With .edit & lp *A&M 75021 7316/ promo/silkscreened pic/ps/'91* $5
I've Got to Go Now edit & lp *A&M 75021 7256/promo/ps/'91* $5
I've Got to Go Now/House of Hope/I Want to Walk With You/Heaven's ... *A&M 75021 7470/ promo/silkscreened/ps/'91* $5
Let the Rain Come Down/Dont Walk Away + 2 *A&M 37582/promo/3"/5" ps/'88* $6
Many Rivers to Cross edit & lp *A&M 17774/promo/ps/'89* $5
Stop Your Fussin' *A&M 17557/promo/ gatefold hardcover ps/'88* $4
Walk and Talk Like.. *A&M 17615/promo/'88* $4

CHILLS, THE
Double Summer/Song For Randy Newman etc. *Slash 5723/promo/'92* $6
Heavenly Pop Hit *Slash 3988/promo/'90* $5
Heavenly Pop Hit/Part Past Part Fiction/ Familiarty Breeds Contempt/Sub.Bells *Slash CHICD 1/promo/ps* $10
Soft Bomb 17 tracks *Slash 5479/promo/'92* $12
The Male Monster From the Id *Slash 5535/promo/silkscreened/'92* $5
Oncoming Day *Slash 4330/promo/rear insert* $5

CHIMES, THE
1-2-3 3:22/6:02 *Columbia 73087/promo/ silkscreened copper/ps/'89* $6
I Still Haven't Found What I'm Looking For (3 versions) *Columbia 73310/promo/ps/'90* $5
True Love 4 vers. *Columbia 73538/promo/ps/'90* $5

CHINA CRISIS
St Saviour Square edit & lp *A&M 17778/promo/silkscreened/'89* $5

CHOIRBOYS
Boys Will Be Boys *WTG 1800/promo/'89* $5
Guilty *WTG 1609/promo/silkscreened/'89* $5
Run To Paradise *WTG 1423/promo/ silkscreened logo/'89* $5

CHRIS & COSEY
Synresthesia 3 versions *Wax Trax 9153/stock/ps/'91* $6

CHRISSY STEELE
Love You Till it Hurts/Try Me/Armed &Dangerous/ Love Don't Last Forever *Chrysalis 23729/promo/silkscreened/'91* .. $5

CHRISTENSEN, MARIA
I've Got to Find a Way radio & lp *Atlantic 5086/promo/ps/'93* $4

CHRISTIANS
Forgotten Town (3 vers.) *Island 2184/promo/ps* .. $4

CHRISTY, LAUREN
You Read Me Wrong edit *Mercury 884/promo/logo on blue/ps/'93* ... $3

CHUBB ROCK
Just the Two of Us vocal & oustrumental *Select 8424/promo/'91* $5
Lost in the Storm 6 versions *Select 8619/promo/logo on purple/'92* $5
The Big Man 4 versions *Select 8586/promo/silkscreened/'92* $5
Yabadabadoo vocal & instrumental/ I'm Too Much 3 versions *Select 8696/promo/silkscreened pic/'92* ... $5

CHUNKY A
Owwww/Ho Is Lazy/Sorry/Very High Key *MCA 18080/promo/silkscreened/ custom stickers (2)/'89* $6

CHURCH
Destination/Under the Milky .. acoustic/Tantalized *Arista 3001/stock/3"/ps/'88* $8
Feel 6 versions *Arista 2436/promo/silkscreened/ps/'92* $7
Life Before Starfish compilation .... *Arista 9724/promo/gatefold ps/'88* $20
Megalopolis ep (Metropolis/Monday Morning/ Much too Much) *Arista 9944/stock/ps/'90* . $6
Metropolis *Arista 9950/promo/ps/'90* $6
Ripple edit & lp *Arista 2389/promo/ps/silkscreened/'92* $6
Russian Autumn Heart/Hunter/Feast/Desert + 1 *Arista 2068/stock/ps/'90* $6
Sum of the Parts interview & live acoustic *Arista 9713/promo/for Atlanta radio only/ps/'88* $35
Under the Milky Way *Arista 9669/promo/ps/'88* .. $8
Under the Milky Way single & lp *Arista 9687/promo/ps/'88* $8
You're Still Beautiful *Arista 2042/promo/rear insert/'90* $5

CHURCH OF EXTACY
Oowee I Am Ready 4 versions *Sonic 2004/ps/stock/logo on red/'92* $5

CINDERELLA
Coming Home edit & lp *Mercury 69/promo/silkscreened/ps/'88* $6
Dont Know What You Got edit/lp *Mercury 25/promo/embossed logo ps/'88* . $6
Hot and Bothered *Reprise 5309/promo/'92* $5

Nobody's Fool (video & audio)/In From Outside/ Push Push/Nothin' For Nothin' (last 3 audio only) *Mercury 080 047/ promo/ps/CD video (1 song)* $15
Shelter Me *Merc. 336/promo/silkscreened/ps/'90* .$5
The More Things Change *Merc.457/promo/ps/'91* $5

CIRCLE OF SOUL
Shattered Faith *Hollywood 8333/promo/ silkscreened/ps/'91* $4

CIRCLE OF SOUL
Stone in My Shoe *Hollywood 8397/promo/ silkscreened/rear insert/'91* $4

CIRCUS OF POWER
Vices (clean edit) *RCA 2632/promo/ps/'90* $4

CLAIL, GARY
Escape no way out mix&on the mix/Human Nature.. *RCA 62147/stock/ps/'91* $6
Human Nature edit & lp *RCA 2855/promo/ logo on green/rear insert/'91* $5
Human Nature edit/something wrong with me edit/ wrong with me mix/lp *RCA 62066/promo* $6

CLANNAD
Harry's Game *Atlantic 4675/promo/cust.sticker*...$5
Hourglass/Theme From Harrys Game/World of Dif./Journeys End *RCA 43876/stock/ps*..$8
I Will Find You *Atlantic 5135/promo* $5
In a Lifetime *RCA 9171/promo/ps/'90* $10
Family Tree Sampler 9 tracks *Atlantic 4945/ promo/ps/silkscreened/'93* $15

CLAPTON, ERIC
Bad Love edit & lp *Reprise 3792/promo/'89* $8
Before You Accuse Me *Reprise 4050/promo/'89*..$8
Crossroads sampler (4 tracks -After Midnight, Presence of the Lord, Further on Up the Road/Layla) *Polydor 10/promo/ps/'88* ..$20
Help Me Up edit & lp *Reprise 5235/promo/'92*..$6
No Alibis edit & lp *Reprise 3797/promo/'89* $7
Pretending edit & lp *Reprise 3789/ promo/silkscreened pic* $12
Rarities on Compact Disc (19 tracks) .... *On theRadio/Westwood One/promo/ps* $35
Run So Far *Reprise 4373/promo/ps/'89* $8
Selections From Lethal Weapon 3 soundtrack (Medley: Riggs and Rogg-Lorna/ Riggs & Rogg/Lorna- A Quiet Evening...) *Reprise 5678/promo/'92* $8
Tears in Heaven *Reprise 5240/promo/'92* $6
Tears in Heaven edit *Reprise 5362/promo/'92* .$6
Watch Yourself/White Room (edit)/Wonderful Tonight (edit) *Reprise 5110/promo/'91* ..$8

CLAPTON, ERIC & JEFF BECK
Farther Up the Road/I Shall Be Released *Rhino 90138/promo/ps/'92*......................$10

CLAPTON, ERIC/DEREK & DOMINOS
Little Wing remix & live *Polydor 298/promo/ silkscreened/gatefold hardcover ps/'90* ..$15

CLARK, GUY
Baton Rouge *Asylum 8667/promo/ logo on white/ps/'92* $5

CLARK, PETULA
Oxygen 2 versions *Scotti Bros 75325/promo/ logo on white/ps/NIK KERSHAW/'92* $7

CLARK, RHONDA
(If Loving You is Wrong) I Don't Want to Be Right lp/edit/instrumental *Tabu 28965 1804/ promo/ps/'92* $5
Must be Real Love 6 vers. *Tabu 31458 8004/ promo/logo on purple/ps/'92* $6
State of Attraction 4 versions *Tabu 1751/ promo/logo on gold/'89* $6
When the Next Tear Drop Falls edit/lp/instrum. *Tabu 31458 8026/promo/silkscreened/ps*.$6

CLARK, SUSAN
Deeper 7" edit & extended *FFRR 637/promo/logo on black/'92* $5

CLARKE, ROZLYNE
Eddy Steady Go 5 versions *Atlantic 3617/promo/rear insert/'90* $6

CLARKE, STANLEY & GEORGE DUKE
Lady *Epic 73422/promo/rear insert/'90*..............$5

CLASH, THE
Clash on Broadway: The Interviews *Epic 4337/promo/silkscreened/ps/'91* $20
Clash on Broadway: The Trailer (14 tracks) *Epic 4274/promo/ps/silkscreened pic* $15
Return to Brixton (3 versions)/The Guns of Brixton ... *Epic 73516/promo/silkscreened/ps/'90* $8

CLASSIC EXAMPLE
Christmas Song/Auld Lang Syne-Lift Every Voice and Sing *Boston Inernation.10260/promo/ silkscreened pic/custom sticker/'92* $6
I Do Care 4 versions/Lift Every Voice and Sing *Boston International 10275/promo/ silkscreened/rear insert/'93* $6
It's Alright edit/lp/remix *Hollywood Basic 10201/ promo/silkscreened pic/rear insert/ custom sticker/'92* $6

CLASSICS IV
Spooky/Traces/Everyday With You Girl/Stormy *Rhino R3 73004/3"/stock/ps/'88* $5

CLAY, ANDREW DICE
Dice's Greatest (Bleeped) Bits From 40 Too Long and Other Jemts (75 tracks) *Def American 5631/promo/ps/'92* $10
Attitude/L.A./Makin' Money + 3 more mini tracks *Def American 3489/promo/'89* $6

CLAYTON-THOMAS, DAVID
The Christmas Song *SRC 17102/promo/ silkscreened/rear insert/'92* $5

CLAYTOWN TROUPE
Wanted It All/How Can Anybody Do This?/Alabama/ Feel Like a Woman *EMI 56235/stock/ ps/silkscreened/'91* $5

CLEGG, JOHNNY
Life is a Magic Thing edit & lp *Capitol 79287/promo/ps/'92* $5
Cruel Crazy Beautiful World (7 versions) *Capitol 79868/promo/silkscreen/ps/'89* $6
I Can Never Be *Capitol 79678/promo/ps/ logo on white/'93* $4
One (Hu)'Man One Vote/Woman Be My Country/ Dela (2 versions each) *Capitol 79387/ promo/gatefold hardcover ps/'90* $6
These Days edit & lp *EMI 79673/promo/silkscreened/ps/'93* $4

CLEMONS, CLARENCE
Quarter to Three *Columbia 1772/promo/ps/'89* . $5

CLEVELAND, ASHLEY
Feel Like Falling/Henry Doesn't Care/Water/ Light at the End of the Tunnel *RCA 62551/promo/silkscreened pic/insert/envelope type ps/'93* $6
Willy *Atlantic 3704/promo/ps/'91* $4

CLIFF, JIMMY
I'm a Winner radio & lp *JRS 808/promo/ps/'92* .. $5
Oneness *JRS 808/promo/logo on black/'92* $5
Peace edit & lp *JRS 808/promo/silkscreened/'92* . $4

CLINTON, GEORGE
Paint the White House Black 3 vers./Picture This street mix/Boot *Paisley Park 41057/stock/ps/'93* $5
Tweakin' edit & lp *Paisley Park 3717/promo/'89* . $6
Why Should I Dog U Out? (3 versions) *Paisley Park 3438/promo/'89* $7

CLIVILLES & COLE
A Deeper Love radio/edit remix/ballad radio edit *Columbia 4345/promo/ps/'91* $8
Pride (In the Name of Love) 3 versions/ A Deeper Love 2 versions *Columbia 44K 74135/stock/ps/'91* $6
Pride (In the Name of Love) 4 versions *Columbia 4344/promo/ps/'91* $8

CLUB NOUVEAU
I Like Your Way radio & radio with piano intro *Quality 19116/promo/ps/'92* $5
No Friend of Mine 7" & fade *WB 3736/promo/'89* .. $4
Oh Happy Day *Quality 19100/promo/ps/'92* $4
Under a Nouveau Groove single & lp *WB 3912/promo/'89* $4

CLUBLAND
Hold On (Tighter to Love) 5 versions *Great Jones 611/promo/custom sticker* $4
Let's Get Busy (3 versions) *Geffen 4159/promo/silkscreened/ps/'90* ... $5

CLUTCH
A Promo Named Marcus (A Shogun Named ../ 12 Ounce Epilogue/Juggernaut) *Eastwest 5177/promo/ps/silkscreened* $5

COCHRANE, TOM
Life is a Highway *Capitol 79135/promo/ps/'91* $5
No Regrets *Capitol 79212/promo/rear insert/'92* .. $4
Washed Away edit & lp *Capitol 79441/promo/rear insert/'91* $5

COCK ROBIN
Biggest Fool of All *Columbia 2849/promo/ps/'87* .. $4
Its Only Make Believe *Columbia 73479/promo/ps/'90* $4

COCKBURN, BRUCE
A Dream Like Mine *Columbia 4192/promo/logo on tan/ps/prod.by T BONE BURNETT/'91* $5
Great Big Love remix/great big rock mix/ great big long rock mix *Columbia 4413/promo/ps/'92*....................$7
If a Tree Falls edit & lp *Gold Castle 79505/promo/'88*...................$6
Nothing But a Burning Light/Primer 23 tracks *Columbia 4222/promo/trifold hardcover/ 2 cds/foldout lyric book/'91*....................$18
Where the Death Squad ../Dont Feel Your Touch *Gold Castle 79623/promo/'88*..................$6

COCKER, JOE
Feels Like Forever *Capitol 79256/promo/'92*.....$5
Love Is Alive *Capitol 79211/promo/logo on gold/ rear insert/'92*...$5
Night Calls *Capitol 79584/promo/ps/'92*............$5
Now That the Magic Has Gone *Capitol 79210/ promo/logo on green/rear insert/'92*..........$5
What Are You Doing With a Fool.. remix & lp *Capitol 79020/promo/silkscreened/ rear insert/'90*...$5
When the Night Comes *Capitol 79710/promo/silkscreened/'89*......$5
When the Night Comes edit & lp *Capitol 79898/promo/silkscreened/'89*......$5
You Can Leave Your Hat On remix/lp/studio *Capitol 79273/promo/ logo on gold silkscreened/'90*..................$5

COCTEAU TWINS
Carolyns Fingers/Ella Megalast Burls Forever *Capitol 79405/promo/'88*........................$12
dj only sampler (Aikea Guinea/High Monkey ../ Sigh's Smell of Farewell/Pearly Dewdrops Drop/Dials/Hazel + 4) *Capitol 79065/ promo/silkscreened/ps/'91*....................$25
Evangline/Mud and Dark/Summer-Blink *Capitol 79259/promo/silkscreen pic/'93*....$7
Heaven in Las Vegas (edit & lp)/Dials *Capitol 79291/promo/custom sticker/'90*...$7
Heaven in Las Vegas (edit & lp)/Dials *Capitol 79291/promo/ps/'90*...................$10
I Wear Your Ring *Capitol 79498/promo/ custom sticker/'90*...................................$12
Iceblink Luck *Capitol 79686/promo/ silkscreened/ps/'90*.................................$10
Iceblink Luck/Mizake the Mizan/Watchlar *Capitol 15626/stock/ps/silkscreened/'90*...$7

COFFEY, DENNIS
Under the Moonlight radio & lp/Yesterday's Girl *Orpheus 4577/promo/ silkscreened/rear insert/'90*.......................$6

COHEN, LEONARD
Closing Time *Columbia 4932/promo/silkscreened/ ps/custom sticker/'92*...............................$6
Democracy *Columbia 4867/promo/silkscreen/ps*.$6
Democracy/First We Take Manhattan/I'm Your Man . *Columbia 44K 74778/stock/ps/'92*............$5
The Future *Columbia 5148/promo/silkscreen/ps*.$6

COHN, MARK
29 Ways *Atlantic 4102/promo/ logo on white/rear insert/'91*......................$4
Paper Walls *Atlantic 5168/promo/ silkscreened/rear insert/'93*.......................$4
Paper Walls *Atlantic 5172/promo*......................$4
Silver Thunderbird edit & lp *Atlantic 3943/promo/ gatefold hardcover ps/silkscreened/'91*....$5
True Companion edit & lp *Atlantic 4213/ promo/custom sticker*...............................$4
Walk Through the World edit & lp *Atlantic 5066/ promo/silkscreened pic/rear insert/'93*......$5
Walking in Memphis *Atlantic 3705/promo/ps/'91*..$5

COIL
Windowpane 3 versions *Wax Trax WAXCDS 9142/stock/ps/'90*.....$5

COLD SWEAT
Let's Make Love Tonight *MCA 1051/promo/rear insert/'90*..............$4

COLDCUT
People Hold On (radio) *Reprise 3658/promo/'89*..$4
Stop This Crazy Thing 7 versions *Tommy 3849/promo/'89*...........................$7

COLE, GARDENER
Live It Up (3 remixes) *WB 3192/promo/ps/'88*.....$4

COLE, HOLLY/TRIO
Calling You/If I Were a Bell/Trust in Me/Purple Avenue *Manhattan 79077/promo/ silkscreened pic/rear insert/'91*................$6
Trust in Me/If I Were a Bell *Manhattan 79370/ promo/silkscreened pic/cust.pic sticker/ rear insert/'92*...$6

COLE, JUDE
Baby, It's Tonight lp *Reprise 4013/promo/'90*....$4
Baby, It's Tonight lp & soft version *Reprise 4007/promo/'90*...........................$4
Compared to Nothing *Reprise 4771/promo/'90*.$4
House Full of Reasons *Reprise 4495/promo/'90*.$4
Start the Car *Reprise 5642/promo/silkscreen pic/'92*.....$6
Start the Car 11 tracks *Reprise 5632/promo/'92*.$10
Tell the Truth edit & lp *Reprise 5842/promo/'92*.$4
Time For Letting Go remix & lp *Reprise 4337/promo/rear insert/'90*..........$4
You Were In My Heart (edit) *WB 2864/promo/ps* $4

COLE, LLOYD
Downtown edit & lp *Capitol 79033/promo/ silkscreened logo on white/rear insert/ custom sticker/'90*..................................$6

Downtown/No Blue Skies/What Do You Know
About Love *Capitol 79003/promo/ gatefold hardcover ps/silkscreen yellow* .$10
No Blue Skies *Capitol 79944/promo/ silkscreened/rear insert/'90* $6
She's a Girl and I'm a Man
Capitol 79834/promo/ps/'91 ....$5
She's a Girl and I'm a Man/Weird on Me/
Children of the Revolution
Capitol 15753/stock/rear insert/'91 ....$5
Tell Your Sister *Capitol 79045/promo/ logo on white/'91* $5
Weeping Wine/The L Word (tell your sister demo)/
Somewhere Out in the East
Capitol 79122/promo/ps/'91 ....$6

COLE, NATALIE

As a Matter of Fact 4 versions *Capitol 04443/ promo/silkscreened/rear insert/'89*...........$7
I Do *EMI 04330/promo/silkscreen/rear insert/'89* .$5
I Live For Your Love
Manhattan 79155/promo/ps/'87 ....$8
Pink Cadillac (4 vers.) *EMI 04020/promo/ps/'88* .$10
Route 66 *Elektra 8439/promo/ logo silkscreened/rear insert/'91* $5
Take a Look *Elektra 8776/promo/silkscreened/ps*$4
The Christmas Song *Elektra 8473/promo/ps/'91* .$5
The Very Thought of You
Elektra 8521/promo/logo on purple/ps/'92 $5
When I Fall in Love 7" & lp
Manhattan 04083/promo/ps/'88 ....$7
Wild Women Do 6 versions *EMI 04467/promo/ silkscreened/rear insert/'90* $7
Wild Women Do (new ric wake power mix)
EMI 4559/promo/silkscreened/ custom sticker/'90 ....$6

COLE, NATALIE & NAT KING COLE

Unforgettable *Elektra 8374/promo/ps/ logo on purple/'91* $6

COLE, NATALIE/MILES DAVIS

The Christmas Song/We Three Kings
A&M 17646/promo/ps/'88 ....$7

COLEMAN, ORNETTE & JERRY GARCIA

3 Wishes/Desert Players
Portrait 1160/promo/ps/'88 ....$8

COLLEGE BOYZ, THE

Humpin' 4 versions
Virgin 12699/promo/rear insert/'92 ....$5

COLLIE, MARK

Even the Man in the Moon is Cryin'
MCA 54448/promo/silkscreened/ gatefold hardcover ps/'92 ....$4

COLLINS, ALBERT

Travellin' South *Virgin 031/promo/ps/'91* $5

COLLINS, BOOTSY

Party on Plastic (6 versions)
Columbia 1245/promo/ps/'88 ....$6

COLLINS, JIMMY

Cowboy Rap (2 versions) *Platinum Edge/ promo/custom sticker/'90* $4

COLLINS, JUDY

Fires of Eden 2 vers. *Columbia 2164/promo/ps*...$5
The Colorado Song edit & lp
Columbia 2288/promo/ps/'91 ....$5

COLLINS, PHIL

Another Day in Paradise single & lp
Atlantic 3048/promo/ps/'89 ....$7
Another Day in Paradise (5:15)/Saturday Night../
Heat on Street *Atlantic 86261/ logo on black/stock/ps/'90* $7
Do You Remember? *Atlantic 3121/promo/ silkscreened logo on black/rear insert/'89* .$6
Hang in Long Enough (lp & club mix)
Atlantic 3616/promo/ps/silkscreened logo on yellow/'89 ....$7
I Wish It Would Rain .. edit & lp *Atlantic 3120/ promo/ps/silkscreened logo on black/'90* ..$6
In the Air Tonight/Take Me Home/Separate Lives
(all live) *Atlantic 3642/promo/ logo on yellow/ps/'90* $15
Profiled! (25:02 interview & more)
Atlantic 3092/promo/ps/'90 ....$15
Something Happened on the Way to Heaven
Atlantic 3392/promo/ps/'90 ....$6
Something Happened on the Way to Heaven (3 vers.) *Atlantic 3503/promo/ps/'90* $8
Two Hearts *Atlantic 2545/promo/rear insert/'88*...$6
Up Close radio special
MediaAmerica 9001/promo/2 cds/ps/'90 $30
Who Said I Would *Atlantic 3758/promo/ps/ logo on white/'90* $6

COLLINS, PHIL & Y KANT TORI READ

Groovy Kind of Love + 2 Y Kant cuts
Atlantic 2452/promo/rear insert/'88 ....$6

COLLINS, TYLER

It Doesn't Matter radio/edit/lp
RCA 62325/promo/ps/'92 ....$4
Just Make Me the One 4 versions
RCA 62203/promo/ps/'92 ....$4

COLLISION

Chains *Chaos 4753/promo/silkscreened/ps/'92*....$4

COLONEL ABRAMS

When Somebody Loves Somebody edit & lp
Scotti Bros 75323/promo/ silkscreened pic/'92 ....$4
You Don't Know (Somebody Tell Me) 8 versions
Scotti Bros 75294/promo/ps/'91 ....$5

COLOR ME BADD
All 4 Love edit & lp *Giant 4900/promo/'91* $7
Color Me Badd *Giant 5111/promo/'91* $6
I Adore Mi Amor 4:27/4:52/4:49 *Giant 4943/ promo/silkscreen color band pic/rear insert/'91* $8
I Wanna Sex You Up 3 versions *Giant 4728/promo/ps/'91* $8
I Wanna Sex You Up 5 versions *Giant 40031/ stock/gatefold hardcover ps/'91* $5
I Wanna Sex You Up 5 versions *Reprise 4916/promo/'91* $8
Slow Motion 7 versions *Giant 40453/stock/ gatefold hardcover ps/'92* $6
Slow Motion 7 versions *Giant 5446/promo/'91* $8
Thinkin' Back edited master/a cappella/lp/ pop mix with piano *Giant 5403/promo/'91* $8
Thinkin' Back edit/XXX versions/more radio edit *Giant 5169/promo/rear insert/'91* $8

COLORTONE
Nothings Gonna Be ...*Pasha 1086/promo/ps* $3

COLVIN, SHAWN
Climb On *Columbia 74972/promo/ps/'93* $4
Diamond in the Rough edit & lp *Columbia 2057/promo/ps/'90* $5
Diamond in the Rough edit & lp *Columbia 73325/promo/ps/'90* $5
Round of Blues edit & lp *Columbia 4828/promo/ps/'92* $4
Steady On edit & lp *Columbia 73061/promo/ps* ... $5

COMMITMENTS, THE
Mustang Sally *MCA 1625/promo/ps/'91* $5
That's the Way Love Is *MCA 2180/promo/ps/'92* . $5
Try a Little Tenderness *MCA 1626/promo/ps/'91* $5

COMPANY B
Boogie Woogie Bugle Boy lp & king B vocal edit *Atlantic 2999/promo/rear insert/'89* $5

COMPANY OF WOLVES
Call of the Wild edit & lp *Mercury 176/promo/silkscreened pic/'90* .. $6
The Distance *Mercury 226/promo/silkscreen/'90* .. $4

COMPTON'S MOST WANTED
Growin' Up in the Hood (censored versions) *Qwest 4901/promo/'91* $5
Def Wish II 3 versions *Epic 4943/promo/'93* $6
Growin' Up in the Hood 4 versions/Driveby Miss Daisy 2 vers. *Epic 73827/promo/ logo on black* $6
Hood Took Me Under 4 vers. *Orpheus 74447/ promo/silkscreened/ps/'92* $6

CONCRETE BLONDE
Caroline (edit) *IRS 67029/promo/'90* $8
Everybody Knows *MCA 18482/promo/ silkscreened yellow/rear insert/'90* $8
Ghost of a Texas Ladies Man *IRS 67082/promo/ gatefold hardcover ps/'92* $8
Ghost of a Texas Ladies Man/Bloodletting extended/Everybody Knows/Ship Song *IRS 13849/stock/ps/'92* $8
God is a Bullet *IRS 8201/promo/silkscreened design/'89* . $8
Joey *IRS 023/promo/ps/logo on red/'90* $8
Scene of a Perfect Crime *IRS 007/promo/silkscreened/ps/'89* $8
Someday? *IRS 67092/promo/silkscreen. clock* $8
Walking in London (edit)/God is a Bullet (live)/ Free/100 Games of Solitaire *IRS 67101/promo/silkscreened/ rear insert/'92* $8

CONDEMNED
To Protect and Serve with & without audience/Condemned Truth all live *Sounds of Seattle 1/promo/ logo on yellow/ps/'92* $6

CONFEDERATE RAILROAD
Queen of Memphis *Atlantic 4707/ promo/rear insert* $4
Queen of Memphis dance versions 6:07 *Atlantic 4922/promo* $5
When You Leave That Way You Can...edit *Atlantic 5006/promo/rear insert* $4

CONNELLS, THE
Hey Wow/Fun & Games *TVT/promo/'89* $5
Scottys Lament/If It Crumbles/Over There *TVT/promo/silkscreened pic/ps/'89* $7
Stone Cold Yesterday *TVT 2580/promo/silkscreened/'90* $5

CONNELLY, CHRIS
July edit & lp/This Edge of Midnight (sparse)/The Last of Joy (secret mix)/Trash (live-spoken word) *Wax Trax 89190/stock/ps/'92* $7

CONNICK, HARRY (JR)
Blue Light, Red Light *Columbia 4207/promo/ logo on red&blue/ps/'91* $6
Everyones Wild About Harry ep (4 songs) *Columbia 1504/promo/ps/'89/ with DR JOHN & CARMEN MCCRAE* $10
It Had to Be You *Columbia 1719/promo/ps/'89* .. $6
It Had to Be You/Stompin at Savoy/But Not For.. *Columbia 1725/promo/ps/'89* $8
Recipe For Love *Columbia 73863/promo/ps/'91* . $6
Stardust single/lp *Columbia 4927/promo/custom sticker/'92* . $6
You Didn't Know Me When *Columbia 4342/promo/ps/'92* $6

CONNORS, NORMAN
Only When She Cries/Naima/Hellies' Theme/ Lush Life *MoJazz 374631093/promo/ logo on black/ps/'93* $6

Remember Who You Are lp & instrumental
Mojazz 374631091/promo/ps/'93 .... $5

CONSOLIDATED

Accept Me For What I Am/You Suck lp & jack bangers mix *Nettwerk 6701/ promo/silkscreened/rear insert/'92* $5
Brutal Equation (4 versions)
Nettwerk Z25G 13822/stock/ps/'91 .... $5
Dysfunctional (3 versions)/Message to the People/ This is a Collective *IRS 74006/stock/ps* .. $5
Unity of Oppression (3 vers.)/Your Body Belongs to the State (unedited mix)
Nettwerk Z25G 13828/stock/ps/'91 .... $5

CONTRABAND

All the Way From Memphis edit & lp *Impact 1393/ promo/silkscreened/rear insert/ MICHAEL SCHENKER/'91* $4
Loud Guitars, Fast Cars.. single remix
Impact 1553/ promo/logo on silver/rear insert/'91 .... $5

CONWELL, TOMMY & YOUNG RUMBLERS

I'm Seventeen pt 1 & 2
Columbia 73500/promo/ps/'90 .... $5
If We Never Meet Again
Columbia 1399/promo/blue CD/'88 .... $5
Im Not Your Man with & without intro
Columbia 1206/promo/ps/'88 .... $5
Let Me Love You... *Columbia 2253/promo/ps/'90* . $5
Loves on Fire (2 versions)/Million Pretty Girls
Columbia 1497/promo/silkscreened pic/'89 .... $6

COODER, RY

Get Rhythm *WB 2934/promo/ps/'87* $8

COODER, RY & JIM KELTNER

King of the Street clean lp *Sire 5923/promo/'92* . $6

COODER, RY & THE PAHINUI BROS

Jealous Guy edit & lp *Private 81008/promo/ps* ... $7

COOKIE CREW

Got to Keep On 3:40/4:35
ffrr 85/promo/silkscreened/'89 .... $6
Secrets (of Success) 3 versions
ffrr 543/promo/silkscreened on black/'91 .. $6

COOL'R

If It Were Me *A&M 17785/promo/silkscreen/'89* ... $4

COOLY LIVE

That's What I Like 5 versions
RCA 62083/promo/silkscreened/ps/'92 .... $5

COOPER, ALICE

Hey Stoopid 2 versions *Epic 73845/promo/ silkscreened/gatefold hardcover ps/'91* $8
House of Fire *Epic 73085/promo/silkscreened/'89* $8
I Got a Line on You *Epic 1355/promo/'88* $8
Love's a Loaded Gun *Epic 73983/promo/ps/'91* . $6
Only My Heart Talkin' lp & radio edit
Epic 73268/promo/silkscreened/'89 .... $5
Poison *Epic 1665/promo/ps/'89* $6

COOPER, ALICE/DEEP PURPLE

Sampler (Muscle of Love/It's Hot Tonight/ From the Inside/Serious/Teenage Lament '74/Burn/Stormbringer/Lady Double .. + 2) *Metal Blade 6454/promo/ps/'90* $25

COOPER, MICHAEL

Let's Get Closer edit & lp
Reprise 5657/promo/'92 .... $4
Shoop Shoop (Never ...) *Reprise 5889/promo* $4
Shoop Shoop (Never Stop...) lp & instrumental/ Fun Fun Fun/Let's Get Closer 7 versions *Reprise 40717/gatefold hardcover ps/stock/'92* $5
Should Have Been You (6 version)
Reprise 3851/promo/'89 .... $5
Should Have Been You edit & lp
Reprise 3812/promo/'89 .... $4

COP SHOOT COP

Suck City (Nowhere/Days Will ../We Shall Be \ Changed + 1) *Interscope 96116/stock /gatefold hardcover ps/silkscreened/'92* ... $5

COPE, JULIAN

Beautiful Love/World Shut Your Mouth/ Trampolene/Charlotte Anne/5 O'Clock World/Love (Luv) (beautiful love mix) *Island 6664/promo/ps/'91* $12
Fear Loves This Place/I Have Always Been Here Before/Sizewell B/Gogmagog *Island 6751/promo/silkscreened/ps/'92* $6
Head 3:34 & 6:07/Love 6:51/Easty Risin' 8:18
Island 422 868 909/stock/ps/'91 .... $6

COPPERHEAD

Born Loser lp & live/Hard Livin'/Whiskey (last 2 live)
Mercury 893/promo/ps/silkscreened/'93 ... $8
Busted *Mercury 768/promo/gatefold hardcover ps/silkscreened/'92* $5

CORBIN/HANNER

I Will Stand By You *Mercury 807/promo/logo on red/rear insert/'92* $4
One More Night *Mercury 426/promo/ silkscreened/rear insert/'91* $4

CORONER

About Life *Noise 44887/promo/silkscreened/ rear insert/'91* $6
Last Entertainment *Noise International CDP 4/ promo/silkscreened/rear insert/'89* $6

CORROSION OF CONFORMITY
Dance of the Dead *Relativity 0139/promo/ logo on black/rear insert/'92* $6

COSTELLO, ELVIS
Let Him Dangle/Coal Trail Robberies/Ugly Things/ You're No Good *WB 3720/promo/ rear insert/'89* $12
Live at New York Town Hall (4 tracks) *WB 6480/promo/ps/'93* $12
Mighty Like a Rose 14 tracks deluxe edition *WB 26593/promo/ps* $25
Spike 15 tracks *WB 3426/promo/gatefold hardcover (with booklet)/silkscreen/'89* $20
The Juliet Letters excerpts (7 track sampler) *WB 6018/promo/ps/'93* $12
The Other Side of Summer *WB 4781/promo/'91* .$4
The Other Side of Summer *WB 4781/promo/silkscreened pic/'91* $6
This Town *WB 3511/promo/rear insert/ with MCCARTNEY, MCGUINN* $4
Veronica *WB 2424/promo/silkscreened green w/graphics/cowritten by McCartney* $8

COTTON, PAUL
Changing Horses *Sisapa/promo/'90* $4

COUNTESS VAUGHN
It's a Man's, Man's, Man's World edit/lp/ instrumental *Charisma 12714/promo/ silkscreened/rear insert/'92* $4

COURSE OF EMPIRE
Coming of the Century *Zoo Entertainment 17074/ promo/silkscreened/rear insert/'92* $4

COVER GIRLS
All That Glitters Isn't Gold (6 versions) *Capitol 79988/promo/logo on gold/ CLIVILLES & COLE/'89* $6
Don't Stop Now single & 12"/Funk Boutique 12" *Epic 73650/promo/ logo on purple/rear insert/'90* $6
Funk Boutique (3 versions) *Epic 73698/promo/rear insert/'90* $6
Thank You edit & lp *Epic 74438/promo/ps/logo on blue/'92* $4
We Can't Go Wrong *Capitol 79850/promo/silkscreened/'89* $5
We Can't Go Wrong edit & lp *Capitol 79883/promo/silkscreened/'89* $5
Wishing on a Star *Epic 74343/promo/logo on black/ps/'92* $4
Wishing on a Star 5 versions *Epic 4652/promo/ ps/silkscreened/custom sticker/'92* $6

COVERDALE/PAGE
Over Now edit & lp *Geffen 4529/promo/ps/'93* ...$5
Pride and Joy *Geffen 4491/promo/ silkscreened/gatefold hardcover ps/'93* $6
Shake My Tree *Geffen 4504/promo/silkscreen/ps* $5
Take Me For a Little While edit & lp *Geffen 4510/promo/silkscreened/ps/'93* ...$5
Take Me For a Little While edit 1 & 2 *Geffen 4535/promo/silkscreened/'93* $6

COWBOY JUNKIES
Cause Cheap is How I ../Dead Flowers/Capt. Kidd *RCA 2612/promo/ps/'90* $8
Floorboard Blues *RCA 62681/ps/silkscreen/'93* ...$4
Live! ep (This Street, That Man, This Life/If You Were the Woman & I Was the Man/Hot Burrito No. 1/Sweet Jane) *RCA 62329/ promo/silkscreened/ps/JOHN PRINE/'92* .$8
Misguided Angel (edit) *RCA 8977/promo/ps/'89* .$6
Misguided Angel (edit)/Sweet Jane + 3 more live *RCA 8958/promo/ps/'89* $18
Murder, Tonight, In the Trailer Park/Black Eyed .. *RCA 62206/promo/silkscreened/ps/'92* $7
Sun Comes Up, Its Tuesday... (edit)/The Truth about The Caution .. (29:04 interview) + open end interview *RCA 9180/promo/ gatefold hardcover ps/'90* $15
Sweet Jane (live) *RCA 8879/promo/ps/'88* $8
This Street, That Man, This Life *RCA 62310/ promo/logo on brown/rear insert/'92* $5

COWBOY JUNKIES & BRUCE HORNSBY
Rock & Bird (remix) *RCA 2701/promo/ rear insert/custom sticker/'90* $6

COX, DEANNA
Never Gonna Be Your Fool .. *WB 5597/promo/'92* $4

CRAAFT
Jane lp & edit *RCA 8884/promo/ps/'89* $4

CRACK THE SKY
From the Greenhouse (4:59) *Grudge 4752/promo*$5
Lost in America/Greenhouse Finale *Grudge 4750/promo/'89* $5
Mr President edit & lp *Grudge 4768/promo/'90*...$5

CRACKER
Happy Birthday to Me
Virgin 4568/promo/rear insert/'92 ....$4
Happy Birthday to Me lp & remix *Virgin 12691/promo/logo on pink/rear insert/'92* $5
I Ride My Bike edit & lp *Virgin 12736/promo/silkscreened/rear insert/'92* $5
Low *Virgin 12813/promo/silkscreen/rear insert* .$5
Teen Angst edit & lp *Virgin 4380/promo/silkscreened/rear insert/'92* $5
This is Cracker Soul
Virgin 12700/promo/silkscreened/'92 ....$5
Tucson ep (River Euphrates/I Ride My Bike/Euro Trash Girl/Bad Vibes Everybody - all live in the studio) *Virgin 12702/promo/silkscreened/ps/'92* $15

CRAMPS & IGGY POP
Miniskirt Blues *Restless 012/promo/silkscreened pic/'91* $8

CRAMPS, THE
Journey to the Center of a Girl/King of Drapes/Teenage Rage/High School Hellcats *Enigma 288/promo/silkscreened logo/custom sticker/'90* $8

CRANBERRIES, THE
Dreams *Island 6757/promo/ps/logo on white/'92* .$4
Still Can't... *Island 6799/promo/silkscreened/'93* ..$4
Sunday edit & lp/Them *Island 6781/promo/ps/logo on black/'93* $4

CRANES
Everywhere 2 versions/Adrift/Underwater *RCA 62550/promo/ps/'93* $5
Tomorrows Tears/Sixth of May/Casa Blanca/Dreamless/interview (24:17) *RCA 62247/promo/ps/ltd edit.of 2000/'92* $12

CRASH TEST DUMMIES
A Portrait of the Artist as a Young Dummy ep (Comin' Back Soon/Superman's Song/Ghosts That Haunt Me/Androgynous/interview (30+ minutes) *Arista 2131/promo/logo on tan/gatefold ps/'91* $10

CRASH VEGAS
Sky *Atlantic 3471/promo/silkscreened logo on white/rear insert/'89* $4
You& Me *London 294/promo/ps/silkscreened/'93* $4

CRASH, JOHNNY
All the Way in Love *WTG 2112/promo/silkscreened logo on purple/rear insert* $4

CRAVEN, BEVERLEY
Holding On *Epic 73963/promo/logo on purple/ps* ..$4
Promise Me/Joey (west coast versions)/Castle in Clouds/Promise Me (last 2 live) *Epic 4464/promo/ps/'92* $5

CRAWFORD, MICHAEL
Only You edit & lp *Atlantic 4303/promo/rear insert/custom sticker/'91* $6
A Lot That You Can..4 vers. *WB 5614/promo/'92* ..$8
A Lot That You... edit & lp *WB 5521/promo/'92* ..$5

CRAWFORD, RANDY
Cigarette in Rain *WB 4364/promo/rear insert/'89* ..$5
I Don't Feel Much Like Crying edit & lp *WB 4031/promo/'89* $5
Knockin' on Heavens Door edit & lp *WB 3635/promo/with ERIC CLAPTON & DAVID SANBORN/'89* $7
Rhythm of Romance/Diamante *WB 5580/promo* ..$5
Shine edit & lp *WB 5779/promo/'92* $5
Shine/If I Were/If You'd Only Believe/Like the Sun Out of Nowhere *WB 5351/promo/'92* $6
Wrap U Up edit & lp *WB 3894/promo/'89* $5

CRAY, ROBERT
Bouncin' Back edit &lp *Mercury 389/promo/silkscreened logo on brown/'91* $4
Consequences *Mercury 343/promo/silkscreened logo on blue/ps/'90* $4
Dont Be Afraid of the Dark
Mercury 21/promo/ps/'88 ....$5
I Was Warned edit & lp *Mercury 806/promo/logo on orange/ps/'92* $4
Interview (30:00) + 4 song segments
Mercury 197/promo/'90 ....$12
Just a Loser *Mercury 732/promo/silkscreened pic/gatefold ps/'92* $5
Midnight Stroll ep & Interview (30:00) + 4 song segments/The Forecast 3 versions *Mercury 197/promo/oversized box container/2 cds/booklet/'90* $20
The Price I Pay edit & lp *Mercury 836/promo/ps* $5
These Things *Merc. 381/promo/silkscreened/'91* $5

CRAZYHEAD
Have Love Will Travel *EMI 04438/promo/silkscreened pic/rear insert/'89* $5

CREEPS, THE
Ooh - I Like It orig. & swingin' radio mix
Atlantic 3384/promo/ps/'90 ....$5

CRENSHAW, MARSHALL
A Collection (13 tracks) *Paradox 1343/promo/ps* $25
Better Back Off *MCA 1344/promo/ps/'91* $5
Don't Disappear *.MCA 1663/promo/rear insert/'91* $5
Some Hearts *WB 3581/promo/silkscreened/custom sticker/'89* $5

CRIME & THE CITY SOLUTION
I Have the Gun (2 versions)
Mute 8236/promo/rear insert/'90 ....$6

CRIMINAL NATION
6 Down Deep 3 vers./Sick to the Brain edit & lp
Nastymix 130/promo/silkscreened/'92 ......$5

Release the Pressure (12 tracks) *Nastymix 70240/ promo/ps/silkscreened/'90* $10

CRO MAGS

See the Signs/Eyes of Tomorrow/The Other Side of Madness *Century Media 7730/ promo/silkscreened* $5

CROKER, BRENDAN

No Money At All *RCA 1252/promo/ps/'89* $4

CRONIN, KEVIN

Hard to Believe *Epic 4000/promo/silkscreen/'91* ...$4

CROSBY STILL & NASH

CSN - Boxed Set Sampler (14 tracks - lots of rare stuff) *Atlantic 4283/promo/ logo on white/ps/'91* $25
(Got to Keep) Open *Atlantic 3508/promo/ps/'90* ..$5
Chippin' Away *Atlantic3144/promo/rear insert/'89* .$5
If Anybody Had a ...*Atlantic 3492/promo/ps/'90* $5
In the Studio radio show *Album Network & Bullet Prod./promo/air date: 6/27/88* $30
Live it Up *Atlantic 3336/promo/ps/ logo silkscreened/'90* $5
Profiled interview... *Atlantic 3446/promo/ps/'90* .$15
selftitled *In the Studio 1/promo/radio show/'88* ..$25

CROSBY STILLS NASH & YOUNG

American Dream *Atlantic 2497/promo/ silkscreened pic/'88* $10
American Dream *Atlantic 2542/promo/rear insert* .$7
American Dream (14 tracks) *Atlantic 2552/promo/ gatefold hardcover/book/silkscreen pic* .$60
Got It Made *Atlantic 2578/promo/rear insert/'88* $5
Woodstock (original version) *Atlantic 2860/promo/ rear insert/cust. "20th Anniv." sticker/'89* ..$6

CROSBY, DAVID

Drive My Car 3:20/3:34 *A&M 17720/promo/silkscreened/ps/'89* $5
In the Wide Ruin *A&M 17814/promo/silkscreened logo/'89* .$4
Lady of the Harbor *A&M 17758/promo/purple CD/'89* $4
Monkey and the Underdog *A&M 17749/promo/silkscreened red/'89* ...$5
Through Your Hands *Atlantic 5179/promo* $5

CROSBY, DAVID & PHIL COLLINS

Hero *Atlantic 5060/promo/silkscreened/ps/'93* ..$5

CROSS, THE

Shove It 9 tracks *Virgin 90857/stock/ps/'88* $15

CROW, SHERYL

Scenes From the Tuesday Night Music Club (Run Baby Run/Strong Enough/All I Wanna Do/ No One Said It Would Be Easy) *A&M 31458 8182/promo/ gatefold hardcover ps/silkscreened/'93* $5

CROWDED HOUSE

Better Be Home .. *Capitol 79341/promo/ps/'88* $7
Chocolate Cake *Capitol 79775/promo/silkscreened/ps/'91* .$5
Chocolate Cake/As Sure As I Am/Anyone Can *Capitol 15738/stock/ps/'91* $6
Fall At Your Feet *Capitol 79849/promo/silkscreened/ps/'91* .$6
Fall At Your Feet/Whispers &Moans/6 Months in a Leaky Boat *Capitol 15757/stock/ps/'91* .$6
I Feel Possessed/Mr Tambourine Man/Eight Miles High/So You Want to Be a RnR Star (last 3 w/ROGER MCGUINN) *Capitol 15490/box/stock/'89* $12
It's Only Natural *Capitol 79738/promo/silkscreen/ rear insert/custom sticker/'91* $5
Weather With You edit & lp *Capitol 79327/ promo/ps/custom sticker/silkscreened/'91* $6
Weather With You edit + 4 live tracks *Capitol 15734/stock/ps/'91* $7
Woodface 14 tracks *Capitol 79759/promo/ elaborate diecut multifold cover with book/outer sleeve (promo comes with outer sleeve)/silkscreened/'91* $25
World Where You Live single & live/Something So Strong/Dont Dream Its Over (last 2 live) *Capitol 79070/promo/ps/'87* $25

CROWELL, RODNEY

It's Not For Me to Judge *Columbia 4642/ promo/ps/silkscreened pic/'92* $6
Keys to the Highway 12 tracks *Columbia 45242/ promo/silkscreened pic/'89* $12
Let's Make Trouble *Columbia 4768/promo/ps* $5
Lovin' All Night *Columbia 74250/promo/ logo on red/rear insert/'92* $4
Many A Long & Lonesome... *Columbia 1881/ promo/silkscreened/rear insert/'89* $6
Now That We're Alone *Columbia 73569/promo/rear insert/'90* $4
Things I Wish I'd ... *Columbia 73760/promo/'91* $4
What Kind of Love *Columbia 4663/promo/ps/'92* ..$4

CRUEL SHOES

Dancing Shoes *Rendezvous Entertainment 62225/ promo/rear insert/'92* $4
Where Are the Angels radio remix *RCA 62353/promo/ps/'92* $4

CRUEL STORY OF YOUTH

You're What You Want to Be *Columbia 1469/ promo/blue silkscreened/'89* $4

CRUISE, JULEE

Falling edit & lp/Twin Peaks Theme *WB 4346/promo/custom sticker/'89* $4
Floating Into the Night full cd *WB 25859/ promo/ps/color pic silkscreened/'89* $12
Rockin' Back Inside My Heart edit & lp *WB 3934/promo/ps/'89* $4

Rockin' Back Inside My Heart (3 versions)/
The World Spins *WB 40027/stock/ gatefold hardcover ps/'91* $6

CRUSADERS
That's How It Is *Profile 7371/promo/ logo on black/rear insert/'92* $4

CRUSH
The Rain edit/lp *Eastwest 4970/promo/ silkscreened/ps/'93* $4

CRY CHARITY
I Want You Back *Morgan Creek 0021/promo/ logo on purple/ps/'92* $4

CRY OF LOVE
Bad Thing edit & lp/Shade Tree *Columbia 5348/promo/ps/'93* $4

CRY WOLF
Pretender 3:57 & 5:25 *I Really Spend 67037/ promo/silkscreened/rear insert/'90* $4

CRYPT KEEPER, THE
The Crypt Jam 4 versions *Giant 5577/promo/rear insert/'92* $6

CUD
Rich & Strange/Purple Love Balloon/Day By Day/ Once Again *A&M 31458 8043/ promo/silkscreened/ps/'92* $5
The Cud Band ep (Magic (farsley mix)/ Robinson Crusoe/Now/Hey Boots/Magic) *A&M 75021 5380/stock/ dj silkscreened/ps/'91* $6
Through the Roof/Undoubtedly Thomas/Prime Cut *A&M 75021 7345/promo/logo on blue/ps* .$6

CUEVAS, CHRIS
Hip Hop Atlantic 3721/promo/logo on black/ps/'91 .$4
I Need You *Atlantic 4515/promo/ silkscreened pic/rear insert/'91* $5
You Are the One *Atlantic 4188/promo/'91* $4

CULT, THE
Edie (Ciao Baby) edit & lp *Reprise 3631/promo/silkscreened/'89* $6
Fire Woman edit/Automatic Blues *Sire 27543/stock/3"/ps/'89* $10
Fire Woman lp & edit *Reprise 3435/promo/'89* ...$6
Heart of Soul edit & lp *Sire 5187/promo/'91* $6
Sonic Temple lmtd promo cover *Sire 25871/ promo/gatefold mirror cover/'89* $25
Sun King edit & lp *Sire 3604/promo/'89* $6
Sweet Soul Sister edit & lp *Sire 3881/promo/'89* $6
The Witch edit & lp *Sire 5708/promo/'92* $6
Wild Hearted Son lp without chant/edit/lp *Sire 5009/promo/silkscreened/'91* $6

CULTURAL REVOLUTION
Nite & Day edit & lp *Epic Soundtrax 77160/promo/ps/'93* $4

CULTURE BEAT
Cherry Lips (4 versions) *Epic 49K 73170/stock/ps/'90* $6
Cherry Lips (6 versions) *Epic 1999/promo/ps/'89* $6
I Like You (5 versions) *Epic 73600/promo/ps/'90* $6
Tell Me That You Wait (5 versions) *Epic 73762/promo/ps/'91* $6

CULTURE CLUB & BOY GEORGE
Generations of Love (land of oz mix) + Do You Really Wanna Hurt Me/I'll Tumble For Ya/ Karma Chameleon + 3 more CC hits *Virgin 3557/promo/silkscreened/'90* $15

CURE
A Letter to Elise *Elektra 8627/promo/logo on red* .$6
A Letter to Elise 4:18/7:06 *Elektra 8638/promo/logo on red/'92* $8
Close to Me radio edit *Elektra 8276/promo/ silkscreened logo/rear insert/'90* $6
Close to Me (closest mix)/Just Like Heaven (dizzy mix)/Primary (red mix) *Elektra 66582/ stock/gatefold hardcover ps/'90* $7
Fascination Street 4:17 & 8:48/Babble/ Out of Mind *Elektra 66702/stock/ps/'89* ..$7
Fascination Street (remix 4:17) *Elektra 8075/promo/'89* $8
Friday I'm in Love *Elektra 8578/promo/logo on red* $6
Friday I'm in Love 2 vers/Halo/Scared of You *Elektra 66416/stock/gatefold hardcover ps/custom sticker/'92* $6
Friday I'm in Love/Halo *Elektra 64742/ps/stock/silkscreened/'92* ...$5
High 2 versions/This Twilight Garden/Play *Elektra 66437/stock/gatefold hardcover ps/'92* $6
High 3:33/Open *Elektra 64766/stock/ps/'92* $5
High single mix *Fiction 8547/promo/silkscreened/ps/'92* ...$7
Hot Hot Hot remix & extended *Elektra 2173/promo/ps/'87* $20
In Between Days (edit) *Elektra 8328/promo/rear insert/'90* $7
Just Like Heaven video & audio/Catch/Hot Hot ../ Why Can't I Be.. 8:04 (last 3 audio only) *Elektra 64002/stock/ps/'87* $15
Love Song *Elektra 8094/promo/'89* $7
Love Song remix & extended remix *Elektra 8102/promo/logo silkscreen/'89* $8
Love Song remix & extended/Late/Fear of Ghosts *Elektra 66687/stock/ps/'89* $7
Lullaby 4:07/7:41/4:08 *Elektra 8125/promo/silkscreened/'89* $12
Lullaby 4:07&7:41/Homesick/Untitled (last 2 live) *Elektra 66664/stock/ps/'89* $8
Never Enough 4:26 & 6:07 *Elektra 8233/promo/rear insert/'90* $8

Never Enough (2 versions)/Harold and Joe/ Lets Go to Bed (milk mix) *Elektra 66604/stock/ps/'90* $6
Pictures of You remix 4:45 *Elektra 8165/promo/ silkscreen logo on orange/rear insert/'90* .. $7
Pictures of You remix/Last Dance/Fascination Street/Prayers For Rain/Disintegration (last 4 live) *Elektra 66639/stock/ps/'90* ... $7

CURIOSITY KILLED THE CAT
Name and Number 3:59/4:21 *Mercury 161/promo/silkscreened/'89* $4

CURRY, MARK
Sorry About the Weather edit & lp *Virgin 12685/ promo/silkscreened/rear insert/'92* $4

CURVE
Fait Accompli 3 versions/Arms Out/Sigh *Anxious 085/promo/silkscreened/ps/'92* ... $6
Frozen ep (Coast is Clear/Colour Hurts/Frozen/ Zoo) *Charisma 96293/stock/ gatefold hardcover ps/'91* $6
Horror Head (remix)/Coast is Clear/Die Like a Dog *Charisma 0100/promo/ps/silkscreened* $7
Horror Head (remix)/Coast is Clear/Die Like a Dog *Charisma 0100/promo/silkscreened/ custom sticker/'92* $6

CUT N MOVE
Get Serious 6 versions *Epic 73878/promo/logo on blue/ps/'91* $5
Spread Love 5 versions *Soulpower 74059/promo/ps/'91* $5

CUTTING CREW
(Between a) Rock & a Hard Place edit & lp *Virgin/promo/silkscreened titles/'89* $6
Big Noise *Virgin 2824/promo/silkscreened/'89* ... $5
Everything But My Pride (edit) *Virgin 2823/promo/silkscreened/'89* $5
I've Been in Love Before edit & lp *Virgin 2076/ promo/silkscreened blue/ps/'87* $5
The Scattering *Virgin PRO CD CREW/promo/ gatefold ps/silkscreened/'89* $6

CYCLE SLUTS FROM HELL
Speed Queen/Dark Ships/By the Balls/I Wish You Were a Beer *Epic 4006/promo/ silkscreened pic/rear insert/'91* $6

CYPRESS HILL
Hand on the Clock *Ruffhouse 4564/promo/rear insert/'92* $6
How I Could Just Kill a Man *Columbia 4486/promo/logo on black/'92* .. $6
Insane in the Brain 3 versions *Ruffhouse 5209/promo/logo on black/ps* .. $8
Latin Lingo prince paul mix & lp *Ruffhouse 4747/promo/ps/'92* $6

Something For the Blunted ep (7 tracks) *Atlantic 4634/promo/silkscreened/ps/'92* .. $6

DAME, DAMIAN
Right Down to It edit & lp *LaFace 4002/promo/ps/silkscreened/'91* .. $4

DAMIAN, MICHAEL
Another You *A&M 75021 7323/promo/ps/'91* ... $4
Christmas Time Without You *Cypress 17970/ promo/silkscreened green & red/'87* $4
Cover of Love power & dance mix *Cypress 17803/ promo/silkscreened pic/'89* $5
Let's Get Into This 6 versions *A&M 75021 7267/ promo/logo on white/ps/'91* $5
Was It Nothing At All *Cypress 17887/ promo/silkscreened pic/'89* $5
What a Price to Pay (4 versions) *A&M 75021 7539/promo/ps/'91* $5

DAMN THE MACHINE
Lonesome God *A&M 31458 8133/promo/ silkscreened/ps/'93* $4

DAMN YANKEES
Bad Reputation *WB 4051/promo/'90* $5
Come Again radio mix/single *WB 4751/promo/'90* $6
Come Again edit & lp *WB 4321/promo/rear insert* . $5
Coming of Age *WB 4000/promo/'90* $5
Don't Tread on M edit & lp *WB 5622/promo/'92* . $5
Fifteen Minutes of Fame *WB 5870/promo/ back "tour date" ps/'92* $5
High Enough single & lp *WB 4416/promo/rear insert/'90* $5
Mister Please *WB 5839/promo/'92* $5
Runaway *WB 4052/promo/'90* $5
Silence is Broken radio mix *WB 5962/promo/'92* ... $5
Silence is Broken remix/Double Coyote *WB 18612/stock/ps/'92* $5

Do you have CDs that belong in the next edition of this guide? If so, we'd like to hear from you. See "How You Can Help" on page xiii.

Where You Goin' Now *WB 5774/promo/'92*.......$5
Where You Goin' Now edit & lp *WB 5739/promo* ..$5

DAN REED NETWORK
Make It Easy *Mercury 117/promo/silkscreened/'89*$4
Tiger in a Dress edit & lp
Mercury 133/promo/silkscreened/'89........$4

DANCING HOODS
Babys Got Rockets *Relativity 88561-8224/promo/rear insert/silkscreened cat/'88*......$4

DANE, DANA
A Little Bit of Dana Tonight radio/clark kent mix
Profile 7314/promo/'90..............................$4

DANGER DANGER
Bang Bang *Imagine 2003/promo/silkscreened logo/ps/'90* $4
Don't Walk Away *Epic 73606/promo/logo silkscreened/rear insert/'90*.......................$4
Down and Dirty Live (5 songs)
Imagine 1996/promo/ps/'90....................$15
I Still Think About You *Epic 74231/promo/logo on blue/rear insert/'92*.......................$4
Monkey Business
Epic 73949/promo/silkscreened/ps/'91 .....$4
Naughty Naughty *Epic 2170/promo/silkscreened/rear insert/'90*..$4

DANGEROUS TOYS
Gimme No Lip *Columbia 4023/promo/ps/'91* $4
Line 'em Up straight up mix & lp
Columbia 4147/promo/ps/'91....................$4
Scared remix & lp *Columbia 1833/promo/ps/silkscreened logo on black/'89*..................$4
Selftitled (lp length) *Columbia 1703/promo/silkscreened/rear insert/'89*..........$10
Sport'n a Woody (3 versions)/Queen of the Nile
Columbia 1950/promo/silkscreened logo on red/ps/'90...................................$6

DANIEL, JEFFREY
She's the Girl vocal & instrumental
Epic 74009/promo/ps/'90.........................$4

DANIELS, CHARLIE
Holiday Radio Special 52+ minutes
Epic 2204/promo/ps/'90..........................$20
Little Folks *Epic 74061/promo/logo silkscreened/rear insert/'91*......................$5

DANZIG
'88 Def American release (10 tracks) *Def American/promo silkcreen issue/'88*.......$20
A Taste of Danzig III ep (How the Gods../Godless/Dirty Black Summer/Sistinas)
Def American 5595/promo/ps/'92.............$8
Dirty Black Summer *Def American 5563/promo/ps* $6
Dirty Black Summer/Bodies/When Death Had No.. ...
Def American 40544/stock/gatefold hardcover ps/'92...$6
Her Black Wing *Def American 4121/promo/ps/'90* $6
Killer Wolf *Def American 4152/promo/ps/custom sticker/'90*..................................$6
Mother 2 vers. *American 6422/promo/ps/'93*....$5
Thrall ep (It's Coming Down/The Violet Fire/Trouble)/Demonsweatlive ep (Snakes of Christ/Am I a Demon/Sistinas/Mother)
Def American 45286/stock/ps/'93.............$5

DAOU, THE
Sympathy Bouquet (remix)/Never Ending Winter/What Are You Guilty Of?
Columbia 4773/promo/ps/'92....................$4

DARE
Abandon *A&M 17622/promo/ps/'88*......................$4
Nothing is Stronger Than .. *A&M 17731/promo*....$4

DARLING BUDS, THE
Crystal Clear (5 vers.) *Columbia 73662/promo/ps* $6
It Makes No Difference *Columbia 2275/promo/blue silkscreened/ps/'90* $6
Long Day in Universe/There's Nothing About You That Makes Me Feel OK/Clearlight/Poppy's Spell *Chaos 4913/promo/ps/'92* $6

DARLING CRUEL
Everythings Over *Polydor 66/promo/silkscreened/custom sticker/'89*................$4

DAS DAMEN
The Promise/Chaindrive/The Outsider/Thrilled to the Marrow/Silence Sings You
Sup Pop 111/stock/ps/'91.......................$10

DAS EFX
If Only edit *Eastwest 4980/promo*....................$4
Straight Out the Sewer 3 versions
Eastwest 4854/promo..................................$6
They Want EFX remix & dead serious
Eastwest 4449/promo/silkscreened/rear insert/'92......................$5

DAVID J
Space Cowboy edit 1/edit 2 *MCA 2473/promo/custom tour date sticker/rear insert/'92*...$7

DAVIS, CARLENE
Dial My Number 4 versions
Gee Street 6729/promo/ps/'92..................$5
Dial My Number 6 versions
Geestreet 422-864 219/stock/ps/'92.........$5
Dial My Number morales radio mix/carlenes radio
Geestreet 559/promo/ps/'92.....................$5

DAVIS, CAROLE
J'Aime You edit & lp
Atlantic 5034/promo/silkscreened/ps/'93 ..$4

DAVIS, MIKE
Ain't No Stoppin' Us Now 7 versions
Jive 42087/promo/rear insert/'92 ....$6

DAVIS, MILES
Jo Jo edit & lp *WB 3659/promo/'89*.................$6
Red/Orange/Blue/Violet *Epic 1869/promo/ silkscreened green/'89*.............................$7
Summertime/Someday My Prince Will Come/ Flamenco Sketches + 2
Columbia 1376/promo/ps/'88...................$8
The Doo Bop Song edit with rap/edit without rap/lp/instrumental *WB 5430/promo/'92* .$7
The Doo Bop Song 3 versions/Mystery/Sonya
WB 5619/promo/'92 ....$7

DAVIS, MILES & MARCUS MILLER
Siesta/Conchita/Claire/Augustine (all edits)
WB 3002/promo/ps/'87 ....$10

DAVIS, MILES & WYNTON MARSALIS & SHIRLEY HORN
Don't Let the Sun Catch You Cryin'/ You Won't Forget Me
Verve PRO HORN/promo/ instruments on red silkscreened $8

DAX, DANIELLE
Big Blue '82 3 versions/Jehovahs Precious Stone 2 versions *Sire 40047/stock/ gatefold hardcover ps/'91* $6
Tomorrow Never Knows (4 versions)/King Crack
Sire 21773/stock/ps/'90 ....$6

DAY ZS, THE
Certainly edit & lp
Reprise 4424/promo/rear insert/'90 ....$4
Certainly (6 versions) *Reprise 4596/promo/'90*...$6

DAY, MORRIS
Gimme Whatcha Got 5 versions
Reprise 5879/promo/'92 ....$6
Gimme Whatcha Got edit/lp/instrumental
Reprise 5782/promo/'92 ....$5

DAYNE, TAYLOR
Can't Get Enough of Your Love *Arista 2582/ promo/logo on blue/ps/'93* $5
Dont Rush Me (4 mixes) *Arista 9723/promo/ps* .$10
Heart of Stone *Arista 2057/promo/silkscreened logo on red/rear insert/'90*........................$6
I'll Be Your Shelter single versions & groove mix
Arista 2006/promo/'90/logo on aqua silkscreened/rear insert..........................$7
With Every Beat of My Heart 4:12/6:25
Arista 9895/promo/ps/'89.......................$10

DBS, THE
Working For Somebody *IRS 17449/promo/ps/'87* $8

DE JOHNETTE, JACK
Jack It/Exotic Isles/Nine Over Reggae/Indigo Dreamscapes (all edits)
MCA 18312/promo/rear insert/'90............$6

DE LA SOUL
A Roller Skating Jam Named Saturdays 8 vers
Tommy Boy 990/promo/'91......................$8
Breakadawn vocal & instr./Stickabush/En Focus vocal & instrumental/Dawn Brings Smoke/Hsubakkits
Tommy Boy 586/promo/'93......................$6
Millie Pulled a Pistol on Santa 2 vers./Keepin' the Faith 6 versions
Tommy Boy 500/stock/ps/'91...................$6
Ring Ring Ring 3 versions/Afro Connections at Hi 5
Tommy Boy 964/stock/ps/silkscreened $6
Ring Ring Ring 4 vers. *Tommy Boy 980/promo/ silkscreened/rear insert/'91* $6
Say No Go (4 versions)/Double Huey Skit/ Mack Daddy on Left *Tommy Boy 934/ promo/silkscreened logo/rear insert/'89*....$6

DEACON BLUE
Real Gone Kid *Columbia 1801/promo/ps/'89*.....$4
Twist and Shout
*Columbia 4247/promo/logo on blue/ps/'91*$4
When Will Yo Make My Telephone Ring edit & lp ...
Columbia 1215/promo/ps/'88...................$4
Your Swaying Arms lp & remix
Columbia 4070/promo/ps/'91...................$4

DEAD MILKMEN
Dollar Signs in Her Eyes
Enigma 316/promo/silkscreened/ps/'90....$6
If I Had a Gun/Dolce/Bitchin' Camaro/Silly Dreams/ The Conspiracy Song (last 3 live)
Hollywood 61409/stock/gatefold hardcover ps/silkscreened/'92 ....$6
Instant Club Hit (3 versions)/Boner Beats/Tugena/ Vince Lombardi Service Center
Restless 72231/stock/ gatefold ps/silkscreened/'87 ....$6
Methodist Coloring Book *Enigma 282/promo/ custom sticker/silkscreened/'90* $6
Punk Rock Girl
Enigma 173/promo/custom sticker/'88......$7
Smokin' Banana Peels (remixed by DON WAS)
Enigma 180/promo/custom sticker/ banana silkscreen/'89..............................$6
The Conspiracy Song/South Bound Saurez
Hollywood 10191/promo/silkscreened/ rear insert/custom sticker/'92...................$6
The Secret of Life *Hollywood 10141/promo/ silkscreened/rear insert*............................$6

DEAD OR ALIVE
Come Home With Me Baby 3:50/6:20/6:24
Epic 1637/promo/logo on pink/'89 .... $15

DEAN, PAUL
Sword & Stone
Columbia 1384/promo/silkscreened/'89 .... $4

DEAN, TRENT
Livin' It Up edit & extended
Chrysalis 23655/promo/ps/'91 .... $4

DEATH ANGEL/D.A.
A Room With a View edit & lp
Geffen 4171/promo/ps/'90 .... $4

DEBURGH, CHRIS
Missing You (remix) *A&M 17640/promo/'88* $5
Tender Hands *A&M 17676/promo/'89* $5
The Simple Truth *A&M 75021 7258/promo/'91* ... $5

DEE, DAISY
Crazy (4 versions) *RCA 2790/promo/ps/'91* $5

DEEE-LITE
ESP *Elektra 8329/promo/silkscreen/rear insert* ... $5
Good Beat turn up radio mix & lp *Elektra 8363/ promo/logo on blue/rear insert/'91* $6
Groove is in the Heart (3 versions)
Elektra 8214/promo/ps/'90 .... $8
Groove is in the Heart (4 versions)/What is Love? (3 versions) *Elektra 66609/stock/ps/'90* .. $7
I Had a Dream I Was Falling Through... edit ....
Elektra 8575/promo/gatefold hardcover ps ... $5
Power of Love (4 versions) *Elektra 8275/ promo/silkscreened/rear insert/'90* $7
Power of Love (6 versions)/Build the Bridge (2 versions) + 2 *Elektra 66592/stock/ gatefold hardcover ps/'90* $6
Runaway sampladelic edit
Elektra 8581/promo/silkscreened/ps/'92 ... $6

DEELE, THE
Imagination 3 versions *Solar 70030/promo/'93* .. $5

DEEP FOREST
Sweet Lullaby 5 vers. *Epic 49K 74919/stock/ps/ custom sticker/'93* $4

DEEP JIMI & THE ZEP CREAMS
Blowup ep (Why/I'm Lookin'/Waiting For My Time/ Middle of the Shoes III)
Technicolor TCH-001/stock/ps/'92 .... $5

DEEP PURPLE
Fire in the Basement *RCA 3030/promo/ps/'90* ... $7
Hush *Mercury 16/promo/ps/'88* $8
King of Dreams lp & edit
RCA 2703/promo/silkscreened/ps/'90 ...... $6
King of Dreams lp & edit
RCA 2744/promo/rear insert/'90 .... $6
Love Conquers All edit & lp
RCA 2810/promo/ps/'91 .... $6
The Battle Rages On
Giant 6359/promo/silkscreened/ps/'93 ..... $5

DEF LEPPARD
Adrenalize interview (with Joe Elliott) *Merc.508/ promo/ps (with questions)/'92* $25
Desert Song/Fractured Love/Ride Into the Sun
Mercury 1055/promo/'93 .... $8
Elected (live) *Mercury 765/promo/custom sticker* $12
Have You Ever Needed Someone So Bad
Mercury 722/promo/gatefold hardcover ps .. $8
I Wanna Touch U
Mercury 938/promo/logo silkscreened/'92 $8
Let's Get Rocked *Mercury 641/promo/ gatefold hardcover ps/silkscreened/'92* .. $12
Make Love Like a Man *Mercury 705/promo/ gatefold hardcover ps/'92* $8
Rocket/Women (live)
Mercury 872 614/3"/ps/stock/'88 .... $12
Stand Up (Kick Love Into Motion)
Mercury 803/promo/ps/'93 .... $8
Tonight 2 versions *Mercury 803/promo/ps/'93* ... $8
Two Steps Behind *Columbia 5235/promo/ps/'93* . $6
Two Steps Behind electric & acoustic
Mercury 1052/promo/custom sticker/'93 . $10
Women lp & edit/Tear It Down
Mercury 02/promo/foldout poster ps/'87 . $20

DEFINITION FX
Something Inside 3 versions/Road Song Fever
RCA 62536/stock/ps/custom sticker/'93 ... $5

DEFINITION OF SOUND
Moira Jane's Cafe live/lp/e-smoove's groovy mix
Cardian 4023/stock/silkscreened/ rear insert/custom sticker/'92 .... $5
Wear Your Love Like Heaven 3 versions
Cardiac 6015/promo/'91 .... $5

DEFRANCESCO, JOEY

Blues For J/Lights Camera Action/Dr Jekyll
Columbia 3045/promo/ps/'91 ....$4

DEJA

Made to Be Together engagement mix
Virgin PRCD XXXX/promo/'88 ....$4
Made to Be Together (3 versions)
Virgin 2668/promo/'88 ....$4

DEL AMITRI

Always the Last To Know remix & lp
A&M 75021 7385/promo/silkscreened pic/ custom sticker (invitation to Whiskey show)/'92 ....$8
Always the Last To Know remix & lp
A&M 75021 7385/promo/ silkscreen pic/gatefold hardcover ps/'92 ...$8
Be My Downfall *A&M 31458 8072/promo/ silkscreened logo/ps/'92* $5
Change Everything 12 tracks *A&M 75021 5385/ promo/silkscreened/ps/'92* $15
Just Like a Man edit & lp *A&M 31458 8008/ promo/logo on gold/ps/'92* $5
Kiss This Thing Goodbye *A&M 17985/promo/ps* ..$6
Stone Cold Sober remix & lp *A&M 75021 8065/ promo/ps/'89* $6
Waking Hours w/intros by JUSTIN CURRIE
A&M 17950/promo/logo silkscreen/'90 ...$20

DEL BARRIO, EDUARDO

Free Play ep (Images of Life/Lament for a Lonely Child/Chaca Rara/Cubana)
A&M 75021 7468/promo/silkscreened/ps ..$5

DEL FUEGOS

Breakaway *RCA 9161/promo/ps/'90* $4
Move With Me Sister *RCA 9075/promo/ps/'89* ...$4

DEL LORDS, THE

About You *Enigma 272/promo/silkscreened/ custom sticker/'90* $4

DEL THE FUNKY HOMOSAPIEN

Dr. Bombay edit & remix edit/Hoodz Come in Dozens sd50 remix & edit
Elektra 8568/promo/ps/'92 ....$4

DELLS, THE

A Heart is a House For Love (2 versions)/ Stay in My Corner *Virgin 3729/promo/'91* $5
Come and Get It edit & lp
Zoo 17071/promo/logo on grey/ps/'92 ......$4
Oh My Love edit & lp
Phil.International 17085/promo/ps/'92 ......$4

DELORY, DONNA

Just a Dream lp/alt.pop mix *MCA 2293/promo/ ps/prod.by MADONNA/'93* $7
Just a Dream 6 versions *MCA 2591/promo/ prod.&cowritten by MADONNA/ps/'93* $6

Praying For Love 4 vers *MCA 2346/promo/ps/'92* .$6

DELTA REBELS

Tattoo Rosie *Polydor 70/promo/silkscreened/'89* .$4

DEMUS, CHAKA & PLIERS

I Wanna Be Your Man lp & hip hop mix
Mango 858/promo/rear insert/'93 ....$6
Murder She Wrote 4 versions
Mango 853/promo/ps/'93 ....$6

DENNIS, CATHY

Everybody Move 3 versions
Polydor 575/promo/logo on green/ps/'91 ..$5
Irresistable (cathy's mix)
Polydor 851/promo/logo on red/'93 ....$5
Irresistible 3:51/3:48
Polydor 816/promo/logo on green/ps/'92 ..$5
Just Another Dream (3 versions) *Polydor 322/ promo/fold out hardcover ps/'90* $6
Moments of Love radio edit/lp
Polydor 899/promo/logo on purple/'93 ......$5
The Cathy Dennis Story *The Weekly Specials/ promo/Unistar/radio show 9/20-22/91* $20
Too Many Walls radio mix & acappella
Polydor 441/promo/silkscreened/ps/'91 ....$5
Touch Me (All Night Long) 7"/4:09/hot mix
Polydor 386/promo/gatefold hardcover ps/logo on green/'91 ....$7
You Lied to Me 3 versions
Polydor 741/promo/logo on purple/ps/'92 .$6
You Lied to Me 4 versions/Nothing Moves Me
Polydor 863 453/stock/ps/'92 ....$5

DENVER, JOHN

The Flower That Shattered The Stone/ Christmas Like a Lullaby
Windstar 557/promo/'90 ....$5
Wish You Were Here (Postcard from Paris)
Windstar 51334/promo/'90 ....$5

DEODATO
Everybody Wants My Girl lp & hot radio edit
Atlantic 3042/promo/rear insert/'89 ....$5

DEPECHE MODE
Behind the Wheel 4 versions/Route 66 3 versions
Sire 40338/gatefold hardcover ps/stock $6
Behind the Wheel (5 versions)/Route 66
Sire 2953/promo/ps/'88 ....$20
Enjoy the Silence single mix/hands&feet mix/ bass line *Sire 3976/promo/'90* $10
Enjoy the Silence (6 versions)/Sibeling/Memphisto ...
Sire 21490-2/stock/ps/'90 ....$8
Everything Counts live & 2 remixes
Sire 3485/promo/'89 ....$15
Everything Counts (3 versions)/Nothing/Sacred/ A Question of Lust (last 3 live)/ Strangelove (remix) *Sire 40331/ stock/gatefold hardcover ps/'92* $8
Halo *Sire 4362/promo/rear insert/'90* $8
I Feel You remix *Sire 6022/promo/logo on black* .$6
Never Let Me Down Again (4 versions)
Sire 2973/promo/ps/'87 ....$20
Never Let Me Down Again 4 versions/ Pleasure Little Treasure 3 vers/ To Have & To Hold *Sire 40329/stock/ gatefold hardcover ps/'92* $6
Personal Jesus 5 versions/Dangerous 3 versions
Sire 21328/ps/stock/'89 ....$8
Policy of Truth (4 versions)
Sire 4027/promo/rear insert/'90 ....$10
Policy of Truth (4 versions)/Kaleid
Sire 21534-2/stock/ps/'90 ....$8
See You (extended)/Now This is Fun (single & extended) *Sire 40292/stock/ gatefold hardcover ps/'92* $6
selections from box set three (14 tracks,all remixes or live) *Sire 5242/promo/ps/'91* $25
Singles 1-6 (6 cd single box set) *Sire 40284/ stock/6 cd set/booklet/box container/'91* .$25
Singles 13-18 (6 cd box set) *Sire 40284/stock/ 6 cd set/booklet/box container/'91* $25
Singles 7-12 (6 cd box set) *Sire 40285/stock/ 6 cd set/booklet/box container/'91* $25
Strangelove 5 vers./PIMPF/Agent Orange/FPMIP
Sire 40328/stock/gatefold hardcover ps ...$6
Strangelove remix edit/Nothing remix edit
Sire 27777/3"/stock/3x6 ps/'87 ....$12
Strangelove (4 versions) *Sire 3213/promo/ps/'88* $15
Walking in My Shoes lp edit/single edit
Sire 6178/promo/silkscreened/'93 ....$6
World In My Eye *Sire 4441/promo/rear insert/'90* ..$8
World In My Eyes (4 versions)
Sire 4531/promo/rear insert/'90 ....$12

DESERT ROSE BAND
Come a Little Closer edit *Curb 54107/promo/ ps/'91/CHRIS HILLMAN* $4
In Another Lifetime edit & lp *Curb 53804/promo/ silkscreened blue/rear insert/'90* $4
She Dont Love Nobody/Running/Glass Hearts + 2
MCA 3004/promo/ps/'88 ....$8
Start All Over Again edit & lp
Curb 53746/promo/rear insert/'89 ....$4
Twilight is Gone (edit)
Curb 54136/promo/logo on brown/ps/'91 ..$4
You Can Go Home *Curb 54188/promo/ silkscreened logo on gold/rear insert/'91* ..$4

DESIYA
Comin' on Strong radio edit *Mute 8528/ promo/logo on black/rear insert/'92* $4

DESKEE
Let There Be House 3 vers.
RCA 2589/promo/rear insert/'89 ....$4

DETROIT'S MOST WANTED
Pop the trunk remix/instrumental/lp
Bryant 124/promo/logo on brown/'92 ....$5

DEVICE
What is Sadness? (radio edit & club mix)
Arista 2186/promo/rear insert/'91 ....$4

DEVILLE, CC
Hey, Good Lookin' *Hollywood 10331/promo/ silkscreen pic/rear insert/custom sticker* $4

DEVO
Baby Doll (4 remixes 3:16/5:44/6:05/3:40)
Enigma 140/promo/ps/'88 ....$8
Baby Doll 5 versions/Agitated hyperextendedmix
Enigma 75515/silkscreened/stock/ps/'88 ..$6
Disco Dancer (4 remixes)
Enigma 75511/ps/3"/stock/'88 ....$6
Post Post Modern Man (If I Had a Hammer)
Enigma 307/promo/silkscreened/ rear insert/'90 ....$6
Post Post Modern (If I Had a Hammer) CHR mix/lp ..
Enigma 306/promo/silkscreened/ rear insert/'90 ....$6

DEVONSQUARE
If You Could See Me Now *Atlantic 4295/promo/ silkscreened/rear insert/'91* $4

DIAMANDA GALAS
The Litanies of Satan/Wild Women With Steak Knives *Restless 71419/stock/ps/'89* ...$12

DIAMOND & PSYCHOTIC NEUROTICS
Sally Got a One Track Mind radio/remix
Chemistry 839/promo/ps/'93 ....$4

DIAMOND RIO
Meet in the Middle
Arista 2182/promo/silkscreened/ps/'91 .....$4
Norma Jean Riley *Arista 2407/promo/ silkscreened/ps/'92* $4

DIAMOND, NEIL
All I Really Need is You studio/live
Columbia 4665/promo/ps/'92 ....$10
Baby Can I Hold You
Columbia 1702/promo/rear insert/'88 ....$8
Don't Turn Around
Columbia 4258/promo/silkscreen/ps/'91 ...$7
If There Were No Dreams
Columbia 4152/promo/silkscreen/ps/'91 ...$7
Morning Has Broken
Columbia 4837/promo/rear insert/'92 ....$6
This Time & All Time Hits (14 song compilation)
Columbia 1352/promo/booklet ps/'88 .....$30

DIAMOND, NEIL & KIM CARNES
Hooked on the Memory of You
Columbia 4372/promo/ps/'91 ....$8

DICKIES, THE
Dummy Up *Enigma 177/promo/cust. sticker/'89* ...$6

DICKINSON, BRUCE
All the Young Dude *Columbia 2145/promo/ps/'90* $6
Bring Your Daughter to the Slaughter
Jive 1261/promo/ps/'89.............................$7
Tattooed Millionaire + 2:22 interview
Columbia 73338/promo/ps/silkscreened.$10

DIDDLEY, BO
Bo Diddley/Say Man/I'm a Man/Diddley Daddy
MCA 37281/stock/3"/ps/'88 ....$7
Who Do You Love/Road Runner/I'm a Man/You Can't Judge a Book By It's Cover
MCA 37326/stock/3"/ps/'89 ....$7

DIE LAUGHING
Humans edit & lp *Curb 79087/promo/ps/ silkscreened logo on white/'90*..................$4

DIESEL
Tip of My Tongue edit/One More Time/Man Alive
Giant 6165/promo/rear insert/'93 ....$4

DIESEL PARK WEST
Walk With the Mountains
EMI 4779/promo/ps/logo on white/'91 ......$4

DIFFIE, JOE
Is It Cold In Here *Epic 74123/promo/rear insert/ silkscreened/'91*..$4

DIG
I'll Stay High *Wasteland 2770/promo/ps/'93* $4

DIGABLE PLANETS
Where I'm From aural g ride radio mix/lp/ chridgnal radio *Pendulum 8749/ promo/silkscreened/ps/'93*........................$6
Where I'm From ohridgnal radio mix
Pendulum 8786/promo/cust. sticker/'93....$6

DIGITAL ORGASM
Guilty of Love 3 versions
Whte Lbls 5826/promo/ps/silkscreened....$4

DIGITAL UNDERGROUND
Kiss You Back 4 vers. *Tommy Boy 993/stock/ps*..$6
No Nose Job ultrafunk mix & ultragroove mix
Tommy Boy 525/promo/cust. sticker/'92...$6
No Nose Job 5 vers. *Tommy Boy 513/stock/ps* $6
Same Song (4 versions)
Reprise 4583/promo/custom sticker/'91 ...$8

DILLINGER
Can It Be Love 3 times *JRS 5800/promo/ silkscreened (like record)/ gatefold hardcover ps/'91* $5
Home For Better Days unplugged
JRS 800/promo/ps/silkscreened/'91 ....$5
Home For Better Days/Can It Be Love/We Had It..
JRS 800/promo/gatefold hardcover ps $6

DILLON FENCE
Christmas/Playful/In the Sound
Mammoth 0031/stock/ps/'91 ....$4

DILLON, DEAN
Hot, Country, and Single *Atlantic 5007/ promo/silkscreened/rear insert/'93*...........$4

DIMEOLA, AL
Kiss My Axe radio edits (The Embrace/One Night Last June/Morocco/No Mystery/ Purple Orchids - 2 versions)
Tomato 9021/promo/rear insert/'91 ....$8

DINO
Gentle edit & lp *Island 6645/promo/ps/'90* $4
Never 2 Much of U *4th B'way 7495/promo/'89* ..$4
Romeo (6 vers.) *Island 422 878 013/stock/ps* $5
Sunshine (edit) *4th B'way 7489/promo/'89* $4
Swingin' (10 tracks) *Island 422 846 481/promo/ trifold hardcover/book (no tape)/'90* $12

DINOSAUR JR
Goin' Home/Quest/Kracked (last 2 live)/Keeblin'
Sire 6328/promo/'93 ....$10
Start Choppin edit & lp
Sire 5915/promo/silkscreened/'93 ....$5
The Wagon *Sire 4704/promo/'91* $5
Whatever's Cool With../Sideways/Not You Again/ The Little Baby/Pebbles & Weeds/ Quick Sand/Thumb/Keep the Glove (last 2 live) *Sire 26761/stock/ps/'91* $6

DIO
Born on the Sun lp & edit *Reprise 4360/ promo/silkscreened logo/ps/'90* $4
Hey Angel edit & lp *Reprise 4476/promo/ rear insert/'90*..$4

Lock Up the Wolves 11 tracks *Reprise 26212/ promo/silkscreened/gatefold leather package/booklet/'90* $20
Wild One *Reprise 4080/promo/silkscreened/'90* $4

DION

And the Night Stood... *Arista 9797/promo/ps/'89* ... $6
Romeo 7" edit *Island 6633/promo/ps/'90* $6
Sea Cruise *Elektra 8191/promo/rear insert/'90* $6

DION, CELINE

(If There Was) Any Other Way *Epic 73665/promo/rear insert/'90* $5
If You Asked Me To *Epic 74277/promo/ gatefold hardcover ps/'92* $5
Love Can Move Mountains *Epic 4875/promo/logo on blue/'92* $5
Love Can Move Mountains 4 vers./(If There Was) Any Other...remix/Unison mainstream mix *Epic 74817/stock/ps/'92* $6
Nothing Broken But My Heart *Epic 74336/promo/ps/'92* $5
The Last to Know *Epic 4141/promo/logo on aqua/ps/'91* $5
Water From the Moon *Epic 74809/promo/silkscreened/ps/'93* $5
Where Does My Heart Beat Now *Epic 73536/ promo/logo on pink/rear insert/'90* $5

DION, CELINE & PEABO BRYSON

Beauty and the Beast *Epic 74090/promo/ logo on purple/ps/'91* $6

DIRE STRAITS

Calling Elvis edit & lp *WB 4953/promo/silkscreened/ps/'91* $6
Heavy Fuel *WB 5126/promo/'91* $5
Heavy Fuel edit & lp *WB 5134/promo/'91* $5
I Think I Love You Too Much *Polydor 330/ promo/silkscreened blue on white/'90* $6
On Every Street edit & lp *WB 5394/promo/'91* $6
The Bug *WB 5183/promo/'91* $6

DIRTY DOZEN BRASS BAND

Thats How You Got Killed Before/ When Im Walking/Inside Straight + 3 *Columbia 2036/promo/ps/'90* $7

DIRTY RHYTHM

Hot n Cold 3 versions *BFE 852/promo/ps* $4

DIRTY WHITE BOY

Lazy Crazy/Hammer on the Heart/Dead Cat Alley *Polydor 221/promo/logo on black/ rear insert/'90* $5

DISNEY

Selections From Fantasia & other Disney Classics (Little Mermaid/Jungle Book/Mary Poppins) *W.Disney PR-CD1/promo/ps* .. $15

DISPOSABLE HEROES OF HIPHOPRISY

Famous and Dandy 5 versions *4th & B'way 557/promo/ps/'92* $6
Television, The Drug of the Nation 3 versions/ Winter of Long Hot Summer/ Language of Violence instrumental *4th B'way 162 440 541/stock/ps/'91* $5
Language of Violence lp & instrumental/ Famous and Dandy instrumental *4th B'way 162 440 551/stock/ps/'92* $5

DISTANCE

Under the One Sky edit & lp *Reprise 4323/promo/rear insert/'89* $4

DIVINE WEEKS

Preachin'/Think/Roll Away *First Warning 72705-75775/stock/ps/'91* .. $4

DIVING FOR PEARLS

Gimme Your Good Lovin' *Epic 1696/promo/ silkscreened/rear insert/'89* $4
Have You Forgotten/Dear Prudence *Epic 2054/promo/rear insert/'90* $4

DIVINYLS

Bless My Soul lp & live/Bullet/Make Out Alright/ Pleasure & Pain (last 3 live) *Virgin 4134/promo/logo on red/'91* $20
I Touch Myself *Virgin 3666/promo/silkscreen/'90* . $6
I'm on Your Side greg royale edit *Virgin 4148/promo/logo silkscreened/'91* .. $6
Make All Aright/I Touch Myself + 8 *Virgin PRCD VINYL/promo/gatefold hardcover/'91* $12
Make Out Alright *Virgin 3911/promo/ silkscreened/rear insert/'91* $5

DIXIE DREGS

Bloodsucking Leeches/Kashmir *Capricorn 5540/promo/'92* $5
Medley (Take It Off the Top) Capricorn 5820/promo/'92 .... $4

DIXON, DON
Bad Reputation *Enigma 226/promo/silkscreen/ custom sticker/'89* $4
Gimme Little Sign *Enigma 284/promo/ custom sticker/'90* $4
Oh Cheap Chatter *Enigma 248/promo/ green silkscreen/custom sticker/'89* $4

DJ JAZZY JEFF & FRESH PRINCE
Boom! Shake the Room 6 vers./From Da South *Jive 42107/promo/silkscreened/ps/'93* $6
I Think I Can Beat Mike Tyson radio/lp/extended *Jive 1278/promo/ps/'89* $6
I Think I Can Beat Mike Tyson radio/lp/extended *Jive 1278/promo/ps/'89* $7
Summertime 7 versions *Jive 1442/promo/silkscreened/ps/'91* $7
The Groove (Jazzy's Groove) (6 versions) *Jive 1313/promo/ps/'89* $6
The Things That U Do 6 versions *Jive 42037/promo/rear insert/'91* $7

DJ MAGIC MIKE
House of Magic 3 versions *Cheetah/promo/ silkscreened pic/ps* $6

DJ QUIK
Jus Lyke Compton *Profile 7372/promo/ rear insert/'92* $4
Quik is the Name radio & remix *Profile 7349/promo/silkscreened/'91* $4

DO
Guilty of Love 6 versions *Whte Lbls 40725/ stock/gatefold hardcover ps/'93* $5
Running Out of Time 7 vers. *White Lbls 40934/ stock/gatefold hardcover ps/'93* $5

DOC, THE
Its Funky Enough (3 versions) *Ruthless 2762/ promo/rear insert/'89* $4

DOE, JOHN
A Matter of Degrees/Worldwide Brotherhood (censored)/Imitation of the Blues/Liars Market/Lets Be Mad (last 3 acoustic) *DGC 4155/promo/ps/'90* $12
I Will Always Love You *WB 5698/promo/'92* $4
Let's Be Mad *DGC 4115/promo/gatefold hardcover ps/silkscreened/'90* $5

DOG, TIM
Step to Me edit *Ruffhouse 4465/promo/ps/'92* ...$4

DOGS D'AMOUR, THE
How Come It Never .. dynamite remix edit & lp .... *Polydor 84/promo/silkscreened/ps/'88* $8
Trail of Tears edit & lp *China 132/promo/silkscreened/'89* $5

DOKKEN
Alone Again live & live extended edit *Elektra 8039/promo/'88* $7
Burning Like a Flame *Elektra 2128/promo/ps* $5
Heaven Sent (2 vers.) *Elektra 2269/promo/'88* ...$5
So Many Tears *Elektra 8018/promo/'87* $6
Walk Away edit & lp *Elektra 8048/promo/silkscreened logo/'88* $5

DOKKEN, DON
Give It Up (3 versions) *Geffen 4214//promosilkscreened/'91* $4
Mirror Mirror *Geffen 4145//promo/ embossed hardcover ps/'90* $6

DOLBY, THOMAS
Airhead (3 versions) *EMI 04039/promo/'88* $8
Aliens Ate My Buick 8 tracks *Manhattan 48075/stock/ps/'88* $15
Close But No Cigar *Virgin 1410/promo/ silkscreened"pipe" pic* $6
Eastern Bloc edit & lp *Giant 5786/promo/'92* $5
I Love You Goodbye bayou mix/n.orleans mix/lp *Giant 5958/promo/'92* $6
I Love You Goodbye/That's Why People Fall in Love (both edit & lp) *Giant 5715/promo/'92* $6

DOMINO THEORY
Radio Driver 4:20/5:54/4:45/7:14 *RCA 9172/promo/ps/'90* $4

DOMINO, FATS
My Blue Heaven *EMI 4668/promo/silkscreened/ rear insert/'90* $6

DON, THE
Big 12 Inch lp/extended/instrumental *Columbia 73916/promo/ps/'91* $4
In There 3 vers. *Columbia 73727/stock/ps/'91* $4

DONALD D
Let the Horns Blow 2 vers. *Sire 5236/promo/'91* ..$4

DONOVAN
Hurdy Gurdy Man *Great Northern Arts 61007/ promo/logo on gold/ps/'91* $7

DONOVAN, JASON
Every Day (I Love You More) *Atlantic 3027/promo/ps/'89* $6
Too Many Broken Hearts edit & extended *Atlantic 2818/promo/rear insert/'89* $7

DOOBIE BROTHERS
Dangerous edit & lp *Capitol 79662/promo/ rear insert/custom sticker/'91* $5
Need a Little Taste of Love *Capitol 79722/promo/silkscreened/'89* $5
One Chain (Don't Make No Prison) *Capitol 79786/promo/silkscreened/'89* $5

Rollin' On *Capitol 79820/promo/logo silkscreened/custom sticker/'91* $5
Something You Said *Capitol 79859/promo/ logo on red/rear insert/'91* $5
The Doctor *Capitol 79600/promo/silkscreened* $5

DOORS
Break On Through *Elektra 8314/promo/ logo on orange/ps/'91* $10
Light My Fire edit/Love Me Two Times *Elektra 45051/stock* $6
Roadhouse Blues (live edit)/Unknown Soldier (live) .. *Elektra 8361/promo/ps/custom sticker* $15

DORFF, STEVE & FRIENDS
Like the Whole World's Watching (edit) (Murphy Brown theme)/Swept Away/Whattley By the Bay/Spenser For Hire *WB 3432/ promo/ps/with TAKE 6, CHRIS CROSS, DEAN PARKS, more* $8
Theme from Growing Pains (As Long As We Got Each Other) vocal & instrumental *Reprise 3256/promo/ps/'88/ with DUSTY SPRINGFIELD* $6

DORO
A Whiter Shade of Pale *Mercury 86/promo/silkscreen pic/ps/'89* ... $7
Only You *Mercury 341/promo/silkscreened/'90* ... $5
Unholy Love *Mercury 264/promo/ silkscreened pic/ps/'90* $6

DOUG E. FRESH
Bustin' Out 3 versions *Bust It 79149/promo/custom sticker/'92* $5
If I Was Your Man 6 versions/Back in the Dayz *Bust It 79361/promo/'92* $5

DOUGHBOYS
Shine/Forward Stop/Good Cop, Bad Cop *A&M 31458 0339/promo/silkscreened/ gatefold hardcover ps/'93* $4

DOVES, THE
Beaten Up in Love Again (edit) *Elektra 8432/ promo/logo on green/ps/'91* $4
I Wouldn't Know You From the Rest (7" edit) *Elektra 8394/promo/ps/red silkscreened* .. $4

DOWNING, WILL
Free *Island 2174/promo/ps* $4
I Go Crazy 4:00 & 4:41 *Island 6674/promo/ps* $4
Test of Time (radio vers.) *Island 2880/promo/'89* . $4

DOWNY MILDEW
Elevator/Cool Nights triple x single versions/ Till I Die/Lady Day and John Coltrane live *High Street 72902 19207/stock/ gatefold hardcover ps* $5

DOZIER, LAMONT
Love in the Rain 2 vers. *Atlantic 3899/promo/ps* $4
Profiled! profile (24:55)/interview answers *Atlantic 3924/promo/ps (with questions)* $15

DR ALBAN
It's My Life 4 versions *Arista 12492/stock/ps/'93* $5
It's My Life single/us club/ragga mix *Arista 2491/ promo/logo on purple/ps/'92* $5

DR DRE
Dre Day radio/lp/inst./club (10:00) *Interscope 6661/promo/'92* $10

DR DRE & SNOOP DOGGY DOGG
Deep Cover edit & uncensored *Solar 74547/promo/ps/'92* $8

DR JOHN
Candy edit & lp *WB 3815/promo/'89* $5
Goin' Back to N.Orleans sampler (Since I Fell For You/Goin' Back to New Orleans/Fess Up/Cabbage Head/Basin Street . + 1) *WB 5582/promo/'92* $15
Makin' Whoopee! *WB 3500/promo/'89* $5
My Buddy *WB 3784/promo/'89* $5

DRAKE, NICK
The Hannibal Sampler 17 tracks *Hannibal 4434/promo/ps/'92* $30

DRAMARAMA
Anything, Anything (I'll Give You) (3 versions) *Chameleon 87/promo/silkscreened/'90* $7
Haven't Got a Clue *Chameleon 8435/promo/ silkscreened like record/die cut ps/'91* $5
Haven't Got a .. edit & lp *Chameleon 8518/promo/ silkscreened record like cd/rear insert/'91* $5
I've Got Spies/On the Streets/Come (To Meet Me)/ Tine Me Down/Convenience Store (demo) *Chameleon 8559/promo/silkscreened (to look like record)/ps/'92* $10
Last Cigarette edit & lp *Chameleon 71/promo/custom sticker/'89* . $7
Live in Wonderamaland 7 tracks *Chameleon 84/promo/silkscreened/'90* .. $15
What Are You Gonna Do lp & acoustic/7 Minutes *Chameleon 8497/promo/ silkscreened record like CD/'91* $7
Wonderamaland *Chameleon 78/promo/silkscreened pic* $6
Work For Food lp & acoustic *Chameleon 8753/ promo/silkscreened/rear insert/'93* $5

DREAD FLIMSTONE
From the Ghetto 6 versions *Acid Jazz 75298/promo/ps/'91* $5

DREAD ZEPPELIN
Heartbreaker (at the End of Lonely Street) (edit)/Hey Hey What Can I Do + :36 interview *IRS 67030/promo/ silkscreened/rear insert/'90* $10
Stairway to Heaven edit *IRS 67057/promo/silkscreened/'91* $5
Your Time is Gonna Come (edit)/All I Want For Christmas... *IRS 67043/ promo/silkscreened/'90* $10

DREAD, MIKEY
The Source (of Your Divorce) *WB 4034/promo/rear insert/'89* $4

DREAM ACADEMY
A Different Kind of Weather 11 tracks *Reprise 26307/promo/silkscreened/ps* ...$12
Angel of Mercy edit/extended/lp *Reprise 4892/promo/'91* $7
Indian Summer edit/lp *Reprise 2841/promo/ps*.$5
Love (4 versions) *Reprise 4411/promo/'90* $6
Love (8 versions) *Reprise 21738/stock/ gatefold hardcover ps/'90* $7

DREAM SYNDICATE
I Have Faith *Enigma 122/promo/cust.sticker/'88* .$7

DREAM WARRIORS
Follow Me Not 3:02 & 4:38/Ludi 5:15/ Very Easy to Assemble.. 4:51 *4th & B'way 545/promo/ silkscreened/custom sticker/'91* $6
My Definition of a Boombastic Jazz Style (UK 7")/ Wash Your Face in My Sink (UK 7") *4th & B'way 526/promo/rear insert/'91*......$7

DREAMS SO REAL
Red Lights (Merry Christmas) (non lp)/ Bearing Witness/Rough Night *Arista 9784/promo/ps/'88*.......................$12

DRED SCOTT
Nutin Ta Lose 4 ver./Duck Ya Head 2 versions .... *A&M 31458 8172/promo/ silkscreened pic/ps/'93*.............................$5

DRIVE, SHE SAID
If This is Love *CBS 000274/promo/ silkscreened logo on blue/'89* $4

DRIVIN N CRYIN
Around the Block Again/Fly Me Courageous (live) *Island 6703/promo/ silkscreened/rear insert/'91* $6
Build a Fire *Island 6668/promo/rear insert/'90* $4
Build a Fire/Toy Never Played With/Wild Dog Moon/Scarred but Smarter (last 3 live) *Island 422 868 535/stock/ps/'91* $7
Cant Promise You the World *Island 2290/promo/ps/'88* $4
Fly Me Courag. *Island 6647/promo/box type ps* ...$5
Honeysuckle Blue *Island 2680/promo/'89*...........$4
Oooeee ep (What's the Differ./Easter European Carny Man/Minnesota Strip/With the People - last 2 live) *Island 6769/promo/ silkscreened (like record)/ps/'93* $8
Smoke *Island 6771/promo/logo on purple/ps/'93*..$4
The Innocent (edit) *Island 6686/promo/silkscreened/ps/'90* $5
Turn It Up or Turn It Off *Island 6758/promo/ silkscreened (like record)/ps/'93* $4
Whiskey Soul Woman/Rockin' in the Free World *Island 6787/promo/logo on purple/'93* $4

DSK
I'll Keep Holdin' On 6 vers. *Active 8620/promo*....$4

DUELING TECHNO
Pood, Bhud n Pflug 7 versions *Zoo 17091/promo/silkscreened/rear insert* $6

DUKE, GEORGE
Fame edit & lp *WB 5880/promo/'92* $4
Guilty lp/pt 2 *Elektra 8056/promo/'89* $5
Love Ballad *Elektra 8082/promo/ silkscreened purple/'89* $5
No Rhyme, No Reason single edit/single mix *WB 5693/promo/'92* $4

DUNN, HOLLY
No One Takes the Train Anymore *WB 5040/promo/recycled foldout cover*.....$5

DUNN, HOLLY/MARCY BROS/ KEVIN WELCH
Are You Gonna Love Me/Cotton Pickin' Time/ I Came Straight.. *WB 3520/promo/'89* ...$4

DURAN DURAN
All She Wants Is *Capitol 79456/promo/'88* $10
Come Undone 4 versions *Capitol 79660/ promo/silkscreened/ps/'93* $8
Come Undone churban mix/12" dub/dub *Capitol 79749/promo/custom sticker/ white & black silkscreened*.....................$10
I Dont Want Your Love 7" mix & big mix (7:25) *Capitol 79246/promo/ps/ silkscreened white/'88*...............................$8
I Dont Want Your Love 7"/lp/big mix *Capitol 44237/stock/3"/plastic ps/'88* $10
Liberty (11 tracks) *Capitol 94292/special promo edition in box w/bonus cassette*..............$25
None of the Above edit & lp *Capitol 79853/promo/silkscreened/ps/'93* .$7
Ordinary World edit/acoustic/lp *Capitol 79588/promo/silkscreened/'92*......$8
Serious edit & lp *Capitol 79299/promo/ silkscreened/rear insert/'90* $8
Too Much Information *Capitol 79767/promo/ silkscreened/custom sticker/'93* $6

Too Much Information 4 churban mixes
Capitol 79256/promo/silkscreened green & black/custom sticker/'93 ....$10
Violence of Summer (4 versions)/Throb (instrum.)
Capitol 15612/stock/ps/'90 ....$8
Violence of Summer (6 vers.)/Throb (instrum.)
Capitol 79235/promo/logo on orange/ps .$10
Violence of Summer edit & lp
Capitol 79288/promo/silkscreened/'90 ......$5

DURAN/KRUSH BROTHERS

The Edge of America-Lake Shore Driving
EMI79451/promo/rubber stamp on ps ..$12

DUSTIN, ALTA

Lookin' For Love (5 versions) *Atlantic 3843/promo/ps/silkscreenedon orange/'91* $5
Tonite radio mix & extended 12" vogue
Atlantic 3055/promo/rear insert/silkscreened lettering/'89 ....$5

DYLAN & THE GRATEFUL DEAD

Slow Train *Columbia 1447/promo/'89* $12

DYLAN, BOB

Blind Willie McTell edit & lp/It Takes a Lot to Laugh..
Columbia 4042/promo/ps/'91 ....$12
Everything is Broken *Columbia 1814/promo/ps* ..$10
Most of the Time edit/lp/live *Columbia 73326/promo/silkscreened logo on grey/ps/'90* .$15
Series of Dreams
Columbia 3041/promo/silkscreen/ps/'91 ...$8
Sittin' on Top of the World/Tomorrow Night/
Canadee-I-O/Hard Times
Columbia 4857/promo/custom sticker $10
Step It Up and Go *Columbia 4922/promo/custom sticker/'92* $7
Unbelievable *Columbia 2138/promo/ps/silkscreened/'90* $10

DYLANS, THE

Godlike/Lemon Afternoon 2 vers./My Hands Are......
RCA 2806/stock/ps/custom sticker/'91 .....$5
Mary Quant in Blue *RCA 62209/promo/silkscreened/rear insert/'91* $4
Planet Love 4 versions *RCA 62187/promo/silkscreened/rear insert/'91* $5

E

A Man Called (E) 11 tracks *Polydor 454/promo/gatefold hardcover/'92* $10
Are You & Me Gonna Happen
Polydor 743/promo/ps/'92 ....$4
Hello Cruel World
Polydor 654/promo/silkscreened/ps/'92 ....$5
Nowheresville/Strawberry Blonde
Polydor 690/promo/ps/'92 ....$4

E, SHEILA

Cry Baby edit & lp *WB 4987/promo/'91* $4
Like Flies 3 versions *WB 4869/promo/silkscreened logo on green/'91* $6
Droppin' Like Flies 4 versions
WB 4456/promo/silkscreened/'91 ....$6
Droppin' Like Flies 5 versions/Heaven
WB 21758/stock/hardcover gatefold ps $5
Sex Cymbal (4 versions) *WB 4651/promo/silkscreened/rear insert/'90* $8
Sex Cymbal 12 tracks *WB 26255/promo/round can package/silkscreened/cymbal & strap* $20
Sex Cymbal (4 versions) + dj video VHS
WB 4651/promo/silkscreened/video/die cut box package/'91 ....$20

E.Y.C. & BOO-YAA TRIBE

Get Some edit/long/dog-rock versions
Gasoline Alley 2444/promo/ps/'93 ....$5

EARL, STACY

Love Me All Up 5 versions *RCA 62115/promo/silkscreened pic/rear insert/'91* $6
Romeo & Juliet *RCA 62191/promo/silkscreened... pic/rear insert/'92* $5
Romeo & Juliet 3:00 AM mix/extended3:00 AM mix .
RCA 62231/promo/silkscreened pic/rear insert/custom sticker/'92 ....$5

EARLE, STEVE

An Interview With - June 1990 *MCA 9042/promo/ps/silkscreened pic/'90* $15
Angry Young Man *MCA 17403/promo/'87* $6
Back to the Wall
Uni 17772/promo/rubber stamped ps/'88 .$6
Billy Austin *MCA 1229/promo/silkscreened light blue/rear insert/'90* $5
Copperhead Road lp & edit
Uni 17681/promo/silkscreen copper/'88 ...$5
Even When I'm Blue
MCA 17820/promo/custom sticker/'89 ......$5

Live Sampler (Guitar Town/Copperhead Road/ Devil's Right Hand/Good Ol Boy/ She's About a Mover)
MCA 1664/promo/ps/'91 ....$8
Nothing But a Child *Uni 18077/promo/'88* $5
Promise You Anything
MCA 1019/promo/rear insert/'90 ....$5
The Other Kind edit & lp
MCA 18399/promo/black silkscreen/ps $5

EARTH WIND & FIRE
For the Love Of You (6 versions)
Columbia 73344/promo/ps/'90 ....$6
Heritage (5 versions) *Columbia 73205/promo/ silkscreened/super fold out cover/'90* $10
Mighty Mighty sampler 9 tracks
Columbia 4750/promo/silkscreened/ps ...$10
Sunday Morning edit *Reprise 6502/promo/'93* ..$4
Sunday Morning edit & lp
Reprise 6286/promo/silkscreened/'93 ....$4
System of Survival (4 versions)
Columbia 2837/promo/ps/'87 ....$8
Thinking of You (4 versions)
Columbia 1002/promo/ps/'88 ....$8
Turn On (the Beat Box) 4 versions
Columbia 1338/promo/'88 ....$8

EARTH WIND & FIRE & MC HAMMER
Wanna Be the Man 4 versions
Columbia 73436/promo/ps/'90 ....$6

EAST 17
Deep breath mix/meaning
London 956/promo/ps/logo on purple/'93 .$4

EAST OF EDEN
From this World edit & lp
Capitol 79888/promo/silkscreened/ rear insert/custom sticker/'89 ....$4

EASTERHOUSE
Come Out Fighting remix & 7" *Columbia 000132/ promo/silkscreened black/'89* $5

EASTON, SHEENA
101 (3 remixes) *MCA 17939/promo/ custom sticker/'89/prod by PRINCE* $8
101 (4:06) *MCA 17807/promo/custom sticker/'89*.$7
A Dream Worth Keeping
MCA 2194/promo/rear insert/'92 ....$6
Days Like This 4:10/6:15
MCA 17745/promo/custom sticker/'89 ....$7
Follow My Rainbow *MCA 18038/promo/'88* $7
No Deposit No Return (3 versions)
MCA 17952/promo/custom sticker/'89 ....$6
The Lover in Me *MCA 17639/promo/ps/'88* $6
To Anyone edit & lp *MCA 1616/promo/rear insert* $5
What Comes Naturally (5 versions)
MCA 1134/promo/rear insert/'91 ....$6
What Comes Naturally (6 versions) *MCA 1346/ promo/silkscreened white/rear insert/'91* ..$8

You Can Swing It lp/edit with rap/edit without rap....
MCA 1512/promo/back title cover/'91 ....$6
You Can Swing It 4 vers. *MCA 1493/promo/'91* .$8

EASTSIDE BEAT
Ride Like the Wind 3 versions
FFRR 633/promo/logo on black/'92 ....$5
(You're My) Heaven short & long remixes
A&M 17650/promo/green silkscreen $4

EASY PIECES
Trust One Another
A&M 17772/promo/silkscreened/'88 ....$4
Whenever You're Ready 7" & 12" version
A&M 17618/promo/'88 ....$4

EBERHARDT, CLIFF
The Long Road ac mix & lp
Windham Hill 90-16/promo/ps/'90 ....$4

ECHO & THE BUNNYMEN
Bedbugs & Ballyhoo (2 versions)
Sire 2926/promo/ps/'88 ....$10
Enlighten Me (3 versions)
Sire 4556/promo/silkscreened logo/'90 ....$6
Lips Like Sugar (2 versions)
Sire 2806/promo/nice custom dj sticker ..$10

ED O. G & DA BULLDOGS
Be a Father to Your Child 4 versions
PWL 551/promo/silkscreened/ps/'91 ....$4
Bug a Boo 3 versions
PWL 483/promo/logo on green/'91 ....$4
I Got to Have It 3 versions
PWL 417/promo/logo on green/'91 ....$4

EDDIE, JOHN
Inbetween Days *Elektra 8279/promo/ps/'90* $4
Swear 7" edit & lp
Columbia 1631/promo/silkscreen/ps/'89 ...$5
Tough Luck *Columbia 1810/promo/ps/'89* $4

EDELWEISS
Bring Me Edelweiss (single)
Atlantic 2698/promo/rear insert/'88 ....$6

EDER, LINDA
A Little Bit of Heaven *RCA 60564/promo/ ps/STANLEY TURRENTINE/'91* $4

EDER, LINDA & PEABO BRYSON
You Are My Home *Angel 79377/promo/ps/'92* ...$4

EDMUNDS, DAVE
Closer to the Flame *Capitol 79938/promo/ silkscreened/rear insert/'90* $4
King of Love *Capitol 79773/promo/silkscreen/'89* .$5

EDWARDS, MARK
Just Having Touched/interview
R&A 10521/promo/ps/'90 ....$5

EEK A MOUSE
Dyer Maker *Island 6669/promo/rear insert/'91* ...$4

EIGHTH WONDER
Baby Baby (radio remix)
WTG 1470/promo/silkscreened pic/'88 .....$7
I'm Not Scared (3 remixes)
WTG 1625/promo/silkscreened red/'89 ....$8

808 STATE
Cubik (3 versions)/In Yer Face
Tommy Boy 959/stock/ps/'90...................$7
Lift 6 versions/Open Your Mind 2 versions
Tommy Boy 989/promo/'91.......................$7
Pacific (6 versions) *Tommy Boy 949/ promo/rear insert/'90*...............................$10
Time Bomb fon mix/Nimbus 7" mix/Reaper Repo short & 12" *Tommy Boy 540/stock/ps/'92*..$6

808 STATE & UB40
One In Ten 5 vers. *Tommy Boy 553/stock/ps/'92*..$6

EL DEBARGE
My Heart Belongs to You 7 versions/You Turn Me ..
WB 40357/stock/gatefold hardcover ps $5
My Heart Belongs to You edit & lp
WB 5264/promo/pic silkscreened/'92 ....$6
Words and Music for "In the Storm" (trt: 28:16)
WB 5416/promo/rear insert/'92..............$15

ELECTRA, CARMEN
Everybody Get On Up 5 versions/ Go Go Dancer edit *Paisley Park 40693/ stock/gatefold hardcover ps/'92* $5
Everybody Get On Up 7 versions
Paisley Park 5933/promo/'92...................$6
Fantasia Erotica 7 versions *Paisley Park 40970/ stock/gatefold hardcover ps/'93* $5
Go Go Dancer 6 versions *Paisley Park 40458/ stock/gatefold hardcover ps/'92* $5

ELECTRIC ANGELS
The Drinking Song
Atlantic 3400/promo/rear insert/'90 ....$4

ELECTRIC BOYS
All Lips n Hips edit & lp *Atco 3282/promo/ps/'90* .$4
Dying to Be Loved *Atco 4693/promo/ silkscreened/gatefold hardcover ps/'92* $4
Mary in the Mystery World pirate edit/nasty edit/lp
Atco 4522/promo/logo on green/ps/'92 .....$5

ELECTRIC LOVE HOGS
Mr Fun (edit)/Holy Halitosis
London 704/promo/silkscreened/ps/'92 ....$4

ELECTRONIC
Disappointed 3 vers/Gangster fbi mix
WB 40562/stock/gatefold hardcover ps/JOHNNY MARR/'92 ....$5
Feel Every Beat 5 versions/Lean to the Inside instrumental *WB 40159/stock/ gatefold hardcover ps/'91* $5
Feel Every Beat single & lp
WB 5019/promo/orange logo on blue/'91 .$6
Get the Message 4 versions/Free Will extended
WB 21832/stock/gatefold hardcover ps $5
Get the Message 5 versions
WB 4678/promo/logo on orange/'91 ....$6

Getting Away With It (5 versions)
WB 3987/promo/rear insert/with JOHNNY MARR & NEIL TENNANT/'90 ...$8
Getting Away With It (7 versions)
WB 21498/stock/ps/'90 ....$6
Tighten Up edit & lp *WB 4958/promo/JOHNNY MARR, BERNARD SUMNER, more/'91* ...$7

ELECTROSET
How Does It Feel 4 versions/Resistance
ffrr 162 350 013/stock/ps/'93 ....$5

ELEVEN
Rainbow's End edit & lp Morgan Creek 0002/
promo/silkscreened/ps/'91 ....$4
Vowel Movement ep (Break the Spell/Burning Your Bed/Down/Message to You)
Morgan Creek 0017/promo/ps/ silkscreened/'91 ....$7

ELEVENTH DREAM DAY
Makin' Like a Rug lp/demo *Atlantic 4978/ promo/silkscreened/rear insert/'93*...........$5

ELFMAN, DANNY
The Batman Theme action mix & edit
WB 3756/promo/rear insert/'89 ....$5

ELIAS, ELIANE
Fantasia edits (Girl From Ipanema/ Cravo E Canela/Bahia/Ivan Lins Medley)
Blue Note 79434/promo/rear insert/'92 .....$5

ELKHARD, SHIRLEY
Someone Else/You're My Weakness/Roll That Rock *Cypress 17566/promo/silkscreened pic* $7

ELLINGTON, LANCE
Pleasure & Pain *A&M 75021 7543/promo/ps/'90* . $4

ELLIOT, RICHARD
Movers & Shakers/Take Your Time *Enigma 309/promo/silkscreened/custom sticker/'90* $4
When a Man Loves a Woman *Enigma 241/promo/silkscreened/ps/'89* $4

ELLIS, T.C.
Miss Thang *Paisley Park 4471/promo/composed & produced by PRINCE/'90* $5
Pussycat (radio edit) *Paisley Park 4909/promo* ... $5

ELO
Destination Unknown + 9 past hits *Epic 2109/promo/silkscreened/rear insert/'90* $25

ELO PART TWO
Honest Men 2 vers. *Scotti Brothers 75284/promo/silkscreened/gatefold hardcover ps/'91* $8

ELY, JOE
Settle For Love/Jazz Street/Rich Man Poor Boy *Hightone 001/promo/silkscreen* $7

EMERGENCY BROADCAST NETWORK
Behavior Modification 2 versions/We Will Rock You/Psychoactive Drugs 2 versions *TVT 3511/stock/ps/'92* $5

EMERSON LAKE & PALMER
Affairs of the Heart *Victory 739/promo/silkscreened mini logos/ps/'92* $7
Black Moon *Victory Music 694/promo/silkscreened/ps/'92* $6
Lucky Man/From the Beginning/Karn Evil/Jerusalem/Still... You Turn Me On/I Believe in Father Christmas *Atlantic 4599/promo/ps/silkscreened* $15

EMF
It's You 4 versions *EMI 04668/promo/ps/logo on purple/'92* ... $7
Lies *EMI 04794/promo/silkscreen/rear insert/'91* .. $6
Lies 3 vers. *EMI 4816/promo/silkscreened/ps* $8
Search and Destroy *EMI 04887/promo/silkscreened/custom sticker/'92* $5
Unbelievable (5 versions)/Live at the Bilson *EMI 56210/stock/ps/'91* $6
Unexplained ep (Getting Through/Far From Me/The Same/Search and Destroy) *EMI 99401/stock/ps/logo on black/'92* $6

EMMETT, RIK
Big Lie *Charisma 023/promo/ps/'90* $4

EN VOGUE
Don't Go (3 versions)/National Anthem *Atlantic 3829/promo/ps/'91* $8
Free Your Mind 3 versions/Hold On marley marl remix/Lies eddie f remix *Eastwest 96128/stock/gatefold hardcover ps/'92* $6
Free Your Mind 4 versions *Eastwest 4791/promo/rear insert* $8
Give It Up, Turn It Loose 5 versions *Eastwest 4843/promo* $8
Giving Him Something He Can Feel *Eastwest 4559/promo/logo on red/ps/'92* . $5
Hold On 2 edits & extended *Atlantic 3171/promo/rear insert/custom sticker/'90* $7
Hold On radio edit & edit *Atlantic 3386/promo/rear insert* $5
Lies (7 versions) *Atlantic 3373/promo/silkscreen logo on black/rear insert/'90* $8
Love Don't Love You *Eastwest 4988/promo* $5
Love Don't Love .. remix edit #1/remix edit #2/lp *Eastwest 5011/promo* $8
My Lovin' (You're Never Gonna Get It) 4 versions *Eastwest 4464/promo/foldout hardcover/silkscreened group pic/insert/'92* $20
Time Goes On 4 versions *Eastwest 4288/promo/silkscreened/rear insert/'91* $8
You Don't Have to Worry (4 vers.) *Atlantic 3592/promo/silkscreened/rear insert/'90* $8

ENEA, LAURA
Better the Devil You Know 3 vers./Take Me Back *Next Plateau 027/promo/silkscreen/'93* $5
Our Love house radio/orig.radio/house club/house bonus beats *Next Plateau 50192/promo/'92* $5
Say I'm Your Number One 4 versions *N.Plateau 162 350 014/stock/rear insert* .. $5

ENERGY ORCHARD
Belfast *MCA 18293/promo/rear insert/'90* $4
Sailortown *MCA 18360/promo/ps/'90* $4

ENGLAND, COLIN
Come Over Baby edit/lp/instrumental *Motown 3746310992/promo/ps/'93* $5
I Got What You.. *Motown 1338/promo/ps/'91* $4
You Took My Love Away 6 versions *Motown 374631122/promo/ps/'93* $5

ENGLISH BEAT
I Confess/Tears of a Clown/Twist and Crawl (last 2 live) *A&M 31016/3"/ps/stock/ps* .. $10
Save It For Later/Doors of Your Heart (5:49)/Best Friend (live) *A&M 31012/ps/3"/stock/'88* $10

ENIGMA
Carly's Song 2 versions *Virgin 12796/promo/ silkscreened/rear insert/'93* $4
Mea Culpa pt 2 catholic vers. *Charisma 039/ promo/logo on brown/rear insert/'90* $5
Sadeness pt 1 4 versions/Introit: Benedicta Sit Sancta Trinitas *Charisma 96395/ stock/gatefold hardcover ps/'90* $6
Sadeness pt 1 (radio edit) *Charisma 032/promo/silkscreened/'90* $5
The Rivers of Belief radio edit *Charisma 078/promo/rear insert/'90* $4

ENO, BRIAN
Fractal Zoom 12 vers (more than 60 min.) *Opal 40539/stock/gatefold hardcover ps* .. $7
Nerve Net Sampler (Juju Space ../Pierre in Mist/ Ali Click darkly mad mix/Distributed Being) *Opal 5886/promo/cust. sticker* ... $15
Words & Music From Wrong Way... *Opal 4691/ promo/silkscreened red/rear insert/'91* ... $15

ENO/CALE
Been There Done That *Opal4493/promo/ silkscreen logo on purple/rear insert/'90* ... $6
One Word edit & lp *Opal Warner 4601/promo/ silkscreened blue on green/'90* $6
One Word (2 versions)/Empty Frame/ You Don't Miss Your Water/ Grandfather's House *Opal 40001/stock/gatefold hardcover/'91* . $6

ENRIQUE, LUIS
Lo Que Es Vivir *Sony 10012/promo/ps/'91* $4

ENSONIC
No 1 Is 2 Blame 4 versions *Chrysalis 23693/ promo/logo on black/rear insert/'91* $5

ENTOUCH
All Nite edit & club mix *Elektra 8134/promo/'89* $4
Drop Dead Gorgeous 3 versions *Elektra 8368/promo/'91* $4
Hype edit, radio & lp *Elektra 8084/promo/'89* ... $4
She Used 2 B My Girl edit & lp *Elektra 8438/ promo/logo on black/ps/'91* $4

ENUFF Z NUFF
Baby Loves You *Atco 4005/promo/ps/'91* $4
Fly High Michelle *Atco 3089/promo/ps/'89* $4
Innocence *Arista 2569/promo/ps/silkscree/'93* $4
Mother's Eyes *Atco 3745/promo/ps/'91* $4
New Thing *Atco 2731/promo/silkscreened peace sign/rear insert/'89* $4
Right By Your Side *Arista 2468/promo/ps/'93* $4

ENYA
Book of Days *Reprise 5491/promo/'92* $4
Caribbean Blue *Reprise 5142/promo/'91* $4
Exile *Geffen 4240/promo/custom sticker/'88* $6
Oiche Chiun/Oriel Window/'S Fagaim Mo Bhaile *Reprise 40660/stock/ gatefold hardcover ps/'92* $5
Oiche Chiun (Silent Night)/Orinoco Flow *Reprise 5851/promo/silkscreened/'92* $5
Orinoco Flow (edit) *Geffen 3389/promo/'88* $8
Storms in Africa remix & lp *Geffen 3499/promo/ps/'88* $5

EON
Basket Case 3 vers./Inner Mind deep thought edit/ Spice morbid vs baron mix *Columbia 44K 74313/stock/ps/'92* $5

EPMD
Crossover lp & instrumental& trunk mix/ Brothers From Brentwood L.I. *Rush Associated 42K 74172/stock/ps/'92* $5
Crossover lp & instrumental/Brothers From Brentwood L.I. *Rush Associated 74173/ promo/silkscreened/ps/'92* $5
Give the People 4 versions *Def Jam 73782/promo/ps/'91* $6
Gold Digger vocal & instru. *Def Jam 73634/promo/ps/'90* $6
Head Banger lp/edit/remix edit *Columbia 42K 74700/stock/ps/'92* $5

EPMD & LL COOL J
Rampage (4 vers.) *Columbia 73701/promo/ps* $6

ERASURE
A Little Respect (lp/remix edit/12" vocal/12" remix) *Sire 3252/promo/'88* $15
Blue Savannah (4 vers.) *Sire 3801/promo/'89* .. $15
Blue Savannah (4 versions)/Runaround on the Underground (12" mix)/Supernature (orbits mix)/No GDM (Zeus held mix) *Sire 21428/ps/stock/'89* $8
Breath of Life 6 versions/Waiting For Sex full vers/Carry on Clangers *Sire 40344/stock/gatefold hardcover ps* ... $6
Chains of Love (4 dif. versions) *Sire 3140/promo/silkscreen/'88* $15
Chorus 5 versions/Snappy/Over the Rainbow *Sire 40123/gatefold hardcover ps/stock* ... $6
Chorus single/single low/lp *Sire 5138/promo/'91* . $8
Chorus (single mix) *Sire 4945/promo/'91* $8
Drama (7" version/Krucial mix/Act 2) *Sire 3737/promo/'89* $12
Drama krucial & 7" mix & act 2/Sweet Baby medi mix & moo moo mix & 7"/ Paradise lost & found mix & 4:08 *Sire 21356/stock/ps/'89* $10
Love to Hate You 3 versions/Vitamin C 2 vers./ La La La *Sire 40218/stock/ gatefold hardcover ps/'91* $6
Star 3:37/6:24/6:27/5:50/Dreamlike State (24 hr tech.mix) *Sire 21558/stock/ps/'90* . $8
Star 3:38/3:59/6:24/5:49 *Sire 4327/promo/rear insert/'89* $15

Take a Chance on Me edit/wyro edit/full versions
Elektra 8645/promo/logo on black/'92 ......$8

ERIC B & RAKIM

Casualties of War 6 versions
MCA 2509/promo/rear insert/'92 ....$7
Casualties of War/Relax With Pep
MCA 2385/promo/rear insert/'92 ....$5
Don't Sweat the Technique 6 versions
MCA 2267/promo/rear insert/'92 ....$6
Don't Sweat the Technique 9 versions
MCA 2192/promo/ps/'92 ....$7
In the Ghetto *MCA 18499/promo/'90* $5
In the Ghetto 4 versions *MCA 53901/stock/ gatefold hardcover ps/'90* $5
Juice main mix & instr. *Soul 2103/promo/ps/'92* .$5
Mahogany 4 versions *MCA 1181/promo/'90* $5
What's on Your Mind 4 versions
MCA 2061/promo/ps/'91 ....$7

ESCAPE CLUB

Call It Poison (3 versions) *Atlantic 3753/ promo/silkscreened/rear insert/'91* $5
Call It Poison (3 vers.)/Keep the Motor Running
Atlantic 86085/stock/'91 ....$5
Call It Poison (AOR mix)
Atlantic 3752/promo/silkscreened/ps/'91 ..$5
So Fashionable edit *Atlantic 4241/promo/ silkscreened pic/rear insert/'91* $5
Twentieth Century Fox *Atlantic 2975/promo/ rear insert/prod by RAY MANZAREK/'89* .$5
Walking Through Walls CHR mix/AOR vocal up .....
Atlantic 2606/promo/rear insert/'88 ....$5
Walking Through Walls CHR mix/AOR vocal up/ mini interview *Atlantic 2657/promo/ ps (front & back)/'88*................................$5
Wild Wild West edit & lp *Atlantic 2353/promo/'88* $6

ESCOFFERY'S, THE

Look Who's Loving Me 5 versions
Atlantic 4132/promo/logo on white/ps/'91 .$5
Unobtainable (Standing in Need) edit & lp
Atlantic 4356/promo/silkscreened pic/ rear insert/'91 ....$4

ESTEFAN, GLORIA

Anything For You English & Spanish
Epic 34K 7759/promo/3"/'88 ....$15
Anything For You (English/Span.-Engish/Spanish)
Epic 1060/promo/ps/'87 ....$15
Can't Forget You *Epic 73864/promo/ps/'91* $6
Christmas Through Your Eyes
Epic 74768/promo/ps/'92 ....$6
Coming Out of the Dark
Epic 73666/promo/ps/silkscreened/'90 .....$8
Cuts Both Ways *Epic 73395/promo/ silkscreened/rear insert/'90* $8
Dont Wanna Lose You english/spanish
Epic 1666/promo/ps/'89 ....$12
Go Away 3 vers./Words Get in ... live/megamix
Epic 49K 74843/stock/silkscreened/ps $7
Here We Are *Epic 73084/promo/ silkscreened logo/rear insert/'89* $12
I See Your Smile/Megamix *Epic 74847/promo/ps*$10
Live For Loving You 4 versions
Epic 73962/promo/silkscreened/ps/'91 .....$8
Oye Mi Canto (English radio mix/Spanish/Latin)
Epic 73269/promo/ps/'90 ....$8
Rhythm is Gonna Get You 7" & 12" versions
Epic 2700/promo/ps/'87 ....$15
Seal Our Fate (edit) *Epic 73769/promo/ps/'91*....$5
The Gloria Estefan Story
The Weekly Specials/Unistar/ promo/radio show 1/31-2/2/92 ....$30

ESTUS, DEON

Heaven Help Me 2 vers. *Polydor 44/promo/ps/'88* $6
Spell 3:59/4:38 *Polydor 74/promo/ps/'89* $4

ETHERIDGE, MELISSA

2001 us remix radio edit/orig.radio edit
Island 6730/promo/silkscreened/ custom sticker/'92 ....$7
2001 edit *Island 6717/promo/logo on red/ps/'92* .$6
2001/Meet Me in the Back/Testify (last 2 live)
Island 422 866 893/stock/ps/'92 ....$5
4 song ep from debut lp (Similar Features/ Bring Me Some Water/Precious Pain/ Don't You ..) *Island 2258/promo/ps/'88* .$10
Ain't It Heavy *Island 6700/promo/ps/'92* $5
Chrome Plated Heart 3:59/live edit
Island 2713/promo/rear insert/'88 ....$8

MELISSA ETHERIDGE

Dance Without Sleeping edit & lp
Island 6733/promo/ps/logo on white/'92 ...$5
Dance Without Sleeping (edit)/Similar Features/ Ain't It Heavy (last 2 live)
Island 422 864 321/stock/ps/'92 ....$5
I'm the Only One edit & lp
Island 6790/promo/ps/silkscreened/'93 ....$5
Let Me Golp & live *Island 3109/promo/rear insert*.$7
Let Me Go lp & live/Occasionally (live)
Island 99127/stock/ps/'89 ....$8

Live ep (Chrome Plated Heart/Late September Dogs/Similar Features/Bring Me Some Water/Like the Way I Do)
Island 2555/promo/ps/'88 .... $15
No Souvenirs lp & live
Island 2879/promo/rear insert/'89 .... $7
No Souvenirs lp & live/Like the Way I Do (live)
Island 99176/stock/ps/'89 .... $7
Similar Features (edit) *sland 2568/promo/ps/'88* .. $6
Skin Deep/Royal Station../You Can Sleep While I Drive/Let Me Go (all live) *Island 3136/ promo/gatefold hardcover/'90* $15
The Angels lp & live/Chrome Plated Heart (live)
Island 3062/promo/rear insert/'89 .... $7
The Angels lp & live/Chrome Plated Heart (live)
Island 99138/ps/stock/'89 .... $7

EU

Ain't Found the Right One Yet 4 versions
Virgin 3702/promo/silkscreened logo/'90 .. $4
Buck Wild (3 remixes)
Virgin 2645/promo/silkscreened/'89 .... $4
Da Butt (2 vers.)/B Boy Dub *EMI 4066/promo/'88* . $6
I Confess (5 versions) *Virgin 3477/promo/'90* $4

EUGENIUS

Buttermilk *Atlantic 4824/promo/silkscreened/ps* . $5

EUROPE

Halfway to Heaven
Epic 74117/promo/logo on red/ps/'91 .... $6
I'll Cry For You edit *Epic 74118/promo/ logo on black/rear insert/'91* $5
Mystery Disc ep (All or Nothing/Little Bit of Lovin'/Halfway to Heaven/Got Your Mind in the Gutter)
Epic 4195/promo/silkscreened/ps/'91 ..... $10
Prisoners in Paradise 3 versions
Epic 4179/promo/silkscreened/ps/'91 .... $5
Superstitious 4:09 & 4:31
Epic 1225/promo/ps/logo on black/'88 ...... $8

EURYTHMICS

(My My) Baby's Gonna Cry single/remix/acoustic
Arista 9939/promo/ps/'90 .... $12
Acoustic Eurythmics Sampler (My My Babys Gonna Cry/Don't Ask Me Why/ When the Day Goes Down)
Arista 9915/ps/'89 .... $20
Angel *Arista 9917/promo/silkscreen black/ps/'89* .. $8
Dont Ask Me Why *Arista 9880/promo/ps/'89* $6
I Need a Man (edit) *RCA 5361/promo/ps* $8
Rough & Tough at the Roxy (4 track live ep)
RCA 5629/ps/'86 .... $25
Sweet Dreams '91 single remix & hot remix
Arista 2243/promo/logo on yellow/ps/'91 $10

EVANGELINE

Bayou Boy *Margaritaville 54408/promo/ps/ silkscreened/JIMMY BUFFETT/'92* $4

EVERLAST

I Got the Knack (3 versions)/Pay the Price
WB 21323/stock/ps $4
Never Missin' a Beat fade&lp *WB 3779/promo* ... $4

EVERLY BROTHERS

Wake Up Little Susie/Bird Dog/Let It Be Me + 1
Rhino 73008/ps/3"/stock/'88 .... $8

EVERY MOTHERS NIGHTMARE

Already Gone edit & lp
Arista 2509/promo/silkscreened/ps/'93 ..... $4
House of Pain edit & lp/Buried Half Alive/Long Haired Country Boy (live)
Arista 2489/promo/logo on black/ps/'92 .... $6
Long Haired Country Boy (3 vers.) *Arista 2052/ promo/silkscreened/rear insert/'90* $4
Love Can Make You Blind (3 vers.) *Arista 2078/ promo/silkscreened/rear insert/'90* $4
Walls Come Down lp & edit *Arista 2012/ promo/silkscreened/rear insert/'90* $4

EVERYDAY PEOPLE

Headline News (4 versions)
SBK 05345/promo/trifold hardcvr ps/'90 ... $4

EVERYTHING BUT THE GIRL

Alison *Atlantic 4745/promo* $6
Driving radio edit & full versions
Atlantic 3173/promo/ps/'90 .... $5
Driving/Meet Me in the Morning/Language of Life
Atlantic 3191/promo/ps/'90 .... $6
I Always Was Your Girl/interview
Sire 3086/promo/ps/'88 .... $10
I Dont Want to Talk... *Sire 3273/promo/ps/'88* $7
Love is Strange
Atlantic 4579/promo/logo/rear insert/'92 ... $5
Old Friends *Atlantic 4207/promo/ silkscreened art/rear insert/'91* $5
Take Me edit, lp, love mix *Atlantic 3345/promo/ps* $8
Understanding *Atlantic 4362/promo/ logo on blue/rear insert/'91* $5

EX-GIRLFRIEND

Why Can't You Come .. 2 vers. *Reprise 4790/ promo/silkscreened full color pic/'91* $5
You (You're the One For Me) edit & lp
Reprise 4981/promo/'91 .... $5

EXODUS

Objection Overruled/Free For All *Capitol 79197/ promo/silkscreened logo/custom sticker* ... $4
Objection Overruled/Free For All *Capitol 79197/ promo/silkscreened logo on red/ps/'90* $5
Lunatic Parade/Good Morning *Capitol 79406/ promo/silkscreened/rear insert/'90* $4
Thorn in My Side
Capitol 79416/promo/ps/logo on black/'92 $4

EXOTIC BIRDS

Imagination (3 vers.) *Alpha International 79482/ promo/silkscreened/ps/'90* $4

EXPOSE

I Wish the Phone Would Ring 4 versions/ I'll Never Get Over You Getting Over Me *Arista 07822-112498/stock/ps/'92* $6

I Wish the Phone Would Ring single & lp *Arista 2466/promo/silkscreened/ps/'92* $5

I'll Never Get Over You *Arista 2518/promo/logo on red/ps/'93* $5

Seasons Change (3 versions)/Megamix (10:00) *Arista 9639/promo/ps/'87* $15

Tell Me Why (4 versions) *Arista 9918/ promo/ps/silkscreened/'89* $8

What You Don't Know (5 remixes) *Arista 9837/promo/ps/'89* $8

Your Baby Never Looked Good in Blue *Arista 2010/promo/silkscreened logo/'90* .. $6

Am I Ever Gonna.. edit & lp *A&M 31458 8123/ promo/silkscreened group pic/'92* $8

EXTREME

Decadence Dance edit & lp *A&M 75021 8102/ promo/silkscreened red logo/'90* $5

Get the Funk Out *A&M 75021 7295/promo/ps/ red & black logo silkscreened/'90* $5

Get the Funk Out *A&M 75021 7431/promo/ps* $5

Get the Funk Out 3 versions *A&M 75021 7320/ promo/ps/logo silkscreened/'91* $8

Get the Funk Out/Lil Jack Horny/Mutha remix *A&M 390 613/stock/ps/'90* $5

Hole Hearted *A&M 75021 7003/promo/ps/ silkscreened logo on black/'90* $6

Kid Ego clean & lp *A&M 17717/promo/silkscreened/ps/'89* $6

Little Girls *A&M 17830/promo/ps/ silkscreened red/'89* $6

More Than Words 4:11 & 3:43 *A&M 75021 7515/ promo/silkscreened pic/ps/'90* $8

Mutha You Dont Wanna Go to School Today *A&M 17874/promo/silkscreened logo/'89* . $5

Rest in Peace edit & lp *A&M 31458 8015/promo/ silkscreened/gatefold hardcover ps/'92* $6

Rest in Peace new radio edit *A&M 31458 8070/ promo/silkscreened/custom sticker/'92* $6

sampler & interview (31 tracks in all) *Foundations/ promo/silkscreened/'92* $18

Stop the World edit & lp *A&M 31458 8030/promo/ silkscreened/gatefold hardcover ps/'92* $6

Stop the World radio/edit/lp *A&M 31458 8097/ promo/logo on black/ps/'92* $6

Tragic Comic radio/lp *A&M 31458 8031/promo/ gatefold hardcover ps/silkscreened/'93* $5

Tragic Comic/Help/Hole Hearted horn mix/ Don't Leave Me Alone *A&M 31458 0117/ stock/ps/silkscreenedpic/'92* $5

EYE & I

Virgin Heart *Epic 74375/promo/ps/logo on red/'92* $4

EZO

Flashback Heart Attack/Here It Comes/Kiss of Fire *Geffen 2696/promo/'87* $4

Million Miles Away *Geffen 3557/promo/ps/'89* $4

F MACHINE

Here Comes the 20th Century 7" & lp *Reprise 3751/promo/'89* $4

Runaway Train fade & lp *Reprise 3547/promo/'89* $4

FABULON

Im in a Mood/Wonderbus/Simple Man/ Love&Affection *Charisma 12695/promo/ gatefold hardcover ps/silkscreened/'92* $4

FABULOUS THUNDERBIRDS

Knock Yourself Out *CBS 1581/promo/'89* $5

Roller Coaster lp & live/Twist of the Knife live *Epic 4203/promo/ps/'91* $10

Stand Back *CBS 2738/promo/ps* $5

Twist of the Knife *Epic 4124/promo/ps/'91* $5

FACE TO FACE

As Forever As You/A Place Called Home/ Shes a Contradiction + 1 *Mercury 13/promo/embossed ps/'88* $5

FAGEN, DONALD

Century's End *WB 2987/stock/3"/3x6 ps/'88* $7

Centurys End (edit) *WB 2987/promo/ps/'88* $6

The New York Rock and Soul Revue ep (Pretzel Logic/Lonely Teardrops (edit)/ Drowing in Sea of Love/At Last) *Giant 5037/promo/logo on white/ trifold diecut hardcover ps/ MICHAEL MCDONALD, PHOEBE SNOW, BOZ SCAGGS, more/'91* $12

Green Flower Street edit & lp *Giant 5316/promo* . $5

Tomorrow's Girls edit & lp *Reprise 6200/promo/silkscreened/ps/'93* .. $5

Tomorrow's Girls single versions
Reprise 6211/promo/ps/'93 .... $5

FAGEN, DONALD & MICHAEL MCDONALD
Pretzel Logic *Giant 5186/promo/'91* $6

FAITH HEALERS, THE
Don't Jones Me/Gorgeous Blue Plower/My Loser/ Oh Baby *Elektra 66327/stock/ gatefold hardcover ps/silkscreened/'93* $5

FAITH NO MORE
A Small Victory 6 versions *Slash 40626/stock/ gatefold hardcover ps/'92* $5
A Small Victory edit & lp *Slash 5564/promo/'92*. $5
Epic (What Is It) edit & lp
Slash 3913/promo/silkscreened/'89 .... $8
Epic (What Is It) radio remix edit
Slash 4071/promo/'89 .... $5
Epic/Zombie Eaters/Edge of the World/ The Real Thing (all live)
Slash 4486/promo/silkscreened/ps/'90 ... $10
Falling to Pieces remix/video/lp
Slash 4409/promo/rear insert/'90 .... $6
From Out of Nowhere *Reprise 3559/promo/'89* .. $6
Land of Sunshine/Caffeine/Kindergarten
Slash 5523/promo/'92 .... $8
Midlife Crisis scream mix *Slash 5498/promo/'92* .. $5

FALCO
Data De Groove 3 vers. *American Sound 79754/ promo/rear insert/'91* $4

FALCON, BILLY
Power Windows *Mercury 465/promo/ silkscreened/gatefold hardcover ps/'91* $4
Pretty Blue World 11 tracks *Mercury 848 800/ silkscreened pic/gatefold hardcover ps* $8

FALL, THE
Ladybird/Paranoia Man in Cheap../Free Range/The Birmingham School of Business/I'm Frank/ So What About It/Bombast/L.A./ Rouch Rumble - live)
Matador 5094/promo/custom sticker $12

FALLING JOYS
Black Bandages lp & slammin' siren mi
Nettwerk 67095/promo/logo on black/ps .. $4
God in a Dustbin/Black Bandages slammin' siren/ Kiss the World Goodbye
Nettwerk 13869/stock/ps/'92 .... $5
You're in a Mess
Nettwerk 67036/promo/rear insert/'90 ...... $4

FAM-LEE
Always On My Mind
Columbia 73979/promo/silkscreened/ps ... $4

FAMILY CAT, THE
Steamroller ep (Steamroller/Tom Verlaine/ Colour Me Grey + 2)
Dedicated 66137/stock/ps/'92 .... $5

FAN CLUB
Dont Let Me Fall Alone radio mix & atomic mix
Epic 73321/promo/ps/'90 .... $4

FARM, THE
All Together Now (3 vers.) *Sire 4798/promo/'91* ... $7
Groovy Train wilson-miniaci mix *Sire 5068/promo* . $6
Groovy Train single mix/club mix radio edit/ alt.12" *Sire 4935/promo/ silkscreened train pic/'91* $6
Love See No Colour edit *Sire 5898/promo/'92* $5
Rising Sun 3 versions/Creepers/History
Sire 40532/stock/gatefold hardcover ps ... $5
Rising Sun single versions
Sire 5594/promo/silkscreened/'92 .... $4

FARNHAM, JOHN
3 songs from Whispering Jack (You're the Voice/ Pressure Down/A Touch of Paradise)
RCA 6310/promo/ps/'86 .... $8
Two Strong Hearts
RCA 8915/promo/silkscreened logo/'88 ... $4
You're the Voice 4:27/5:30 *RCA 9086/promo/ps* $4
You're the Voice new Australian mix (5:05)
RCA 2513/promo/rear insert/'90 .... $4

FARROW, CEE
Imagination 4 vers. *Graphite 1003/promo/ps/'91* . $4

FASTER PUSSYCAT
House of Pain edit & lp *Elektra 8139/promo/'89* . $5
Nonstop to Nowhere chr edit/aor edit/lp
Elektra 8610/promo/silkscreened/ps/'92 ... $5
Nonstop to Nowhere/Too Tight/Charge Me Up/ You're So Vain *Elektra 66396/stock/ gatefold hardcover ps/'92* $5
Poison Ivy edit & lp *Elektra 8105/promo/ps/'89* . $5
The Body Thief *Elektra 8661/promo/logo on white* $4
Where Theres a Whip Theres a Way
Elektra 8213/promo/rear insert/'90 .... $5
You're So Vain *Elektra 8222/promo/ps/'90* $5

FASTWAY
A Fine Line *Enigma 168/promo/cust. sticker/'89* .. $5

FAT BOYS
Lie Z 4:25/5:13
Mercury 106/promo/silkscreened pic/'89 .. $5
Whip It On Me/Fly Car *Emperor 86/promo/'91* $4

FAT LADY SINGS, THE
Man Scared *Atlantic 3907/promo/ silkscreened logo on purple/ps/'91* $4

FAT TUESDAY
Califuneral/Joy-Locoweed/Rio
Columbia 4823/promo/logo on red/ps/'92 .$4

FATES WARNING
Eye to Eye *Reprise 5289/promo/'91* $5
Nothing Left ../Anarchy Divine/Exodus/Damnation ...
Metal Blade 281/promo/ps/'90 ....$8
Point of View *Metal Blade 42493/promo/ps/'91* .$5

FATHER M.C.
I've Been Watching You 5 versions
Uptown 1507/promo/rear insert/'90 ....$5
One Nite Stand 4 vers. *Uptown 2294/promo/ps* ...$5

FATIMA MANSIONS, THE
Blues For Ceausescu edit & lp *Radioactive 2029/ promo/ps/custom sticker/'91* $4
Blues For Ceausescu/Chemical Cosh (both 2 vers.)
Radioactive 54152/stock/ gatefold hardcover ps/'91 ....$6
Tima Mansio Dumps the Dead 10 tracks
Radioactive 2109/promo/ps/'92 ....$8
Tima Mansio Dumps t.. ep (Only Losers Take the Bus/Stigmata/Shiny Happy People/ Hive/Behind the Moon)
Radioactive 54344/stock/ps/'92 ....$6

FAVORITE ANGEL
Only Women Bleed *Columbia 73476/promo/ ps/silkscreened/'90* $4

FEAR OF GOD
Betrayed (edit)/Emily *WB 4776/promo/'91* $4

FEELIES, THE
Doin' it Again mix *Coyote 75021 7537/promo/ps* ..$5
Higher Ground/Dancing Barefoot/Everybodys Got Something/Egyptian Reggae (last 2 live)
A&M 17712/promo/silkscreened/'89 ....$10
Higher Ground/Egyptian Reggae/Everybodys Got Something to Hide (last 2 live)
A&M 17675/promo/ps/'88 ....$8
Invitation remix *A&M 75021 7225/promo/ silkscreened/ps/'91* $5
Sooner or Later *A&M 75021 7519/promo/ps/'91* ..$5

FEINSTEIN, MICHAEL
Both Sides Now *Elektra 8223/promo/ps/'90* $5
Moondance/Soon *Elektra 8706/promo/gatefold hardcover ps/'91* $5

FEIVEL & FRIENDS
Diddy Diddy Dum Dum *MCA 2076/promo/ "American Tail" ps/silkscreened/'91* $5

FELDER, WILTON
Since I Fell For You radio & lp
Par 9007/promo/logo on blue/'91 ....$4

FELDER, WILTON & BOBBY WOMACK
Forever *Par 9018/promo/silkscreened pic/'93* $4

FEMME FATALE
Falling in & out of Love *MCA 17700/promo/ps/'88* .$4
Rebel *MCA 17787/promo/custom sticker/'88* $4

FENDER, FREDDY
It's All in the Game *Reprise 5049/promo/'91* $5

FERRELL, RACHELLE
Till You Come Back to Me radio/lp
Capitol 79371/promo/ps/'92 ....$4
Welcome to My Love edit & lp *Capitol 79541/ promo/silkscreened/rear insert/'92* $4
Welcome to My Love edit & lp & ac edit
Manhattan 79603/promo/rear insert/'92 ....$4

FERRY, BRYAN
I Put a Spell on You edit & lp
Reprise 6078/promo/logo on red/'93 ....$4
Kiss & Tell edit/lp *Reprise 2909/promo/ps/'87* $6
Limbo (4 versions) *Reprise 2910/promo/ps/'88* .$10
Right Stuff *Reprise 2853/promo/gatefold ps/'87* ..$8
Will You Love Me Tomorrow 2 vers./Crazy Love/ Feel the Need *Reprise 40949/stock/ gatefold hardcover ps/'93* $5

FETCHIN' BONES
Love Crushing *Capitol 79684/promo/silkscreen* ..$4

FIERCE RULING DIVA
Get Funky With.. 8 vers. *Medicine Label 40828/ stock/gatefold hardcover ps/'93* $5

FIFTH PLATOON
The Partyline (4 vers.) *SBK 05381/promo/ps/'91* .$4

54-40
One Day in Your Life *WB 2912/promo/ps* $3

FIGHT
Nailed to the Gun/Kill It 2 vers.each *Epic 5353/ promo/ps/ROB HALFORD/silkscreened* ...$6

FIGURES ON A BEACH
Accidentally 4th Street 7" remix/lp/12" remix *Sire 3614/promo/'89* ...$4
You Aint Seen Nothing Yet (4 versions) *Sire 3523/promo/custom sticker/'89* ...$4
You Aint Seen Nothing Yet (rock mix) *Sire 3486/promo/'89* ...$4

FINAL CUT, THE
Testament radio relevation edit/ I Believe in You 2 versions *Nettwerk 13864/stock/ps/'92* ...$4

FINE YOUNG CANNIBALS
Don't Look Back *IRS 17895/promo/cust.sticker* ...$4
Don't Look Back 7" & ext. *IRS 17997/promo/'89* $5
Good Thing *IRS 17831/promo/cus. sticker/'89* ...$4
I'm Not Satisfied *MCA 18142/promo/'88* ...$4
Im Not the Man I Used .. *IRS 17957/promo/'89* ...$4
Im Not the Man I Used to Be 12" remix/ Cook II Soul mix/lp *IRS 18098/promo* ...$7
She Drives Me Crazy 3:35/7:39 *IRS 17720/rubber stamp ps/'88* ...$15

FINN, TIM
Crescendo *Capitol 79556/promo/silkscreen/'89* ..$6
How'm I Gonna Sleep *Capitol 79573/promo/silkscreened/'89* ...$5
Not Even Close *Capitol 79860/promo/silkscreen* ..$5
Persuasion lp/acoustic *Capitol 79766/promo/silkscreened/ps/'93* .$5

FIONA
Ain't That Just Like Love *Geffen 4378/promo/ gatefold hardcover ps/'92* ...$4
Don't Come Cryin' single/single mix edit/rock vers. *Geffen 4426/promo/logo on black* ...$4
Everything You..(You're Sexing ..) *Atlantic 2911/ promo/ps/'89/duet with KIP WINGER* ...$4
Little Jeannie *Atlantic 3277/promo/ps/'89* ...$4
Where the Cowboys Go edit & lp *Atlantic 3161/promo/ps/'89* ...$4

FIORILLO, ELISA
On the Way Up (3 versions) *Chrysalis 23599/promo/ps/'90* ...$6
Oooh This I Need *Chrysalis 23670/promo/ps/ prod & writ.by PRINCE/'91* ...$5

FIRE TOWN
She Reminds Me of You *Atlantic 2767/promo/ rear insert/silkscreened blue/'89* ...$4

FIREHOSE
Down With the Bass *Columbia 4036/promo/ps* ...$4
Down With the Bass remix *Columbia 4069/promo/ps/'91* ...$4
Witness 3 vers. *Columbia 5173/promo/ps/'93* ...$4

FIREHOUSE
All She Wrote *Epic 73984/promo/logo on red/ps* ...$4
Don't Treat Me Bad *Epic 73676/promo/rear insert/'90* ...$4
Love of a Lifetime 4:13 & 4:47 *Epic 73771/promo/ps/'90* ...$6
Reach For the Sky edit & lp *Epic 74335/promo/logo on black/ps/'92* ...$4
Shake & Tumble *Epic 2165/promo/logo on red/ rear insert/'90* ...$4
Sleeping With You *Epic 74323/promo/logo on black/ps/'92* ...$4
Sleeping With You acoustic & lp *Epic 4874/promo/logo on red/rear insert* ..$5
When I Look Into Your Eyes *Epic 74440/promo/ps/logo on black/'92* ...$4

FISCHER, LISA
Colors of Love *Elektra 8773/promo/logo on red/ rear insert/'93* ...$4
How Can I Ease the Pain *Elektra 8312/promo/ps* .$5
Save Me 4 versions *Elektra 8402/promo/ps/'91* .$6
So Intense 7" radio mix *Elektra 8474/promo/rear insert/'91* ...$5

FISHBONE
Bonin' in the Boneyard (new vers.)/In the Name of Swing/Love & Bullsh*t/Hide Behind My Glasses/Bonin' in the Jungle *Columbia 44K 73549/stock/ps/'90* ...$5
Everyday Sunshine edit & lp *Columbia 73859/promo/ps/'91* ...$5
Fight the Youth edit/remix/lp/extendedremix *Columbia 74045/promo/ps/'91* ...$7
Servitude edit & lp *Columbia 5285/promo/ps (w/LOLLAPALOOZA tour dates)/'93* ...$5
Sunless Saturday *Columbia 3035/promo/ps/silkscreen/'91* ...$5
Sunless Saturday/Fishy Swa Ska/Understand Me *Columbia 44K 73668/stock/ps/'91* ...$5
Swim single & lp *Columbia 5180/promo/ps/'93* ...$4

FIVE STAR
Shine 6 versions *Epic 74111/promo/ps/'91* $5
Shine edit & new jack mix edit
Epic 4335/promo/logo on red/ps/'91 .... $5
Treat Me Like a Lady (4 ver.)
Epic 73394/promo/rear insert/'90 .... $5

FIVE THIRTY
13th Disciple lp & edit
Atco 4159/promo/silkscreened/ps/'91 .... $4

FIVE XI
Say It Isn't Over 4 versions
RCA 62539/promo/rear insert/'93 .... $4

FIXX, THE
All is Fair/Shut It Out/Crucified/Still Around
Impact 1287/promo/silkscreened/rear insert/'91 $6
Crucified *Impact IMDP 6/promo/silkscreened/'91* $4
Driven Out *RCA 8841/promo/ps/'88* $5
How Much is Enough edit & lp
Impact 1298/promo/rear insert/'91 .... $5
How Much is Enough single, lp, Jeff Lorber vers. ....
Impact 1331/promo/rear insert/'91 .... $5
Live From Electric Ladyland 4/29/91
Album Network/promo/dj live show/'91 ... $25
Precious Stone *RCA 8932/promo/ps/'89* $5
Shut It Out *Impact IMPD-1/promo/*
logo on silkscreened design/'91 .... $5

FLACK, ROBERTA
Friend extended *Atlantic 4484/promo/*
silkscreened pic/rear insert/'92 .... $6
Oasis edit, lp & radio version
Atlantic 2510/promo/rear insert/'88 .... $6
Shock to My System (4 versions)
Atlantic 2717/promo/rear insert/'88 .... $6
Uh Uh Ooh Ooh Look Out edit & lp
Atlantic 2624/promo/rear insert/'88 .... $4
When Someone Tears Your Heart in Two
Atlantic 4614/promo/
silkscreened/rear insert/'91 .... $4
You Make Me Feel Brand New edit & lp
Atlantic 4321/promo/silkscreened
pic/rear insert/'91 .... $4

FLACK, ROBERTA & MAXI PRIEST
Set the Night to Music edit & lp *Atlantic 4164/*
promo/silkscreened pic/rear insert/'91 ...... $5

FLAME
One Way Lover (5 versions) *Epic 73060/promo/*
silkscreened logo on yellow/'89 .... $4
Wild One/Rain/Never Say Die
Giant 5423/promo/rear insert/'92 .... $4

FLAMIN' GROOVIES
Sealed With a Kiss *National NAT-031/promo/*
ps/logo on purple/'92 .... $6

FLAMIN' GROOVIES/MARTHA VELEZ
Shake Some Action/Its Take a Lot to Laugh
Sire 3762/promo/'89 .... $8

FLAMING LIPS
Everyone Wants to Live Forever
WB 5401/promo/logo on pink/'92 .... $4
Frogs *WB 5726/promo/'92* $4
Turn It On edit & lp *WB 6270/promo/silkscreen* ... $4
Wastin' Pigs ep (Talkin' 'bout the Smiling ..porn../
All That Jazz-Happy Death Men/
Jets demo versions *WB 40244/*
stock/gatefold hardcover ps/'91 .... $5

FLAVOR UNIT MCS, THE
Roll Wit tha Flava clean edit/instrum./a cappella
Epic 5006/promo/logo on black/ps/'93 ...... $5

FLECK, BELA & THE FLECKTONES
Sex in a Pan/Bonnie & Slyde (edit)/Seresta
WB 5618/promo/'92 .... $4
The Sinister Minister (video edit)/Sea Brazil/
Sunset Road *WB 3978/promo/'90* $4

FLEETWOOD MAC
As Long As You Follow *WB 3351/promo/'88* $5
As Long As You Follow/Oh Well (live)
WB 27644/stock/3"/ps/'88 .... $8
Behind the Mask 13 tracks *WB 26206/*
silkscreened/ps/oversized outer box/
booklet/transparency/'90 .... $25
Big Love *WB 2710/promo/custom dj sticker/'87* $6
Don't Stop *WB 5934/promo/ps/'92* $6
Family Man *WB 2948/promo/ps/'87* $7
Hard Feelings edit & lp *WB 4504/promo/'90* $4
Little Lies lp & extended
WB 2818/promo/3"/3x6 package $12
Little Lies (2 versions)
WB 2821/promo/custom sticker $10
Love is Dangerous *WB 4302/promo/'90* $4
Paper Doll *WB 5872/promo/logo on yellow/'92* ... $4
Save Me fade & lp *WB 4011/promo/'90* $4
Skies the Limit *WB 4010/promo/'90* $4
The Chain sampler 18 tracks *WB 5905/custom*
sticker/rear insert/logo on black/'92 .... $22

FLEETWOODS, THE
Mr Blue/Come Softly to Me/Tragedy/Runaround
Rhino R3 73009/stock/3"/ps/'88 .... $5

FLESH FOR LULU
Every Little Word (6 versions)
Capitol 79994/promo/silkscreened/'90 ...... $6
Every Little Word (edit & lp)
Capitol 79943/promo/silkscreened/'90 ...... $4
She Was *MCA 2041/promo/ps/'91* $4
Siamese Twist/Postcards From Paradise
Capitol 79293/promo/ps/'87 .... $6
Time and Space remix & lp *Capitol 79772/*
promo/silkscreened logo on pink/'89 .... $5

FLIES ON FIRE
Babtize Me Over Elvis Presley's Grave *Atco 3138/ promo/silkscreened/rear insert/'89* $4
C'mon *Atco 2898/promo/ silkscreened pic/rear insert/'89* $4
Cry to Myself *Atco 3925/promo/silkscreen/ps/'91* . $4

FLIPPER
American Grafishy 10 tracks *Def American/promo/custom sticker/'92* . $12

FLOCK OF SEAGULL
Magic 4:11/5:43/7:58/6:16 *GNP Crescendo 1208/ps/stock/'89* $5

FLOTSAM & JETSAM
The Master Sleeps/interview (25:17) *MCA 18515/promo/ps/'90* $8

FLOWERHEAD
Acid Reign *Zoo 17095/promo/silkscreened pic/ rear insert/custom sticker/'92* $5
Thunderjeep/What?!/Acid Reign *Zoo 0054/ promo/silkscreened pic/rear insert/'92* $5

FLUID, THE
Mister Blameshifter *Hollywood 10296/ promo/silkscreened/"sparkly" ps/'93* $6
Pill/Cell/Waves/Pill (last 3 demo versions) *Hollywood 10328/promo/silkscreened/ rear insert/custom sticker/'93* $8

FLUKE
Out (In Essence) (Pan Am Into Philly/Pearls of Wisdom/The Bells/Heresy & Garden of Blighty/Philly techno rose mix) *Circa 96218/stock/gatefold hardcover ps* . $5

FOGELBERG, DAN
4 song CD ep from Exiles *Epic 2728/promo/ps* .. $8
Anastasia's Eyes *Full Moon-Epic 2273/promo/ rear insert/'90* $5
Rhythm of the Rain-.. *Epic 73513/promo/ps/'90* ... $5

FOLEY
... If It's Positive 4 versions *Mojazz 374631090/promo/ps/'93* $5

FONKE SOCIALISTIKS
You Are My Heaven 3 versions *Priority 07297/promo/silkscreened/'91* $4
You Are My Heaven remix & extended *Priority 07299/promo/logo oon blue/'91* $4

FORBERT, STEVE
Baby, Don't *Geffen 4372/promo/ gatefold hardcover ps/'91* $4
Running on Love *Geffen 3114/promo/ps* $4
The American In Me/Romeo's Tune *Geffen 4413/promo/silkscreened/'92* $4

FORBIDDEN, THE
Candyman 3 versions (from the soundtrack) *Acid Jazz/stock/ps/'92* $4

FORCE MDS
Couldn't Care Less (5:26 & 3:58)/House of Love medley(9:43) *Tommy Boy 909/promo/'88* . $5
Your Love Drives Me Crazy vocal & instrumental/ House of Love medley 9:43 *Tommy Boy 516/promo/'92* $5

FORCE ONE NETWORK
Somethin' About Youedit & lp *Qwest 5558/promo* $4
Spirit 6 versions *Qwest 5201/promo/'91* $4
Spirit 6 versions *Qwest 40263/stock/ gatefold hardcover ps/'91* $4

FORD, LITA
Back to the Cave mix *RCA 8664/promo/ps/'88* . $10
Falling In and Out of Love remix & lp *RCA 9008/promo/ps/'89* $7
Hungry *RCA 2607/promo/silkscreened yellow/ps* . $7
Larger Than Life/What Do Ya Know About Love/ Hellbound Train/Playin' With Fire *RCA 62097/promo/silkscreened pic/ rear insert/'91* $8
Lisa fade & lp *RCA 2673/promo/ silkscreened pic/ps/custom sticker/'90* $8
Playin' With Fire top 40 mix/fire mix/lp *RCA 62189/ promo/logo on orange/rear insert/'91* $6
Shot of Poison *RCA 62074/promo/ silkscreened pic/rear insert/'91* $6
Shot of Poison remix & lp *RCA 62096/promo/ silkscreened/rear insert/'91* $6
Shot of Poison remix/Kiss Me Deadly lp & radio/ Close My Eyes Forever remix *RCA 62164/ promo/silkscreened/rear insert/'91* $10

FORD, LITA & OZZY OSBOURNE
Close My Eyes Forever (remix) *RCA 8899/promo/ps/'89* $8

FORD, ROBBEN
Born Under a Bad Sign *WB 3600/promo/'89* $4
Wild About You/interview *WB 3139/promo/ps/'88* $8

FORDHAM, JULIA
Comfort of Strangers *Virgin 2669/promo/silkscreened/'88* $4
Happy Ever After *Virgin 2404/promo/'88* $4
Lock and Key (edit) *Virgin 3320/promo/silkscreened/'89* $4
Manhattan Skyline (edit) *Virgin 3030/promo/silkscreened/'89* $4
Manhattan Skyline (edit) + 4 *Virgin PRCDJULIA/promo/beautiful die cut open up package/silkscreened/'89* $15
Mysterious Ways edit & full *Virgin 4195/promo/logo on gold/'91* $4
Talk, Walk, Drive edit & lp *Virgin 4379/promo/rear insert/'91* $4

The Genius of Julia Fordham ep (6 songs)
Virgin 3514/promo/silkscreened logo on white/multi fold out cover/'89 ...... $12

FOREIGNER
Heart Turns to Stone remix/lp
Atlantic 2385/promo/'87 .... $6
I'll Fight For You edit & lp *Atlantic 4141/promo* $4
Lowdown & Dirty lp & edit *Atlantic 3999/promo/ nifty car deck stereo type package/'91* ... $15
Only Heaven Knows *Atlantic 4242/ promo/silkscreened/rear insert/'91* $4
Profiled! *Atlantic 4007/promo only interview/ps* .. $15
Say You Will *Atlantic 2160/promo* $4
Soul Doctor edit & lp
Atlantic 4786/promo/silkscreened/ps/'92 .. $4
With Heaven on Our Side edit
Atlantic 4869/promo/silkscreened/ps/'92 .. $4

FORESTER SISTERS
That Makes One of Us
WB 5123/promo/recycle fold out package $4
Dont You/I Fell in Love Again Last Night
WB 3561/promo/'89 .... $4

FORTRAN 5
Heart on the Line 4 versions
Elektra 66491/stock/ps/'91 .... $4
Heart on the Line vince clark mix & hp saucey mix
Mute 8451/promo/logo on red/rear insert . $5
Love Baby (2 versions)/Midnight Trip/Crazy Earth (2 versions) *Elektra 66587-2/stock/ gatefold hardcover ps/'90* $5

45 GRAVE
Only the Good Die Young 16 tracks
Restless 72259/stock/silkscreened/ps $15

FOSTER, DAVID
Grown-Up Christmas List *Atlantic 3647/promo/ logo on white/rear insert/'90* $4
River of Love remix
Atlantic 3778/promo/rear insert/'90 .... $4
Winter Games *Atlantic 2200/promo/'88* $4

FOUR HORSEMEN, THE
Nobody Said It Was Easy
Def American 4882/promo/ps/'91 .... $4
Nobody Said It Was Easy 12 tracks
Def American 26561/promo/ps/'91 .... $10
Rockin' Is Ma Business (clean)
Def American 5089/promo/ps/'91 .... $4
Tired Wings edit & lp
Def American 5286/promo/ps/'91 .... $4

4 NON BLONDES
Dear Mr President *Interscope 4690/promo/ silkscreened/ps/'92* $4

4 OF US, THE
Drag My Bad Name Down
Columbia 73243/promo/ps/'89 .... $4

FOURPLAY
Between the Sheets lp/instru./chaka khan radio edit/fourplay radio edit *WB 6444/ promo/CHAKA KHAN/'93* $6
Between the Sheets single/lp/instru.
WB 6285/promo/silkscreened/'93 .... $6
Fourplay ep (Monterey/Flying East/Between the Sheets vocal & instr.)
WB 6396/promo/custom sticker/'93 .... $8
Live - Authorized Bootleg (Moon Jogger/October Morning/Max-O-Man/Wish You Were Here-Quadrille/After the Dance)
WB 5413/promo/custom sticker/'92 .... $15
Words & Music (music & interview)
WB 5140/promo/ps/BOB JAMES, LEE RITENOUR, more/'91 .... $15

FOURPLAY & EL DEBARGE
After the Dance edit & lp *WB 4976/promo/'91* ... $6

4 SEASONS, THE
Sherry/Working My Way Back to You/Rag Doll + 1
Rhino 73010/stock/3"/ps/'88 .... $5

FOUR SURE
Try and Find a Way radio/lp/instrumental
Ruffhouse 77123/promo/ps/'93 .... $5

FOUR TOPS
Indestructible 4:30/7:48 *Arista 9706/promo/ps* ... $6

4 WAY! with all my love
PROMOTION ONLY NOT FOR RESALE

4 WAY
With All My Love 3 vers./4way 1 *Nastymix 76100/ promo/gatefold hardcover ps/'90* $4

FOX, BRITNY
Dream On edit #2/remix edit/lp
Columbia 1965/promo/silkscreen/ps/'90 ... $4
Girlschool 3:59/4:43 *Columbia 1269/promo/'88* . $4

Long Way to Love 2 vers. *Columbia 1159/promo* $4
Louder *East West 4286/promo* $4
Save the Weak 2 vers. *Columbia 1442/promo* ... $4

FOX, SAMANTHA
(Hurt Me Hurt Me) But the Pants Stay On 5 vers. *Jive 1441/promo/custom sticker/ poster cover/silkscreened pic/'91* $8
I Only Wanna Be With You single edit/spec. single edit/extended mix *RCA 1195/promo/ps/'89* $8
I Wanna Have Some.. UK single edit&extended *RCA 1165/stock/ps/'88* $8
Just One Night edit & lp *Jive 42100/promo/ps/custom sticker/'91* ... $7
Love House (4 vers.) *Jive 1234/promo/ps/'89* $8
Naughty Girls (Need Love to) 4:20/4:10/6:34/5:52 *Jive 1102/promo/rear insert/'88* $8

FOXWORTHY, JEFF
You Might Be a Redneck sampler (46 mini tracks) *WB 6514/promo/ps/custom sticker/'93* $8

FRAMES, THE
The Dancer *Island 6725/promo/ps/'92* $4

FRAMPTON, PETER
Holding On to You *Atlantic 2917/promo/ps/'89* .. $4
More Ways Than One edit & lp *Atlantic 3130/promo/ps/'89* $4

FRAMPTON, PETER & STEVE MARRIOTT
The Bigger They Come/I Won't Let You Down/ Show Me the Way/Lines on My Face *A&M 31458 8059/promo/ps/logo on black* $10

FRANKE, CHRISTOPHER
The London Concerts ep (Private Diary/Cloudburst Flight/Dolphin Dance/Mountain Heights) *Sonic Images 5399/promo/ps/'92* $15

FRANKLIN, ARETHA
Aretha Sampler 12 tracks *Rhino 90126/promo/ gatefold hardcover ps/'92* $15
Everyday People 3 versions *Arista 2239/ promo/silkscreened/ps/'91* $8
Someday We'll All Be Free 4:39/8:21 *Qwest 5861/promo/'92*.............................. $6
Someone Else's .. edit & lp *Arista 2350/promo/ purple & white logo on black/ps/'91* $5
What You See is What You See *Arista 2380/ promo/silkscreened/rear insert/'91*............ $5

FRANKLIN, ARETHA & ELTON JOHN
Through the Storm *Arista 9809/promo/Peter Max ps/'89* $8

FRANKLIN, ARETHA & JAMES BROWN
Gimme Your Love 4:19/10:44 + 6 min. of interview *Arista 9906/promo/silkscreened/ps/'89* ... $15

FRANKLIN, ARETHA & MICHAEL MCDONALD
Ever Changing Times edit/lp *Arista 2394/promo/silkscreened pic/ps* $5

FRANKLIN, ARETHA & WHITNEY HOUSTON
It Isn't, It Wasn't... edit & lp *Arista 9850/promo/ps/'89* $6

FRANKS, MICHAEL
Camera Never Lies *WB 2933/promo/ps/'87* $5
Dr. Sax *WB 2900/promo/ps* $4
Speak to Me (4 vers) *Reprise 4564/promo/'90* .. $6
The Art of Love *Reprise 4084/promo/'90* $4
Woman in the Waves edit & lp *Reprise 4716/promo/'90* $4

FRAZIER CHORUS
Cloud 8 (3 versions) *Charisma 030/promo/silkscreened/'90* $6
Cloud 8 (2 versions/Dream Kitchen 12"/Typical 12"/Anarchy in the UK *Virgin 96378/ stock/gatefold hardcover ps/'91* $5
Nothing 4:21/4:06/4:27 *Charisma 045/promo/'91* $6

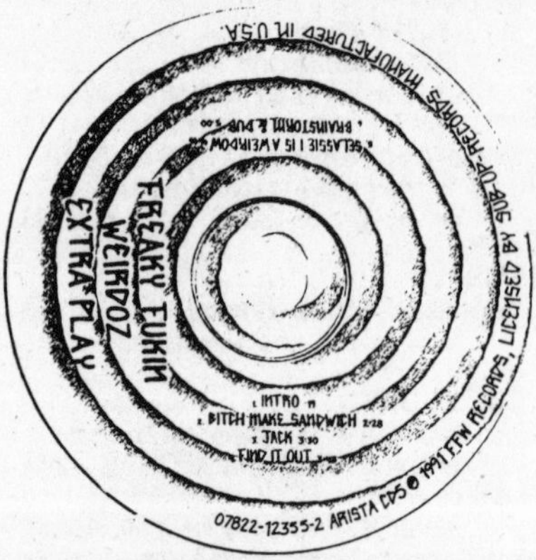

FREAKY FUKIN WEIRDOZ
Extra Play ep (Intro/Bitch Make Sandwich/Jack/ Find It Out + 2) *Arista 12355/stock/ps/silkscreened/'91* $4

FREEEZE
I.O.U. extended/dub *Warlock 801/stock/ps/'91* $6

FREELOVE, LAURIE
Smells Like Truth/Eyes/Arms of a Dream/ Heaven on Hearth *Ensign 23720/promo/ps/silkscreened/'91* . $5

FREESTYLE FELLOWSHIP
Hot Potato blow-up club edit *4th B'way 569/promo/ logo on red/custom sticker/'93* $4

FREEWHEELERS, THE
No More Booze *DGC 4317/promo/silkscreened/ gatefold hardcover ps/'91* $4

FREEZE
Voulez Vous lp/house *Profile 7357/promo/ red on blue silkscreened/'92* $4

FREHLEY, ACE
Do Ya *Megaforce 3010/promo/rear insert/'89* $8
Its Over Now remix & lp
Megaforce 2434/promo/rear insert/'88 ...... $8

FRESH BUSH & THE INVISIBLE MAN
Hard Times *IRS 67104/promo/silkscreened pic (of G.Bush with guitar)* $6
Hard Times *IRS X25E 0777-7 13872 27/ silkscreened/rear insert/stock/'92* $5

FREY, GLENN
I've Got Mine single edit & edit lp
MCA 2276/promo/ps/'92 .... $4
Livin' Right remix *MCA 17762/promo/stamped ps* $5
Love in the 21st Century edit & lp
MCA 2266/promo/ps/'93 .... $4
Part of You, Part of Me edit & lp
MCA 1358/promo/back title cover/'91 .... $4
River of Dreams edit *MCA 2279/promo/ps/'92* ... $4
Some Kind of ... *MCA 17941/promo/cust. sticker* .. $4
Strange Weather - Live in Dublin (6 tracks)
MCA 2469/promo/rear insert/'92 .... $10
True Love edit & lp *MCA 17589/promo/ps/'88* ... $5

FRIDAY, GAVIN
I Want to Live 3:45/4:03 *Island 6746/promo/ps* ... $4
King of Trash *Island 6739/promo/ps/'92* $4

FRISELL, BILL
Have a Little Faith ep (The Open Prairie/Street Scene../I Can't Be Satisfied/Little Jenny Down/Just Like a Woman) *Elektra 8710/ promo/silkscreened pic/rear insert/'93* $5

FRONT 242
Gripped by Fear 3 versions *Epic 2297/promo/ silkscreened logo on white/rear insert/'91* . $6
Masterhit pt 1,2,3 *Wax Trax 036/stock/ps/'89* ... $6
Never Stop 2 versions/Work 242 N.Off is N.Off/ Agony/Work 242
Wax Trax 9070/stock/ps/'89 .... $7
Quite Unusual/Aggressiva *Wax Trax 016/ps/stock* $7
Religion 7" & bitch slapper mix/Crapage
Epic 5146/promo/silkscreened/rear insert $5
Rhythm of Time 3:32/3:52/5:13/7:46
Epic 3091/promo/ps/logo on black/'91 ...... $6
Rhythm of Time 3:52/5:13/7:46
Epic 73767/stock/ps/'91 .... $5
Sampler (Operating Tracks/U-Men/No Shuffle/ Body to Body/Quite Unusual/Masterhit/ Headhunter V3.0 + 9)
Epic 4488/promo/r--/'92 .... $15

Tragedy (For You) (7 versions)
Epic 49K 73594/stock/ps/'90 .... $6

FRONT, THE
Fire edit & lp *CBS 73222/promo/ps/'89* $4
Le Motion *Columbia 2025/promo/ps/'90* $4
Pain/Fire/Violent World *Columbia 1915/promo/ps* $4

FU SCHNICKENS & SHAQUILLE O'NEAL
What's Up Doc? 4 vers. *Jive 42127/promo/ps/'93* . $6

FU-SCHNICKENS
Ring the Alarm 4 versions
Jive 42019/promo/rear insert/'92 .... $6
True Fuschnick 3 versions/Props/ Ring the Alarm steely & clevie extended
Jive 01241-42078/stock/ps/'92 .... $5

FU2
Boomin' in Ya Jeep lp/radio/instrumental
JDK 2275/promo/ps/'92 .... $5

FUDGE TUNNEL
Creep Diets (Grey/Tipper Gore/Ten Percent/ Face Down/Grit/Don't Have Time ...+ 5)
Earache MOSH64CD/promo/ps/silkscr/'92 . $6
Sunshine of Your Love edit & lp/Cat Scratch Fever..
Relativity 0131/promo/logo on black/ps $6

FULL FORCE
All In My Mind/The Mind (the Slow Dance)/ The Mind (the FF Mellow mix)
Columbia 1009/promo/ps/'88 .... $6
Friends B4 Lovers (4 versions)
Columbia 73025/promo/ps/'89 .... $6
Kiss Those Lips 5:30/7:37/4:11/All I Wanna Do 5:10 & 4:04 *Columbia 73227/ promo/blue silkscreen/ps/'90* $6

FUNKDOOBIEST
Bow Wow Wow 3 versions/I'm Flippin' on Em
Epic 4969/promo/ps/custom sticker/'93 .... $5
The Funkiest lethal dose remix/Freak Mode triple x remix & lp *Epic 5240/promo/ps* ... $5

FUZZBOX
Self 3:43/8:20 *Geffen 3688/promo/'89* $8

G LOVE E
Dance Baby (edit) *Chrysalis 23485/promo/ps* $4

G, KENNY
Forever in Love single & lp
Arista 2482/promo/logo on black/ps/'92 .... $6
Silhouette edit & lp *Arista 9751/promo/ps/'88* $6
Theme From Dying Young *Arista 2267/promo/ps* .. $6

G, KENNY & PEABO BRYSON
By the Time This Night is Over edit & lp
Arista 2565/promo/ps/logo on green/'93 ... $6

GABLE, ERIC
Straight From Heart edit & lp *Orpheus 74160/ promo/silkscreened/rear insert/'91* $4

GABRIEL, ANA
Evidencias *Sony Discos 10037/promo/ps/'92* ... $4

GABRIEL, PETER
Before Us: a Brief History (10 tracks including "In Your Eyes" - live) *Geffen 4412/promo/ps/'92* $20
Come Talk to Me clearmountain mix/lp *Geffen 4537/promo/ps/'93* $5
Digging in the Dirt edit & lp *Geffen 4446/promo/silkscreened/ps/'92* $5
Digging in the Dirt lp & instrumental/Quiet Steam/ Bashi-Bazouk *Geffen 21816/stock/silkscreened/ps/'92* $6
From Us to You interview *Album Network/promo/silkscreened pic* .. $25
Kiss That Frog edit & lp *Geffen 4495/promo/silkscreened/ps/'93* $5
Secret World edit & lp *Geffen 4519/promo/ silkscreened/ps/custom sticker/'93* $5
Selections from Passion (The Feeling Begins + 3) *Geffen 3558/promo/ps/'89* $10
Shaking the Tree edit & lp *Geffen 4217/promo* $4
Shaking the Tree/16 Golden Greats 16 tracks *Geffen 24326/promo silkscreened on stock/ps/'90* $12
Steam edit & lp *Geffen 4479/promo/ps/ silkscreened/'92* $5
Steam edit/let off steam 7"/let off steam 12" *Geffen 4484/promo/silkscreened/ps/'92* $6
Us 10 tracks *Geffen 24473/promo silkscreened on stock/ps/'92* $12

GABRIEL, PETER & KATE BUSH
Don't Give Up 5:26/6:30 *Geffen 2680/promo/ps/'86* $20

GABRIEL, PETER & YOUSSOU N DOUR
Shakin' the Tree (edit) *Virgin 2789/promo/silkscreened/'89* $5

GABRIELLE
Dreams 7"/dignity mix/the red underground mix *Go! Discs 1011/promo/ps/'93* $5

GAINES, JEFFREY
Headmasters of Mine 3:59 & 5:40/In Your Eyes live . *Chrysalis 24815/stock/ps/'92* $4
Headmasters of Mine rock & lp *Chrysalis 04631/ promo/silkscreened/rear insert/'92* $4
Hero in Me/Scares Me More *Chrysalis 23854/stock/ps/'92* $4
Scares Me More lp & live/In Your Eyes live *Chrysalis 05481/promo/ps/logo on tan/'92* $6
The Hero in../Why/Scares Me ../Love Disappears/ Headmasters of Mine *Chrysalis 23811/ promo/logo on black/ps/'91* $6

GALACTIC COWBOYS
I Do What I Do edit & lp *DGC 4517/ promo/ps/silkscreened pic/'93* $4
I'm Not Amused edit & lp *DGC 4403/promo/ gatefold hardcover ps/'92* $4
If I Were a Killer/Circles in the Fields *DGC 4514/promo/gatefold hardcover ps/ logo on black/'93* $4

GALES, ERIC
Resurrection *Elektra 8434/promo/ silkscreened/rear insert/'91* $4
Sign of the Storm single versions *Elektra 8377/promo/ps/logo on white/'91* .. $4

GALLAGHER, RORY
Kid Gloves edit *IRS 87052/promo/silkscreen* ... $10

GALLIANO
Jus' Reach 4 versions *4th B'way 162-440 552/stock/ps/'91* $5

GAMBALE, FRANK
The Final Frontier *JVC 020/promo/ silkscreened/rear insert/'93* $4

GAMILAH SHABAZZ
America's Living in a War Zone edit/street/instrum. *RCA 62405/promo/JOHNNY MARRS, ICE CUBE, more/rear insert/'92* $5

GANG OF FOUR
Cadillac 4:29 & 5:28/Favorites *Polydor 421/ promo/silkscreened/rear insert/'91* $6
Damaged Goods/Not Great Men/To Hell With Poverty/I Love a Man... *WB 4547/promo/ps/'90* $8
Don't Fix What Ain't Broke *Polydor 424/promo/ silkscreened orange/ps/'91* $5
Satellite 4:05/6:15/3:56 *Polydor 440/promo/silkscreened/ps/'91* $6
Satellite 4:05/6:15/3:56/I Love a Man in Uniform live *Polydor 867 503/stock/ps/'91* $7
Satellite single & lp/I Love a Man in a ..(live) Polydor 500/promo/logo on blue green $4

GANG STARR
Lovesick/Whos Gonna Take the Weight *Chrys. 23676/promo/silkscreened/ps/'91* .. $5

GAP BAND, THE
Addicted to Your Love (7 versions) *Capitol 79942/promo/silkscreened/'89* $6
We Can Make It Alright (6 versions) *Capitol 79046/promo/'90* $5

GARBAREK, JAN
I Took Up the ../Molde Canticle (pt 2,4,5) *ECM JG 2/promo/silkscreened/ps/'90* $6
Legend of Seven Dreams sample (6 songs - edits) .. *ECM/promo/ps/'89* $6

GARCIA, JERRY
Deal 3 vers./Waiting For a Miracle *Arista 2343/ promo/silkscreened pic/rear insert/'91* $10

GARRETT, SIEDAH
Kissing (3 vers.) *Qwest 3123/promo/ps/silkscreen* $7

GATTON, DANNY
Funky Mama (edit) *Elektra 8362/promo/'91* $4
Funky Mama/Blues Newburg/In My../ Simpsons *Elektra 8305/promo/ps/'91* $5
The Simpsons *Elektra 8303/promo/rear insert/'90*.$4

GAYE, MARVIN
My Last Chance (3 vers.) *Motown 1169/promo* $5

GAYE, NONA
The Things That We All Do For Love 5 versions *Third Stone 4930/promo/ silkscreened logo/ps/'92* $4

GAYLE, CRYSTAL
Nobody's Angel *WB 3166/promo/ps/'88* $6

GEAR DADDIES
Color of Her Eyes (elec. & acoustic)/The Tide is High/My Maria/Party Stomp *Polydor 346/promo/silkscreened/ps/'90* $8
Shes Happy/Cut Me Off/Statue of Jesus/Strength *Polydor 253/promo/silkscreened/'90*.........$8

GELDOF, BOB
Love or Something *Atlantic 3507/promo/ps/silkscreened/'90* ..$5
The Great Song of Indifference *Atlantic 3493/promo/ps/'90* $5
Yeah, Definitely *Polydor 904/promo/silkscreened/ps/'92*....$5

GENE LOVES JEZEBEL
Break the Chain edit & lp *Savage 50040/promo/silkscreened/'93*.....$6

Jealous *Geffen 4125/promo/ps/silkscreen red*.....$8
Josephina edit/lp/extended *Savage 50028/ promo/silkscreened/custom sticker/'92*.....$6
Jospehina lp & extended/Life Without Love/ Tomorrow's Colours *Savage 74785 50024/ stock/gatefold hardcover ps/'92*................$5
Remix Sampler (Desire/Heartache/Twenty Killer Hurts/Suspicion/Jealous) *Geffen 4192/promo/ps/'90* $15
Suspicion (3 vers.) *Geffen 3051/promo/ps/'88*....$10
Tangled Up in You (3 versions) *Geffen 4173/promo/ps/'90* $8
Tangled Up in You/Jealous (Francois mix & house) *Geffen 4157/promo/ps/'90* $8

GENESIS
Domino pt 2 *Atlantic 4848/promo/rear insert* $6
Driving the Last Spike edit & lp *Atlantic 4616/promo* $6
Hold On My Heart *Atlantic 4533/promo/ logo on black/ps/'92* $6
I Can't Dance 4:00/7:00 *Atlantic 4412/ promo/ps/logo silkscreened/'92* $8
Jesus He Knows..single mix *Atlantic 4680/promo* $6
Live - The Way We.. 11 tracks *Atlantic 82452/ promo/gatefold hardcover ps/'92* $20
Live The Way We Walk: Volume Two: The Longs (trt: approx.70:00) *Atlantic 82461/ promo/gatefold hardcover ps/'92* $20
Never a Time *Atlantic 4864/promo/'92*................$6
Never a Time/Tonight Tonight../Invisible Touch (last 2 live) *Atlantic 87411/stock/ps/'92*..$6
Never a Time/Tonight Tonight../Invisible Touch (last 2 live) *Atlantic 87411/promo/ custom stickers (2)/'92*..........................$10
No Son of Mine *Atlantic 4277/promo/silkscreened/ps/'91* ..$6
No Son of Mine/Living Forever *Atlantic 87571/stock/ps/silkcr./'91* $5
Rarities/Two Songs From the Longs (Domino/ The Lamb Lies Down on Broadway)/ interview with Phil & Mike *Atlantic 4997/promo/custom sticker*........$22

GENTLEMEN WITHOUT WEAPONS
Unconditional Love edit/lp *A&M 17576/promo/ps* .$3

GEORGIA SATELLITES
Another Chance edit *Elektra 8113/ promo/silkscreened logo/'89* $4
Another Chance/Saddle Up/That Woman/Nights of Mystery/Im Waiting for the Man (last 4 non lp) *Elektra 66678/stock/ps/'89* .$7
Dont Pass Me By *Elektra 8024/promo/ps/'88* $4
Hippy Hippy Shake *Elektra 8030/promo/'88* $4
Open All Night *Elektra 8007/promo/'88*.............$4
Shake That Thing edit & lp *Elektra 8159/promo/silkscreen logo/'90*....$4
Sheila remix/Hippy Hippy Shake *Elektra 9 69328/stock/3"/ps/'88* $6

Sheila remix/lp *Elektra 8045/promo/'88* $5

GEORGIO
Rollin' 7 versions *RCA 62031/promo/ps/'91* $4

GERARDO
Here Kitty Kitty 4 versions
Interscope 4714/promo/rear insert............$5
Here Kitty Kitty 8 versions
Interscope 4711/promo/ps/'92 ....$6
Latin Till I Die
Interscope 4253/promo/logo on red/ps $5
Rico Suave spanglish & spanish
Interscope 3679/promo/rear insert/'90......$7
We Want the Funk 5 versions/Fandango
Interscope 96357/stock/
gatefold hardcover ps/'91 ....$5
We Want the Funk edit & lp *Interscope 3846/*
promo/logo on white/rear insert/'91 ....$4
When the Lights Go Out dr freeze mix & lp
Interscope 4103/promo/rear insert............$5

GERMANO, LISA
You Make me Wanto Wear Dresses radio
Capitol 79747/promo/silkscreened/ps/'93 .$4

GET THE FIST MOVEMENT
Get the Fist edit & street versions
Mercury 771/promo/silkscreened/ps/'92 ...$4

GETO BOYS
Straight G-Ing 4 versions
Rap A Lot 7017/promo/logo on black/'93..$6

GETZ, STAN
Apasionado 8 tracks *A&M 75021 5297/*
stock/ps/dj silkscreened/'90 ....$15
Apasionado/Waltz For Stan/Espanola/Amorous Cat
(all edits) *A&M 75021 7430/promo/*
silkscreened logo on purple/'90 ....$7

GHOST OF AN AMERICAN AIRMAN
Honeychild *Hollywood 8524/promo/*
silkscreened/rear insert/'92 ....$4

GIANT
Chained 4:36/6:59 *Epic 4433/promo/ps/'92*.......$4
I'm a Believer edit & lp *A&M 5272/promo/ps* $4
I'm a Believer (hitmakers top 40 mix) *A&M/promo* $4
Ill See You in My Dreams edit & lp
A&M 18010/promo/silkscreened/ps/'89 ....$4
Innocent Days remix & edit *A&M 18004/promo/*
logo silkscreened/'89 ....$4
It Takes Two edit & lp
A&M 75021 8088/promo/ps/'89 ....$4
Time to Burn *Epic 4690/promo/silkscreened/ps* ...$4

GIANT SAND
Shadow to You
Atlantic 3863/promo/silkscreened/ps/'90 ..$5

GIANT STEPS
Another Lover (3 vers) *A&M 17597/promo/ps/'88*.$4
Into You lp version & 7" hot mix
A&M 17649/promo/'88 ....$4

GIBSON, DEBBIE
(This So-Called) Miracle (edit)
Atlantic 3770/promo/ps/'90 ....$6
Anything is Possible (3 versions)
Atlantic 3638/promo/ps/'90 ....$8
Anything is Possible + Live Around the World video :
Atlantic 50176/promo/
video & cd/in box package $15
Electric Youth *Atlantic 2671/promo/rear insert*....$6
Electric Youth (5 vers.)/We Could Be Together
(campfire mix) *Atlantic 86427/stock/ps* ...$8
Electric Youth 7" house edit & alt. latin edit & lp
Atlantic 2689/promo/ps/'89 ....$10
Electric Youth lp + 2 remixed songs
Atlantic 81932/promo/gatefold ps/'89 ....$6
How Can This Be? *Atlantic 5092/promo* $5
Losin' Myself 5 versions *Atlantic 4917/promo/*
silkscreened pic/ps/'92..............................$6
Lost in Your Eyes
Atlantic 2562/promo/gatefold ps/'89 ....$8
No More Rhyme *Atlantic 2749/promo/ps/'89* $6
One Hand, One Heart *Atlantic 3836/promo/ps* $6
One Step Ahead 6 versions
Atlantic 3944/promo/rear insert/'91 ....$10
Profiled! (31 minute story + interview)
Atlantic 2850/promo/
fold out cue sheet ps/'89 ....$15
Shock Your Mama edit & lp *Atlantic 5050/promo/*
silkscreened pic/rear insert/cust. sticker ...$6
We Could Be Together (4 versions)
Atlantic 2724/promo/ps/'89 ....$10

GIBSON/MILLER BAND
WhereThere's Smoke..11 tracks *Epic 52980/*
promo/silkscreened/matchbook t
ype ps/'92 ....$10

GILBERT, BRUCE
This Way to the Shivering Man ep (Work for Do You
Me.. - 3 versions/Hommage/Shivering
Man/Here Visit + 2)
Restless 71432/stock/ps/'87 ....$12

GILL, JOHNNY
Fairweather Friend (6 versions)
Motown 1026/promo/'90 ....$6
I Got You 16 versions
Motown 374631119/promo/ps/'93 ....$10
I'm Still Waiting master mix & instrumental
Giant 4912/promo/'91 ....$5
My, My, My "Live" record breaking versions/
Wrap My Body Tight 12" remake & remix
Motown 4756/stock/
gatefold hardcover ps/'91 ....$5
Rub You the Right Way 7" edit/radio edit/
extendedhype *Motown 18229/promo/'90*.$6

Rub You the Right Way lp & edit
Motown 18130/promo/'90 .... $6
The Floor 10 vers. *Motown 374631110/promo* $8
The Floor 7 versions *Motown 374631095/promo/ silkscreened pic/ps/'93* $7
The Floor 8 versions *Motown 374631102/ promo/silkscreened pic/ps/'93* $7
Wrap My Body Tight (6 versions)
Motown 1014/promo/ps/'91 .... $6

GILL, VINCE
I Still Believe in You *MCA 2366/promo/'92* $5
I Still Believe in You *MCA 54406/promo/'92* $5
I Still Believe in You/intro *MCA 2296/promo/ps* $5
Pocket Full of Gold *MCA 54026/promo/'91* $5
Take Your Memory With You *MCA 54282/promo* . $5

GILLIS, BRAD
Honest to God/Stampede/If Looks Could ..(all edits) .
Guitar 9714 99203/promo/silkscreened pic/custom sticker/GREGG ALLMAN/'93 .. $4

GILMORE, JIMMIE DALE
My Mind's Got a Mind of Its Own
Elektra 8522/promo/ps/'92 .... $4

GIN BLOSSOMS
Allison Road *A&M 75021 5169/promo/ silkscreened/'91* $4
Found Out About You *A&M 31458 8055/ promo/logo on white/'92* $4
Hey Jealousy *A&M 75021 7602/promo/ silkscreened/ps/'92* $6
Hey Jealousy lp & edit *A&M 31458 8005/ promo/silkscreened/ps/'92* $6
Lost Horizons *A&M 31458 8061/promo/ silkscreened/ps/'92* $4
Mrs. Rita *A&M 31458 8056/promo/ ps/silkscreened/'92* $4
Shut Up and Smoke ep (Soul Deep/Heart Away/ Cold River Dick/Christine Irene)
A&M 31458 8107/promo/silkscreened/ps . $8

GINN, GREG
Payday remix & origin./Pig MF *Cruz028/stock/ps* $5

GIPSY KINGS
Baila Me *Elektra 8393/promo/'91* $4
Bamboleo *Elektra 8041/promo/'88* $4
Bamboleo latin remix & latin extended
Elektra 8083/promo/'88 .... $5
Djobi Djoba single & 12" remix & extended club
Elektra Musician 8091/promo/'88 .... $5
Hotel California *Elektra 8217/promo/ps/'90* $4
Vamos a Bailar edit, lp, extended
Elektra 8131/promo/'89 .... $5
Volare *Elektra 8143/promo/silkscreened/'89* $4

GIRLS NEXT DOOR, THE
Hes Gotta Have Me
Atlantic 3001/promo/rear insert/'89 .... $4

Maybe You Wouldn't Be Missin' Me Tonight
Atlantic 3251/promo/rear insert/'89 .... $4

GIRLSCHOOL
Fox on the Run *Enigma 169/promo/cust.sticker* .. $5
Head Over Heels *Enigma 179/promo/ logo on purple/custom sticker/'89* $5

GLAMOUR CAMP
She Did It For Love single/lp *EMI 04272/promo/ rear insert/silkscreened lettering/'89* $4

GLASS TIGER
Far Away From Here *EMI 04103/promo/ps/'88* $4
Im Still Searching edit/lp *EMI 04011/promo/ps/'88* $4
My Town *Capitol 572/promo/'90* $4

GLASS, PHILIP
1000 Airplaines on the Roof interviewed by SUZ.VEGA *Virgin 2708/promo/'89* $10

GLORIES
Aurora ep (Nothing to Believe/Dry Season/ What Do You Expect?/Blackened Eyes)
Aurora AU010/promo/ps/'92 .... $4

GO WEST
Don't Ever Let Em See You Sweat
EMI 04881/promo/logo silkscreened/ custom sticker/'92 .... $4
Faithful/I Want You Back/King of Wishful Thinking
EMI 56259/stock/ps/'92 .... $5
King of Wishful Thinking (3 versions) *EMI 04569/ promo/"Pretty Woman" silkscreened/ rear insert/'90* $8
King of Wishful Thinking (wake up mix) *EMI 04621/ promo/"Pretty Woman" silkscreened/'90* ... $7
What You Won't Do For Love 4 versions
EMI 56262/stock/ps/silkscreened/'92 .... $7
What You Won't Do For Love beat appella/ a cappella/ragga mix *EMI 04707/promo/ silkscreened/custom sticker/'93* $5

GOATS, THE
Typical American 4 vers./Burn the Flag 3 versions
Ruffhouse 44K 74726/stock/ps/'92 .... $5

GOD MACHINE, THE
Home 7" UK & 5:20/What Time is Love?
Fiction 870/promo/logo on black/ps/'93 .... $4

GODDESS
In My Bed lp & 7" *Big Beat 5054/promo/ silkscreened/ps/'93* $4
Sexual 5 versions *Atlantic 4877/promo* $5

GODFATHERS
Birth School Work Death 11 tracks
Epic 2896/promo/ps/'88 .... $15
More Songs About Love & Hate 13 tracks
Epic 1545/promo/logo on black/'89 .... $15

She Gives Me Love lp/high octane mix/extended
Epic 1639/promo/silkscr. logo on red/'89 .. $8
Texas Chainsaw Massacre - Reverse 2
(9 tracks live) *Epic 1761/promo/ reverse lettering silkscreened/'89* $25
Unreal World *Epic 3043/promo/silkscreened/ rear insert/'91* $5

GODFLESH
Mothra/Spite *Relativity 0152/promo/ silkscreened/ps/'92* $5

GOFFIN, LOUISE
Bridge of Sighs (edit)/Interview
WB 3021/promo/ps/'88 .... $8

GO GOS
Cool Jerk (6 versions)
IRS 75021 7478/promo/silkscreened/'90 $10
Cool Jerk edit & lp
IRS 75821 7439/promo/silkscreened/ps ... $5

GOLDEN EARRING
I Can't Sleep Without You
First Quake 4488/promo/logo on gold/'93 . $6
The Naked Truth live acoustic show 15 tracks
First Quake 4481/stock/'93 .... $15
Twilight Zone acoustic edit w.intro/without intro/lp ....
First Quake 4489/stock/silkscr. pic/'93 ..... $6

GOLDEN PALOMINOS, THE
Dying From the Inside Out edit
Virgin 081/promo/silkscreened/'91 .... $5

GOLDEN, WILLIAM LEE
Louisiana Red Dirt Highway
Mercury 275/promo/silkscreened/'90 .... $4

GOLDSTEIN, GIL & ROMERO LUBAMBO
My Foolish Heart Big World 2008/
promo/silkscreened/rear insert/'93 .... $4

GOO GOO DOLLS
I'm Awake Now
Metal Blade 5053/promo/rear insert/'91 .... $4
Just the Way You Are/Just the Way You Are/Hey/ You Know What I Mean (last 3 live)
Metal Blade 4711/promo/ps/'91 .... $10
There You Are *Metal Blade 4520/promo/ps/'90* ... $4
We Are the Normal *WB 6043/promo/'93* $4

GOOD GIRLS
It Must be Love edit & lp
Motown 374631083/promo/ps/'92 .... $4
Just Call Me 4 versions
Motown 374310512/promo/ps/'92 .... $5

GOOD QUESTION
Got a New Love (4 remixes) *Paisley Park 3119/ promo/silkscreened/ps/'88* $5

Listen To Your Heart (edit)
Paisley Park 3545/promo/'88 .... $4

GOODBYE MR MACKENZIE
Blacker Than Black *Radiactive 1269/promo/ silkscreened/ps/'91* $4
The Rattler/Open Your Arms/Down to the Minium/ Fridays Child/Goodbye Mr MacKenzi
Radioactive 54173/stock/ps/'91 .... $5

GORDON, LONNIE
Gonna Catch You 4 versions
SBK 05406/promo/silkscreened/ps/'91 ..... $6

GORKY PARK
Bang *Mercury 109/promo/silkscreened/'89* $4
Bang edit & lp *Mercury 120/promo/silkscreen* ... $4
Peace in Our Time edit & lp
Mercury 173/promo/silkscreened/'89 .... $4
Try to Find Me edit & lp *Mercury 174/ promo/silkscreened pic/'90* $5

GOTHIC SLAM
Who Died and Made You../Thunder and Lightning
Epic 1843/promo/silkscreened/'89 .... $4

GOWAN
All the Lovers in the World *Atlantic 3415/promo/ ps/'90/with ALEX LIFESON* $5
Lost Brotherhood *Atlantic 3736/promo/ps/'90* $4

GRACES, THE
50,000 Candles Burning *A&M 17971/ promo/silkscreened logo/'89* $6
Lay Down Your Arms *A&M 17822/promo/ps/ '89/with CHARLOTTE CAFFEY* $6
Perfect View *A&M 17911/promo/ps/'89* $6
Perfect View lp length *A&M 17844/promo/ pic disc/rear insert/'89* $10
Perfect View remix
A&M 17968/promo/silkscreened/'89 .... $6

GRAMM, LOU
Angel With a Dirty Face edit & lp *Atlantic 3309/ promo/rear insert/silkscreened logo./'89* ... $4
Just Between You and Me edit & lp
Atlantic 3025/promo/ps/'89 .... $4
True Blue Love edit & lp
Atlantic 3059/promo/ps/'89 .... $4

GRAND PUBA & MARY J BLIGE
Check It Out 3 versions
Elektra 8733/promo/silkscreened/'92 .... $4

GRAND PUBA 360º
What Goes Around 4 vers. *Elektra 8602/promo* ... $4

GRANDMASTER SLICE
Thinking of You *Jive 42034/promo/custom sticker/rear insert/'91* $4

GRANT LEE BUFFALO
Blue Plate Special ep (Dixie Drug Store/America Snoring/Jupiter and Teardrop/ Wish You Well/Burning Love - last 3 live) *Slash 6339/promo/ps/'93* $8
Fuzzy *Slash 6030/promo/silkscreened group pic/ rear insert/custom sticker/'93* $5
Jupiter and Teardrop single & lp *Slash 6029 promo/silkscreened/rear insert/'93* $4

GRANT, AMY
Baby 7" heart in motion mix/12"/Lead Me On *A&M 75021 2397/stock/ps/'91* $6
Baby Baby (5 versions) *A&M 75021 7512/promo/ps/'91* $12
Every Heartbeat (5 versions) *A&M 75021 7541/promo/silkscreened/ps* . $7
Good For Me 4 versions *A&M 75021 7264/ promo/silkscreened logo/ps/'91* $8
Grown Up Christmas List edit & lp *A&M 31458 8065/promo/silkscreened/ps* . $7
Hope Set High *Myrrh 9010807207/promo/ps/'91* . $7
I Will Remember You rhythm remix/lp remix/lp *A&M 75021 7339/promo/ logo on green/ps/'92* $7
Lead Me On edit & lp *A&M 17580/promo/silkscreened pic/ps* $7
Smash Hits (I Will Remember You - rhythm remix/ Baby Baby7" no getting over you & heart in motion mix/Every Heartbeat 7" body & soul mix + 3) *A&M 75021 7387/ promo/gatefold hardcover ps/'91* $20
That's What Love is For 4 versions *A&M 75021 7233/promo/ps/'91* $7

GRANT, DAVID
Wake Up Everybody *4th & B'way 546/promo/ custom sticker/'90* $4

GRANT, EDDY
Gimme Hope Jo'Anna *Enigma 276/promo/ silkscreened/custom sticker/'90* $4

GRANT, TOM
Monkey Magic/Mambo to the Moon/Show Me the Way/In My Wildest Dreams/I've Just Begun to Love You *Verve 543/promo/silkscreened/'92* $6
Need to Heart Say I Love../Bernies Groove (edit)/ Night on the Town *Verve/promo/silkscreened/'90* $5

GRANT, TOM & ART PORTER
The Christmas Song/seasons greetings *Verve VXMAS-2/promo/logo on green/gatefold hardcover ps/'92* $5

GRANT, TOM & SHARON BRYANT
I've Just Begun to Love You/In My Wildest Dreams (both radio edits) *Verve 555/ promo/logo on red/rear insert/'92* $4

GRAPES OF WRATH, THE
All the Things I Wasn't *Capitol 79937/promo/ '89/silkscreen logo on yellow/rear insert* ... $4
I Am Here 3 versions/All the Time/See Emily Play *Capitol 75268/stock/ps/'91* $5
I Am Here rock mix & lp *Capitol 79881/promo/ps* $4
Stay *Capitol 79914/promo/'89* $4
You May Be Right aor mix/Down So Close/ Let Me Roll It/Peace of Mind (live) *Capitol 79169/promo/ps/'91* $10
You May Be Right rock remix & lp *Capitol 79047/ promo/silkscreened/rear insert/'91* $4

GRASS ROOTS, THE
Let's Live For Today/Things I Should Have Said/ Sooner of Later/Glory Bound *MCA 37293/stock/3"/ps/'88* $5
Midnight Confessions/Where Were You When I Needed ../Tempt.Eyes/The Runway *MCA 37311/3"/stock/ps/'89* $5

GRATEFUL DEAD
Ante Up - The Built to Last interview *Arista 9921/ promo/interview & music/ps/'89* $18
Foolish Heart *Arista 9899/promo/ps/'89* $10
Touch of Grey 2 vers. *Arista 9606/promo/ps* $15

GRAVEYARD TRAIN, THE
Down to the Wire edit & lp *Geffen 4493/promo/ps/'93* $4

GREAT PLAINS
A Picture of You *Columbia 73961/promo/ rear insert/'91* $4

GREAT WHITE
Back Tracks 1986-1991 (Rock Me/Face the Day 7:04/House of Broken Love live/ Congo Square/Train to Nowhere + 2) *Capitol 79286/promo/logo on blue/ps* $15
Big Goodbye 5:55/4:18 *Capitol 79433/promo/ silkscreened pic/ps/'92* $6
Call It Rock n Roll *Capitol 79500/promo/silkscreen/ps/'91* $4
Desert Moon *Capitol 79741/promo/logo on blue* ... $4
Hooked 10 tracks *Capitol 95330/stock/ "girl on hook" ps/'91* $15
House of Broken Love edit & lp *Capitol 79784/promo/silkscreened/'89* $6
Live at the Ritz 2/2/88 *Capitol 79305/promo/ps* $15
Live in London (Move It/House of Broken Love/ Once Bitten...) *Capitol 79034/promo/silkscreened/'90* $15
Lovin' Kind *Capitol 79858/promo/'91* $4
Mista Bone edit & lp/Wasted Rock Ranger *Capitol 79682/promo/silkscreened/'89* $6
Mistreater/Rock Me (live)/Save Your Love (remix) *Capitol 79280/promo/ps/'87* $10
Old Rose Motel edit & lp *Capitol 79578/promo/ silkscreened/custom sticker/'92* $4

Once Bitten Twice Shy *Capitol 004647/ promo/silkscreened pic/'89* $10
Rock Me/Face the Day (extended) *Capitol 79061/promo/ps* $8
The Angel Song 7" & lp *Capitol 79753/promo/ silkscreened logo on red/'89* $6
Original Queen of Sheba *Capitol 79883/promo/'91* $4

GREAT WHITE + 2

Move It/House of Broken .. + 4 non G. White tunes *Capitol 79017/promo/silkscreened/'90*....$10

GREEN JELLO

Cereal Killer (11 tracks) *Zoo 72445-11038/ stock/original name on cover/ps/'93* $15
Suxx! ep (Green Jello Theme Song/3 Little Pigs/ Obey the Cowgod + 2) *Zoo 14057/ silkscreened/stock/ps/'92* $5
Three Little Pigs edit & lp *Zoo 17111/ promo/silkscreened/rear insert/'93*...........$4

GREEN JELLY

Electric Harley House rock/edit *Zoo 17136/ promo/silkscreened/rear insert/'93*...........$4

GREEN ON RED

Reverend Luther/This Time Around *Polydor 258/promo/silkscreened/'89*.........$6

GREEN, AL

As Long As Were Together memphis mix & remix *A&M 17784/promo/silkscreened logo/'89* .$7
Love is Reality 4 versions *Word-Epic 74232/ promo/logo on brown/ps/'92* $7

GREENE STRING QUARTET

Welcome to the Jungle edit & cd *Virgin 3997/promo/silkscreened/'91*..........$4

GREENWOOD, LEE

God Bless the USA *MCA 1335/promo* $5

GREGSON, CLIVE & CHRISTINE COLLISTER

This is the Deal edit & lp *Rhino 90031/promo/ ps/silkscreened pic/'90*.............................$5

GRETA

Love is Dead/There'll Be No Teardrops Tonight *Stardog 862 196/stock/ps/logo on purple* .$4
Rocking Chair/Insomnia *Stardog 885/promo/silkscreened/ps/'93* ...$4

GRIFFITH, NANCI

A Portrait of An Artist (Late Night Grande Hotel/ Its a Hard Life../Love at Five & Dime/ From a Distance/Gulf Coast Highway + 7) *MCA 1693/promo/ps/'91* $15
Across the Great Divide *Elektra 8777/promo/silkscreened/'93*........$4
Heaven *MCA 2069/promo/'91* $4
Its a Hard Life Wherever You Go *MCA 17961/promo/custom sticker/'89*......$4
Late Night Grande Hotel *MCA 2002/promo/'91* ...$4
Present Echoes 12 track sampler with 6 Nanci songs + 6 songs that she really likes (!) (included DYLAN, JOHN PRINE, WOODY GUTHRIE, more) *Elektra 8711/promo/gatefold hardcover/ extensive booklet/silkscreened/ pic insert/INDIGO GIRLS, more/'93*........$20
Speed of the Sound of Loneliness *Elektra 8714/promo/silkscreened/ps/'93*...$4
Storms/Wooden Heart/Deadwood, S.Dakota/ There's a Light Beyond These Woods *MCA 18092/promo/ps/'89* $8

GRIFFITHS, MARCIA

Electric Boogie *Mango 126/promo/'89* $5
Electric Boogie 4 versions *Mango 7832/promo/ silkscreened/rear insert/'89* $8
Electric Boogie 4 vers. *Mango 7832/stock/ps/'90* .$6

GRIMACE

Tomorrow's Gonna Suck ep (Nothing/She Turns to Favor/I Try/Away Be Gone/Time/ Here Comes John + 1) *Gift 003/stock/ps/silkscreened/'92* $5

GRIMES, SCOTT

I Dont Even Mind *A&M 17762/promo/ps/ '89/prod by RICHARD CARPENTER* $4

GRISSOM, RICH

It Must be Love *Merc. 232/promo/silkscreen/'90* ...$4

GRONEMEYER, HAROLD

Full Moon *SBK 05315/promo/ps/'88* $4

GROOVE B CHILL

Hip Hop Music (4 versions) *A&M 75021 8087/promo/silkscreened/'90* $4

GROUND ZERO

Lettin Ya Know radio & extended p-mix *Lethal Beat LBR116/stock/ BOOTSY COLLINS/'90*............................$5

GRUSHECKY, JOE

How Long *Rounder 1003/promo/silkscreen/ps/'89* $4

GUADACANAL DIARY

Always Saturday single/lp *Elektra 8055/promo*...$4
Pretty Is As Pretty Doe *Elektra 8081/promo/silkscreened/'89*........$4

GUESSS

Shu-B 4 versions *WB 6414/promo/'93* $4

GUILTY

Tora Tora *A&M 17905/promo/silkscreen logo/'89*.$4

GUMBALL
Accelerator *Columbia 4960/promo/ps/'93* $4
Real Gone Deal lp & malco mix *Columbia 5145/promo/ps/'93* $4

GUN
Money edit & lp *A&M 18033/promo/silkscreened/ps/'89* $4
Steal Your Fire edit & lp *A&M 75021 7373/promo/ps/'92* $4
Watching the World Go By edit & lp *A&M 31458 8040/promo/silkscreened/ps* . $4
Welcome to the Real World edit & lp *A&M 75021 7336/promo/ps/silkscreened* . $4

GUNS N ROSES
14 Years *Geffen 4418/promo/silkscreened/ gatefold hardcover ps/'92* $8
Dead Horse *Geffen 4511/promo/silkscreened/ps* $7
Don't Cry orig./alternate lyrics/demo versions *Geffen 4232/promo/ die cust ps/foil innerwrap/'91* $10
Garden of Eden *Geffen 4366/promo/silkscreen* ... $10
Knockin' on Heavens Door (remix) *DGC 4140/promo/silkscreened/ rear insert/'90* $10
Live and Let Die *Geffen 4352/promo/ps/'91* $8
Nightrain *Geffen 3625/promo* $8
November Rain 8:53 *Geffen 4387/promo/ logo on blue/gatefold hardcover ps/'92* ... $10
Patience *Geffen 3437/promo/'88* $10
Pretty Tied Up *Geffen 4386/promo/ carboard gatefold/tied with string/'91* $15
Sweet Child o' Mine (3 versions) *Geffen 3077/promo/ps/'87* $15
Sweet Child of Mine edit remix *Geffen 3147/promo/'87* $10
Use Your Illusion 1 16 tracks *Geffen 24415/ promo silkscreened on stock/ps/'91* $15
Use Your Illusion 1 & 2 (11 tracks) *Geffen 4441/promo/ps/'91* $20
Use Your Illusion 2 14 tracks *Geffen 24420/ promo silkscreened on stock/ps/'91* $15
Use Your Illusion I & II sampler (Locomotive/Don't Cry/Live and Let Die/The Garden/14 Years/November Rain + 2) *Geffen 4328/promo/custom sticker/'91* ... $25
Welcome to the Jungle *Geffen 2668/promo/ps* .. $12
Yesterdays lp/live in Vegas *Geffen 4470/promo/ silkscreened/custom sticker/'92* $12
You Could Be Mine *Geffen 4253/promo/ps/'91* ... $8

GURU & DONALD BYRD
Loungin'/Transit Ride (BRANFORD MARSALIS)/ Trust Me *Chrysalis 04711/promo/ps/'93* . $5

GURU JOSH
Infinity (5 versions) *RCA 2570/promo/ps/'90* $5

GUTHRIE, GWEN
Miss My Love edit & lp *Reprise 4332/promo/rear insert/'90* $4
Say It Isn't So edit & lp *Reprise 4616/promo/'90* . $4
Sweet Bitter Love 2 vers. *Reprise 4786/promo/'90* . $4

GUTTERBALL
Trial Separation Blues *Mute 8756/promo/ silkscreened/rear insert/'93* $4

GUTTERBOY
A Rainy Day on Mulberry St. *DGC 4142/promo/ silkscreened/gatefold hardcover/'90* $4
Every Other Night *Mercury 643/promo/ logo on white/gatefold hardcover ps/'92* ... $4

GUY
D-O-G Me Out 7 versions *MCA 1541/promo/'91* $7
Do Me Right *MCA 1382/promo/'90* $4
I Wanna Get With U 3 versions *MCA 1096/promo/logo on green/'90* $7
I Wanna Get With U 4 vers. *MCA 53931/ stock/gatefold hardcover ps/'90* $6
Let's Chill lp/edit/instru. *MCA 1264/promo/rear insert/'91* $5
Let's Stay Together 9 versions *MCA 2086/promo/rear insert/'91* $8
Let's Stay Together 7 versions *MCA 2052/promo/ps/'91* $7
Spend the Night with rap/without/extended *Uptown 17930/promo/custom sticker* $6
Teddy's Jam 2 6 versions *MCA 2205/promo/'92* $7
The Future (16 tracks) *MCA 1193/promo/tri fold hardcover ps/logo on white/'90* $15

GUY, JASMINE
Don't Want Money 6 versions/ Johnny Come Lately *WB 40228/stock/ gatefold hardcover ps/'91* $5
Don't Want Money 7 versions *WB 4940/promo/'90* $5
Just Want to Hold You *WB 4787/promo/'90* $4
Try Me slammin' remix/slammin' remix edit/ext. *WB 21597/stock/ps/'90* $5
Try Me edit & lp *WB 4344/promo/ silkscreened pic/rear insert/'90* $5
Try Me (edit)/Just Want to Hold You *WB 18892/stock/'92* $4

GUYS NEXT DOOR
I Was Made For You edit & lp *SBK 05350/ promo/silkscreened/ gatefold hardcover ps/'90* $4

GYPSY ROSE
Poisoned by Love *RCA 2657/promo/ps/'90* $4

H TOWN
Lick U Up 4 versions *Luke 469/promo/ silkscreened pic/'93* $6

H.E.A.L.
Heal Yourself lp & instrumental *Elektra 8414/promo/ps/'91* $4

HAGAR, SAMMY
Give to Live *Geffen 2750/promo/ gatefold hardcover ps/'87* $8
Returns Home/interview for I Never Said Goodbye *Geffen 2832/promo/ps/'87* $15

HAGGARD, MERL
When It Rains It Pours/Me & Crippled Soldiers *Curb 79049//promo logo on tan silkscreened/rear insert/'90* $5

HALEY, BILL
Rock Around the Clock + 3 *MCA 37294/ 3"/promo/custom sticker/'88* $8

HALFORD, ROB
Light Comes Out of Black *Columbia 4713/promo/ps/'92* $6

HALL & OATES
Don't Hold Back YOur Love single & lp *Arista 2157/promo/rear insert/'90* $5
Everything Your Heart Desires (6 versions *RCA 9685/promo/ps/'88* $10
Love Train 7"/lp/12" remix *Sire 3505/promo/'89* $6
So Close single, lp, unplugged *Arista 2086/ promo/ps/silkscreened/'90* $6
Starting All Over Again radio remix & unplugged vers. *Arista 2217/promo/ silkscreened pic/rear insert/'91* $10

HALL AFLAME
One Time Winner *IRS 67061/promo/silkscreened/'91* $4

HALL, AARON
Don't Be Afraid 8 versions *Soul 2147/promo/rear insert/'92* $7

HALL, DARYL
Dreamtime RCA 14386/promo/ps/'86 .... $10
Three Hearts in the Happy.. (10 tracks) *RCA 7196/stock/ps/'86* $15

HALL, JENNIFER
Ice Cream Days edit/lp *WB 3071/promo/ps* $5

HALL, KRISTEN
Empty Promises/Just So You Know/It Ain't Me Babe/Very Busy Man *High Street 93-13/promo/ silkscreened/ps/'93* $5

HALLIGAN, BOB
Could've Been You *Atco 3923/promo/trifold hardcover ps/green logo on white/'91* $4

HALLYDAY, DAVID
Tears of the Earth *Scotti Bros 5279/promo/ blue on green silkscreened/ps/'90* $4

HAMILTON, SCOTT
Groovin' High 10 tracks *Concord 4509/stock with promo silkscreened/ps/'92* $12

HAMMER
2 Legit 2 Quit 7:52 & 10:16/Addams Groove lp & instrumental *Capitol 15791/stock/ps/'91* $5
Addams Groove lp & instrum. *Capitol 79029/ promo/logo on black/ps/'91* $4
Do Not Pass Me By edit/lp/instrumental *Capitol 79196/promo/ silkscreened logo/'91* $5
Do Not Pass Me By single vers *Capitol 79236/ promo/silkscreened logo/'91* $4
Gaining Momentum 6 versions *Capitol 79093/promo/'91* $6
Gaining Momentum edit/moment.jam/hip hop mix *Capitol 79465/promo/'91* $5
Good to Go 6 vers. *Capitol 79319/promo/'91* $6

HAMMER, MC
Have You Seen Her lp & instrumental *Capitol 79146/promo/silkscreened* $5
Help the Children vocal & instrumental *Capitol 79892/promo/silkscreened* $5
Here Comes the Hammer (5 versions) *Capitol 79445/promo/lsilkscreened* $7
Pray (3 versions) *Capitol 79285/promo/ silkscreened logo/rear insert/'90* $6
Pray (5 versions)/U Can't Touch This *Capitol 15661/stock/ps/'90* $5
Pray (6 versions) *Capitol 79459/ promo/silkscreened logo/'90* $7
U Can't Touch This (3 versions) *Capitol 79071/ promo/silkscreened/'90* $8
U Can't Touch This/Pray (jam the hammer mix)/Let's Get It Started (edit)/ Have You Seen Her/ Turn This Mutha Out (edit) + 4 *Capitol 79651/promo/logo on green* $10

HAMMERBOX
Hed/Starring Matter *A&M 31458 8119/ promo/gatefold hardcover ps/ silkscreened/'93* $4

Hole *A&M 31458 8104/promo/silkscreened/ps* $4
When 3 is 2/Rain/No acoustic
A&M 31458 8120/promo/ gatefold hardcover ps/'93 ..... $5

HAMMOND, JOHN
I've Got Love If You Want It
Charisma 092/promo/rear insert/ prod.by JJ CALE/'92 ..... $5

HAMPTON, BRUCE
A Conversation With *Capricorn 5248/promo/ silkscreened pic/rear insert/'91* $10
Time is Free edit & lp
Capricorn 5464/promo/ps/'92 ..... $4
Working on a Building/Yield Not to Temptation/ Planet Earth *Capricorn 5866/ promo/ps/'92* $5

HANCOCK, HERBIE
Beat Wise (7" edit)
Columbia 1241/promo/ps/'88 ..... $5
Vibe Alive edit/extended/bonus beats
Columbia 1097/promo/ps/'88 ..... $6

HANGMEN, THE
Rotten Sunday *Capitol 79718/ promo/silkscreened/'89* $4

HANOI ROCKS
Malibu Beach Nightmare/Taxi Driver/Oriental Beat/Tragedy
Uzi Suicide 3738/promo/ps/'89 ..... $10

HAPPY MONDAYS
Angel *Elektra 8671/promo/silkscreened/ps* $4
Hallelujah 2:38/6:26 *Elektra 8160/promo/ silkscreened logo on purple/'90* $4
Hallelujah (2 versions)/Clap Your Hands/ Rave On (2 versions)/WFL (future mix)
Elektra 60945/stock/ps/'90 ..... $5
Kinky Afro (radio mix) *Elektra 8254/promo/ logo on yellow/rear insert/'90* $4
Loose Fit 3:53/6:15 *Elektra 8310/ promo/silkscreened/rear insert/'91* $5
Loose Fit edit 7" *Elektra 8382/ promo/silkscreened logo/'90* $4
Step On stuff it in mix/twistin my melon mix
Elektra 8192/promo/silkscreened logo/rear insert/'90 ..... $7
Step On ('91 edit remix) *Elektra 8309/ promo/rear insert/blue silkscreened* $6
Stinkin' Thinkin' 3 versions *Elektra 8634/ promo/silkscreened/ps/'92* $4
Sunshine & Love 2 versions/Judge Fudge/ Staying Alive/24 Hour Party People
Elektra 66353/stock/ gatefold hardcover ps/'92 ..... $5
Wrote For Luck radio, dance & club mixes
Elektra 8060/promo/ ps/silkscreened/'89 ..... $5

HAPPYHEAD
Digital Love Thing 3:00/3:54/4:40
Eastwest 4631/promo/ silkscreened/rear insert/'92 ..... $4
Digital Love Thing lp & extended/Love Kills bryce mix/Get Out the Cab, Babe xrated dub/Hand on My Heart live
Eastwest 4602/promo/rear insert $4
Fabulous 4 versions *East West 4433/ promo/silkscreened/ps/'92* $4
Fabulous 5 versions *Eastwest 96196/ stock/gatefold hardcover ps/'92* $5

HARD CORPS, THE
Hard Corps *Interscope 4137/promo/ logo on red/ps/'91* $4

HARDLINE
Can't Find My Way edit & lp *MCA 2404/ promo/NEAL SCHON/ps/'92* $4
Takin' Me Down *MCA 2207/promo/NEAL SCHON/ps/'92* $4

HARFORD, CHRIS
Living End *Elektra 8631/promo/ps/ silkscreened/'92* $4
Road With You/Living End/Raise the Roof/ Blanket of Snow *Elektra 8644/ promo/custom sticker/silkscreened* $5

HARLOW
Chain Reaction *Reprise 3961/ promo/silkscreened* $4
When You Love Someone
Reprise 4384/promo/rear insert/'90 ..... $4

HARMONY
Your Love Ain't Right 3 versions
Virgin 3727/promo/silkscreened/'91 ..... $4

HARP, EVERETTE
Let's Wait Awhile 4 versions *Manhattan 79310/ promo/silkscreened pic/rear insert/ custom sticker/'92* $4
More Than You'll Ever Know edit & cd *Manhattan 79628/promo/ silkscreened pic/rear insert/'92* $4

HARPER BROTHERS, THE
You Can Hide Inside the Music 12 tracks *Verve HAR-2/promo/ gatefold hardcover ps/'92* $10

HARRELL, GRADY
Fun (3 versions) *RCA 9010/promo/ps/'89* $4

HARRIET
Temple of Love 3:57/3:19/6:40 *East West 3701/promo/ps/'90* $4

HARRIS, EMMYLOU
Heartbreak Hill *Reprise 3370/promo/'88* $6
Never Be Anyone Else But You *Reprise 4400/promo/rear insert/'90* $5
Rollin' and Ramblin' *Reprise 4854/promo/'90* $5
Wheels of Love *Reprise 4535/promo/'90* $5

HARRIS, EMMYLOU & WILLIE NELSON
Gulf Coast Highway *Reprise 4002/promo/'90* $5

HARRIS, ROBIN
Special Radio Edits (24 mini tracks) *Wing 365/promo/ps/silkscreened/'90* $8

HARRISON, GEORGE
Best of Dark Horse 1976-1989 *Dark Horse WB 25726/stock with promo only silkscreen/'89* $35
Cheer Down *WB 3647/promo/'89* $6
Cloud 9 *Dark Horse 2924/promo/ps* $20
Cloud Nine 11 tracks *D.Horse 25643/promo/ silkscreened George/rear insert/'87* $50
Got My Mind Set On You *Dark Horse 2846/ promo/ps/'87/with booklet & special die cut envelope* $100
Live in Japan sampler 5 tracks *Dark Horse 5555/promo/ps/ custom sticker/'92* $25
Masters of Rock radio show (7/17/89) *Radio Today Entertainment/promo/ cue sheets/55 minute show* $40
Poor Little Girl edit & lp *Dark Horse 3775/promo/'89* $10
Rock Stars #35 (1/15/90) *Radio Today Entertainment/promo/2 CDs/ music from all eras/cue sheets* $50
This Is Love *Dark Horse 3068/promo/ps* $12

HARRISON, JERRY & CASUAL GODS
Cherokee Chief *Sire 3095/promo/ps/'88* $4
Flying Under Radar *Sire 4067/promo/'90* $4
Kick Start *Sire 4439/promo/rear insert/'90* $4
Rev It Up *Sire 2941/promo/ps* $4

HARRY, DEBORAH
Def Dumb & Blonde *Sire 25938/ stock with promo only "flicker" cover/'89* $20
I Can See Clearly single/lp *Sire 6336/promo/silkscreened/'93* $6
I Want That Man *Sire 3680/promo/silkscreened/'88* $8
I Want That Man (3 versions)/Bike Boy (CD versions) *Sire 21322/stock/ps/'89* $8
I Want That Man 3 vers./Bike Boy *Sire 21322/stock/ps/'89* $6
Liar Liar *Reprise 3206/promo/'88* $10
Prelude to a Kiss *RCA 62324/promo/ rear insert/logo on purple/'92* $6
Sweet and Low (5 versions)/Lovelight *Sire 21492/stock/ps/'89* $8

HART, COREY
A Little Love *EMI 4461/promo/ silkscreened/ps/'90* $4
Always *Sire 5662/promo/'92* $4
Baby When I Call Your .. *Sire 5368/promo/'92* $4
Bang! (Starting Over) *Aquarius 6050/promo/ silkscreened/rear insert/'90* $4
Chase the Sun *EMI 04642/promo/ logo on pea green/rear insert/'90* $4
In Your Soul *EMI 04076/promo/ps/'88* $4

HART, MICKEY
#4 for Gaia/Skywater (excerpt)/Cougar Run/ Pigs in Space *Ryko/promo/ rear insert/'90* $6

HARTMAN, DAN & DENISE LOPEZ
The Love You Take *A&M 17668/promo/ps/'88* $5

HARVEY, P.J.
50 Ft. Queenie/Reeling/Man-Size/ Hook (last 2 demo versions) *Island 6770/promo/silkscreened/ps* $8
50Ft. Queenie/Reeling/Man-Size/Hook (last 2 demo) *Island 6770/promo/ ps/silkscreened/'93* $8
Dry *Island 6779/promo/ silkscreened pic/custom sticker/'93* $5
Man-Size/Wang Dang Doodle (J.Peel session)/ Daddy *Island 6786/promo/ps/'93* $8

HASLAM, ANNIE
The Angels Cry *Epic 73219/promo/ps/'89* $8

HATHAWAY, LALAH
Baby Don't Cry (edit) *Virgin 3601/promo/'90* $4
Heaven Knows (3 versions) *Virgin HEAVEN/ promo/'90* $4
It's Somethin' (4 versions) *Virgin 3803/ promo/silkscreened/'91* $5

HATTON, SUSIE
Blue Monday *Giant 4621/promo/rear insert* $4

HAUNTED GARAGE
976-Kill *Metal Blade 976/promo/ps/'91* $4

HAVALINAS, THE
High Hopes *Elektra 8153/promo/ silkscreened logo/'90* $4
Not alot to Ask For *Elektra 8181/promo/rear insert/'90* $4

HAVANA 3 AM
Reach the Rock (edit) *IRS 67048/promo/ GARY MYRICK, PAUL SIMENON/ silkscreened/rear insert/'91* $6

HAVANA BLACK
Freedom Child *Hollywood 8429/promo/ silkscreened/rear insert/'91* $4

HAWKES, CHESNEY
Feel So Alive *Chrysalis 23799/promo/ rear insert/'91* $4
The One and Only single/US remix/rock remix *Chrysalis 23730/promo/silkscreened/ rear insert/'91* $6

HAWKINS, EDWIN
If at First You Dont Succeed (3 versions) *Lection 177/promo/silkscreened/'90* $4
Like Him *Lection 302/promo/silkscreened/ps* $4
Pieces *Lection 235/promo/silkscreened/'90* $4

HAWKINS, SOPHIE B.
California Here I Come *Columbia 4594/ promo/ps/'92* $4
Damn I Wish I Was Your Lover edit & lp *Columbia 74164/promo/ps/'92* $4
Damn I Wish I Was Your ../Don't Stop Swaying *Columbia 38K 74164/stock/ps/'92* $5
I Want You edit *Columbia 4807/promo/ps/'92* $4
Tongues and Tails 11 tracks *Columbia 4501/ promo/trifold diecut hardcover ps/'92* $15

HAY, COLIN
Help Me *MCA 18373/promo/'90* $4
Into My Life *MCA 18070/promo/'89* $4

HAYES, ISAAC
Showdown (4 versions) *Columbia 1250/ promo/ps/'88* $6

HAYNES, WARREN
Fire in the Kitchen edit & lp *Megaforce 888/ promo/logo on black/ps/ prod.by CHUCH LEAVELL/'93* $4
I'll Be the One edit & lp/Movers & Shakers live *Megaforce 962/promo/ custom sticker/'93* $6

HAZA, OFRA
Ya Ba Ye (4 versions)/Da'Asa/Da'ale Da'Ale (razor maid mix) *Sire 21382/ps/stock/'89* $5

HE SAID
Could You US edit/German edit/lp version *Enigma 174/promo/custom sticker* $8
Take Care/Could You *Enigma/promo/ps* $8

HEALEY, JEFF
Angel Eyes (newly recorded) long version/ single version/Hideaway *Arista 9808/ promo/ps/'89/with tour dates* $6
Cruel Little Number *Arista 2467/promo/ps* $4
Full Circle lp & remix *Arista 2115/promo/ silkscreened/rear insert/'90* $5
Heart of an Angel edit & lp *Arista 2516/promo/rear insert/'92* $4
Hell to Pay (11 tracks) *Arista 8632/promo/ silkscreen/oversize box package/'90* $15
How Long Can a Man Be Strong short & lp *Arista 2116/promo/logo on black/ps* $5
I Think I Love You Too Much edit & lp *Arista 2031/promo/silkscreened/ rear insert/'90/MARK KNOPFLER* $4
Lost in Your Eyes edit & lp *Arista 2521/ promo/ps/logo on black/'93* $4
Roadhouse Blues *Arista 9839/promo/ps/'89* $5
While My Guitar Gently Weeps edit & lp *Arista 2065/promo/silkscreened/ rear insert/with GEORGE HARRISON, JEFF LYNNE, more* $8

HEART
All I Wanna Do Is Make Love to You edit & lp *Capitol 79909/promo/silkscreened/ ps/'90* $8
Alone *Capitol 79024/promo/ps/'87* $10
Brigade (full lp) *Capitol 79967/promo/dj only box container/silkscreen/booklet* $25
Dreamboat Annie In the Studio *radio show/ promo/cue sheet 7/11/90* $40
I Didn't Want to Need You *Capitol 79073/promo/ps/'90* $8
Secret *Capitol 79468/promo/ps/'90* $8
Stranded *Capitol 79270/promo/logo on black silkscreened/mini box ps/'90* $12
You're the Voice edit & lp *Capitol 79010/ promo/silkscreened/ps/'91* $8
You're the Voice/Call of the Wild/Barracuda live *Capitol 15748/stock/silkscreened/ps* $8

HEART AND FIRE
Go For It (4 versions) *Capitol 79467/ promo/silkscreened/'90* $4

HEART THROBS, THE
Dreamtime/I See Danger/This Man/White Laughter (alpha angel mix) *Elektra 8201/promo/ps/cust.sticker* $8

I Wonder Why *Elektra 8302/promo/rear insert/ silkscreenedred/'90* $5
Outside *A&M 75021 7390/promo/ logo on yellow/ps/'92* $4
She's in a Trance (3 versions) *Elektra 8245/ promo/silkscreened logo on red/'90* $5

HEART THROBS, THE/DEEE LITE
Dreamtime/I See Danger/This Man/White Laughter/Grooves in the Heart (minds mix)/ESP/What is Love (holograp. mix) *Elektra 8198-2-8/promo/ 2 CDs/gatefold hardcover/'90* $15

HEAVEN'S EDGE
Find Another Way edit & lp *Columbia 2134/ promo/ps/logo on blue/'90* $4

HEAVY BONES
The Hand That Feeds/4AM T.M./Light of Day *Reprise 5674/promo/'92* $4

HEAVY D & THE BOYZ
Big Tyme 3 versions/More Bounce 3 versions........ *Uptown 18300/promo/'89* $5
Don't Curse *Uptown 2210/promo/rear insert/'92* $4
Don't Curse (5:43)/You Can't See What I Can.. *MCA 54420/stock/ps/'92* $5
Peaceful Journey 4 versions *Uptown 2094/promo/rear insert/'92* $6
Somebody For Me 2 vers. *Uptown 18093/promo/'89* $5
Truthfull vocal & tv/Blue Funk vocal & tv *MCA 2553/promo/rear insert/'93* $4
We Got Our Own Thang 3:50 & 5:45 *MCA 17976/promo/custom sticker* $5
Who's the Man 4 versions *Uptown 2464/promo/rear insert/'92* $5

HEIGHTS, THE
How Do You Talk to An Angel lp & ac edit *Capitol 79526/promo/logo on blue/ custom sticker/'92* $5
I'm Still On Your Side single/edit/lp *Capitol 79560/promo/ logo on gold/rear insert/'92* $4

HELIX
The Storm *Grudge 4771/promo/'90* $4

HELLOWEEN
Keeper of the Seven Keys (10 tracks) *RCA 8529/promo/custom sticker* $10

HELMET
Give It *Interscope 4847/promo/silkscreen/ps* $5
In the Meantime *Interscope 4592/promo/ logo on white/ps/'92* $5
Unsung *Interscope 4687/promo/ logo on black/ps* $5
Unsung/FBLA/FBLA II/Bad Mood (last 3 live) *Interscope 4788/promo/ps/'92* $10

HELMET & HOUSE OF PAIN
Just Another Victim 5 versions *Immortal 5259/promo/ps/'93* $8

HENDERSON, SCOTT & TRIBAL TECH
Nomad edit & lp *Relativity 0106/promo/ silkscreened/ps/'89* $4

HENDRIX, JIMI
Between the Lines ep (10 second narration/ Hey Joe/Im a Man (live - '65)/ Red House (live '67) + 6 more) *Reprise 4541/promo/ silkscreened logo/ps/'90* $25
Radio Radio ep (Day Tripper/Hoochie Koochie Man/Hound Dog/Hear My Train a Comin'/Stone Free) *Ryko 0078/ promo/ps/silkscreened Jimi/'89* $25
Stages '67-'70 Sampler 8 tracks *Reprise 5194/promo/'91* $20

HENDRYX, NONA
Women Who Fly edit & extended *Private 2055/promo/silkscreened/'89* $5

HENLEY, DON
Building the Perfect Beast In the Studio *radio show/promo/cue sheet 7/2/90* $25
End of the Innocence In the Studio *radio show/ promo/cue sheet 6/21/89* $20
How Bad Do You Want It *Geffen 4103/ promo/silkscreened/ps/'90* $5
New York Minute edit & lp *Geffen 4158/ promo/silkscreened/ps/'90* $5
The End of the Innocence *Geffen 3555/promo/ gatefold hardcover ps/ silkscreened black/'89* $6

The End of the Innocence (lp length)
Geffen 24217/promo/ special cloth bound cover with book/ silkscreened $25
The Heart of the Matter edit remix/lp/ac edit
Geffen 3955/promo/'89 ....$5
The Last Worthless Evening (2 edit versions)
Geffen 3734/promo/'89 ....$5
The Last Worthless Evening (new mix)
Geffen 3834/promo/'89 ....$5

HENRY, JOE
Here and Gone *A&M 17716/promo/ps/'89* $4

HERE AND NOW
Are You Ready 8 versions *Third Stone 5029/ promo/silkscreened/ps/'93* $5

HERICANE ALICE
Wild Young and Crazy edit & lp
Atlantic 3122/promo/rear insert/'90 ....$4

HEWITT, HOWARD
Forever & Ever *Elektra 8032/promo/'88* $4
How Fast Forever Goes
Elektra 8734/promo/silkscreened/'92 ....$4
If I Could Only Have That Day Back (4 versions)
Elektra 8199/promo/rear insert/'90 ....$5
Let Me Show You How to Fall..
Elektra 8250/promo/rear insert/'90 ....$4
Save Your Sex For Me edit & lp *Elektra 8675/ promo/silkscreened/ps/'92* $4
Show Me edit & lp *Elektra 8156/promo/'90* $4
Strange Relationship (4 versions)
Elektra 2210/promo/'88 ....$4

HEYMAN, RICHARD X.
Call Out the Military *Cypress 79062/promo/ silkscreened/'90* $4

HEYWARD, NICK
You're My World (3 versions)
Reprise 3245/promo/ps/'88 ....$6

HI FIVE
I Just Can't Handle It 7" & lp
Jive 1386/promo/ps/custom sticker $4
Just Another Girlfriend 4 versions
Jive 42041/promo/logo on green/ rear insert/custom sticker/'91 ....$5
Just Another Girlfriend 6 versions
Jive 42029/promo/rear insert/'91 ....$5
Mary Mary 7 vers. *Jive 42118/promo/ps/'93* $5
She's Playing Hard to Get 5 versions
Jive 42066/promo/poster ps/ custom sticker/'92 ....$6

HI TEK 3 & YA KID K
Spin That Wheel flick/extended/dub
SBK 05332/promo/ps/'90 ....$4

HIATT, JOHN
Bring Back Your Love to Me *A&M 75021 7415/ promo/logo on black/ps/'90* $4
Child of the Wild Blue Yonder
A&M 75021 8078/promo/ps/'90 ....$4
Drive South *A&M 17707/promo/silkscreened* $4
Paper Thin *A&M 17647/promo/silkscreened* $4
Perfectly Good Guitar edit & lp
A&M 31458 8188/promo/gatefold hardcover ps/silkscreened/'93 ....$5
Slow Turning *A&M 17611/promo/ps/'88* $6
The Rest of the Dream 4:26 & 4:45
A&M 75021 7420/promo/ps/'90 ....$4
Your Love to Me *A&M 75021 7415/promo/ps* $4

HICKMAN, SARA
Blue Eyes Are Sensitive to the Light (edit)
Hollywood 8209/promo/'90 ....$4
Equal Scary People *Elektra 8120/promo/'89* $4
I Couldn't Help Myself lp & remix
Elektra 8246/promo/rear insert/'90 ....$4
In the Fields (edit) *Elektra 8307/ promo/rear insert/logo on pink/'90* $4
The Very Thing *Elektra 8335/promo/'90* $4

HICKS, MARVA
I Got You Where I Want 4 vers
Polydor 452/promo/ps/'91 ....$4

HIGHWAY 101
Honky Tonk Heart (edit) *WB 3526/promo/'89* $4
The Blame *WB 4944/promo/'91* $4
Who's Lonely Now *WB 3730/promo/'89* $4

HIJACK
The Badman is Robbin' (3 versions)/Hold No Hostage/Doomsday of Rap
Epic 73079/promo/ps/'89 ....$4

HILL, BENNY
Ernie (The Fastest Milkman in the West)/ Yakety Sax *Continuum 12206/ promo/silkscreened pic/'92* $6
I Cant Help Myself *Reprise 3842/promo/'89* $4
Too Much Month at the End of the Money
Reprise 3563/promo/'89 ....$4

HILL, BRYAN
Take It Easy 3 versions/Underground Bass 2 versions *Sam 5016/promo/'91* $3

HILL, DAN
Hold Me Now *Quality 19107/promo/ps/ logo on gold/'92* $4
I Fall All Over Again *Quality 15180/promo/ logo on brown/ps/'91* $4

HILL, KIM
Satisfied lp/chr remix/ac remix
Geffen 4300/promo/ps/'91 ....$4

HILL, WARREN
The Passion Theme edit & lp *RCA 62442/ promo/rear insert/custom sticker/'92* $4

HIMMELMAN, PETER
245 Days (remix 4:28) *Island 2869/promo/rear insert/'89* $4
Beneath the Damage and the Dust lp/acoustic *Epic 4732/promo/ps/'92* $4
Only Innocent/7 Circles/Blind Ambition/ A Million Sides/Trembles (last 2 live) *Epic 4105/promo/ps/silkscreened* $10
Waning Moon *Island 2120/promo/ps* $4
Woman With the Strength of 10,000 Men *Epic 4003/promo/silkscreened/ps/'91* $4
You Know Me Better Than I Do *Epic 5009/promo/ps/ silkscreened pic/'93* $6

HINDU LOVE GODS
Raspberry Beret *Giant 4414/promo/ silkscreened/rear insert/ custom sticker/'90* $7
Raspberry Beret (record mix) *Giant 4414/promo/silkscreened/ custm sticker/WARREN ZEVEN, PETER BUCK, MIKE MILLS, more/rear insert/'90*.................................$8
Selftitled (10 tracks) *Giant 24406/ promo/silkscreened/ps/'90* $15
Selftitled (10 tracks) *Giant 24406/ stock/promo silkscreened/ps/'90*.............$15

HINES, GREGORY & PATTI AUSTIN
The Gershwins in Hollywood 14 tracks *Philips 274/promo/silkscreened/ps* $10

HIROKO
My Love's Wating (3 versions) *Enigma 205/promo/custom sticker/silkscreened logo/'89* $4

HIROSHIMA
Come to Me lp & single *Epic 000147/promo/ silkscreened pic/'89* $5
The Story of a Thousand Cranes/Thousand Cranes edit & live/Hawaiian Electric (live)/Tabo (live) *Epic 1918/ promo/rear insert/'89*.............................$15

HIS NAME IS ALIVE
In Every Ford/Lip/Drink, Dress and Ink/Can't Go Wrong Without You/The Dirt Eaters *4AD 6069/promo/silkscreened/'93*............$6

HITCHCOCK, ROBYN
Balloon Man/Globe of Frogs/The Ghost Ship *A&M 000052/ps/3" stock* $6
Balloon Man/Globe of Frogs/The Ghost Ship *A&M 75021 2374/ps* $7
Driving Aloud (Radio Storm) *A&M 31458 8099/ promo/logo on white/ps*............................$4
Driving Aloud/Allright Yeah *A&M 31458 8102/ promo/silkscreened/ gatefold hardcover ps/'93* $8
Live Death (Clean Steve/Glass Hotel/My Wife and My Dead Wife/Arms of Love/ When I Was Dead + 2) *A&M 31454 8000/promo/logo on white/gatefold hardcover ps/'92* $25
Madonna of the Wasps edit & lp *A&M 17773/promo/silkscreened logo & art/'89*..$5
Madonna of the Wasps/intro/One Long Pair of Eyes (acoustic)/More Than This *A&M 17718/promo/ps/'89* $12
Oceanside *A&M 75021 7297/promo/ps/'91* $5
One Long Pair of Eyes edit & lp *A&M 17812/promo/silkscreened/'89* $5
So You Think You're in Love *A&M 75021 7268/ promo/ps/logo on purple/'91* $4
So You Think You're in Love/Watch You Intelligence/Eight Miles High *A&M 75021 2392/promo/ps/'91* $7
The Yip Song/The Live-In Years/Bright Fresh Flower *A&M 31458 8134/gatefold hardcover ps/'93* $12
Ultra Unbelievable Love/Dark Green Energy *A&M 75021 7273/promo/ silkscreened/ps/'91* $7

HOFFNER, HELEN
Summer of Love *Atlantic 4734/promo/ silkscreened/ps/'92* $4

HOFFS, SUSANNA
My Side of the Bed *Columbia 73529/promo/ps* ...$8
Only Love edit & lp *Columbia 73899/promo/ logo on brown/ps/'91*...................................$8
Unconditional Love *Columbia 73752/promo/ silkscreened/ps/'91* $8
When You're a Boy (12 tracks) *Columbia 3027/ promo/silkscreened/gatefold hardcover ps/lyric book*..........................$18

HOLCOMB, ROBIN
Nine Lives (edit) *Elektra 8240/promo/ps/'90* $4

HOLE, DAVE
The Bottle/Keep Your Motor Running/ Dark Was the Night *Alligator/promo/ silkscreened pic/custom sticker/'92* $6

HOLLIDAY, JENNIFER
I'm on Your Side single & lp *Arista 2238/promo/ logo on pink/ps/'91* $4

HOLLOW MEN, THE
November Comes 3:14 & 6:00/Thanks to the Rolling Sea *Arista 2174/promo/ silkscreened/rear insert/'91* $4

Strong Enough 5 versions
Active 8625/promo/silkscreened/'92 .... $6

Strong Enough 6 versions
Active 8491/promo/silkscreened/'92 .... $6

HOMEWORK

Special Kind of Lady *Epic 73454/promo/ps* $4

HONEYMOON SUITE

Love Changes Everything edit/lp
WB 3039/promo/silkscreened pic/'88 .... $4

HONEYS, THE

How Low (Can You Go) edit & instrumental
J & J 79915/promo/'91 .... $4

HOODOO GURUS

1,000 Miles Away + 1 *RCA 2854/promo/ps/silkscreened/'91* $5

Come Anytime *RCA 9082/promo/ps/'89* $5

Come Anytime/Hallucination/Wheres That Hit?
RCA 8998/promo/ps/'89 .... $5

Miss Freelove '69/Stomp the Tumbarumba/Brainscan *RCA 2805/stock/ps/'91* $5

HOOKER, JOHN LEE

Boom Boom *Pointblank 12739/promo/rear insert/'92* $5

Mr. Lucky *Charisma 061/promo/logo on yellow* ... $5

The Healer edit & lp *Chameleon 69/promo/ps/silkscreened/'89/with SANTANA* $5

This is Hip *Charisma HOOK1/promo/'91* $5

HOOKER, JOHN LEE & ROBERT CRAY

Baby Lee *Chameleon/promo/'90* $5

HOOTERS

500 Miles *Columbia 73013/promo/silkscreened* ... $4

Brother, Dont You Walk Away edit & lp
Columbia 73235/promo/silkscreened/ps/'90 .... $4

Heaven Laughs *Columbia 73320/promo/ps/'90* ... $4

Twenty-Five Hours a Day *MCA 2657/promo/rear insert/'93* $4

Zig Zag (10 tracks) *Columbia 1832/promo/ps/silkscreened full color pic* $10

HORN, JIM

Neon Nights/Divided Soul (both fades)
WB 3348/promo/'88 .... $4

Nightshift *WB 4016/promo/'90* $4

HORN, JIM/MARK O'CONNOR

Silver Bells/What Child is This
WB 3379/promo/'88 .... $4

HORN, SHIRLEY

Here's to Life 11 tracks *Verve HORN 2/promo/diecut gatefold ps/'92* $12

The Secret of Christmas/What Are You Doing New Year's Eve *Verve XMAS 2/promo/gatefold hardcover ps/'91* $6

HORNSBY, BRUCE

A Night on the Town (AOR remix) *RCA 2686/promo/silkscreened pic/ps/'90* $5

Across the River edit & lp *RCA 2621/promo/silkscreened red on black/ps/'90* $4

Defenders of the Flag lp & live/Look Out any Window (live) *RCA 8706/promo/ps/'88* $10

Fire on the Cross lp & live/Lost Soul (edit)
RCA 2715/promo/ps/'90 .... $5

Harbor Lights radio/long/space *RCA 62486/promo/ps/silkscreened/'93* $5

Live the Way It Is Tour 1986-87 (7 songs live)
RCA 6275/promo/ps/'87 .... $25

Lost Soul edit & short edit
RCA 2704/promo/ps/'90 .... $4

Masters of Rock radio show *Radio Today Entert. 90-11/promo/cue sheets/air date: 11/29-30/90/2 cds* $30

Set Me In Motion single & lp
RCA 2846/promo/ps/'91 .... $4

The Valley Road *RCA 7647/promo/ps/'88* $6

HORSE FLIES, THE
Life is a Rubber Rope/I Live Where It's Gray/ Oh Death (last 2 live) *MCA 1492/promo/'91* $6

HOT TUNA
Eve of Destruction *Epic 2224/promo/ps/'90* $5

HOTHOUSE FLOWERS
Give It Up lp & edit *London 256/promo/ silkscreened/ps/'90* $4
I Can See Clearly Now (edit) *London 310/promo/silkscreened/'90* $4
Live ep (6 songs - Give It Up/Christchurch Bells/I Can See Clearly Now/Giving it All Away/Movies/If You Go) *London 334/promo/rear insert/ logo on blue/'90* $15
Movies (edit)/Kansas City/Better Days Ahead/ Strange Feeling (last 3 live) *London 307/promo/silkscreened/'90* $8
One Tongue *London 908/promo/ logo on aquamarine/ps/'93* $4
Thing of Beauty edit *London 860/promo/ silkscreened/ps/'93* $4

HOUSE OF FREAKS
Rocking Chair *Giant 4815/promo/ gatefold hardcover ps/'91* $4

HOUSE OF LORDS
Cant Find My Way Home 3:45 & 4:53 *RCA 2658/promo/ps/'90* $4
Heart on the Line 3:50 & 4:00 *RCA 2804/promo/rear insert/'91* $4
I Wanna Be Loved *RCA 8737/promo/ps/'88* $4
Love Dont Lie remix/Looking For Strange *RCA 8900/promo/ps/'89* $4
O Father edit & lp *Victory 659/promo/ps/'92* $4
Remember My Name edit & lp *RCA 2736/promo/ps/'90* $4
What's Forever For *Victory 714/promo/silkscreened/'92* $4
What's Forever For/Demons Down *Victory 383 483 002/stock/ps/'92* $5

HOUSE OF LOVE
Beatles and the Stones edit & lp *Fontana 270/ promo/silkscreened/rear insert/'90* $4
Hollow/Sweet Anatomy/Shining On *Fontana 987/promo/ps/'93* $4
I Don't Know Why I Love You *Fontana 213/ promo/silkscreened pic/'89* $5
Live (Never/Road/Beatles & Stones/ In a Room/Christine) *Fontana 189/ promo/silkscreened/rear insert/'90* $15
Marble *Fontana 429/promo/ps/'91* $4
Safe/Love II/Shine On (second mix) *Fontana 518/promo/silkscreened logo* $8
You Don't Understand *Fontana 731/promo/ps* $4

HOUSE OF PAIN
Jump Around blood stain remix/instrumental *Tommy Boy 539/promo/'92* $6
Jump Around orig.mix & master mix/ House of Pain Anthem orig.mix & master mix *Tommy Boy 526/stock/ps* $6

HOUSE, JAMES
Spoken intro/Hard Times For An Honest Man *MCA 53731/promo/ps/'89* $4

HOUSEMARTINS
Caravan of Love *Elektra 2162/promo/ps/'87* $6

HOUSTON, THELMA
High 4 versions *Reprise 4475/promo/'90* $5
Out of My Hands (radio remix) *Reprise 4487/promo/rear insert/'90* $4
Throw You Down 5 versions/What He Has 12" versions *Reprise 40080/stock/ gatefold hardcover ps/'91* $5

HOUSTON, WHITNEY
All the Man I Need *Arista 2156/promo/ silkscreened gold/ps/'90* $8
I Belong to You lp/single/international remix *Arista 2369/promo/silkscreen logo/ps* $8
I Have Nothing *Arista 2527/promo/logo on pink/ps/'93* $6
I Have Nothing/Where You Are/Lover For Life *Arista 12527/stock/logo on pink/ps* $5
I Wanna Dance With Somebody (single, 12" remix edit, 12" remix) *Arista 9599/promo/ps/'87* $15
I Will Always Love You *Arista 2490/promo/ logo on black/ps/'92* $7
I Will Always Love You/Jesus Loves Me/Do You Hear What I Hear? *Arista 12503/stock/ps/'92* $6
I'm Every Woman *Arista 2519/promo/ logo on black/ps/'92* $7
I'm Every Woman 5 versions/Who Do You Love *Arista 07822-12520/stock/ps/'93* $6
I'm Your Baby Tonight *Arista 2108/promo/ silkscreened/die cut ps/'90* $8
Love Will Save the Day (4 versions) *Arista 9721/promo/ps/'88* $10
Miracle *Arista 2222/promo/ps/'91* $7
My Name is Not Susan 4 versions *Arista 2259/promo/ps/'91* $7
Run to You *Arista 2570/promo/ps/ logo on white/'93* $7
So Emotional 6 versions *Arista 9641/promo/ps/'87* $10
Star Spangled Banner/America the Beautiful *Arista 2207/stock/ps/'91* $6
We Didn't Know remix edit/lp edit/extended *Arista 2420/promo/ps/'92* $8

Where Do Broken Hearts Go single mix
Arista 9674/promo/ps/'88 .... $12

HOWARD, CHERYL
If I Can't Have You 4 versions *Atlantic 4465/promo/rear insert/'92* $5

HOWARD, MIKI
Ain't Nobody Like You 4 versions
Giant 5539/promo/rear insert/'92 .... $5
Femme Fatale sampler (Good Morning Heartache/This Bitter Earth/Hope That We Can Be Together Soon/Shining Through/But I Love You)
Giant 5682/promo/rear insert/'92 .... $8
Love Under New Management 4:12/6:44/instrum.6:44 *Atlantic 3066/promo/silkscreened logo/rear insert/'89* $5
Release Me edit & lp
Giant 5824/promo/rear insert/'92 .... $4

HOWE, STEVE
Turbulence *Relativity 0130/promo/logo on yellow/ps/'91* $8

HUBBARD, FREDDIE
Spanish Rose/Back to Lovin' Again/Times R Changin' (all edits)
Blue Note 79644/promo/'89 .... $6

HUDSON, LAVINE
Intervention (3 versions)
Virgin 2371/promo/ps/'88 .... $5

HUE & CRY
Labor of Love lp/remix
Virgin 2345/promo/ps/'88 .... $4

HUGH, GRAYSON
Talk It Over lp/edit *RCA 8802/promo/ps/'88* $4

HUMAN LEAGUE
Dare to Be Romantic ep (Heart Like a Wheel/Kiss the Future + 3) *A&M 75021 8055/promo/silkscreened/ps/custom sticker/'90* $8
Heart Like a Wheel *A&M 75021 7406/promo/gatefold die cut dial cover/'90* $8

HUMAN RADIO
Me & Elvis *Columbia 73330/promo/silkscreened/die cut ps/'90* $4
My First Million *Columbia 2154/promo/ps/'90* $4

HUMPHREY, BOBBI
Let's Get Started radio & extended
WB 4354/promo/rear insert/'90 .... $4

HUNTER, IAN & MICK RONSON
American Music *Mercury 127/promo/silkscreened pic/'89* $8
Womens Intuition *Mercury 171/promo/silkscreened pic/'89* $8

HUNTERS & COLLECTORS
Blind Eye (Walk Away) *Atlantic 3427/promo/logo on black silkscreened/ps* $5
When the River Runs Dry new single & lp
Atlantic 3328/promo/silkscreened logo/rear insert/'89 .... $4
When the River Runs Dry single & lp
Atlantic 3280/promo/ps/'89 .... $4
When the River Runs Dry single & lp/The Price of Freedom/Two Roads
Atlantic 86202/stock/ps/'89 .... $5

HURRICANE
I'm On to You (3 versions)
Enigma 114/promo/ps/'88 .... $4
I'm On to You (video & audio)/Baby Snakes/The Girls Are Out Tonight (last 2 audio only) *Enigma 72300/ps/CD video/stock/'88* $8
I'm On to You radio edit & lp
Enigma 080/promo/ps/'88 .... $4
Little Sister edit & complete
Enigma 267/promo/ps/'90 .... $4
Livin' Over the Edge radio edit & lp
Enigma 119/promo/custom sticker $4
Young Man/In the Fire/Lock Me Up
Enigma 297/promo/cust. sticker/'90 .... $4

HUTCH, WILLIE
I Choose You *Sire 5345/promo/'92* $4

HUTCHINS, BRENT
Arachnophobia *Hollywood 8210/promo/rear insert/'90* $4

HYMAN, PHYLLIS
Don't Wanna Change the World no rap/rap/extendedrap *Zoo 17013/promo/silkscreened pic/ps/'91* $6

Living in Confusion edit & lp *Zoo 17040/ promo/silkscreened/ps/'91* $5
When You Get Right Down to It edit & lp *Zoo 17047/promo/silkscreened pic/ rear insert/'91* $4

I LOVE YOU

2 *Geffen 4284/promo/custom tour date sticker/ps/'91* $4
Hang Straight Up *Geffen 4225/promo/ps/'91* $4
The Lamb/Angles/Hungry Wolf/JAMF *Geffen 4338/promo/tour date sticker/'91* .. $5

I MOTHER EARTH

Levitate/The Mothers/Basketball/No One *Capitol 79776/promo/silkscreened/ps* $4
Rain Will Fall edit & lp *Capitol 79788/ promo/ps/silkscreened/'93* $4

I NAPOLEON

Go To Pieces fade & lp *Geffen 4227/promo/ps/'91* $4
Perfect Abosolution *Geffen 4194/promo/ps/'90* $4

I START COUNTING

Million Headed Monster *Mute 8378/promo/ silkscreened/rear insert/'91* $5
Still Smiling fortran 5 mix radio edit & 7" mix *Mute 8290/promo/ silkscreened/rear insert/'91* $6

IAN, JANIS

Days Like These *Mercury 627/promo/ prod.by JOHN MELLENCAMP/ps/'92* $5

ICE CUBE

It Was a Good Day clean top 10 edit/ smooth instrumental *Priority 6651/ promo/silkscreened pic/ps/'92* $6
Steady Mobbin' (clean)/No Vaseline *Priority 6610/promo/ silkscreened pic/'92* $6
Wicked 3 versions/U Ain't Gonna Take My Life 2 versions *Priority 6637/ promo/silkscreened/ps/'92* $6

ICE MC

Easy edit, lp, extend. *Chrysalis 23525/promo/ silkscreened logo/rear insert/'90* $4

ICE T

Dick Tracy (4 versions) *Sire WB 21704/stock/ps/'90* $5
High Rollers remix/instrumental *Sire 3415/ promo/sexy picture CD/'89* $6
I'm Your Pusher (5 versions) *Sire 3308/promo/ps/'88* $6
Lethal Weapon *Sire 3686/promo/'89* $4
Lifestyles of the Rich and Infamous (RV radio versions) *Sire 4931/promo/ silkscreened/'91* $4
Lifestyles of the Rich and Infamous 3 versions/ The Tower edit & instrumental .... *Sire 40161/stock/gatefold hardcover ps/'91* $5
Midnight evil edit vocal & inst./Body Count/ Escape From Killing Fields (last 2 edits) *Sire 5020/promo/'91* $6
Mind Over Matter clean radio mix *Sire 5392/promo/'91* $4
New Jack Hustler censored radio edit *Giant 4853/promo/rear insert/'91* $4
New Jack Hustler radio/instru./dub *Giant 4643/promo/rear insert/'91* $5
O.G. Original Gangster 23 tracks (radio vers.) *Sire 4959/promo/cleaned up airplay versions/custom sticker/'91* $25
O.G. Original Gangster (radio versions) *Sire 4761/promo/'91* $4
Ricochet 3 versions/Mind Over Matter 4 vers. *Sire 40210/stock/gatefold hardcover ps/'91* $5
Ricochet 3 vers./Mind Over Matter 5 versions *Sire 5143/promo/custom sticker/'91* $5
The Girl Tried to Kill Me (radio remix) *Sire 3970/promo/'89* $4
What Ya Wanna Do? (Party) edit & instrum. *Sire 3898/promo/'89* $5
You Played Yourself lp & instrumental *Sire 3865/promo/'89* $4

ICEHOUSE

Great Southern Land edit & lp *Chrysalis 23396/promo/ps/'89* $8
Play Crazy For Me (advance for Man of Colours) with 2 remixes of Crazy *Chrysalis 41592/promo/full length* $25
Touch the Fire *Chrysalis 23414/promo/ custom sticker/rear insert/'89* $6

ICON

Forever Young *Megaforce 3201/promo/ silkscreened logo/rear insert/'89* $4
Taking My Breath Away *Atlantic 2889/promo/ps/'89* $4

ICY BLU

Pump It (4 versions) *Giant 4725/promo/rear insert/'91* $4

IDEOLA

Is It Any Wonder *A&M 17447/promo/ gatefold hardcover ps/'87* $4

IDOL, BILLY

Charmed Life (11 songs) *Chrysalis 21762/ stock/limited open up edition/'90* $18
Cradle of Love single & lp *Chrysalis 23509/ promo/trifold die cut package/'90* $8

L.A. Woman (edit & lp)
Chrysalis 23571/promo/ps/'90 .... $5
L.A. Woman (edit)/License to Thrill/Lovechild
Chrysalis 23571/ps/stock/'90 .... $5
No Religion 4 versions *Chrysalis 04567/promo/ silkscreened/custom sticker/'93* $6
Prodigal Blues edit & lp
Chrysalis 23603/promo/ps/'90 .... $4
Shock to the System *Chrysalis 04718/promo/ silkscreened/trifold hardcover ps/ bonus hard disc (for color Mac)/insert/'93* $20

IDOLLS, THE
Give a Dog a Bone (4 versions)
Atlantic 3453/promo/ps/'90 .... $4

IGLESIAS, JULIO
Ae, Ao (3 vers.) *Columbia 1238/promo/ps/'88* $5
Can't Help Falling in Love *Columbia 2222/ promo/logo on white/ps/'90* $5
Y Aunque Te Haga Calor
Sony 10041/promo/ps/'92 .... $5

IGLESIAS, JULIO & STEVIE WONDER
My Love *Columbia 1102/promo/ps/'88* $5

IGUANAS, THE
Fortune Teller *MCA 2618/promo/silkscreened/ exec.prod.JIMMY BUFFETT/'93* $4

II CLOSE
Call Me Up 6 versions *Tabu 31458 8161/ promo/silkscreened/ps/'93* $5
My Conscience Says No 4 versions
Tabu 31458 8106/promo/ silkscreened/ps/'93 .... $5
So What 5 versions
Tabu 31458 8084/promo/ps/'93 .... $6
So What! 5 versions
Tabu 31458 8002/promo/ps/'92 .... $5

II D EXTREME
Cry No More 4 versions *Gasoline Alley 2675/ promo/rear insert/'93* $4
Cry No More 4 versions
Gasoline Alley 54651/stock/ps/'93 .... $5

ILLSAY, JOHN
I Want to See the Moon *WB 3130/promo/ps* $4

IMATURE
Da Munchies 4 vers. *Virgin 12746/promo/'92* $4

IMMACULATE FOOLS
Stand Down/Thanks, But No Thanks
Continuum 12209/promo/ silkscreened pic/rear insert/'92 .... $5
The Prince edit & lp
Epic 2045/promo/silkscreened ps/'90 .... $4

IMMATURE/BEBE'S KIDS
Tear It Up/Straight Jackin' *Capitol 79443/ promo/silkscreened/'92* $4

IMPEDANCE
Tainted Love (4 versions)
Epic 73206/promo/silkscreened/'89 .... $5

IN TUA NUA
All I Wanted *Virgin 2349/promo/ps/'88* $7
Seven Into the Sea remix & lp
Virgin 2683/promo/silkscreened/'89 .... $6

INCOGNITO
Radio Vibes 5 versions *Talkin' Loud 617/ promo/silkscreened/rear insert/'92* $4

INDIA
Right From the Start (4 versions)
Reprise 3859/promo/'89 .... $4
The Love Who Rocks... (5 vers.)/Steppin' Out *Reprise 21524/stock/ps/'90* $5

INDIGO GIRLS
Closer to Fine *Epic 1634/promo/ green silkscreened/'89* $8
Galileo *Epic 4434/promo/silkscreened/ps/'92* $6
Galileo *Epic 74326/promo/silkscreened/ gatefold hardcover ps/'92* $8
Get Together *Epic 73255/promo/ silkscreened logo on black/'90* $6
Ghost *Epic 4863/promo/logo on white/ rear insert/'92* $6
Hammer and a Nail *Epic 2200/promo/ silkscreened/ps/'90* $8
Holiday Greetings intro/Get Together
Epic 1939/promo/silkscreened red $10
Joking *Epic 4550/promo/silkscreened/ps/'92* $6
Kid Fears/Closer to Fine/Center Stage/Prince of Darkness *Epic 1486/promo/ps* $12
Land of Canaan *Epic 73003/promo/ silkscreened blue/'89* $8
Loves Recovery/Secure Yourself/Kid Fears
Epic 1490/promo/'89 .... $10
Reverse 1 - Live (7 live songs & 2 studio)
Epic 1670/promo/weird reverse letter silkscreen/'89 .... $35
Rites of Passage 13 tracks *Epic 4552/ promo/silkscreened/rear insert/'92* $15
Rites of Passage13 tracks *Epic 4570/promo/ diecut trifold cover/silkscreened/'92* $25
Shades of Indigo (interview & music - some live & unrel.) *Epic 2201/promo/ps/'90* $15
Watershed lp & live/All Along Watchtower (live)
Epic 2284/promo/ps/'90 .... $8

INDIGO GIRLS/ALLMAN BROTHERS
Welcome Me/Galileo/Joking/Ghost/Three Hits/Closer to Fine/Water is Wide/ Come On In My Kitchen/Seven Turns/ Midnight Rdier/Southbound/In Memory of Elizabeth Reed + 2 (all acoustic from 6/11/92)
Epic 4632/promo/ps/'92 .... $50

INDIO
Hard Sun *A&M 17808/promo/ silkscreened/ps/'89* $4

INFECTIOUS GROOVES
Infectious Grooves *Epic 4432/promo/ silkscreened/rear insert/'92* $5
Therapy *Epic 4238/promo/silkscreened/ rear insert/'91* $5
What's a Party Without Freaks/These Freaks Are Here to Party/Jama Wama, Make Ya Wanna Have Sex *Epic 4949/promo/ logo on green/ps/'93* $5

INFECTIOUS GROOVES/ SUICIDAL TENDENCIES
Busload of Freaks 27 tracks
Epic 5004/promo/ps/'93 .... $12

INFIDELS
100 Watt Bulb *IRS 67067/promo/ silkscreened/gatefold hardcover ps/ lightbulb package type package/'91* $6

INFORMATION SOCIETY
Going, Going, Gone 6 versions/Strength
Tommy Boy 555/promo/'93 .... $6
Going, Going, Gone edit/saber tooth mix/ mindwarp mix
Tommy Boy 6012/promo/'92 .... $6
How Long (3 versions) *Tommy Boy 4639/ promo/silkscreened/ps/'91* $6
How Long 4 versions
Tommy Boy 966/stock/ps/'90 .... $5
Lay All Your Love on Me (3 versions)
Reprise 3449/promo/'89 .... $6
Peace & Love, Inc. 4 versions *Tommy Boy 5686/ promo/silkscreened/'92* $6
Peace & Love, Inc. lp & passion mix/To the City disco mosh pit mix & radio remix
Tommy Boy 544/promo/ silkscreened/ps/'92 .... $6
Repetition lp/edit
Tommy Boy 3333/promo/'88 .... $8
Think (4 versions)
Tommy Boy 4422/promo/ps/'90 .... $6
Walking Away (4 versions)
Tommy Boy 3253/promo/ps/'88 .... $10
What's on Your Mind (4 versions)
Tommy Boy 3143/promo/ps/'88 .... $10

INGRAM, JAMES
(You Make Me Feel Like) A Natural Man edit & lp
WB 3638/promo/'89 .... $4
I Don't Have the Heart fade & lp
WB 3939/promo/'89 .... $4
I Wanna Come Back fade & 12" extended
WB 3726/promo/'89 .... $5
It's Real single & lp *WB 3509/promo/'89* $4
One More Time *Qwest 5807/promo/'92* $4
Remember the Dream edit & lp
WB 5363/promo/'91 .... $4
When Was the Last Time Music Made You Cry fade & lp *WB 4311/promo/'90* $4
Where Did My Heart Go *WB 4957/promo/'91* $4

INNER CIRCLE
Bad Boys (Theme from Cops) 5 versions
Atlantic 5016/promo/custom sticker $6
Bad Boys (Theme from Cops) 5 versions
Big Beat 5053/promo/rear insert $6
Sweat 5 versions *Big Beat 5167/promo/ps/ silkscreened/'93* $5

INNER CITY
Do You Love What You Feel (3 versions)
Virgin 2694/promo/silkscreened/'89 .... $5
Follow Your Heart 3 versions *Virgin 12719/ promo/logo on purple/'92* $6
Follow Your Heart 6 versions *Virgin 12603/ stock/gatefold hardcover ps/ custom sticker/'92* $5
Good Life radio mix & magic juan mix
Virgin 2622/promo/silkscreened/'88 .... $5
That Man (He's All Mine) 4 versions
Virgin 3814/promo/logo on green/'90 .... $6
Whatcha Gonna Do With My Lovin' edit with sax/def radio mix
Virgin 3210/promo/'89 .... $6
Whatcha Gonna Do With My Loving (4 versions)
Virgin 3101/promo/silkscreened/'89 .... $6

INNOCENCE
Let's Push It 5 versions
Chrysalis 23597/promo/rear insert/'91 ...... $6
Silent Voice 3 versions/Let's Push It 3 versions
Chrysalis 23714/stock/ps/'91 .... $5

INNOCENCE MISSION
And Hiding Away *A&M 75021 7260/ promo/logo on white/ps/'91* $4
Black Sheep Wall *A&M 17875/ promo/silkscreened/ps/'89* $5
I Remember Me
A&M 17936/promo/silkscreened/'89 .... $3
selftitled 13 tracks
A&M 5274/promo/silkscreened/ outer box/insert/transparency $15
Sorry and Glad Together/An Old Sunday
A&M 75021 7293/promo/ps/'91 .... $5
Umbrella 12 tracks *A&M 75021 5362/ promo/silkscreened/ps/'91* $12

Wonder of Birds *A&M 17932/promo/ silkscreened/ps/'89* $4

INSIDERS

Ghost on the Beach *Epic 2786/promo/silkscreened/'87* $4

INSPIRAL CARPETS

Caravan (3 versions) *Elektra 8352/promo/ silkscreened purple/rear insert/'91* $6
Commercial Rain lp & snatch mix *Elektra 8232/promo/rear insert/ silkscreened logo on yellow/'90* $5
Commercial Rain lp & snatch mix/Sackville/ Seeds of Doubt *Elektra 66606/stock/ps/'90* $5
Generations *Mute 8642/promo/ps/'92* $5
Please Be Cruel remix *Mute/Elektra 8398/promo/'91* $5
Smoking Her Clothes *Mute 8727/promo/ silkscreened/rear insert/'93* $5
This Is How it Feels (extended)/God Top (2 versions)/Biggest Mountain (kammer mix) *Mute 66581/stock/gatefold hardcover ps/silkscreened/'90* $5
This Is How it Feels (radio mix)/She Comes in the Fall *Elektra 8281/promo/ silkscreened gold/'90* $5

INTELLIGENT HOODLUM

Arrest the President 3 versions *A&M 75021 7497/promo/ silkscreened/ps/'90* $6
Back to Reality (4 versions) *A&M 75021 7424/promo/ps/'90* $6
Black and Proud (remix) *A&M 75021 8063/ promo/silkscreened logo on white/'90* $5
Grand Groove 6 versions *A&M 31458 8042/ promo/logo on green/ps/'93* $5

INTRO

Let Me Be the One 3 versions *Atlantic 5093/promo* $4

INTVELD, JAMES

Doin' Time For Bein' Young *MCA 18292/ promo/custom sticker/'90* $4

INXS

Beautiful Girl *Atlantic 4888/promo/ps/'92* $5
Bitter Tears *Elektra 3740/promo/gatefold ps* $5
Bitter Tears lp & lorimar dance mix *Atlantic 3860/promo/gatefold hardcover ps/'90* $7
Bitter Tears 3 vers./Disappear alt.12"/ Other Side *Atlantic 86080/ stock/ps/'90* $6
Compilation 10 tracks *Atlantic 3416/promo/ps/'90* $25
Disappear *Atlantic 3655/promo/ poster ps/custom sticker* $6
Disappear *Atlantic 3655/promo/ps/'90* $5
Disappear lp & extended/Middle Beast/ What You Need coldcut force mix *Atlantic 86093/stock/ gatefold hardcover ps/'90* $5
Heaven Sent *Atlantic 4600/promo/ gatefold hardcover ps/'92* $5
Live Baby Live *Atlantic 82294/stock/ ltd.edition package/gatefold hardcover ps* $12
Masters of Rock 10/15-31/90 *Radio Today Entertainment/ promo/2 CDs/cue sheets* $45
Mystify *Atlantic 2549/promo/rear insert/'88* $5
Need You Tonight *Atlantic 2132/promo/'87* $5
Never Tear Us Apart *Atlantic 2399/promo/ silkscreened pic/'88* $8
Not Enough Time *Atlantic 4721/promo/ gatefold hardcover ps/'92* $5
Not Enough Time 4 tracks *Atlantic 85819/stock/ps* $6
Not Enough Time/Light the Planet *Atlantic 87437/stock/ps* $5
Profiled! *Atlantic 3675/promo/dj only interview/ps/'90* $20
Shining Star *Atlantic 4248/promo/ silkscreened/ps/'91* $6
Shining Star 4 tracks *Atlantic 85942/stock/ps/'91* $6
Suicide Blonde *Atlantic 3460/promo/ps/'90* $6
Suicide Blonde 5 vers./Everybody Wants U Tonight *Atlantic 86139/stock/ps/'90* $6
Taste It lp/radio/club *Atlantic 4729/promo/ gatefold hardcover ps/'92* $7
Taste It/Questions *Atlantic 87409/stock/ps* $5
The Gift 3 vers./Born to Be Wild/Heaven Sent live *Atlantic 85722/stock/ps/'93* $6
The Gift 4:05 *Atlantic 5286/promo/ps* $5
X (11 tracks) *Atlantic 82140/promo/ gatefold pop up cover/poster* $12

IRON MAIDEN

Be Quick or Be Dead/Nodding Donkey Blues/ Space Station #5 *Epic 4551/promo/ silkscreened/ps/'92* $10
Bring Your Daughter to the Slaughter *Epic 4007/promo/silkscreened/'91* $15
From Here to Eternity/Public Enema Number One/No Prayer For the Dying (last 2 live) *Epic 4758/promo/ logo on yellow/rear insert/'92* $10
Holy Smoke *Epic 2194/promo/ps/logo on red* $8
No Prayer For the Dying/Communication Breakdown/Im a Mover *Epic 73695/promo/silkscreened pic/ rear insert/'90* $15
Tailgunner *Epic 2233/promo/Eddie silkscreened/ rear insert/'90* $8
Wasting Love *Epic 4640/promo/ silkscreened/ps/'92* $8

IRWIN, RUSS
I Need You Now edit&lp/interview *SBK 05401/ promo/gatefold hardcover ps/'91* $6

ISAAK, CHRIS
Blue Spanish ... edit & lp *Reprise 5035/promo* ...$6
Can't Do a Thing *Reprise 6000/promo/ silkscreened pic/'93* $6
Dont Make Me Dream About You *Reprise 3567/promo/'89* $6
Solitary Man *Reprise 6284/promo/ silkscreened pic/'93* $6
Wicked Game edit/lp/instrumental *Reprise 4408/promo/rear insert/'89* $6

ISIS
Rebel Soul *4th B'way 513/promo/ps/'90* $4

ISLEY BROTHERS
Come Together edit *WB 4070/promo/'89* $4
Spend the Night/Colder Are My Nights/ Smooth Sailin' Tonight (all edits) *WB 5411/promo/'89* $5
You'll Never Walk Alone edit & lp *WB 3771/promo/'89* $4

ISLEY, ERNEST
Back to Square One edit *Elektra 8184/promo/ rear insert/silkscreened purple/'90* $4
High Wire single edit & extended *Elektra 8121/promo/silkscreened logo* $4
Rising From the Ashes *Elektra 8163/promo/ silkscreened/rear insert/'90* $4

IT BITES
Calling All the Heroes *Geffen 3785/promo/ps* $4

ITALS, THE
Could You Be Loved 5 versions *Rhythm Safari 6603/promo/rear insert/'91* $5

J
Come Over Here edit & lp *A&M 42286 1860/promo/ gatefold hardcover ps/'92* $4
Keep the Promise/First They Came *Polydor 42286 1425/promo/ps/ silkscreened/'92* $4

J GEILS BAND
Bloodshot radio show *In the Studio 100/ promo/cue sheet/hosted by P.Wolf* $25

J, DAVID
Candy on the Cross/Antartica Starts Here 2:36 & :50/Memphis Ghosts *MCA 54424/stock/ps/ custom sticker/'92* $5
Fingers in the Grease remix & orig./This Town *RCA 2717/promo/custom sticker/ rear insert/'90* $6
I'll Be Your Chauffeur radio edit *RCA 2687/promo/ps/'90* $7
I'll Be Your Chauffeur lp & orig./The Moon in the Man *RCA 2613/promo/ps/'90* $8
Some Big City 4 versions *MCA 2261/promo/ps/'92* $6

J.T.
Swing It edit & long mix *Eastwest 3900/ promo/silkscreened/rear insert/'91* $4

JABULANI
Shine Your Light radio & lp *Giant 5433/promo/ps/'92* $4

JACK RUBIES, THE
Book of Love *TVT/promo/silkscreened/'90* $4

JACKSON 5, THE
Who's Lovin' You live edit/live lp/orig. *Motown 374631066/promo/ps/'92* $7

JACKSON, ALAN
I'd Love You All Over Again *Arista 2166/promo/ps/'90* $5
She's Got the Rhythm (And I Got the Blues) *Arista 2463/promo/logo on black/ps* $5
Tonight I Climbed the Wall *Arista 2514/promo/ logo on blue/ps/'93* $5
Don't Rock the Jukebox 3 versions *Arista 2220/promo/ps/logo on black* $6

JACKSON, FREDDIE
All Over You lp & instrumental *Orpheus 4531/ promo/silkscreened/rear insert/'90* $4
Can I Touch You 8 versions *Capitol 79480/promo/'92* $6
I Could Use a Little Love (Right Now) 4 vers. *Capitol 79374/promo/ps/ logo on white/'92* $5
Love Me Down (3 versions) *Capitol 79351/promo/rear insert/'90* $5
Main Course 8 versions *Capitol 79496/promo/ custom sticker/rear insert/'90* $5
Me and Mrs Jones edit & lp *Capitol 79581/promo/ps/'92* $4
Nice n Slow edit & lp/You Are My Love *Capitol 79352/promo/ps/'88* $5

JACKSON, FREDDIE & IRENE CARA
Love Survives *Curb 10570/promo/ silkscreened baby blue/ps/'89* $4

JACKSON, JANET
Alright 7" remix/7" r&b mix/lp *A&M 17978/ promo/ps/silkscreened blue/'89* $12
Alright (7 versions) *A&M 17981/promo/ ps/silkscreened orange/'89* $12
Black Cat (9 versions) *A&M 75021 7972/ promo/silkscreened/ps/'90* $12

Come Back to Me (6 vers.) *A&M 75021 7939/ promo/tan silkscreened/ps/'89* $12
Escapade *A&M 18000/promo/silkscreened green/'89* $6
Escapade (8 versions) *A&M 18002/promo/ silkscreened blue/'89* $12
If 6 versions *Virgin 12800/promo/ps/'93* $10
Love Will Never Do (10 versions) *A&M 75021 7444/promo/ silkscreened purple/ps/'90* $12
Miss You Much (3 versions)/You Need Me *A&M 12325/stock/ps/'89* $8
Miss You Much (5 versions) *A&M 17917/promo/'89* $10
Miss You Much 7" edit & mama mix *A&M 17885/promo/ps/'89* $8
Miss You Much 7" slammin' r&b mix & s lammin' r&b mix/You Need Me *A&M 75021 2398/stock/ps/'89* $8
Remixes (remixes of 8 songs) *A&M 17966/promo/ps/'89* $20
Rhythm Nation (3 versions) *A&M 17915/promo/ps/'89* $12
Rhythm Nation (4 versions) *A&M 12330/ps/stock/'89* $8
Rhythm Nation (7 versions) *A&M 17928/ promo/silkscreened black/'89* $12
Rhythm Nation (lp, cassette & special pin) *A&M 6720/promo/ special box container* $25
State of the World (8 versions) *A&M 75021 7514/promo/ps/'90* $12
That's the Way Love Goes Shocklee remixes (3) *Virgin 12783/promo/silkscreened/ custom sticker/'93* $10
That's the Way Love Goes 5 versions *Virgin 12773/promo/ps/'93* $10
That's the Way Love Goes 6 versions *Virgin 12654/promo/ps/'93* $10

JACKSON, JANET & LUTHER VANDROSS

The Best Things In Life Are Free 4:37 & instrum. *Perspective 28968 1713/ promo/logo on green/ps/'92* $8
The Best Things in Life Are Free 9 versions *Perspective 31458 8003/promo/ logo on black/'92* $10
The Best Things in Life Are Free cd/lp/ instrumental *no label or #/promo testpressing/custom sticker* $12
The Best Things in Life are Free vocal & instrum. *Perspective 28968 1713/ promo/silkscreened/ps/'92* $8
The Best Things In Life Are Free without rap *Perspective 28968 1715/ promo/silkscreened green logo/'92* $8

JACKSON, JERMAINE

Daddy's Home/That's How Love Goes/ Let's Get Serious/Let Me Tickle Your Fancy *Motown 70005/stock/3"/ps* $4
Don't Take It Personal *Arista 9875/promo/ps/'89* $4
I'd Like to Get to Know You *Arista 2018/ promo/silkscreened logo on black/ rear insert/'89* $4
Word to the Badd!! *LaFace 4011/promo/ silkscreened pic/ps/'91* $4
You Said, You Said edit/pump it to the max/ dub *LaFace 4010/promo/ logo silkscreened/'91* $5
You Said, You Said 6 versions *LaFace 4003/promo/ps/logo on gold* $5

JACKSON, JOE

Down to London *A&M 17831/promo/ silkscreened titles/'89* $4
He's a Shape in a Drape *A&M 15792/promo/ps/'88* $4
He's a Shape in a Drape/Soul Kiss/Monday Papers *A&M 31008/3"/stock/ 3" gatefold ps/'88* $5
I'm the Man/Look Sharp/Slow Song (all live) *A&M 17550/promo/3"/ps/'88* $8
Me and You (Against the World) *A&M 17910/promo/silkscreened pic* $6
Nineteen Forever early fade/lp *A&M 17766/promo/ps/'89* $4
Obvious Song edit & lp *Virgin 3844/promo/ silkscreened logo on red/rear insert* $4
Oh Well *Virgin 4015/promo/'91* $4
Stranger Than Fiction *Virgin 4131/promo/ logo on orange/'91* $4

JACKSON, KEISHA

U Needa Lover 5 versions *Epic 73260/promo/logo on red/'90* $4

JACKSON, MICHAEL

Another Part of Me (5 versions) *Epic 1200/promo/ps/'88* $10
Bad (5 versions) *Epic 2808/promo/ps/'87* $12
Black or White vocal & instrumental *Epic 34K 74100/stock/trifold hardcover ps/silkscreened/'91* $6
Dirty Diana vocal/instrumental *Epic 1110/promo/ps/'88* $12
Heal the World 7" edit with intro/6:25 *Epic 74790/promo/ps/'92* $8
Heal the World 7" edit/7" edit with intro *Epic 74708/promo/ps/'92* $8
I Just Can't Stop .. *Epic 2750/promo/ps* $10
In the Closet 4 versions/Remember the Time (new jack jazz) *Epic 74267/stock/ ps/logo on black/'91* $6
In the Closet 5 versions *Epic 74266/promo/ logo on blue/custom sticker/ rear insert/'91* $10

Jam 7 versions *Epic 74333/promo/ps/ custom sticker/'92* $10
Jam 5 versions *Epic 49K 74334/stock/ silkscreened/ps/'92* $6
Jam 8 versions *Epic 4583/promo/silkscreened/ ps/custom sticker/'92* $12
Man in the Mirror 4:55/5:17 *Epic 1006/promo/'88* $12
Remember the Time *Epic 74200/promo/ logo on white/ps/'91* $8
Remember the Time 5 vers/Black or White 4 versions *Epic 74201/stock/ps/'91* $6
Remember the Time 7 versions *Epic 4456/ promo/silkscreened/rear insert/'92* $10
Remember The Time silky soul 7"/new jack radio mix/silky soul 12"/12" main mix/ e smoove's late nite mix *Epic 4457/ promo/silkscreened/rear insert/'92* $10
Smooth Criminal (6 different mixes) *Epic 1274/promo/ps/'88* $12
Way You Make Me Feel (5 versions) *Epic 2862/promo/ps* $12
Who Is It 4 versions *Epic 74406/promo/ logo on black/ps/'92* $10

JACKSON, MILLIE

Young Man, Older Woman no rap/half rap/lp *Jive 42016/promo/rear insert/'91* $6

JACKSON, PAUL (JR)

Preview of Coming Attractions/Alain/End of the Road/East From Wes *Atlantic 5048/promo* $5

JACKSON, REBBIE

Plaything 7"/extended/dub *Columbia 2915/promo/ps/'89* $4

JACKSONS, THE

Nothin (That Compares 2 U) 7 versions *Epic 1515/promo/ps/'89* $12
Private Affair *Epic 1889/promo/ silkscreened/ps/'89* $8

JACKYL

Dirty Little Mind *Geffen 4505/promo/ logo & cat on black/ps/'93* $5
Down on Me *Geffen 4487/promo/ silkscreened pic/ps/'92* $5
I Stand Alone *Geffen 4437/promo/ps/'92* $4
The Lumberjack *Geffen 4478/promo/ silkscreened/ps/'92* $4
When Will It Rain *Geffen 4516/promo/ silkscreened/ps/'93* $4
When Will It Rain 4 versions *Geffen 4534/ promo/ps/custom sticker/'93* $6
When Will It Rain 5 versions *Geffen 21927/stock/ps/'93* $5

JADE

Don't Walk Away edit/lp/instrumental *Giant 5803/promo/silkscreened/ rear insert/'92* $6
I Wanna Love You 4 versions *Giant 5393/promo/rear insert/'92* $6
I Wanna Love You 5 versions *Giant 40595/stock/'92* $6
One Woman ghetto flava radio/instrumental *Giant 6288/promo/rear insert/'92* $6

JAGGED EDGE UK

Out in the Cold *Polydor 509/promo/ logo on blue/ps/'90* $4

JAGGER, MICK

Don't Tear Me Up *Atlantic 5015/promo* $6
Let's Work single/lp/dance edit/dance *Columbia 2771/promo/ps/'87* $5
Let's Work 3:58/4:49/5:04/7:20 *Columbia 2771/promo/ps/'87* $15
Out of Focus lp & 7" nipgrass mix *Atlantic 5152/promo/ silkscreened/rear insert/'93* $8
Sweet Thing 6 versions *Atlantic 85775/stock/ps/'93* $6
Sweet Thing/Don't Tear Me Up *Atlantic 4929/ promo/silkscreened/ps/custom sticker* $8
Sweet Thing/Wandering Spirit *Atlantic 87410/stock/ps/'93* $5
Wired All Night/Out of Focus *Atlantic 5020/promo* $8

JAM, THE

Jam Covers ep (And Your Bird Can Sing/I Got You (I Feel Good)/Move on Up/ Disguises/So Sad About Us/ Stoned Out of My Mind) *Polydor 491/promo/'92* $15

JAMES

Born of Frustration *Fontana 653/ promo/gatefold hardcover ps/'92* $4
Born of Frustration/All My Sons/Sunday Morning/Sit Down (live) *Fontana 866 495/custom sticker/ stock/ps/'92* $4
Born of Frustration/All My Sons/Sunday Morning/Sit Down (live) *Fontana 866 495/promo/ custom sticker/'90* $5
Live ep (Protect Me acoustic/Lose Control acoustic/Sound/Heavens/Don't Wait That Long/How Was It For YOU?/ Seven) *Fontana 561/promo/ps/'92* $15
Seven/Be My Prayer/Fight *Fontana 702/promo/ps/'92* $4
Sit Down *Fontana 510/promo/ silkscreened dark blue/ps/'91* $4

JAMES, BOB
Bare Bones *WB 4333/promo/rear insert/'90* $4
Restoration edit & lp *WB 4473/promo/ rear insert/'90* $4
Rosalie/Ashante (both edits) *WB 3257/promo/ps/'88* $4
The Bob James Radio Special *WB 4516/ promo/dj only interview & more/'90* $15

JAMES, BOB & EARL KLUGH
As It Happens edit & lp *WB 6089/promo/custom sticker/'92* $4
Movin' On 3 versions/Handara *WB 5639/promo/'92* $6

JAMES, COLIN
Five Long Years *Virgin 2517/promo/ silkscreened pic/'88* $4
Voodoo Thing *Virgin 2401/promo/ps/'88* $4
Why'd You Lie edit & lp *Virgin 2666/ promo/silkscreened/'88* $4

JAMES, ELMORE
King of the Slide Guitar sampler (The Sky is Crying/Dust My Broom + 6) *Capricorn 5831/promo/ps/'92* $10

JAMES, ETTA
Beware *Island 6621/promo/rear insert/'90* $5

JAMES, RICK
This Magic Moment Dance With Me radio edit & 12" remix *WB 3231/promo/'89* $5
This Magic Moment-Dance With Me (remix) *Reprise 3649/promo/'89* $4

JAMES, TOMMY
You Take My Breath Away *Aegis 2/promo/'90* $5

JAMES, TOMMY & SHONDELS
Crimson & Clover/Sweet Cherry Wine/ Crystal Blue Pers./Draggin' the Line *Rhino 73046/3"/stock/ps/'88* $5

JAMES, VINNIE
All American Boy *Cypress 2387/promo/ silkscreened/gatefold hardcover/book/'91* $4

JAMISON, JIM
Rock Hard edit & lp/interview *Scotti Bros 75296/promo/ps/'91* $8
Taste of Love *Scotti Bros 75285/promo/ps* $4
Ever Since the World Began *Scotti Bros 1782/ promo/silkcreened/'89* $4

JANATA
The River (radio edit) *Mercury 188/promo/ps/ silkscreened/'90* $4

JANES ADDICTION
Been Caught Stealing *WB 4523/promo/ gatefold, embossed hardcover/ with handcuffs/'90* $25
Been Caught Stealing (12" & lp)/ Had a Dad (demo versions) *WB 21736/stock/gatefold hardcover ps/'90* $10
Classic Girl *WB 4633/promo/silkscreened/ rear insert/'90* $15
Classic Girl ep (Then She Did/Aint No Right/ No One's Leaving/LA medley (last 3 live)/Classic Girl) *WB 40129/promo/ gatefold hardcover ps/'91* $10
Had a Dad *WB 3324/promo/ps/'88* $15
Jane Says *WB 3445/promo/'88* $15
Stop lp without intro & with *WB 4038/promo/silkscreened pic/ rear insert/'90* $20
Stop/I Would For You (demo)/Three Days *WB 21559/stock/ps/sol/'90* $10
Three Days *WB 4037/promo/silkscreened pic* $20

JANZ, PAUL
Believe in Me *A&M 15723/promo/'88* $4
Send Me a Miracle *A&M 5156/promo/ custom sticker* $4

JARBOE
Red 4 versions *Hyperium 5066/stock/ps/'92* $5

JARREAU, AL
All or Nothing at All (7" remix & lp) *Reprise 3513/promo/'89* $4
Blue Angel 11 versions *Reprise 40531/ stock/gatefold hardcover ps/'92* $5
Classic Hits sampler (Take Five/Were in This Love Together/Breakin' Away/Teach Me Tonight/Roof Garden + 6) *Reprise 5412/promo/'90* $12
Heaven and Earth edit & lp *Reprise 5322/promo/'92* $4
It's Not Hard to Love You edit & lp *Reprise 5486/promo/'92* $4
One Way/All or Nothing at All/Hearts Horizon *Reprise 3429/promo/'88* $5

Since I Fell For You *MCA 17413/promo* $4
So Good fade & lp *Reprise 3341/promo/'89* $4
The Christmas Song *Reprise 5219/promo* $4

JARRETT, KEITH
Blues/The Wind *ECM CD PRO KJ 2/promo/ blue & white logo on red/'90* $5

JASON & THE SCORCHERS
Find You *A&M 17823/promo/silkscreened/ matchbook like cover/'89* $15
Find You *A&M 17823/promo/silkscreened/ps*......$4
Try Me/Hardluck Boy/Feels So Right/Letter of Love *Liberty 79186/promo/ logo on blue/custom sticker/'92* $8
When the Angels Cry *A&M 17903/promo/silkscreened/'89* $5

JASPER, CHRIS
One Time Love (2 versions) *Gold City 1124/promo/ps/'88* $4

JAVIER
Rave It Up 6 versions *Rampart 80921/ stock/trifold hardcover ps/'92* $4

JAYHAWKS
Scrapple ep (Take Me With You/Leave No Gold/Keith and Quentin/Up Above My Head) *Def American 007/promo/ps/'93* $8
Settled Down Like Rain/Reason to Believe/ Sister Cry/Ain't No End/Martins Song-Settled Down (last 4 live) *Def American 6207/promo/ps/'93* $12
Take Me With You (When You Go) *Def American 6040/promo/ps/'93* $4
Waiting For the Sun *Def American 5867/promo/ps/'92* $4

JAYMES, JESSE
Body Heat radio versions & mac mix *Delicious 6688/promo/rear insert/'91* $4

JAZ A GROOVE, THE
This is What U Rap 2 (5 versions) *EMI 4770/promo/silkscreened/ps/'91* $4

JAZZ BUTCHER, THE
She's a Yo Yo edit & lp *Sky 7-5081/promo/ps* $6

JAZZI P
Feel the Rhythm (4 vers.) *A&M 75021 7506/ promo/yellow silkscreened/ps/'90* $4

JAZZMASTERS, THE
Sound of Summer edit & lp *JVC 102/promo/ silkscreened pic/rear insert/'93* $4

JEFFERSON AIRPLANE
... Loves You sampler 11 tracks *RCA 66113/ promo/custom sticker/'92* $15
Planes *Epic 1769/promo/silkscreened logo/'89* $5
Surrealistic Pillow/In the Studio *radio show/promo/hosted by MARTY BALIN, PAUL KANTNER, GRACE SLICK/cue sheet* $25
True Love *Epic 73080/promo/silkscreened logo/'89* $5

JEFFREYS, GARLAND
Hail Hail Rock n Roll 5 versions *RCA 62175/promo/silkscreened/'91* $5
Hail Hail Rock n Roll boilerhouse radio mix/ I Was Afraid of Malcolm/ The Answer 12" & extended *RCA 62212/stock/ps/'92* $4
The Answer 5 versions *RCA 62295/ promo/logo on red/rear insert/'92*.............$5

JELLYBEAN
Spillin' the Beans 5 versions *Atlantic 3890/ promo/ps/logo on black/'91* $4

JELLYBEAN & NIKI HARIS
What's It Gonna Be (5 versions) *Atlantic 3668/promo/ps/'90* $5

JELLYFISH
Baby's Coming Back (remix) *Charisma 008/ promo/silkscreened/ps/'91* $5
Comes Alive ep (No Matter What/The King is Half Undressed/Now She Knows She's Wront/Let Em In-That is Why/Jet) *Charisma 084/promo/ ps/logo silkscreened/'91* $15
I Wanna Stay Home *Charisma 042/promo/ silkscreened/ps/'91* $4
I Wanna Stay Home/Jet/Now She Knows She's Wrong (last 2 live) *Charisma CUSDG 4/stock/ gatefold hardcover ps/'91* $6
New Mistake *Charisma 12786/promo/ silkscreened/rear insert/'93* $4
That is Why (edit) *Charisma 019/promo/ silkscreened pic/weird waterfilled outer package/'90* $12
The Ghost at Number One edit & lp *Charisma 12753/promo/ silkscreened/rear insert/'93* $4
The King is Half Undressed *Charisma 012/promo/silkscreened/'90* $5

JENKINS, TOMI
Telling You How It Is edit & lp *Elektra 8074/promo/'89*..................................$4

JENNINGS, WAYLON
Just Talkin' *Epic 74403/promo/ logo on blue/rear insert/'92* $4

Too Dumb For New York City
Epic 74705/promo/rear insert/'92 ....$4

JENNINGS, WAYLON & WILLIE NELSON

If I Can Find a Clean Shirt *Epic 73832/ promo/rear insert/silkscreened/'91* $4

JESUS & MARY CHAIN

10 Smash Hits/1985-1992
Def American 5336/promo/ps/'92 ....$20
Almost Gold *Def American 5606/promo/ps/'92* ...$7
April Skies *WB 2955/promo/ps* $10
Far Gone and Out
Def American 5513/promo/ps/'92 ....$8
Far Gone and Out lp & arc weld mix/Why'd You Want Me?/Sometimes
Blanco Y Negro 40422/ stock/ps/silkscreened/'92 ....$6
Head On *WB 3868/promo/silkscreened pic* $10
Her Way of Praying *WB 4058/promo/'89* $6
Reverence lp/jim & william reid mix/ al jorgensen mix *Def American 5340/ promo/logo on black/ps/'92* $7
Reverence lp/jim & william reid mix/ al jorgensen mix/mark stent mix/ Guitarman *Def American 40375/ stock/gatefold hardcover ps/'92* $6

JESUS & MARY CHAIN/CURVE/ SPIRITUALIZED

Teenage Lust 3 vers/Clipped/Medication
Def American 5834/promo/ps/'92 ....$8

JESUS JONES

A Perverse Conversation With 16 tracks (half interview/half music)
Food 04704/promo/silkscreened/ps........$15
Real Real .. 3:06/4:19/6:16 /Interview (1:30)
SBK 05402/promo/ps/ blue logo on gold/'91 ....$12
Real Real Real rock mix & lp/interview (1:30)
SBK 05405/promo/blue logo on gold/ps/'91 ....$12
Right Here, Right Now 3 versions
SBK 19734/stock/ps/'91 ....$6
Right Here, Right Now righteous radio mix & lp/Move Me *SBK 05376/promo/ps* $8
Right Here, Right Now righteous radio mix/ hit radio mix/m.phillips 12"
SBK 05387/promo/silkscreened logo/ps/'91 ....$8
The Right Decision edit/lp *SBK 04722/ promo/silkscreened/ps/'93* $5
The Right Decision klanger mix/single edit
SBK 04733/promo/silkscreened/ custom sticker/'93 ....$5
Welcome Back Victoria 3:29 & 3:24
SBK 05423/promo/red logo on black/custom sticker/'91 ....$6

JESUS LOVES YOU

Generations of Love (3 versions)
Virgin 3469/promo/'90 ....$6

JET RED

Not the Only One *Relativity 88561-1001/ promo/silkscreened logo on red/'89* $4

JETBOY

Heavy Chevy *MCA 18291/promo/ silkscreened pic/rear insert/'90* $4
Stomp It *MCA 1076/promo/silkscreened/ rear insert/'90* $4

JETHRO TULL

20 Years of Jethro Tull sampler 21 tracks
Chrysalis 21655/stock/ps/'88 ....$12
A Christmas Song *Chrysalis 04657/ promo/silkscreened/ps/'92* $6
Another Christmas Song/intro-A Christmas Song/Cheap Day Return-Mother Goose/ Outro-Locomotive Breath (last 3 live in dressing room)
Chrysalis 23471/promo/ps/'89 ....$15
Aqualung radio show *In the Studio 126/ promo/cue sheet/ hosted by Ian Anderson*.........................$30
Doctor to My Disease/Night in the Wilderness/ Jump Start (live) *Chrysalis 23801/ promo/silkscreened logo on black/ rear insert/'91* $8
Kissing Willie *Chrysalis 23418/promo/ps/'89* $6
Rocks on the Road lp & live/Bouree live/ Jack a Lynn demo/Night in the Wilderness/Jump Start live
Chrysalis 23818/stock/ps/'91 ....$7
The Rattlesnake Trail/Another Christmas Song
Chrysalis 23457/promo/ rear insert/silkscreened logo/'89 ....$8
This is Not Love *Chrysalis 23760/promo/ silkscreened/rear insert/'91* $6

JETS, THE

Special Kinda Love radio edit/chr edit
MCA 1005/promo/logo on blue/'90 ....$4
You Better Dance 3:50/strauss remix 3:50/7:27 *MCA 17874/ promo/custom sticker/'89* $5

JETT, JOAN

Backlash *Epic 73985/promo/logo on black/ps* $6
Dirty Deeds *CBS Associated 73215/promo/ silkscreened/rear insert/'89* $6
Dirty Deeds (spec. hit radio version
Epic Associated 1976/promo/ silkscreened logo on red/ps/'90 ....$6
Don't Surrender edit & most excellent mix
Epic 74067/promo/ps/'91 ....$6
Little Liar (baby tush mix)
Blackheart 1324/promo/'88 ....$6

Love Hurts special A/C only mix
Epic 9999/promo/silkscreened logo/custom sticker/'90 .... $6
Love Hurts special hit radio versions/lp
Epic 2013/promo/silkscreened/ rear insert/'89 .... $6

JIBRI WISE ONE

I'll Be There For You radio & extended
Ear Candy 38007/promo/ps/'91 .... $4

JIMENEZ, FLACO

Eres Un Encanto *WB 5817/promo/'92* $4
Me Esta Matando *Reprise 5429/promo/'92* $4

JIVE BUNNY AND THE MASTERMIXERS

Swing the Mood 4:05/6:00/3:55
Atco 3039/promo/ps/'89 .... $4

JODECI

Come & Talk to Me 4 versions/ Gotta Love r&b edit
Uptown 54354/stock/ps/'92 .... $5
Come & Talk to Me 6 versions
Uptown 1595/promo/rear insert/'92 .... $6
Gotta Love 6 versions *MCA 1259/promo/'91* $6
I'm Still Waiting lp/jazz/instrumental
MCA 2153/promo/ps/'92 .... $5
I'm Still Waiting swing mob radio mix/ swing hip hop mix/daddy's jeep mix/ daddy hip hop *Uptown 2441/promo/ rear insert/'92* $6
Lately 5 versions *Uptown 2740/promo/ps/'93* $5
Lately pop edit/pop edit without intro
Uptown 2777/promo/rear insert/'93 .... $5
Lately radio & lp *Uptown 2679/promo/ps/'93* $4
Let's Go Through the Motions
Uptown 2598/promo/ps/'93 .... $4
Let's Go Through the Motions edit & lp
Uptown 2732/promo/rear insert/'93 .... $4
Stay cool crossfade edit & mccartney slick orig.
Uptown 2209/promo/ps/'92 .... $5
Stay 6 versions *Uptown 2053/promo/ps/'91* $6

JOE PUBLIC

Do You Everynite *Columbia 4793/promo/ps* $4
I Miss You 4 versions/Live and Learn 12" remix
Columbia 44K 74322/stock/ps/'92 .... $5
I Miss You remix single/12"/lp
Columbia 74321/promo/ps/'92 .... $5
I've Been Watchin' 4 versions
Columbia 4734/promo/ps/'92 .... $5
Live and Learn radio with rap/without rap/ 12" remix *Columbia 74012/promo/ps* $5
Live and Learn edit/radio versionswith rap/ public dance mix
Columbia 4428/promo/ps/'91 .... $5

JOEL, BILLY

All Shook Up *Epic 74422/promo/ps/ silkscreened/'92* $4
And So It Goes *Columbia 73602/promo/ silkscreened logo on white/'90* $4
Glass Houses In the Studio
radio show/promo/cue sheet/'90 .... $25
I Go To Extremes *Columbia 73091/promo/ps/ silkscreened/'90* $4
The Downeaster Alexa *Columbia 73333/promo/ silkscreened/ps/'90* $5
The Storm Front Tour CD (16 tracks including 4 live songs)
Columbia 2127/promo/ps/'90 .... $20
We Didn't Start the Fire *Columbia 73021/ promo/silkscreened pic/ps/'89* $6

JOESKI LOVE

I Know She Likes Joe 4 versions
Columbia 73480/promo/ps/'90 .... $4

JOHN CONNELLY THEORY

Aggressive/Hold Your Head Up
Relativity 0125/promo/silkscreened/'91 .... $4

JOHN WESLEY HARDING

Cathy's New Clown lp, live, & acoustic live *Sire 4087/promo/ silkscreened/rear insert/'90* $5
Collected Stories 1990-1991 *Sire 4698/ silkscreened pic/booklet/'91* $15
Crystal Blue Persuasion edit & lp
Sire 4773/promo/silkscreened/'90 .... $4
Kill the Messenger
Sire 5636/promo/silkscreened/'92 .... $4
Scared of Guns/If You Have Ghosts *Sire 4498/ promo/silkscreened pic/rear insert* $5
The Devil in Me edit & lp *Sire 3893/promo/'90* $4
The Person You Are lp & remix
Sire 4700/promo/'90 .... $4
Why We Fight 12 tracks *Sire 5695/promo* $10

JOHN, ELTON

A Word in Spanish *MCA 17640/promo/ps/'88* $8
Club at the End of the Street *MCA 18303/ promo/rear insert/'89* $5
Durban Deep *MCA 18060/promo/ps/'89* $8
Goodbye Marlin Brando *MCA 17641/promo/'88* $5
Healing Hands *MCA 17873/promo/ custom sticker/'89* $6
I Don't Wanna Go On With You Like That 3:57/4:00
MCA 17535/promo/ps/'88 .... $8
Madman Across the Water edit & lp
Polydor 819/promo/'92 .... $5
Rare Masters-The Elton John Collection sampler (25 tracks) *Polydor 535/promo/ gatefold hardcover ps/2 cds/'92* $25
Sacrifice *MCA 18061/promo/'89* $5
Simple Life hot mix/orig. mix/lp
MCA 2539/promo/rear insert/'93 .... $6
The Last Song *MCA 2425/promo/ps/'92* $6
The One *MCA 2263/promo/ps/'92* $5

The One short edit/early faded
MCA 2302/promo/ps/'92 .... $6
The One/Suit of Wolves/Ugly Girls and Fat Boys
MCA 54435/stock/ps/'92 .... $5
You Gotta Love Someone 4:23 & 4:5
MCA 1135/promo/rear insert/'90 .... $6

JOHN, ELTON & BERNIE TAUPIN
Two Rooms - The Elton John & Bernie Taupin Interview
Polygram 866 233/promo/ps/'91 .... $25

JOHN, ELTON & ERIC CLAPTON
Runaway Train *MCA 2305/promo/ps/'92* $6

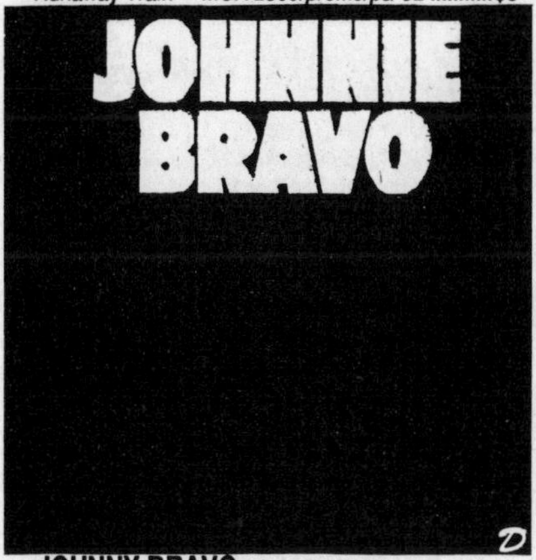

JOHNNY BRAVO
Social Grooming ep (I See Right Through You + 3)
Dkema 10010/stock/ps/'92 .... $20

JOHNNY HATES JAZZ
I Dont Want to Be a Hero 3:29/6:35
Virgin 2367/promo/ps/'88 .... $6
Shattered Dreams (2 versions)
Virgin 2177/promo/ps $6

Turn Back the Clock 7" single & 12" extended
Virgin 2348/promo/silkscreened/'88 .... $6

JOHNSON & BRANSON
Jockin' Me edit, lp, a capella screamapella
A&M 18006/promo/ logo on silkscreened purple/'90 .... $4
Lets Get to Know Each Other Better (4 vers.)
A&M 17906/promo/logo on green/'89 .... $4

JOHNSON, ERIC
Cliffs of Dover *Capitol 79159/ promo/silkscreened/rear insert/'90* $4
Cliffs of Dover live & lp *Capitol 79524/ promo/silkscreened/'90* $6
Desert Rose *Capitol 79342/ promo/silkscreened/rear insert/'90* $4
East West/Trademark/Forty Mile Town/ Song For George *Capitol 79043/ promo/silkscreened logo/'90* $6
Forty Mile Town edit & lp *Capitol 79458/ promo/logo on purple/'90* $4
High Landrons edit & lp *Capitol 79876/ promo/rear insert/'90* $4
Righteous *Capitol 79457/promo/ logo on black/rear insert/'90* $4
Trademark *Capitol 79567/promo/rear insert* $4

JOHNSON, HOLLY
Americanos 3:30/6:44 *Uni 17986/promo/'89* $5
Love Train 3:59/6:52 *Uni 17837/promo/ custom sticker/'89* $5

JOHNSON, JESSE
Love Struck dance & 7" edit *A&M 17547/ promo/silkscreened pic/ gatefold hardcover ps/'88* $7

JOHNSON, JOHNNIE
Tanqueray *Elektra 8437/promo/'91* $4

JOHNSON, MICHAEL
One Honest Tear *Atlantic 4181/promo/ logo on brown/ps/'91* $4

JOHNSTONE, DAVEY/WARPIPES
Back a Ma Buick *Artful Balance 7224/ promo/silkscreened/'91* $4

JOMANDA
I Like It 5 versions *Big Beat 5113/promo* $5

JONES, BOOKER T
The Cool Dude edit *MCA 3014/promo/'89* $4

JONES, DAVID LYNN
Lonely Town *Mercury 168/promo/ silkscreened brown/'90* $4

JONES, GEORGE

Honky Tonk Myself to Death
MCA 54370/promo/rear insert/'91 .... $5

I Don't Need Your Rockin' Chair edit & lp
MCA 54470/promo/ps/GARTH BROOKS, TRAVIS TRITT, ALAN JACKSON, VINCE GILL, CLINT BLACK, more/'92 .... $6

She Loved a Lot In Her Time
MCA 54272/promo/'91 .... $4

Six Foot Deep... *Epic 73424/promo/'90* $5

Walls Can Fall *MCA 54687/promo/'92* $4

Wrong's What I Do Best *MCA 54604/promo* $4

You Couldn't Get the Picture with & without spoken intro *MCA 54187/promo/ps/silkscreened logo/'91* $6

JONES, GLENN

Every Step of the Way *Jive 42089/promo/custom sticker/'92* $4

JONES, GRACE

Love on Top of Love (single versions)
Capitol 79759/promo/silkscreened $10

JONES, HOWARD

Everlasting Love 4:18/6:32
Elektra 8066/promo/'89 .... $6

Lift Me Up *Elektra 8526/promo/ps/'92* $4

Tears to Tell edit *Elektra 8612/promo/logo on black/'92* $4

The Prisoner *Elektra 8089/promo/'89* $4

The Prisoner (portmeirion mix)/Rubber Morals/Have You Heard the News
Elektra 66695/stock/ps/'89 .... $6

JONES, MARTI

Any Kind of Lie *RCA 2545/promo/ps/'90* $4

JONES, MICK

4 Wheels Turnin' *Atlantic 3018/promo/rear insert/'89* $4

Everything That Comes Around
Atlantic 2592/promo/ps/'89 .... $4

Everything That Comes Around *Atlantic 3096/promo/silkscreened logo/rear insert* $4

Just Wanna Hold *Atlantic 2854/promo/ps/'89* $4

JONES, QUINCY

Back on the Black 10+ tracks *WB 26020/promo/embossed clothbound book/booklet/silkscreened/'89* $25

Listen Up *Qwest 4496/promo/gatefold hardcover ps/SIEDAH GARRETT, AL B SURE, KARYN WHITE, ICE T, RAY CHARLES, more/'90* $10

Listen Up (3 vers.) *Qwest 4444/promo/ps/with SIEDAH GARRETT, AL B SURE, KARYN WHITE, ICE T, RAY CHARLES, more/'90* $6

The Secret Garden vocal remix/Tomorrow
Qwest 18893/stock/AL B. SURE, JAMES INGRAM, BARRY WHITE, more/'92 .... $6

The Secret Garden pt 1 & 2/lp *Qwest 3890/promo/'89/with AL B SURE, JAMES INGRAM, EL DEBARGE, B.WHITE* $5

Wee B. Dooinit *Qwest 4048/promo/'89* $5

JONES, QUINCY FEATURING RAY CHARLES & CHAKA KHAN

I'll Be Good to You (7 versions)
Qwest 21408/stock/'89 .... $5

I'll Be Good to You single mix & instrumental
Qwest 3832/promo/'89 .... $6

JONES, QUINCY FEATURING SIEDAH GARRETT

I Don't Go For That (7 versions)
Qwest 21594/stock/ps/'90 .... $5

I Don't Go For That (7 versions)
Qwest 4343/promo/rear insert/'89 .... $5

JONES, QUINCY FEATURING SIEDAH GARRETT & CHAKA KHAN

The Places You Find Love edit/long
Qwest 4458/promo/'89 .... $4

The Places You Find Love (edit)
Qwest 4569/promo/'89 .... $4

JONES, QUINCY FEATURING TEVIN CAMPBELL

Tomorrow (A Better You, A Better Me)
WB 3986/promo/'89 .... $4

Tomorrow (A Better You, A Better Me) (bigger choir vers.) *WB 4028/promo* $5

Tomorrow (A Better You, A Better Me) 4 vers.
Qwest 21504/stock/ps/'90 .... $6

JONES, RICKIE LEE

Don't Let the Sun Catch You Crying
Geffen 3924/promo/silkscreened/'89 .... $4

Don't Let the Sun Catch You Crying/
Easter Parade (live) *Geffen 3956/ promo/ps/with THE BLUE NILE/'89* $8
Flying Cowboys special edition *Geffen 005561/ promo/2 cds/interview/ 6x12 box/booklet/'89* $25
Flying Cowboys/The Horses *Geffen 4113/ promo/ps/silkscreened/'89* $4
Pop Pop/A Special Open Ended Conversation For Radio *Geffen 4320/promo/ gatefold hardcover ps/'91* $15
Satellites edit & lp *Geffen 3715/promo/ gatefold hardcover ps/'89* $5

JONES, STEVE

Fire and Gasoline/Wild Wheels/God in Louisiana/ Freedom Fighter (all live) *MCA 18179/promo/'90* $10
Freedom Fighter *MCA 17953/promo/ custom sticker/'89* $4
Freedom Fighter *MCA 17991/promo/'89* $4

JONES, TOM

Move Closer *Jive 1230/promo/'89* $6

JONES, WILLI

Love Me Up *Geffen 4124/promo/ gatefold hardcover ps/'90* $4

JONESES, THE

Don't You Know edit & lp *Atlantic 3176/promo/ps/'90* $4
Let's Live Together *Atlantic 3421/promo/ logo on red/rear insert/'90* $4
Steppin Out edit & lp *Atlantic 3311/promo/ps/'90* $4

JORDAN, JEREMY

The Right Kind of Love 3 versions *Giant 5746/promo/ps/'92* $5
Try My Love edit/lp/instrumental *Giant 6323/promo/rear insert/'93* $4

JORDAN, MARC

3 song sampler from lp *RCA 6549/promo/ps* $4
Catch the Moon remix *RCA 6931/promo/ps* $4
Edge of the World (3 versions) *RCA 2547/ promo/silkscreened/rear insert/'90* $4

JORDAN, RONNY

After Hours edit & lp *4th B'way 536/ promo/silkscreened/custom sticker* $4
Cool ep (After Hours/Show Me/So What! jazz mix) *4th B'way 558/promo/ silkscreened/ps/'92* $5
Get to Grips edit & cool mix *4th & B'way 570/ promo/logo on purple/rear insert/'92* $4
So What! lp/dance/jazz *4th B'way 554/ promo/ps/logo on black/'92* $5

JORDAN, SASS

Tell Somebody *Atlantic 2892/ promo/rear insert/'89* $4
You Don't Have to Remind Me *Impact 2306/promo/rear insert/'92* $4

JORDAN, STANLEY

What's Going On single/short/lp *Capitol 79983/promo/logo on cream/* rear insert/'90 .... $6

JORDY

Dur Dur D'Etre Bebe! english versions *Columbia 5191/promo/ps/'93* $4

JOURNEY

A Test of Time sampler 10 tracks *Columbia 4880/promo/ps/'92* $15
Lights edit (live) & lp *Columbia 4920/ promo/custom sticker/'92* $6
Lights studio & live *Columbia 4882/promo/ps/'92* $6

JUDAS PRIEST

A Touch of Evil edit & lp *Columbia 2218/ promo/silkscreened logo/ps/'90* $8
Blood Red Skies *Columbia 1249/promo/ silkscreened/'88* $7
I Am A Rocker *Columbia 1149/promo/silkscreened* $7
Night Crawler edit & lp *Columbia 3030/promo/ps/'91* $8
The Sharpest Cuts 10 tracks *Columbia 2133/ promo/with background card/'90* $30
The Sharpest Cuts 9 tracks *Columbia 2133/promo/'90* $20

JUDD, WYNONA

Wynona (full lp) *Curb 2171/ promo only silkscreened pic/'92* $15
My Strongest Weakness *Curb 54516/promo/rear insert/'92* $5
No One Else on Earth *Curb 2373/promo/rear insert/'92* $5
No One Else on Earth *Curb 54449/promo/rear insert/'92* $5
Only Love *Curb 54689/promo/rear insert/'93* $5
Tell Me Why *Curb 54606/promo/ps/'93* $5

JUDDS, THE

John Deere Tractor *RCA 62038/promo/ rear insert/'91* $5

JUDYBATS

Being Simple single/edit/simple versions *Sire 5982/promo/silkscreened/ rear insert/'93* $4
Daylight/Alliwannadois F*ck Your Hair (live)/ Cars *Sire 40134/stock/ gatefold hardcover ps/'91* $5

Is Anything (radio versions)
Sire 5439/promo/'92 .... $4
Saturday *Sire 5265/promo/silkscreened dog* $4
She Lives/When Southern Bells Ring/
Kindness Kills Me *Sire 21772/stock/gatefold hardcover ps/'90* $5

JUNGLE BROTHERS
Beyond This World *WB 3804/promo/'89* $4
What U Waitin' 4? (5 versions)
WB 4001/promo/'89 .... $5

JUNIOR
Better Part of Me 6 versions
MCA 1262/promo/'91 .... $5

JUNK MONKEY
Bliss/Boys Don't Cry
Metal Blade 5986/promo/ps/'93 .... $5

JUNKYARD
All the Time in the World edit & lp
Geffen 4237/promo/ps/'91 .... $4
Hollywood *Geffen 3514/promo/ps/'89* $4
Nowhere to Go But Down/Give the Devil His Due (demo versions) *Geffen 4303/promo/custom sticker/'91* $6
Simple Man edit & lp *Geffen 3858/promo/silkscreened logo/'89* $4
Slippin' Away edit & lp
Geffen 4339/promo/ps/'91 .... $4

K 9 POSSE
Get Wild Go Crazy 4:33 & 7:38 *Arista 2196/promo/logo on white/ps/'91* $4

KAM
Peace Treaty edit *Eastwest 4867/promo/silkscreened/ps/'92* $4

KAMEN, MICHAEL
Sasha edit & lp *WB 4544/promo/silkscreened/rear insert/'90* $4

KAMEN, NICK
I Promised Myself single & extended
Atlantic 3404/promo/ps/'90 .... $4

KANSAS
In the Spirit of Things 12 tracks
MCA 6254/promo/ps/'88 .... $15
Stand Beside Me *MCA 17657/promo/ps/'88* $5

KANTER, HILARY
Best Kept Secrets 11 tracks *ESP 00001/promo/trifold hardcover ps/insert* $10

KAOMA
Jambe Finete remix/dub/lp *Epic 73511/promo/silkscreened green/rear insert/'90* $4
Lambada vocal & instrumental *Epic 73090/promo/silkscreened logo/ps/'89* $5

KASHIF & MELLISA MORGAN
Love Changes/Midnight Mood
Arista 9626/promo/ps/'87 .... $5

KASTLE, RICHARD
Streetwise (9 tracks) *Virgin PRCD KASTLE/promo/gatefold hardcover ps/'91* $12

KATMANDU
Selftitled (special limited edition) (12 tracks)
Epic 2216/promo/ps/silkscreened green $10
The Way You Make Me Feel
Epic 4008/promo/ps/'91 .... $4

KATRINA & THE WAVES
Rock n Roll Girl 7" & lp
SBK 05318/promo/ps/'89 .... $5
That's the Way *SBK 06304/promo/ps/'89* $5

KATRINA & THE WAVES & ERIC BURDON
We Gotta Get Out of this Place lp & single
SBK 05331/promo/ps/custom sticker/'90 .... $6

KATT, JEANNETTE
Girl Noise 4 vers. *A&M/promo/logo on pink/'92* ... $4
Girl Noise remix & lp *A&M 75021 7397/promo/silkscreened pic/ps/'92* $4
When I Do Wrong I Do It So Right G-rated/lp
A&M 31458 8066/promo/logo on green/ps/'92 .... $4

KATYDIDS
Heavy Weather Traffic *Reprise 4094/promo/'90/prod by NICK LOWE* $4
Lights Out (Read My Lips) (2 versions)/Disappointed/Another August Night
Reprise 21732/stock/ps/'90 .... $5

KAY, JOHN & STEPPENWOLF
We Like It, We Love It (edit) *IRS 024/promo/ps/silkscreened blue/'90* $7

KC & THE SUNSHINE BAND
Game of Love regular edit/rox edit
Sisapa 75782/promo/'90 .... $4

KCM
All n All edit & lp *Virgin 4595/promo/rear insert/'92* $4

KEAGGY, PHIL
Be In My Heart radio mix/Strong Tower rock/60 second radio spot *Myrrh 901 0754 154/promo/silkscreened/ps* $8

KEEDY
Save Some Love (3 versions)
Arista 2194/promo/ps/'91 .... $4

KEENE, TOMMY
Our Car Club *Geffen 3414/promo/ps/'89* $4

KELLY, PAUL
Dumb Things *A&M 17578/promo/ps/'88* $4
Sweet Guy *A&M 17849/promo/silkscreened* $4
To Her Door *A&M 17624/promo/silkscreened* $4

KELTNER, LANCE
The Party's Over edit & lp
Eastwest 4477/promo/ silkscreened pic/rear insert/'92 .... $4

KEMP, TARA
Hold You Tight (3 versions) *Giant 4617/ promo/silkscreened/rear insert/'90* $5
Piece of My Heart (3 versions)
Giant 4743/promo/rear insert/'91 .... $5
Too Much edit & lp *Giant 5006/promo/ rear insert/'91* $4

KENNEDY-ROSE
Love Like This *IRS PAND 013/promo/ps/'90* $4

KENTUCKY HEADHUNTERS
Dumas Walker
Mercury 179/promo/silkscreened/'90 .... $4
It's Chitlin' Time *Mercury 524/promo/ps/'91* $4
Let's Work Together *Mercury 553/promo/ logo on brown/gatefold hardcover ps/'91* $4
Oh Lonesome Me *Mercury 246/promo/ silkscreened/'89* $4
Only Daddy That'll Walk the Line
Mercury 565/promo/silkscreened/ rear insert/'91 .... $4

KENTUCKY HEADHUNTERS & JOHNNY JOHNSON
Stumblin' *Nonesuch 8826/promo/ps/'93* $4

KENYATTA
I Wanna Do Something Freaky to You
Delic.Vinyl 0111/promo/rear insert $4

KEROSENE
Worthless/Sink/In My Head/Heart
Sire 40884/stock/gatefold hardcover ps/silkscreened/'93 .... $4

KEROUAC, JACK
Sampler (6 tracks) *Rhino Word Beat 90044/ promo/silkscreened pic/ps/'90* $10

KERSHAW, SAMMY
Anywhere But Here *Mercury 749/promo/ silkscreened/rear insert/'91* $4
Cadillac Style/introducing Sammy (12:53)
Mercury 511/promo/logo on black/ps $8
Don't Go Near the Water *Mercury 598/ promo/logo on grey/rear insert/'91* $4
She Don't Know She's Beautiful *Mercury 825/ promo/silkscreened pic/rear insert* $4

KETCHUM, HAL
Small Town Saturday Night/I Miss My Mary/ Five O'Clock World/Past the Point of Rescue *Curb 054/promo/ps/'91* $4

KHAN, CHAKA
Don't Look at Me That Way edit & lp
WB 5742/promo/'92 .... $4
End of a Love Affair/I'll Be Around
WB 3439/promo/ps/'88 .... $6
I Want edit & lp *WB 5783/promo/'92* $4
It's My Party edit & lp
WB 3316/promo/ps/'88 .... $6
Love You All My Lifetime 10 versions
WB 40377/stock/gatefold hardcover ps/'92 .... $5
Love You All My Lifetime edit & lp
WB 5338/promo/silkscreened pic/'92 .... $6
Love You All My Lifetime edit & lp
WB 5338/promo/with bonus video/ oversized custom box (holds video & cd)/'92 .... $20
You Can Make the Story Right edit & lp
WB 5485/promo/'92 .... $4

KHAN, STEVE & R. MOUNSEY
Local ep (4 songs edited)
Denon DA 002/promo/ps/'89 .... $5

KID CREOLE & COCONUTS
I Love Girls remix & edit
Columbia 73452/promo/ps/'90 .... $4
People Will Talk lp & club mix
Musician 8069/promo/'89 .... $4
The Sex of It (4 versions) *Columbia 73256/ promo/silkscreened/ps/'90* $4

KID FROST
La Raza (3 versions) *Virgin 3339/ promo/silkscreened/'90* $4
La Raza (3 vers.) *Virgin GRINGO/promo/'90* $4
No Sunshine edit & lp *Virgin 4471/promo/ silkscreened/rear insert/'92* $4

KID N PLAY
Funhouse 5 versions *Select 002/promo/'90* $6
Slippin'/Friendz 3 versions each
Select 8484/promo/'91 .... $6

KIHN, GREG
Kihn of Hearts 10 tracks
Riot 2001/stock/ps/'92 .... $15

KIK TRACEE
Don't Need Rules *RCA 2795/promo/ps/'91* $4
Don't Need Rules ep (Screamer/No Scream) *RCA 62023/promo/rear insert/'91* $5
You're So Strange *RCA 2856/promo/ps/'91* $4

KIKI
One Thing 3 versions *Turnstyle 4541/promo/rear insert/'92* $4

KILL FOR THRILLS
Brothers Eyes edit & lp *MCA 17900/promo/custom sticker/'89* $4
Motorcycle Cowb./Paisley Killers/Brothers Eyes *MCA 18198/promo/'89* $5

KILLER DWARFS
Dirty Weapons *Epic 1936/promo/3"/'89* $4
Dirty Weapons *Epic 2034/promo/silkscreened logo on yellow/'90* $4
Driftin' Back *Epic 4797/promo/ps/'92* $4
Driftin' Back *Epic 74351/promo/rear insert* $4
Hard Luck Town *Epic 4608/promo/logo on red/ps/'92* $4

KILLING JOKE
Money Is Not Our God video edit & lp *Noise 4877/promo/silkscreened logo on black/'90* $7

KILZER, JOHN
Hands edit & lp *Geffen 4293/promo/ps/'91* $4
Marilyn Dean and James Monroe *Geffen 4349/promo/ps/'91* $4
Memory in the Making *Geffen 3302/promo/ps (w/tour dates)/'88* $4

KIMMEL, TOM
A Small Song *Polydor 218/promo/silkscreened/gatefold hardcover ps (w/transparency)* $4

KING MISSILE
(Why Are) Trapped edit & lp *Atlantic 4960/promo/ps/silkscreened/'93* $5
(Why Are We) Trapped edit & lp/I'm Sorry *Atlantic 4960/promo/silkscreened/ps/'93* $5
My Heart is a Flower 7 versions *Atlantic 4118/promo/ps/'91* $6
My Heart is a Flower/The Story of Willy/Indians *Atlantic 3854/promo/ps/'91* $6

KING OF FOOLS
Eat Your Heart Out *Imago 28002/promo/ps* $4
Sad in Wonderland/Rising Sun/Love is Blind/No Man's Land/Sacco and Vanzetti *Imago 28015/promo/ps/'91* $5

KING OF KINGS
Burning Horn *DGC 4224/promo/silkscreened/custom sticker/'91* $4

KING OF THE HILL
If I Say (3 versions) *SBK 05394/promo/silkscreened/ps/'91* $4
If I Say 3 versions *SBK 05415/promo/silkscreened/cust.stickr/'91* $4

KING SWAMP
Blown Away *Virgin 2839/promo/silkscreened logo on purple/'89* $4
Interview *Virgin 2696/promo* $8
Is This Love? lp & 12" 3:59 & 7:19 *Virgin 2684/promo/silkscreened/'89* $4
One Step Over the Line interview + 4 songs *Virgin 2997/promo/ps/'89* $8
Wiseblood (orig.rock mix) *Virgin 3515/promo/silkscreened/'90* $4

KING TEE
At Your Own Risk (5 versions) *Capitol 79470/promo/silkscreened/rear insert/'90* $4

KING, BB
Back in L.A. edit & lp *MCA 2010/promo/'91* $5
Joe Cool edit *GRP 9925/promo/ps/Snoopy & BB cover/'89* $5
King of the Blues sampler (Into the Night/Right Time, Wrong Place/Never Make a Move too Soong/Aint Nobody Home + 8) *MCA 2428/promo/silkscreened pic/ps/'92* $12
Peace to the World *MCA 18450/promo/silkscreened yellow/rear insert/'90* $5
The Blues Come Over Me 3 versions *MCA 2131/promo/rear insert/'92* $6

KING, BEN E.
You've Got All of Me/It's Allright *Ichiban 097/promo/ps/'92* $5

KING, BEN E. & BO DIDDLEY
Book of Love radio & lp-dance versions
Atlantic 3535/promo/rear insert/'90 .... $5

KING, CARL
I Love You *Scotti Brothers 75326/promo/ silkscreened logo/'92* $4

KING, CAROLE
City Streets *Capitol 79555/promo/ silkscreened vermillion/'89* $5
City Streets special edition *Capitol 79575/ promo/nice cloth bound with book/silkscreened* $20
Lay Down My Life edit & lp *King's X 6644/ promo/silkscreened pic/rear insert* $5
Now and Forever *Columbia 4667/promo/ps/'92* $4
Someone Who Believes in You *Capitol 79742/ promo/silkscreened logo/'89* $5

KING, EVELYN
Flirt (5 versions) *EMI 04067/promo/ps/'88* $5

KING, EVELYN CHAMPAGNE
Shame '92 4:20 & 5:00/Shame '77 3:45 & 6:27
RCA 62350/promo/rear insert/'92 .... $5

KINGDOM COME
Do You Like It *Polydor 51/promo/ fold out die cut ps/silkscreened/'89* $8
Get It On + 3 audio *Polydor 870 720/stock/ video & audio cd/'88* $8
Overrated *Polydor 105/promo/silkscreenpic* $5
Should I *Polydor 466/promo/silkscreened/ gatefold hardcover ps/'91* $4
Who Do You Love *Polydor 90/promo/ silkscreened/die cut ps/'89* $4
You're Not the Only .. I Know
Polydor 526/promo/logo on green/ps $4

KINGMAKER
Really Scrape the Sky lp & thompson-barbiero mix *Chryalis 05471/promo/ silkscreened/custom sticker/'92* $4
When Lucy's Down/Hard Times
Chrysalis 04632/promo/silkscreened/ custom sticker/'92 .... $4

KINGS OF SWING
Nod Your Head to This 4 versions
Bum Rush 3406/promo/silkscreened $5
U Know I Love Ya Baby 3 versions
Bumrush 3728/promo/logo on red/'91 ...... $5

KINGS OF THE SUN
Drop the Gun *RCA 2518/promo/ps/'90* $4
Drop the Gun edit & lp *RCA 2611/promo/ silkscreened/rear insert/'90* $4

KINGS X
Black Flag *Atlantic 4461/promo/ silkscreened/ps/'92* $7
Dream in My Life edit & lp
Atlantic 4738/promo/rear insert $7
I'll Never Get Tired of You
Megaforce 3922/promo/rear insert $7
It's Love fade & lp *Megaforce 3612/ promo/logo on black/ps/'90* $7
Over My Head edit & lp
Atlantic 2779/promo/ps/'89 .... $7
Summerland *Atlantic 3041/promo/ rear insert/'89* $7
We Are Finding Who We Are *Megaforce 3765/ promo/silkscreened/ps/'90* $7

KINISON, SAM
Under the Thumb *WB 4033/promo/'90* $6
Wild Thing edit & lp + comic bits from lp
WB 3327/promo/ps/'88 .... $10

KINKS
Did Ya/Gotta Move (live)/Days/New World/ Look Through Any Doorway
Columbia 44K 74050/stock/ps/'91 .... $7
Down All the Days edit & lp
MCA 18294/promo/rear insert/'89 .... $4
Drift Away edit & lp *Columbia/promo/ps/'93* $4
Entertainment *MCA 18168/promo/'89* $4
Hatred (A Duet) edit/lp
Columbia 5076/promo/ps/'93 .... $5
How Do I Get Close edit & lp
MCA 17969/promo/'89 .... $3
Masters of Rock 4/11-23/90 *2 hour/promo/ 2 CD/with cue sheets radio show* $45
Scattered *Columbia 74872/promo/ps/'93* $5
Still Searching edit & lp
Columbia 5276/promo/rear insert/'93 .... $4

KINSEY REPORT, THE
Image Maker (edit) *Charisma 028/promo/'91* $4
Midnight Drive/Nowhere to Go...
Alligator ALA10/promo/ps/'89 .... $4

KIRSCH, RANDELL & PIGS ON CORN
Midnight Cowboy (3 versions)/ Something to Remember Me By
Pigs on Corn VS001/stock/ps/'92 .... $5

KISS
Crazy Crazy Nights *Merc. 04/promo/ps/'87* $15
Crazy Crazy Nights/No No No/When Your Walls Come Down/Thief in the Night
Mercury 870 709/stock/ps/ video (on first track) & audio/'88 .... $20
Domino radio edit & radio eq *Mercury 681/ promo/silkscreened logo/ps/'92* $10
Forever (remix) *Mercury 195/promo/ neat silkscreened group pic/'89* $15

God Gave Rock and Roll to You edit & lp
Interscope 4076/promo/ silkscreened/rear insert/'91 .... $8
Hide Your Heart
Mercury 140/promo/silkscreened/'89 .... $8
Hot in the Shade full CD
Mercury 838 913/stock/ promo silkscreened/'89 .... $15
I Love It Loud (live) *Mercury 882/promo/ logo on red/gatefold hardcover ps/'93* $8
Let's Put the X in Sex
Mercury 35/promo/ps/'88 .... $10
Let's Put the X in Sex (audio & video) + 3 (audio only) *Mercury 870 750/stock* $10
Lick It Up (audio & video)/Dance All Over Your Face/Gimme More/Fits Like a Glove (last 3 audio only) *Mercury 080 045/ promo/ps/CD video (1 song)* $20
Rise to It *Mercury 242/promo/silkscreen/ps/'90* .. $8
Tears Are Falling video & audio/Anyway You Slice It/Who Wants to Be Lonely/ Secretly Cruel
Mercury 870 710/stock/ps/'88 .... $15
Turn on Night (audio & video) + 3 (audio only)
Mercury 870 724/stock/'88 .... $10
Unholy (radio eq versions)/Creatures of the Night/War Machine/I Still Love You
Mercury 666/promo/ps/custom sticker/logo on black/'92 .... $20

KISS OF THE GYPSY

Whatever It Takes lp & remix *Atlantic 4423/ promo/logo silkscreened/ rear insert/'92* $4

KISS THE SKY

Living For You 4 versions
Motown 3746310312/promo/ps/'92 .... $4

KITA, TOMI

Life in Disguise 5 track ep *Ra Falcon 20365/ stock/silkscreened/rear insert/ custom sticker* $4

KITARO

Sundance/Moondance
Geffen 2837/promo/custom sticker $6
The Eight Headed Dragon/The Festival/The New Dawn *Geffen 4100/promo/ ps/silkscreened/'90* $6

KITCHENS OF DISTINCTION

4 Men/Goodbye Voyager/Skin
A&M 31458 8038/promo/ silkscreened/gatefold hardcvr ps/'92 .... $5
Drive That Fast edit & lp
A&M 75021 7488/promo/ps/'90 .... $4
Gorgeous Love/Prize demo/Concede/Innocent ....
A&M 75021 7226/promo/ silkscreened/ps/'90 .... $6
Smiling *A&M 75021 7603/promo/ silkscreened/ps/'92* $4

KITTEN

Dance With Me dance pop radio edit/radio edit/ dance extended *Atlantic 4231/promo/ silkscreened/rear insert/'91* $4

KIX

Blow My Fuse *Atlantic 2573/promo/ rear insert/'88* $4
Cold Blood *Atlantic 2463/promo/'88* $4
Don't Close Your Eyes (edit)
Atlantic 2674/promo/rear insert/'88 .... $4
Get It While It's Hot *Atlantic 2711/promo/'88* $4
Girl Money *East West 3988/promo/ps/ logo on black/'91* $4
Girl Money 3 versions *East West 4026/ promo/ps/logo on red/'91* $5
Hot Wire/Blow My Fuse/Cold Blood (last 2 live)
East West 3885/promo/ silkscreened/rear insert/'91 .... $8
Rock Profile interview & music
Eastwest 4091/promo/ps/'91 .... $15
Same Jane edit & lp *East West 4252/ promo/silkscreened/rear insert/'91* $4
Tear Down the Walls 4 versions *Eastwest 4218/ promo/ps/custom sticker/ red logo on black/'91* $5

KLF, THE

3 AM Eternal (4 versions)
Arista 2230/promo/ps/silkscreened $10
Stand By the Jams single & 12" (w/TAMMY WYNETTE)/The White Room vers./ All Bound For Mu Mu Land/ Let Them Eat Ice Cream
Arista 2403/promo/ps/'92 .... $10
Stand by the Jams single & 12"/The White Room/All Bound For Mu Mu Land/ Let Them Eat Ice Cream
Arista 07822-12403/stock/ps/'92 .... $6
What Time is Love? remix & live at transcentral mix *Arista 2365/ promo/silkscreened/ps/'91* $8

KLUGH, EARL

Days of Wine and Roses/I Say a Little Prayer
WB 5189/promo/'91 .... $4
Midnight in San Juan edit/Kissin' on the Beach edit/Jamaican Winds
WB 4813/promo/'91 .... $4
Prelude/Goldfinger/Now We're One/ Jo Ann's Song *WB 6064/promo/'93* $4

KLYMAXX

When You Kiss Me *MCA 1143/ promo/logo on white/'90* $4

KMD
Peachfuzz/Gasface Refill (both lp & instrum.)
Elektra 8336/promo/silkscreened/'90 ....$5
Who Me? lp & instrumental/Humrush lp & instrum. *Elektra 8338/promo/ps/'91* $5

KMFDM
Money 4 versions/Bargeld 3 versions
Wax Trax 9172/stock/ps/ dj silkscreened/'92 ....$6
Sex on the Flag *Wax Trax PROMOCD6/promo/ silkscreened/rear insert/'92* $4
Sucks 4 versions/More n Faster
TVT 8703/stock/ps/'92 ....$5

KNACK, THE
One Day at a Time 3:57 & 3:59
Charisma 043/promo/silkscreened/ps $5
Rocket o' Love *Charisma 025/promo/ silkscreened/ps/'91* $5

KNIGHT, GLADYS
Licence to Kill *MCA 17885/promo/ custom sticker/'89* $5
Love Overboard 4:25/5:25 *MCA 17442/ promo/envelope ps/pic insert/'87* $15
Meet Me in the Middle 4 versions
MCA 1678/promo/ps/'91 ....$6
Meet Me in the Middle 7 versions
MCA 2075/promo/ps/'91 ....$6
Men 5 versions *MCA 1463/promo/'91* $6
Where Would I Be vocal/instrumental/suite
MCA 4638/promo/ps/'91 ....$5

KNIGHT, GLADYS & DIONNE WARWICK & PATTI LABELLE
Superwoman 3 versions *MCA 1670/promo/'91* ...$6

KNIGHT, HOLLY
Heart Dont Fail Me Now 4:15/5:07/5:33
Columbia 1199/promo/ps/'88 ....$5

KNOPFLER, DAVID
Whispers of Gethsemane/To Feel That Way .
Cypress 17638/promo/ silkscreened pink/'88 ....$5

KNUCKLES, FRANKIE
The Whistle Song 3:24/4:08/6:54
Virgin 4013/promo/logo on black/'91 ....$4

KON KAN
(Could've Said) I Told You So
Atlantic 3702/promo/ps/ black silkscreened/'90 ....$4
Liberty! (5 versions) *Atlantic 3598/promo/ silkscreened orange/ps/'90* $6
Puss n Boots-These Boots Are Made For Walkin' (5 versions)
Atlantic 2901/promo/rear insert/'89 ....$6

KONITZ, LEE
Ocean Song/Rainy Afternoon/Samba Zezita + 1
M.A. 737/promo/ps/'89 ....$5

KOOL & THE GANG
Raindrops 3 versions *Mercury 85/promo/ silkscreened/ps/'89* $5
Unite 4 versions *JRS 820/promo/ silkscreened/ps/'93* $5

KOOL MOE DEE
Can U Feel It remix edit/remix/instrumental
Jive 42145/promo/rear insert/'93 ....$5
Death Blow radio edit & lp
Jive 42015/promo/rear insert/'91 ....$5
God Made Me Funke new & original
Jive 1352/promo/rear insert/'90 ....$5
How Kool Can One Blackman Be 5 versions
RCA 1453/promo/ps/'91 ....$5
They Want Money *Jive 1217/promo/ps/'89* $5

KOOL MOE DEE & KRS ONE & CHUCK D
Rise n Shine long/short/instrumental
Jive 1438/promo/rear insert/ custom sticker/'91 ....$5

KOPPES, PETER
The Lost Peace *TVT/promo/ silkscreened pic/'89* $4

KOZ, DAVE
Lucky Man sampler (You Make Me Smile/ Tender is the Night/After Dark/ Wait a Little While) *Capitol 79746/ promo/ps/silkscreened/'93* $5
Tender is the Night quiet storm edit/edit/lp
Capitol 79836/promo/ps/'93 ....$4

KRAFTWERK
The Robots single edit & kling klang mix
Elektra 8392/promo/rear insert/'91 ....$6
The Robots single edit & kling klang mix & kling klang extended *Elektra 66526/stock/ gatefold hardcover ps/'91* $5
Trans Europe Express (2 versions)/ Les Mannequins/Showroom Dummies
Capitol 15620/stock/ps/'90 ....$5

KRAVITZ, LENNY
Are You Gonna Go My Way
Virgin 12755/promo/ps/'93 ....$4
Believe edit & lp *Virgin 12781/promo/ silkscreened/rear insert/'93* $5
Fields of Joy *Virgin America 3981/promo/ silkscreened/'91* $5
I Build This Garden For Us edit & lp
Virgin PRCD WEED/promo/ silkscreened/'90 ....$5

Is There Any Love in Your Heart censored/
Let Love Rule/I Build This Garden../
Stop Draggin' Around + 2
Virgin 12803/promo/rear insert/
custom sticker/'93 .... $8

It Ain't Over Til It's Over *Virgin 3883/promo* $4

Let Love Rule (edit) *Virgin 2864/promo/*
silkscreened logo & title/'89 .... $5

Mama Said sampler (Always on the Run/
Fields of Joy/What the.. Are We
Saying? clean/Stop Draggin'
Around + 2) *Virgin 3941/promo/'91* $10

Mr Cab Driver (radio edit)
Virgin 3272/promo/silkscreened logo $6

Stand By My Woman edit & lp
Virgin 4099/promo/logo on black/'91 .... $5

Stop Draggin' Around/Light Skin Girl From
London/Stop Draggin' Around/Always
on the Run (last 2 live in Japan)
Virgin 4377/promo/custom
sticker/rear insert/'91 .... $12

The Sampler With Soul ep (It Ain't Over Til
Its Over/What Goes Around Comes
Around/Stand By My Woman + 2)
Virgin 3869/promo/logo on
purple/ps/'91 .... $15

What Goes Around Comes Around
Virgin 4274/promo/logo on tan/'91 .... $5

KREATOR

Betrayer *Epic 1687/promo/silkscreened logo* $4

People of the Lie/When the Sun Burns Red
Epic 2215/promo/
silkscreened/rear insert/'90 .... $4

KRIS KROSS

I Missed the Bus 3 versions/The Way of the
Rhyme (live) *Columbia 4761/promo/ps* .. $7

It's A Shame lp/watch your back mix/
playin' the game mix/instrumental
Ruff House 4914/promo/ps/'92 .... $7

Jump 4 versions *Ruffhouse 44K 74193/*
stock/ps/'92 .... $5

Jump edit/extended/instrumental
Columbia 74197/promo/ps/'92 .... $7

Warm It Up dupri's mix/lp/butcher mix
Ruff House 74376/promo/ps/'92 .... $7

KRUSH

Let's Get Together 4 versions
Perspective 31458 8058/promo/
silkscreened pic/'92 .... $6

KWS

Please Don't Go 4 versions/Different Man
afternoon of rhino mix
Next Plateau 50187/promo/'92 .... $5

KYLE, JAIME

Ragged Heart *Atco 4544/promo/ps/'92* $4

KYPER

Conceited (3 versions)
Atlantic 3631/promo/rear insert/'90 .... $4

Spin the Bottle 3 versions *Atlantic 10057/*
promo/silkscreened/
rear insert/custom sticker/'92 .... $4

KYUSS

Green Machine *Dali 8726/promo/silkscreened/*
custom sticker/'93 .... $4

Thong Song *Dali 8693/promo/*
silkscreened/rear insert/'92 .... $4

KYZE

Stomp 3:28/5:01/4:21 *WB 3719/promo/'89* $4

L'TRIMM

Cuttie Pie edit & lp *Atlantic 2564/*
promo/rear insert/'88 .... $4

Low Rider lp & acappella *Atlantic 4264/*
promo/silkscreened/rear insert/'91 .... $5

L. KAGE

My Heads on Fire *A&M 31458 8116/*
promo/ps/'93 .... $4

L.A. STYLE

James Brown is Dead 4 versions
Bounce IND 616.2/stock/ps/'92 .... $6

James Brown is Dead 9 versions
Arista 2387/promo/ps/'92 .... $8

L7

Everglade/Wargasm/Scrap/Mr Integrity
Slash 5371/promo/silkscreened/'92 .... $7

Lose Your Dignity ep (Pretend We're Dead/
Everglade/Sh*tlist/Fast and
Frightening + 2) all live *Slash 5871/*
promo/silkscreened pic/'92 .... $15

Pretend We're Dead
Slash 5518/promo/silkscreened/'92 .... $6

LA GUNS

Cuts ep (Night of the Cadillacs/Suffragette
City/Ain't the Same '92/Papa's Got a
Brand New Bag/Killer Mahari)
Polydor 314 517 623/stock/ps/
silkscreened/'92 .... $6

Holiday Foreplay (Dirty Luv/Some Lie 4 Love/
Rip and Tear/Sex Action - last 3
live/holiday greetings) *Polydor 601/*
promo/silkscreened/ps/'91 .... $12

I Wanna Be Your Man (3 vers.) *Vertigo 283/*
promo/silkscreened/rear insert/'90 .... $5

It's Over Now remix & lp
Polydor 603/promo/logo on red/ps $5

Kiss My Love Goodbye edit *Polydor 490/*
promo/silkscr/3D cover & glasses/'91 .... $8

Never Enough edit & lp
Vertigo 165/promo/neat silkscreen $5

Over the Edge edit & lp *Polydor 708/ promo/silkscreened/ps/'92* $5
Rip and Tear *Vertigo 111/promo/silkscreened/'89* $5
Some Lie 4 Love *Polydor 456/promo/silkscreened/ps* $5
The Ballad of Jayne *Vertigo 210/promo/ gatefold hardcover ps/silkscreened* $7

LA STYLE
I'm Raving 5 versions/Balloony 3 versions *Arista 12525/stock/ps/'93* $5

LA'S, THE
There She Goes *London 403/promo/ silkscreened/custom sticker/'91* $4
There She Goes *London 403/promo/ silkscreened/gatefold hardcover ps* $4
There She Goes 4 versions *London 547/promo/logo on white/'91* $5
Timeless Melody/There She Goes/I Can't Sleep (all live)/I Can't Sleep (lp versions) *London 564/promo/logo on white* $8

LAAZ ROCKIT
Leatherface *Enigma 242/promo/ custom sticker/'89* $4

LABELLE, PATTI
All Right Now 4 versions *MCA 54541/stock/ps/'92* $6
All Right Now 7 versions *MCA 2434/promo/ps/'92* $8
All Right Now 7 versions *MCA 2535/promo/rear insert/'92* $8
Feels Like Another One 7 versions *MCA 1672/promo/'91* $6
I Can't Complain 4:08 & 5:08 *MCA 18298/ promo/custom sticker/'90* $5
I Don't Like Goodbyes-Over the Rainbow/ If Only You Knew/Wind Beneath My Wings (all from "Patti Labelle Live") *MCA 2555/promo/rear insert/'93* $7
If You Asked Me To (3:56) *MCA 17769/promo/ custom sticker/'89* $5
Somebody Loves You Baby *MCA 2072/promo/ps/'91* $6
Twas Love/Reason For the Season *MCA 1120/promo/logo on blue/ rear insert/'90* $6
We Haven't Finished Yet *Virgin 3875/promo/ silkscreened logo on red/'91* $5
When You Love Somebody edit & lp *MCA 2358/promo/ps/'92* $5
When You've Been Blessed (Feels Like Heaven) remix 7"/remix lp/suite/instrumental *MCA 2157/promo/rear insert/'92* $5
Yo Mister 7"/radio edit/12" *MCA 18024/promo/'89* $6

LACE
Why It Gotta Be Like That (5 versions) *Wing 182/promo/silkscreened/'90* $4

LADY SOUL
Don't Forget About Me edit & lp *Boston International 8567/promo/ silkscreened/rear insert/'92* $4

LAGRENE, BIRELI
Made in France (cd versions) *Blue Note 79630/promo/silkscreened/ custom sticker/'91* $4

LAIBACH
Sympathy For the Devil (6 versions) *Restless 71404/ps/stock/'88* $6

LAINE, PAUL
Dorianna edit & lp *Elektra 8158/promo/ silkscreened logo on yellow/'90* $4
We Are the Young edit *Elektra 8186/promo/ silkscreened logo/'90* $4

LAING, SHONA
Fear of Falling/Soviet Snow *Epic 4834/ promo/logo on black/ps/'92* $4
Glad I'm Not a Kennedy/Soviet Union/Bishop *TVT 2472/stock/3"/3x6 ps/'89* $10

LAKESIDE
I Want to Hold Your Hand 7" edit & instrum. *Epic 74004/promo/ps/'89* $4
Party Patrol 5 versions *Solar 2213/ promo/logo on red/rear insert/'90* $5

LAMOND, GEORGE & BRENDA K STARR
No Matter What *Epic 73603/promo/ps/'90* $4

LANDRETH, SONNY
When You're Away *Praxis 17080/promo/ silkscreened pic/ps/cust.sticker/'92* $4

LANG, K.D.
Constant Craving edit & lp *Sire 5400/promo/silkscreened pic/'92* $6
Making of Shadowland (interview & music) *Sire 3120/promo/ps/'88* $15
Miss Chatelaine *Sire 6002/promo/'92* $6
Miss Chatelaine 4 versions/Outside Myself *Sire 40792/stock/gatefold hardcover ps/'93* $7
Pullin' Back the Reins (remix) *Sire 3907/promo/'89* $6
Ridin' the Rails *Sire 4098/promo/ "Dick Tracy" ps/'90* $7
The Mind of Love *Sire 5806/promo/'92* $6
Trail of Broken Hearts (video version) *Sire 3747/promo/'89* $6

LANOIS, DANIEL
Acadie 12 tracks *Opal 25969/stock with dj only silkscreened/ps/'89* $15
Jolie Louise *WB 3948/promo/'89* $4
Lotta Love to Give/interview (7:56) *WB 6127/promo/'93* $8
Still Water remix/live/lp *Opal 3942/ promo/rear insert/'89* $8
The Maker *WB 3760/promo/'89* $4
The Messenger edit & lp/Rain Weather/ Elle Est Bonne Et Belle/ Another Silver Morning *WB 6316/promo/'93* $7

LANZ, DAVID
A Whiter Shade of Pale edit lp & special solo piano version (non lp) with intros *Narada Lotus 17611/promo/ps/'88* $6
Dark Horse/Nights in White Satin/Vesuvius/ The Crane + 2 *Narada 18363/promo/ logo on black/rear insert/'90* $6

LARIN, LIZ
The Color Red *Atlantic 4919/promo/ silkscreened/rear insert/'93* $4

LASALLE, DENISE
Don't Jump My Pony *Malaco 2181/promo/silkscreened/'92* $4

LAST CRACK
Energy Mind/My Burning Time *Road Racer 30/ promo/silkscreened pic/ps/'91* $4

LAST GENTLEMEN
Miss Sympathy radio remix & dub *Zoo 17059/ promo/silkscreened/ps/'92* $4

LATIN ALLIANCE
Lowrider (on the Boulevard) *Virgin 4044/ promo/silkscreened/WAR/'91* $4
With My House 4 versions *Third Stone 5070/ promo/silkscreened/ps/'93* $5

LATOUR
Allen's Got a New Hi Fi lp & picchiotti mix *Smash 489/promo/silkscreened/'91* $4
Cold 3 versions/Blue *Smash 865 525/ stock/ps/silkscreened/'92* $5
Craziaskowboi 2 versions *Smash 009/promo/ silkscreened/rear insert/'93* $5
People Are Still Having Sex radio edit *Smash 406/promo/ps/'91* $5

LAUPER, CYNDI
A Night to Remember *Epic 73031/promo/'89* $6
Hole in My Heart/Boy Blue (live) *Epic 34K 07940/stock/3"/'88* $8
I Drove All Night *Epic 1564/promo/ pic of Cyndi silkscreened/'89* $7
I Gotta Hole in My Heart *Epic 1194/promo/ps/'88* $6
My First Night Without You *Epic 1640/promo/silkscreened Cyndi* $8
Who Let in the Rain *Epic 74942/promo/ps/'93* $5

LAVA HAY
Baby/My Friend *Polydor 303/promo/ gatefold hardcover/silkscreened/'90* $4
Baby/My Friend/Midnight Sun *Nettwerk 3048/stock/ps/'90* $4
Won't Matter *Polydor 219/promo/silkcreened* $4

LAW, JOHNNY
Too Weak to Fight *Metal Blade 4754/promo* $4

LAW, THE
Laying Down the Law *Atlantic 3718/promo/ps/'91* $4
Miss You in a Heartbeat *Atlantic 3933/promo/ gatefold hardcover ps/'91* $4
Profiled interview *Atlantic 3880/promo/ps* $10

LAWRENCE, JOEY
Nothin' My Love Can't Fix 5 versions *Impact 2498/promo/rear insert/'93* $4
Stay Forever *Impact 2674/promo/ps/'93* $4
Stay Forever 4 versions *Impact 2748/ promo/rear insert/'93* $4

LAWRENCE, TRACY
Can't Break It To My ... *Atlantic 5107/promo* $4

LAZY, DOUG
Let It Roll 4:10/5:40 *Atlantic 2891/ promo/rear insert/'89* $4

LEADERS OF THE NEW SCHOOL
Case of the PTA lp & instrumental *Elektra 8299/promo/ps/'91* $4

LEARY, DENIS
Asshole remix & lp *A&M 31458 0150/ promo/silkscreened pic/ps/'93* $6
Asshole/Rehab *A&M 31458 0142/promo/ silkscreened/custom sticker/'93* $5

LEATHERWOLF
Hideaway *Island 2642/promo/ps/'89* $4

LED ZEPPELIN
Baby Come on Home *Atlantic 5255/promo/ps/ silkscreened pic/'93* $12
Profiled (interview) *Atlantic 3629/promo/ps/'90* $25
Remasters 26 songs & interview *Atlantic 82371/stock/ps/3 cds/'90* $25
Stairway to Heaven *Atlantic 4424/promo/ picture folder with pop-up zeppelin* $15
Travelling Riverside Blues *Atlantic 3627/ promo/logo on black/ps/'90* $15

LEE, BRENDA
Your One and Only *WB 4702/promo/'91* $4

LEEDS, ERIC
Little Rock *Paisley Park 4947/promo/'91* $4
The Dopamine Rush edit & lp
Paisley Park 4705/promo/
prod & composed by PRINCE/'91 .... $5
Woman in Chains edit
Paisley Park 6157/promo/'93 .... $4

LEEK, ANDY
Please Please edit/lp *Atlantic 2359/promo* $4

LEFT WING FASCISTS
K Mart Shopper *Cellar Door 90076/promo/*
silkscreened/'91 .... $4

LEILA K
Got to Get single/extended/swemix
Arista 9932/promo/silkscreened/ps $5

LEMANS, TONY
Forever More edit & lp
Paisley Park 3895/promo/'89 .... $4
Higher That High *Paisley Park 3585/promo* $4
Higher That High (6 versions)
Paisley Park 3748/promo/
silkscreened pic/'89 .... $8

LEMONHEADS
Confetti remix & acoustic *Atlantic 4743/*
promo/silkscreened/rear insert/'92 .... $5
Favorite Spanish Dishes ep (Different
Drum/Paint/Ride With Me/Step By
Step/Skulls) *Atlantic 86088/stock/*
gatefold hardcover ps/'91 .... $5
Half the Time *Atlantic 3500/promo/ps/'90* $4
It's a Shame About Ray *Atlantic 4587/*
promo/logo on yellow/rear insert/'92 .... $5
It's a Shame About Ray/Rudderless/Ceiling Fan
in My Spoon *Atlantic 4581/promo/*
logo on white/rear insert/'92 .... $6
Mrs. Robinson *Atlantic 4862/promo/ps/*
silkscreened/'92 .... $4

LENNON, JOHN
Jealous Guy *Capitol 79417/promo/ps/*
silkscreened logo on white/'88 .... $10

LENNON, JULIAN
Help Yourself remix edit & remix
Atlantic 4488/promo/ps/'91 .... $5
Listen edit & lp *Atlantic 4151/promo/ps/'91* $5
Mother Mary edit & lp *Atlantic 2910/*
promo/rear insert/'89 .... $5
Now, You're in Heaven
Atlantic 2653/promo/ps/'89 .... $5
Saltwater edit/lp/spanish
Atlantic 4114/promo/silkscreened $8
Saltwater lp & edit *Atlantic 4113/promo/*
gatefold hardcover diecut
ps/silkscreened/'91 .... $6
You're the One edit & lp
Atlantic 2741/promo/ps/'89 .... $5

LENNON, MARK
A Wonderful Life *A&M 17667/promo/*
"Scrooged" ps/'88 .... $4

LENNOX, ANNIE
Little Bird single remix & edit
Arista 2508/promo/ps/'92 .... $6
Love Song For a Vampire *Arista 2507/promo/*
silkscreened/rear insert/'92 .... $6
Walking on Broken Glass single & lp
Arista 2452/promo/logo on blue/ps $6
Why *Arista 2419/promo/logo on black/ps/'92* $6

LENNOX, ANNIE & AL GREEN
Put A Little Love in Your Heart 7" mix &
12" vocal mix *A&M 17645/promo/*
"Scrooged" ps/'88 .... $8

LETTAU, KEVYN
An Acoustic Sampler (Spring/Forever Lover
and Friend - both live & lp)
JVC 016/promo/rear insert/'93 .... $7

LEVEL 42
Guaranteed edit & lp *RCA 62178/*
promo/logo on black/rear insert/'91 .... $7
Heaven in My Hands *Polydor 28/promo/ps/'88* $6
Leaving Me Now *Polydor 172/promo/*
silkscreened logo/'89 .... $6
Tracie (7" remix) *Polydor 42/promo/ps/'89* $6

LEVELLERS
Fifteen Years/Hard Fight acoustic/
The Devil Went Down to Georgia
Elektra 8680/promo/silkscreened/ps $5

One Way remix edit *Elektra 8572/promo/ ps/logo on yellow/'92* $4

LEVELLERS/ROBIN HOLCOMB

One Way/Far From Home/World Freak Show (live)/When Was the Last Time/ When I Stop Crying/Deliver Me *Elektra 8597/promo/gatefold hardcover package/2 cds/'92* $12

LEVERT

ABC - 123 pop edit/radio edit/lp *Atlantic 5030/promo/ps/'93* $6
Do the Thangs edit & lp *Atlantic 5159/promo/ps/'93* $5
Give a Little Love 5 versions *Atlantic 3990/promo/rear insert/'90* $6
Good Ol' Days edit/remix/lp *Atlantic 4947/promo* $5
Rope a Dope Style 6 versions *Atlantic 3563/ promo/logo on yellow/rear insert/'90* $6

LEVERT, GERALD

Baby Hold On To Me edit/radio/lp *Eastwest 4333/promo/ps/'91* $4
Can U Handle It remix edit & remix *Eastwest 4710/promo* $4
Can You Handle It remix edit & remix *Eastwest 4698/promo/silkscreened/ps* $4
School Me 4 vers *Eastwest 4496/promo* $5

LEWIS, EPHRAIM

Drowning In Your Eyes WYRO edit *Elektra 8656/promo/logo on white/'92* $4
It Can't Be Forever single vers. & single remix *Elektra 8560/promo/logo on gold/'92* $4
It Can't Be Forever single vers. & single remix *Elektra 8580/promo/logo on gold/ps* $4

LEWIS, HUEY

Build Me Up *EMI 04776/promo/'91* $4
Couple Days Off aor, lp, edit *EMI 04752/promo/ps/'91* $6
He Don't Know *EMI 4807/promo/ps/'91* $5
Perfect World *Chrysalis 1165/promo/'88* $4
It Hit Me Like a Hammer lp/single/a-c mix *EMI 04777/promo/silkscreened/ps* $6

LEWIS, JERRY LEE

Great Balls of Fire/Breathless *Polydor 76/promo/ps/'89* $6
It Was the Whiskey Talkin' 2 versions *Sire 4077/promo/"Dick Tracy" ps* $6

LEWIS, RAMSEY

Eye on You 4 versions *Columbia 1747/promo/ps/'89* $5
People Make the World Go Round *GRP 5103/promo/ps/'93* $4

LEWIS, SHIRLE

You Can't Hide (7 versions) *A&M 18001/ promo/silkscreened logo/'89* $5

LFO

Love is the Message beware of bass remix & lp/ Tan Ta Ra moby remix & lp *Tommy Boy 501/stock/ps/'91* $5
We Are Back 2 versions/LFO 2 versions/ We Are Happy *Tommy Boy 994/promo/'91* $4

LIA

Tell Me It's Not Too Late (4 versions) *Virgin 2453/promo/silkscreened/'88* $4

LIEBERT, OTTMAR

Poets & Angels (15 tracks) *Higher Octave 7030/promo/ oversized "greeting card" ps/inserts* $12

LIFE SEX & DEATH

Tank *Reprise 5596/promo/'92* $4
Tank/Jawohl Asshole/F*ckin' Sh*t Ass/ Big Black Bush *Reprise 5548/promo* $6
Telephone Call lp & live/Fuckin' Shit Ass/ Tank (last 2 live) *Reprise 6149/promo/ silkscreened/rear insert/'93* $6

LIGHTER SHADE OF BROWN

Spill the Rhyme radio & extended/ Spill the Wine muggs wine mix *Pump 19105/promo/ps/silkscreened* $4

LIGHTNING SEEDS, THE

All I Want 3:01 & 4:29 *MCA 18447/promo/ silkscreened purple/rear insert/'90* $4
All I Want 3:01 & 6:11 *MCA 1018/promo/rear insert/'90* $4
Blowing Bubbles *MCA 2190/promo/ps/'92* $4
Joy remix & bonus mix *MCA 1148/promo/ silkscreened logo on white/ rear insert/'90* $4
Pure *MCA 18265/promo/ps/'90* $4
Sense *MCA 2278/promo/ps/'92* $4
Sense/The Life of Riley (radio mix)/ Flaming Sword/Lucifer Sam *MCA 54431/stock/ps/'92* $5
Sweet Dreams/Hang onto a Dream/ Flaming Sword *MCA 1105/ promo/logo on blue/ps/'90* $6
The Life of Riley *MCA 1584/promo/'92* $4

LIKKLE WICKED

Perfidia lp & instrm./Mi Pistol *Luke 467/promo/'93* $4

LIL LOUIS & THE WORLD

Club Lonely 7 versions *Epic 49K 74282/ stock/ps/custom sticker/'92* $4

LILAC TIME, THE
American Eyes electric & acoustic
Fontana 149/promo/silkscreened/'89 .... $5

LILLIAN AXE
True Believer *IRS 67081/promo/ silkscreened logo/'91* $4

LIMBOMANIACS
Butt Funkin' edit & lp
In Effect 0619/promo/ps $4

LINCOLN, ABBEY
Devil's Got Your Tongue ep (The Music is the Magic/A Child is Born/People in Me)
Verve ABY-2/promo/silkscreened pic/trifold hardcover ps/'93 .... $5
You Gotta Pay the Band 10 tracks
Verve LIN 2/promo/ color silkscreened pic/ps/'91 .... $10

LINDEN, HAL
Meet Me at Jacks *JP 0001/promo/ silkscreened pic/ps/'93* $5

LINDLEY, DAVID
Never Knew Her/Papa Was a Rolling Stone
Elektra 8022/promo/'88 .... $6

LINEAR
Sending All My Love radio mix/hot radio mix/ 1990 club mix *Atlantic 3221/ promo/rear insert/'90* $5
Something Going On (5 versions)
Atlantic 3559/promo/ps/'90 .... $5

LINS, IVAN
Love Dance *Reprise 3910/promo/'89* $4
You Moved Me to .. *Reprise 3527/promo/'89* $4
You Moved Me to This/Whos in Love Here/ Marlena *Reprise 3457/promo/ silkscreened pic/'89* $5

LIONS & GHOSTS
Arson in Toyland *EMI 4248/promo/ silkscreened green with logo/ '89/rear insert* $4
Too Shy *EMI 04363/promo/silkscreened/ rear insert/'89* $4

LIQUID JESUS
Better or Worse/The Light/7 and 7 Is
MCA 2001/promo/rear insert/'91 .... $5

LISA LISA & CULT JAM
Forever *Columbia 74096/promo/ps/'91* $4
Go For Yours 7" & lp & FF Hole in One mix & Instrum. *Columbia 1222/promo/ps/'88* $6
Just Git It Together (5 versions)
Columbia 1700/promo/ps/'89 .... $6
Kiss Your Tears Away
Columbia 1788/promo/ps/'89 .... $4
Let the Beat Him 'em 6 versions
Columbia 44K 73834/stock/ps/'91 .... $5
Let the Beat Hit em 6 versions
Columbia 4334/promo/ps/'91 .... $6
Little Jackie Wants to Be a Star lp & edit/ Star/Jackies Theme
Columbia 1500/promo/ps/'89 .... $6
Someone to Love Me For Me/Someone (full Force Harmony)/Spanish Fly 8:22
Columbia 2835/promo/ps/'87 .... $8
Where Were You When I Needed You (edit)
Columbia 74010/promo/ps/'91 .... $6

LITTLE AMERICA
Where Were You *Geffen 3430/promo/ps/'89* $4

LITTLE ANGELS
From the Start *DGC 4151/promo/ gatefold hardcover ps/'90* $4
Kickin' Up Dust *Polydor 202/promo/ silkscreened/'89* $4
Young Gods radio edit *Polydor 610/promo/ logo & devil character silkscreened/'91* $4

LITTLE CAESAR
Chain of Fools (3 versions) *WB 4102/promo/ silkscreened/fold out, pop up hardcover ps/'90* $5
Chain of Fools CHR edit/hit groove edit *DGC 4105/promo/silkscreened logo on blue/ps/'90* $4
From the Start *DGC 4151/promo/ gatefold hardcover ps/'90* $4
In Your Arms *CHR remix & lp DGC 4180/promo/ps/'91* $4
In Your Arms *CHR remix & lp DGC 4202/promo/'90* $4
Name Your Poison/Tastes Good to Me/ God's Creation/Tears Don't Lie
Metal Blade 72418/stock/ps/'89 .... $5
Selftitled (12 songs) *DGC 24288/promo/ gatefold pop up hardcover/'90* $15
Slow Ride edit & lp *DGC 4442/promo/ps/'92* $4
Stand Up *DGC 4424/promo/silkscreened/ps* $4

LITTLE CHARLIE & THE NIGHTCATS
The Big Break/Dont Do It/Thats OK + 1
Alligator 11/promo/silkscreened/'89 .... $4

LITTLE FEAT
Fast & Furious *Morgan Creek 0008/promo/'91* $4
Hate to Lose Your Lovin'
WB 3180/promo/ps/'88 .... $5
Long Time Till I Get Over You
WB 3297/promo/ps/'88 .... $5
Loved and Lied to *Morgan Creek 0026/ promo/silkscreened/rear insert/'91* $4
One Clear Moment *WB 3296/promo/ps/'88* $5
One Clear Moment (edit) *WB 3410/promo/'88* $4

Quicksand & Lies edit & lp *Morgan Creek 0025/ promo/"White Sands" movie ps/ silkscreened/'92* $5
Shake Me Up edit & lp *Morgan Creek 0005/ promo/silkscreened/ps/'91* $5
Texas Twister *WB 4022/promo/'90* $4
That's Her, She's Mine *WB 4465/promo/rear insert/'90* $4
Things Happen edit & lp *Morgan Creek 0007/ promo/silkscreened/ps/'91* $4
Things Happen/Loved and Lied To/Fast & Furious/Oh Atlanta/Rocket in My Pocket *Morgan Creek 0015/ promo/ps/silkscreened/'92* $10
Waiting For Columbus radio show *In the Studio 114/promo/cue sheet/ hosted by Bill Payne & Paul Barrere* $25
Woman in Love *WB 4307/promo/rear insert* $4

LITTLE RICHARD

Good Golly Miss Molly Little Richard/ John Goodman *Polydor 399/promo/ silkscreened/ps/'91* $5
Grand Slam *Grudge 4758/promo/ silkscreened/'89* $5
Tutti Frutti/Good Golly Miss Molly + 2 *Rhino 73014/stock/3"/ps/'88* $5

LITTLE RIVER BAND

If I Get Lucky edit & lp *MCA 18079/promo* $4
Listen to Your Heart *MCA 17894/promo/ custom sticker/'89* $4
Love is a Bridge *MCA 17576/promo/ps/'88* $4
Worldwide Love ac versions *Curb 057/promo/ logo silkscreened/rear insert/'91* $4

LITTLE TEXAS

First Time For Everything *WB 5293/promo* $4
Some Guys Have All the.. *WB 4967/promo/'91* ... $4

LITTLE VILLAGE

Dont Go Away Mad *Reprise 5533/promo/ JOHN HIATT, RY COODER, NICK LOWE/'92* $5
She Runs Hot *Reprise 5228/promo/ silkscreened/ps/JOHN HIATT, RY COODER, NICK LOWE, more/'92* $4
Solar Sex Panel *Reprise 5222/promo/ JOHN HIATT, RY COODER, NICK LOWE/'92* $5

LIVE

Four Songs ep (Operation Spirit/ Good Pain/Heaven Wore a Shirt/ Negation) *Radioactive 54236/ stock/ps/prod.by Jerry Harrison/'91* $5
Mirror Sing *Radioactive 2320/promo/ rear insert/'91* $4
Operation Spirit *Radioactive 2088/promo/ps/'91* $4
Pain Lies on the Riverside edit & lp *Radioactive 2089/promo/ps/'92* $6
The Beauty of Gray (edit & live)/Good Pain/ Pain Lies on Riverside/Operation Spirit.. (last 3 live) *Radioactive 54442/stock/ps/'92* $5

LIVIN' LARGE

Livin' Large (4 versions) *Virgin 3029/promo/silkscreened/'89* $4

LIVING COLOUR

Auslander 5 versions/17 Days *Epic 74955/stock/ps/custom sticker* $5
Bi edit & lp/Middle Man/Auslander (last 2 live 4/24/93) *Epic 5308/promo/rear insert/'93* $8
Biscuits ep (Talking Loud & Sayin' Nothing/ Desperate People (live)/Love & Happiness/Memories Can't Wait (live)/Burning of the Midnight Lamp/ Money Talks) *Epic 4098/promo/ silkscreened/ps/'91* $12
Cult of Personality *Epic 1473/promo/ logo on black/rear insert/'89* $6
Elvis is Dead/Memories Can't Wait (live)/ Love and Happiness *Epic 2237/ promo/silkscreened/rear insert/'90* $8
Funny Vibe (remix 4:59) *Epic 73010/promo/ silkscreened logo on yellow/'89* $6
Glamour Boys lp & live/Whats Your Favorite Color (medley - live - 13:52) *Epic 1746/promo/silkscreened tour dates on purple/'88* $10
Leave It Alone/17 Days *Epic 4952/promo/silkscreened/ps/'93* $5
Love Rears Its Ugly Head (2 versions)/ Elvis is Dead (2 versions)/ Zans is Dead dub *Epic 49K 73677/ stock/ps/custom sticker/'91* $6
Love Rears Its Ugly Head (3 versions) *Epic 73660/promo/ silkscreened/rear insert/'90* $6
Nothingness lp/radio/acoustic *Epic 5151/promo/ps/'93* $8
Open Letter 5:30 & 4:46/Broken Hearts/ Cult of Personality/Should I Stay of Should I Go (last 3 live) *Epic 1491/promo/ps/'88* $12
Open Letter (To a Landlord) 4:46/5:30 *Epic 1636/promo/silkscreened/'88* $6
Open Letter (To a Landlord) 5:05/4:19 *Epic 1685/promo/silkscreened/'88* $6
Pride/Middle Man (live)/Sailin' On *Epic 2241/promo/silkscreened/'90* $6
Solace of You *Epic 73800/promo/ logo/rear insert/'90* $5
Time's Up (12 tracks - banded) *Epic 2171/promo/ps/'90* $15
Time's Up (15 tracks) *Epic 2151/promo/ silkscreened/tri fold hardcover/'90* $15

Type edit & lp *Epic 2146/promo/ps/'90* $5
Type edit & lp/Final Solution/Sailin' On (live)
Epic 2147/promo/ps/'90 .... $7

LIVING IN A BOX
Blow the House Down 4:02/7:08/6:22
Chrysalis 23364/promo/ custom sticker/'89 .... $5
Room in Your Heart new mix & lp
Chrysalis 23420/promo/rear insert $5

LL COOL J
6 Minutes of Pleasure radio remix/lp edit
Def Jam 73820/promo/ps/'91 .... $6
Around the Way Girl lp vers & untouch. remix
Def Jam 73609/promo/ps/'90 .... $6
Around the Way Girl (3 vers.)/Murdergram - Live *Def Jam 44K 73610/stock/ps* $6
Go Cut Creator Go/Kanday
Def Jam 2836/promo/ps/'87 .... $8
Going Back to Cali 7" & lp
Def Jam 2922/promo/ps/'87 .... $6
How I'm Comin' lp/short/instrumental
Def Jam 74811/promo/ps/ logo on red & black/'93 .... $6
I'm That Type of Guy 3:23/5:16
Def Jam 1605/promo/ps/'89 .... $6
Jingling Baby 5:07/4:16
Def Jam 73207/promo/ps/'90 .... $6
Mama Said Knock You Out orig.recipe/hot mix short/7 AM mix/for steering pleasure
Def Jam 73706/promo/ps/'91 .... $6
One Shot at Love *Def Jam 1806/promo/ps/ silkscreened logo on green/'89* $5
Pink Cookies in a Plastic Bag.. 3 versions/ Back Seat (Of My Jeep
Def Jam 74984/promo/silkscreened $6
Strictly Business 4 versions
MCA 2012/promo/ps/'91 .... $6
The Boomin' System (3 versions)
Def Jam 73457/promo/ps/'90 .... $6
To Da Break of Dawn (4 versions)
Motown 18376/promo/'90 .... $6

LLOYD, CHARLES
Notes From Big Sur ep (Sam Song/When Miss Jessye Sings/Sister)
ECM CHARLES 2/promo/ silkscreened/gatefold hardcover ps $4

LO-KEY
Attention: The Shawanda Story 6 versions
Perspective 28968 1705/promo/ logo on black/ps/'91 .... $6
Hey There Pretty Lady 5 versions
Perspective 31458 8151/promo/ logo on green/ps/'92 .... $5
I Got a Thang 4 Ya!
Perspective/promo/silkscreened pic $5
I Got a Thang 4 Ya! 3 versions
Perspective 28968 1712/promo/ silkscreened/ps/'92 .... $5
I Got a Thang 4 Ya! edit/extended/instrum.
Perspective 31458 8076/promo/ custom sticker/logo on green/'92 .... $5
Sweet on U 5 versions
Perspective 31458 8081/promo/ps $5

LOCK UP
24 Hour Man (2 versions)
Geffen 4167/promo/ps/'90 .... $4
Nothing New *Geffen 4004/promo/ gatefold ps/'90* $4

LOFGREN, NILS
Drunken Driver single & lp/Crooked Line ext.
Ryko 1029/stock/ps/'92 .... $5
Just a Little single versions/No Mercy/ Across the Tracks (last 2 live)
Ryko 1026/stock/ps/'92 .... $5
Trouble's Back/Keith Don't Go/Just a Little
Ryko 1022/stock/ps/'91 .... $5
Valentine edit & lp *Ryko 9014/promo/ ps/silkscreened on white/ SPRINGSTEEN/'90* $7

LOGAN, ANDREW
Love Can Be Enough edit/lp/edit remix
Motown 374631085/promo/ps/'92 .... $4

LOGGINS, KENNY
Conviction of Heart radio edit 1/radio edit 2/lp
Columbia 74029/promo/ps/'91 .... $5
If You Believe *Columbia 74320/promo* $4
Nobody's Fool *Columbia 1205/promo/ silkscreened/'88* $4
Now Or Never edit & lp
Columbia 4810/promo/rear insert/'92 .... $4
The Real Thing single & lp
Columbia 74186/promo/ps/'91 .... $4

LONDON BOYS
London Nights 7", extended & instrumental
Atlantic 2972/promo/rear insert/'89 .... $4

LONDON QUIREBOYS
7 O'Clock *Capitol 79016/promo/ silkscreened/ps/'90* $4
7 O'Clock *Capitol 79016/promo/silkscreened/ ps/special oversize hardcover package/ booklet/ribbons/'90* $10
7 O'Clock *Capitol 79910/promo/rear insert* $4
Hey You *Capitol 79271/promo/ silkscreened logo on blue/'90* $4
I Don't Love You Anymore edit & lp
Capitol 79145/promo/silkscreened $4

LONDONBEAT
A Better Love *Radioactive 1397/promo/'90* $4

I've Been Thinking About You lp/c'est wot mix/ def 12" mix *MCA 1230/promo/'90* $8
I've Been Thinking About You (4 versions) *Anxious 1377/promo/rear insert/'91* $8
No Woman No Cry chr & ac versions *Radioactive 1623/promo/'91* $4

LONESOME ROMEOS
Selftitled 10 tracks *Curb 77268/ps/ promo silkscreened on stock/'90* $10
U.S. Male *Curb 10533/promo/ custom sticker/'89* $4

LONGHOUSE
She Don't Wanna Go Home Tonight *WB 3115/promo/ps/'88* $4

LOOSE BRUCE & ARC MOE ROCK
Brick House 3 versions *Arista 2357/ promo/logo on green/ps/'91* $4

LOPEZ, DENISE
Don't You Wanna Be Mine (5 versions) *A&M 75021 7432/promo/ silkscreened logo on white/ps/'90* $4
If You Feel It 7" pop & 7" hot *A&M 17635/promo/silkscreened/'88* $4
Too Much Too Late edit & remix *A&M 17719/promo/silkscreened/'89* $4

LORAIN, A'ME
Follow My Heartbeat radio & dance *RCA 2637/promo/custom sticker/'90* $4
Whole Wide World 3:50/6:04/5:35/7:15 *RCA 9099/promo/rear insert/'90* $5

LORBER, JEFF
Coffee Clutch with Your Host Dave Koz trt: 30 min. *Verve 701/promo/ silkscreened/interview cd/'93* $12

LORDS OF ACID
I Must Increase My Bust 8 versions *Caroline 2525/stock/ps/silkscreened* $5
Rough Sex 3 versions/Take Control 2 versions *Caroline 2518/stock/ps/'92* $5
Take Control 4:42 & 3:31/Let's Get High *Caroline 2512/stock/ps/'91* $5

LORDS OF THE UNDERGROUND
Funky Child 3 versions *Pendulum 8682/ promo/logo on black/ps/'92* $4

LORENZ, TREY
Just to Be Close to You edit/soul convention hip hop/acappella *Epic 74934/ promo/silkscreened pic/ prod.by MARIAH CAREY/ps/'93* $6
Photograph of Mary 5 versions *Epic 74783/ promo/logo on blue/ps/'92* $6
Photograph of Mary speech remix *Epic 4939/promo/ps/logo on black* $5
Someone to Hold *Epic 74482/promo/ logo on white/ps/'92* $5
Someone to Hold/Find a Way *Epic 34K 74482/stock/ps/'92* $5

LORENZO
Let Me Show U single/extended/instrumental *Alpha International 79399/ promo/rear insert/'90* $6
Make Love 2 Me 5 versions *Alpha International 786/promo/ logo on brown/'92* $6
Real Love radio mix/extendedradio *Alpha International 698/ promo/logo on red/ps/'92* $6
Tik Tok single/ruff mix *Alpha International 79584/promo/ silkscreened/ps/'90* $6

LOS LOBOS
Beautiful Maria of My Soul *Elektra 8490/ promo/logo on blue/ps/'91* $4
Bertha edit & lp *Arista 2226/promo/ silkscreened/rear insert/'91* $4
Down on the Riverbed *Slash 4440/promo/ silkscreened pic/rear insert/'90* $6
Dream in Blue *Slash 5645/promo/ tour date back ps/'92* $4
I Can't Understand *Slash 4548/promo/rear insert/'90* $4
Jenny's Got a Pony *Slash 4443/promo/'90* $4
One Time One Night (remix & lp version) *Slash 2879/promo/ps* $5
Reva's House *Slash 5494/promo/'92* $4
The Wolf Pack/An AOR Sampler 6 tracks *Slash 6578/promo/'93* $12

LOST TRIBE
Letter to the Editor remix/T.A. the W./ Mofungo/Eargasm *WD 93-07/promo/ gatefold hardcover ps/ prod.by WALTER BECKER* $4

LOUD FLOWER
Heart To Heart 4 versions *Invasion 36007/stock/ps/'91* $4

LOUD SUGAR
Faith & Hope & Love hit radio edit & l *SBK 05428/promo/silkscreened/ps/'91* $4
Instant Karma Coffee House (3 versions) *SBK 05385/promo/gatefold hard cover ps/silkscreened/'91* $6

LOUDHOUSE
Super Soul Killer/Loudhouse edit *Virgin 4299/promo/'91* $4

LOUDNESS
A Lesson in Loudness (mini compilation (5 songs)
Atco 2916/promo/ps/'89 ....$12
Sleepless Nights studio/orig.studio/live
Atco 4119/promo/rear insert/'91 ....$7

LOUIE LOUIE
The Thought of It 5 versions
The Hardback Recording Co. 5909/ promo/logo on black/'92....................$5
The Thought of It 8 versions
The Hardback Recording Co. 40745/ promo/gatefold hardcover ps/stock...........$6

LOVE & ROCKETS
Jungle Law + 9 *Beggars Banquet 9715/ neat limited black can package/ silkscreened heart/stock/'89* $15
Mirror People '88 versions re-recorded & edit
RCA 6072/promo/rear insert/'88 ....$12
No Big Deal *RCA 9045/promo/'89* $6
No Big Deal 7" & 12" club mix
RCA 9045/promo/ps/'89 ....$8
Selftitled *Bigtime 9041/promo/10 song comp. (2 live - No New Tale to Tell & Ball of Confusion)/ps/'89* $18
So Alive *RCA 8908/promo/ps/'89* $6
Waiting For the Flood/Mirror People '88 versions re-recorded & edit
Beggars Banquet 6072/ promo/rear insert/'88....................$10

LOVE AND MONEY
Strange Kind of Love 7" & lp *Fontana 56/ promo/silkscreened/ps/'88* $4

LOVE DROPS
Feel 4 versions/Monster Sound 3 versions
WB 40186/stock/ gatefold hardcover ps/'91 ....$4
Super Hero 6 vers/Siento 2 versions
WB 40438/stock/ gatefold hardcover ps/'92 ....$4

LOVE TRACTOR
Crash *DB/silkscreened/promo*....................$5

LOVE, DARLENE
All Alone on Christmas
Fox 003/promo/silkscreened/ps/'92 ....$6
Hes Sure the Man I Love
Columbia 1259/promo/'88....................$5

LOVE, MONIE
Born 2 B.R.E.E.D. 6 versions *WB 40641/ stock/gatefold hardcover ps/'93* $4
Born 2 B.R.E.E.D. paisley park versions/radio/ hip hop *WB 5801/promo/rear insert*........$5
Down 2 Earth 3 versions *WB 4862/promo/'90* $5
In a Word or 2 *WB 6117/promo/'93* $4
In a Word or 2/Wheel of Fortune 3 vers.each
WB 40832/stock/ gatefold hardcover ps/'93 ....$5
It's a Shame (My Sister) (5 versions)
WB 4528/promo/rear insert/'90 ....$5
It's a Shame (My Sister) 3 versions/Race Against Reality *WB 21791/ stock/gatefold hardcover ps/'91* $5
Monie in the Middle *WB 4415/promo/ silkscreened pic/'90* $5
Monie in the Middle (8 versions)/Roots
WB 21737/stock/ gatefold hardcover ps/'90 ....$5

LOVE/HATE
Black Out in the Red Room
Columbia 2048/promo/ps/'90....................$4
Happy Hour *Columbia 4360/promo/ps/'92*.........$4
Wasted in America *Columbia 4529/promo/ logo on red/ps/'92* $4
Why Do You Think They Call It Dope broadcast vers. *Columbia 2143/promo/ps/'90* $4

LOVELESS, PATTY
Don't Toss Us Away *MCA 53477/ promo/silkscreened pic/'88* $6
Hurt Me Bad *MCA 54178/promo/ silkscreened color pic/rear insert/'91* $6
I'm That Kind of Girl *MCA 53977/promo/'90* $4
Jealous Bone *MCA 54271/promo/'91* $4
On Down the Line *MCA 79004/promo/ logo on black/rear insert/'90*....................$4

LOVEMONGERS, THE
Battle of Evermore/Love of the Common Man/ Papa Was a Rollin' Stone/Crazy on You
Capitol 15953/stock/ps/'93....................$5

LOVENOTES
Lithium ep (The Candy Butcher/A Thousand Things/Avalanche/Epiphany/Nirvana Twitch/Wrecking Crew)
Tripindicular/stock/ps/silkscreened $5

LOVERBOY
Too Hot edit & lp *Columbia 73066/promo/ps* $4

LOVETT, LYLE
Here He Is (15 tracks) *MCA 18455/promo/ ps/dj only sampler/'90* $15
Here I Am *MCA 17815/promo/ custom sticker/'89* $4
If I Had a Boat with & without Kiss my Ass
MCA 3002/promo/silkscreened pic $7
Nobody Knows Me *MCA 17841/promo/ custom sticker/'89* $5
North Dakota *Curb 2754/promo/rear insert*..........$4
She Makes Me Feel Good
Curb 2354/promo/ps/'92 ....$4
She's Already Made Up Her Mind
Curb 2166/promo/ps/'92 ....$4

Stand By Your Man
MCA 2617/promo/rear insert/'89 .... $5
You Can't Resist It re-recorded/M-O-N-E-Y remix/Once is Enough remix/If I Had a Boat/Simple Song
MCA 54153/stock/ps/'91 .... $5
You Can't Resist It single & lp
MCA 1357/promo/'91 .... $4
You've Been So Good Up to Now
Curb 2319/promo/ps/'92 .... $4

LOW POP SUICIDE

Kiss Your Lips 2 versions/Hey You! 16-track-demo *World Domination 79608/promo/silkscreened/custom sticker/'93* $5
My Way 3 vers./Hunger Smiles 16 track demo *World Domination 79689/promo/silkscreened/custom sticker/'93* $5

LOWE, NICK

All Men are Liars *Reprise 4057/promo/'90* $4
You Got the Look I .. *Reprise 3975/promo/'90* $4

LUCIEN, JON

Listen Love words & music *Mercury 411/promo/ps/lots of interview/'91* $12
Nothin' Lasts Forever edit & lp
Mercury 472/promo/ps/'91 .... $4
Sweet Control love edit & lp
Mercury 415/promo/ps/'91 .... $4

LUKE

I Wanna Rock clean versions *Luke 4397/promo/logo on yellow/rear insert/'92* $4

LULABOX

Full Blood ep (Ride On/Ivory Hill/Innocent Love/Gift alt.versions) *Radioactive 10703/stock/ps/silkscreened/'92* $5
I Believe 2 versions *Radioactive 2595/promo/logo on black/ps/'93* $4

LULU & BOBBY WOMACK

I'm Back For More 4 versions *SBK 04723/promo/logo on black/ps/'93* $7

LUNA

Anesthesia *Elektra 8632/promo/silkscreened pic/custom sticker/'92* $4
Slash Your Tires radio edit/radio eq *Elektra 8662/promo/silkscreened pic/custom sticker/'92* $4
Slide/Indian Summer/Ride Into the Sun/That's What You Always Say/Hey Sister demo *Elektra 61472/promo/silkscreened* $5

LUSH

De-Luxe (3 versions) *4AD 4662/promo/'90* $5
For Love *4AD 5299/promo/logo on black/'92* $4
Nothing Natural 2 versions/God's Gift/Monochrome *4AD Reprise 40231/stock/gatefold hardcover ps/'91* $5
Spooky 12 tracks *Reprise 26798/stock/ps/dj embossed velvet sleeve/'92* $15
Superblast remix & lp/Starlust/Fallin' in Love *Reprise 5471/promo/logo on blue/'92* $8
Sweetness and Light single & lp
Reprise 4568/promo/ps/'90 .... $4

LYNCH MOB

Dream Until Tomorrow fade & lp *Elektra 8616/promo/silkscreened logo/'92* $4
No Bed of Roses edit & lp *Elektra 8356/promo/silkscreened/'90* $4
River of Love *Elektra 8301/promo/ps/'91* $4
Tangled in the Web *Elektra 8558/promo/silkscreened/ps/'92* $4
Wicked Sensation edit & lp *Elektra 8243/promo/silkscreened logo on black/rear insert/'90* $4

LYNN, CHERYL

Everytime I Try to Say Goodbye (3 versions)
Virgin 2838/promo/silkcreened logo $6
Upset 3 versions
Virgin 3238/promo/silkscreened/'89 .... $6
Whatever It Takes edit, lp, instr. *Virgin 3036/promo/silkscreened logo/'89* $5

LYNNE, JEFF

Armchair Theatre (11 tracks) *Reprise 26184/stock/promo silkscreen/ps/'90* $15
Every Little Thing *Reprise 4088/promo/'90* $5
Lift Me Up *Reprise 4091/promo/rear insert* $4

LYNNE, SHELBY

Feelin' Kind of Lonely Tonight lp/dance *Morgan Creek 0034/promo/ps/silkscreened pic/'93* $6
The Hurtin' Side *Epic 1060/promo/silkscreened pic/rear insert/'89* $6
The Very First Lasting Love
Epic 73904/promo/rear insert/'91 .... $4

LYNYRD SKYNYRD

All I Can Do Is Write About It (acoustic)
MCA 1681/promo/'91 .... $8
Born to Run edit & lp *Atlantic 5051/promo* $5
Double Trouble/Free Bird *MCA 17823/promo/custom sticker/'89* $6
Good Lovin's Hard to Find/Outta Hell in My .. *Atlantic 4953/promo/silkscreened pic/ps/'93* $6
Pure & Simple *Atlantic 4240/promo/logo on white/rear insert/'91* $5
Ten From the Swamp (Sweet Home Alabama/All I Can Do Is Write About It acoustic/What's Your Name/I Aint the One demo + 6) *MCA 2033/promo/ps/'91* $15

LYNYRD SKYNYRD 1991
Keeping the Faith edit & lp *Atlantic 4117/ promo/silkscreened/rear insert/'91* $5

M & M
Get to Know Ya 4 versions *Atlantic 4691/ promo/logo on black/rear insert* $4

M.C. SHAN
It Dont Mean a Thing fade & lp *Cold Chillin' 3992/promo/'90* $4

MacAlpine

Eyes Of The World

MACALPINE
The World We Live In *Squawk 222/promo/silkscreened pic/'90* $4

MACCOLL, KIRSTY
All I Ever Wanted/All the Tears That I Cried *Charisma 067/promo/'91* $7
The Real MacColl ep (Tread Lightly/They Dont Know/A New England/Innocence - guilt mix + 1) *Charisma 3564/promo/silkscreened/ps/'90* $15
Walking Down Madison 5 versions *Charisma 96342/stock/ gatefold hardcover ps/'91* $5
Walking Down Madison edit *Charisma 062/promo/JOHNNY MARR/'91* $6

MACHINES OF LOVING GRACE
Rite of Shiva 3 versions/All I Really Need *Mammoth 0026/stock/ps/'91* $5

MACK, JACK
It Don't Bother Me *Voss 5004/promo/'90* $4

MAD COBRA
Flex 3 versions *Columbia 74373/promo/ps/'92* $5
Legacy classic radio/smoove groove/joker mix *Columbia 74917/promo/ps/'93* $5

MADKAP
Da Whole Kit and Kaboodle vocal & instrumental /Ph*ck What Ya Heard *Loud 62445/promo/rear insert/'93* $4

MADONNA
Bad Girl edit *Maverick 5888/promo/'92* $8
Bad Girl edit & extended/Fever 4 versions *Maverick 40793/stock/gatefold hardcover ps/custom sticker/'92* $5
Cherish fade & lp *Sire 3608/promo/'89* $10
Deeper and Deeper edit/dave's radio edit/ shep's deep makeover edit *Maverick 5896/promo/'92* $8
Erotic *Sire 5648/cd that came with book/ zip-lock tin foil sleeve/'93* $15
Erotica edit/lp/edit *Maverick 5665/promo/ silkscreened/rear insert/'92* $8
Erotica 7 versions *Maverick 40585/ gatefold hardcover ps/stock/'92* $5
Erotica lp/instrumental *Sire 18782/stock/ps/'92* $6
Express Yourself (4:30/4:50/7:54/6:20) *Sire 3541/promo/'89* $15
Hanky Panky *Sire 4304/promo/rear insert/'90* $8
Hanky Panky (2 versions)/More *Sire 21577/stock/ps/'90* $6
I'm Breathless (12 songs) *Sire 26209/ promo only silkscreen/ps/'90* $25
Justify My Love 4 versions/Express Yourself shep's 'spressin' himself remix *Sire 21820/stock/ gatefold hardcover ps/'90* $7
Justify My Love (5 versions) *Sire 4613/ promo/custom sticker/'90* $10
Keep It Together 4:35/4:45/7:50/7:20 *Sire 3791/promo/'89* $10
Like a Prayer 5:06/5:41/5:19/7:50/6:35 *Sire 3448/promo/ps/'89* $15
Like a Prayer 11 tracks *Sire 25844/stock/ promo only silkscreen design/ps/'89* $25
Oh Father (edit) *Sire 3798/promo/'89* $8

Rescue Me *Sire 4577/promo/'90* $8
Rescue Me (6 versions) *Sire 4710/promo/'90*.....$12
This Used to Be My Playground single/long versions/instrumental *Sire 5588/promo/'92* $12
Vogue 4 ver. *Sire 21513/stock/ps/'90* $8
Vogue/Like a Virgin *no label or #/promo/ ps/'90/for Q Sound promotion*................$15
You Can Dance 45 edits of remixes (7 tracks) *Sire 2892/promo/silkscreened/ps/'87*.....$25

MAESTRO FRESH WES

Another Funky Break vocal & instrumental *Polydor 649/promo/logo on white/ps/'92*......$4
Louie Rap/Louie Vocal Attack/ Louie Louie House Mix *Cypress 79069/ promo/silkscreened/'90*............................$4

MAGGIE'S FARM

Glory Road *JRS 807/promo/gatefold hardcover ps/silkscreened like record/'91*....$4
Change For Better/Dear Simone (special mix) *Capitol 79818/promo/ silkscreened/custom sticker/'91* $4
Dear Simone edit & AOR mix *Capitol 79817/ promo/silkscreened/custom sticker/'91*....$4
Its a Sin 7 vers. *Capitol 79634/promo/c ustom sticker/'90*......................................$4
Love & Tears edit & lp *Capitol 79327/promo/ silkscreened/rear insert/'90*.......................$4

MAGNOLIAS, THE

Hung Up On... ep (When Im Not/Hello or Goodbye remix/Way Out/Fathers and Sins/ Last Train to Clarksville/Stole Your Love) *Alias 31/stock/ps/'92*..............................$5

MAHAL, TAJ

Don't Call Us *Private Music 81000/ promo/logo on gold/rear insert/'91*............$4
Love Up/Take All the Time You Need/ Squat that Rabbit *Private 2086/promo/silkscreened/'91*........$6

MAHARRY, WENDY

All That I've Got edit & lp *A&M 17990/promo/silkscreened/'90*.........$4
California (edit) *A&M 75021 8103/promo/ silkscreened/ps/'90*...................................$4
How Do I Get Over You edit/lp/remix *A&M 75021 7335/promo/ps/'91*..............$5

MAHOGANY BLUE

Affair final versionswith rap/without/instrm *MCA 2673/promo/rear insert/'93*..............$4

MAIN ATTRACTION, THE

I Love You Baby/Sweet Harmony/You've Lost That Lovin' Feeling/Mama alt.take *Satin 1303/stock/gatefold hardcover ps/'92*..$5

MAIN INGREDIENT, THE

Nothings too Good For My Baby (3 versions) *Polydor 190/promo/silkscreened/'90*.........$5

MAJEK FASHEK

Spirit of Love/So Long/Majek Fashek in N.York *nterscope 4186/promo/ps/ prod.by LITTLE STEVEN/'91*...................$4

MALAIKA

Gotta Know (Your Name) 5 versions *A&M 31458 8135/promo/ps/'93*...............$6
Introducing ep (Gotta Know/Sugar Time/ Lead Me Into Temptation/ Easy to Love/This Will Be) *A&M 31458 8166/promo/gatefold hardcover ps/silkscreened/'93*.................$8
So Much Love 5 versions *A&M 31458 8034/ promo/silkscreened/'92*............................$6

MALCOLM X

Excerpts from Music, Speeches and Dialogue from the Historic 1972 Documentary Film (10 tracks) *WB 5943/promo/rear insert/'93*..............$10

MALLOY, MITCH

Anything at All *RCA 62197/promo/ silkscreened pic/ps/'91*.............................$4
Nobody Wins In This War lp & unplugged *RCA 62297/promo/ps/'92*..........................$5

MALMSTEEN, YNGWIE

Bedroom Eyes *Polydor 284/promo/silkscreened*...$5
Dragonfly *Elektra 8570/promo/logo on gold/custom sticker/'92*...................................$5
Live in Leningrad (6 tracks) *Polydor 126/ promo/silkscreened pic/'89*....................$12
Making Love edit & lp/Eclipse *Polydor 238/promo/silkscreened/'90*........$5
Making Love (extended guitar mix)/ Devil in Disguise/Eclipse *Polydor 237/promo/silkscreened/'90*........$6
Teaser single versions *Elektra 8514/ promo/logo on blue/ps/'92*.......................$5

MALONE, MICHELLE

Big Black Bag/interview *Arista 2043/promo/ps/'90*..........................$7
Live Building Fires Over Atlanta (5 tracks) *Arista 2155/promo/silkscreened/ps/'91*......$12

MANCHESTER, MELISSA

Walk on By *Polydor 130/promo/silkscreened*......$5

MANDRELL, BARBARA

I'll Leave Something Good Behind *Capitol 79475/promo/silkscreened/'90*.....$4

MANDY
Victim or Pleasure (3 versions)/
Say Its Love (remix)
Altantic 2649/promo/rear insert/'89 ....$4

MANHATTAN TRANSFER
A World Apart 3:29/3:42
Columbia 4239/promo/ps/'91 ....$5
The Offbeat of Avenues edit & lp/10 Minutes
Til the Savages Come/The Quietude (edit)
Columbia 4129/promo/ps/'91 ....$6

MANIC STREET PREACHERS
Slash n Burn *Columbia 4506/promo/ps/'92* $4
Slash n Burn/Motown Junk/Sorrow 16/
Ain't Goin Down *Columbia 657873/stock/*
gatefold hardcover ps/custom sticker/'92 ....$5
Stay Beautiful *Columbia 74195/promo/*
ps/logo on blue/'92 ....$4
Stay Beautiful/Motown Junk/Sorrow 16/
R.P.McMurphy/Star Lover
Columbia 44K 74036/stock/ps/'91 ....$5

MANIFESTO
Pattern 26/Afterthought/Cut & Dry
Eastwest 4965/promo/
silkscreened/ps/'93 ....$5

MANILOW, BARRY
Another Life *Arista 2473/promo/ps/'92* $6
Christmas Sampler (Jingle Bells/Because Its
Christmas/Joy to the World-Have Yourself../
Baby, It's Cold Outside) *Arista 2096/*
promo/logo on black/ps/'90 ....$15
Excerpts from the Complete Collection and
Then Some... ep (16 tracks)
Arista 2496/promo/ps/'92 ....$15
If You Remember Me *Arista 9948/promo/*
silkscreened logo on black/ps/'90 ....$6
Keep Each Other Warm
Arista 9838/promo/ps/'89 ....$8
Where or When *Arista 2386/promo/*
silkscreened/rear insert/'91 ....$6

MANITOBAS WILD KINGDOM
Fired Up *MCA 18180/promo/'90* $4
Haircut and Attitude remix & lp *MCA 18454/*
promo/silkscreened/rear insert/'90 ....$5
New York, New York edit & lp *MCA 18518/*
promo/rear insert/'90 ....$4
The Party Starts Now edit & lp
MCA 18347/promo/rear insert/'90 ....$4

MANN, AIMEE
I Should've Known 2 edits & lp
Imago 28048/promo/ps/'93 ....$5
Say Anything 3 versions/Jimmy Hoffa Jokes/
Baby Blue *Imago 28061/promo/*
rear insert/'93 ....$8

MANNHEIM STEAMROLLER
The Seven Metals of Alchemy
American Gramaphone 7771/promo/ps/'90 ....$6

MANNSFIELD, RODNEY
Wanna Make Luv 2 U 2 vers. *A&M 31458 8088/*
promo/silkscreened pic/ps/'93 ....$4

MANO NEGRA
King Kong Five 5:20 & 2:09/Soledad
Virgin 3212/promo/silkscreened logo/'90 ......$4
Rock and Roll Band (lp & live)/Rebel Spell/
Mad House *Virgin 3468/promo/silkscreened* $5

MANOWAR
Kills ep (8 tracks) *Atlantic 4858/*
promo/logo on black/ps/'92 ....$10

MANTRONIX
Don't Go Messin' With My Heart 8 versions
Capitol 79697/promo/rear insert/'91 ....$5
Got to Have Your Love (6 versions)
Capit.ol 79946/promo/silkscreened/'89 .....$5
Step to Me 4 versions *Capitol 79499/*
promo/logo on orange/ps/'91 ....$5
Take Your Time 7 versions *Capitol 79044/*
promo/logo on white/'90 ....$5

MANUFACTURE
Control Yourself/A Measured Response/
World Control/Many Machines (all remixes)
Nettwerk 13820/stock/ps/'90 ....$5

MANZANERA, PHIL
A Million Reasons Why
Agenda 747772/promo/ps/'91 ....$6

MARC V.
Let Them Stare *Elektra 8053/promo/'89* $4

MARCH ON
The Dream *Reprise 6421/promo/'93* $4

MARCY BROS, THE
You're Not Even Crying *WB 3761/promo/'89* $4

MARDONES, BENNY
I Never Really Loved You.. with & without
drum intro *Curb 10554/promo/'89* $4
I'll Be Good to You *Curb 10562/promo/ps/'89* $4

MARGITZA, RICK
Recess *Blue Note 79485/promo*
/silkscreened/rear insert/'90 ....$4

MARIE, TEENA
Here's Looking at You (6 versions) *Epic 73494/*
promo/silkscreened/rear insert/'90 ....$5
If I Were a Bell (3 vers.) *Epic 2236/promo/'90* $5
Just Us Two 5 versions *Epic 3049/*
promo/rear insert/'91 ....$5

Since Day One 5 versions *Epic 4082/ promo/rear insert/'91* $5
Work It 7"/12"/lp/instrumental/accapella *Epic 1133/promo/silkscreen/'88* $6

MARIENTHAL, ERIC
One Touch ep (Ouch/Walk Though the Fire/ That's the Way/Where Are You?) *GRP 5118/promo/gatefold hardcover ps/JEFF LORBER, more/'93* $5

MARILLION
Cover My Eyes *IRS 67084/promo/ silkscreened/'91* $4
Hooks in You *Capitol 79751/promo/ silkscreened logo on orange/'89* $6
The Uninvited Guest *Capitol 79922/promo/ silkscreened/rear insert/'89* $6

MARILLION/FISH
Credo 4:02 & 6:37/Poet's Moon *Polydor 728/promo/silkscreened/ps/'91* $5

MARK, MARKY
Gonna Have a Good Time 5 versions *Interscope 4895/promo/rear insert* $6
Gonna Have a Good Time edit/edit with solo/lp *Interscope 4885/promo/ps/logo on black/'92* $6
Wildside lp & radio *Interscope 4254/promo/ps/'91* $6

MARK, MARKY & L.HOLLOWAY
Good Vibrations/So What Chu Sayin' *I nterscope 4055/promo/silkscreened/ps/'91* $8

MARKIE, BIZ
Spring Again mix *Cold Chillin' 3911/promo/'89* $4

MARLEY MARL
Check the Mirror 6 versions/At the Drop of a Dime 3 versions *Cold Chillin' 40310/ stock/gatefold hardcover ps/'92* $5
The Symphony pt 2 radio remix *Cold Chillin' 4919/promo/'91* $4

MARLEY, BOB
Get Up Stand Up *Tuff Gong 6651/promo/rear insert/'91* $6
Iron Lion Zion 3:21/7:04 *Tuff Gong 6749/promo/ps/'92* $6
Iron Lion Zion 3:38/3:13/7:04 *Island 6762/ promo/custom sticker/'92* $6
Songs of Freedom 15 track sampler *Tuff Gong 6740/promo/ps/ 2 cds/custom sticker/'92* $25
Could You Be Loved *Tuff Gong 6624/ promo/rear insert/'90* $6

MARLEY, ZIGGY
All Love (KRS One mix & edit)/Lee & Molly (live) *Virgin 3472/promo/silkscreened logo/'89* $8
Black My Story *Virgin 3245/promo/ silkscreened/ps/'89* $5
Brothers and Sisters *Virgin 12804/promo/ silkscreened/rear insert/'93* $4
Good Time 4 versions *Virgin 4100/promo/'91* $6
Kozmik 4 versions *Virgin 3837/ promo/rear insert/'91* $6
Kozmik aor edit *Virgin 3973/promo/'91* $4
Look Who's Dancing 3 versions/Rat Race (live)/ Pains of Life *Virgin 96541/ stock/custom sticker/'89* $10
Look Who's Dancing (3 remixes) *Virgin 2841/promo/silkscreened/'89* $6
Look Who's Dancing (edit) *Virgin 2826/promo/silkscreened/'89* $4
One Bright Day single edit & alternative edit *Virgin 3103/promo/silkscreened/'89* $5
One Bright Day (full length) *Virgin PROCDZIGGY/promo/ gatefold hardcover/silkscreened* $10
Tomorrow People (4 versions) *Virgin 9347/promo/ps/'88* $6
Tumblin' Down 7" & lp *Virgin 2391/promo/ps* $5
Tumblin' Down 7" remix (4:04)/12" remix (5:52)/dub (4:28)/live version (6:08) *Virgin 2494/promo/'88* $8
Who Will Be There *Virgin 2996/promo/ silkscreened/'89* $4

MARLEY, ZIGGY/REDHEAD KINGPIN
Look Who's Dancing (2 versions)/ Do the Right Thing (2 versions) *Virgin 2928/promo/silkscreened/'89/ remixed by JAZZIE B* $8

MARS, CHRIS
Monkey Sees/Dawn Dawn *Smash 6722/promo/ silkscreened/ps/custom sticker/'92* $5
Popular Creeps/Before It Began *Smash 650/ promo/silkscreened/ps/'92* $5
Public Opinion/Monkey Sees/Outer Limits/ Popular Creeps/Get Out of My Life *Smash 005/promo/ps/silkscreened/'93* $10

MARSALIS, BRANFORD
Housed From Edward/Stardust/Makin' Whoopee + 3 *Columbia 1654/promo/ps/'89* $10

MARSALIS, WYNTON
Standard Time Vol. 3 sampler (Where or When/Flamingo + 5) *Columbia 2073/promo/ps/'90* $10
Majesty of the Blues/Hickory Dickory Dock + 1 *Columbia 1594/promo/silkscreened blue/'89* $8

MARSH, HUGH
Purple Haze radio/lp/interview (19:28) *Soundwings Duke Street 5001/promo/'89* $8

MARSHALL TUCKER BAND

Driving You Out of My Mind edit & lp *Cabin Fever 103/promo/ps/'92* $4
Southern Spirit (12 tracks) *Sisapa/promo/rear insert/'90* $12
Stay in Country *Sisapa/promo/rear insert/'90* $4
Tan Yard Road 4 versions *Cabin Fever 101/promo/ps/'92* $5

MARTHA'S VINEYARD

Old Beach Road *RooArt 240/promo/ps/'90* $4
Old Beach Road/3 AM/Skin on Skin/Sweet Love *rooArt 309/promo/silkscreened/ps/'89* $5

MARTIKA

Coloured Kisses single & lp *Columbia 74194/promo/ps/'91* $5
I Feel the Earth Move (5 versions) *Columbia 1744/promo/ps/'89* $8
Love ... Thy Will Be Done *Columbia 73853/* promo/silkscreened/writ.&prod. by *PRINCE/ps/'91* $5
Martika's Kitchen single & lp *Columbia 74094/promo/ps/'91* $6
Toy Soldiers single & lp *Columbia 1563/promo/ps/'89* $8

MARTIN, GEORGE & ANDY LEEK

Say Something questions & answers *Atlantic 2373/promo/'88* $10

MARTIN, MARILYN & DAVID FOSTER

And When She Danced *Atlantic 2421/promo* $4

MARTINEZ, NANCY

Everlasting remix *A&M 17999/promo/ silkscreened logo/'89* $4
Save Your Love For Me (4 versions) *A&M 17962/promo/silkscreened green logo on purple/'89* $5

MARVIN

The Firecracker Sweet (The Needle/Star Spangled Banner/You Believe in Money/You Gotta Eat/500,000 Firecrackers)*Regional 018/ promo/logo on white/rear insert/'92* $4
Train of Love hit single edit & lp *Regional 024/promo/'92*...........................$4
Vanishing Breed edit & lp *Regional 021/promo/silkscreened/'92*.......$4

MARX, RICHARD

Angelia single & lp *EMI 04426/promo/ silkscreened/rear insert/'89*.....................$6
Chains Around My Heart remix 1 edit/ remix 2 edit/lp *Capitol 79085/ promo/silkscreened/ps/'91* $5
Chains Around My Heart ac remix *Capitol 79582/promo/logo on green/'91* $4
Children of the Night single & lp *EMI 04522/ promo/silkscreened/rear insert/'90*............$6
Hazard edit & lp *Capitol 79095/promo/ silkscreened/ps/'91* $5
Keep Comin' Back 3rd world edit *Capitol 79102/promo/logo silkscreened/'91* $5
Keep Coming Back 4 versions *Capitol 79945/ promo/ps/silkscreened pic/'91* $8
Keep Coming Back 4 versions *Capitol 79957/ promo/silkscreened/ps/'91* $6
Marx sampler (Playing With Fire 2 versions/ Keep Coming Back 2 versions/Don't Mean Nothing/Satisfied/Have Mercy + 1) *Capitol 79956/promo/silkscreened pic/ps* ...$15
Playing With Fire aor edit/ Keep Coming Back aor mix *Capitol 79958/promo/silkscreen pic/ps/'91* ..$6
Right Here Waiting *EMI 04358/promo/ silkscreened/rear insert/'89* $5
Satisfied single, lp & AOR mix *EMI 04254/ promo/silkscreened/rear insert/'89*............$6
Take This Heart *Capitol 79170/ promo/logo on blue sky/'91* $5
Take This Heart ez mix/radio/lp *Capitol 79355/promo/'91* $6
Too Late to Say Goodbye *EMI 04368/promo/ silkscreened/rear insert/'89* $5
Too Late to Say Goodbye (4 versions) *EMI 04447/promo/ silkscreened/rear insert/'89* $8

MARY MY HOPE

Suicide Kings ep (5 songs - 2 live) *Silvertone 1302/promo/ps/'89* $12
Wildman Childman *RCA 1255/promo/ps/'89* $4

MARY'S DANISH

Don't Crash the Car Tonight *Chameleon 66/ promo/silkscreened/ps/'89* $5
Foxey Lady 3:43 & 3:57 *Chameleon 89/promo/silkscreened/'90* $5
Julie's Blanket *Morgan Creek 0003/promo/ ps/logo on brown/'91*...............................$4
Live ep (5 songs) *Chameleon 81/promo/ silkscreened/rear insert/'90* $12
Underwater edit & acoustic & live/interview *Morgan Creek 0032/promo/silkscreened/ rear insert/custom sticker/'92* $10
Underwater 3 versions/Big Block/Ships in the Sky/Much Too Young.../interview *Morgan Creek 0030/promo/rear insert/custom sticker/'92* $10
Yellow Creep Around/Friends of the Friendless *Morgan Creek 0004/promo/ silkscreened/ps/'91* $4

MASEKELA, HUGH

If You Don't Know Me By Now edit & lp *RCA 3081/promo/ps/'89* $5

MASON, DAVE

Dreams I Dream *MCA 17412/promo/ps/'87* $6

MASSEY, WILL T.
I Ain't Here *MCA 2068/promo/'91* $4

MASSIVE ATTACK
Be Thankful for What You've Got
Virgin 4284/promo/'91 .... $4
Be Thankful for What You've Got 3 versions
Virgin 4381/promo/'91 .... $5
Safe From Harm 4 versions
Virgin 4014/promo/silkscreened/'91 .... $5

MASTERS OF REALITY
100 Years *Chrysalis 04728/promo/ps/ silkscreened/'93* $4
Ants in the Kitchen *Chrysalis 04545/promo/ silkscreened/custom sticker/'93* $4
Domino *Del.Vinyl 6641/promo/rear insert/'90* $4
John Brown (live - 3 versions)
Delicious 0001/promo/rear insert/'91 .... $6
The Blue Garden *Def American 3405/promo* $4
The Candy Song *Delicious Vinyl 6625/promo/ black silkscreened/rear insert/'90* $4

MATERIAL ISSUE
11 Supersonic Hit Explosions (Very First Lie/ Crazy/Renee Remains the Sam/Diane (acoustic)/The Boxer (live)/Valerie Loves Me (live) + 5
Mercury 390/promo/logo on white/custom sticker/'91 .... $15
Diane lp & live *Mercury 420/promo/ silkscreened/rear insert/'91* $6
Diane/Valerie Loves Me (live)/Cowboy Song/ Diane (live)
Mercury 868 165/stock/ps/'91 .... $5
Everything electric & acoustic/She Was An Actress/Don't You Think I Know acoustic *Mercury 808/ promo/logo on red & black/'92* $8
Valerie Loves Me *Mercury 368/promo/ silkscreened/rear insert/'91* $5
What Girls Want radio/lp/love mix
Mercury 685/promo/ gatefold hardcover ps/silkscreened $7
What Girls Want/Bad Time/Next Big Thing (acoustic) *Mercury 679/promo/ gatefold hardcover ps/prod.by JEFF MURPHY/silkscreened/'92* $10
When I Get This Way (Over You)/ Who Needs Love (acoustic)
Mercury 718/promo/ps/logo on blue $5

MATHIS, JOHNNY
Better Together (duet with REGINA BELLE)
Columbia 4286/promo/ps/'91 .... $5
In the Still of the Night
Columbia 69092/promo/ps/'89 .... $6
You Brought Me Love *Columbia 4182/promo/ ps/PATTI AUSTIN/'91* $5

MATTEA, KATHY
A Few Good Things Remain *Merc.301/promo/ silkscreened/rear insert/'90* $5
Asking Us to Dance *Merc.525/promo/ps/'91* $5
Come From the Heart *Mercury 48/promo/ps* $5
Lonesome Standard Time
Mercury 750/promo/rear insert/'92 .... $5
Seeds radio remix *Mercury 876/promo/ps* $5
She Came From Fort Worth
Mercury 199/promo/silkscreened/'89 .... $5
Standing Knee Deep in a River *Mercury 826/ promo/silkscreened/rear insert/'92* $5
Where've You Been with intro & lp
Mercury 146/promo/ silkscreened pic/ps/'89 .... $8
Whole Lotta Holes *Mercury 444/promo/ silkscreened/rear insert/'91* $5

MATTEA, KATHY & TIM O'BRIEN
The Battle Hymn of Love
Mercury 268/promo/silkscreened/'90 .... $5

MAURICE & DA POSSE
All Because of You (7 versions)
A&M 17929/promo/silkscreened/'89 .... $4

MAW & COMPANY
Gonna Get Back to You radio edit
Esquire 74347/promo/custom sticker $4

MAX Q
Sometimes (3 remixes) *Atlantic 3086/ promo/ps/silkscreened/'89* $6
Sometimes straight rock mix
Atlantic 3085/promo/ps/'89 .... $5
Way of the World 7" & 12" mixes
Atlantic 2851/promo/rear insert/'89 .... $6
Way of the World (2 versions)/Zero 2-0 (T.Terry mix)/Ghost of the Year (T.Terry mix) *Atlantic 86317/ stock/ps/'89* $5

MAX, CHRISTOPHER
Serious Kinda Girl single/extended/club mix
EMI 04421/promo/rear insert/ silkscreened/'89 .... $5

MAXI PRIEST
Close to You (edit) *Charisma 006/promo/ silkscreened pic/ps/'90* $5
Goodbye to Love Again 3:55/5:18
Virgin 2623/promo/silkscreened/'89 .... $5
Groovin' in the Night 4 vers. *Charisma 12721/ promo/logo on black/rear insert/'92* $6
Just a Little Bit Longer edit
Charisma 021/promo/ps/'90 .... $5
One More Chance 4 versions
Charisma 12768/promo/'92 .... $6
One More Chance edit/quiet storm/lp
Charisma 12757/promo/silkscreened $5

Some Guys Have All the Luck
Charisma 074/promo/ps/'91 .... $5
Wild World 7" & long & saxy
Virgin 2485/promo/'88 .... $6

MAY MAY
Life's a Test 4 versions *Scotti Bros 75308/ promo/logo on black/ps/'92* $4

MAY, BRIAN
Too Much Love Will Kill You lp/live/instrum.
Hollywood 10343/promo/silkscreened/ rear insert/'93 .... $8

MAY, BRIAN & COZY POWELL
Resurrection edit & lp *Hollywood 10320/ promo/silkscreened/rear insert/'93* $8

MAY, RAYMOND
Romantic Guy *Elektra 8003/promo/'88* $3

MAYFIELD, CURTIS & ICE T
Superfly 1990 (7 versions)
Capitol 79204/promo/rear insert/'90 .... $5

MAYS, LYLE
Feet First *Geffen 3266/promo/ps/'88* $4

MAZE
Can't Get Over You fade *WB 3595/promo/'89* $4
Can't Get Over You fade & Maze is soul mix
WB 3769/promo/'89 .... $4
Love's on the Run *WB 3897/promo/'89* $4
Silky Soul edit & lp *WB 3780/promo/'89* $4
Twilight/In Time/Love Is/What Goes Up
WB 6385/promo/'93 .... $5

MAZELLE, KYM
Don't Scandalize Me (6 versions)
Capitol 79337/promo/'89 .... $7

MC 900 FT JESUS
Killer Inside Me 5 versions
Nettwerk 13835/stock/ps/'91 .... $5

MC 900 FT JESUS & DJ ZERO
Truth is Out of Style (4 versions)
IRS 74005/promo/ps/'90 .... $6

MC BRAINS
Everybody's Talking About M.C. Brains edit/lp/ instrumental
Motown 3746310322/promo/ps/'92 .... $5

MC EIHT
Streiht Up Menace (from Menace II Society) 3 versions *Jive 42138/promo/ custom sticker/rear insert/'93* $5

MC LYTE
Act Like You Know remix/lp/acapella
Atlantic 4823/promo/rear insert $5
Ice Cream Dream 4 versions
Perspective 31458 8067/promo/'92 .... $5

MC PILLSBERRY & THE 4 LARGE CREW
Me So Hungry (3 versions)
Atlantic 3348/promo/rear insert/'90 .... $4

MC SERCH
Back to the Grill *Def Jam 74760/promo/ silkscreened/ps/'92* $4

MC SHAN
Time For Us to Defend .. edit/remix/lp
Cold Chillin' 4550/promo/'90 .... $4

MCAULEY SCHENKER GROUP
This is My Heart edit & lp *Capitol 79122/ promo/silkscreened logo/'90* $5

MCCARTER, JENNIFER & T HE MCCARTERS
Quit While Im Behind *WB 3743/promo/'89* $4

MCCARTERS, THE
Timeless and True Love *WB 2911/promo/ hardcover gatefold ps/'87* $6
Up and Gone *WB 3433/promo/'89* $4

MCCARTNEY, PAUL
Birthday *Capitol 79392/ promo/rear insert/'90* $12
Figure of Eight 7" & 12" *Capitol 79871/ promo/silkscreened/rear insert/'89* $15
Hope of Deliverance *Capitol 79579/ promo/silkscreened/ps/'92* $8
Hope of Deliverance/Big Boys Bickering/ Long Lethal Coat/Kicked Around No More *Capitol 15950/ stock/ps/silkscreened/'92* $6
My Brave Face *Capitol 79590/promo/ silkscreened/'89* $6
Ou Est le Soleil? (Shep Pettibone edit)
Capitol 79836/promo/ silkscreened blue/'89 .... $10
Paul McCartney Rocks (10 song sampler)
Capitol 79987/promo/ silkscreened pic/ps/'90 .... $35
Save the Child/The Drinking Song
EMI Classics 15796/stock/ps/'91 .... $6
We Got Married edit & lp *Capitol 79979/ promo/silkscreened/'89* $8

MCCLINTON, DELBERT
Every Time I Roll the Dice edit & lp
Curb 1001/promo/ps/BONNIE RAITT, MELISSA ETHERIDGE, more/ logo on green/'92 .... $6

Everytime I Roll the Dice/Why Me?/Blues As Blues Can Get/Good Man, Good Woman *Curb 1006/promo/silkscreened pic/ rear insert/'92* $8
I Want to Love You *Curb 042/promo/ps/'90* $6
I'm With You *Curb 015/promo/ silkscreened pic/ps/'90* $6
Little Bitty Pretty .. *A&M 17846/promo/'89* $5
My Baby's Lovin' *Curb 79187/promo/ rear insert/'90* $5
Weatherman edit & lp *Epic 5028/promo/ logo on blue/rear insert/'93* $4
Why Me? *Curb 1024/promo/silkscreened pic/ rear insert/'92* $5

MCCOO, MARILYN
Warrior for the Lord/Against the Wall/ Love Understands *WB 5005/promo* $4

MCCRAY, LARRY
I Don't Mind/Nobody Never Hurt Nobody../ Sally's Got a Friend... *Point Blank 040/ promo/gold silkscreened/ps/'91* $4

MCCULLOCH, IAN
Candleland single & extended/Big Days/ The World is Flat/Wassailing in Night *Sire 21567/stock/ps/'90* $6
Faith and Healing single & rock mix *Sire 3793/promo/'89* $5
Honey Drip *Sire 5323/promo/silkscreened/'92* $5
Honeydrip/Proud to Fall (acoustic)/Vibor Blue (acoustic)/The Ground Below *Sire 40376/stock/ps/'92* $5
Lover Lover Lover lp & indian dawn remix *Sire 5515/promo/'92* $6
Lover Lover Lover lp & indian dawn remix/ Ribbons & Chains/Birdy *Sire 40435/ stock/gatefold hardcover ps/'92* $5
Proud to Fall lp & extended *Sire 3768/promo/'89* $5
Unravelled 15 track sampler (solo & ECHO) *Sire 5330/promo/logo on black/ps* $20

MCDERMOTT, MICHAEL
A Wall I Must Climb *Giant 4739/promo/ silkscreened/rear insert/'91* $4

MCDONALD, MICHAEL
All We Got (3 versions)/Show Me *Reprise 21734/stock/ps/'90* $6
All We Got (4 versions) *Reprise 4395/ promo/custom sticker/'90* $8
I Stand For You edit *Reprise 6264/promo/silkscreened/'93* $4
Take it to Heart edit fade *Reprise 4054/promo/'90* $5
Tear It Up *Reprise 4398/promo/rear insert* $4

MCENTIRE, REBA
Fallin' Out of Love *MCA 54108/promo/rear insert/'91* $6
Fancy lp & edit *MCA 54042/promo/rear insert/'90* $6
Is There Life Out There (edit) *MCA 54319/promo/rear insert/'91* $6
It's Your Call *MCA 54496/promo/'92* $5
Rumor Has It *MCA 53970/promo/ rear insert/'90* $6
The Greatest Man I Never Knew *MCA 54441/promo/'92* $5
The Night the Lights Went Out in Georgia *MCA 54386/promo/rear insert/'92* $5

MCENTIRE, REBA & LINDA DAVIS
Does He Love You *MCA 54719/promo/ logo on purple/ps/'93* $5

MCENTIRE, REBA & VINCE GILL
The Heart Won't Lie *MCA 54599/promo/ logo on purple/embossed gatefold hardcover ps/'93* $7

MCFERRIN, BOBBY
Baby *EMI 04711/promo/ silkscreened/rear insert/'91* $5
Good Lovin'/Dont Worry Be Happy (edit) *Manhattan 04167/promo/ps/'88* $6

MCFERRIN, BOBBY & CHICK COREA
Spain/Autumn Leaves (both edits) *Blue Note 79223/promo/logo on yellow/custom sticker/'92* $6

MCGARRIGLE, KATE & ANNA
Heartbeats Accelerating *Private 2070/promo/ps/'90* $8

MCGHEE, JACCI
It Hurts Me 4 versions *MCA 2450/promo/rear insert/'92* $4
Skeeza 7 versions *MCA 2290/promo/ps/'92* $5
Something's on My Mine *MCA 2559/promo/ps* $4

MCGREGOR, FREDDIE
(Playing) Hard to Get 6 versions *Pow Wow 479/promo/silkscreened/ rear insert/'93* $5

MCGUINN, ROGER
Back From Rio (10 tracks) *Arista 8648/ promo/silkscreened/hardcover open up box type ps/'91* $20
King of the Hill edit & lp *Arista 2154/ promo/ps/logo on baby blue/'90* $5
Someone to Love *Arista 2214/promo/ps/'91* $5

MCKAGAN, DUFF
Believe in Me edit & lp *Geffen promo/gatefold hardcover ps/silkscreened* $6

MCKEE, LONETTE
Watch the Birds *Columbia 74469/promo/ps* $4

MCKEE, MARIA
Breathe/Nobodys Child/To Miss Someone *Geffen 3599/promo/ps/'89* $6
I'm Gonna Soothe You *Geffen 4512/promo/silkscreened pic/gatefold hardcover ps/'93* $6
I've Forgotten What It Was In You *Geffen 3556/promo/ps/'89* $6
Selftitled 11 tracks *Geffen 24229/promo issue with box cover/pic insert/'89* $20
Show Me Heaven *Geffen 4156/promo/silkscreened/ps/'90* $6
To Miss Someone edit & lp *Geffen 3666/promo/'89* $5

MCKENNITT, LOREENA
The Lady of Shalott edit & lp/Between the Shadows/Tango to Evora *WB 5671/promo/'91* $7
The Visit music & interview (trt: 26:30) *WB 5809/promo/rear insert/'92* $12

MCKNIGHT, BRIAN
One Last Cry single edit *Mercury 880/promo/ps/'93* $4

MCKONE, VIVIENNE
Get to Know You/Beware *London 958/promo/ps/'93* $4

MCLACHLAN, SARAH
Into the Fire extended/john fryer mix/dub/lp *Arista 2402/promo/'92* $8
Into the Fire john fryer mix & lp *Arista 2390/promo/ps/'92* $6
Solace 10 tracks *Arista 18631/promo/exotic package with book/silkscreened/'91* $25
The Path of Thorns remix & edit *Arista 2423/promo/logo on tan/ps/'92* $6

MCLAREN, MALCOLM
Romeo and Juliet (justy my groove mix)/Il Be or Not Il Be *Virgin 3667/promo/silkscreened/'91* $6
Waltz Darling (3 versions) *Epic 1775/promo/silkscreened/'89* $6

MCLEAN, DON
And I Love You So (newly recorded)/American Pie (orig. versions 8:33) *Curb 099/promo/rear insert/'92* $6

MCM
Xmaz n the Hood (Chris Kringle is a Black Man/Ebony's a Scrooge/This Christmas/Xmaz n the Hood/Brighter Daze) *Priority 6611/promo/logo on brown/censored versions/custom sticker/'91* $5

MCMURTRY, JAMES
Candyland *Columbia 4760/promo/ps/'92* $4
Too Long in the Wasteland (full length) *Columbia 1734/promo/ps/with booklet/'89* $12
Where's Johnny *Columbia 4589/promo/ps/'92* $4

MCQUEEN STREET
In Heaven *SBK 05422/promo/ps/'91* $4

MCVIE, JOHN
Now I Know *WB 5553/promo/'92* $4
One More Time With... *WB 5854/promo/'92* $4

ME PHI ME
Pu Sho Hands 2Getha 6 versions *RCA 62277/promo/rear insert/logo on black/'92* $5
Sad New Day 5 versions *RCA 62306/promo/logo on black/ps/'92* $5

MEAT BEAT MANIFESTO
Circles remix *Mute 8764/promo/silkscreened/rear insert/'93* $5
Edge of No Control 4 versions/The Circular Cosmic Spot/DJ Interruptus *Mute 66375/stock/ps/'92* $5
Mindstream 5 versions/Original Control *Mute 66343/stock/ps/'93* $5
Mindstream lp edit/stream of consciousn.edit *Mute 8689/promo/logo on red/rear insert/'92* $6

MEAT LOAF
Bat Out of Hell II: Back Into Hell *MCA 10699/promo/logo on black/custom sticker* $10
I'd Do Anything For Love 5 versions *MCA 2637/promo/ps/'93* $6
Paradise by the Dashboard Light edit & lp *MCA 2492/promo/rear insert/'92 (for soundtrack to Leap of Faith)* $6
Two Out of Three Ain't Bad/Paradise By the Dashboard Light *Epic 34K 02371/stock/3"* $6

MEAT LOAF & TANGERINE DREAM
A Time For Heroes vocal, instru. & extended *Orpheum 060187/ps/stock/'87* $8

MEAT PUPPETS
Forbidden Places 10 tracks *London 481/promo/silkscreen/trifold hardcover* $15
Sam *London 485/promo/ps/silkscreened/'91* $5
Whirlpool/Funnel of Love/Rock and Roll *London 531/promo/silkscreened/ps* $7

MEDEIROS, GLENN
She Ain't Worth It (3 versions) *MCA 18331/promo/rear insert/'90* $4

MEDICINE
Selftitled 9 tracks *Def American/promo/'91* $10

MEDLEY, BILL
Don't Let Go *Curb 072/promo/logo on black/ rear insert/'91* $5
Don't You Love Me Anymore? *Curb 79321/promo/rear insert/'90* $5
Rude Awakening (edit) *Elektra 8101/promo* $5

MEGADETH
Angry Again *Columbia 5234/promo/ps/'93* $5
Foreclosure of a Dream edit & lp *Capitol 79391/promo/logo on grey/ps/'92* .$6
Hangar 18 lp & aor edit *Capitol 79462/ promo/silkscreened/rear insert/'90*..........$6
Hangar 18 aor edit & lp/The Conjuring/Hook in Mouth (last 2 live) *Capitol 15662/stock/ps/'90*..........$7
Holy Wars.. The Punishments Due *Capitol 79292/promo/ silkscreened logo/rear insert/'90* $6
Interview music & interview *Capitol 79396/ promo/logo on black/rear insert/'92* $20
Maximum Megadeth (Peace Sells/Hangar 18 live/In My Darkest Hour/Holy Wars../Anarchy in UK live/Wake Up Dead/Hook in Mouth/Lucretia) *Capitol 79757/promo/silkscreen/ps/'91* ...$30
Skin o' My Teeth *Capitol 79363/ promo/silkscreened/'92*..........$6
Sweating Bullets edit & lp *Capitol 79592/ promo/ps/logo on black/'93*..........$5
Sweating Bullets lp & live/Ashes in Your Mouth/Countdown to Extinction (last 2 live) *Capitol 15946/stock/ps* $5
Symphony of Destruction radio mix *Capitol 79339/promo/ps/'92*..........$6
Various sampler (UGLY KID JOE, RAMONES, EXTREME, more) & interview (35 tracks in all *Foundations/promo/ silkscreened/'92* $25

MEKONS
Wicked Midnite/All I Want/The Curse/Waltz/ Amnesia (last 3 live) *Loud Music 89014/stock/ps/'92* $5
Makes No Difference/Sheffield Park/ Having a Party/One Horse Town *A&M 75021 5325/promo/ silkscreened/ps/'90* $7

MELENDEZ, LISETTE
Never Say Never 3 versions *Fever 74144/promo/ps/'91*..........$5
Together Forever 6 versions *Fever 73629/promo/ps/'90*..........$5

MELIAH RAGE
No Mind/The Witching *Epic 2108/promo/ps/ silkscreened red/'90* $5

MELIDIAN
Lost in the Wild 9 tracks *CBS Associated 1671/promo/ silkscreened pics (of GRANDPA MUNSTER!)/rear insert/'89* $10

MELLENCAMP, JOHN
Again Tonight *Mercury 616/promo/ red logo on yellow/ps/'91* $5
Again Tonight/Get a Leg Up live/Love and Happiness radio & london club mix *Mercury 866 415/stock/ps/'92* $5
Get a Leg Up lp & family versions *Mercury 546/ promo/logo on red/gatefold hardcover ps/'91* $6
Jackie Brown *Mercury 102/promo/'89*..........$5
Last Chance *Mercury 709/promo/ logo on red/custom sticker/'91* $5
Let It All Hang Out/Country Gentleman/ Pop Singer (ext.) *Mercury 874 933/ promo/silkscreened/ps/'89* $10
Love and Happiness *Mercury 612/ promo/logo on red/ps/'91* $5
Now More Than Ever *Mercury 657/promo/'92* $5
Paper in Fire *Mercury 03/promo/ps* $5
Paper in Fire (audio & video)/Never Too Old/ Under the Boardwalk/Cold Sweat (last 3 audio only) *Mercury 870 707/ video & audio/stock/ps/'88* $12
Pop Singer *Mercury 52/promo/ps/ pic silkscreened/'89* $7
Rave On *Elektra 8029/promo/ Tom Cruise ps/'88*..........$6
Rave On/Tutti Frutti *Elektra 69370/3" stock w/ps*..........$6

MELLOW MAN ACE
If You Were Mine (3 versions)/Hip Hop Crature (remix)/Rap Guanco (remix) *Capitol 79293/promo/silkscreened* $6
Mentirosa (2 versions)/Welcome to My Groove (5 versions) *Capitol 79130/ promo/silkscreened/'90*..........$6
What's It Take to Pull a Hottie edit *Capitol 79984/promo/ps/ logo on orange/'92* $5

MEN AT LARGE
So Alone edit/radio/lp *Eastwest 4861/promo* $5
Um Um Good 4 versions *Eastwest 5085/promo* ..$5
Use Me remix edit/remix w'out rap/single/ extended/3 way street mix *Eastwest 4549/promo/ps/'92* $5
Would You Like to Dance (With Me) edit & lp *Eastwest 4951/promo/ps/'93* $5

MEN AT WORK
Business as Usual/In the Studio *dj radio show/promo/ hosted by COLIN HAY/cue sheet* $20

MEN THEY COULDN'T HANG, THE
Great Expectations *RCA 1410/promo/ps/'90* $6

MEN WITHOUT HATS
Hey Men 3:37/5:03
Mercury 151/promo/silkscreened/'89 .... $4
Pop Goes the World *Mercury 06/promo/ps/'87* $6
Pop Goes the World audio & video/The End (of the World)/Jenny Wore Black/ Lose My Way (last 3 audio only)
Mercury 870 718/stock/ps/'88 .... $12

MEN, THE
Church of Logic, Sin & Love *Polydor 662/ promo/silkscreened/ps/'92* $4

MENDES, SERGIO
Mas Que Nada (4 versions) *A&M 17817/ promo/silkscreened/'89* $4

MENTAL AS ANYTHING
Rock and Roll Music/You're So Strong
Columbia 1790/promo/'89 .... $6

MERCHANTS OF VENUS
Say Ahh edit &lp *Elektra 8359/promo/ silkscreened/ps/'91* $4

MERCURY, FREDDIE
Love Kills *Hollywood 10235/promo/ logo on black/rear insert/'92* $8
Time lp & radio *Hollywood 10308/promo/ silkscreened/rear insert/'92* $8

MERRITT, SCOTT
Are You Sending (edit) *IRS 020/promo/ silkscreened/ps/'90* $4

MESSIAH
Temple of Dreams 5 vers./You're Going Insane
Def American 40655/stock/ gatefold hardcover ps/'92 .... $5

METAL CHURCH
Badlands (edit) *Elektra 8078/promo/'89* $4
Date With Poverty video & lp *Epic 4022/ promo/logo on black/rear insert/'91* $4
Fake Healer edit/lp *Elektra 8051/promo/'89* $4
In Mourning/Date With Poverty live
Epic 4133/promo/silkscreened/ rear insert/'91 .... $6
The Human Factor *Epic 3067/promo/ silkscreened/rear insert/'91* $4

METALLICA
...And Justice For All edit & lp
Elektra 8099/promo/logo on green $20
15 Pieces of Live Sh*t 15 tracks
Elektra 8879/promo/2 cds/'93 .... $60
Don't Tread on Me *Elektra 8728/promo/ silkscreened logo/'91* $10
Enter Sandman *Elektra 8407/promo/ silkscreened/ps/'91* $8
Enter Sandman edit *Elektra 8421/ promo/silkscreened/'91* $15
Eye of the Beholder *Elektra 8028/promo/'88* $20
Garage Days Re-Visited (Helpless/The Small Hours/The Wait/Crash Course../ Last Caress-Green Hell)
Elektra 60757/stock/ps/'87 .... $30
Kill em All 10 tracks
Megaforce 069/stock/ps/'86 .... $30
Kill em All 12 tracks *Elektra 60766/stock/ ps/'83 recorded/reissued in '89* $20
Mandatory Metallica (7 song compilation)
Elektra 8020/promo/ps $55
Mandatory Metallica (8 song compilation)
Elektra 8071/promo/ps/'89 .... $50
Nothing Else Matters *Elektra 8534/promo/ logo on black/rear insert/'91* $15
Nothing Else Matters 6:29 *Elektra 8530/ promo/logo on black/rear insert/'91* $12
One edit/lp *Elektra 8044/promo/ silkscreened logo/'88* $25
One/The Prince *Elek.69329/stock/3"/ps/'88* $15
Sad But True *Elektra 8646/promo/ logo on black/ps/'92* $8
Stone Cold Crazy *Elektra 8224/promo/ps* $25
The Unforgiven edit *Elektra 8479/promo/ silkscreened/ps/'91* $12
Wherever I May Roam (edit)
Elektra 8592/promo/silkscreened/'92 .... $8

METHENY, PAT
A Special Conversation With.. (30 interview segments) *Geffen 4438/promo/ gatefold hardcover/silkscreened/'92* $15
Beat 70 edit & lp *Geffen 3847/promo/ps/'89* $5
Change of Heart edit, lp, remix/Three Flights Up *Geffen 4129/promo/ps/ silkscreened/'90* $6
Last Train Home long/short *Geffen 2767/ promo/gatefold hardcover ps/'87* $6
Slip Away edit-fade
Geffen 3617/promo/ps/'89 .... $5
The Longest Summer (edit)/Facing West (edit)
Geffen 4439/promo/ps/'92 .... $5

METHOD OF DESTRUCTION
Intruder *Megaforce 818/promo/'92* $4

MIAMI SOUND MACHINE
Betcha Say That *Epic 2789/promo/ps/'87* $12
Cuts Both Ways audio cue card (music & interview) *Epic 1707/promo/ps/'89* $25

MICHAEL, GEORGE
Freedom lp & edit *Columbia 73559/promo/ps* $8
Freedom (2 versions)/Fantasy
Columbia 44K 73584/stock/ps/'90 .... $6
I Believe (When I Fall In Love..) edit & lp
Columbia 4429/promo/ps/'91 .... $10

I Want Your Sex rhythm 1 lust/rhythm 2 brass in love *Columbia 38K 07164/ 3"/stock/'87* $15
Kissing a Fool lp & instrumental *Columbia 1297/promo/'87* $15
Listen Without Prejudice (profile & interview) *Columbia 2226/promo/ps/'90* $25
Monkey (6 versions) *Columbia 1186/promo/ps/'87* $20
One More Try *Columbia 1091/promo/ps/'87* $15
Papa Was a Rollin' Stone urban radio single *Hollywood 10341/promo/ logo on black/custom sticker/'93* $10
Praying For Time *Columbia 73512/promo/ps* $8
Soul Free *Columbia 73799/promo/ps/ logo on black/'91* $8
Soul Free special radio edit/Cowboys and Angels radio edit *Columbia 4059/ promo/logo on white/'91* $10
Too Funky *Columbia 4622/promo/ps/ custom sticker/'92* $8
Too Funky 4 versions/Crazyman Dance *Columbia 44K 74352/stock/ps/'92* $6
Waiting For That Day/Mother's Pride *Columbia 73663/promo/ps/'90* $10

MICHAEL, GEORGE & ARETHA FRANKLIN

I Knew You Were .. lp & edit remix *Arista 9560/promo/ps/'87* $20

MICHAEL, GEORGE & ELTON JOHN

Don't Let the Sun Go Down On Me (live) *Columbia 74086/promo/ps/'91* $8
Don't Let the Sun Go Down On Me (live)/ I Believe When I Fall in Love../ Freedom back to reality mix/ If You Were My Woman *Columbia 74130/stock/ps/'91* $8

MICHAEL, GEORGE & QUEEN

Somebody to Love *Hollywood 10307/promo/ silkscreened pic/rear insert/'93* $10

MICHAELIS, LISA

Rain Falls 4:01/10:41 *Virgin 4609/ promo/logo on blue/'91* $5

MICHAELS, LAZET

Kraze 6 versions *Zoo 17005/promo/ silkscreened pic/rear insert/'91* $5

MICHEL'LE

Keep Watchin' (5 versions) *Ruthless 3482/promo/silkscreened logo on purple/rear insert/'90* $6
Nicety (4 versions) *Ruthless 3258/promo/rear insert/'89* $6
No More Lies (4 versions) *Atco 3013/promo/ps/'89* $6
Something in My Heart edit & lp *Ruthless 3654/promo/logo on purple/rear insert/'89* $4

MIDI MAX & EFTI

Ragga Steady edit/lp/ragga steady mix *Columbia 4682/promo/logo on red/ps* $5
Bad Bad Boys lp/edit/extended *Columbia 74215/promo/ps/'92* $6
Bad Bad Boys 6 versions *Columbia 44K 74138/stock/ps/'92* $5
Bad Bad Boys kcs mix *Columbia 4596/ promo/ps/logo on red/'92* $5
Bad Bad Boys radio mix edit/mischief mix edit *Columbia 4584/promo/ps/'92* $5

MIDI RAIN

Shine 3 versions *Vinyl Solution 44K 74948/stock/ps* $4

MIDLER, BETTE

Best Bettes ep (One More For My Baby/ Boogie Woogie Bugle Boy/The Rose/ Wind Beneath My Wings/From a Distance) *Atlantic 5154/promo/ custom sticker/rear insert* $15
From a Distance *Atlantic 3528/promo/ps/'90* $5
In My Life *Atlantic 4267/promo/rear insert/'91* $5
Moonlight Dancing (4 versions) *Atlantic 3853/ promo/silkscreened/ps/'91* $8
Moonlight Dancing (edit mix w/a cappella) *Atlantic 3879/promo/ logo on white/ps/'90* $6
Night and Day edit & lp *Atlantic 3583/ promo/ps/logo on black/'90* $5
The Gift of Love *Atlantic 4078/promo/ rear insert/'91* $5
Under the Boardwalk (edit) *Atlantic 2547/promo/ ... rear insert/'88* $5
Under the Boardwalk (new mix) *Atlantic 2772/ promo/rear insert/'88* $5
Wind Beneath My Wings edit & lp *Atlantic 2615/promo/rear insert/'88* $5

MIDNIGHT OIL

Beds Are Burning *Columbia 1058/promo/ps* $8
Blue Sky Mining *Columbia 73250/promo/ silkscreened logo on purple/ trifold textured hardcover ps/'90* $10
Drums of Heaven *Columbia 5071/promo/ps* $5
Forgotten Years *Columbia 73336/promo/ silkscreened/ps/'90* $7
Forgotten Years/You May Not Be Released/ Blue Sky Mine (food on table mix)/ Power & Passion (spec. versions) *Columbia 44K 73192/stock/ps/'90* $6
King of the Mountain 12" nixmix *Columbia 2172/promo/'90* $8
Outbreak of Love edit & lp *Columbia 5257/promo/ps/'93* $5

Screaming in Blue/Live
Sony 4556/promo/silkscreened/'92 .... $8
Sometimes *Columbia 4560/promo/ silkscreened/ps/'92* $5
The Dead Heart long & short & short w/intro *Columbia 1219/promo/\ silkscreened pic./rear insert/'88* $10
Truganini *Columbia 74933/promo/ silkscreened/ps/'93* $5
Who's Gonna Save Me (15 song comp. - 2 unrel. songs) *Columbia 2038/promo/ silkscreened green/die cut fold out \ package/insert/'90* $25

MIDNIGHT STAR

Do It 6 versions *Epic 74509/promo/ rear insert/'90* $5
Luv U Up (4 vers.) *Solar 2156/promo/ps/'90* $5
Red Roses *Epic 74530/promo/ logo silkscreened/'90* $4

MIGHTY LEMON DROPS

Another Girl../We Love You/Too High (3 vers.) *Reprise 5057/promo/logo on yellow* $5
Fall Down (remix)/Mighty Lemon Talk/ Inside Out (live) *Sire 3103/promo/rear insert/'88* $8
Inside Out (7" & 12" version) *Sire 2963/promo/ps/'88* $6
Into the Heart of Love edit & lp *Reprise 3751/promo/rear insert/'89* $4
Into the Sun *Sire 5574/promo/silkscreened/'92* ... $4
Sound (11 tracks) *Sire 26512/ promo only color silkscreened/ps/'91* $15
Unkind remix & lp *Reprise 4755/promo/ silkscreened pic/'91* $6
Where Do We Go From Heaven? (7" remix/ full length remix) *Sire 3880/promo* $6

MIGHTY MIGHTY BOSSTONES, THE

Someday I Suppose *Mercury 900/promo/ silkscreened/ps/'93* $4
Someday I Suppose/Issachar *Mercury 901/promo/ps/silkscreened* $4
Where'd You Go?/Sweet Emotion/Enter Sandman/ Do Something Crazy/Ain't Talkin' Bout Love *Taang T-48/stock/ps* $8

MIGUEL, LUIS

Mucho Corazon *WEA Latina 501/promo/ps/'92* $4

MIKE & MECHANICS

Everybody Gets a Second Chance *Atlantic 3930/promo/ps/'91* $5
Nobodys Perfect lp & edit *Atlantic 2521/promo/rear insert/'88* $5
Revolution *Elektra 8097/promo/'89* $5
Seeing is Believing *Atlantic 2658/promo/rear insert/'88* $5
Stop Baby *Atlantic 4177/promo/silkscreened/ rear insert/'91* $5
The Living Years lp & edit *Atlantic 2577/promo/rear insert/'88* $5
Word of Mouth edit & lp *Atlantic 3835/promo/ ps/silkscreened/'91* $5

MILIRA

One Man Woman edit/lp/instrumental *Motown 3746310302/promo/ps/'92* $5
Three's a Crowd edit/lp/instrumental *Motown 374631068/promo/ps/'92* $5

MILLER, DENNIS

Excerpts from the Off White Album (12 short cuts) *WB 3210/promo/ps/'88* $6

MILLER, STEVE

Blue Eyes edit & lp *Sailor 979/promo/logo on blue/'93* $4
Born 2 B Blue interview & music *Capitol 79420/promo/cust.sticker* $20
Just a Little Bit lp & extended *Capitol 79439/promo/'88* $7
Wide River *Polydor 924/promo/silkscreened/ ps/'93* $4
Ya Ya *Capitol 79389/promo/ps/'88* $6

MILLI VANILLI

Blame It on the Rain (lp/single/extended) *Arista 9904/promo/ps/'89* $8
Girl I'm Gonna Miss You 4:19 & 3:57 *Arista 9870/promo/ps/'89* $10
Mega Mix (4:19) (Girl You Know.., Baby Dont Forget,..Blame it On Rain, Cant You Feel My Love) *Arista 2048/promo/ silkscreened/rear insert/'90* $10

MILLI VANILLI/ROB & FAB

We Can Get It On 4 versions *Taj 63191/stock/silkscreened/ps/'92* $6

MILLIONS LIKE US

Guaranteed for Life (2 versions) *Virgin 9412/promo/ps* $4

MILLIONS, THE

Sometimes edit & lp *Smash 545/promo/silkscreened/ps* $4

MILLS, STEPHANIE

All Day, All Night 8 versions *MCA 2487/promo/rear insert/'92* $6
All Day, All Night edit & lp *MCA 2345/promo/ps/'92* $4
Comfort of a Man 4:39 & 5:49 *MCA 18285/ promo/custom sticker/'89* $5
Home *MCA 17992/promo/'89* $4
Never Do You Wrong 9 versions *MCA 2529/promo/ps/'93* $6
Real Love 3 versions *MCA 18339/promo/'90* $5

MILLTOWN BROTHERS
Apple Green lp & remix *A&M 75021 7265/ promo/logo on green/ps/'91* $4
Which Way Should I Jump *A&M 75021 7004/promo/ps/'91* $4

MIND BOMB
Do You Need Some? 4 versions/Segue *Mercury 862 009/stock/ps/'93* $4
Segue *Mercury 862/promo/silkscreened/ps* $4
Segue 5:44/4:00 *Mercury 925/promo/silkscreened/'93* $5

MIND FUNK
Sugar Ain't So Sweet *Epic 3099/promo/ silkscreened logo/rear insert/'91* $4

MINER, TIM
Heart lp & instrumental *Motown 374631086/promo/ps/'92* $4

MINISTRY
JESUS BUILT MY HOTROD
COMPACT DISC MAXI-SINGLE

MINISTRY
Jesus Built My Hotrod 2 versions/TV Song *Sire 40211/stock/ gatefold hardcover ps/'91* $5
Just One Fix *Sire 5766/promo/'92* $4
N.W.O. 4:40/5:30/8:34 *Sire 5589/promo/silkscreened/'92* $7

MINNELLI, LIZA
Losing My Mind *Epic 73011/promo/ps/'89/ prod by the PET SHOP BOYS* $7
Love Pains 3:54/5:04 *Epic 73355/promo/ps* $8

MINOGUE, DANNII
Jump the Beat 3 versions/Hallucination *MCA 2034/promo/ps/'91* $5
Success 5 versions *Savage 2231/promo/ ps/logo on cream/'92* $5

MINOGUE, KYLIE
Better the Devil You Know *MCA 1369/ promo/logo on grey/rear insert/'90* $5
I Still Love You *Geffen 3477/promo/'88* $5
It's No Secret (edit) *Geffen 3412/promo/'88* $5
Locomotion *Geffen 3254/promo/ps/'88* $7
Tears on My Pillow *Geffen 4020/promo/ silkscreened/ps/'90* $6
Wouldn't Change a Thing lp/Espagna mix edit/ Espagna mix/Your Thang mix *Geffen 3714/promo/ps/'89* $8

MINT CONDITION
Are You Free 7 versions *Perspective 28968 1703/promo/ silkscreened/ps/'91* $7
Breakin' My Heart 7 versions *Perspective 28968 1707/promo/ps/'91* $6
Forever in Your Eyes 7"/lp/instru. *Perspective 28968 1711/promo/ps/'91* $7
Single to Mingle live/Forever in Your Eyes/ Breakin' My Heart teardrop edit/ My Dear *Perspective 31458 8073/ promo/silkscreened/'92* $7

MIRACLE LEGION
Snacks and Candy 2 versions *Morgan Creek 0012/promo/ps/'92* $5
We Are All Lost ep (Everything is Rosy/ Sea Hag/Waiting Room/The Sounds of Drenched) *Morgan Creek 0011/ promo/silkscreened/ps/'92* $7

MIRANDA SEX GARDEN
Sunshine edit & lp *Mute 8772/promo/ silkscreened/ps/'93* $5

MISS WORLD
The First Female Serial Killer *Atlantic 4733/ promo/silkscreened/rear insert/'92* $4

MISSION UK, THE
Amelia lp & live/Stay With Me/Tower of Strength (last 2 acoustic) *Mercury 878 335/stock/ silkscreened/ps/'90* $5
Butterfly on a Wheel lp, 7", edit *Mercury 251/promo/silkscreened/ gatefold hardcover ps (with popout butterfly)/'90* $15
Deliverance edit & lp *Mercury 192/promo/ silkscreened logo on black/'90* $6
Deliverance/Butterfly on a Wheel/Paradise/ Grapes of Wrath *Mercury 203/promo/ silkscreened logo on black/ps/'89* $8
Hands Across the Ocean *Mercury 354/promo/ silkscreened/rear insert/'90* $5
Like a Child Again 4 versions/All Tangled Up in You *Mercury 864 109/ stock/ps/logo on purple/'92* $5
Words Upon the Sand interview + six songs *Mercury 169/promo/ silkscreened/ps/'90* $15

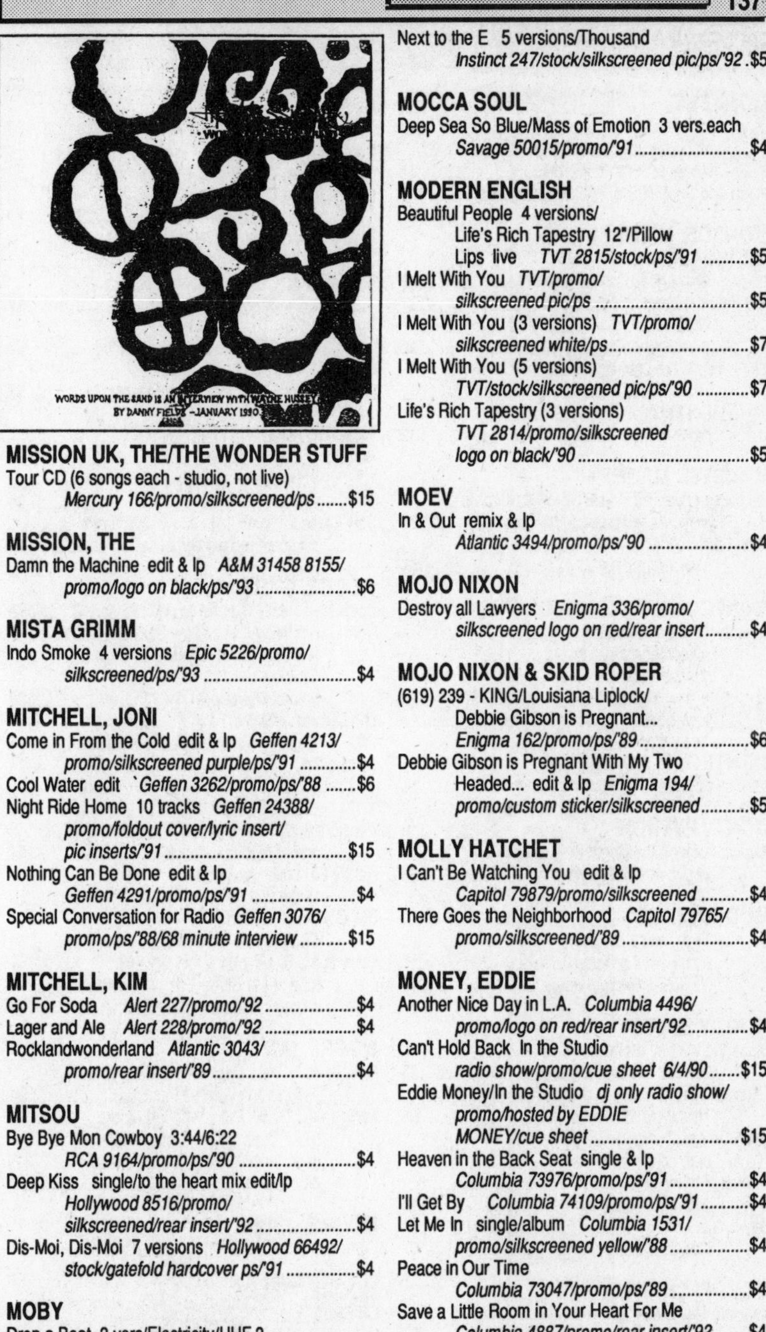

WORDS UPON THE SAND IS AN INTERVIEW WITH WAYNE HUSSEY
BY DANNY FIELDS - JANUARY 1990

MISSION UK, THE/THE WONDER STUFF
Tour CD (6 songs each - studio, not live)
Mercury 166/promo/silkscreened/ps $15

MISSION, THE
Damn the Machine edit & lp *A&M 31458 8155/ promo/logo on black/ps/'93* $6

MISTA GRIMM
Indo Smoke 4 versions *Epic 5226/promo/ silkscreened/ps/'93* $4

MITCHELL, JONI
Come in From the Cold edit & lp *Geffen 4213/ promo/silkscreened purple/ps/'91* $4
Cool Water edit *Geffen 3262/promo/ps/'88* $6
Night Ride Home 10 tracks *Geffen 24388/ promo/foldout cover/lyric insert/ pic inserts/'91* $15
Nothing Can Be Done edit & lp *Geffen 4291/promo/ps/'91* $4
Special Conversation for Radio *Geffen 3076/ promo/ps/'88/68 minute interview* $15

MITCHELL, KIM
Go For Soda *Alert 227/promo/'92* $4
Lager and Ale *Alert 228/promo/'92* $4
Rocklandwonderland *Atlantic 3043/ promo/rear insert/'89* $4

MITSOU
Bye Bye Mon Cowboy 3:44/6:22 *RCA 9164/promo/ps/'90* $4
Deep Kiss single/to the heart mix edit/lp *Hollywood 8516/promo/ silkscreened/rear insert/'92* $4
Dis-Moi, Dis-Moi 7 versions *Hollywood 66492/ stock/gatefold hardcover ps/'91* $4

MOBY
Drop a Beat 2 vers/Electricity/UHF 2 *Instinct 240/stock/ps/silkscreened* $5
Next to the E 5 versions/Thousand *Instinct 247/stock/silkscreened pic/ps/'92* .$5

MOCCA SOUL
Deep Sea So Blue/Mass of Emotion 3 vers.each *Savage 50015/promo/'91* $4

MODERN ENGLISH
Beautiful People 4 versions/ Life's Rich Tapestry 12"/Pillow Lips live *TVT 2815/stock/ps/'91* $5
I Melt With You *TVT/promo/ silkscreened pic/ps* $5
I Melt With You (3 versions) *TVT/promo/ silkscreened white/ps* $7
I Melt With You (5 versions) *TVT/stock/silkscreened pic/ps/'90* $7
Life's Rich Tapestry (3 versions) *TVT 2814/promo/silkscreened logo on black/'90* $5

MOEV
In & Out remix & lp *Atlantic 3494/promo/ps/'90* $4

MOJO NIXON
Destroy all Lawyers *Enigma 336/promo/ silkscreened logo on red/rear insert* $4

MOJO NIXON & SKID ROPER
(619) 239 - KING/Louisiana Liplock/ Debbie Gibson is Pregnant... *Enigma 162/promo/ps/'89* $6
Debbie Gibson is Pregnant With My Two Headed... edit & lp *Enigma 194/ promo/custom sticker/silkscreened* $5

MOLLY HATCHET
I Can't Be Watching You edit & lp *Capitol 79879/promo/silkscreened* $4
There Goes the Neighborhood *Capitol 79765/ promo/silkscreened/'89* $4

MONEY, EDDIE
Another Nice Day in L.A. *Columbia 4496/ promo/logo on red/rear insert/'92* $4
Can't Hold Back In the Studio *radio show/promo/cue sheet 6/4/90* $15
Eddie Money/In the Studio *dj only radio show/ promo/hosted by EDDIE MONEY/cue sheet* $15
Heaven in the Back Seat single & lp *Columbia 73976/promo/ps/'91* $4
I'll Get By *Columbia 74109/promo/ps/'91* $4
Let Me In single/album *Columbia 1531/ promo/silkscreened yellow/'88* $4
Peace in Our Time *Columbia 73047/promo/ps/'89* $4
Save a Little Room in Your Heart For Me *Columbia 4887/promo/rear insert/'92* $4

She Takes My Breath Away *Columbia 74107/ promo/silkscreened/ps* $4

MONKEES
Daydream Believer/For Pete's Sake/ You May Just Be the One *Arista 3009/3"/stock/'88* $6
Heart and Soul *Rhino PRCD 1/promo/ps/'87* $10

MONROE, MICHAEL
Man With No Eyes *Mercury 193/promo/silkscreened/'89* $5
Not Fakin' It/Dead, Jail or RnR/While You Were Looking... *Mercury 107/promo/ silkscreened/gatefold hardcover ps* $6
While You Were Looking At Me/Love is Thicker Than Blood/Dead, Jail or Rock n Roll/ Not Fakin' It (live) *Mercury 224/ promo/silkscreened/ps/'90* $12

MONSTER MAGNET
Face Down/Unsolid *A&M 31458 8143/promo/ silkscreened/gatefold hardcover ps* $4
Twin Earth *A&M 31458 8108/promo/ silkscreened/ps/'93* $4

MONTGOMERY, JOHN MICHAEL
Beer and Bones *Atlantic 5108/promo/ silkscreened/rear insert/ custom sticker/'93* $4
I Love the Way You Love Me *Atlantic 4907/ promo/silkscreened/rear insert/'92* $4

MONTROSE, RONNIE
Telstar *Enigma 110/promo/custom sticker* $6

MONTY PYTHON
Always Look on the Bright Side of Life (edit) *Virgin 4160/promo/rear insert/'89* $8

MOODSWINGS
Spiritual High edit & single *Arista 2458/promo/CHRISSIE HYNDE/silkscreened/ps/'92* $4

MOODY BLUES
Bless the Wings orchestral & lp *Polydor 529/promo/ps/'91* $7
I Know You're Out There Somewhere edit & lp *Threshold 15/promo/ps/'88* $8
Lean On Me (Tonight) *Polydor 710/ promo/logo on white/'91* $8
Question (new '89 version) *Threshold 154/ promo/silkscreened/'89* $10
Say It With Love *Polydor 453/promo/logo on blue/gatefold hardcover ps/'91* $7

MOORE, CHANTE
As If We Never Met edit/remix vocal/suite *MCA 2689/promo/rear insert/'93* $6
It's Alright 7 versions (jazz & hip hop remixes) *Silas 2611/promo/custom sticker/ rear insert/'93* $6
It's Alright 6 versions *Silas 2494/promo/rear insert/'93* $7
It's Alright 8 versions *Silas 2610/promo/rear insert/'93* $7
Love's Taken Over 10 versions *Silas 2260/promo/ps/'92* $7
Love's Taken Over 5:17/6:34 *MCA 2416/promo/ps/'92* $6
Love's Taken Over 6 versions *Silas 2091/promo/ps/'92* $7
Who Do I Turn To 4 versions *MCA 2794/promo/rear insert/'93* $7
Who Do I Turn To 7 versions *Silas 2810/promo/rear insert/'93* $7

MOORE, DOROTHY
Be Strong Enough to Hold On/If You'll Give Me Your Heart *Malaco 2172/promo/ logo on black/'91* $4
Stay Close to Home *Malaco 2190/promo/ silkscreened pic/'93* $4

MOORE, GARY
Cold Day in Hell *Charisma 087/promo/'92* $5
Cold Day in Hell/All Time Low/Stormy Monday (live)/Key to Love/Woke Up This.. *Charisma 96199/stock/ gatefold hardcover ps/'92* $6
Led Clones edit & lp *Virgin 714/promo/silkscreened/'88* $5
Moving On *Virgin 027/promo/ps/'90* $4
Oh Pretty Woman *Charisma 003/promo/ silkscreened/ps/'90* $5
Parisienne Walkways edit & lp *Charisma 12789/ promo/logo on black/'93* $4
Ready For Love lp & edit *Virgin 2597/promo/'88* $5
Still Got the Blues (edit) *Charisma 014/promo/ps/'90* $4
Story of the Blues edit & lp & dry mix/ King of the Blues live *Charisma 099/ promo/silkscreened/ps/'92* $5

MOORE, IAN
How Does It Feel *Capricorn 6246/promo/ ps/logo on silver/'93* $4
Intro: Texas Radio Talks With Ian Moore (How Does It Feel/2 interview segments/Nothing) *Capricorn 6243/ promo/silkscreened/ps/'93* $10

MOORE, JOHN
Perfect End *Polydor 404/promo/ps/'91* $4

MOORE, MELBA
Lift Every Voice and Sing (6 versions) *Capitol 79895/promo/'90* $5

Moore Love Songs ep (Im in Love/First Love/ I Dont Know No One Else../ Love Always Finds a Way) *Capitol 79369/promo/custom sticker* $5

MOORE, MELBA & FREDDIE JACKSON

I Can't Complain edit & lp *Capitol 79313/promo/ps/'88* $5

MOOSE

Jack *Virgin 4319/promo/logo on green/'91* $4

MORALES, MICHAEL

I Don't Wanna See... *Wing 470/promo/ps/'91* $4
I Don't Know *Wing 155/promo/ silkscreened pic/'89* $4
What I Like About You *Mercury 103/ promo/silkscreened pic/'89* $4
Who Do You Give Your Love To 3 versions *Wing 50/promo/silkscreened logo/ps* $4

MORDRED

Esse Quam Videri remix/Killing Time/Every Days a Holiday (last 2 live)/Lion's Den/Johnny the Fox Meets Jimmy the Weed *Noise International 3612-44888/ stock/gatefold hardcover ps/'91* $5
Every Day's a Holiday/Superfreak *Noise International 3/promo/ silkscreened/rear insert/'89* $5

MORGAN, LORRIE

Something in Red edit single *RCA 62219/promo/'92* $4
We Both Walk *RCA 2748/promo/ps/'91* $5

MORGAN, MELI'SA

Can You Give Me What I Want 5 versions *Capitol 79976/promo/rear insert/'90* $7
I Don't You Know 3 versions *Capitol 79211/ promo/logo on yellow/'90* $6
I'm Gonna Be Your Lover (Tonight) 3 versions *Pendulum 8659/promo/ silkscreened/ps/'92* $6
Still in Love With You edit/radio edit/ still in love mix *Pendulum 8536/ promo/logo on blue/ps/'92* $6

MORICE, TARA & MARK WILLIAMS

Time After Time *Columbia 5106/promo/ps* $4

MORRIS, GARY

Full Moon on an Empty Heart *Capitol 79816/ promo/silkscreened/'91* $4

MORRIS, JENNY

She Has to Be Loved (2 versions)/ Giant 30 second sampling *Giant 4508/ promo/rear insert/custom sticker/'90* $4
She Has to Be Loved (4 versions)/ Saved Me (2 versions) *Giant 4387/promo/rear insert/'89* $5

MORRISON, VAN

Ball & Chain/It Fills You Up/And the Healing Has Begun (last 2 live) *Polydor 989/ promo/logo on black/'93* $8
Have I Told You Lately *Mercury 108/promo/ silkscreened swan/'89* $6
I'm Not Feeling It Anymore edit & lp *Polydor 623/promo/ps/logo on cream* $5
Orangefield *Mercury 167/promo/silkscreened* $5
Ordinary Life *Polydor 656/promo/ logo on gold/ps/'92* $5
Real Real Gone *Mercury 340/promo/ps/'90* $5
Songs From Hymns to the Silence ep (Why Must I Explain/Prof.Jealousy/Im Not Feeling It Anymore + 3) *Polydor 560/promo/ps/'91* $8
Whenever God Shines His Light *Mercury 79/promo/silkscreened/ps/'89* $6
Why Must I Always Explain *Polydor 491/ promo/logo on white/ps/'91* $5
Youth of 1,000 Summers *Mercury 387/promo/ps/'91* $5

MORRISSEY

At KROQ (3 tracks live) *Sire 40184/stock/ps/'91* $8
Everyday is Like Sunday *Sire 3112/promo/ps/'88* $12
Glamorous Glue *Sire 5752/promo* $6
My Love Life/I've Changed My Plea to Guilty/ Skin Storm *Sire 40163/stock/ gatefold hardcover ps/'91* $6
November Spawned a Monster/He Knows Id Love to See Him/Girl Least Likely To *Sire 21529/stock/ps/'90* $6
Ouija Board, Ouija Board/Yes Im Blind/East West *Sire 21424/stock/ps/'89* $8
Our Frank *Sire 4732/promo/'91* $6
Our Frank/Journalists Who Lie/Tony the Pony .... *Sire 40043/stock/ gatefold hardcover ps/'91* $6
Sing Your Life/That's Entertainment/The Loop *Sire 40084/stock/ gatefold hardcover ps/'91* $6
Suedehead *Sire 3013/promo/ps/'88* $12
Tomorrow *Sire 5649/promo/'92* $6
Tomorrow remix & lp *Sire 5637/promo/ logo on brown/'92* $8
Tomorrow/Let the Right One Slip In/ Pashernate Love *Sire 40580/ stock/gatefold hardcover ps/'92* $6
We Hate It When Our Friends Become Success./ I've Changed My Plea to Guilty/ Pregnant For the.../Alsatian Cousin (last 3 live) *Sire 40560/stock/ gatefold hardcover ps/'92* $6

MORSE, STEVE

Battle Lines *MCA 1611/promo/'91* $4
Endless Waves/Country Colors/Modoc/Ghostwind *MCA 18047/promo/'89* $5
Morning Rush Hour *MCA 2182/promo/'92* $4
Simple Simon *MCA 1378/promo/ green silkscreened/rear insert/'91* $4
Tumeni Notes *MCA 17965/promo/'89* $4

MOTHER LOVE BONE

Stardog Champion 4:30/4:58 *Mercury 763/ promo/silkscreened/ gatefold hardcover ps/'92* $6
Stardog Champion/Gentle Groove *Polygram 244/promo/ silkscreened/ps/'90* $6
Stargazer *Mercury 849/promo/ silkscreened/ps/'93* $5
This is Shangrila *Polydor 348/promo/ silkscreened logo on pink/ps/'90* $6

MOTHERS FINEST

Cry Baby 3 versions *Scotti Bros 75334/ promo/logo on black/ps/'92* $5
Generator *Scotti Bros 75316/promo/ps/'92* $4
Im in Danger (5 versions) *Capitol 79676/ promo/silkscreened/'89* $5
Like a Negro/Head Bangin' and Booty Shakin'/ The Wall/Police on My Back *Scotti Bros 75339/promo/ logo on black/ps/'92* $5

MOTHERS, THE

Miracle Man *Elektra 8331/promo/ps/'91* $4

MOTLEY CRUE

Angela *Elektra 8513/promo/ps/'92* $6
Crucial Crue (10 song compilation) *Elektra 8116/promo/ps/ silkscreened logo on green/'89* $25
Dont Go Away Mad edit & lp *Elektra 8176/ promo/silkscreened logo/rear insert*..........$8
Dr Feelgood *Elektra 8108/promo/ps/'89* $8
Home Sweet Home *Elektra 8463/ promo/logo on blue/'91* $8
Kickstart My Heart *Elektra 8128/promo/ silkscreened logo/'89* $8
Primal Scream edit & lp *Elektra 8418/ promo/logo silkscreened/ps/'91* $6
Same Ol Situation (S.O.S.) *Elektra 8204/ promo/silkscreened logo/rear insert*..........$8
Without You *Elektra 8152/promo/ silkscreened logo/'89* $8

MOTORHEAD

Angel City/Going to Brazil/No Voices in Sky/ I'm So Bad/Ramones (last 4 live) *WTG 4169/promo/ logo on red/rear insert/'91* $20
Bad Religion *WTG 4903/promo/ silkscreened/ps/'92* $6
Hellraiser *Epic 4588/promo/silkscreened red&black logo/ps/custom sticker/'92* $7
It's Almost... 1916 (The One to Sing the Blues/ I'm So Bad/interview with Lemmy + additional musical segments) *WTG 2295/promo/ps/'91* $12
No Voices in the Sky/Eagle Rock *WTG 4010/promo/ silkscreened/rear insert/'91* $7
You Better Run *WTG 4789/promo/ silkscreened/ps/'92* $6

MOTORHEAD/TRIUMPH

Hellraiser/Hell on Earth/Troublemaker *Dimension 558/promo/silkscreened*..........$7

MOTORPSYCHO

Midnite Sun *Hollywood 10165/promo/ silkscreened/rear insert/'92* $4
Truth *Hollywood 10108/promo/ silkscreened/ps/'92* $4

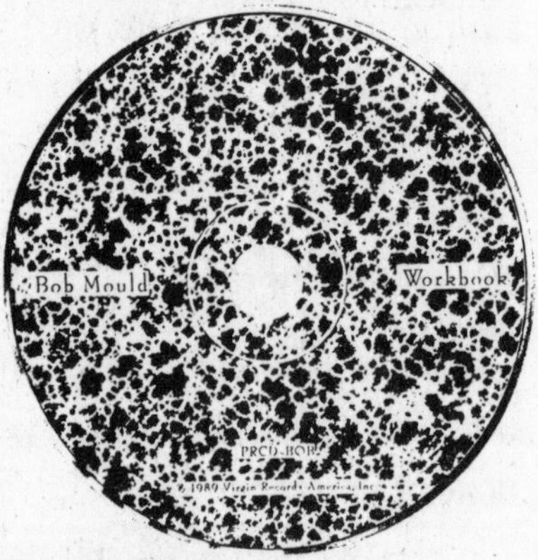

MOULD, BOB

It's Too Late *Virgin 3471/promo/ silkscreened logo/'90* $5
Out of Your Life/Stop Your Crying *Virgin 3665/promo/silkscreened/'90*..........$5
See a Little Light *Virgin 2685/promo/silkscreened/'89*..........$4
Stand Guard/Stop Your Cryin'/Hanging Tree/ One Good Reason + 1 *Virgin 3513/promo/'90*....................$10
Wishing Well/If You're True/Poison Years/ Brasilia Crossed../Shoot Out the Lights (last 4 live) *Virgin 2929/promo/'89*....................$15
Workbook lp in special cover *Virgin PRCD-BOB/ promo/silkscreened/ super package!!/'89* $15

MOUSKOURI, NANA

Even Now *Philips PRO 2/promo/ silkscreened/rear insert/'91* $4

Falling In Love Again sampler (Beauty & the Beast/Falling in Love Again/Wind Beneath My Wings/Over the Rainbow) *Philips 629/promo/silkscreened/ gatefold hardcover ps/'93* $8

MOVEMENT, THE

Bingo 6 versions *Arista 2500/promo/ps/ silkscreened/'92* $4
Jump! 7 versions *Arista 2456/ promo/logo on purple/ps/'92* $4

MOVING PICTURES

What About Me lp & live *Geffen 3723/promo* $4

MOYET, ALISON

Hoodoo lp & single remix/Situation/ State Farm/Invisible/Love Resurrect./ Glorious Love *Columbia 4080/promo/ps/'91* $12
It Won't Be Long edit & lp *Columbia 73872/ promo/ps/silkscreened/'91* $5

MOZART

Japan is Calling lp & edit *SBK 05450/ promo/silkscreened/ps/'92* $4

MR. BIG

Addicted to That Rush *Atlantic 2780/promo/ps/'89* $4
Big Love *Atlantic 3080/promo/ custom tour date sticker/rear insert* $4
Green Tinted Sixties Mind *Atlantic 3796/promo/ps/'91* $4
Green Tinted Sixties Mind *Atlantic 3796/promo/ps/'91* $4
Just Take My Heart edit & lp *Atlantic 4445/ promo/silkscreened pic/rear insert* $4
Lucky This Time *Atlantic 4022/promo/ps/'91* $4
To Be With You *Atlantic 4211/promo/ silkscreened pic/rear insert/'91* $4
Wind Me Up *Atlantic 2966/promo/ps/'89*..............$4

MR. BUNGLE

Quote Unquote edit & lp *WB 4993/promo/'91* $4

MR. FIDDLER

Cool About It (edit) *Elektra 8226/ promo/rear insert/'90*................................$4
So You Wanna be a Gangster 3 versions *Elektra 8383/promo/ps/'91* $4

MR. FINGERS

What About This Love 6 versions *MCA 2393/promo/rear insert/'92*...............$4

MR. LEE

Hey Love 2 versions *Jive 42017/promo/ps/'92* $4

MR. MISTER

Something Real (Inside Me Inside You) *RCA 6601/promo/rear insert/'87* $6
Stand & Deliver (2 versions) *RCA 7667/promo/ps/'87* $6

MR. REALITY

Anonymous SBK 04675/promo/ps/ *silkscreened/'92* $4

MS. ADVENTURES

Undeniable (4 versions) *Atco 3428/promo/ silkscreened/ps/'90* $4

MSG

Crazy/Eve/Paradise/Never Ending Nightmare *Impact 2122/promo/logo on black/ back title cover/'91* $7
Follow the Night (2 versions) *EMI 79281/ promo/laser etched/rear insert*..................$5
Never Ending Nightmare chr/aor/lp *Impact 2243/promo/ silkscreened/rear insert/'92* $5

MUDHONEY

Blinding Sun/Deception Pass/King Sandbox/ Baby o Baby *Reprise 40741/promo/ gatefold hardcover ps/'93* $5
Into the Drink *Sub Pop/promo/logo on brown* $8
Let It Slide/Ounce of Deception/Paperback Life/The Money Will Roll Right In/ Checkout Time (alt.versions) *Sub Pop 95/logo on orange/stock/ps*........$8
Suck You Dry *Reprise 5771/promo/ silkscreened (like old tan labels)/'92* $6

MUFFS, THE

Lucky Guy remix & lp *WB 6212/promo/ silkscreened group shot/'93*.....................$5

MULDAUR, JENNI

Black Clouds *WB 5830/promo/logo on purple* $4

MURDOCK, SHIRLEY

Found My Way edit & remix *Elektra 8043/promo/'88*.............................$4
In Your Eyes *Elektra 8337/promo/ logo on white/ps/'91* $4
Stay With Me Tonight edit & lp *Elektra 8428/promo/ps/'91* $4

MURPHEY, MICHAEL MARTIN/ SOUTHERN PACIFIC

Never Givin' Up on Love/Any Way the Wind . *WB 3498/promo/'89* $4

MURPHY'S LAW

Monster Mash/Beer Bath/Big Spliff *Relativity 88561 1062/stock/ps/'91* $5

MURPHY, EDDIE
I Was a King edit/lp/instrumental/percapella *Motown 374631075/promo/ps/silkscreened/'92* $5
Put Your Mouth on Me (4 versions) *Columbia 1616/promo/ps/'89* $6
Till the Moneys Gone (5 versions) *Columbia 1896/promo/ps/'89* $6
Wahtzupwitu lp & instrumental *Motown 374631100/promo/ps/'93* $4
Whatzupwitu 6 versions *Motown 374631111/promo/'93* $4

MURPHY, PETER
Cuts You Up edit & lp *RCA 9140/promo/fold out cover/silkscreened/'89* $10
Deep (lp length) *RCA 9877/limited fold out cover/stock/'89* $12
Strange Kind of Love (3 versions)/All Night Long (live) *RCA 2625/promo/silkscreened pic/ps/'90* $12
The Line Between the Devils Teeth 5:34/7:57 *RCA 9108/promo/ps/'89* $8
The Sweetest Drop edit & lp/Low Room/All Night Long/The Line Between the Devil's Teeth (last 2 live) *RCA 62239/promo/ps/silkscreened* $10
You're So Close edit & lp *RCA 62285/promo/silkscreened pic/rear insert/'92* $4
You're So Close/Line Between the Devil's ../Cuts You Up/All Night .. (last 3 live) *RCA 62302/stock/ps/silkscreened pic/'92* . $5

MURRAY, ANNE
New Way Out *Capitol 79600/promo/silkscreened red/'91* $5

MURRAY, ANNE & KENNY ROGERS
If I Ever Fall in Love Again *Capitol 79747/promo/silkscreened logo on blue/'89* $5

MUSTO & BONES
Dangerous on the Dancefloor 4 versions *RCA 62058/promo/rear insert/'91* $4

MY BLOODY VALENTINE
Only Shallow edit & lp *Sire 5191/promo/'91* $4
Soon/Glider/Dont Ask Why/Off Your Face *Sire 26313/stock/ps/'90* $6
To Here KnowsWhen/Swallow/Honey Power/Moon Song *Sire 40024/stock/gatefold hardcover ps/'91* $6
When You Sleep *Sire 5303/promo/logo on metallic red/'91* $4

MY LIFE WITH THE THRILL KILL KULT
Sex on Wheelz 4 versions/Farout 1 *Interscope 4621/promo/silkscreened/rear insert* $7
Sexplosion 4 versions *Wax Trax 9180/stock/silkscreened/ps/'92* $6

MY LITTLE FUNHOUSE
I Want Some of That *Geffen 4459/promo/silkscreened/gatefold hardcover ps* $4

MYLES, ALANNAH
Black Velvet *Atlantic 2884/promo/rear insert* $4
Living on a Memory edit & lp *Atlantic 4985/promo* $4
Love Is *Atlantic 2673/promo/ps/89* $4
Lover of Mine *Atlantic 3419/promo/ps/'90* $4
Our World edit & lp *Atlantic 4846/promo* $4
Song Instead of a Kiss edit *Atlantic 4775/promo/silkscreened/ps/'92* $4

N-JOI
Mindflux hot mind edit & full length *RCA 62238/promo/rear insert/cust.sticker* $4

N/MOTION
Love is Not a Dinosaur *WB 5304/promo/'92* $4

NAIL, JIMMY
Ain't No Doubt *Atlantic 4736/promo/silkscreened pic/rear insert/'92* $5

NAJEE
All I Ever Ask edit & lp *EMI 04720/promo/ps/custom sticker/logo on black/'93* $6
I Adore Mi Amor lp/edit/non vocal *EMI 04882/promo/silkscreened/ps/'92* $6
I'll Be Good to You 7" edit/12" remix/lp/instrumental remix *EMI 4612/promo/silkscreened logo/rear insert/'90* $6
I'll Be Good to You 7" good sax mix/extended/good sax instrumental *EMI 4672/promo/silkscreened/rear insert/'90* $6
Tokyo Blue 7" & lp/Gina *EMI 04356/promo/silkscreened/rear insert/'90* $6

NAKED SOUL
Inside Out lp/ep/acoustic *Scotti Bros 75361/promo/logo on white/ps/'93* $4
Lonely Me, Lonely You *Scotti Bros 75343/promo/logo on black/ps/'92* $4

NASA
Magic Jewelled Limousine/Power to Love (both edits) *Sire 4066/promo/'90* $4
Shah Shah (4 versions)/Raag Murubihag../Cruisin' Persian *Sire 21434/stock/ps/'90* . $4

NASHVILLE CHILDREN'S CHORUS
It's Beginning to Look a Lot../Jingle Bell Rock/Carole of the Bells/O Holy Night *WB 4571/promo/'90* $5

NATURAL SELECTION
Hearts Don't Think remix edit/radio remix *Eastwest 4305/promo* $5

NAUGHTY BY NATURE

Everything's Gonna Be Alright 4 versions
Tommy Boy 508/promo/'91 .... $7
Hip Hop Hooray 3 versions/The Hood Comes First lp & instrumental
Tommy Boy 554/stock/ps/'93 .... $5
It's On 4 versions *Tommy Boy 574/promo/'93* $7
Naughty by Numbers ep (OPP clean versions/ Everything's Gonna Be Alright radio/ Uptown Anthem video/Hip Hop Hooray/It's On kay gee remix/ Written on Ya Kitten)
Tommy Boy 1079/promo/ logo on white/ps/'93 .... $10
O.P.P. 3 versions/Wickedest Man Alive 2 vers.
Tommy Boy 988/stock/ps/'91 .... $6

NAUMANN, JEFF & PIGS ON CORN

They're Coming to Take Me Away Ha-Haa/ Naumannclature
POC International 003/stock/ps/'93 .... $4

NEAR, HOLLY

Singer in the Storm *Chameleon 92/promo/ silkscreened/'90* $4

NED'S ATOMIC DUSTBIN

Happy/23 Hour Toothache/Aim at the Civic/ 45 Second Blunder
Columbia 4050/promo/ps/'91 .... $6
Kill Your Television lp & censored versions
Columbia 4475/promo/ps/'91 .... $5
Kill Your Television/Terminal Groovie/Sentence/ Kill Your Remix
Columbia 44K 74202/stock/ps/'92 .... $5
Not Sleeping Around/Cut Up tartan shoulders mix/Scrawl *Chaos 74718/stock/ps* $5
Saturday Night *Chaos 5239/promo/ps/'93* $4
Walking Through Syrup/Prostrate/Swiss Legoland (live) *Chaos 4931/promo/ ps/silkscreened/'93* $5

NEIGHBORHOODS, THE

Prettiest Girl *Third Stone 4104/promo/ silkscreened shadow pic/rear insert* $4

NEIL, VINCE

Can't Change Me *WB 6275/promo/ silkscreened pic/'93* $6
Can't Have Your Cake *WB 6151/promo/'93* $4
Sister of Pain *WB 6100/promo/ps/ silkscreened group pic/'93* $6
Various w/interview + other groups songs (MINDBOMB, CATHEDRAL, THE FLUID, ANTHRAX, WASP, TOOL, more) *Foundations/ promo/die cut ps/'93* $15
You're Invited *Hollywood 10164/promo/ logo on black/rear insert/'92* $5

NELSON

After the Rain *DGC 4161/promo/ gatefold hardcover ps/'90* $5
Love and Affection *DGC 4126/promo/ gatefold hardcover ps/'90* $5
More Than Ever
DGC 4200/promo/gatefold ps/'90 .... $5
More Than Ever 4 versions *DGC 4210/ promo/ps/custom sticker/'91* $8
Only Time Will Tell
DGC 4229/promo/logo on blue/ps/'91 .... $5

NELSON, LOEY

Only the Shadows Know (3 versions)
WB 4076/promo/'90 .... $4
To Sir With Love edit & lp *WB 4451/promo* $4

NELSON, WILLIE

A Horse Called Music (lp length)
Columbia 45046/promo/silkscreened/ rear insert/special dj only edition/'89 .... $15
Across the Borderline 14 tracks
Columbia/promo/trifold hardcover/ booklet/DYLAN, SINEAD O'CONNOR, BONNIE RAITT, more/'93 .... $15
Graceland *Columbia 74993/promo/ silkscreened/rear insert/'93* $5
Is the Better Part Over
Columbia 73374/promo/'90 .... $4
Who'll Buy My Memories
Sony Music Special Products 22364/ promo/ps/logo on blue/'91 .... $6

NELSON/CASH/JENNINGS/ KRISTOFFERSON

Highwayman 2 (full length) *Columbia 45240/ promo only silkscreened group pic/ rear insert/'90* $20

NEMESIS

I Want Your Sex 3:59/3:35/6:05
Profile 7341/promo/logo on black/'91 .... $4
Temple of Boom 3:16/3:40 *Profile 7397/ promo/silkscreened/rear insert/'93* $4

NEVADA BEACH

Waiting For an Angel *Metal Blade 4427/ promo/rear insert/'90* $4

NEVIL, ROBBIE

For Your Mind powerhouse mix
EMI 4824/promo/rear insert/'91 .... $4
Somebody Like You single/TJ mix/ radio dance mix + 2 more mixes
EMI 4223/promo/ps/'89 .... $5

NEVILLE BROTHERS

A Change is Gonna Come/The Christmas Song/ People Say/Tell It Like It is/Yellow Moon/Shake Your Tambour.(last 4 live)
A&M 17931/promo/silkscreened/'89 .... $15

A Change is Gonna Come/With God On Our Side (edit) *A&M 18011/promo/ps/'90* $5
Bird on a Wire edit & lp *A&M 18036/ promo/Goldie & Mel ps/'90* $5
Bird on a Wire/Yellow Moon/Healing Chant *A&M 75021 2331/ps/stock/'90* $5
Fearless (3 versions) *A&M 75021 7425/promo/ps/'90* $5
Fire and Brimstone *A&M 17739/promo/silkscreened/'89* $4
Fly Like an Eagle 8 versions *A&M 75021 7349/promo/logo on blue/gatefold hardcover ps/'92*.................$5
Fly Like an Eagle/One More Day/Day to Day .. *A&M 75021 7376/promo/ps/'92* $5
Mystery Train *A&M 75021 7445/promo/ps* $5
One More Day 5 versions *A&M 75021 7381/promo/'92* $6
River of Life edit & lp *A&M 75021 7402/promo/ps/'90* $4
Sister Rosa 3:22/3:30 *A&M 17732/ promo/embossed black CD/'89*................$5
Sister Rosa 3:42/5:58/4:54/3:29 *A&M 17769/promo/cust. sticker/'89* $5
Take Me to Heart single versions *A&M 31458 8035/promo/ silkscreened/ps/'92* $5
The Evolution of Groove 1981 to Now 11 tracks *A&M 75021 7350/promo/ ps/logo on black/'92* $25
With God On Our Side (edit) *A&M 17980/promo/silkscreened/'89* $5
Yellow Moon *A&M 17782/promo/silkscreened* ...$5

NEVILLE, AARON

Don't Fall Apart on Me Tonight radio/lp *A&M 31458 8169/promo/logo on blue/ps* .$5
Don't Take Away My Heaven remix/lp/ remix with intro *A&M 31458 8118/ promo/silkscreened/ gatefold hardcover ps/'93* $5
Everybody Plays the Fool 5 versions *A&M 75021 7001/promo/ silkscreened/ps/'91* $6
Somewhere, Somebody *A&M 75021 7275/ promo/ps/silkscreened/'91* $4
The Grand Tour *A&M 31458 8170/promo/ gatefold hardcover ps/silkscreened* $4
Warm Your Heart 13 tracks *A&M 75021 5354/promo/silkscreened*....$15

NEVILLE, IVAN

Not Just Another Girl 7" & lp *Polydor 22/promo/ps/'88* $4
Primitive Man remix & lp *Polydor 53/promo/ps/'89* $4
Why Can't I Fall in Love *MCA 1049/promo/rear insert/'90*..............$4

NEW ATLANTIC

I Know 4 vers. *Big Beat 10049/stock/ps/'91*........$4
I Know 4 vers. *Big Beat 4521/promo/ rear insert*...$4

NEW EDITION

Boys to Men 4 vers. *MCA 1632/promo/ps/'91* $5

NEW FAITH

You Were Always There (edit)/Love is the Bottom LIne/You Are My Refuge/ Kum Ba Yah *WB 5383/promo/'91* $4

NEW FAST AUTOMATIC DAFFODILS

Bong/It's Not What You Know/Head On/ Beautiful/Cannes *Mute 61438/ stock/custom sticker/'92*...........................$5
Get Better (3 versions) *Mute 8341/promo/ silkscreened/rear insert/'91* $5
It's Not What You Know *Mute 8750/promo/ silkscreened/ps/'93* $4
Stockholm radio & lp *Mute 8703/promo/ logo on green/ps/'92* $4

NEW KIDS ON THE BLOCK

Call It What You Want C&C Pump mix & edit *Columbia 3061/promo/silkscreen/ps*.........$6
Cover Girl *Columbia 1815/promo/ps/'88* $6
Didn't I (blow Your Mind) *Columbia 68960/promo/ps/'89* $6
Games edit & extended *Columbia 73620/promo/ps/'90* $6
If You Go Away *Columbia 4462/promo/ps/'92* $5
Let's Try It Again *Columbia 73443/promo/ps* $5
Please Don't Go Girl (7" version) *Columbia 1184/promo/ps/'88* $6
Step by Step radio edit/lp/club remix *Columbia 73343/promo/ oversized "locker" ps w/lock*....................$12
Step by Step radio edit/lp/club remix *Columbia 73343/promo/ps/'90* $6
Tonight *Columbia 73461/promo/ps/'90* $5
You Got It (The Right Stuff) (3 versions) *Columbia 1328/promo/'88*.........................$5

NEW LEGEND

Angel of Mercy *RCA 2622/promo/ps/'90*..............$4

NEW MODEL ARMY

Here Comes the War *no label or #/promo/sticker/'93*..................$6

NEW ORDER

Blue Monday (single, dub & 12" mix) *Qwest 3053/promo/ps/'88* $15
In Order 7 track sampler *Qwest 5970/promo/ps/'93* $15
Regret 2 versions *Qwest 18586/stock/ps* $4
Regret 4 versions *Qwest 40760/stock/ps* $6
Regret lp & new order mix *Qwest 6006/ promo/silkscreened/rear insert* $4
Republic 11 tracks *Qwest 6190/promo/rear insert* $12

Row 1: *EMI Legends of Rock n' Roll Series* (Various artists. Includes 24 baseball-type cards); *Finally* (Ce Ce Peniston); *Happy Holidays—1992* (Various artists). **Row 2:** *The Smithereens Live* (Smithereens); *Selections from Elton John Rare Masters* (Elton John); *Selections from "House of Hope"* (Toni Childs); *Pretty Blue World* (Billy Falcon). **Row 3:** *My Happiness* (Elvis Presley) *Cream* (Prince and the New Power Generation); *Queen of Soul—Sampler* (Aretha Franklin); *Dead Horse* (Guns N' Roses); *Demolition Man* (Sting). **Row 4:** *Everything in the World* (Squeeze); *Workbook* (Bob Mould); *The Yardbirds* (Yardbirds); *The Koo* (The Koo); *Paint the White House Black* (George Clinton). **Row 5:** *Haunted By Real Life* (Schascle. Includes video cassette); *There's a Spy (In the House of Love)* (Animal Logic); *Live from Leeds* (Burning Tree); **Row 6:** *Green* (R.E.M.).

Row 1: *The Apple EP* (Various artists); *Foreign Affair* (Tina Turner); *Bankstatement* (Bankstatement); *Rhythm of the Saints* (Paul Simon). **Row 2**: *Mighty Like a Rose* (Elvis Costello); *Dis-moi, Dis-moi* (Mitson); *MTV Unplugged* (10,000 Maniacs); *Behind the Mask* (Fleetwood Mac); **Row 3:** *Do the Bartman* (Simpsons); *Where There's Smoke* (Gibson/Miller Band); *Find You* (Jason and the Scorchers); *You Don't Have to Go Home Tonight* (Triplets). **Row 4:** *100 Watt Bulb* (Infidels); *NFL Goes Motown (Songs from the Big Thrill)* (Various artists); **Row 5:** *Capitol's 50th Anniversary* (Various artists. Eight CDs plus book); *Recycler* (ZZ Top); **Row 6:** *Charmed Life* (Billy Idol).

Row 1: *7 O'Clock* (London Quireboys); *The Christmas Song* (David Clayton-Thomas); *Why Believe in You* (Texas); *Songs for Drella* (Lou Reed & John Cale). **Row 2:** *What's Forever For* (House of Lords); *Shut Up and Smoke* (Gin Blossoms); *Ghost of an American Airman* (Honey Child) *Goodnight Song* (Tears for Fears); **Row 3:** *Just for Tonight* (Vanessa Williams); *Someday* (Concrete Blonde); *Nobody Said It Was Easy* (Four Horsemen); *Raw Like Sushi* (Neneh Cherry). **Row 4:** *Demolition Man (Five Phat Versions)* (Sting). *Heart Like a Wheel* (Human League); *Bang!* (Gorky Park); *What You Do to Me* (Teenage Fanclub). **Row 5:** *Desire Walks On* (Heart); *Clash on Broadway—The Trailer* (Clash); *Dogs of Lust* (The The); *If At First You Don't Succeed (Try Again)* (Edwin Hawkins).

Row 1: *This Is Love* (George Harrison); *Groovy Train* (The Farm); *Animal Nitrate* (Suede); *Joesphina* (Gene Loves Jezebel) **Row 2:** *Red Rover* (The Tribe); *Come to My Window* (Melissa Etheridge); *Bertha* (Los Lobos); *Dick Tracy* (Ice-T). **Row 3:** *A Life with Brian* (Flowered Up); *The Thanksgiving Song* (Adam Sandler); *Something Wild* (John Hiatt); *You Make Me Feel Brand New* (Roberta Flack). **Row 4:** *Jurassic Park* ("Weird Al" Yankovic); *Run So Far* (Eric Clapton); *I'm Your Baby Tonight* (Whitney Houston); *Foolish Heart* (Grateful Dead). **Row 5:** *Dear Mr. President* (4 Non Blondes); *The Gershwins in Hollywood* (Hollywood Bowl Orchestra with Gregory Hines and Patti Austin); *Love U More* (Sunscreem); *Live in London* (Great White).

Row 1: *Erotic* (Madonna); *Putumayo Presents The Best of World Music* (Various artists); *Get the Wow* (Shonen Knife); *En-Tact* (The Shamen). **Row 2:** *Collected Stories: 1990-1991* (John Wesley Harding); *Beatfish* (Beatfish); *Back on the Black* (Qunicy Jones); Listen Love (Jon Lucien. With body oil, bubble bath and loofah). **Row 3:** Robin Holcomb/Levellers (Robin Holcomb/Levellers. Has one disc by each artist); *Love Me Do* (Beatles); **Row 4:** *Out of Time* (R.E.M.); *Liberty* (Duran Duran); *Shock to the System* (Billy Idol); *Let's Get Rocked* (Def Leppard). **Row 5:** Double Features (Elvis Presley. Four CDs in film canister); *Stress* (Stress); **Row 6:** *These People Are Nuts* (Various artists).

Row 1: *Will You Be There (In the Morning)* (Heart); *Zig Zag* (Hooters) *Rudolph the Red Nosed Reindeer* (Smithereens); *Cloud Nine* (George Harrison). **Row 2:** *What's an Aquarium Rescue Unit* (Col. Bruce Hampton, Ret.); *Steam* (Peter Gabriel); *Too Much Information* (Duran Duran); *Estranged* (Guns N' Roses). **Row 3:** *Postcard* (Widespread Panic); *Jenny Ondioline (Part 1)* (Stereolab); *The Green Disc* (Midnight Oil); *Directified* (Sweet n Lo). **Row 4:** *Baby-Baby-Baby* (TLC); *As Long As I Can Dream* (Expose); *Dry* (PJ Harvey); *Everything Is Broken* (Bob Dylan). **Row 5:** *Vamp* (Transvision Vamp); *Here I Am (Come and Take Me)* (UB40); *57 Channels (And Nothin' On)* (Bruce Springsteen); *Lita's Big Ones* (Lita Ford).

Row 1: *Sex Cymbal* (Sheila E. Includes brass cymbal); *One Bright Day* (Ziggy Marley and the Melody Makers); *These Are Crazy Days* (Boom Crash Opera. Includes cassette); *If Looks Could Kill* (Transvision Vamp). **Row 2:** *7 O'Clock ("It's Time to Party" Choir Book)* (London Quireboys); *Love and Happiness* (John Mellencamp); *Chic-ism* (Chic). **Row 3:** *From the Heart* (Tommy Page); *Blues Masters—The Essential Blues Collection (Sampler)* (Various artists); *Brigade* (Heart). **Row 4:** *Valentine Heart* (Tanita Tikaram) *On the Greener Side* (Michelle Shocked); *Get a Grip* (Aerosmith); *The Sharpest Cuts* (Judas Priest). **Row 5:** *Ferrington Guitars* (Various artists. Includes book); *Born into the 90's* (R. Kelly and Public Announcement. With cassette and velvet pouch); *Tumbleweed* (Tumbleweed). *Pump* (Aerosmith); *Love Hurts* (Cher. Includes 13 tarot-type cards).

Row 1: *The Last Drag* (Samples); *RCA Nashville—Sixty Years: 1928-1988* (Various artists); *Mondo Supremo* (Various artists); *Daylight* (Judy Bats). **Row 2:** *Mercury Menu* (Various artists); *Tom's Album* (Various artists); *Otis! (The Definitive Otis Redding Sampler)* (Otis Redding); *Garth Brooks Interview for a World Premier of "In Pieces"* (Garth Brooks). **Row 3:** *Message for the Mess Age* (NRBQ); *Flat Duo Jets in Stereo* (Flat Duo Jets); *Sweet Leaf* (Ugly Kid Joe); *The Only Way Is Up* (Yazz). **Row 4:** *Sentimental Journey (Pop Vocal Classics Sampler)* (Various artists); *Red Hot & Blue (All Time Great Rhythm & Blues Songs)* (Various artists); *Again Tonight* (John Mellencamp); *Who's Watching You* (Vain); **Row 5:** *This Is Not the Age of Aquarius* (Various artists); *Tasty New Doo Wop* (Various artists); *Chrome* (Catherine Wheel); *Tease Me, Please Me* (Scorpions).

Round & Round (4 versions)
Qwest 3463/promo/'89 .... $10
Ruined in a Day single/sly & robbie edit/lp
Qwest 6318/promo/rear insert/'93 .... $5
True Faith (3 versions) *Qwest 2899/ promo/silkscreened/'87* $16
World (The Price of Love) 5 versions/ Ruined in a Day 2 versions
Qwest 40966/stock/ gatefold hardcover ps/'93 .... $6
World (The Price of Love) edit/perfecto edit/lp/perfecto mix *Qwest 6276/ promo/logo on blue/rear insert/'93* $5
World (The Price of Love)/Ruined in a Day
Qwest 18432/stock/ps $4
World in Motion 4 versions
Qwest 21582/stock/ps/'90 .... $6

NEWBURY, MICKEY
An American Trilogy/San Francisco Mabel Joy
Airborne 0101/promo/'88 .... $4

NEWMAN, COLIN
Provisionally Entitled.. & Not To 25 tracks
Restless 72397/stock/ps $12

NEWMAN, RANDY
Falling in Love *Reprise 3397/promo/'89* $5
I Love to See You Smile (edit)/End Title (I Love to see..) (long edit)
Reprise 3707/promo/'89 .... $5
It's Money That Matters
Reprise 3272/promo/ps/'88 .... $5

NEWMAN, TROY
I Can Feel It single remix *East West 4074/ promo/logo silkscreened/'91* $4

NEWTON, WAYNE
At This Moment *Curb 025/promo/'90* $5
I Know So *Curb 085/promo* $5

NEWTON-JOHN, OLIVIA
Can't We Talk It Over in Bed *MCA 17673/ promo/silkscreened blue/'88* $8
Deeper Than a River radio/lp
Geffen 4449/promo/'92 .... $7
Deeper Than a River single/urban/lp
Geffen 4448/promo/ silkscreened pic/ps/'92 .... $8
I Need Love 5 versions
Geffen 4406/promo/ gatefold hardcover ps/'92 .... $8
Reach Out For Me (5 versions)
Geffen 3782/promo/die cut trifold hardcover ps/silkscreened/'89 .... $12
The Rumour remix edit & 12" remix ext. & lp version *MCA 17594/promo/ps/'88* $10
Warm and Tender (15 tracks)
Geffen 242572/promo/ die cut round booklet ps/'89 .... $15

NEXT ISSUE
Dear Mr President 4 versions *Epic 74397/ promo/silkscreened/ps/'92* $4

NFL GOES MOTOWN
Songs From the Big Thrill Single
Motown 822/promo/ps/ silkscreened(to look like vinyl 7")/'92 .... $4

NICE & SMOOTH
Cake & Eat It Too 3 versions *Columbia 74365/ promo/logo on blue/rear insert/'92* $4
Hip Hop Junkies 6 versions *Columbia 73784/ promo/logo on black/ps/'91* $4

NICKS, STEVIE
Love's a Hard Game to .. remix & edit of remix
Modern 4282/promo/ silkscreened pic/rear insert/'91 .... $10
Rooms on Fire *Modern 2691/promo/ gatefold hardcover ps/'89* $6
Rooms on Fire remix & remix edit
Modern 2744/promo/rear insert/'89 .... $8
Sometimes *Modern 4021/promo/silkscreened/p* .. $8
Two Kinds of Love (duet with BRUCE HORNSBY) *Modern 2875/promo/ silkscreened logo/rear insert/'89* $8
Whole Lotta Trouble (edit remix)
Modern 2977/promo/ps/'89 .... $10

NICKS, STEVIE & RICK VITO
Desiree *Modern 4413/promo/silkscreened/ps* $8

NIGHT RANGER
Reason to Be *MCA 17728/promo/'88* $4

NIKITA
Sweet as it Comes edit/lp/instrumental
Motown 374631088/promo/ps/'92 .... $4

NIKKI
If You Wanna *Geffen 3549/promo/ps/'89* $4

NIKKI D
Freak Out clean/instrumental *Epic 5192/ promo/rear insert/logo on black/ custom sticker/'93* $4
Hang On Kid 4 versions
Def Jam 73811/promo/ps/'91 .... $4

NILE, WILLIE
Everybody Needs a Hammer *Columbia 4055/ promo/silkscreened pic/ps/'91* $4
Heaven Help the Lonely
Columbia 73730/promo/ps/'91 .... $4

NILSSON, HARRY
How About You edit & lp
MCA 1582/promo/ps/'91 .... $6

NINE INCH NAILS

Down in It (3 versions)
TVT 2611/ps/stock/silkscreened/'89 .... $6
Happiness in Slavery *Interscope 4795/ promo/rear insert/'92* $5
Head Like a Hole (4 versions)/Terrible Lie (2 vers.)/Down In It (3 versions) + 1
TVT 2615/stock/ps/'90 .... $8
Sin (3 versions)/Get Down Make Love
TVT 2617/stock/ps/'90 .... $6

9 WAYS TO SUNDAY

Come Tell Me Now long & short
Giant 4538/promo/ silkscreened/rear insert/'90 .... $4
Come Tell Me ../Midnight Train/Get Back Home
Giant 4403/promo/ps/'90 .... $5
Selftitled (10 tracks) *Giant 24402/ promo/silkscreened/ps/'90* $12

NIRVANA

Come as You Are *DGC 4375/promo/ silkscreened/gatefold hardcover ps* $6
Heart-Shaped Box *DGC 4545/promo/ gatefold hardcover ps/'93* $5
In Bloom *DGC 4463/promo/silkscreened/'92* $6
Lithium *DGC 4429/promo/logo on green/'92* $6
Lithium/Been a Son (live)/Curmudgeon
DGC 21815/stock/ps/silkscreened (with promo)/'92 .... $8
Nevermind 13 tracks *DGC 24425/ with 13th hidden track/ps/'91* $15
Nevermind, its an Interview
DGC 4382/promo/ gatefold hardcover ps/'92 .... $15
On a Plain *DGC 4354/promo/logo on blue/'91* $6
Smells Like Teen Spirit edit & lp
DGC 4308/promo/silkscreened/ps $8
Smells Like Teen Spirit edit/Even in His Youth/Aneurysm *DGC 21673/ gatefold hardcover ps/ silkscreened/stock/'91* $8

NITTY GRITTY DIRT BAND, THE

From Small Things (Big Things One Day Come)
MCA 79013/promo/rear insert/'90 .... $5
Mr Bojangles *Capitol 79755/promo/ps/ silkscreened logo on black/'91* $5
The Rest of the Dream (edit-remix)
MCA 53964/promo/rear insert/'90 .... $5
You Made Life Good Again
MCA 79075/promo/rear insert/'90 .... $5

NITTY GRITTY DIRT BAND, THE w/ROSANNE CASH & JOHN HIATT

One Step Over the Line
MCA 53795/promo/silkscreened logo on cream/rear insert/'89 .... $5

NITZER EBB

All States Promo (Godhead purified/I Give to You pestilence/Join in the Chant/ Control Im Here/Fun to Be Had +1)
Geffen 4374/promo/ gatefold hardcover ps/'92 .... $10
Ebbhead 10 tracks *Geffen 24456/stock/ promo silkscreened/ps/'91* $10
Family Man/Lovesick/Come Alive/Higher
Geffen 21658/stock/ gatefold hardcover ps/'91 .... $6
Family Man/Lovesick/Come Alive/Higher
Mute 21658/promo/logo on black/'91 .... $6
Fun to Be Had (6 versions)/Out of Mind
Geffen 4137/promo/ silkscreened logo on green/'90 .... $6
Godhead purified&alt.purified&live&lp/ Let Your Body Learn-Murderous live medley/Join In the Chant live
Geffen 21705/stock/gatefold hardcvr ps ... $6
Godhead purified/alt.purified/l
Geffen 4384/promo/custom sticker $6
I Give to You lp & elemental/Family Man remix
Geffen 4334/promo/logo on black/ps $6
Lightning Man (2 versions)/Getting Closer (3 versions)/Fun to Be Had (2 vers.)
Geffen 21602/stock/ps/'90 .... $6

NO TWO

Tourist radio/club/beverly hills (remixes)
A&M 17736/promo/'89 .... $4

NOISEWORKS

Hot Chilli Woman *Columbia 4263/promo/ps* $4

NOISY MAMA

Eyes on the Prize/Dirty Love/Heart of Stone
Atco 3865/promo/silkscreened/ps $4

NOMAD

(I Wanna Give You) Devotion (8 versions)
Capitol 79766/promo/'91 .... $4

NOONE, PETER

I'm Into Something Good *Cypress 17714/ promo/silkscreened "Naked Gun" art* $6

NORMAL, THE

TVOD/Warm Leatherette
Mute 71400/stock/3"/5" ps/'88 .... $6

NORTHERN PIKES, THE

Dream Away edit radio/radio/lp
Scotti Bros 75301/promo/ps $4
GirlWithaProblem remix & lp *ScottiBros 75311/ promo/ps/custom sticker* $4
She Ain't Pretty *Scotti Bros 75287/ promo/silkscr/ps/'90* $4

NORTHSIDE
My Rising Star/Tour De World edit & lp
Geffen 4353/promo/cust.sticker/'91 .... $4
Take 5 edit & lp *Geffen 4257/promo/ silkscreened/ps/'91* $4

NOTORIOUS
The Swalk edit & lp *DGC 4107/promo/ silkscreened/die cut gatefold hardcover ps/'90* $5

NOTTING HILLBILLIES
Bewildered *WB 4340/promo/rear insert/'90* $8
Will You Miss Me *WB 4092/promo/'90* $8
Your Own Sweet Way fade & lp
WB 3943/promo/silkscreened/'90 .... $7
Your Own Sweet Way fade & lp
WB 3943/promo/silkscreened/'90 .... $8

NOVA MOB
Admiral of the Sea 2 versions/The Last Days of Pompeii (single)/Getaway in Time/ I Just Want to Make Love to You (live)
Rough Trade 267/stock/ps/'91 .... $5

NOVA, ALDO
Blood on the Bricks *Mercury 436/ promo/silkscreened/ gatefold box type ps/'91* $4
Someday edit & lp *Mercury 571/promo/ gatefold hardcover ps/logo on blue* $4

NRBQ
If I Don't Have You (edit) *Virgin 3115/promo/ silkscreened logo & more/'89* $6
It's a Wild Weekend edit & lp
Virgin 2866/promo/silkscreened/'89 .... $6
The One and Only (comp. from Wild Weekend + other lps - 14 songs)
Virgin 2962/promo/ps/'89 .... $15

NU COLOURS
Fallin' Down 4 versions
Polydor 896/promo/ps/'93 .... $4

NU GIRLS
Rush On Me radio/extendedhip hop/street
Atlantic 2937/promo/ silkscreened/rear insert/'89 .... $4

NU SHOOZ
Should I Say Yes 3 versions
Atlantic 2273/promo/'88 .... $4
Time Will Tell 5 versions *Atlantic 4719/promo/ silkscreened/rear insert/'92* $4

NUCLEAR VALDEZ
(Share a Little) Shelter
Epic 4112/promo/ps/'91 .... $4
(Share a Little) Shelter mancuban mix & lp
Epic 74159/promo/ps/ custom sticker/'91 .... $4
Dream Another Dream (10 tracks)
Epic 4121/promo/ps/'91 .... $10
Hope/Summer (live) *Epic 2027/promo/ps/'90* $5
Summer lp & acoustic/Save Me & Dont Believe a Word (both acoustic)
Epic 1891/promo/ps/'89 .... $8

NUDESWIRL
F Sharp *Megaforce 641/promo/'93* $4
F Sharp *Megaforce 974/promo/ silkscreened/ps* $5

NUNN, TERRI
89 Lines club mix edit/blurring the line remix/ edit *DGC 4428/promo/'92* $5
89 Lines edit & lp *DGC 4347/promo/ gatefold hardcover ps/'91* $4
Let Me Be the One chr mix/ac mix/soft ac mix
DGC 4330/promo/ps/'91 .... $6
Take My Breath Away (remix)/Desire Me/ For What It's Worth
DGC 21704/stock/ps/'91 .... $7
Take My Breath Away/No More Words/ Sex (I'm a ..)/Let Me Be the One/ 89 Lines/Who's Gonna Take../ Fly By Night *DGC 4337/promo/ gatefold hardcover ps/'91* $15

NWA
Appetite For Destruction clean/lp
Ruthless 6613/promo/ silkscreened pic/'91 .... $12

NYLONS, THE
Don't Look Any Further with & without rap
Scotti Bros 75350/promo/'92 .... $5
Poison Ivy/same
Windham Hill 17709/promo/ps/'89 .... $5
Wildfire single edit & hot radio mix
Windham Hill 17807/promo/ps/'89 .... $5

NYMPHS
Imitating Angels *DGC 4385/promo/ silkscreened logo on black/ gatefold hardcover ps/'91* $4
Sad and Damned *DGC 4342/promo/ silkscreened/foldout cover/'91* $4

O POSITIVE
Back of My Mind *Epic 2032/promo/ silkscreened/rear insert/'90* $4
Back of My Mind/I Call Your Name/ Gotta Stop Sometime
Epic 2026/promo/ps/'90 .... $4
Imagine That *Epic 2122/promo/silkscreened logo on blue/rear insert/'90* $4

O'CONNELL, MAURA
A Real Life Story (10 tracks) *WB 4638/ promo/silkscreened/rear insert/'91* $10
Guns of Love *WB 4715/promo/'90* $4

O'CONNOR, MARK
Bowtie single versions *WB 5103/promo/ recycled foldout cover/'91* $4
Restless single fade/video fade/lp fade *WB 4717/promo/'91* $4

O'CONNOR, SINEAD
My Special Child vocal & instr./Nothing Compares 2 U/Emperors New Clothes (last 2 live video versions) *Chrysalis 23733/stock/ps/'91* $6
Nothing Compares 2 U *Chrysalis 23488/promo/ps/'90* $8
The Emperors New Clothes edit & lp *Chrysalis 23528/promo/ps/'90* $8
The Emperors New Clothes lp & main mix/ What Do You Want?/Mandinka (jakes remix) *Chrysalis 23585/stock/ps/'90* $6

O'HARA, MARY MARGARET
Body's in Trouble *Virgin 2863/promo/silkscreened/'88* $4

O'HEARN, PATRICK
Black Delilah 4 versions *Private 2076/promo/ps/'90* $6

O'JAYS
Don't Let Me Down edit & lp *EMI 04665/ promo/silkscreened/rear insert/'90* $4
Emotionally Yours (4 vrs.) *EMI 04738/ promo/silkscreened/ps/'91* $5
Have You Had Your Love Today 4 versions *EMI 04273/promo/silkscreened/ rear insert/'89* $5
I Can Hardly Wait Til Christmas *EMI 4828/promo/ps/silkscreened logo on red & gold/'91* $5
Keep on Lovin' Me 4:38 & 4:05 *EMI 4782/ promo/silkscreened logo/ps/'91* $5
Out of My Mind 5 versions *EMI 04364/ promo/silkscreened/rear insert/'89* $6

O'KANES, THE
Tell Me I Was Dreaming *Columbia 73445/ promo/logo on black/'90* $4

O'NEAL, ALEXANDER
All True Man (3 versions) *Tabu 3032/promo/ps/'90* $6
All True Man (4 versions) *Tabu 73626/promo/rear insert/'91* $6
Aphrodisia radio/lp/instrumental *Tabu 31458 8174/promo/ps/'93* $5
In the Middle edit/lp/instrumental *Tabu 31458 8113/promo/ps/'93* $5
In the Middle no rap mix/brown mix/brown surround mix/beats *Tabu 31458 8154/ promo/silkscreened/'93* $5
Love Makes No Sense 5 versions *Tabu 31458 8082/promo/ gatefold hardcover ps/'93* $6
Love Makes Sense For Quiet Storm Radio ep (Aphrodisia/Lady/Your Precious Love/Home is Where the Heart is - all edits) *Tabu 31458 8149/promo/ silkscreened/gatefold hardcover ps* $7
The Little Drummer Boy/My Gift to You/ Sleigh Ride *Tabu 1871/promo/ps/'89* $6
The Yoke 5 vers *Tabu 73880/promo/rear insert/'91* $6
What is This Thing Called Love? (6 versions) *Epic 73810/promo/ps/ purple silkscreened/'90* $6

O'NEAL, ALEXANDER & CHERELLE
Never Knew Love Was Like This (5 versions) *Tabu 1003/promo/ps/'88* $7

OAK RIDGE BOYS
Baby, You'll Be My Baby (edit) *MCA 79006/promo/rear insert/ silkscreened logo on blue/'89* $4

OAKTOWNS 357
Hickeys on Your Chest 10 versions *Capitol 79138/promo/ps/silkscreened* $6
Honey lp/extended/dub *Capitol 15776/stock/ps/'91* $5
Honey lp/extended/dub *Capitol 79928/ promo/silkscreened/ps/'91* $5
It's Not Your Money 6 vers. *Capitol 79021/ promo/logo silkscreened/'91* $6
Juicy Gotcha Krazy vocal, lp, instrumental *Capitol 79949/promo/ silkscreened logo/'90* $6
Turn It Up 3 versions *Capitol 15729/ stock/ps/silkscreened logo/'91* $5
Turn It Up 3 versions *Capitol 79744/ promo/ps/silkscreened/'91* $5
We Like It (3 versions) *Capitol 79172/ promo/silkscreened/'90* $5

OCASEK, RIC
Rockaway *Reprise 4833/promo/ silkscreened pic/'91* $5
The Way You Look Tonight edit & lp *Reprise 5100/promo/'91* $3

OCEAN BLUE, THE
Ballerina Out of Control *Sire 5106/promo/'91* $4
Between Something and Nothing *Sire 3627/promo/'89* $4
Cerulean *Sire 5032/promo/custom sticker/'91* $4
Drifting, Falling *Sire 3963/promo/'89* $4
Mercury *Sire 5257/promo/silkscreened/'90* $4
Sublime *Sire 6384/promo/silkscreened/'93* $4

OCEAN COLOUR SCENE
Do Yourself a Favour/Yesterday Today/ Sway/Do Yourself a Fav. (last 3 live) *Fontana 859/promo/ps/'92* $6
Selftitled 12 tracks *Fontana 314 512 269/ promo/booklet ps/'92* $10
Sway *Fontana 738/promo/ps/'92* $6

OCEAN, BILLY
Everything's So Different Without You *Jive 42135/promo/silkscreened/ps* $5
I Sleep Much Better (In Someone Elses Bed) (3 versions) *Jive 1311/promo/rear insert/'89* $5
License to Chill 7" & extended *RCA 1279/promo/ps/'89* $5

ODDS
Heterosexual Man *Zoo 17127/promo/ silkscreened/rear insert/'93* $4
Love is the Subject edit & lp *Zoo 17028/ promo/ps/silkscreened/'91* $4

OFF SHORE
I Can't Take the Power 4 versions *Epic 73751/ promo/silkscreened/ps/'90* $4

OINGO BOINGO
Out of Control *MCA 18147/promo/'90* $4
Out of Control (6 versions) *MCA 18250/promo/rear insert/'90* $8
Skin (edit) *MCA 18385/promo/rear insert/'90* $4
When the Lights Go Out *MCA 18112/promo/ 3 color silkscreen pic/custom sticker* $10
Winning Side (remix) + 7 (all from live lp) *MCA 17671/promo/'88* $25

OLDFIELD, MIKE
Hostage *Virgin 3208/promo/ logo on orange silkscreen/'89* $8
Sentinel edit *Reprise 5800/promo/'92* $7
The Bell (edit)/Sentinel Restructure 5 versions *Reprise 40749/stock/ gatefold hardcover ps/'92* $6
Tubular Bells (edit) *Virgin 3572/promo/ silkscreened logo* $8
Tubular Bells II 14 tracks *Reprise 5705/ promo/rear insert/'92* $15
Virgin Compilation 11 songs *Virgin 2113/promo/ps* $25

OLIVER WHO?
Clever 5 versions *Zoo 17086/promo/ silkscreened/rear insert/'92* $4

OMAR & THE HOWLERS
Rattlesnake Shake *Columbia 1223/promo/ps* $4

OMARTIAN, MICHAEL
Let My Heart Be the First to Know *Word Epic 4167/promo/ logo on purple/rear insert/'91* $4

OMD
Dream Of Me 7" remix *Virgin 14097/promo/'93* $5
Dreaming (3 versions) *A&M 17541/ promo/trifold hardcover ps/'88* $15
Dreaming/Gravity Never ../Secret (12" mix) *A&M 31004/ps/stock/3"* $8
Dreaming/Gravity Never Failed/Secret (12" mix) *A&M 7502-12373/stock/ps/'88* $8
Forever Live & Die *A&M 17422/promo/ gatefold hardcover ps/ silkscreened/'86* $12
Pandora's Box 2 versions/Sugar Tax/All She Wants is Everything *Virgin 96338/ stock/gatefold hardcover ps/'91* $6
Pandora's Box 4 versions *Virgin 3949/ promo/silkscreened/'91* $7
Stand Above Me single & lp *Virgin 12777/ promo/logo on blue/rear insert/'93* $5

ONE 2 MANY
Downtown 7" edit & way downtown mix *A&M 17743/promo/ps/'89* $4

ONE 2 ONE
Memory Lane *A&M 75021 7344/promo/ps/'92* $4
Peace of Mind *A&M 75021 7325/promo/ gatefold hardcover ps/poster/'92* $4
Peace of Mind/Memory Lane/Keeping Faith *A&M 75021 7952/promo/ logo on brown/ps/'92* $5

ONE CAUSE ONE EFFECT
Up With Hope, Down With Dope (4 versions) *Capitol 79228/promo/ silkscreened/rear insert/'90* $4

ONLY CHILD
I Believe in You *Rampage 70835/promo/ps/'88* $4

ONO, YOKO
An Xmas Message From Yoko *Ryko VRCD ONO/promo/ps/'91* $12
Walking on Thin Ice sampler 19 tracks *Rykodisc 0230/promo/ silkscreened/ps/'92* $15

ONYX
Slam 5 versions *Chaos 42K 77039/stock/ps* $5

OPUS III
I Talk to the Wind *Eastwest 4803/ promo/rear insert* $5
I Talk to the Wind 4 versions *Eastwest 4832/promo/ silkscreened/rear insert/'92* $7

It's a Fine Day edit & lp
Eastwest 4498/promo/ps/'92 ....$5

OR N MORE

Everyotherday *EMI 4764/promo/ trifold hardcover ps/'91* $4

ORB, THE

Blue Room edit & remix & full length/ Assassin oasis of rhythms mix
Mercury 804/promo/silkscreened/'92 ....$7

Little Fluffy Clouds dance mix mk I edit
Big Life 591/promo/logo on white/'91 ....$7

Perpetual Dawn 4 versions/Star 6 & 7
Big Life 867 547/stock/ps/'91 ....$6

ORBISON, ROY

(All I Can Do Is) Dream of You
Virgin 2755/promo/'89 ....$8

(All I Can Do Is) Dream of You
Virgin 2843/promo/'89 ....$6

California Blue *Virgin 2756/promo/'89* $10

Heartbreak Radio *Virgin 12731/promo/ logo on black/rear insert/'92* $6

I Drove All Night *MCA 2025/promo/ produced by JEFF LYNNE/ps/'91* $6

I Drove All Night/Line of Fire (TRIXTER)
MCA 54419/stock/ps/'92 ....$5

In Dreams *Virgin 2044/promo/ps/'87* $15

Mystery Girl 10 tracks *Virgin PROCD-ROY/ promo/gatefold textured hardcover ps/'89* $25

Oh Pretty Woman edit & lp *Virgin 2964/ promo/silkscreened lettering/'89* $8

Polaroy (16 tracks) *Virgin POLAROY/promo/ silkscreened/ps/'89/with KD LANG, ELVIS COSTELLO, SPRINGSTEEN, TOM WAITS, more* $25

She's a Mystery to Me *Virgin 2667/promo/ silkscreened pic/'89* $8

You Got It *Virgin 2593/promo/ silkscreened logo/'89* $6

ORBITAL

Halcyon 11:05/The Naked & the Dead 6:23 & 11:51/Sunday 7:10/Chime edit
FFRR 162 350 009/ps/stock/'92 ....$6

ORGANIZED KONFUSION

Who Stole My Last Piece of Chiken/ Drumstick Mix/Rough Side of Town/ OK Mood Swing *Hollywood 8384/ promo/silkscreened/ps/'91* $4

ORIGIN, THE

Bonfires Burning
Virgin 4320/promo/logo on tan/'92 ....$4

Growing Old (remix) *Virgin 3263/promo/ silkscreened yellow/'90* $4

ORIGINAL BROADWAY CAST

Tommy ep (Overture/Eyesight to the Blind-Acid Queen/Sensation/Pinball/ Listening to You-Finale)
RCA 61874/promo $8

ORLANDO, TONY

With Every Yellow Ribbon orig.mix & remix
Quality 15159/promo/'91 ....$7

ORRALL, ROBERT ELLIS

Boom! It Was Over *RCA 62335/ promo/rear insert/'92* $4

ORUP

My Earth Angel 4:10 & 5:15 *Atlantic 4023/ promo/ps/custom sticker/'91* $4

OSBORNE, JEFFREY

Can't Go Back on a Promise
A&M 17616/promo/'88 ....$4

If My Brother's in Trouble single & r&b vers.
Arista 2212/promo/ps/silkscreened $5

Only Human *Arista 2127/promo/ps/ logo on black/'90* $4

She's On the Left 7" edit & 12" versions
A&M 17596/promo/ps/'88 ....$5

The Morning After I Made Love to You
Arista 2236/promo/ logo on purple/rear insert/'91 ....$5

OSBORNE, PHIL RYAN

Memorial Album 27 tracks *no label or #/ ltd edition (only 200 made)/ silkscreened pic/ps/'94* $16

OSBOURNE, OZZY

Crazy Babies/You Said It All
CBS Associated 1345/promo/ pic silkscreened/rear insert/'88 ....$12

Live & Loud 21 tracks *Epic 48973/stock/ ltd metal grill cover/'93* $15

Live & Loud Sampler 12 tracks
Epic 5247/promo/ps/'93 ....$15

Mama, I'm Coming Home 3:23 & 4:09
Epic 74093/promo/ps/'91 .... $6

Miracle Man/The Liar *CBS 1344/*
promo/silkscreened pic/rear insert $12

Mr Tinkertrain *Epic 4605/promo/*
silkscreened/ps/'92 .... $6

No More Tears *Epic 73973/promo/ps/*
logo on black/'91 .... $6

Road to Nowhere/Party With the Animals
Epic 4493/promo/ps/'92 .... $6

Ten Commandments compilation
Priority 57129/stock/ps/'90 .... $30

Time After Time *Epic 4742/*
promo/logo on black/ps/'92 .... $6

War Pigs (live)/Breaking All the Rules
CBS Associated 1948/promo/
silkscreened pic/rear insert $10

OSBOURNE, OZZY & RANDY RHOADS

Tribute sampler (9 songs)
CBS 2699/promo/ps/'87 .... $20

OSBOURNE, OZZY

(misnamed as J. Osbourne)
Crazy Babies *CBS 1426/promo/rear insert* $8

OSBY, GREG

Mr. Gutterman 4 versions *Blue Note 79626/*
promo/silkscreened/rear insert/'93 .... $4

OSCAR

I'm Calling You edit/lp/12"/instrumental
Epic 74732/promo/silkscreened/
rear insert/'92 .... $4

OSLIN, K.T.

Cornell Crawford (edit)
RCA 62053/promo/ps/'91 .... $4

New Way Home radio *RCA 62499/*
promo/silkscreened/rear insert/'93 .... $4

Two Hearts *RCA 2567/promo/*
silkscreened/rear insert/'90 .... $4

OSMOND BOYS

Hey Girl *Curb 79140/promo/*
silkscreened logo/'90 .... $5

Reverse Psychology edit & lp
Curb 79263/promo/rear insert/'90 .... $5

OSMOND, DONNY

Hold On 7" & club mix *Capitol 79752/*
promo/silkscreened/'89 .... $5

I'll Be Good to You half guitar/extended guitar
Capitol 79885/promo/silkscreened $6

Love Will Survive edit & lp *Capitol 79689/*
promo/logo on red/custom sticker/'90 .... $6

My Love is a Fire (3 versions) *Capitol 79332/*
promo/silkscreened/rear insert/'90 .... $6

My Love is a Fire (3 versions)
Capitol 79332/promo/
special limited "invitation" ps/'90 .... $12

Sure Lookin' 6 versions *Capitol 79456/promo/*
logo on yellow/custom sticker/'90 .... $6

OSMOND, MARIE

Boogie Woogie Bugle Boy *Curb/promo/'91* $5

Steppin' Stone *Capitol 79719/promo/'89* $5

OSMOND, MARIE/BUCK OWENS

Let Me Be the First/Tijuana Lady
Capitol 79903/promo/'90 .... $5

OTCASEK, CHRISTOPHER

Real Wild Child (3 versions) *EMI 04604/*
promo/silkscreened/rear insert/'90 .... $4

OTTMAR LIEBERT & LUNA NEGRA

A Special 4 Track Sampler (Albatross/
Snakecharmer/Ten Piedad De../Bombay)
Epic 5299/promo/ps/silkscreened/'93 .... $5

OUR HOUSE

Our House 6 versions *Turnstyle 4741/promo/*
silkscreened/rear insert/'92 .... $4

OUTFIELD, THE

Closer to Me *MCA 2168/promo/ps/'92* $4

For You 4:05 & 4:25 *MCA 1138/promo/*
silkscreened on white/rear insert/'90 .... $4

For You lp & aor mix *MCA 1101/promo/'90* $4

My Paradise edit & lp
Columbia 1669/promo/ps/'89 .... $4

Take It All *MCA 1250/promo/rear insert/'91* $4

Voices of Babylon *Columbia 1493/promo/*
silkscreened/'89 .... $4

Winning It All *MCA 2277/promo/rear insert* $4

OVERKILL

I Hear Black lp & edit *Atlantic 4977/promo/*
silkscreened group pic/rear insert/'93 .... $5

Infectious *Atlantic 4125/promo/*
silkscreened/rear insert/'91 .... $4

Spiritual Void/Killogy *Atlantic 5064/promo/*
silkscreened/rear insert/'93 .... $4

OVERWEIGHT POOCH
Ace is a Spade 4 versions *A&M 75021 7544/ promo/silkscreened/ps/'91* $5

OVERWHELMING COLORFAST
Bender ep (You Keep Me Hangin' On/For Emily/ Roy Orbison/Rollo the Head/ She Said, She Said) *Relativity 0178/ promo/ps/logo on blue/'92* $5
It's Tomorrow *Relativity 0160/promo/ silkscreened/rear insert/'92* $4

OWENS, BUCK
Kickin' In *Curb-Capitol 79396/promo/'90* $5

PAGE, JIMMY
An Interview with (53 minute) *Geffen 3099/promo/ps/'88* $20
Prison Blues edit/lp *Geffen 3286/promo/ps* $7
Wasting My Time/Interview intro version *Geffen 3083/promo/ps/'88* $12

PAGE, TOMMY
23 minute interview (by Martika) *Sire 3616/promo/'89* $8
A Shoulder to Cry on *Sire 3350/promo/'88* $5
A Zillion Kisses (5 vers.) *Sire 3566/promo/'88* $7
From the Heart (11 tracks) *Sire 26583/ promo/silkscreened pic/ 3D box package/'91* $12
I'll Be Your Everything *Sire 3908/promo/'90* $5
My Shining Star old phones edit & versions *Sire 5054/promo/'91* $5
Turn on the Radio (3 versions) *Sire 4383/promo/rear insert/'90* $5
Turn on the Radio (6 versions) *Sire 4461/promo/rear insert/'90* $6
When I Dream of You *Sire 4032/promo/'90* $4
Whenever You Close Your Eyes radio mix & smooth mix *Sire 4797/ promo/silkscreened pic/'91* $6
You Make Christmas Feel Like Heaven *Sire 4529/promo/'90* $5

PAHINUI BROS, THE
Jealous Guy lp & video edit *Private 81008/ promo/prod.by RY COODER/'92* $6

PAJAMA PARTY
Got My Eye on You (5 versions) *Atlantic 3768/promo/rear insert/'91* $4
Hide and Seek (4 vers.) *Atlantic 3196/promo/ silkscreened logo/rear insert/'89* $4
Over and Over (4 versions) *Atlantic 2986/promo/rear insert/'89* $4

PALADINS
Follow Your Heart/Lets Buzz *Alligator 13/promo/silkscreened/'90* $5

PALE DIVINE
Something About Me 3:51 & 4:12 *Atco 4158/promo/logo on purple/ rear insert/'91* $4

PALE FOUNTAINS
Throwing Back the Apple *4AD 5467/promo/ silkscreened/ps/'92* $4

PALE SAINTS
Blue Flower (edit) *4AD 5546/promo/ silkscreened/rear insert/'92* $4
Throwing Back the Apple *4AD 5467/ promo/silkscreened/ps/'92* $5

PALEFACE
Burn and Rob 2:40 & 2:23 *Polydor 528/ promo/silkscreened/ps/'91* $4
World Full of Cops/Paleface's Jingle Jingle #1 Smash Hit Christmas Single *Polydor 602/promo/silkscreened/'91* $5

PALMER, KEITH
Don't Throw Me in the Briarpatch *Epic 73988/promo/rear insert/'91* $4

PALMER, ROBERT
Addicted to Love (edit)/I Didn't Mean to Turn You On/Bad Case of Loving You *Island 422-875 925/stock/ps/'90* $6
Bad Case of Loving You *Island 3045/ promo/rear insert/'89* $5
Can We Still Be Friends? *Island 6741/promo/ps/'92* $4
Early in the Morning single version/get up mix/west coast mix *EMI 04211/ promo/dj custom sticker/'88* $6
Early in the Morning single/album/extended *Manhattan 04153/promo/ps/'88* $6
Every Kinda People remix *Island 6714/ promo/ps/logo silkscreened/'92* $5
I'll Be Your Baby Tonight lp & ext. *EMI 4747/ promo/ps/silkscreened logo/'91* $5
Life in Detail *EMI 04514/promo/ silkscreened/rear insert/'90* $5

Mercy Mercy Me (The Ecology)-I Want You (3 versions) *EMI 4714/promo/ red silkscreened/ps/'91* $6
Mercy Mercy Me (The Ecology)-I Want You (4 versions) *EMI 4742/promo/ silkscreened/rear insert/'91* $6
More Than Ever lp/live *EMI 04193/promo/custom sticker/'88* $6
Simply Irresistable *EMI 04075/promo/ps/'88* $6
Simply Irresistable (7" & extended) *Manhattan 04140/promo/ps/'88* $8
Simply Palmer (30 minute interview) *EMI 04121/promo/ps/'88* $12
Sweet Lies *Island 2190/promo/ps/'88* $6
Tell Me Im Not Dreaming (6 versions) *EMI 04307/promo/silkscreened/ rear insert/'89* $6
You Can't Get Enough of a Good Thing edit & lp *EMI 4743/promo/rear insert/'91* $5
You're Amazing *EMI 4651/promo/box type hardcover ps/silkscreened logo on black/'90* $7
You're Amazing remix & edit *EMI 4699/ promo/logo on black/rear insert/'90* $5

PALUMBO, JOHN

Drifting Back to Motown *Grudge 4762/promo/'89* $4
Walk on the Wild Side 3:47/5:15 *Grudge 4760/promo/'89* $5

PANDORAS, THE

Nymphomania Live (full length - 9 songs) *Restless 72318/ps/stock/'89* $10

PANTERA

A Not So Vulgar Display of Power *Atco 4538/promo/ps/'92* $6
Cemetary Gates edit & lp *Atco 3965/promo/rear insert/'90* $4
F#cking Hostile 2 versions/By Demons Be Driven biochem.mix/ Walk decranial mix *Atco 4990/ promo/ps/silkscreened/'92* $5
Mouth For War *Atco 4414/promo/ silkscreened pic/rear insert/'92* $5
Psycho Holiday/Cowboys From Hell/ Heresy (last 2 live) *Atco 3871/promo/ps/'90* $8
This Love aor edit/video edit/lp *Atco 4651/ promo/silkscreened/ps/'92* $4
Walk lp & live *Atco 4866/promo/ silkscreened group pic/rear insert/'92* $6

PAPA'S CULTURE

Swim edit & lp/Top 40/Sometimes *Elektra 8719/promo/ gatefold hardcover ps/silkscreened* $4

PAPERBOY

Bumpin' 5 versions *Next Plateau 021/promo/silkscreened* $5

PARADIS, VANESSA

Be My Baby *Polydor 784/promo/ silkscreened/ps/'92* $4
I'm Waiting For the Man *Polydor 754/promo/ logo on white/ps/'92* $4

PARENTAL ADVISORY

Lifeline vocal/clean vocal/instrumental *MCA 2503/promo/rear insert/'93* $5

PARIAH

Powerless *Geffen 4532/promo/gatefold hardcover ps/silkscreened/'93* $5

PARIS

Assata's Song 3 versions/Guerrillas in the Mist remix/Coffee, Donuts & Death piggy on platter mix *Scarface 102/stock/ps/'93* $5
The Days of Old vocal & instrumental/ Bush Killa hellraiser mix *Scarface 101/promo/logo on black* $5

PARIS BY AIR

C'mon and Dance With Me 5 versions *Columbia 73261/promo/ps/'90* $4
Voices in Your Head 4 vers. *Columbia 1886/ promo/silkscreened/ps/'89* $4

PARIS, MICA

Breathe Life Into Me altered album mix & breathless edit *Island 2870/ promo/rear insert/'89* $7
Contribution 3 vers *Island 6666/promo/ rear insert/custom sticker/'91* $5
Contribution 4 versions *Island 6652/ promo/ps/custom sticker/'91* $5
I Wanna Hold On to You edit & lp *Island 6774/promo/ps/'93* $4
My One Temptation *Island 2567/promo/ps/'88* $6

PARKER, GRAHAM

Big Man on Paper/Green Monkeys *RCA 9114/promo/ps/'89* $5
Everything Goes (3:28)/That Thing Is Rockin' *RCA 9178/promo/ps/'90* $5
Release Me *Capitol 79390/promo/ silkscreened/ps/'92* $5

PARKER, MACEO

Galactic Grooves ep (Shake Everything You've Got/Pass the Peas/I Got You/ Addicted Love/Soul Power) *Verve PAR-2/promo/ logo on red/rear insert/'92* $8
Let em Out (edit) *4th & B'way 515/ promo/rear insert/'90* $5
Mo Roots 10 tracks *Polygram MAC 2/promo/ silkscreened pic/ps/'91* $12

PARKER, RAY (JR)
She Needs to Get Some damions groove *MCA 1646/promo/'91* $4
She Needs to Get Some with rap, without rap, instrumental *MCA 1464/promo/ rear insert/'91* $5

PARKER, RICK
Salesgirl Blues *Geffen 4313/promo/ silkscreened/custom sticker/'91* $4
Salesgirl Blues edit & lp *Geffen 4367/ promo/logo silkscreened/ gatefold hardcover ps/'92* $4

PARKS, JOHN ANDREW
Ten Gallon Dreams/The Way I Feel/Do a Little Dance/Veronica *Capitol 79110/ promo/silkscreened/ps/'90* $4

PARNELL, LEE ROY
Tender Moment/The Rock/What Kind of Fool../ Love Without Mercy *Arista 2523/ promo/logo on maroon/ps/'93* $5
The Rock *Arista 2400/promo/silkscreened/ps* $4
What Kind of Fool Do You Think I Am *Arista 2431/promo/ps/silkscreened/'92* $4

PARSONS, ALAN
Turn It Up edit/shorter edit/lp *Arista 2623/promo/ps/'93* $6

PARTON, DOLLY
Slow Healing Heart *Columbia 73498/ promo/logo silkscreened/'90* $5
Straight Talk single & lp *Hollywood 10129/ promo/rear insert/silkscreened/'92* $6
Why'd You Come In Here Lookin' Like That *Columbia 1588/promo/ rear insert/silkscreened/'89* $5

PARTON, DOLLY & RICKY VAN SHELTON
Rockin' Years *Columbia 73711/promo/ rear insert/'91* $5

PARTON, RONSTADT, HARRIS
Telling Me Lies edit & lp *WB 2735/promo/'87* $6

PARTY, THE
I Found Love (2 versions) *Hollywood 8231/ promo/silkscreened/ps/'90* $4
In My Dreams *Hollywood 8440/promo/ rear insert/silkscreened/'92* $4
Private Affair remix & remix with rap *Hollywood 8498/promo/logo silkscreened/rear insert/'92* $4
Summer Vacation remix *Hollywood 8366/ promo/silkcreened on black/'91* $4
Summer Vacation single & ext. *Hollywood 8200/ promo/silkscreened/'90* $4
That's Why (4 versions) *Hollywood 8293/ promo/silkscreened/'91* $4
The No Excuse 11 versions *Hollywood 10083/ promo/silkscreened/'91* $5

PASADENAS
Riding on a Train (4 versions) *Columbia 1618/promo/ps/'88* $5
Tribute 4:25/5:11 *Columbia 1438/promo/ silkscreened blue/'89* $6

PAT & MICK
Use It Up and Wear It Out *Charisma 024/promo/silkscreened/'90* $4

PATTI, SANDI
Another Time, Another ... *Word 9011095154/ promo/color pic silkscreened/'90* $6
Another Time, Another Place *Word Epic 4420/promo/ps/'91* $5
Exalt Thy Name/One - Spirit to Spirit *Word/promo/silkscreened color pic* $5

PAUL, LES & MARY FORD
How High the Moon/World is Waiting for Sunrise/Mockin' Bird Hill/Vaya Con Dios *Rhino 73039/stock/3"/ps/'88* $5

PAW
Jessie/Gasoline *A&M 31458 8129/ promo/silkscreened/ gatefold hardcover ps/'93* $4

PAYCHECK, JOHNNY
Next of Kin *Playback 20/promo/rear insert* $4

PC QUEST
After the Summer's Gone 5 versions *RCA 62075/promo/rear insert/'91* $4

PEARL JAM
Alive *Epic 4188/promo/silkscreened/ rear insert/'91* $6
Alive/Wash/I've Got a Feeling *Epic 4041/promo/silkscreened/ps/'91* $8
Even Flow/Dirty Frank *Epic 4469/promo/ps* $8
Jeremy *Epic 4606/promo/ps/logo on white* $6
Why Go/Deep/Alive (live) *Epic 4285/promo/ ps with tour dates/'91* $10

PEASTON, DAVID
Two Wrongs (Don't Make It Right) (edit) *Geffen 3504/promo/ silkscreened color pic/rear insert/'89* $4
Two Wrongs (Dont Make It Right) (edit) *Geffen 3504/promo/'89* $4
We're All in This Together 7" remix/club mix edit/club mix *Geffen 3964/promo/'89* $4

PEBBLES
Girlfriend/Mercedes Girl (remix) *MCA 17591/ promo/silkscreened pic/'88* $10
Giving You the Benefit (4 versions) *MCA 18517/promo/rear insert/ silkscreened logo on white/'90* $6
Giving You the Benefit (4 versions) *MCA 24075/stock/ gatefold hardcover ps/'90* $6
Love Makes Things Happen 4:28 & 5:10 *MCA 1151/promo/logo on white/'90* $6

PEBBLES & SALT N PEPA
Backyard 2 versions *MCA 1182/promo/rear insert/'90* $6

PEEPLES, NIA
Faces of Love (edit) *Charisma 095/promo/ ps/silkscreened/'92* $5
Kissing the Wind 4 versions *Charisma 088/promo/ps/'92* $5
Kissing the Wind edit *Charisma 080/promo/ps/'92* $4
Street of Dreams (edit) *Charisma 063/ promo/gatefold hardcover with poster ps/'91* $5
Trouble (4 vers.) *Mercury 11/promo/ps/'88* $6

PENDERGRASS, TEDDY
2 A.M. edit & instrumental *Elektra 69422/stock/3"/ps/'88* $6
How Can You Mend a Broken Heart edit & lp *Elektra 8257/promo/rear insert/'90* $5
I Find Everything in You 3 versions *Elektra 8357/promo/ps/'91* $6
It Should've Been You *Elektra 8323/ promo/ps/'90* $5
It Should've Been You (4 versions) *Elektra 8300/promo/ps/ silkscreened purple/'90* $6
Joy (2 versions) *Elektra 1001/promo/'88* $4
Love is the Power *Elektra 8035/promo/'88* $4
Make It With ..(edit) *Elektra 8218/promo/'90* $4
This is the Last Time edit & lp *Elektra 8062/promo/'88* $4

PENDERGRASS, TEDDY & LISA FISHER
Glad to Be Alive edit remix/remix *Elektra 8178/ promo/rear insert/'90* $5

PENISTON, CE CE
Finally 9 versions *A&M 75021 7281/ promo/silkscreened/ps/'91* $7
We Got a Love Thang 10 versions *A&M 75021 7330/promo/ silkscreened logo/ps/'92* $7
Crazy Love 6 versions *A&M 31458 8017/ promo/ps/'92* $7
Inside That I Cried edit & lp *A&M 31458 8020/ promo/logo on brown/ps/'92* $5
Keep on Walkin' 10 versions *A&M 75021 7337/ promo/silkscreened/ps/'92* $8
We Got a Love Thang 6 vers. *A&M 75021 2395/ stock/ps/silkscreened/'92* $5

PENN, MICHAEL
Brave New World *RCA 2647/promo/ps/'90* $4
Free Time remix/Rising Steam (live)/By the Book (live)/Seen the Doctor (acoustic) *RCA 07863 62457/stock/ ps/custom sticker/'93* $5
Long Way Down *RCA 62417/promo/ silkscreened/ps/'92* $5
No Myth 4:11/4:45 *RCA 9111/promo/ps/'89* $7
No Myth (acoustic) *RCA 2550/promo/'90* $8
Seen the Doctor pg versions/Brave New World acoustic *RCA 62339/promo/ps* $6
Seen the Doctor pg versions/No Myth *RCA 62356/promo/silkscreened/ps* $6
Strange Season/Rising Steam *RCA 62340/ promo/silkscreened/ps/'92* $6
This & That *RCA 9200/promo/rear insert/'90* $5
This & That/No Myth (acoustic) *RCA 2512/promo/ps/'90* $7

PERE UBU
Breath edit & lp *Fontana 125/promo/ silkscreened/'89* $4
Kathleen edit & lp/interview *Imago 28058/promo/rear insert/'93* $12
Sleepwalk edit & lp *Imago 28045/promo/ps/ "Story of Pere Ubu" floppy disc for the Mac/'93* $25
Waiting For Mary *Fontana 98/promo/ silkscreened/'89* $6
We Have the Technology (2 versions)/ Postman Drove a Caddy/The B Side *Restless 72340/stock/3"/5" ps/'88* $7
Worlds In Collision lp & live/Goodnite Irene (live)/I Hear They Smoke the Barbecue (live)/Over the Moon (live)/ Final Solution (live) *Fontana 514/ promo/logo on purple/'91* $12

PEREGRINS
True Believer *MCA 17862/promo/ custom sticker/'89* $4

PERFECT GENTLEMEN
Ooh lala (I Can't Get Over You) 3 version *Columbia 73211/promo/ps/ prod.by MAURICE STARR/'90* $4

PERFORMANCE GUARANTEED
Peace/Love is a Cile Thing (both radio) *Hollywood 8342/promo/ silkscreened (peace sign)/'91* $4

PERKINS, CARL
Blue Suede Shoes/Honey Don't/Matchbox + 1 *Rhino 73015/3"/ps/stock/'88* $6

Pink Cadillac *Platinum Records/promo/JOAN JETT, CHARLIE DANIELS../ps/'92* $8

PERRY, PHIL

Amazing Love *Capitol 79706/promo/ silkscreened/rear insert/'91* $4

Call Me lp & instrumental *Capitol 79552/ promo/ps/silkscreened/'91* $4

PESCO, PAUL

Black is Black edit & lp *Sire 3678/promo/ silkscreened black/'89* $4

PET SHOP BOYS

Always On My Mind 7"/julian mendelsohn 12"/ p.harding 12" *Manhattan 04037/ promo/ps* $25

Always On My Mind extended dance & lp/ Do I Have To *Manhattan 04058/promo/ps/'88* $10

Can You Forgive Her? 5 versions/I Want to Wake Up *EMI 56281/stock/ps/'93* $6

Can You Forgive Her? 7"/mk remix edit/ rollo remix edit *EMI 04539/promo/ps* $6

Domino Dancing 7"/12" disco/12" alternative *Manhattan 04155/promo/ps/'88* $20

Go West 6 versions/Shameless *EMI 58084/stock/ps/'93* $6

Go West radio/lp *EMI 04619/promo/ps/'93* $6

How Can You Expect to Be Taken Seriously? 3 vers. + 3 other tracks *EMI 56205/stock/ps* $6

How Can You Expect to Be Taken Seriously? lp/7" perf.attitude mix/12" mix/ classical reprise/perfect mood mix *EMI 4698/promo/rear insert/'91* $10

Left to My Own Devices lp & disco mix/ Sound of Atom Splitting *EMI 04180/promo/ps/'88* $15

So Hard 3 versions/It Must Be Obvious/ Paninaro 12" *EMI 56195/stock/ps* $6

So Hard (4 versions) *EMI 4650/promo/ silkscreened/box type cover/ history of PSB booklet/'90* $12

Was It Worth It 2 vers/Miserablism electro mix/Music For Boys pt 3/Overture to Performance *EMI 56244/stock/ps/'91* $6

Where the Streets Have No Name 3 versions/ Bet She's Not Your Girlfriend/I Want a Dog techno funk mix *EMI 56217/stock/live shot ps/'91* $6

Where the Streets Have No Name 3 versions/ Bet She's Not Your Girlfriend/I Want a Dog techno funk mix *EMI 56217/stock/Neil & Chris ps/'91* $7

Where the Streets Have No .. 7" & extended *EMI 04753/promo/rear insert/'91* $10

PETERSON, RICKY

Livin' It Up *WB 4045/promo/'90* $4

PETTY, TOM

A Face in the Crowd *MCA 18113/promo/'89* $5

Free Fallin' *MCA 18056/promo/'89* $5

Free Fallin' (live) *MCA 18073/promo/'89* $8

Full Moon Fever lp w/Free Fallin' (live) *MCA 6253/promo/ps/'89* $25

I Won't Back Down *MCA 17822/promo/ custom picture sticker/'89* $6

Into the Great Wide Open *MCA 1485/promo/ silkscreened pic/rear insert/'91* $6

Kings Highway *MCA 2067/promo/ silkscreened/rear insert/'91* $6

Learning to Fly *MCA 1482/promo/ silkscreened/rear insert/'91* $6

Makin' Some Noise *MCA 2110/promo/ps/ prod.by JEFF LYNNE/'92* $6

Out in the Cold *MCA 1627/promo/silkscreened/ ps/prod.by Tom & JEFF LYNNE/'91* $6

Peace in L.A. 4:59/4:42 *MCA 2286/promo/ps/'92* $8

Runnin' Down a Dream with fade/lp *MCA 17938/promo/cust.sticker/'89* $6

The Gone Gator Sampler (American Girl/ Breakdown/Strangered in the Night/ I Need to Know/Listen to Her Heart) *MCA 1478/promo/ps/'91* $20

Yer So Bad *MCA 18335/promo/rear insert* $5

PFEIFFER, MICHELLE

Makin' Whoopee *GRP 9924/promo/ps/'89* $6

PHALON

Dance Floor of Life (6 versions) *Elektra 8207/promo/ silkscreened logo/rear insert/'90* $4

Don't Cha Wanna *Elektra 8272/promo/rear insert/'90* $4

Ready or Not (4 versions) *Elektra 8315/promo/ps/'90* $4

Rising to the Top (6 versions) *Elektra 8189/promo/'90* $4

PHARCYDE, THE

Ya Mama cosby mix *Delicious Vinyl 4758/promo/ps/'92* $5

PHATIGAN, SUZANNE

To Hell With Love *Imago 28027/promo/ps/'92* $4

PHIL PHILLIPS & TWILIGHTS

Sea of Love *Mercury 158/promo/ silkscreened logo on red/'89* $4

PHILLIPS, SAM

Holding On to the Earth *Virgin 2621/ promo/silkscreened logo/'88* $4

I Don't Know How to Say Goodbye to You *Virgin 2378/promo/silkscreen/'88* $4

Where the Colors Don't Go *Virgin 4135/promo/logo on blue/'91* $4

PHISH
Chalk Dust Torture *Elektra 8511/promo/ silkscreened/ps/'92* $4
Fast Enough For You *Elektra 8707/promo/ logo on blue/ps/'93* $4
The Wedge *Elektra 8768/promo/'93* $4

PHRANC
'64 Ford/Surfer Girl 4:22 & 1:48 *Island 6675/ promo/custom sticker/'91* $5
Bloodbath *Island 2944/promo/rear insert/'89* $4
I'm Not Romantic *Island 6656/promo/ rear insert/'91* $4

PIECE DOGS
Devil Dog/Ridin High/Death Chant *Energy PRO 3/promo/ silkscreened/rear insert/'92* $4

PINE, COURTNEY
Closer to Home 10 tracks *Antilles 001/ promo/silkscreened/ps/'92* $8
Psalm *4th & B'way 571/promo/silkscreened/ rear insert/'92* $4

PINK FLOYD
Another Brick in the Wall pt 2/One of My Turns *Columbia 38K 03118/stock/3"* $8
Comfortably Numb/Learning to Fly/Time/ Another Brick (pt 2) *Columbia 1375/ promo/silkscreened/'88* $15
Dark Side of the Moon *In the Studio 7/ promo/dj only show/'88* $25
Dark Side of the Moon 9 tracks *EMI 0777-7-81479-2-3/stock/20th anniversary edition/box cover/postcards/'93* $20
Momentary Lapse tour CD (2 unreleased live tracks) *Columbia 1100/promo/ps* $25
Shine On sampler 9 tracks *Columbia 4848/ promo/ps/silkscreened/'92* $20

PIRATES OF THE MISSISSIPPI
Georgia Peaches/Nashville Nights-Redneck Blues (11:09)/Honky Tonk Highway *Capitol 79087/promo/logo on black* $4

PIXIES
Alec Eiffel *Elektra 8519/promo/ps/'92* $4
Alec Eiffel/Letter to Memphis (instrumental)/ Build High/Evil Hearted You *Elektra 66444/stock/silkscreened/ gatefold hardcover ps/'92* $6
Allison *Elektra 8287/promo/ silkscreened logo/rear insert/'90* $4
Dig For Fire 3:02/2:46 *Elektra 8251/promo/ silkscreened pic/rear insert/'90* $5
Dig For Fire/Velvety instru./Winterlong/Santo *Elektra 66596/stock/ gatefold hardcover ps/'90* $6
Head On *Elektra 8476/promo/ logo on green/ps/'91* $6
Head On remix *Elektra 8535/promo/ logo on green/ps/'91* $4
Here Comes Your Man *Elektra 8090/promo/'89* ...$4
Here Comes Your Man/Wave of Mutilation/ Into the White/Baileys Walk *Elektra 66694/stock/ps/silkscreened* $6
Letter to Memphis *Elektra 8441/promo/ silkscreened/ps/'91* $5
Monkey Gone to Heaven *Elektra 8073/promo* $4
Monkey Gone to Heaven/Manta Ray/Weird at My School/Dancing the Manta Ray *Elektra 66707/stock/ps/'89* $5
Velouria/Make Believe/I've Been Waiting For You/Thing *Elektra 66616/stock/ps* $5
Velouria/Make Believe/I've Been Waiting For You/The Thing *Elektra 8202/ promo/logo on brown silkcr./ps/'90* $6

PLANET P PROJECT
Planet P Project 12 tracks *Geffen 4000/ promo silkscreened on stock/ custom sticker/ps* $12

PLANT, ROBERT
29 Palms edit & lp *Es Paranza 5097/promo/ ps/logo on black/'93* $4
29 Palms/Whole Lotta Love (acoustic) *Es Paranza 98388/stock/ps/'93* $5
Calling to You edit/lp *Esparanza 5082/promo/ logo on black/ps/'93* $4
Heaven Knows (2 versions) *Esperanza 2221/promo* $4
Hurting Kind *Esparanza 3186/promo/ps/'90* $4
Hurting Kind/I Cried/Oompah *Esparanza 96483/stock/ps/'90* $5
Manic Nirvana - world premiere broadcast *Album Network/Esparanza 3301/ promo/ps/'90* $15
Nirvana *Esparanza 3636/promo/cust.sticker* $4
Profiled (interview) *Esparanza 3297/promo/ps/'90* $12
SSS & Q *Esparanza 3449/promo/ps/ silkscreened purple/'90* $4
Walking Towards Paradise *Esparanza 2551/ promo/rear insert/'88* $4
Your Ma Said You Cried In Your Sleep Last Night clean & scratchy versions *Esparanza 3349/promo/rear insert* $5

PLANT, ROBERT/DEBBIE GIBSON + 1
Ship of Fools edit & lp/Staying Together lp-new vocal/remix + 1 *Atlantic 2436/promo/'88* $6

PLEASURE BOMBS
Love Takes a Walk *Atco 3968/promo/ logo on black/ps/'91* $3

PLEASURE THIEVES
Blue Flowers *Hollywood 10151/promo/ silkscreened/rear insert/'92* $3

PLUNKETT, STEVE

Louie, Louie radio & club
Quality 15178/promo/ps/'91 .... $3

PM

Piece of Paradise edit/lp
WB 3218/promo/ps/'88 .... $3
Say It Again *WB 3452/promo/'88* $3

PM DAWN

A Watcher's Point of View 3:58/6:05
Island 6671/promo/ps/'91 .... $4
Comatose *Gee Street 6712/promo/ps/'91* $4
I'd Die Without You 4 versions *LaFace 4036/ promo/silkscreened/ps/'92* $5
I'd Die Without You 5 versions
LaFace 73008 24039/stock/ps/'92 .... $4
I'd Die Without You edit/passion mix/lp
LaFace 4034/promo/logo on blue/'92 .... $5
Looking Through Patient Eyes radio & extended & instrumental/Plastic radio mix
Gee Street 422-862 025/stock/ silkscreened/ps/'93 .... $5
Paper Doll 3 versions/For the Love of Peace
Island 422 866 375/stock/ps/'91 .... $5
Paper Doll radio/club/instrumental
Island 6699/promo/ps/'91 .... $5
Plastic radio/extended/funk u tomorrow/ instrumentaldub *Gee Street 6766/ promo/silkscreened/custom sticker* $4
Reality Used to Be a Friend of Mine 3 versions
Gee Street 6711/promo/ps/'91 .... $4
Set Adrift On Memory Bliss edit *Island 6690/ promo/logo on white/custom sticker* $4

POCO

Call It Love edit & lp *RCA 9039/promo/ die cut trifold cover/silkscreened/'89* $4
Nothin' to Hide edit & l
RCA 9131/promo/ps/'89 .... $4
The Nature of Love/The Open Ended Interview (14:43) *RCA 9183/promo/ps/'90* $10
What Do People Know edit & lp
RCA 2623/promo/ps/'90 .... $4

POETS, THE

Subversive (2 versions/the Danube Stops Me/ Dont Waste Your Roses
RCA 2726/promo/ps/'91 .... $4

POI DOG PONDERING

Be the One single & lp
Columbia 74203/promo/ps/'92 .... $4
Everybody's Trying/Pulling Touch (live)/ Everybody's Trying "Memphis"/You Think too Much (acoustic)
Columbia 2093/promo/ps/'90 .... $5
Fruitless (remix)/I Had to Tell You/Wood Guitar-Falling (live)/Love Vigilantes/ Going Up Country/Thanksgiving (live)
Columbia 44K 73533/stock/ps/'90 .... $4

Get Me On remix/extended/lp *Columbia 4610/ promo/logo on red/ps/'92* $4
Jack Ass Ginger 4:35 & 5:30/Fever/Take Care of Your Thing/Mele Kalikimaka
Columbia 44K 74083/stock/ps/'91 .... $4

POINDEXTER, BUSTER

All Night Party (3 versions)
RCA 9007/promo/ps/'89 .... $4
Hit the Road Jack *RCA 8914/promo/ps/'89* $4
Under the Sea *RCA 9195/promo/ custom sticker/rear insert/'90* $4
Friends Advice edit/dance/video
Motown 90003/promo/'90 .... $5

POINTER, JUNE

Tight on Time (8 versions) *Columbia 000145/ promo/silkscreened pink/'89* $5

POISON

(Flesh & Blood) Sacrifice *Capitol 79815/ promo/silkscreened/'90* $5
Life Goes On *Capitol 79995/promo/ silkscreened logo & snake-heart/'91* $5
Nothin' But a Good time *Capitol-Enigma 79301/ promo/ps/'88* $6
Ride the Wind *Capitol 79275/promo/ silkscreened/rear insert/'90* $5
So Tell Me Why *Capitol 79007/promo/ logo on dark blue/ps/'91* $5
Something to Believe In *Capitol 79272/promo/ silkscreened/mini box type ps/'90* $6
Stand chr edit/edit/lp *Capitol 79585/ promo/silkscreened/ps/'93* $5
Talk Dirty to Me (audio & video)/Cry Tough/ I Want Action (last 2 audio only)
Capitol 5686/promo/ps/CD video $12
The Real Me *Capitol 79507/promo/ silkscreened/'89* $5
Unskinny Bop *Enigma 79133/promo/ rear insert/logo on green/'90* $5
Until You Suffer Some *Capitol 79658/ promo/logo on brown/ps/'93* $4

POISON/AEROSMITH

Rock and Roll all Nite/Rocking Pneumonia & Boogie Woogie Flu *Def Jam 2892/ promo/silkscreened wreath/'87* $12

POLAND, CHRIS

Return to Metaloplis (10 tracks)
Enigma 73590/stock/ps/'90 .... $4

POLICE

Don't Stand So Close to Me '86 *A&M 17435/ promo/gatefold hardcover ps/'86* $15

PONTY, JEAN LUC

In the Fast Lane/Tender Memories/The Gift of Time/Faith in You
Columbia 1835/promo/ps/'89 .... $6

POOL, GRACE
Stay *Reprise 3398/promo/'88* $4

POORBOYS, THE
The Spider and the Fly *Hollywood 8221/promo/ silkscreened logo on purple/'90* $4

POP WILL EAT ITSELF
Another Man's Rhubarb (2 versions)/ 92 (2 versions) *RCA 2834/promo/ custom sticker/rear insert/'90* $8
Can U Dig It (8 versions) *RCA 9087/promo/ps/'89* $8
Dance of the Mad (2 versions)/Preached to the Perverted (remix)/Touched by the Hand of Cicciolina *RCA 2732/promo/ps/'90* $8
Dance of the Mad (2 versions)/Preached to the Perverted (remix)/Touched by the Hand of Cicciolina *RCA 2732/ stock/ps/silkscreened/'90* $6
I've Always Been a Coward Baby/ Bulletproof! 5:17&5:45 *RCA 62416/ promo/silkscreened/ps/'92* $8
Inside You/Shes Surreal/Hit the Hi Tech Groove *Def Con 001/promo/ps/'88* $8
Karmadrome 3:52 & 5:04/Eat Me, Drink Me../ PWEI-Zation *RCA 07863 62321/stock/ps/'92* $6
X Y & Zee (3 vers.) *RCA 2763/promo/ps/'91* $8

POP, IGGY
Butt Town + 10 demo versions (Butt Town/ Foolish Dreams/Beggar/When Dreaming Fails ...) *Virgin PRCD BUTT/promo/'90* $18
Candy *Virgin 3575/promo/silkscreened/'90* $4
Candy (3 versions) *Virgin PRCD IGGY/promo/ '90/with KATE PIERSON* $6
Cold Metal *A&M 17573/promo/ps/ silkscreened/'88* $6
High on You *A&M 17632/promo/'88* $4
Home (sanitized edit) *Virgin 3364/promo/ silkscreened/'90* $4
Livin' on the Edge of the Night edit & lp *Virgin 3072/promo/silkscreened* $5
Livin' on the Edge of the Night/Lust For Life/ China Girl/The Passenger *Virgin 3204/promo/silkscreened logo* $6
Livin' on the Edge of the Night/Lust For Life/ China Girl/The Passenger *Virgin 96497/stock/ps/'90* $6
The Raw Trax ep (Pussy Power/Butt Town/ Home/My Baby Wants..) *Virgin 3365/ promo/silkscreened pic/'90* $12

POPINJAYS
Monster Mouth/Something About You/ Helicopter People (disco sex mix) *Epic 4672/promo/silkscreened/ps/'92* $4
Vote Elvis/Doctor Fell/Thinking About the Weather/Hey!/Fine Lines *Alpha International 73021/stock/ps* $6

POPS COOL LOVE
Buzz edit & soul house remix *Elektra 8388/ promo/silkscreened/ps/'91* $4
Free Me live radio edit *Elektra 8486/promo/ps/'91* $4

PORNO FOR PYROS
Pets edit & lp *WB 6167/promo/silkscreened* $5

PORTER, ART
Straight to the Point/Someone Like You/ Free Spirit/Skirt Chaser *Verve Forecast 686/promo/ silkscreened/ps/'93* $5

PORTRAIT
Day by Day 7 versions *Capitol 79714/ promo/logo on brown/rear insert/'92* $5
Here We Go Again! 7 versions *Capitol 79392/ promo/logo on green/ps/'92* $5

POSIES
Definite Door *DGC 4548/promo/ silkscreened/ps* $4
Dream All Day *DGC 4520/promo/ ps/silkscreened/'93* $4
Golden Blunders *DGC 4154/promo/ silkscreened/ps/'90* $5
Solar Sister/Ever Since I .. demo/Start a Life *DGC 4551/promo/'93* $6
Suddenly Mary edit & lp *DGC 4206/promo/ps/'91* $4
Suddenly Mary edit/Feel/Spite & Malice *DGC 21631/stock/ gatefold hardcover ps/'91* $5
Suddenly Mary (edit) *DGC 4205/promo/'90* $4

POSITIVE K
Ain't No Crime 4 versions *Island 6761/ promo/silkscreened/ps/'93* $5
I Got a Man 3 versions *Island 6764/promo/ silkscreened/custom sticker/'93* $5

POSTER CHILDREN
Clock Street *Sire 6034/promo/'93* $4
Clock Street/Blatant Dis/In My Way/ Everything Burns *Sire 5969/promo/ps* $6

POWER TRIO FROM HELL, THE
Go to Hell ep (Nineteen/Lost Souls - live/ Reach ../Thrash Epic/interview 21:23) *Reprise 6038/promo/silkscreened/ps* $8

POWERMAD
Slaughterhouse edit & lp *Reprise 4431/promo/ custom sticker/rear insert/'89* $5

Terminator/Hunter Seeker/Gimme Gimme Shock Treatment + 1 *Reprise 3345/promo/silkscreened/'88* $6

POWERULE

Pass the Vibes 3 versions *Interscope 4426/ promo/silkscreened/ps/'92* $5

That's the Way It Is edit & lp *Interscope 4090/promo/ps/'91* $4

PRAISE

Easy Way Out (radio mix)/Solitude/Brand New Day *Giant 5627/promo/rear insert* $4

Easy Way Out 7 versions *Giant 40536/stock/ gatefold hardcover ps/'92* $5

PRAXIS

Animal Behavior edit/lp/video *Axiom 6726/ promo/silkscreened/rear insert/'92*...........$4

PRAYERS

Alleluia (3 versions)/Make It Groovy *WB 40040/stock/ gatefold hardcover ps/'90* $4

PRECIOUS METAL

Downhill Dreamer/Mr Big Stuff/ Eazier Than You Think/Nasty Habits *Chameleon 96/promo/silkscreened/'90* $5

Mr Big Stuff single & lp *Chameleon 95/promo/silkscreened/'90* $4

PREFAB SPROUT

All the World Loves Lovers/Carnival 2000/ Wild Horses + 1 *Epic 2187/promo/ silkscreened/rear insert/'90*......................$6

I Remember That/Enchanted/Manhattan *Epic 1145/promo/ps/'88* $7

If You Don't Love Me 4 versions *Epic 4940/promo/ps/'92* $7

Looking For Atlantis (2 versions)/Wicked Things/Til the Cows../Dublin *Epic 2196/promo/ps/'90* $7

Machine Gun Ibiza/Couldn't Bear to Be../Don't Sing/Cruel *Epic 2276/promo/ps* $6

We Let the Stars Go *Epic 2271/promo/ silkscreened/ps/'90* $4

PRESLEY, ELVIS

Elvis *RCA PCD11382/stock/ reprocessed stereo issue (quickly pulled)/ps/'84* $500

Elvis 15th Anniversary 6 cds *Creative Radio Network/ 6 hour radio program/promo* $150

Elvis Double Features 4 cds *RCA 61835/ silkscreened/with booklet & pin in metal film cannister/mail order only* $100

Elvis Gold Records Vol. 2 *RCA PCD1-5197/ stock/ps/(only 50 copies made!)/ silkscreened/'84* $3000

Elvis Gold Records Vol. 2 *RCA PCD12075/ stock/reprocessed stereo issue (quickly pulled)/ps/'84* $500

Elvis Golden Records *RCA PCD11707/ stock/reprocessed stereo issue (quickly pulled)/ps/'84* $500

Elvis Presley *RCA PCD11254/stock/ reprocessed stereo issue (quickly pulled)/ps/'84* $500

Elvis Presley Radio Special program (4 tracks 54+minutes)/promos (3)/soundbites (8) *RCA 66121/promo/ps/'92* $50

Gold Standard Singles 5 disc set *RCA 8990-8994/stock/ps/'89* $75

Legend of a King 2 cds *Associated Broadcasters ABI 2CD/ promo/ps/silkscreened/numbered & limited edition/'89* $100

My Happiness *RCA 2654/promo/ps/'90* $40

Out of the Box ep (Don't Be Cruel/Hound Dog/Jailhouse Rock/All Shook Up) *RCA 62328/promo/ silkscreened pic/rear insert/'92* $35
Shake, Rattle & Roll sampler *RCA 6382/promo/ps/'92* $50
The Honeymoon Companion sampler *RCA 661242/promo/silkscreened/ps/'92* $50
Vintage 1955 *Oak 1003/stock/ps/'90* $75

PRESLEY, ELVIS/LIEBER & STOLLER - THE FIFTIES
w/ELVIS (8), ROBINS (3), COASTERS (8), THE DRIFTERS (2), RUTH BROWN, many more (26 in all) *Lieber & Stoller music publishing issue/promo/ps* $25

PRETENDERS, THE
Hold a Candle to This *Sire 4072/promo/'90* $4
I'm Not in Love vocal/instrumental *MCA 2625/promo/ps/'93* $5
Never Do That *Sire 4061/promo/'90* $3
Sense of Purpose *Sire 4089/promo/'90* $3

PRETTY IN PINK
Dreams edit/lp/instrumental *Motown 1005/promo/rear insert/'91* $4

PRETTY MAIDS
In Santa's Claws/A Merry Jingle/Eye of the Storm/Red Hot & Heavy + 1 (last 3 live) *CBS 467744/stock/ps/'90* $4

PRETTY POISON
Nightime 7" & 12" *Virgin 8350/promo/ps/'88* $4
When I Look In Your Eyes *Virgin 2346/promo/ps/'88* $4

PRICE, LOUIS
Flesh and Blood 5 versions *Motown 1538/promo/rear insert/'91* $4

PRIMAL SCREAM
Damaged edit & lp *Sire 5278/promo/'91* $3
Movin' on Up *Sire 5063/promo/'91* $3
Movin' On Up/Dont Fight It Feel It (3 vers.)/ You're Just Too Dark to Care *Sire 40193/stock/ gatefold hardcover ps/'91* $4
Slip Inside This House *Sire 5262/promo/'91* $3

PRIME MINISTER PETE NICE & DADDY RICH
Kick the Bobo 3 vers. *Def Jam 4966/promo/ps/'93* $4

PRIMITIVES
All the Way Down (beat versions)/ As Tears Go By/Really Stupid *RCA 9187/promo/custom tour date sticker/rear insert/'90* $7
Secrets *RCA 9135/promo/ps/'89* $5
Sick of It *RCA 9088/promo/ps/'89* $5

PRIMUS
Seas of Cheese/Jerry Was a Race Car Driver/ Those Damned Blue Collar Workers *Interscope 3881/promo/ logo on gold/rear insert/'91* $4
Seas of Cheese/Jerry Was a Race Car Driver/ Tommy the Cat/Those Damned Blue Collar Workers/Intruder/Making Plans For Nigel *Interscope 4340/ promo/ps/logo on red/'91* $6

PRINCE
"Symbol" special promo edition *Paisley Park 45121/promo/ color pic silkscreened/ps* $25
7 7 versions *Paisley Park 5581/promo/'92* $10
7 6 versions *Paisley Park 40574/stock/ gatefold hardcover ps/'92* $6
7 acoustic *Paisley Park 5981/promo/'92* $8
7 lp/acoustic *Paisley Park 18824/stock/ps* $5

Alphabet St. (4 versions) *Paisley Park 3079/ promo/custom sticker/'88* $15
Batdance lp & edit *WB 3579/promo/ps/'89* $10
Batdance (the batmix)/Batdance (vicki vale mix)/200 Balloons *WB 21257/ stock/ps/'89* $8
Batman (9 tracks) *WB 25978/stock/can/ book/silkscreened/'89* $15
Black Box *WB/technically not released (pulled at last minute)/stock* $10,000

Cream *Paisley Park 4985/promo/'91* $8
Damn U *Paisley Park 5890/promo/'92* $8
Damn U/2 Whom It May Concern *Paisley Park 18700/stock/ps/'92* $6
Diamonds and Pearls 13 tracks *Paisley Park 25379/promo/ps/ hologram on ps/silkscreened pic/'91* $25
Diamonds and Pearls edit & lp *Paisley Park 5148/promo/'91* $8
Gett Off 4 versions/Violet the Organ Grinder/ Gangster Slam/Clockin' the Jizz (instrum) *Paisley Park 40138/ gatefold hardcover ps/stock/'91* $6
Gett Off 6 versions *Paisley Park 4977/promo/'91* $14
Glam Slam edit/lp *Paisley Park 3181/promo/'88* $10
Graffiti Bridge (17 tracks) *Paisley Park 27493/promo only silkscreened pic/ps/'90* $20
I Wish U Heaven *Paisley Park 3242/promo/'88* .. $10
If I Was Your Girlfriend *Paisley Park 2747/promo/dj sticker* $12
Insatiable edit & lp *Paisley Park 5141/promo* $8
Money Don't Matter 2 Night edit & lp *Paisley Park 5298/promo/'91* $7
My Name is Prince edit & lp *Paisley Park 5770/promo/'92* $8
My Name is Prince 4 vers./Sexy M.F. 12" remix *Paisley Park 40700/stock/ gatefold hardcover ps/'92* $6
My Name is Prince/Sexy M.F. *Paisley Park 18707/stock/ps/'92* $5
New Power Generation funky weapon remix 5:01 *PaisleyPark 4578/promo/rear insert* $10
New Power Generation pt 1 & 2 *Paisley Park 4515/promo/rear insert* $8
Partyman *WB 3705/promo/ silkscreened Batman logos/'89* $10
Pink Cashmere vocal/guitar/lp *Paisley Park 5993/promo/rear insert* $8
Scandalous edit & lp *WB 3704/promo/ silkscreened Batman logos/'89* $10
Scandalous Sex Suite (5 tracks) *WB 21422/stock/ps/'89* $8
The Morning Papers *Paisley Park 5985/promo/'92* $6
The Morning Papers/Live 4 Love *Paisley Park 18583/stock/ps* $4
Thieves in the Temple *Paisley Park 4345/ promo/rear insert/'90* $8
Thieves in the Temple (3 versions) *Paisley Park 21598/stock/ps/'90* $7
Willing and Able edit & lp *Paisley Park 5301/promo/'91* $10

PRINCE & SHEENA EASTON
The Arms of Orion edit & lp *WB 3787/promo/'89* $8

PRINCE MARKIE DEE
Trippin Out edit/summer cool mix/hip hop mix *Columbia 74379/promo/ps/'92* $4

PRIVATE LIFE
Domino remix & lp *WB 4374/promo/ rear insert/'90* $4
Last Heartbeat *WB 3425/promo/silkscreened/ prod by EDDIE VAN HALEN* $4
Put Out the Fire *WB 3278/promo/ps/ '88/prod. by EDDIE VAN HALEN* $4
Touch Me *WB 4036/promo/silkscreened pic* $4

PROCLAIMERS, THE
I'm On My Way *Chrysalis 04555/promo/ logo on green/ps/'93* $5

PROCOL HARUM
A Dream in Ev'ry Home edit & lp *Zoo 17051/ promo/silkscreened/rear insert/'91* $5
All Our Dreams Are Sold *Zoo 17026/ promo/silkscreened/ps/'91* $15
Best of/In the Studio *show #169/ promo/aired 9/16/91* $20
The Return of Procol Harum: The Interview *Zoo 17044/promo/ps/silkscreened* $5
The Truth Won't Fade Away *Zoo 17041/promo/silkscreened/ps* $5

PROCOL HARUM & more

The Prodigal Stranger 12 tracks + 16 tracks by other artists *Album Network Tuneup In Store Play Edition #4/ promo/2 CDs/silkscreened + special lyric booklet for Procol CD* $25

PRODIGY, THE

Charly (2 versions)/Everybody in the Place (2 versions)/Your Love/G-Force *Elektra 66411/gatefold hardcover ps/stock/'92* $5

Fire 2 versions/Jericho 2 vers./Pandemonium *Elektra 66370/stock/gatefold hardcover ps/custom sticker/'92* $5

Out of Space 4 versions/Ruff in the Jungle Bizness/Jericho (live) *Elektra 66346/ stock/gatefold hardcover ps/'92* $5

Wind It Up 5 versions/We Are the Ruffest/ Weather Experience top buzz remix *Elektra 66319/stock/ gatefold hardcover ps/'93* $5

PROFESSOR GRIFF

Blackdraft 4 versions + 3 *Luke 465/promo* $5

Jail Sale 4 versions *Luke 4024/promo/ silkscreened/rear insert/'91* $5

Verbal Intercourse 2 versions/Living Proof lp & a-KKK-apella versions *Luke 4452/promo/rear insert/ logo on black/'91* $5

PRONG

For Dear Life/Defiant *Epic 2244/promo/ silkscreened/rear insert/'90* $4

Live at CBGBs (Third From the Sun/Dying Breed/Intermenstrual D.S.B.) *Epic 1951/promo/ silkscreened/rear insert/'90* $15

Lost and Found *Epic 2117/promo/ silkscreened/rear insert/'90* $4

Prove You Wrong/Talk Talk *Epic 4371/ promo/silkscreened deep blue logo on black/rear insert/'91* $4

Unconditional *Epic 4187/promo/ps/'91* $4

Whose Fist Is this Anyway ep (Prove You Wrong 2 versions/Get a Grip.. harm mix/Hell If I Could dub/Irrelevant Thoughts safety mix/Talk Takl) *Epic 74264/stock/ps/'92* $5

PROPAGANDA

Heaven Give Me Words *Charisma 005/promo/ silkscreened logo on blue/'90* $4

Only One Word (edit) *Charisma 009/promo/ ps/silkscreened logo/'90* $4

Mexican Power refried remix/One Summer Night remix *Skanless 90122/promo/ps/'92* $4

PROPER GROUNDS

Mind Tempest/I'm Drowning/Downtown Circus/ G.O.D. *Maverick 5788/promo/ custom sticker/'92* $4

PROPHET

Sound of a Breaking Heart *Megaforce 2197/promo/'88* $4

PROVEN INNOCENT

I'm Not the One lp/clark kent supermix *First Priority 4500/promo/ silkscreened/rear insert/'92* $4

PRYOR, STEVE

Spellbound *Zoo 17012/promo/silkscreened/ps* $4

PSYCHEDELIC FURS

Don't Be a Girl 4 versions *Columbia 4193/promo/ps/'91* $7

House (4 vers.) *Columbia 1944/promo/ps/'89* $8

Shock *Columbia 2739/promo/ps/'87* $10

Until She Comes single & lp *Columbia 4065/ promo/silkscreened/ps/'91* $6

Until She Comes (2 versions)/Make It Mine/ Sometimes *Columbia 44K 73855/stock/ps/'91* $6

World Outside 10 tracks *Columbia 47303/ promo/silkscreened/ gatefold hardcover/lyric poster/'91* $12

PSYCHEFUNKAPUS

We are the Young edit & lp *Atlantic 3285/promo/ps/'90* $4

PSYCHEFUNKAPUS & DICK DALE

Surfin on Jupiter *Atlantic 4360/promo/ silkscreened/rear insert/'91/ prod.by JERRY HARRISON* $4

PSYCHIC TV PRESENTS ULTRAHOUSE

BonE (do e rave mix)/Tempter hard dub mix & phallic rub mix *Wax Trax 9188/ stock/ps/'91* $6

PSYKOSONIK

Silicon Jesus 5 versions *TVT 8696/stock/ps/custom sticker* $5

PUBLIC ENEMY

911 is a Joke vocal & instrumental *Def Jam 73309/promo/ silkscreened green/ps/'90* $8

Bring the Noise (3 versions) *Columbia 2916/promo/ps/'88* $12

Brothers Gonna Work It Out 4 versions *Def Jam 73390/promo/ps/'90* $8

Brothers Gonna Work Out (3 versions)/ Anti-N*gger Machine/Powersaxx/ Power to the People (2 versions)/ The Enemy Assault Vehicle mix
Columbia 44K 73391/stock/ps/'90 .... $5
By the Time I Get to Arizona 3 versions
Def Jam 4358/promo/ps/'91 .... $10
Can't Do Nuttin' For Ya Man (3 versions)/ Burn Hollywood Burn (extended, censored versions)
Def Jam 44K 73612/stock/ps/'90 .... $6
Can't Do Nuttin' For Ya Man (3 versions)/ Burn Hollywood Burn (extended, censored versions)/Get the F** Out of Dodge (censored escapism versions)
Def Jam 73611/promo/ps/'90 .... $8
Can't Truss It 3 versions/Move! (censored radio versions) *Def Jam 73870/ promo/ps/'91* $8
Hazy Shade of Criminal vocal/instrumental
Def Jam 74488/promo/ silkscreened pic/ps/'92 .... $7
Nighttrain 4 versions
Def Jam 74272/promo/ps/'92 .... $8
Shut Em Down 4 versions
Def Jam 4351/promo/ps/'91 .... $8
Welcome to the Terrordome (4 versions)
Def Jam 73086/promo/silkscreened green logo on black/ps/'90 .... $10

PUBLIC IMAGE LTD

Acid Drops edit & lp
Virgin 4551/promo/silkscreened/'92 .... $4
Disappointed lp, edit & 12" versions
Virgin 2709/promo/silkscreened/'89 .... $4
Don't Ask Me + 12:00 of interview
Virgin 3573/promo/silkscreened/'90 .... $12
Happy lp & live/Disappointed live
Virgin 2927/promo/silkscreened $8
That What is Metal ep (Acid Drops edit & lp/Luck's Up/Love Hope/Emperor)
Virgin 4383/promo/ps (with furry piece) .. $10
Warrior lp & edit
Virgin 3031/promo/silkscreened/'89 .... $4

PURE

Blast *Reprise 5947/promo/silkscreened/'93* $4
Greedy morphine mix/Laughing Like a Fiend/ Tall Grass live acoustic/So Wrapped Up demo *Reprise 45003/ stock/ps/silkscreened/'92* $6
Spiritual Pollution *Reprise 6184/promo/ prod.by JERRY HARRISON/'92* $4

PURSUIT OF HAPPINESS, THE

Cigarette Dangles *Mercury 840/promo/ silkscreened/ps/'93* $4
Two Girls in One *Chrysalis 23508/promo/ rear insert/'90* $4

PYLON

Sugarpop/Interview (20:43)
Sky/promo/silkscreened/'90 .... $15

Q FEEL

Dancing in Heaven short & long intro/GZ edit/ext.
Jive 1221/promo/rear insert $8

QUADROPHONIA

Schizofrenia 4 vers. *RCA 62232/stock/ps/'92* $5

QUEEN

Bohemian Rhapsody *Hollywood 10145/ promo/rear insert/custom sticker/'92* $8
Breakthru *Capitol 79720/promo/'89* $10
Breakthru (4 vers.) *Capitol 79746/promo* $12
Classic (lp length comp. 14 tracks)
Capitol 79591/promo/ps/'89 .... $20
Headlong edit & lp/Under Pressure
Hollywood 8262/promo/ps/'91 .... $8
I Can't Live Without You *Hollywood 8367/ promo/rear insert/'91* $8
Innuendo (6:31) *Hollywood 8319/promo/ps/'91* ... $8
One Year of Love/We Are the Champions/ Barcelona *Hollywood 10196/promo/ silkscreened/rear insert/'92* $12
Queen Rocks Volume 1 6 tracks
Hollywood 8263/promo/ logo on black/rear insert/'91 .... $20
Queen Rocks Volume 2 (Keep Yourself Alive/ Modern Times Rock n Roll/ Crazy Little Thing../One Vision + 3) *Hollywood 8296/promo/ logo on black/rear insert/'91* $20
Queen Rocks Volume 3 (Bohemian Rhapsody/ You're My Best Friends '91 remix/ Im in Love With My Car '91 remix/ Seven Seas + 4) *Hollywood 8297/ promo/logo on red/rear insert/ custom sticker/'91* $20
Queen Rocks Volume 4 (One Vision/Killer Queen/ Play the Game/We Will Rock You/ We Are the Champions/Dragon Attack + 2) *Hollywood 8298/ promo/rear insert/'91* $20
Scandal *Capitol 79785/promo/silkscreened* $8
Stone Cold Crazy 2:12 & 3:49/We Will Rock You-We Are the Champions
Hollywood 10193/promo/logo on blue/ rear insert/custom sticker/'92 .... $12
Talks (interview) (BBC Radio One Interview with Mike Read (53:32)/Thank God It's Christmas) *Hollywood 8674/ promo/logo on green/'92* $25
These are the Days of Our Lives
Hollywood 8390/promo/ silkscreened/rear insert/'91 .... $8
These are the Days of Our Lives edit & lp
Hollywood 10061/promo/ silkscreened/rear insert/'91 .... $8

We Are the Champions/We Will Rock You-
We Are Champions/We Will Rock You r.rubin remix *Hollywood 10192/ promo/logo on red/rear insert/'92* $15
We Will Rock You + versions/We Are the Champions + 2 versions *Hollywood Basic 66573/stock/ gatefold hardcover ps* $7

QUEEN LATIFAH
Fly Girl 7"/sax mix/piano mix/12" club *Tommy Boy 502/promo/'91* $5
Fly Girl vocal & instrumental *Tommy Boy 995/promo/'91* $5
How Do I Love Thee 6 versions *Tommy Boy 524/stock/'92* $5

QUEENSRYCHE
Another Rainy Night *EMI 4808/promo/ silkscreened/ps/'91* $8
Anybody Listening? edit & lp *EMI 4863/promo/ps/silkscreened/'92* $8
Anybody Listening? 7:40/Scarborough Fair *EMI 50388/stock/ps/'92* $6
Best I Can edit & lp *EMI 04674/promo/ silkscreened white/ps/'90* $8
Breaking the Silence *Manhattan 04049/promo/ps/'88* $15
Empire (edit) *EMI 4640/promo/silkscreen/ps/'90* $12
Evolution Calling (Silent Lucidity/Best I Can/ I Don't Believe in Love/Revolution Calling/Walk in the Shadows + 4) *EMI 04760/promo/gatefold hardcover ps/silkscreened/'91* $25
Eyes of a Stranger *EMI 04200/promo/ps/'88* $15
I Don't Believe in Love *EMI 04344/promo/ silkscreened/rear insert/'89* $10
Jet City Woman *EMI 04756/promo/ silkscreened white/ps/'91* $8
Last Time in Paris *Elektra 8190/ promo/rear insert/'90* $8
Operation Live Crime 15 tracks *EMI 4811/ promo/with bonus video/'91* $25
Real World lp/edit with intro/edit without intro *Columbia 5271/promo/ "Last Action Hero" ps/'93* $6
Revolution Calling *Manhattan 04142/promo/ps/'88* $15
Silent Lucidity *EMI 4700/promo/silkscreened/ps/'91* $8
The Sound of Building Empires sampler 5 tracks *EMI 04658/promo/ps/'92* $20

QUESTIONNAIRES
(That Love is a) Killin' Kind 4:30 & 5:10 *EMI 4812/promo/silkscreened/ trifold hardcover ps/'91* $4
Window to the World edit & lp *EMI 4463/ promo/silkscreened/rear insert/'89* $4

QUICKSAND
Dine Alone edit & lp/How Soon is Now? *Polydor 841/promo/ silkscreened/custom sticker/'93* $4
Fazer *Polydor 856/promo/logo on black/ps* $4
Omission/Clean Slate/Unfulfilled/Hypno Jam With Dan *Revelation/stock/ps/'90* $5

R. KELLY & PUBLIC ANNOUNCEMENT
Born Into '90s 11 tracks *Jive 01241 41469/ promo issue with cloth bag/ bonus cassette* $15
Dedicated short intro & long intro *Jive 42115/ promo/custom sticker/rear insert/'92* $6
Honey Love radio & lp *Jive 42031/promo/ps* $6
She's Got That Vibe 6 versions *Jive 42025/ promo/rear insert/custom sticker/'91* $6
Slow Dance (Hey Mr. DJ) *Jive 42092/promo/rear insert/'92* $6

R.J.'S LATEST ARRIVAL
Rich Girls (5 versions) EMI 04397/ promo/silkscreened/rear insert/'89 .... $4

RABIN, TREVOR
Can't Look Away 12 tracks *Elektra 60781/ stock/ps/custom sticker/'89* $12
I Can't Look Away edit & lp *Elektra 8146/ promo/silkscreened logo/'89* $6
Something to Hold on To *Elektra 8086/promo* $6
Sorrow (Your Heart) edit *Elektra 8123/promo/'89* $6

RADIO ACTIVE CATS
Bed of Roses *WB 5277/promo/silkscreened* $4
Shotgun Shack edit & lp *WB 4963/promo/ silkscreened group pic/'91* $5

RADIOHEAD
Anyone Can Play Guitar *Capitol 79773/promo/ps/'93* $4
Creep edit & lp *Capitol 79684/promo/ps/'92* $6
Stop Whispering *Capitol 79243/promo/ logo on black/ps/'93* $4

RAGE AGAINST THE MACHINE
Killing in the Name *Epic 4791/promo/ps/silkscreened/'92* $4

RAGING SLAB
A Taste O' Slab ep (Anywhere But Here/ Take a Hold/So Help Me/What Have You Done?/Lynne/National Dust) *Def American/promo/ps/'93* $6
Anywhere But Here lp & edit *Def American 6125/promo/ps/'93* $4
Bent For Silver/Workin' For RCA (live)/ Dont Dog Me (live) *RCA 9177/ promo/ps/custom sticker/'90* $8
Don't Dog Me *RCA 9036/promo/ps/'89* $4
Selftitled 11 tracks *RCA 9680/stock/ps* $12

Take a Hold lp & acoustic
Def American 6369/promo/ps/'93 ....$5

RAHIEM, EMANUEL
Spend a Little Time 8 versions
Capitol 79647/promo/ps/'91 ....$4

RAILWAY CHILDREN, THE
Every Beat of Heart *Virgin 3358/promo/'90* $4
Music Stop *Virgin 3606/promo/ silkscreened logo/'90* $4

RAIN PEOPLE
Distance 3:58/4:30
Epic 1475/promo/silkscreened/'89 ....$4
Baby Doll *Atco 4183/promo/rear insert/'91* $4
I'm Not Scared *Atco 2971/promo/ silkscreened logo/rear insert/'89* $4
Let's Work Together *Atco 3940/promo/ps* $4

RAINDOGS
May Your Heart Keep Beat. *Atco 3313/promo/ silkscreened logo/rear insert/'90* $4
Some Fun/Dance of the Freaks/Carry Your Cross
Atco 3938/promo/ps/'91 ....$5

RAINMAKERS
Small Circles *Mercury 09/promo/ps/3"/'88* $4
Snakedance *Mercury 07/promo/ps/'87* $4
Spend it On Love/Reckoning Day/Battle of Roses + 1 *Mercury 58/promo/ps/'89* $4

RAITT, BONNIE
Have a Heart
Capitol 79897/promo/rear insert/'89 ....$5
I Can't Make You Love Me edit & lp
Capitol 79768/promo/ logo on black/rear insert/'91 ....$5
Love Letter *Capitol 79127/promo/ silkscreened/'89* $5
Nick of Time *Capitol 79721/promo/'89* $5
Not the Only One edit & lp
Capitol 79115/promo/rear insert/'91 ....$5
Slow Ride *Capitol 79949/promo/silkscreened/ rear insert/'91* $5
Something to Talk About *Capitol 79748/ promo/ps/silkscreened/'91* $5
Something to Talk About/One Part Be My Lover/I Ain't Gonna Let You Break My Heart Again
Capitol 15736/stock/ps/'91 ....$5
Thing Called Love *Capitol 79554/promo/ silkscreened/'89* $5

RAITT, BONNIE & DELBERT MCCLINTON
Good Man, Good Woman *Capitol 79336/promo/ logo on green/rear insert/'91* $5

RAITT, BONNIE & JOHN LEE HOOKER
'Im in the Mood *Chameleon 72/promo/ silkscreened logo on black/'89* $5

RAITT, BONNIE & WAS NOT WAS
Baby Mine *A&M 17625/promo/ps/'88* $5

RAM JAM
Black Betty (3 versions) *Epic 73195/promo/ silkscreened green/rear insert/'90* $6

RAMONES
Pet Sematary 2 vers. *Sire 3569/promo/'89* $5
Poison Heart *Radioactive 2343/promo/ps/'92*....$4
Talkin' Mondo Bizarro 26:16 interview + 4 live tracks (Take It As It Comes/Censorshit/ Poison Heart/Strength to Endure)
Radioactive 2658/promo/ps/'93 ....$20
Touring *Radioactive 2584/promo/rear insert*......$4

RANDY & THE GYPSYS
Love You Honey lp & 7" *A&M 17973/promo/ silkscreened logo/'89* $5
Perpetrators (5 vers.) *A&M 17904/promo/ silkscreened green/'89* $5

RANKIN, LOUIE
Typewriter lp & instrumental/Monster Move lp & hip hop & instrumental *Mesa 76004/ stock/gatefold hardcover ps/'92* $4

RANKS, SHABBA
Muscle Grip 4 versions *Epic 74797/promo/ silkscreened pic/ps/'92* $6
Trailor Load of Girls 5 versions
Epic 73808/promo/ps/'91 ....$6
What 'cha Gonna do? 6 versions *Epic 5114/ promo/silkscreened/rear insert/'92*............$6

RAPINATION & KYM MAZELLE
Love Me the Right Way 3:25/5:48 *Logic 62491/ promo/silkscreened/rear insert/'93*............$4

RAPPIN IS FUNDAMENTAL
Rappin' is Fundamental 3 versions
A&M 75021 7496/promo/ps/'91 ....$4

RASPBERRIES
Go All the Way/I Wanna Be With You/Let's Pretend/Tonight
Rhino 73016/stock/3"/ps/'88 ....$6

RATT
Givin' Yourself Away *Atlantic 3697/promo/ silkscreened logo on yellow/rear insert*.....$4
Givin' Yourself Away (CHR versions)
Atlantic 3762/promo/ps $4
I Want a Woman
Atlantic 2635/promo/rear insert/'88 ....$4
Lovin' Yous a Dirty Job
Atlantic 3495/promo/ps/'90 ....$4

Nobody Rides For Fre
MCA 1533/promo/rear insert/'91 .... $4
Shame Shame Shame lp & lp with intro
Atlantic 3624/promo/ps/silkscreened $4
Way Cool Jr. *Atlantic 2531/promo/'88* $4

RATTLEBONE
X-Ray Eyes/Society Dog/Cities on Flame/
Panther Sweat/Do Your Thing
Hollywood 61405/stock/
gatefold hardcover ps/'92 .... $4

RAVE UPS, THE
A Chance Coversation with Jimmer Podrasky
Epic 2010/promo/ps/'90 .... $10
Respectfully King of Rain *Epic 2015/promo/*
rear insert/silkscreened purple/'90 .... $4
Respectfully King of Rain/Train to Nowhere/
The Night Before Christmas
Epic 1909/promo/ps/
2000 limited edition/'89 .... $10
She Says (Come Around)
Epic 2061/promo/ps/'90 .... $4

RAW FUSION
Throw Your Hands in the Air/Do My Thang
both vocal & instrumental
Hollywood Basic 66546/stock/
gatefold hardcover ps/'91 .... $4

RAW YOUTH
Tame Yourself 3 versions *RNA 90067/*
promo/silkscreened/ps/'91 .... $4

RAWLS, LOU
Don't Let Me Be Misunderstood/All Around the
World *Blue Note 79671/promo/*
custom sticker/'90 .... $4
It's Supposed to Be Fun (3 versions)
Blue Note 79316/promo/rear insert $4

RAWLS, LOU & DIANNE REEVES
At Last *Blue Note 79816/promo* $4
A Lover's Question *Manhattan 79700/promo/*
silkscreened/rear insert/cust. sticker $4

RAYE, COLLIN
Every Second *Epic 74242/promo/*
silkscreened/rear insert/'92 .... $4

REA, CHRIS
Auberge *Atco 3839/promo/ps/'91* $5
Chris Rea Interview Summer 1991
Atco 4147/promo/ps/'91 .... $15
Looking For the Summer edit & lp
Atco 3995/promo/ps/'91 .... $4
On the Beach edit & lp *Geffen 3442/promo/ps/'88* $4
Texas edit & lp/Working on It (live)
Geffen 4110/promo/
silkscreened logo/ps/'90 .... $6

Road to Hell (11 tracks) *Geffen 24276/promo/*
gatefold hardcover/silkscreened/'89 .... $15
Working on It *Geffen 3404/promo/ps/'88* $4

READY FOR THE WORLD
Can He Do It edit & extended
MCA 2013/promo/rear insert/'91 .... $4

REAL LIFE
God Tonight (3 versions) *Curb 79014/promo/*
silkscreened/rear insert/'90 .... $5
Kiss the Ground *Curb 026/promo/*
silkscreened/rear insert/'90 .... $4
Send Me an Angel '89 edit & dance mi
Curb 10303/promo/custom sticker $6

REAL PEOPLE, THE
The Truth single & 12"/Words/Easy
Relativity 657 698/stock/
gatefold hardcover ps/'91 .... $4
Window Pane 3 vers/Love/Come O
Relativity 88562-1086/stock/ps/'91 .... $4

REAL SEDUCTION, THE
Ain't Nuthin Wrong 6 versions
Atlantic 5191/promo $4

REBEL MC
Street Tuff (4 versions)
Desire 209/promo/silkscreened/'89 .... $4

REBEL PEBBLES, THE
Dream Lover lp & fade
IRS 67054/promo/silkscreened/ps $4
How Do You Feel *IRS 67063/*
promo/logo on gold/ps/'91 .... $4

RECKLESS SLEEPERS
If We Never Meet Again single & lp/Jules Shear
interview *IRS 17638/promo/ps/*
'88/CYNDI LAUPER & BANGLES $12

RECOIL
Bloodline 7 tracks *Sire 26850/stock/ps/'92* $5
Faith Healer 7 versions *Sire 40345/stock/*
gatefold hardcover ps/'92 .... $4

RED DEVILS, THE
Selftitled 12 tracks *Def American/promo* $12

RED FLAG
Machines 8 versions *IRS 13863/stock/ps/'92* $5
Russian Radio fresh radio mix & single radio
Enigma 164/promo/cust.sticker/'89 .... $6
Russian Radio (3 versions)/Broken Heart (3
vers.) + 2 *Enigma 71310/ps/stock* $5

RED HOT & BLUE

All the Great Rhythm & Blues Songs 13 tracks *Curb 77264/stock with promo silkscreened/ps/ISAAC HAYES, CHUCK JACKSON, CARLA THOMAS, BILLY PRESTON, more/'90* $12
People Get Ready/Bad Boy/I'm in the Mood *Curb 79030/promo/insert/ISAAC HAYES, CHUCK JACKSON, CARLA THOMAS, BILLY PRESTON.../'90* $6

RED HOT CHILI PEPPERS

Abbey Road ep (Fire/Backwoods/Catholic School Girls Rule/Hollywood (Africa)/ True Man Don't Kill Coyotes) *WB 40992/stock/ gatefold hardcover ps/'93* $8
Bloodsugarsexmagik (17 track censored edit.) *WB 5170/promo/custom sticker/ sanitize strip/logo on white/'91* $25
Breaking the Girl edit *WB 5274/promo/'91* $8
Fight Like a Brave lp & mofo mix/Fire/True Men Don't Kill Coyotes/Jungle Man *EMI 31492/promo/ps/'87* $20
Give It Away *WB 5042/promo/ silkscreened/rear insert/'91* $8
Give It Away 4 versions/Search and Destroy *WB 40261/gatefold hardcover ps/stock/'91* $6
Give It Away edit & lp *WB 5048/promo/'91* $8
Higher Ground 3:12/3:21 *EMI 04389/promo/ silkscreened/rear insert/'89* $10
Knock Me Down/Millionaires Against Hunger/ Fire/Punk Rock Classic *EMI 4380/ promo/rear insert/silkscreened/'89* $12
Show Me Your Soul *EMI 04513/promo/ silkscreened/rear insert/'90* $8
Soul to Squeeze *WB 6393/promo/ silkscreened/rear insert/'93* $6
Suck My Kiss radio & lp *WB 5234/promo/'91* $7
Taste the Pain aor & lp *EMI 04507/promo/ silkscreened/rear insert/'90* $8
Taste the Pain/Castles/Special Secret Song/ F.U. (live) *EMI 07502/promo/ silkscreened/rear insert/'89* $18
Taste the Pain/Millionaires Against Hunger/ Castles live/High.Ground daddy-o mix *EMI 50285/stock/silkscreened/ps* $10
Under the Bridge *WB 5255/promo/ red logo on black/'91* $8

RED HOUSE PAINTERS

Mistress remix & piano versions/ Grace Cathedral Park/Strawberry Hill *4AD 6108/promo/silkscreen/rear insert* $5

RED HOUSE, THE

I Said a Prayer *SBK 05343/promo/silkscreened/ hardcover gatefold ps/'90* $4

RED SIREN

One Good Lover *Mercury 67/promo/ps/'89* $4

REDD KROSS

1976 *Atlantic 3734/promo/rear insert/'90* $4
Annie's Gone *Atlantic 3565/promo/ silkscreened logo/ps/'90* $4

REDD, JEFF

I Found Lovin' 7"/lp/extended *Uptown 18214/promo/'89* $4
You Called & Told Me 5 versions *Uptown 1597/promo/ps/'91* $4

REDDING, OTIS

The Definitive Otis Redding Sampler 12 tracks *Rhino 7011/promo/ps/ logo silkscreened/'93* $20

REDHEAD KINGPIN

3-2-1 Pump edit/power mix/lp *Virgin 4447/promo/'91* $4
Get It Together 5 versions *Virgin 3724/ promo/silkscreened logo/'91* $5
It's a Love Thang 3 versions *Virgin 3952/promo/rear insert/'91* $5
We Don't Have a Plan B lp & extended/All About Red *Virgin 3725/promo/ silkscreened/'90* $5
We Rock the Mic Right 7" remix/12" remix/lp *Virgin 3228/promo/silkscreened/'89* $5

REED, DAN

Long Way to Go *Mercury 587/promo/ logo on red/gatefold hardcover ps/'91* $4
Mix It Up edit & lp *Mercury 493/promo/ gatefold hardcover ps/'91* $4

REED, LOU

Busload of Faith edit & lp *Sire 3510/promo* $5
Dirty Blvd radio version/lp version *Sire 3359/promo/'88* $7
Magic & Loss 14 tracks *Sire 26662/promo* $20
Power and Glory/Harry's Circumcision/Dream/ Power and Glory Part II *WB 5454/ promo/silkscreened pic/rear insert* $10
Romeo Had Juliette lp & 7" *Sire 3619/promo/silkscreen Lou/'89* $8
Selections From Between Thought & Expression: The Lou Reed Anthology (Satellite of Love/Walk on the Wild Side/Heroin 0 live 12/1/76)/Lisa Says/Downtown Dirt/Sweet Jane/Metal Machine Music) *RCA 62284/promo/silkscreened/ps* $15
Tarbelly and Featherfoot *Columbia 5440/promo/ps/'93* $5
What's Good edit & lp *Sire 4988/ promo/silkscreened/rear insert/'92* $6

REED, LOU & JOHN CALE

Nobody But You *Sire 4056/promo/'90* $6

Songs For Drella 15 tracks *Sire 26205/promo/ fuzzy gatefold hardcover with booklet/silkscreened/'90* $30

REEVES, DIANE

Never Too Far 4:09 & 5:19/Better Days *EMI 04451/promo/silkscreened/ rear insert/'89* $5

Afro Blue *Blue Note 79687/promo/ logo on yellow/custom sticker/'91* $5

REEVES, MARTHA

Wild Night *MCA 1445/promo/rear insert/'91* $4

REEVES, RONNA

Sadly Mistaken *Mercury 231/promo/ silkscreened/'90* $4

We Can Hold Our Own *Mercury 778/promo/rear insert/'92* $4

REID, JUNIOR

Actions Speak Louder Than Words (4 versions) *Big Life 400/promo/ps/'91* $5

REID, TERRY

If You Let Her edit & lp *WB 5410/promo/'91* $4

The Whole of the Moon *WB 5566/promo/'91* $4

REM

(Should We Talk About the Weather) *WB 3377/ promo/ps/interview & songs/'88* $40

An AOR Radio Staple (11 song Greatest Hits compilation) *IRSD 7/promo/ps/'87* $40

Drive *WB 5700/promo/silkscreened/ps/'92* $6

Drive/Winged Mammal Theme *WB 18729/stock/ps/'92* $5

Everybody Hurts/Mandolin Strum *WB 18638/stock/ps/silkscreened* $5

Get Up/Orange Crush & Turn You Inside .. (live) *WB 3716/promo/'89* $15

Green full lp *WB 3292/promo/cloth bound with book/silkscreened pic/'88* $25

Ignoreland *WB 5844/promo/silkscreened/'92* $6

It's the End of the World As We Know It (lp & edit) *IRS 17476/promo/ps/'87* $30

Losing My Religion *WB 4707/promo/ps/ silkscreened/'91* $10

Losing My Religion live *WB 4881/promo/'91* ... $10

Man on the Moon edit & lp *WB 5894/promo/silkscreened/'92* $6

Man on the Moon/New Orleans Instrumental #2 *WB 18642/stock/ps/silkscreened* $5

Music From Tourfilm video: Get Up/audio only: World Leader Pretend/It's the End of the World... *WB 4460/promo/ gatefold hardcover ps/cd video/'90* $20

Near Wild Heaven *WB 5058/promo/'91* $6

Orange Crush *WB 3306/promo/ps/ silkscreened pic/'88* $12

Out of Time full length *WB/booklike package/promo* $25

Pop Song *WB 3357/promo/'88* $8

Radio Song *WB 4808/promo/'91* $6

Radio Song (tower of luv bug mix)/Love is All Around/Belong (last 2 live) *WB 40229/ stock/gatefold hardcover ps/'91* $6

Shiny Happy People *WB 4888/promo/silkscreened/'91* $6

Shiny Happy People music mix/pop mix/hip mix *WB 5060/promo/'91* $15

Stand *WB 3353/promo/'88* $7

Texarkana *WB 4826/promo/silkscreened/'91* $8

The Sidewinder Sleeps Tonite *WB 5903/promo/silkscreened/'92* $5

The Sidewinder Sleeps .../Lion Sleeps Tonight *WB 18523/stock/ps/silkscreened* $5

Turn You Inside-Out *WB 3446/promo/'88* $7

REMBRANDTS

Chase the Clouds Away edit & lp *Atco 5068/promo* $5

Chase the Clouds Away edit & lp *Atco 5069/ promo/ps/logo on blue/'93* $5

Johnny Have You Seen Her *Atco 4728/promo/ silkscreened/ps/'92* $4

Just the Way it Is Baby (acoustic) *Atco 3926/promo/rear insert/'90* $5

Just the Way It Is/lp medley (7:50) *Atco 3532/promo/rear insert/'90* $7

Maybe Tomorrow edit & lp *Atco 4925/ promo/silkscreened/ps/'92* $4

Save Me *Atco 3749/promo/silkscreened/ rear insert/'91* $4

Selftitled (13 tracks) *Atco 91412/stock/ps/ promo only picture frame outer box/'91* .. $12

Someone *Atco 3448/promo/gatefold hardcover/custom sticker/'91* $4

Someone *Atco 3448/promo/rear insert/'90* $4

REMEDY

Closer fade & lp *Hollywood 10316/promo/ silkscreened/'93* $4

REN & STIMPY

Little Eediot! (Happy Happy Joy Joy/Kilted Yaksmen Anthem/Don't Whiz..) + interview *Sony 5473/promo/ps/2 cds/'93* $15

RENEGADE SOUNDWAVE

Biting My Nails vocal & instrumental club mix/ Cocaine Sex/Kray Twins *Enigma 75525/ ps/stock/silkscreened/'89* $8

Thunder (2 versions)/Manphibian/Mash Up/ Biting My Nails (2 versions) *Mute 66589/stock/ gatefold hardcover ps/'90* $7

RENO, MIKE

Whenever Theres a Night *Cypress 17760/ promo/silkscreened pic/'89* $5

REO SPEEDWAGON

All Heaven Broke Loose lp & single *Epic 4186/ promo/logo on black/rear insert/'91* $4
Halfway (special versions) *Epic 73659/ promo/silkscreened/rear insert/'90* $5
Here With Me *Epic 1139/promo/ps/'88* $6
Live It Up *Epic 2140/promo/silkscreened/ rear insert/'90* $4
Love is a Rock (3 versions) *Epic 73540/ promo/silkscreened/rear insert/'90* $6
You Won't See Me *Epic 2270/promo/ logo on tan/rear insert/'90* $4

REPLACEMENTS

Achin' to Be *Sire 3606/promo/'89* $5
Back to Back *Sire 3496/promo/'89* $5
Cruella De Ville *A&M 17673/promo/'88* $7
Don't Buy Or Sell It's Crap ep (When It Began/Kissin' in Action/Ought to Get Love/Satellite/Like a Rolling Pin) *Sire 4632/promo/silkscreened/ps* $20
Happy Town edit & lp *Sire 4574/promo/'90* $4
I'll Be You *Sire 3419/promo/'89* $5
Live Inconcerated (Talent Show/Answering Machine/Anywheres Better Than Here/Another Girl, Another Planet/ Here Comes a Regular)+Achin' to Be *Sire 3633/promo/ps/'89* $25
Merry Go Round *Sire 4466/promo/ silkscreened logo/rear insert/'90* $5
Someone Take the Wheel fword edit & lp *Sire 4472/promo/'90* $4
When It Began *Sire 4666/promo/'90* $4

RESTLESS HEART

Big Iron Horses 10 tracks *RCA 66049/promo/ silkscreened pic/foldout ps/'92* $12
Flame It On Love/Big Iron Horses *RCA 62389/promo/ps/'92* $5
Til I Loved You pop remix & lp *RCA 62150/ promo/logo on red/rear insert/'91* $4
When She Cries *RCA 62334/promo/ rear insert/'92* $4

RESTLESS HEART & WARREN HILL

Tell Me What You Dream 4 vers *RCA 62467/promo/ps/'93* $5

REV, MERCURY

Car Wash Hair edit & lp *Columbia 4948/promo/ logo on black/'93* $4

REVENGE

Gun World Porn ep (Little Pig/Cloud Nine/ State of Shock 3 versions/Deadbeat 2 versions) *Capitol 98479/stock/ps/'92* $5
Pineapple Face (3 versions)/Bleach Boy *Capitol 15559/stock/ps/'90* $5
Pineapple Face (4 versions) *Capitol 79092/ promo/custom sticker/'90* $6
Slave (3 versions)/Kiss the Chrome/Jesus I Love You *Capitol 15610/promo/ silkscreen logo on black/cust. sticker/'90* .. $6

REY

Love Don't Come in a Minute lp & extended *Chrysalis 23648/promo/ps/'90* $4

RHATIGAN, SUZANNE

To Hell With Love 4 versions *Imago 28035/promo/ps/'92* $4

RHINO BUCKET

Beat to Death Like a Dog *Reprise 5765/ promo/custom sticker/'92* $4
Blood on the Cross *Reprise 4490/promo/ rear insert/'90* $4
One Night Stand pmrc single versions/live censored versions *Reprise 4615/ promo/gatefold hardcover/'90* $6

RHYTHM CORPS

Satellites *Pasha 2266/promo/ silkscreened/rear insert/'91* $4

RHYTHM SYNDICATE

I Wanna Make Love to You 4 versions *Impact 2315/promo/ps/'92* $5
P.A.S.S.I.O.N. 7"/hip hop/power mix *Impact 1416/promo/'91* $5

RHYTHM TRIBE

Gotta See Your Eyes 4:10/4:34/3:58 *Zoo 17001/promo/silkscreened/ rear insert/'91* $4

RICHARD, ZACHARY

Come On, Sheila *A&M 31458 8023/promo/ silkscreened/ps/'92* $4
One Kiss single & single with intro *A&M 31458 8105/promo/ps/'92* $4
Snake Bite Love 12 tracks *A&M 31454 8003/ promo/gatefold hardcover ps/silkscreened/'92* $10
Too Many Women *A&M 75021 7513/ promo/silkscreened/ps/'90* $4
Who Stole My Monkey *A&M 75021 8083/promo/ silkscreened red/'90* $4

RICHARDS, KEITH

999 edit & lp *Virgin 12770/promo/logo on white/rear insert/'92* $6
Eileen edit & lp *Virgin 12745/promo/ logo on brown/rear insert/'92* $6
Eileen/Gimme Shelter/Wicked As It Seems/ How I Wish (last 3 live)/Key to the Highway *Virgin 12647/promo/ ps/custom sticker/'93* $12
Make No Mistake edit & lp *Virgin 2633/ promo/silkscreened pic/'88* $12
Struggle Virgin 2633/promo/'89 .... $8

Take It So Hard *Virgin 2396/promo/ps/'88* $10
Wicked As It Seems edit & lp *Virgin 12715/ promo/logo on black/rear insert/'92* $6
You Dont Move Me *Virgin 2557/promo/silkscreened/'88* $10

RICHIE, LIONEL
Do It To Me edit/lp/instr. *Motown 374631034/ promo/silkscreened pic/ gatefold box ps/'92* $6
Do It To Me edit/lp/instr. *Motown 374634818/ stock/ps/silkscreened pic/'92* $5
Do It To Me 6 versions *Motown 3746310532/ promo/'92* $8
My Destiny 5 versions *Motown 3746310712/promo/'92* $8
My Destiny edit & lp *Motown 374631057/ promo/ps/silkscreened/'92* $5

RIDE
Kaleidoscope/Seagull/Dreams Burn ../ Vapour Train/In a Different Place/ Nowhere/Drive Blind (last 6 live) *Reprise 4961/promo/silkscreened* $12
Leave Them All Alone 4:36/8:17 *Sire 5369/promo/'92* $6
Leave Them All Behind/Chrome/Waves/ Grasshopper *Sire 40332/stock/ gatefold hardcover ps/'92* $5
Taste *Sire 4659/promo/'90* $4
Twisterella/Going Blank Again/Howard Hughes/ Stampede *Sire 40448/stock/ gatefold hardcover ps/'92* $5
Vapour Trail *Sire 4744/promo/ silkscreened red/'91* $4
Vapour Trail/Unfamiliar/Sennen/Beneath *Sire 40055/stock/gatefold hardcover/'90* ..$5

RIDGELEY, ANDREW
Red Dress 4:08/6:39/5:09 *Columbia 73451/ promo/silkscreened red/ps/'90* $6
Shake 3:29/6:03 *Columbia 73337/promo/ps* $6

RIDGWAY, STAN
Fly on the Wall: Music and Commentary from S.R. (7 songs & interview) *Geffen 3508/promo/ps/'89* $15
Goin' Southbound *Geffen 3502/promo/ps/'89* $4
I Wanna Be a Boss edit & lp *Geffen 4283/ promo/silkscreened/ps/'91* $4

RIFF
Christmas medley 3:47/same (accapella) *SBK 05420/promo/ gatefold hardcover ps/'91* $4
Everytime My Heart Beats narley marley mix & d.lambert lp remix *SBK 05418/promo/ logo on blue/ps/'91* $4
White Men Can't Jump 4 versions *SBK 05446/ promo/gatefold hardcover ps/ silkscreened basketball/'92* $5

RIGHT SAID FRED
Don't Talk Just Kiss 6 vers. *Charisma 96200/ gatefold hardcover ps/stock/'92* $5
I'm Too Sexy 7 versions *Charisma 96256/ stock/gatefold hardcover ps/'91* $6

RIGHTEOUS BROTHERS
Rock and Roll Heaven *Curb 043/promo/ps/'91* $6
Unchained Melody newly recorded (august '90) *Curb 024/promo/logo on blue/ rear insert/'90* $6

RILEY, CHERYL PEPSII
Ain't No Way lp/jazz house overhaul *Columbia 73955/promo/ps/'91* $4
How Can You Hurt the One You..edit & with intro *Columbia 73766/promo/ps/'91* $4

RILEY, JEANNIE C.
Here's to the Cowboys *Laurie 143/promo* $4

RILEY, TEDDY & TAMMY LUCAS
Is It Good to You 5 vers. *Soul 2102/promo/'92* $6

RIPPINGTONS
Indian Summer *GRP 9992/promo/ps/'92* $5
Welcome to the St James Club *GRP 9940/promo/rear insert/'90* $5

RISE ROBOTS RISE
All Sewn Up 5 versions *TVT 3212/promo/silkscreened/'92* $5
If I Only Knew 7 versions/All Sewn Up 2 vers. *TVT 3213/stock/ps/'92* $5
Talk is Cheap/Back Talk/Flowers & Birds 4:47 & 6:00 *TVT 3211/stock/ps/'91* $5

RITENOUR, LEE & MAXI PRIEST
Waiting in Vain edit *GRP 5116/promo/ps/'93* $3

RIVER CITY PEOPLE
(What's Wrong With) Dreaming *Capitol 79929/ promo/silkscreened/rear insert/'90* $4
(What's Wrong With) Dreaming (edit)/ California Dreamin'/Under the Rainbow (live)/Say Something Good (live) *Capitol 79386/promo/silkscreen/ps/'90* $8

RIVERDOGS
I Believe *Epic 2055/promo/ps/'90* $4
On Air ep (12 tracks recorded on radio) *Epic 2202/promo/ps/'90* $15
Special In-Store Advance (Whisper/Toy Soldier/ Big House/Holy War/Baby Blue/I Believe/ Water From the Moon/Rain Rain+2) *Epic Associated 2065/promo/ps/'90* $12
Toy Soldier *Epic 2064/promo/ps/'90* $4

ROACHFORD
Cuddly Toy *Epic 1517/promo/silkscreened/'89* $4

ROBB, ROBBIE
In Time *A&M 17771/promo/'89* $3

ROBERTS, JULIET
Free Love 7 versions *WB 40529/stock/ gatefold hardcover ps/'92* $4

ROBERTS, KANE
Does Anybody Really Fall in Love Anymore? ac edit remix *DGC 4282/promo/'91* $3
Does Anybody Really Fall in Love Anymore? edit & lp *DGC 4219/promo/ps/ silkscreened pic/'91* $4

ROBERTS, MARCUS
Let it Snow../Silent Night/Come All Ye Faithful *RCA 3108/promo/ps/'90* $5

ROBERTSON, NICK
Show Me a Sign (edit) *Charisma 029/ promo/logo on black/'91* $3

ROBERTSON, ROBBIE
Breakin' the Rules edit & lp *Geffen 4415/promo/ gatefold hardcover ps/'92* $4
Christmas Must be Tonight *A&M 17661/promo/ps/'88* $8
Go Back to Your Woods edit & lp *Geffen 4357/promo/gatefold hardcvr ps* ... $4
Interview for college radio *Geffen 2877/promo/ps/'88* $18
Shake This Town edit & lp *Geffen 4362/ promo/gatefold hardcover ps/'92* $4
Showdown at Big Sky *Geffen 2839/promo/ps/'87* $6
Somewhere Down the Crazy River remix & edit remix *Geffen 3035/promo/ps/'87* $8
What About Now edit & lp *Geffen 4312/promo/ps/'91* $4
What About Now edit, edit-remix & lp *Geffen 4343/promo/ps/'91* $4

ROBINSON, SMOKEY
(It's the) Same Old Love (3 versions) *Motown 17806/promo/'89* $5
Double Good Everything *SBK 05414/promo/ logo on white/gatefold hardcover ps* $5
Everything You Touch 3:57/4:14/4:05 *Motown 90001/promo/'89* $6
I Love Your Face *SBK 05436/promo/ps/'92* $5
Rewind edit & smokey's club *SBK 05454/ promo/ps/logo on white/'92* $6

ROCHES, THE
Big Nuthin' *MCA 18036/promo/ custom sticker/'89* $5
Big Nuthin' (edit) *MCA 18102/promo/'89* $5
Everyone is Good *MCA 18230/promo/ silkscreened devils/rear insert/'90* $5

ROCK CITY ANGELS
6 song ep from Young Mans Blues *Geffen 3247/promo/group pic silkscreened/rear insert/'88* $5
Deep inside My Heart *Geffen 3239/promo/ps* $4

ROCKERS REVENGE
Walking on Sunshine 4 versions *Warlock 801/stock/ps/'91* $5

ROCKET FROM THE CRYPT
Pac Man Fever *Interscope 92273/promo/ ps/silkscreened/'93* $5

ROCKY HILL
I Wont Be Your Fool (3 versions) *Virgin 2183/promo/ps/'88* $4

RODGERS, PAUL
Louisiana Blues/Feel Like Making Love (live) *Victory 951/promo/ps/silkscreened* $6
The Hunter *Victory 892/promo/ps/ SLASH/silkscreened/'93* $6

RODRIGUEZ, JOSE LUIS & JULIO IGLESIAS
Torero *CBS Sony 10019/promo/ps/'92* $4

ROGER
(Everybody) Get Up 8 versions *Reprise 40259/ stock/gatefold hardcover ps/'91* $4
(Everybody) Get Up edit & lp *Reprise 5080/promo/'91* $4
Take Me Back edit & lp *Reprise 5203/promo* $4
You Should Be Mine edit & lp *Reprise 5059/promo/'91* $4

ROGERS, CE CE
Never Give Up radio/lp/time mix *Atlantic 4374/promo/rear insert/'91* $4

ROGERS, KENNY
(Something Inside) So Strong *Reprise 3653/promo/'89* $4
Crazy in Love *Reprise 4567/promo/ custom sticker/'90* $4
If You Want to Find Love *Reprise 5159/ promo/recycled foldout cover/'91* $5
Planet Texas *Reprise 3305/promo/ps/'89* $5

ROGERS, KENNY & GLADYS KNIGHT
If I Knew Then What I Know Now *Reprise 3965/promo/'89* $5

ROGERS, KENNY (JR)
Take Another Step Closer *Cypress 17876/ promo/silkscreened pic/'89* $4

ROGERS, ROY
On Track ... With Roy Rogers (interview)
RCA 61053/promo/silkscreened pic/rear insert/'91 .... $15

ROLLING STONES
Almost Hear You Sigh remix & lp
Columbia 73093/promo/ps/'89 .... $20
Flashpoint + Collectibles 27 tracks
Rolling Stone C2K 47880/stock/ ltd. leather package/'91 .... $20
Highwire edit & lp
Rolling Stone 73742/promo/ps/'91 .... $12
Mixed Emotions (3 versions)
Rolling Stone 1755/promo/ silkscreened/ps/'89 .... $16
Rock and a Hard Place 4:05/5:20
Rolling Stones 73057/promo/ps/'89 .... $15
Sexdrive single edit/dirty hands mix/ 12" (6:00) *Rolling Stone 73789/ promo/logo on red/'91* $12
Singles Collection - London Years (6 songs)
Abkco 12183/promo/silkscreened logo on black/rear insert/'89 .... $30
Steel Wheels full length *Rolling Stone 46009/ stock/ltd edition "steel case"cover* $40
The Interview (11 tracks - interview & songs)
Rolling Stone 1910/promo/ps/'89 .... $30

ROLLING STONES

SAY AHHH!

ROLLINS BAND
Low Self Opinion edit & lp
Imago 28017/promo/ps/'92 .... $4
Tearing edit & lp *Imago 28026/promo/ps/'92* $5
The End of Silence: Hammer of the Rok Godz mostly live - (Earache My Eye/Do It/ Jam With the Butthole Surfers/Ghost Rider/ I Know You/Breaking Up is Hard to Do)
Imago 28024/promo/ps/'91 .... $15
You Didn't Need *Imago 28037/promo/logo silkscreened/rear insert/'92* $5

ROLLINS, HENRY
21 excerpts from Rollins Speaks
Imago 28041/promo/ps/'92 .... $12

ROMEO AND
For You I'll Do Anything 5 versions
Elektra 8695/promo/ps/'93 .... $4

ROMEOS DAUGHTER
Heaven in the Backseat (single edit)/I Like What I See *Jive 1256/promo/ps/'88* $4
I Cry Myself to Sleep at Night
Jive 1176/promo/ps/'88 .... $4

RONSTADT, LINDA
Adios *Elektra 8203/promo/ silkscreened/rear insert/'89* $5
Dreams to Dream (finale versions) *MCA 2028/ promo/"Fievel Goes West" ps/'91* $6
Entre Abismos
Elektra 8684/promo/silkscreened/'92 .... $5
Frenesi *Elektra 8626/promo/ps/silkscreened* $5
Gritenme Piedras Del Campo/Siempre Hace Frio
Elektra 8485/promo/logo on red/'91 .... $6
Perfidia *Elektra 8552/promo/'92* $4
Perfidia edit *Elektra 8550/promo/ps/'92* $5
Retrospective (10 tracks)
Elektra 8174/promo/ps/'90 .... $15

RONSTADT, LINDA & AARON NEVILLE
All My Life *Elektra 8148/promo/'89* $6
Close Your Eyes
A&M 75021 73332/promo/ps/'91 .... $5
Don't Know Much *Elektra 8118/promo/ silkscreened logo/'89* $6
When Something is Wrong With My Baby
Elektra 8170/promo/rear insert/'89 .... $6

ROSS, DIANA
Bottom Line *Motown 18078/promo/'89* $6
Waiting in the Wings remix edit/extended/lp
Motown 3746310112/promo/'92 .... $6
When You Tell Me That You Love Me
Motown 1648/promo/ps/'91 .... $6
Workin' Overtime radio edit/extended/ 7" version *Motown 17824/promo/ silkscreened/ps/'89* $6
You're Gonna Love.. 4 vers. *Motown 374634812/ stock/gatefold hardcover ps/'91* $5

ROSS, DIANA & AL B. SURE!
No Matter What You Do 3 versions/ Al'I Justify Your Love/Justi-Muzak (instrum)/Missunderstanding
WB 21843/stock/ gatefold hardcover ps/'91 .... $5
No Matter What You Do 4:4
WB 4627/promo/'90 .... $5

ROSS, DIANA/TEDDY RILEY
This House/My Fantasy
Motown 18006/promo/'89 .... $6

ROTH, DAVID LEE
A Lil Ain't Enough
WB 4622/promo/silkscreened/ps/'91 .... $5
A Little Ain't Enough (12 tracks)
WB 26477/promo/silkscreened/ tri fold hardcover/booklet/'90 .... $20
A Little Ain't Enough world premier broadcast
WB/Album Network/ promo/rear insert/'91 .... $15
Damn Good *WB 3017/promo/ps/'88* $6
Just Like Paradise *WB 2920/ promo/ps/silkscreened/'87* $8
Knucklebones *WB 2956/promo/ps/'88* $8
Sensible Shoes (3 vers.) *WB 4738/promo/'91* $6
Skyscraper *WB 25671/promo/full length/ silkscreened/'88* $20
Skyscraper *WB 2978/promo/ps/'88* $8
Stand Up dj fade out & lp
WB 2929/promo/ps/'88 .... $8
Tell the Truth edit & lp *WB 4868/promo/'91* $5

ROXANNE
Ya Brother Does/Mama Can I Get Some
3 vers.each *Select 8502/promo/'92* $5

ROXETTE
Almost Unreal lp/ac mix *Capitol 79748/ promo/ps/logo on blue/'93* $8
Church of Your Heart *EMI 4837/promo/ logo on yellow/ps/'92* $5
Dressed for Success single ver. & look sharp
EMI 04295/promo/ps/silkscreened logo on white/rear insert $7
Fading Like a Flower lp & ac mix *EMI 04755/ promo/gatefold hardcover ps/'91* $7
How Do You Do 7" & bomkrash us edit/Fading Like a Flower live
EMI 56252/stock/ps/'92 .... $5
It Must Have Been Love single & lp *EMI 4515/ promo/silkscreened/rear insert/'90* $5
Joyride (4 versions)
EMI 04696/promo/silkscreened/ps $8
Joyride (AC mix) *EMI 04724/promo/ silkscreened/rear insert/'91* $5
Listen To Your Heart edit & lp *EMI 4399/ promo/rear insert/custom sticker/silkscreened/'89* $6
Listen To Your Heart remix/remix edit/lp
EMI 04417/promo/silkscreened logo on red/rear insert/'89 .... $8
Spending My Time lp & a/c mixes *EMI 04802/ promo/silkscreened/ps/'91* $8
The Look *EMI 04255/promo/ps/'89* $7

ROXX GANG
No Easy Way Out edit & lp
Virgin 2661/promo/silkscreened/'88 .... $4
Scratch My Back (edit)
Virgin 2862/promo/silkscreened/'88 .... $4

ROXY BLUE
Luv on Me edit & lp *Geffen 4431/promo/ps* $4
Rob the Cradle edit & lp with guitar intro
Geffen 4377/promo/ gatefold hardcover ps/'92 .... $4
Rob the Cradle/Talk of the Town *Geffen 4376/ promo/silkscreened/'92* $4
Want Some? 12 tracks *Geffen 24471/ promo only silkscreened/different cover than stock copy/'91* $10

ROYAL COURT OF CHINA
Geared & Primed
A&M 17770/promo/silkscreened/'89 .... $4
Half the Truth *A&M 17677/promo/ silkscreened/ps/'88* $5

ROYAL CRESCENT MOB
Hungry/Corporation Enema
Sire 3524/promo/custom sticker/'89 .... $4
Konk (3 versions) *Sire 4681/promo/'91* $4
Nanana *Sire 3710/promo/'89* $3
Timebomb 4 versions/Mt Everest *Sire 40066/ stock/gatefold hardcover ps/'91* $5

ROYAL, BILLY JOE
A Ring Where a Ring Used to Be *Atlantic 3431/ promo/rear insert/'90* $4
Funny How Time Slips Away *Atlantic 4641/ promo/silkscreened color pic/ rear insert/'92* $6
If the Jukebox Took Teardrops *Atlantic 3699/ promo/silkscreened logo/rear insert* $4
Till I Can't Take It Anymore
Atlantic 2912/promo/rear insert/'89 .... $4

ROYALTY
Baby Gonna Shake (4 versions)
Sire 3484/promo/'89 .... $4

ROZALLA
Are You Ready to Fly? 7" & smooth rave mix
Epic 74728/promo/logo on blue/ps $8
Are You Ready to Fly? 4 versions
Epic 74729/stock/ps/'92 .... $5
Everybody's Free (To Feel Good) 3 version
Epic 74444/stock/ps/custom sticker $8
Everybody's Free (To Feel Good) m&m edit
Epic 74388/promo/logo on blue/ rear insert/'92 .... $5

RTZ
Face the Music AOR & CHR
Giant 4859/promo/rear insert/'91 .... $3
Until Your Love Comes Back Around edit & lp
Giant 5233/promo/'91 .... $3

RUDE BOYS
Miss You So Much edit & lp *Atlantic 5009/ promo/silkscreened pic/rear insert* $5
My Kinda Girl edit & lp *Atlantic 4636/promo/ silkscreened pic/ps/'92* $5

RUFF, MICHAEL
That's Not Me/Love's Got a Hold on Me/Poor Boy/More Than Ever/Think About You/ More Than You'll Ever Know/I'd Still Be Loving You *NPE/promo/ps/'88* $5

RUFFNER, MASON
Gypsy Blood 10 tracks *CBS 40601/promo/ps/'87* $12

RUMBLEFISH
Everything Electrical *Eastwest 4557/promo/ silkscreened/ps/'92* $4
Everything Electrical/Don't Leave Me/Sing Slim/Knock on Wood/Won't You Ever Come Down? *Eastwest 96181/stock/ gatefold hardcover ps/'92* $4

RUN DMC
Down With the King radio/vocal/instrumental *Profile 7391/logo on black/ rear insert/stock/'93* $5
Ghostbusters 6:00 & dub/Pause 3 versions *Profile 7262/promo/'89* $7
Ghostbusters with & without siren *MCA 17929/promo/cust. sticker/'89* $5
Ooh, Whatcha Gonna Do *Profile 7400/promo/ silkscreened/rear insert/'93* $4
Run's House/Beats to the Rhyme *Profile 5202/promo/'88* $8
What's It All About/The Ave *Profile 7315/ promo/logo on black/'90* $5

RUNDGREN, TODD
2nd Wind 10 tracks *WB 26478/ps/ promo only silkscreened/'91* $15
Can't Stop Running edit & lp *WB 3643/promo/'89* $5
Change Myself edit & lp *WB 4551/promo/'91* $4
Fascist Christ 4 versions *Forward 7005/ promo/silkscreened/rear insert/'93* $6
I Saw the Light/We Gotta Get You a Woman/ Hello It's Me/Can We Still Be Friends *Rhino 73025/stock/3"/ps/'88* $15
No World Order 16 tracks *Forward 71266/promo/ps/'93* $15
Parallel Lines *WB 3632/promo/'89* $4
Public Servant edit & lp *WB 4553/promo/'91* $4
The Want of a Nail edit & lp/2:33 interview *WB 3538/promo/'89* $8

RUPAUL
Supermodel 4 versions/House of Love 3 vers. *Tommy Boy 542/logo on red/stock/ps/'92* . $5

RUSH
Bravado edit *Atlantic 4580/promo/ silkscreened pic/rear insert/'91* $8
Dreamline *Atlantic 4120/promo/ logo on black/ps/'91* $8
Ghost of a Chance edit & lp *Atlantic 4458/ promo/silkscreened/rear insert/'91* $8
Profiled! (27+ minutes interview) *Atlantic 3200/promo/ps/'90* $15
Show Don't Tell *Atlantic 3082/promo/ps/'89* $10
Show Don't Tell edit & lp *Atlantic 3125/ promo/rear insert/'89* $8
Superconductor *Atlantic 3331/promo/rear insert* $10
The Pass edit & lp *Atlantic 3165/promo/ silkscreened logo/ps/'89* $10
Time Stands Still long/short *Mercury 05/promo/ps* $8
Where's My Thing *Atlantic 4126/promo/ silkscreened/rear insert/'91* $8

RUSH, DONELL
If Only You Knew 6 versions *RCA 62482/promo/rear insert/'93* $4
Symphony heavies mix/symphony in e smoove/ hurleys symph. soul *D 62421/promo/ silkscreened/rear insert/'92* $5

RUSSELL, BRENDA
Get Here edit/lp *A&M 17612/promo/ps/'88* $4
Stop Running Away edit *A&M 75021 5274/ promo/silkscreened/slick glossy cover/insert/'90* $8
Stop Running Away edit & lp *A&M 75021 8097/promo/ps/'90* $4

RUSSELL, LEON
Anything Can Happen edit & lp *Virgin 4470/promo/'92* $4
Faces of the Children/Anything Can Happen/ Black Holes/Angel Ways *Virgin 4475/promo/'92* $8

Leon Russell's Country Sampler (Heartbreak Hotel/Roll in My Sweet Babys Arms/ Im So Lonesome I Could Cry + 2) *Virgin 4569/promo/silkscreened pic/ps* ...$10
No Man's Land *Virgin 4382/promo/ silkscreened/rear insert/'92* $6
Slipping Into Christmas/Christmas in Chicago *Shelter 002/promo/silkscreened logo on yellow/'89* $8
The Leon Russell Appetizer (Tightrope/ Stranger in a Strange Land/Roll Away the Stone/Beware of Darknes + 3) *Virgin 4402/promo/ps/'92* $12

RUTHERFORD, PAUL

Oh World radio edit *4th & B'way 7494/promo/ rear insert/'89* $5

RYAN, TIM

Seventh Direction *Epic 73959/promo/rear insert/'91* $4

S'EXPRESS

Music Lover (6 versions) *Capitol 79551/ promo/silkscreened/'89* $6
Nothing to Lose (6 versions)/My Laser/Find Time to Be Yourself (2 versions) *Rhythm King 21789/stock/ gatefold hardcover ps/'91* $5

S, ROBIN

Love For Love radio edit/radio edit with intro/ stone's extendedmix *Atlantic 5180/promo/ps/'93* $6
Show Me Love 4 vers. *Big Beat 5003/promo* $6
Show Me Love 5 versions *Big Beat 5091/promo/custom sticker* $6

S.O.U.L. S.Y.S.T.E.M., THE

It's Gonna Be a Lovely Day 8 versions *Arista 07822 12488/stock/ps/'92* $4

SACRED REICH

31 Flavors *Enigma 317/promo/ silkscreened/rear insert/'90* $4
A Question/Let's Have a War/Who's to Blame *Hollywood 66518/stock/ gatefold hardcover ps/'91* $5
Free *Hollywood 10340/promo/silkscreened/ rear insert/custom sticker/'93* $4
Independent *Hollywood 10258/promo/ silkscreened/rear insert/'93* $4
The American Way *Enigma 290/promo/ custom sticker/'90* $4
The American Way edit *Enigma 322/promo/cust.sticker/'90* $4

SADE

Cherish the Day 5 versions *Epic 74980/promo/ps/'93* $8
Feel No Pain 4 versions *Epic 74903/promo/ps/'93* $8
No Ordinary Love edit & lp *Epic 74734/promo/ps/'92* $6
No Ordinary Love/Paradise remix *Epic 34K 74734/stock/ps/'92* $5
Paradise 7" radio edit/12" extended remix *Epic 1143/promo/ps/'88* $10
Smooth Operator/Hang on To Your Love *Epic 15K 68665/stock/3"/ 3x9 diecut sleeve/'89* $10
Turn My Back on You (edit remix/lp remix/ extended remix) *Epic 1381/promo/ rear insert/silkscreened logo/'88* $10

SAFFRON

One Love 5 versions/Solitaire 2 versions *Reprise 40567/stock/ps/'92* $4
Boy, I've Been Told video & audio/Gonna Make It/Together/Boy I've Been Told 7" (last 3 audio only) *Cutting 870 743/ stock/video & audio/ps/'88* $12
Gonna Make It (4 versions) *Mercury 82/ promo/silkscreened/ps/'88* $5
I Will Survive pop edit, rap version, lp .... *Mercury 162/promo/silkscreened/'89* $5
Made Up My Mind (4 versions) *Mercury 377/ promo/silkscreened/gatefold hardcover/foldout poster/'91* $8

SAHM, DOUG

You're Gonna Miss Me *Sire 4735/promo/'90* $6

SAIGON KICK

All I Want *Third Stone 4844/promo/ silkscreened pic/ps/'92* $5
All I Want radio remix *Third Stone 4644/ promo/silkscreened pic/ps/'92* $5
Feel the Same Way *Third Stone 5033/promo* $4
Freedom/Love Is on the Way *Third Stone 4834/ promo/silkscreened/rear insert/'92* $4
Hostile Youth *Third Stone 4591/promo/ silkscreened/ps/'92* $4
Love is On the Way edit & lp *Third Stone 4645/ promo/silkscreened/ps/'92* $4
New World edit & lp *Third Stone 3766/ promo/logo on black/ps/'91* $4
What You Say *Third Stone 3767/promo/ ps/logo on black/'91* $4

SAINT ETIENNE

Nothing Can Stop Us 5 versions/Speedwell *WB 40395/stock/gatefold hardcover ps/'92* $4
Nothing Can Stop Us 6 versions *WB 5337/promo/'91* $5
Only Love Can Break Your Heart 4 versions *WB 5161/promo/'91* $5

Who Do You Think You Are 6 versions/ Hobart Paving uk single versions/ Your Head My Voice *WB 40910/ stock/gatefold hardcover ps/'93* $4
Who Do You Think You Are lp/radio *WB 6265/promo/'93* $4
You're in a Bad Way lp & alt./St Etienne speaks.. *WB 5948/promo/logo on green/'93* $8

SAINTE-MARIE, BUFFY
The Big Ones Get Away/Fallen Angels/Bad End/I'm Going Home *Ensign 23816/promo/ps/'92* $5

SAINTS & SINNERS
Walk That Walk edit & lp *Savage 50020/promo/ rear insert/silkscreened/ prod.by ALDO NOVA/'92* $4

SAKAMOTO, RYUICHI & JILL JONES
You Do Me (2 versions) *Virgin DO ME/promo/silkscreened/'89* $5
You Do Me (4 versions) *Virgin 3227/promo/silkscreened/'89* $7

SALT N PEPA
Do You Want Me (3versions)/I Gotcha *Next Plateau 50137/promo/'90* $6
Let's Talk About Sex radio/club *Next Plateau 50157/promo/ silkscreened logo/'91* $5
Shake Your Thang 4 versions/Spinderellas Not a Fella 3 vers. *Next Plateau 50077/ promo/silkscreened pic/'88* $8
Shoop 5 versions *Next Plateau 1825/promo/ silkscreened/ps/'93* $5
Start Me Up 4 versions *Next Plateau 50189/ promo/custom sticker/'92* $5
Start Me Up edit *Next Plateau 758/ promo/logo on purple/'92* $4

SALTY DOG
Come Along without ass edit/with ass edit/ the hole ass *Geffen 3957/promo/'90* $4
Lonesome Fool *Geffen 4112/promo/ps/'90* $4

SALUZZI, DINO
Mojotoro/Tango a Mi Padre/Lustrin *ECM DINO 2/promo/ps/'92* $5

SAMBORA, RICHIE
One Light Burning vocal mix edit/lp edit/lp *Mercury 592/promo/ps/'92* $7
Stranger in This Town lp & edit *Mercury 595/ promo/logo on brown/'91* $7

SAMPLE, JOE
Ashes to Ashes words & music *WB 4712/promo/ps/'91* $12
Born to Be Bad/Ashes to Ashes/I'll Love You *WB 4530/promo/'90* $4

Leading Me Back to You edit & lp *WB 3783/promo/'89* $4
Seven Years of Good Luck edit &lp *WB 3537/promo/'89* $4
Somehow Our Love Survives *WB 3754/ promo/'89/with AL JARREAU* $5
Spellbound *WB 3466/promo/'89* $4
Spellbound *WB 3949/promo/'89* $4

SAMPLES, THE
Waited Up *Arista 2161/promo/ps/'91* $3

SANBORN, DAVID
Bang Bang *Elektra 8599/promo/ silkscreened/'92* $4
Benny edit *Elektra 8683/promo/'92* $4
Hobbies *Musician 8389/promo/silkscreened/ps* $4
Lesley Ann edit & lp *Reprise 3521/promo/'89* $4
Slam (2 versions) *Reprise 3122/promo/ps/'88* $5
Snakes edit *Elektra 8563/promo/ps/ silkscreened/'92* $4
So Far Away edit & lp *Reprise 3274/promo/ps/'88* $5
Soul Serenade *Elektra 8686/promo/'92* $4
The Dream remix/edit *WB 2880/promo/ps* $4

SANCTUARY
Into the Mirror live (Future Tense/Long Since Dark/Battle Angels + 3) *Epic 2188/promo/ps/'90* $12

SAND RUBIES
Goodbye/Santa Maria Street/Interstate/ Paper Thin Line *Atlas 832/promo/ silkscreened/ps/'92* $5
Guns in the Churchyard/Drugged/Primeval Love *Polygram 931/promo/silkscreened* $4
Santa Maria Street/Black Eyes... *Polygram 897/ promo/silkscreened/'93* $4

SANDEE
Love Desire 5 versions *Columbia 73755/promo/ps/'91* $4

SANDLER, ADAM
They're All Gonna Laugh At You 17 tracks *WB 6593/promo/rear insert/ custom sticker/'93* $8

SANDMEN, THE
House in the Country *A&M 17747/promo/'88* $4
Western Blood (The G Arden mix) *A&M 17827/promo/'89* $4

SANDOVAL, ARTURO
Dream Come True ep (Giant Steps/Little Sunflower/Dahomey Dance/Blue) *GRP 5115/promo/ps/silkscreen pic/'93* $6
Mambo Caliente *Elektra 8489/promo/ "Mambo Kings" ps/silkscreened/'92* $5

SANDRA
Everlasting Love (3 versions)
Virgin 2334/promo/'88 .... $5

SANDY B
Feel Like Singin' 3 versions
Mercury 848/promo/silkscreened/'93 .... $4

SANTANA
Bella *Columbia 1011/promo/ps/'88* $6
Gypsy Woman *Columbia 73477/promo/ps/'90* $4
Mother Earth tour CD (15 tracks)
Columbia 2099/promo/ps/'90 .... $15
Right On (edit)/Saja-Right On
Polydor 668/promo/ps/silkscreened $5
We Don't Have to Wait *Polydor 724/ promo/logo on black/'92* $4

SARAYA
Love Has Taken Its Toll edit/lp *Polydor 45/ promo/silkscreened/ps/'89* $4
Seducer (3 versions) *Polydor 430/promo/ gatefold hardcover ps/logo on black* $4
Timeless Love single edit & lp
SBK 05321/promo/ps/'89 .... $4

SATRIANI, JOE
Big Bad Moon radio & lp mixes *Relativity 0103/ promo/silkscreened/ gatefold hardcover ps/'89* $7
Friends *Relativity 0164/promo/ logo on green/ps/'92* $6
I Believe radio edit & lp *Relativity 0107/ promo/silkscreened/ps/'89* $6
I Believe single & video/Flying in a Blue Dream
Relativity 88561 1038/stock/ps/'90 .... $5
I Believe (single edit) *Relativity 0105/ promo/silkscreened/ps/'89* $6
Speed of Light *Capitol 79759/promo/ logo on green/ps/'93* $4
Summer Song *Relativity 0159/promo/ gatefold hardcover ps/'92* $5
Surfing With the Alien *Relativity 88561-8193/ promo/silkscreen pic/rear insert/'87* $8

SAUNDERS, FERNANDO
Come a Little Closer remix/edit/lp
A&M 31458 8139/promo/silkscreened pic/gatefold hardcover ps/'93 .... $4

SAUNDERS, MERL
Someplace to Boogie ep (Sugaree/(Finders) Keepers/Harder They Come/You Can Leave Your Hat On/Wondering Why)
Sumertone/promo/silkscreened/ps $10
Blues From the Rainforest - a Musical Suite 6 tracks *Sumertone/silkscreened pic (with Jerry Garcia)/stock/ps/'90* $10

SAVATAGE
Edge of Thorns lp & edit/Forever After
Atlantic 5022/promo $5
Gutter Ballet edit & lp *Atlantic 3220/promo/ silkscreened logo/rear insert/'89* $4
Jesus Saves edit
Atlantic 4453/promo/rear insert $4
Sammy and Tex
Atlantic 4219/promo/rear insert/'91 .... $4

SAVOY BROWN
Deep In My Heart *Crescendo PRO 8/3"/promo* .. $5

SAWYER BROWN
All These Years *Curb 1031/promo/ silkscreened/rear insert/'92* $4
It Wasn't His Child *Capitol 79422/ promo/silkscreened/ps/'88* $4
Thank God For You *Curb 1053/promo/ logo on red/rear insert/'93* $4

SAXON
Requiem 4:41 & 5:16 *Charisma 038/promo/ silkscreened logo/'90* $4

SCARLETT & BLACK
Let Yourself Gogo (2 vers.) *Virgin 2329/promo/ps* $4
You Dont Know 7"/12" *Virgin 9405/promo/ps/'87* $4

SCATTERBRAIN
Big Fun *Elektra 8459/promo/silkscreened/ps* $4
Don't Call Me Dude *In Effect 0614/promo/ps/ silkscreened logo on yellow/'90* $4

SCHENKER, MICHAEL
Follow the Night (2 versions) *EMI 79281/ promo/ps/lazer etched logo/'88* $5

SCHILLING, PETER
The Different Story single & instrumental
Elektra 69307/stock/3"/ps/'89 .... $6
The Different Story (World of Lust etc) (long /lp/instrumental) *Elektra 8067/ promo/silkscreened "S"/'89* $7

SCHMIT, TIMOTHY
Something Sad edit & lp
MCA 1117/promo/logo on green/'90 .... $4
Was It Just the Moonlight (3 versions)
MCA 18332/promo/rear insert/'90 .... $5

SCHMITT, ADAM
Can't Get You on My Mind *Reprise 4872/promo/ silkscreened color pic/'91* $5
Illiterature Sampler (Waiting to Shine/Catching Up/Three Faces West/Rip It Off/Me and You) *Reprise 6181/promo/ps/'93* $5

SCHNEIDER, FRED
Monster edit & lp *Reprise 4875/promo/'91* $6

SCHNELL-FENSTER
Love-Hate Relationship lp & extended
Atlantic 3232/promo/rear insert/'90 .... $6
Love-Hate Relationship lp & extended
Atlantic 3232/promo/rear insert/'90 .... $6
Whisper (langer & winstanl. mix) *Atlantic 3525/ promo/logo on black/rear insert/'90* $6

SCHNITT ACHT
Rage/Random Funk
Cheetah 9110/promo/silkscreened/ps $4

SCHON, NEAL
I'll Cover You edit/lp
Columbia 000117/promo/'89 .... $6

SCHOOL OF FISH
3 Strange Days 3 versions/Where Have I Been/Let's Pretend Were Married dub
Capitol 15675/stock/ps/'91 .... $6
Everyword *Capitol 79709/promo/ silkscreened/custom sticker/'93* $4
Jump Off the World *Capitol 79840/ promo/ps/silkscreened/'93* $4
King of the Dollar *Capitol 79699/promo/ silkscreened/rear insert/'91* $4
Live in LA 8/22/91 (Father Figure/That's All Right/Takin' Care of Business/King of the Dollar/Talk Like Strangers/ Deep End) *Capitol 79995/promo/ silkscreened/custom sticker/'91* $15
Strange Days edit & lp *Capitol 79612/promo/ silkscreened/custom sticker/'91* $4
Take Me Anywhere edit & lp *Capitol 79621/ promo/silkscreened/ps/'93* $4
The Greatest Living Englishman/The Turtle Song/Disconnected/This Is Where I Belong/Wrong *Capitol 79776/ promo/silkscreened/rear insert/'91* $8
Wrong edit & lp *Capitol 79713/promo/ silkscreen/rear insert/custom sticker/'91* ... $4

SCHOOLLY D
Where'd You Get That Funk From 6 versions
Capitol 79787/promo/ps/silkscreened $4

SCHUUR, DIANE
Touch/Nobody Does Me (both edits)
GRP 9943/promo/ps/'90 .... $4

SCORN
Lick Forever Dog (edit)/On Ice (disembodied dub)/Heavy Blood (2 versions)
Relativity 88561-1154/stock/ps/'92 .... $4

SCORPIONS
Don't Believe Her *Mercury 379/promo/ silkscreened pic/rear insert/'91* $8
Hit Between the Eyes
Morgan Creek 0016/promo/'90 .... $4
Holiday/The Zoo (both remixed)
Mercury 208/promo/silkscreened/'90 .... $6
I Can't Explain
Mercury 145/promo/silkscreened/'89 .... $5
I Can't Explain/Blackout/Hey You
Mercury 876 191/promo/ps/ silkscreened/'89 .... $6
Send Me an Angel *Mercury 536/promo/ silkscreened/'90* $5
Tease Me, Please Me *Mercury 332/promo/ silkscreened/box-like ps/'90* $6
Wind of Change *Mercury 423/promo/ silkscreened/ps/'91* $4

SCOTT, CASEY
5 Tracks from Creep City ep (Sharp Metal Objects/7th of November/Watch/ Creep City/Ryan) *Capitol 79697/ promo/ps/logo on white/'93* $6
7th of November edit & lp *Capitol 79719/ promo/silkscreened/ps/'93* $4

SCOTT, MIKE
Interview & music (55:35) *Chrysalis 23719/ promo/silkscreened/rear insert/'91* $15

SCOTT, TOM
If You're Not the One For Me *GRP 9957/ promo/ps/BILL CHAMPLIN, BRENDA RUSSELL/'91* $5

SCOTTI, NICK
Get Over 3 versions/Alone With You 4 vers.
Reprise 40711/stock/ gatefold hardcover ps/'93 .... $4

SCREAM, THE
Father, Mother, Son lp/acoustic
Hollywood 8515/promo/ logo on black/rear insert/'92 .... $4
I Believe in Me *Hollywood 8444/promo/ silkscreened/rear insert/'91* $4

SCREAMING JETS
Better *Mercury 567/promo/silkscreened/ gatefold hardcover ps/'91* $4
Better *rooArt 567/promo/gatefold hardcover ps/silkscreened/'91* $4
Blue Sashes/Sister Tease/F.R.C.
Mercury 868 249/stock/ps/'91 .... $4
C'mon *Mercury 451/promo/gatefold hardcover ps/silkscreened/'91* $4
Stealth Live ep (Needle/Starting Out/Rocket Man/FRC/High Voltage) *rooArt 539/ promo/silkscreened/ps/'91* $12

SCREAMING TREES
Bed of Roses *Epic 2296/promo/ silkscreened/rear insert/'91* $6
Butterfly/Morning Dew *Epic 5286/promo/ ps/logo on black/'93* $6

Dollar Bill/Tomorrow's Dream/(There'll Be) Peace in the Valley *Epic 4771/promo/ gatefold hardcover ps/'92* $6
Nearly Lost You edit & lp *Epic 4942/promo/ logo on black/ps/'93* $5
Nearly Lost You/E.S.K./Song of a Baker *Epic 4604/promo/ps/'92* $6
Something About Today ep (Uncle Anaestesia/ Who Lies in ../Ocean of Confusion + 1) *Epic 49K 73539/stock/ps/'90* $6
Something About Today/This Perfect Day/ New Day Yesterday *Epic 3092/promo/ silkscreened/rear insert/cust.sticker* $8

SCREAMING TRIBESMEN

I've Got a Feeling/Igloo/You Better Run *Ryko/promo/3"/5" ps/'90* $5

SCREWTRACTOR

Eye (Throb/Cowboy Spit/Afterlife/Stupid Humans/Crusader/Twitch) *Gravel 10715/stock/ps/silkscreened* $5

SCRITTI POLITTI

Boom There She Was (3 versions) *WB 2981/promo/ps/'88* $7
Oh Patti edit/lp/ext. *WB 3311/promo/'88* $4

SEAL

Crazy *Sire 4832/promo/'90* $4
Crazy radio/instrumental/dub *Sire 4879/promo/'90* $6
Crazy 8 versions *Sire 41003/stock/ gatefold hardcover ps/'90* $4
Killer 4 versions *ZTT 5085/promo/ custom sticker/'91* $8
The Beginning 4 vers. *Sire 5043/promo/'91* $6
The Beginning 6 versions/Deep Water *ZTT 40200/stock/ gatefold hardcover ps/'91* $4

SEALS, DAN

Sweet Little Shoe *WB 4984/promo/ recycled foldout cover/'91* $4

SEASE, MARVIN

Show Me What You Got edit & lp/Don't Cum.. *Mercury 620/promo/logo on black/'91* $4
Tonight 3 versions *Mercury 557/promo/ gatefold hardcover ps/logo on black* $4

SEASON TO RISK

Mine Eyes/Don't Cry *Red Decibel 74888/promo/ps/'93* $4

SEAWEED

Bill/Squint *Sub Pop PRO 4/promo/rear insert* $5

SECADA, JON

Just Another Day 4 versions *SBK 05483/promo/'92* $5

SECOND SELF

Lose Those Shadows 4:00 & 4:05 *EMI 4616/ promo/silkscreened/rear insert/'90* $4
Mood Ring (11 songs) *EMI 4518/promo/ps* $12

2ND II NONE

Let the Rhythm Take You radio versions *Profile 7373/promo/logo on green/ rear insert/'92* $4

SEDAKA, NEIL

My Friend full length *Polydor 831 235/stock/ps/'86* $15

SEDUCTION

Breakdown (5 vers.) *A&M 75021 8039/promo/ps* .. $6
Could This Be Love (3 versions) *A&M 75021 8082/promo/ silkscreened logo on white/ps/'89* $6
Heartbeat clivilles-cole radio/clivilles cole lp *A&M 17937/promo/silkscreened/'89* $7
Heartbeat 3:29/4:56/7:26 *A&M 18020/promo/silkscreened/'90* $6

SEE NO EVIL

Scream Bloody Murder *Epic 2176/promo/silkscreened/'90* $4
Witchdoctor/Scream Bloody Murder/ Never on Your Knees/Crosses *Epic 2175/promo/silkscreened/'90* $5

SEERS, THE

Psych Out (4 versions) *Relativity 0118/promo/ silkscreened/rear insert/'91* $5

SEGER, BOB

Interview 25 tracks of various lengths *Capitol 79227/promo/ logo on black/back "cue" ps/'92* $15

Silver Seger Sampler (Ramblin' Gamblin' Man/ If I Were a Carpenter/Get Out of Denver/Lucifer/Nutbush City Limits/Beautiful Loser) *Capitol 79622/promo/'93* $15
The Fire Inside edit & lp *Capitol 79025/ promo/logo on black/ps/'91* $5
The Real Love edit & lp *Capitol 79836/promo/ silkscreened/ps/'91* $5

SEIKO
Who's That Boy *Columbia 73523/promo/ps* $4

SENSELESS THINGS
Everybody's Gone/Mystery Train/I'm on Black and White *Epic 4415/promo/ps/ logo on blue/'92* $6
Got It At the Delmar/Beat to Blondie/ Fishing at Tescos/Can't Remember *Epic 4590/promo/silkscreened/ rear insert/'92* $6

SERMON, ERICK
Hittin' Switches radio & lp *Uptown 2681/promo/rear insert/'93* $4

SETZER, BRIAN
Rebelene *EMI 04116/promo/ps/'88* $7
When the Sky Comes Tumbling Down *Manhattan 04009/promo/ps/'88* $7

SEVELLE, TAJA
Love is Contagious edit/lp *Paisley Park 2812/ promo/custom sticker* $5
Trouble Having You Near 4 versions/ Fountains Egg *Reprise 40172/stock/ gatefold hardcover ps/'91* $5
Trouble Having You Near radio mix & edit *Reprise 4921/promo/'91* $4

7 SECONDS
I Can Sympathize *Restless 223/promo/ silkscreened/custom sticker/'89* $5

700 MILES
Messages *RCA 62549/promo/ps/'93* $4

SEVERINSEN, DOC
I Can't Get Started *Amherst 12/promo/ silkscreened pic/rear insert/'92* $6

SEXTANTS, THE
I Don't Lie ep (Morrissey/Read All about It/ Gunslinger/Hungry Wolf/Every Day/Radio Boy/I Heard a Train) *Imago 28036/ promo/gatefold hardcover ps/'92* $6
Sand Dollar Girl *Imago 28021/promo/ps/'92* $4

SEXTON, CHARLIE
Don't Look Back edit & lp *MCA 17718/promo/ps/'89* $5

Tennessee Plates *MCA 1436/promo/rear insert/'91* $5

SGH MOCCA SOUL
Losing You 5 versions *Savage 2143/promo/ logo on orange/ps/'92* $5

SHA'DASIOUS
I'ma Put My Thing Down 5 versions *RCA 62472/promo/rear insert/'93* $4

SHABBA RANKS
Housecall 6 versions *Epic 49K 73929/stock/ps/'91* $4
Mr. Loverman 5 versions *Epic 74257/promo/ logo on black&red/ps/'92* $6

SHABBA RANKS & KRS 1
The Jam 6 versions *Epic 74069/promo/ps/'91* $6

SHADES OF LACE
Smoovin' With ep (Whisper of the Heart/ Love A Little Bit More/Will You Be There/So Deep, So ../I Wanna Be ..) *Wing 184/promo/silkscreened/ps/'90* $6

SHADOW KING
I Want You *Atlantic 4214/promo/LOU GRAMM/ ps/custom sticker/'91* $4

SHADOWLAND
Garden of Eden (10 tracks) *Geffen 24826/ promo/gatefold die cut "wheel" cover/ silkscreened/'91* $12
Garden of Eden/Heroin Eyes/My Escape/ Down By the Seaside *Geffen 4120/ promo/silkscreened pic/'90* $5
The Beauty of Escaping (10 songs) *Geffen 24286/promo/custom pinwheel die cut hardcover ps/silkscreened* $12

SHAFFER, PAUL
Late Night *Capitol 79830/promo/ silkscreened logo on blue/'89* $4
The World's Most Dangerous Sampler 4 tracks *EMI 04562/promo/custom sticker* $10
When the Radio is On (5 versions) *Capitol 79662/promo/'89* $6

SHAI
Baby I'm Yours 5 versions *Gasoline Alley 2532/promo/ps/'93* $6
Comforter radio remix & smoove vocal mix *Gasoline Alley 2571/promo/ rear insert/'93* $6
If I Ever Fall in Love 4 versions *Gasoline Alley 54546/promo/ps/'92* $6
If I Ever Fall in Love 4 versions *Gasoline Alley 54546/stock/ps/'92* $4
If I Ever Fall in Love 6 vers. *Gasoline Alley 2437/promo/rear insert* $7

SHAKA
Steppin' (On the Wild Side) 3 versions
Arista 2354/promo/silkscreened/ps $4

SHAKATAK
Mr Manic & Sister Cool
Mercury 138/promo/silkscreened/'88 .... $5
Perfect sampler (Please Don't Go/China Bay/ Perfect Smile/One Love)
Verve Forecast SHAK 2/ promo/logo on blue/'90 .... $10

SHAKESPEARS SISTER
Break My Heart radio/lp/copa mix *FFRR 214/ promo/silkscreened/'89* $7
Goodbye Cruel World/E-Hello Cruel World
London 533/promo/cust.sticker/'92 .... $7
Hello (Turn Your Radio On) 7" *London 845/ promo/ps/logo on white/'92* $6
I Don't Care edit/Stay acoustic
London 869 946/stock/ps/'92 .... $5
I Don't Care lp & live/Catwoman lp & live
London 795/promo/logo on white/'92 ...... $10
Stay *London 658/promo/logo on dark blue/ps* ... $6
Stay acoustic & lp *London 733/promo/ logo on blue/'92* $7
Stay/Remember My Name + brief edits of Cat Woman/Goodbye Cruel World/I Don't Care *London 869 731/stock/ps/'92* $5
You're History edit & lp
FFRR 110/promo/silkscreened/'89 .... $5
You're History/Run Silent/Sacred Heart/ Primitive Love *FFRR SS1/promo/ps* $12

SHAKING FAMILY
Hold On *Elektra 8187/promo/rear insert/'90* $3
Tic Toc *Elektra 8140/promo/'89* $3

SHALAMAR
Caution: This Love Is Hot (4 versions)
Epic 74518/promo/ps/'90 .... $5
Come Together 4 versions
Solar 74531/promo/rear insert/'91 .... $5

SHAMEN, THE
En Tact 15 tracks *Epic 4283/promo/ gatefold fuzzy cover edition/'91* $20
Love Sex Intelligence 7 versions
Epic 49K 74401/stock/ps/'92 .... $5
LSI 7" radio/7" edit/lp *Epic 74437/promo/ logo on black/ps/custom sticker/'92* $6
Make It Mine 3:30 & 3:13/Purple Haze/ Slip Inside *Epic 74176/promo/logo on purple/rear insert/'92* $6
Make It Mine 9 versions *Epic 74236/ stock/ps/logo on purple/'92* $5
Make It Mine oh moby 7" edit/lp/alt.radio edit
Epic 4548/promo/ silkscreened/rear insert/'92 .... $6

Move Any Mountain 6 versions *Epic 74044/ promo/silkscreened/ps/'91* $6

SHANICE
I Love Your Smile 3 versions
Motown 1000/promo/'91 .... $5
I Love Your Smile hak's radio edit/lp/hak's remix/hak's instrumental
Motown 1009/promo/'91 .... $6
I'm Cryin' edit/lp/instrumental
Motown 3746310262/promo/ps/'92 .... $6
Lovin' You lp & instrumental
Motown 374631056/promo/ps/'92 .... $6
Saving Forever For You edit/lp/instrumental
Giant 5745/promo/ps/'92 .... $6

SHANICE/BIG HAT RAY RAY
It's For You 9 versions/Ain't Nobody Bad Like Meteor Man edit & lp
Motown 374631113/promo/'93 .... $6

SHANNON, DEL
Walk Away *MCA 1453/promo/'91* $5

SHANTE
Dance to This 8 versions
Livin' Large 108/promo/'92 .... $5

SHANTE, ROXANNE
Independent Woman *Reprise 3928/promo/'89* $4
Live on Stage (6 versions)
Reprise 3663/promo/'89 .... $5

SHARK ISLAND
Paris Calling lp & live *Epic 1813/promo/ps/'89* $4
Paris Calling/Ready or Not/Shake For Me/ Get Some Strange + 2 (all live)
Epic 1767/promo/silkscreened/ps $12

SHARKEY, FEARGAL
If This is Love (2 vers.)
Virgin 9339/promo/ps/'88 .... $5

SHARP
Playboy (4:18/7:27/5:28/7:07)
Elektra 8047/promo/'89 .... $4

SHEAR, JULES
The Great Puzzle 12 tracks
Polydor 450/promo/ps/'91 .... $12
The Sad Sound of the Wind edit & lp
Polydor 613/promo/ps/'92 .... $5
The Trap Door/His Audience Has Gone to Sleep/ She Makes Things Happen/Nothing is Left Behind *Polydor 678/promo/ silkscreened/ps/'92* $8
Unplug This (Following Every Finger/All Through the Night/Whispering Your Name/If She Knew What She .. + 4)
Polydor 443/promo/logo on black/ gatefold hardcover ps/'91 .... $8

We Were Only Making Love edit
Polydor 677/promo/silkscreened/ps $5

SHEEP ON DRUGS
Motorbike/Mary Jane/Radio *Smash 162-880 007/ stock/ps/silkscreened/'93* $4

SHELLEYAN ORPHAN
Waking Up sampler (Burst/Dead Cat/ Supernature on a Superhighway/Late Night/Shatter/Summer Flies + 2) *Columbia 4657/promo/ gatefold hardcover ps/'92* $8

SHELTER, LORI CARSON
Selftitled (12 songs) *DGC 24256/ promo/booklet cover/'90* $12

SHENANDOAH
Long Time Comin' 10 tracks
RCA 66011/promo/fold out ps/'92 .... $12
When You Were Mine *Columbia 73957/promo/ silkscreened/rear insert/'91* $4

SHEPARD, VONDA
Baby, Don't You Break My Heart Slow edit & lp
Reprise 4017/promo/'89 .... $4
Don't Cry Ilene edit & lp *Reprise 3731/promo* $4
I Shy Away (6 versions)
Reprise 4396/promo/rear insert/'89 .... $4

SHEPPARD, T.G.
Born in a High 2 versions
Curb Capitol 79566/promo/'91 .... $4

SHINAS, SOFIA
One Last Kiss radio remix & lp edit
WB 5920/promo/silkscreened/'92 .... $4
The Message 5 versions *WB 40534/stock/ gatefold hardcover ps/'92* $5
The Message radio remix *WB 5805/promo/'92* $4

SHINEHEAD
Family Affair (4 vers.) *Elektra 8188/promo/ silkscreened red/rear insert/'90* $5
Gimme No Crack 3:34/4:54/4:05/4:48/4:23
Elektra 8061/promo/'89 .... $5
Jamaican in New York radio without rap & urban radio *Elektra 8716/promo/ custom sticker/'93* $5
Jamaican in New York without rap/single
Elektra 8774/promo/'92 .... $4
Reggae Christmas Medley
Elektra 8130/promo/silkscreened/'89 .... $6
The Real Rock (4 versions)
Elektra 8238/promo/rear insert/'90 .... $6
Try My Love *Elektra 8613/promo/ps/'92* $4

SHOCKED, MICHELLE
Come a Long Way (edit)/Worth the Weight/ Over the Waterfall/Shaking Hands (last 3 live) *Mercury 680/promo/ silkscreened/ps/'92* $10
Jump Jim .../Contest Coming/Shaking Hands/ 33 RPM Soul *Mercury 642/promo/ silkscreened pic/gatefold hardcvr ps* $8
Looks Like Mona Lisa *Mercury 223/promo/ silkscreened logo on white/'89* $5
My Little Sister *Mercury 217/promo/ silkscreened pic/'90* $5
On the Greener Side *Mercury 142/promo/ silkscreened/hardcover ps (with fake grass coating)/'89* $15

SHOMARI
If You Feel the Need 4 versions *Mercury 672/ promo/logo on cream/ps/'92* $5
Let It Be Me *Mercury 781/promo/ps/ logo on red & black/'92* $4

SHOOTING GALLERY
House of Ecstasy *Mercury 648/promo/logo on black/gatefold hardcover ps/'92* $4
Selftitled 12 tracks *Mercury 479/promo/ silkscreened/ps/'92* $12
Teenage Breakdown lp/edit *Mercury 713/ promo/silkscreened/gatefold ps/'92* $4

SHOOTING STAR
Believe in Me *JRS 803/promo/ps/'91* $4
Christmas Together *Enigma 245/promo/ silkscreened/custom sticker/'89* $4
Hollywood *Enigma 262/promo/ custom sticker/silkscreened/'89* $4
It's Not Over (10 tracks)
V&R/promo/silkscreened/'91 .... $12
Rebel With a Cause *V&R 0777/promo/ silkscreened pic/'91* $6

Touch Me Tonight *Enigma 227/promo/ silkscreened/custom sticker/'89* $4

SHORE, PAULY
Future of America sampler (9 tracks) *WTG 3093/promo/ logo on green/rear insert/'91* $10

SHOTGUN MESSIAH
Heartbreak Blvd *Relativity 0148/ promo/silkscreened/rear insert/'91* $6
I Want More/Search and Destroy/53rd and 3rd/Babylon/Nobody's Home *Relativity 88561 1151/stock/ps/'92* $5
Shout It Out *Relativity 88561-1021/promo/ ps/silkscreened/'89* $4

SHOWBIZ & A.G.
Fat Pockets radio & street versions *London 792/promo/silkscreened/ps* $4

SHRIEKBACK
Get Down Tonight *Island 2407/promo/ps/'88* $6
Psycho Drift/Cayenne Sisemen live *World Domination 79609/promo/ silkscreened/custom sticker/'93* $6
The Bastard Sons of Enoch 3 vers/Below/ 3 AM *World Domination 15899/stock/ ps/custom sticker/'92* $4

SHUMAN, MORT
Promised Land (radio edit) *Atlantic 4093/promo/ps/'91* $4

SHY ENGLAND
Give It All You Got edit & lp *MCA 18115/ promo/silkscreened/cust.sticker/'90* $4

SIBERRY, JANE
Bound by the Beauty edit & lp *Reprise 3752/promo/'89* $4
Ingrid (and the Footman) *Reprise 2954/promo/ps/'88* $5
The Life is the Red Wagon special remix/ remix fade/lp *Reprise 3944/ promo/silkscreened pic/'89* $6

SIBERRY, JANE & KD LANG
Calling All Angels edit & lp *Reprise 5398/promo/'91* $5

SIDEWINDERS
Bad Crazy Sun edit & lp *RCA 9035/promo/ps/'89* $4
Doesn't Anyone Believe/I'm Not With You/ Signed DC/If I Can't Have You + 3 (last 6 acoustic) *RCA 2700/promo/ps/'90* $10
We Don't Do That Anymore *RCA 2638/promo/ps/'90* $4
What am I Supposed to Do? *RCA 8968/promo/ps/'89* $4
Witchdoctor (remix) *RCA 8883/promo/ps/'89* $4

SIDRAN, BEN
Shine a Light on Me (edit)/On the Cool Side (fade)+2 *Windham Hill 17666/promo* $6

SIEGEL, DAN
Hometown/Hold On To Your Heart *CBS Associated 1612/ promo/logo on blue/ps/'89* $4
On the Road/Rhapsody *CBS Associated 1111/promo/'88* $4

SIFFRE, LABI
I Will Always Love You extended & other/ Tragical History Tour/Listen to the Voices (piano versions) *Polydor 143/ promo/silkscreened/'89* $6
Nothin's Gonna Change lp & extended *Polydor 100/promo/silkscreened/'89* $5
So Strong edit & lp *Polydor 59/promo/ps* $4

SIGHS, THE
Think About Soul *Charisma 098/promo/ gatefold hardcover ps/silkscreened* $4

SIGUE SIGUE SPUTNIK
Success 4 versions *EMI 04249/promo/ silkscreened/rear insert/'88* $10

SILENCERS, THE
I See Red 3:28 & 4:22 *RCA 6739/promo/ps/'87* $4
Razor Blades of Love edit & lp *RCA 9160/promo/ps/'89* $4
Sampler (Bulletproof Heart/Hey Mr Bank Manager + 2) *RCA 2852/promo/ps* $6

SILENT RAGE
Rebel With a Cause *RCA 8979/promo/rear insert/'89* $3

SILK
Freak Me lp/remix/jeep beat mix *Elektra 8732/ promo/logo on white/'92* $6
Girl U For Me *Elektra 8757/promo/ silkscreened/rear insert/'93* $4
Happy Days edit/lp/12" *Elektra 8637/promo/ps/'92* $6
Happy Days pop mix *Elektra 8698/promo/silkscreened/'92* $4

SILK TYMES LEATHER
New Jack Thang radio remix & alt.radio remix *Geffen 4177/promo/silkscreened/ps* $4

SILKY SLIM
Sistersister radio *Profile 7377/promo/ silkscreened/rear insert/'92* $4

SILOS, THE

(We'll Go) Out of Town remix *RCA 2670/ promo/silkscreened/rear insert/ custom sticker/'90* $4
I'm Over You *RCA 2565/promo/ps/ custom sticker/'90* $4

SILVEIRA, RICARDO

Small World 13 tracks *Verve Forecast RIC 2/promo/ps/'92* $12

SILVERFISH

Crazy 2 versions/Scrub Me Mama/Petal/ F.S.W.T.G.A. *Chaos 42K 74923/ stock/ps/'93* $4

SIMON & GARFUNKEL

Bookends/In the Studio *dj radio show/promo/ hosted by SIMON & GARFUNKEL* $25

SIMON, CARLY

All I Want Is You *Arista 9653/promo/ps/'87* $7
Better Not Tell Her *Arista 2083/promo/ silkscreened pic/ps/'90* $7
Coming Around Again *Arista 9525/promo/ps* $8
Let the River Run *Arista 9793/promo/ps/'88* $7
Life is Eternal edit & lp *Arista 2165/promo/ silkscreened/ps/'91* $6
Love of My Life radio versions *Qwest 5356/promo/'92* $5
My Romance *Arista 9947/promo/ps/'90* $6
The Night Before Christmas *Qwest 5804/promo/'92* $5

SIMON, PAUL

1964/1993 Boxed Set Sampler 16 tracks *WB 6577/promo/'93* $15
Born at the Right Time *WB 4626/promo/'90* $5
Boy in the Bubble (extended & 7" remix) *WB 2659/promo/ gatefold hardcover ps/'86* $12
Concert in the Park sampler (You Can Call Me Al/Born at the Right Time/Diamonds on the Soles edit/America) *WB 5220/promo/'91* $8
Greatest Hits, etc. *Columbia 35032/ stock/ps/'85* $15
Proof (remix) *WB 4604/promo/'90* $5
The Obvious Child *WB 4480/promo/ silkscreened/rear insert/'90* $5
The Rhythm of the Saints *WB/promo/ special box packaging/'90* $20

SIMPLE MINDS

Don't You (Forget About Me) live/Bass Line/ American *A&M 31006/ps/3"/stock* $6
Don't You (Forget About Me) live/Bass Line/ The American *A&M 75021 2375/promo/ps* $6
Glittering Prize 12 tracks *A&M 31454 0052/ promo silkscreened on stock cd/'92* $12
Let There Be Love 4:23/4:44 *A&M 75021 7532/promo/ps/'91* $8
Mandela Day edit & lp *A&M 17882/promo/silkscreened/'89* $5
See the Lights *A&M 75021 7540/promo/ silkscreened/'91* $5
See the Lights (5 versions) *A&M 75021 7546/promo/ps/'91* $8
Stand By Love *A&M 75021 7222/promo/ silkscreened/ps/'91* $5
Take a Step Back *A&M 17824/promo/silkscreened/'89* $5
This Is Your Land edit & lp *A&M 17779/promo/silkscreened/'89* $6

SIMPLE PLEASURE

Givin' You All I've Got to Give edit & lp *Reprise 6168/promo/'92* $4
Never Before edit & lp *Reprise 5891/promo* $4

SIMPLY RED

For Your Babies english & french *Eastwest 4523/promo/logo on blue/ps* $5
If You Don't Know Me By Now *Elektra 8079/promo/'89* $5
If You Don't Know Me By Now + 3 non lp *Elektra 66701/ps/stock/'89* $8
It's Only Love valentine mix/Turn It Up *Elektra 69317/stock/3"/ps/'89* $6
Its Only Love (edit remix 3:59)/(remix 5:44) *Elektra 8054/promo/'89* $6
Something Got Me Started edit *Eastwest 4168/promo/ps/'91* $6
Stars 3 versions *Eastwest 4343/promo/ ps/logo on blue/'91* $6
Stars comprende edit & full comprende *Eastwest 4460/promo/custom sticker* $5
You've Got It *Elektra 8112/promo/'89* $5
You've Got It/Holding Back the Years (live acoustic)/I Know You Got Soul/I Wish *Elektra 66663/stock/ps/'89* $8

SIMPSON, RAY

Crazy Pictures 4 versions *Virgin 4455/promo/rear insert/'92* $5

SIMPSONS, THE

Deep, Deep Trouble (3 versions)/ Sibling Rivalty *Geffen 21633/stock/ gatefold hardcover ps/ custom sticker/'91* $5
Deep, Deep Trouble (4 versions) *Geffen 4208/promo/ps/'91* $7
Do the Bartman (8 versions) *Geffen 4170/ promo/gatefold hardcover/flip cartoon book/silkscreened pic/ lyric innersl./'90* $20
God Bless the Child *Geffen 4218/promo/'91* $4
Sing the Blues 10 tracks *Geffen 24308/ stock with promo silkscreened/ps* $12

SINATRA, FRANK
Fly Me to the Moon *Reprise 4753/promo/'90* $6
It Was a Very Good Year
Reprise 4654/promo/'90 .... $6
It Was a Very Good Year
Reprise 5937/promo/'92 .... $5
The Reprise Collection sampler (10 tracks)
Geffen 4540/promo/ps/'90 .... $20

SINATRA, NANCY
These Boots Are Made For Walkin'/How Does
That Grab You Darlin'/Sugar Town/
Somethin' Stupid
Rhino 73026/stock/3"/ps/'88 .... $12

SINBAD
I Ain't Lyin' 7" edit & 12" edit/Half Naked
Women... *Wing 278/promo/ps/'90* $6

SINGLE GUN THEORY
Surrender edit & extended/From a Million
Miles/Take Me Back unreleased mix
Nettwerk 13850/stock/ps/'91 .... $5

SINITTA
Hitchin' a Ride 3:41 & 6:36
Atlantic 3288/promo/rear insert/'91 .... $6

SIOUXSIE & BANSHEES
(Fear) Of the Unknown/Spiral Twist/I Could Be
Again *Geffen 21702/stock/gatefold
hardcover ps/custom sticker/'91* $6
Face to Face *WB 5567/promo/'92* $5
Fear (Of the Unknown) *Geffen 4306/promo/
silkscreened/custom sticker/'91* $5
Fear (Of the Unknown) 7 versions
Geffen 4345/promo/silkscreened/ps $10
Kiss Them For Me 7" & kathak mix/Starting
Back/Return *Geffen 21650/stock/
gatefold hardcover ps/'91* $6
Kiss Them For Me 7" versions
DGC 4239/promo/silkscreened/ps $6
Kiss Them For Me edit & 7"
Geffen 4260/promo/ps/'91 .... $7
My Last of My Heart (live)/Overground (live)/
This Wheel's on Fire/Cities in Dust
Geffen 4469/promo/ps/logo on black $15

SIOUXSIE & BANSHEES/ THE CREATURES
Fury Eyes (3 versions)/Abstinence/Standing
There (andalucian mix)/Divided
*Geffen 21479/silkscreened blue/
stock/ps/'90* $6

SIR MIX-A-LOT
Baby Got Back
Def American 5213/promo/ps/'92 .... $7
One Time's Got No Case edit/lp/bass mix
Def American 5878/promo/'92 .... $5
Swap Meet Louie 5 vers. *Def American 40559/
gatefold hardcover ps/stock/'92* $5
Swap Meet Louie remix & lp
Def American 5468/promo/ps/'92 .... $5

SIREN
All Is Forgiven lp & edit
Mercury 43/promo/ps/'89 .... $4
All Is Forgiven/One Good Lover/
Dont Let Go/Stand Up
Mercury 36/promo/ps/'88 .... $4

SISKIN, SKEW
If the Walls Could Talk *Giant 5536/promo/
silkscreened/ps/custom sticker/'92* $6

SISTER DOUBLE HAPPINESS
Hey Kids/Wheels a Spinning/Sweet Talker
acoustic/Lightning Struck
*Reprise 40356/stock/
gatefold hardcover ps/'92* $5

SISTER MACHINE GUN
Addiction 4 versions/Degenerate extended
Wax Trax 8691/stock/ps/'92 .... $5

SISTER PSYCHIC
Birdhouse leisuRemix/Little Bird/Lucifer Sam
Restless 025/promo/custom sticker $5

SISTER RED
I'd Love to Change the World *Vision 3325/
promo/logo on red/rear insert/'91* $4

SISTER SOULJAH
Killing Me Softly: Deadly Code of Silence
3 versions *Epic 74289/promo/
silkscreened/rear insert/ICE CUBE* $6
The Final Solution: Slaverys Back in Effect
4 versions *Epic 74018/promo/
rear insert/logo on red/'91* $6

The Hate That Hate Produced 3:02/4:20
Epic 74206/promo/logo on black & red/rear insert/'92 .... $6

SISTERS OF MERCY

Detonation Boulevard (remix)
Elektra 8308/promo/logo on black/rear insert/'90 .... $8
I Was Wrong 3:12 & 6:03/interview with Andr. Eldritch (32:52) *Elektra 8412/ promo/ps/silkscreened/'91* $20
Lucretia My Reflection (3 version)
Elektra 8019/promo/'87 .... $12
More 4:44 & 8:30/You Could Be the One
Elektra 66595/stock/ gatefold hardcover ps/'90 .... $8
More 4:44 & 8:30/You Could Be the One 3:58
Elektra 8253/promo/rear insert/ logo on white/'90 .... $8
More radio edit *Elektra 8252/promo/logo on black/rear insert/'90* $8
This Corrosion edit *Elektra 1003/promo/'87* $10
Tour Thing '91 (8 tracks) *Elektra 8343/ promo/rear insert/silkcr./'90* $25
When You Don't See Me remix *Elektra 8364/ promo/rear insert/'90* $8

SIX FINGER SATELLITE

Weapon/Niponese National Anthem/Shimkus Yell/Polish the Shine *Sub Pop 143/ stock/silkscreened/ps/'91* $5

SKAGGS, RICKY

The Ricky Skaggs Story/Radio Special
Epic 2022/promo/ps/'90 .... $18

SKEW SISKIN

Livin' on the Redline/Purple Haze demo/In Another World *Giant 5813/ promo/silkscreened/ps/'92* $6

SKID ROW

18 and Life *Atlantic 2752/promo/ps/'89* $5
Delivering the Goods *Atlantic 4792/promo/ rear insert* $5
I Remember You faded & lp *Atlantic 2748/ promo/silkscreened/rear insert/'89* $5
Little Wing *Atlantic 4777/promo/ps/ silkscreened pic/'92* $6
Monkey Business *Atlantic 3957/promo/ps/ silkscreened member pics/'91* $6
Piece of Me *Atlantic 2688/promo/ps/'89* $5
Quicksand Jesus *Atlantic 4444/promo* $5
Slave to the Grind *Atlantic 4157/promo/ silkscreened/rear insert/'91* $5
Slave to the Grind 12 tracks *Atlantic 82242/ with "Get the F— Out"/stock/ps* $15
Wasted Time edit & lp *Atlantic 4262/promo/ logo on black/rear insert/'91* $5
Youth Gone Wild *Atlantic 2579/promo/ps/'89* $5

SKINNY PUPPY

Testure (SF mix & 12" mix)/Serpents/Cage
Capitol 44322/3"/ps/stock/'89 .... $5
Tormentor ext./Bark/Natures Revenge dub
Nettwerk 15644/stock/ps/ custom sticker/'90 .... $5
Worlock 6:42 & 5:00/Tin Omen/Brak Talk
Capitol 15535/stock/ps/'90 .... $5

SKRAPP METTLE

Star Hag/Shoot the Sherbert
Par 9005/promo/silkscreened pic/DWEEZIL ZAPPA $6

SKY CRIES MARY

2000 Light Years From Home 2 vers./ The Movement of Water
World Domination 79640/promo/ silkscreened/custom sticker/'93 .... $5

SKYY

Let's Touch edit & long
Atlantic 3269/promo/rear insert/'89 .... $4
Up and Over edit & extended
Atlantic 4431/promo $5

SLASH & MICHAEL MONROE

Magic Carpet Ride *WB 6391/promo/ silkscreened/rear insert/'93* $8

SLAUGHTER

Days Gone By edit & lp/medley of Do Ya Know-Days Gone By-Fly to the Angels (live)
Chrysalis 4641/promo/ps/silkscreened/ custom sticker/'92 .... $8
Do Ya Know edit & lp *Chrysalis 04638/ promo/logo on black/'92* $5
Fly to the Angels (3 versions)
Chrysalis 23527/promo/ps/'90 .... $8
Mad About You edit & lp
Chrysalis 23699/promo/ps/'91 .... $5
Real Love *Chrysalis 05473/promo/ silkscreened group pic/ps/'92* $7
Real Love hot mix & lp *Chrysalis 05479/ promo/silkscreened band pic/ps/'92* $7
Shout It Out edit & lp *Interscope 4071/promo* $5
Spend My Life/Fly to the Angels/Up all Night (last 2 live) *Chrysalis 23605/ promo/logo on black/ps/'90* $12
The Wild Life *Chrysalis 23812/promo/ box cover/custom sticker* $12
The Wild Life 2 vers. *Chrysalis 23812/promo/ trifold hardcover/silkscreened/'92* $6
Up All Night edit & cass-CD versions
Chrysalis 23486/promo/silkscreened/ gatefold hardcover ps/'90 .... $8

SLAVE

She's Just That Kinda Girl radio & boom mix
Ichiban 126/promo/logo on pink/'92 .... $4

SLAYER
Decade of Aggression compilation *Def American 26792/stock/2 cds/ metal case (only 10,000 made)/'91* $40
Seasons in the Abyss (blood pack cd) *Geffen 4664/promo/custom sticker/special package* $18
South of Heaven *Def Jam 3263/promo/ps* $5

SLEDGE, KATHY
All of My Love edit & lp *Epic 74372/ promo/logo on yellow/ps/'92* $4
Heart 3 versions *Epic 74463/promo/ silkscreened/rear insert/'92* $8
Take Me Back to Love Again 4 versions *Epic 4474/promo/logo on orange/ps* $6

SLEEZE BEEZ
I Don't Want to Live Without You *Atlantic 5026/ promo/silkscreened/ps/'93* $4
Raise a Little Hell *Atlantic 4916/promo/ silkscreened/rear insert/'92* $4
Stranger Than Paradise *Atlantic 3233/promo/ps/'90* $4

SLICK RICK
I Shouldn't Have Done It 4 versions *Def Jam 73739/promo/ red & gold silkscreened/ps/'91* $6
It's a Boy edit & remix *Def Jam 74120/promo/ps/'91* $5
Mistakes Of a Woman in Love With Other Men 3 vers. *Def Jam 73914/promo/ps* $6

SLIDE
Why Is It a Crime *Mercury 189/promo/ silkscreened pic/'89* $4

SLIK TOXIK
Big F*ckin' Deal/Riff Raff/Mass Confusion/ Rachel's Breathing *Capitol 15781/stock/ps/'91* $4
Helluvatime *Capitol 79202/promo/ps/'92* $4

SLIPSTREAM
We Are Raving destructo edit/12" *Great Jones 627/promo/cust.sticker* $4

SLOAN
Take It In/Rag Doll/Laying Blame *DGC 4523/ promo/silkscreened/ps/'93* $7
Underwhelmed *DGC 4477/promo/ silkscreened/ps/'92* $4

SLY & ROBBIE
Dance Hall (edit) *Island 3088/promo/'89* $6

SMALL CHANGE
Teardrops 4:32/5:40/5:04/4:22 *Mercury 521/promo/silkscreened/'91* $4
This Must Be Love edit & lp *Mercury 585/ promo/silkscreened/custom sticker* $4
Why 4:10/4:38/5:03/3:38 *Mercury 432/ promo/silkscreened/ps/'91* $4

SMART E'S
Loo's Control 3 versions/F*ck the Law *Big Beat 10096/stock/ps/'92* $4
Sesame's Treet 5 versions *Big Beat 4794/ promo/logo on yellow/rear insert/'92* $4

SMASHED GLADYS
Lick It Into Shape *Elektra 1002/promo/ps/'88* $3

SMASHING PUMPKINS
Drown *Epic 4733/promo/ps/'92* $5
Lull/Rhinoceros/Blue/Slunk/Bye June *Caroline 1465/stock/ps/'91* $6

SMITH, DARDEN
Frankie & Sue *Columbia 4039/promo/ps/'91* $4
Midnight Train & interview & acoustic perf. (16 segments in all) *Columbia 3034/promo/ps/'91* $15

SMITH, G.E. & THE SATURDAY NIGHT LIVE BAND
Fattenin' Frogs For Snakes *Liberty 79597/ promo/logo on green/rear insert/'92* $4
Get A Little 10 tracks *Liberty 99955/promo/ silkscreened/rear insert/'92* $12
Sloozy *Liberty 79716/promo/ silkscreened/rear insert/'93* $4

SMITH, MICHAEL W.
For You 5 vers. *Reunion 4301/promo/ps/'91* $4
Picture Perfect 6 versions *Geffen 4452/promo/ps/'92* $4
Somebody Love Me *Reunion 62466/promo/ silkscreened/rear insert/'92* $4

SMITH, O.C.
The Best Out of Me *Triune 629/promo/ logo silkscreened/'93* $4

SMITH, PATTI
CD Sampler (6 songs) *Arista 9683/promo/ps/'88* $20
Looking For You (I Was) rock edit/pop edit/lp *Arista 9762/promo/ fold-out poster ps/'88* $12
People Have the Power lp/edit *Arista 9689/promo/ps/'88* $6

SMITHEREENS
A Girl Like You 7" & lp *Enigma 79776/ promo/silkscreened pic/'89* $6
Blue Period *Capitol 79051/promo/ silkscreened/rear insert/'89* $5
Blues Before and After *Capitol 79916/ promo/silkscreened/'89* $4

Get a Hold of My Heart 2 vers. *Capitol 79267/ promo/ps/silkscreened logo/'91* $5
Girl in Room 12 *Capitol 79148/promo/ rear insert/logo silkscreened/'91* $5
Live 6 tracks *Restless 72242/stock/ps/'88* $12
Rudolph the Red Nosed Reindeer *Capitol 79572/promo/ps/silkscreened/'92* .$6
Too Much Passion edit & lp *Capitol 79935/ promo/ps/logo on purple/'91* $5
Too Much Passion/World Keeps Going Round/ It Don't Come Easy/If You Want the Sun to Shine (instrumental) *Capitol 15818/stock/ps/'91* $5
Top of the Pops fade & lp *Capitol 79933/ promo/silkscreened/ps/'91* $5
Yesterday Girl *Capitol 79131/ promo/silkscreened/'89* $5

SMITHS

This Charming Man 8 versions *Sire 40583/ stock/gatefold hardcover ps/'92* $6
This Charming Man manchester/Jeane/Accept Yourself *Sire 40591/stock/ gatefold hardcover ps/'92* $6

SMUDGE

Don't Want to Be Grant ../Stranglehold/ Dabble/Spawn *Shock 8004/stock/ps/ silkscreened/'91* $5

SMYTH, PATTI

I Should Be Laughing edit & lp *MCA 2638/promo/rear insert/'93* $4
No Mistakes fade & lp *MCA 2423/promo/rear insert/'92* $5
Sometimes Love Just Ain't Enough *MCA 2235/promo/rear insert/'92* $5

SNAKES, THE

Pay Bo Diddley *Curb 10569/promo/ silkscreened/ps/'89/BO DIDDLEY* $4
Walkaway *Curb 10535/promo/cust.sticker/'89* $4

SNAP

Exterminate! 4 versions *Arista 07822-12545/stock/ps/'93* $4
Mary Had a Little Boy (3 versions) *Arista 2143/promo/ silkscreened/rear insert/'90* $6
Ooops Up (3 versions) *Arista 2071/promo/ silkscreened/rear insert/'90* $7
Ooops Up radio edit *Arista 2092/promo/silkscreened/'90* $5
The Boner single/switch mix/remake bonus dub *Arista 2014/promo/ silkcreened/rear insert/'90* $6

SNOW

Girl, I've Been Hurt 4 versions *Eastwest 4971/ promo/silkscreened/ps/'93* $6
Informer edit without rap *Eastwest 5001/promo* $5
Informer edit/drum mix edit/clark's super radio mix *Eastwest 4830/ promo/silkscreened pic/rear insert* $6
Runway 3 vers. *Eastwest 5162/promo/ps/'93* $5

SNOW, PHOEBE

If I Can Just Get Through the Night *Elektra 8070/promo/'89* $4
Something Real *Elektra 8087/promo/'89* $4
Speak to My Heart *Epic 73505/promo/ rear insert/'90* $4

SO

Are You Sure edit/lp *EMI 243/promo/ps/'88* $4

SOCIAL DISTORTION

1945/Under My Thumb/Playpen *Triple X 51021/ stock/ps/silkscreened/'89* $12
Bad Luck *Epic 4348/promo/silkscreened/ps* $7
Ball and Chain edit & lp/Shame on Me *Epic 2051/promo/ps/'90* $10
Born to Lose/Ready For Love (live) *Epic 4689/promo/ps/silkscreened* $10
Cold Feelings/Alone and Forsaken *Epic 4530/promo/ps/'92* $8
Let It Be Me/Its All Over Now/Pretty Thing *Epic 1969/promo/ps/'90* $10
Ring of Fire/Lonesome Train *Epic 2120/promo/ps/silkscreened* $10
Story of My Life (2 versions)/Back Street Girl/1945/Mommys Little Monster/ It Wasn't a Pretty Picture (last 4 live) *Epic 2198/promo/ps/'90* $15
Story of My Life (single versions)/1945/ Mommys Little Monster/(last 4 live)/Pretty Thing/Shame on Me (last 2 new recording) *Epic 49K 73571/gatefold hardcover ps/stock/'90* $8
When She Begins (edit)/Mainliner 1992 *Epic 4600/promo/logo on red/ps/'92* $8

SOHO

Freaky (4 versions) *Atco 3845/promo/rear insert/'90* $5
Freaky pump edit & lp edit *Atco 3920/promo/ silkscreened/rear insert/'91* $4
Hippychick (5 versions) *Atco 96428/stock/ gatefold hardcover ps/'90* $5
Hippychick edit & extended *Atco 3526/promo/ silkscreened/ps/'90* $4
Love Generation edit *Atco 3653/promo/ silkscreened/rear insert/'90* $4
Ride 3:37/6:20 *Atco 4613/promo/ps/ logo on yellow/'92* $4

SOMETHING HAPPENS

Hello, Hello, Hello../Liverpool Sands
Charisma 004/promo/ silkscreened pic/ps/'90 .... $5
Suffer It edit & lp *Charisma 097/promo/ silkscreened/'92* $4

SOMETHING SPECIAL

I Wonder Who She's Lovin' 4 versions
Epic 73306/promo/logo on pink/'90 .... $4
U Can Get Me Anytime 7"/12"/dub
Epic 73487/promo/logo on black/ rear insert/'90 .... $5

SONIA

You'll Never Stop Me Loving You 3:22/6:40
Chrysalis 23385/promo/rear insert $4

SONIA DADA

New York City 3 versions *Chameleon 8615/ promo/silkscreened/ps/'92* $4

SONIC YOUTH

100% *DGC 4433/promo/ps/'92* $4
100%/Creme Brulee/Genetic/Hendrix Necro
DGC 21735/stock/ps/'92 .... $6
Dirty Boots/White Kross/Eric's Trip/ Cinderellas Big Score/Dirty Boots/ The Bedroom (last 5 live)
DGC 21634/stock/ gatefold hardcover ps//'91 .... $6
Dirty Boots/White Kross/Eric's Trip/ Cinderellas Big Score/Dirty Boots/ The Bedroom (last 5 live)
Geffen 4209/promo/ps/'91 .... $8
Disappearer (2 versions)/Thats All I Know/ Dirty Boots (demo versions)
DGC 21623/stock/ gatefold hardcover ps/'90 .... $6
Disappearer (3 versions) *DGC 4122/promo/ silkscreened pic/multi fold out hardcover/'90* $10
Kool Thing *DGC 4123/promo/ silkscreened logo/ps/'90* $6
Sugar Kane (edit)/The Destroyed Room/ Purr acoustic/End of the End of Ugly
DGC 21818/promo/silkscreened/'93 .... $5
Sugar Kane (edit)/The Destroyed Room/ Purr acoustic/End of the End of Ugly
DGC 21818/stock/silkscreened/'93 .... $6
Youth Against Racism clean & lp
DGC 4472/promo/logo on black/ps $5

SONNIER, JO-EL

You May Change Your Mind
Capitol 79601/promo/'91 .... $4

SONS OF ANGELS

Lonely Rose *Atlantic 3521/promo/ silkscreened/ps/'90* $4

SONZ OF A LOOP DA LOOP ERA & THE SCRATCHADELIC EXPERIENCE

Peace & Loveism 3 versions/Freedomism/Far Out
Pyrotech 10093/stock/ps/'92 .... $4

SOS BAND

Broken Promises lp/instrumental/edit
Tabu 28965 1800/promo/ silkscreened/ps/'91 .... $4
I'm Still Missing Your Love 4 versions
Tabu 1752/promo/silkscreened/ps $6
Secret Wish (7 versions) *Tabu 73089/ promo/silkscreened/rear insert/'89* $5
Sometimes I Wonder 8 versions
Tabu 28965 1702/promo/ps/'91 .... $6

SOUL ASYLUM

And the Horse They Rode In On (15 tracks total - 3 bonus tracks)
A&M 75021 8053/promo/ silkscreened pic/custom sticker/'90 .... $20
Black Gold shortest/shorter/lp/live
Columbia 4910/promo/ps/'93 .... $6
Cartoon *A&M 17574/promo/ps/'88* $8
Easy Street *A&M 75021 7429/ promo/silkscreened/ps/'90* $6
Runaway Train *Columbia 5016/promo/ps/'93* $6
Somebody to Shove
Columbia 4730/promo/ps/'92 .... $6
Something Out of Nothing/Freaks/To Sir With Love/Marionette (last 3 live)
A&M 75021 7409/promo/ silkscreened/ps/'90 .... $18
Spinnin' *A&M 75021 7423/promo/ silkscreened logo/'90* $6
Summer of Drugs *Chaos 5260/promo/ps/'93* $5
Without a Trace *Columbia 5274/promo/ps/'93* $5

SOUL II SOUL

2 Sides of (10 tracks of instrum. & remixes)
Virgin 12686/promo/rear insert/'92 .... $25

A Dreams a Dream (3 versions) *Virgin 3344/ promo/silkscreened logo/'90* $6
A Dreams a Dream (edit) *Virgin DREAM/promo/logo silkcr./'90* $4
Back to Life (3 versions) *Virgin 2844/ promo/silkscreened pic/'89* $8
Get a Life 3 versions/Fairplay 12" mix *Virgin 96481/stock/rear insert/'89* $6
Get a Life (3 versions) *Virgin 3256/promo/ silkscreened lettering/'90* $5
Jazzie's Groove 3:23/3:55/5:03 *Virgin 3033/ promo/silkscreened logo/'89* $6
Joy radio mix/new vibrations mix/spag n joy dub/7" club edit *Virgin 4401/promo* $6
Keep on Movin 6 versions *Virgin 96556/ stock/silkscreened/custom sticker/'89* $5
Keep on Movin' (4 remixes) *Virgin/promo/silkscreened brown/'89* $6
Missing You (5 versions) *Virgin 3600/promo/silkscreened/'90* $7
Move Me No Mountain 5 versions *Virgin 4628/promo/rear insert/'92* $6
People (5 versions) *Virgin 3470/promo/silkscreened/'90* $6

SOUL KITCHEN

Rosie Jones edit & lp *Giant 5691/promo/rear insert/'92* $4

SOULED OUT INTERNATIONAL

Shine On 6 versions *Columbia 73926/ promo/logo on white/ps/'91* $4

SOUND FACTORY

2 the Rhythm 6 versions *RCA 62569/stock/ps/'93* $4
Understand This Groove 3 versions/ Take Me 2 the Top (orig.mix) *Logic 62371/stock/ps/silkscreened* $4
Understand This Groove edit/xtatic mix/ original mix *RCA 62477/promo/ custom sticker/rear insert/'93* $4

SOUND ON SOUND

Time to Feel 5 versions *Sire 40396/stock/ gatefold hardcover ps/'92* $5

SOUNDGARDEN

Get On the Snake *A&M 17811/promo/silkscreened/'89* $5
Get On the Snake *A&M 18029/promo/silkscreened/'89* $5
Hands All Over edit/Come Together *A&M 17969/promo/silkscreened/'89* $6
Into the Void/Girl U Want/Stray Cat Blues/ She's a Politician/Slaves & Bulldozers (live) *A&M 75021 5401/promo/ silkscreened/'92* $12
Jesus Christ Pose *A&M 75021 7284/ promo/logo on orange/ps/'91* $6
Loud Love *A&M 17893/promo/silkscreened/'89* ... $5
Loud Love (full length lp) *A&M/promo only silkscreened pic/'89* $20
Outshined edit & lp *A&M 75821 7383/ promo/silkscreened/ps/'91* $6
Rusty Cage edit & lp *A&M 75021 7342/ promo/silkscreened/ps/'91* $6
Rusty Cage edit & lp/Girl U Want/Show Me/ Into the Void *A&M 75021 7334/ promo/logo on brown/ps/'91* $12

SOUNDS OF BLACKNESS, THE

Optimistic (6 vers.) *Perspective 28968 1702/ promo/ps/silkscreened/'91* $7
Soul Holidays edit & lp/It's Christmas Time/ We Give You Thanks + 6 dif.holiday greetings *Perspective 31458 8064/ promo/silkscreened/ps/'92* $8
Testify 8 versions *Perspective 28968 1708/ promo/ps/logo on black/'91* $7
The Pressure pt 1 9 versions *Perspective 28968 1704/ promo/logo on black/ps/'91* $7

SOUNDTRACK

Bill & Ted's Bogus Journey sampler (with SLAUGHTER, MEGADETH, PRIMUS) *Interscope 3914/promo/logo silkscreened/rear insert/'91* $6
Ghosts of the Civil Dead with NICE CAVE, MICK HARVEY, BLIXA BARGELD *Restless 71433/stock/ps/'88* $12
Highlights from Jekyll & Hyde ep (Someone Like You/Love Has Come of Age/ A New Life) *RCA 60422/promo/ gatefold hardcover/'90* $8
Nutcracker Prince ep (Always Come Back to You) *Atlantic 3677/promo/ custom sticker/rear insert/'91* $5
Robin Hood excerpts *Morgan Creek/promo/'91* $6
Tales From the Crypt ep (title theme/ Threes a Crowd/The Man Who Was Death) *Big Screen 5775/promo/ rear insert/custom sticker/'92* $8
Teenage Mutant Ninja Turtles sampler (MC HAMMER, SPUNKADELIC, JOHNNY KEMP, more) *SBK 05352/promo/ custom sticker/silkscreened orange* $6
The Civil War sampler (Sullivan Ballou Letter/Ashokan Farewell/same (edit)) *Elektra 8260/promo/ps/'90* $6
The Fly 23 tracks *Varese Sarabande 47272/promo/ps/ HOWARD SHORE/'86* $12
Theme From Northern Exposure *MCA 2463/promo/rear insert/'92* $6
Thirtysomething main title theme (radioactive mix) *Geffen 4255/promo/ps/'91* $6
Tresspass 12 tracks *Sire 5823/promo/ICE CUBE & ICE T, PUBLIC ENEMY, SIR MIX A LOT, RY COODER.../'92* $12

Twin Peaks (11 tracks) *WB 26316/promo/ps/silkscreened "donut"/'90* $18

SOUP DRAGONS

Backwards Dog (3 versions) *Big Life 352/promo/silkscreened/'90* $6
Divine Thing 3 versions/Driving/Electric Blues *Big Life 865 765/stock/ps/silkscreen* $6
I'm Free (3 versions) *Big Life 308/promo/silkscreened/'90* $6
I'm Free (3 versions)/Backwards Dog/ Way Brain *Big Life 877 843/stock/silkscreened/ps/'90* $6
Mother Universe 3:50 & 7:30 *Mercury 380/promo/silkscreened/'91* $5
Mother Universe 3:50 & 7:30/Sweetmeat 6:14/ Softly live *Big Life 879 545/stock/ps/silkscreened/'91* $5
Pleasure 7" & lp/Dive Bomber *Big Life 721/promo/ps/logo on blue/'92* $6
Running Wild edit & revisited & lp/Stand Loud *Mercury 801/promo/logo on blue/'92* $7
The Majestic Head/interview *Sire 2965/promo/ps/'88* $12

SOUTH CENTRAL CARTEL

Papa Was a Rolling Stone radio/house/ext. *Pump 19125/promo/logo on black/ps* $6
U Gotta Deal Wit Dis *G.W.K./promo/'91* $4

SOUTHERN PACIFIC

All Is Lost *WB 3465/promo/'88* $4
I Go to Pieces *WB 4015/promo/'90* $4
Memphis Queen *WB 4525/promo/'90* $4
Side Saddle (remix) *WB 4342/promo/rear insert/'89* $4
Thing About You/Perfect Stranger/Reno Bound/Dont Let Go My Heart (remix) + 2 *WB 3374/promo/'88* $8

SOUTHERN PACIFIC & CARLENE CARTER

Time's Up (edit) *WB 3809/promo/'89* $4

SOUTHERN PACIFIC/CHRIS AUSTIN

Honey I Dare You/I Know Theres a Heart in There ... *WB 3304/promo/ps/'88* $5

SOUTHSIDE JOHNNY

Aint That Peculiar *A&M 17637/promo/silkscreened/'88* $4
Coming Back single & lp *Impact 2123/promo/rear insert/'91* $4
I've Been Working To Hard edit & lp *Impact 2120/promo/'91* $4
It's Been a Long Time edit & l *Album Network JUKEUP 1/promo/weird AN like package with repeats of the above/'91* $5
It's Been a Long Time edit & lp *Impact 1688/promo/rear insert/'91* $4

Little Calcutta *Cypress 17705/promo/silkscreened* $4
Your Precious Love *Cypress 17820/promo/'89* $4

SPACEMEN 3

Big City/Drive (2 versions each) *RCA 2801/promo/silkscreened/rear insert/'91* $6

SPARKS

Just Got Back From Heaven 3:59/3:54/6:45 *Rhino 70413/promo/silkscreened/embossed jewel box* $7
So Important (single & extend. important mix) *Rhino 90002/promo/ps/'88* $6
So Important 2 versions *Rhino 90006/promo/ps/'88* $8

SPECIAL GENERATION

Lift Your Head (And Smile) edit/lp/extended/instrumental *Bust It 79499/promo/silkscreened/'92* $4
The Right One edit & lp *Bust It 79690/promo/silkscreened/'92* $4

SPECTOR, PHIL

Back to Mono sampler 8 tracks *Phil Spector 711831/promo/silkscreened/rear insert/'91* $15
Christmas (Baby Please Come Home)/ Silent Night *Phil Spector 711832/promo/silkscreened brick look/'91* $10

SPENCE, JUDSON

Hot & Sweaty edit & lp *Atlantic 2477/promo/ps/'88* $4

SPENCER, TRACIE

Save Your Love 7 versions *Capitol 79179/promo/rear insert/'90* $5

SPENT POETS, THE

Dogtown edit & lp *Geffen 4392/promo/gatefold hardcover ps/'92* $4

SPICE 1

187 Proof 3 versions *Jive 42040/promo/ps/custom sticker/'91* $4
In My Neighborhood 4 versions *Jive 42057/promo/custom sticker/rear insert/'92* $4

SPIN DOCTORS

Jimmy Olsen's Blues *Epic 4658/promo/logo on pink/ps/'92* $6
Little Miss Can't Be Wrong lp/live *Epic 4571/promo/silkscreened/ps/'92* $8
Little Miss Can't Be Wrong no reason to bitch versions *Epic 4845/promo/'91* $6
Two Princes *Epic 3086/promo/silkscreened/ps/'91* $8

Two Princes edit & lp *Epic 74804/promo/ silkscreened/ps/'92* $6
What Time is It? *Epic 5112/promo/silkscreened/ps/'93* $5

SPINAL TAP
Bitch School *MCA 2169/promo/ps/'92* $5
The Majesty of Rock *MCA 2185/promo/ps/'92* $5

SPIREA X
Speed Reaction *4AD 5547/promo/'92* $5

SPIRIT
Nature's Way '91/Darlin' If/Genetic Dreams/ Fallen Hero/Tent of Miracles/interview (23:14) *Crew 22002/promo/ps/'91* $15

SPIRITUALIZED
I Want You/Feel So Bad (13:20) *RCA 62327/promo/logo on blue/rear insert/'92* . $6
Run/Angel Sigh *RCA 62269/promo/ silkscreened/ps/'92* $5

SPLASH
Dizzy Miss Lizzy 3:30/4:10 *Grudge 4753/promo/'89* $4

SPOT 1019/THIS WORLD OWES ME A BUZZ
Promo for 10/22/91 release of both groups 12 tracks *Frontier 34634/promo* $12

SPREAD EAGLE
Back on the Bitch *MCA 1077/promo/ps/'90* $4

SPRINGER, DENNIS
Rio 9 versions *Nastymix 70310/promo/ silkscreened/ps/'91* $12

SPRINGFIELD, DUSTY & PET SHOP BOYS
Nothing Has Been Proved single edit/ dance mix/instrum. *Enigma 181/promo/ silkscreened red/custom sticker/'89* $8
Stand By My Woman 4 vers. *Tabu 28965 1806/ promo/silkscreened/ps* $5

SPRINGHOUSE
Eskimo ep (Eskimo dark mix/That Was Before/ Get it Going/Angels/Layers) *Caroline 1466/stock/ps/'91* $5

SPRINGSTEEN, BRUCE
57 Channels *Columbia 4599/promo/ps/'92* $8
57 Channels little steven mix vers.1/versions2 *Columbia 4670/promo/ logo on blue/custom sticker/'92* $12
57 Channels 2 vers/Theres a Riot Goin' On/ Part Man Part Monkey *Columbia 44K 74416/stock/ps/'92* $5
57 Channels/Part Man Part Monkey *Columbia 38K 74354/stock/ps/'92* $5
Better Days *Columbia 74274/promo/ps/'92* $8
Born in the USA/Shut Out the Light *Columbia 38K 04680/stock/3"* $15
Born to Run/Spirit in the Night *Columbia 13K 68658/stock/3"/ps* $18
Chimes of Freedom ep 4 tracks *Columbia 44K 44445/stock/3"/'88* $10
Cover Me/Pink Cadillac *Columbia 38K 07946/ 3"/stock/custom sticker* $15
Cover Me/Pink Cadillac *Columbia 38K 07946/ stock/custom sticker* $15
Human Touch edit & lp *Columbia 74273/ promo/ps/logo on orange/'92* $8
Leap of Faith *Columbia 4703/promo/ logo on red/'92* $8
One Step Up *Columbia 1031/promo/ps/'87* $25
Rarities on Compact Disc *Westwood One #15/promo/ps/'93* $30
Tougher Than the Rest/Chimes of Freedom/ Be True/Born to Run (all live) *Columbia 000125/promo/3"/'88* $10
Tunnel of Love Express tour CD (5 songs) *Columbia 1046/promo/ps/'88* $40
Tunnel of Love Express Tour CD Cont'd (All That Heaven Will Allow/One Step Up/Roulette/Be True/Pink Cadillac) *Columbia 1108/promo/ps/'88* $40

SPRINGSTEEN, BRUCE/ MIGHTY MAX & FRIENDS
Summer on Signal Hill *Hard Ticket 01612 6../ promo/ps/LITTLE STEVEN, JON BON JOVI, BEACH BOYS../'91* $8

SPUNKADELIC
Boomerang 4:14/6:58 *SBK 05366/promo/ silkscreened/gatefold hardcover ps* $5
Take Me Like I Am (3 versions) *SBK 05336/promo/ps/'90* $5

SQUEEZE
Annie Get Your Gun (live) *IRS 022/promo/ silkscreened/ps/'90* $6
Annie Get Your Gun (live)/Is It Too Late (live)/Backtrack/Cat on the Wall/ Night Ride *IRS 74007/stock/ps/'90* $6
Crying In My Sleep *Reprise 5130/promo/'91* $3
Everything in the World *A&M 31458 8197/ promo/logo on green & black/ps/'93* $5
Footprints/Black Coffee in Bed/Take Me Im Yours (last 2 live) *A&M 31002/ stock/3"/ps/'88* $6
Footprints/Black Coffee in Bed/Take Me Im Yours (last 2 live) *A&M 31002/stock/ps/'88* $6
If It's Love *A&M 17884/promo/silkscreened* $6
Play 12 tracks *Reprise 26644/stock with promo only silkscreened/ps/'91* $15

Satisfied edit & lp *Reprise 4930/promo/ ps/silkscreened/'91* $5
Three From Babylon and On (3 songs) *A&M 17490/promo/ps/3" CD/'87* $10

SQUIER, BILLY

Angry/The Truth Is (preview of "Tell the Truth" lp) 8:26 *Capitol 79659/ promo/silkscreened/ps/'93* $8
Don't Let Me Go edit & lp *Capitol 79789/ promo/silkscreened/'89* $5
Don't Say You Love Me 7" & lp *Capitol 79635/promo/'89* $5
Facts of Life 2 versions/Young at Heart/ Don't Talk Like That *Capitol 15746/stock/ps/'91* $5
Facts of Life edit & lp *Capitol 79632/ promo/logo on black/rear insert/'91* $4
Hear, Then & Now (comp.) (Lonely is the Night/ Stroke/Everybody Wants You/Calley Oh/Shes a Runner (live)/Shot of Love/ Learn how to Live (live)/Rock Me Tonite/In the Dark/Don't Say You Love Me) *Capitol 79769/promo/ ps/silkscreened red/'89* $15
Love edit & lp *Capitol 79996/promo/ logo on red/'91* $5
She Goes Down *Capitol 79609/promo/ silkscreened/rear insert/'91* $5

STACEY Q

Don't Make a Fool of Yourself (3 versions) *Atlantic 2206/promo/'88* $8
Favorite Things edit/lp *Atlantic 2518/promo/rear insert/'88* $4
Give You All My Love 3:32/4:23/5:47 *Atlantic 2735/promo/rear insert/'89* $6

STAGE DOLLS

Love Cries edit & lp *Chrysalis 23366/ promo/custom sticker/'88* $4
Love Don't Bother Me edit *Polydor 625/ promo/ps/logo on white/'92* $4

STAIRS, THE

Flying Machine/Fall Down the Rain *London 745/promo/logo on purple/'92* $4

STAMOS, JOHN

Forever ac/chr/cd *Brother Entertainment. PROCD-3/promo/ gatefold hardcover ps/'92* $8

STANSFIELD, LISA

A Little More Love *Arista 2449/promo/ps/'92* $5
All Woman lp & edit *Arista 2398/promo/ps/'92* ..$5
Change single mix/radio mix edit/ultim.club mix *Arista 12363/stock/ps/'91* $5
Change single mix/radio mix edit/ultim.club mix *Arista 2362/promo/silkscreened/ps* $6

In All the Right Places edit & lp *MCA 2685/promo/ps/'93* $4
This is the Right Time 4:30 & 7:51 *Arista 2069/promo/silkscreened stripes/rear insert/'90* $6
You Can't Deny It *Arista 2024/promo/logo on black/rear insert/'90* $5
You Can't Deny It/Lay Me Down/Something's Happenin' *Arista 2025/stock/ps/'90* $6

STAPLES, MAVIS

20th Century Express edit & lp *Paisley Park 3506/promo* $4
Melody Cool edit & lp *Paisley Park 4397/promo/'90* $4
The Voice *Paisley Park 5991/promo/'93* $4
Time Waits For No One edit & lp *Paisley Park 3813/promo/ prod & cowritten by PRINCE/'89* $5

STAR STAR

Science Fiction Boy radio & lp *Roadrunner 061/promo/ps/'92* $4

STARCLUB

Hard to Get *Island 6755/promo/ silkscreened/ps/'92* $4

STARLIN

That's It You're In Trouble/Sick Puppy *Atlantic 4961/promo/ps/'92* $4

STARPOINT

I Want You - You Want Me (6 versions) *Elektra 8155/promo/silkscreen blue/'90* $5
Midnight Love (3 versions) *Elektra 8185/promo/rear insert/'90* $5
Tough Act to Follow edit/lp *Elektra 8057/promo/'88* $4

STARR, RINGO

Don't Go Where the Road Don't Go *Private 81007/promo/silkscreened/ prod.by JEFF LYNNE/'92* $10
Rocky Mountain Way/Act Naturally/It Don't Come Easy/The Weight *Ryko 1019/stock/ps* ..$6
Weight of the World *Private 81003/ promo/silkscreened/ps/'92* $10
Weight Of the World/After All These Years/ Don't Be Cruel *Private 01005 81003/ stock/ps/logo on red/'92* $6
You Never Know *Giant 5153/promo/rear insert/'91* $8

STARR, RINGO & BUCK OWENS

Act Naturally/The Keys in the Mailbox *Capitol 79650/promo/'89* $8

STARSHIP

Good Heart *RCA 2796/promo/ps/'91* $4
Good Heart ac mix & lp *RCA 2851/promo/'91* $4

Good Heart/Don't Lose Any Sleep
RCA 2847/promo/rear insert/ custom sticker/'91 .... $4
I Didn't Mean to Stay All Night 4:35/4:51
RCA 9109/promo/ps/'89 .... $4
I'll Be There edit & extended solo edit
RCA 9195/promo/rear insert/'89 .... $5
It's Not Enough remix & lp *RCA/promo/'89* $4
Its Not Over (2 vers.) *Grunt 6478/promo/ps* $5
Wild Again edit & remix *Elektra 8040/promo* $5

STATEN, KEITH
Miracles (3 versions) *Polydor 285/promo/ silkscreened/ps/'90* $4

STATLER BROTHERS
Let's Get Started If We're..
Mercury 29/promo/ps/'88 .... $4
Put It On the Card *Mercury 580/promo/ silkscreened/rear insert/'91* $4
Walking Heartache in Disguise
Mercury 200/promo/silkscreened/'90 .... $4

STEADY B
Pay Me Baby 4 vers. *Jive 1456/promo/ps/'91* $5

STEEL PULSE
Soul of My Soul 5 versions
MCA 1274/promo/rear insert/'91 .... $6
Taxi Driver 4 versions
MCA 2551/promo/rear insert/'93 .... $6

STEELE, CHRISSY
Love You Til It Hurts/Try Me/Armed & Dangerous/.... Love Don't Last Forever
Chrysalis 23729/promo/ silkscreened/ps/'91 .... $4

STEELE, JEVETTA
Calling You edit *Great Jones 622/ promo/rear insert/'92* $4

STEELE, TERR
Tonights the Night (3 versions)
SBK 05380/promo/ps/'91 .... $5

STEELHEART
Electric Love Child 4 versions
MCA 2322/promo/ps/'92 .... $5
Sticky Side Up edit & lp
MCA 2269/promo/ps/'92 .... $4

STEEN, NIKOLAJ
The New Message 5 versions
Imago 72787-25013/stock/ps/'92 .... $4

STEMS, THE
At First Sight *A&M 17837/promo/silkscreen/ with YAHOO SERIOUS intro & commentary/'89* $4

STEPHANIE
Winds of Chance/You Don't Die From Love/ Born Blue/interview *Epic 3029/ promo/ps/logo on red/'91* $5

STEREO MCS
Connected edit & full length
Gee Street 6756/promo/ps/'92 .... $4
Elevate My Mind (3 versions) *4th & B'way 519/ promo/rear insert/'90* $6
Lost in Music edit/USA extended/ultimatum remix *4th B'way 544/promo/ custom sticker/'91* $6
Lost in Music radio edit
4th B'way 534/promo/ps/'91 .... $4
Step It Up 4 versions
Gee Street 6772/promo/ps/'92 .... $5
What is Soul?/On 33/Bring it On/ Neighbourhood/Gee Street
4th B'way 444 026/stock/ps/'90 .... $4

STETSASONIC
Talkin' All That Jazz 5 versions
Tommy Boy 918/promo/ps/'88 .... $6

STEVE STEVENS ATOMIC PLAYBOYS
Action 7" & lp *WB 3778/promo/'89* $4
Atomic Playboys *WB 3652/promo/ silkscreened pic/'89* $5
Atomic Playboys single edit, video edit, lp
WB 3744/promo/'89 .... $4

STEVIE B
Because I Love You (radio edit) *RCA 2724/ promo/rear insert/custom sticker/'90* $4
Forever More 3 versions *Lefrak Moelis 62112/ promo/logo on blue/rear insert/'91* $5
I'll Be By Your Side *RCA 2758/promo/ps/'91* $4
Love & Emotion (6 versions)
RCA 2645/promo/ps/'90 .... $6
Love & Emotion/Spring Love/Girl I Am Searching For You + 3 *RCA 2693/ promo/custom sticker/'90* $5
Who's Lovin' You Tonight? radio & lp
RCA 2705/promo/ps/'90 .... $4

STEVIE V
Dirty Cash (4 versions) *Mercury 295/ promo/silkscreened yellow/'89* $6
Dirty Cash (Money Talks) 4:16 & 8:04
Mercury 269/promo/silkscreened/'89 .... $5
Jealousy 4 versions *Mercury 355/promo/ logo silkscreened/'90* $6

STEWART, AL
King of Portugal 4 versions
Enigma 1877 75025/stock/ps/'88 .... $6
King of Portugal lp version + 2 remixes/15:40 interview *Enigma 123/promo/ custom sticker/'88* $12

Year of Cat/Time Passages/Midnight Rocks
Arista 3014/stock/3"/'88 .... $6

STEWART, DAVE

Crown of Madness remix & lp/Motorcycle Mystics live *Arista 2352/promo/ silkscreened/ps/'91* $6
Love Shines *Arista 2113/promo/logo on yellow/rear insert/'90* $6
Party Town 4:30/4:21/6:42
Arista 2046/promo/silkscreened/ps $6
Party Town (3 versions)/Love Calculator/ Suicidal Sid *Arista 2073/promo/ps* $7

STEWART, DAVE & BARBARA GASKIN

Subterranean Homesick Blues 3:39/6:43
Ryko 9004/promo/silkscreened/'90 .... $5

STEWART, DAVE & CANDY DULFER

Lily Was Here *Arista 2188/promo/ps/ silkscreened white/'89* $6
Lily Was Here radio edit & extended
Arista 2253/promo/ps/'91 .... $7

STEWART, JERMAINE

Set Me Free 5 versions *Reprise 40635/ stock/gatefold hardcover ps/'92* $4

STEWART, JERMAINE/KASHIF

Say It Again/Love Me All Over/Kathryn
Arista 9668/promo/ps/'88 .... $5

STEWART, POINDEXTER

College Rock/Reality/College Jelly Brain/ Reality Groove *SST 299/stock/ps* $5

STEWART, ROD

Broken Arrow *WB 4864/promo/'91* $4
Crazy About Her (3 remixes)
WB 3612/promo/custom sticker/'88 .... $7
Crazy About Her remix & lp
WB 3334/promo/'89 .... $5
Downtown Train (fade) *WB 3836/promo/ silkscreen lettering/'89* $4
Dynamite *WB 3146/promo/ps/'88* $6
Forever Young *WB 3169/promo/ps/'88* $6
Forever Young/Days of Rage
WB 27796/stock/3"/ps/'88 .... $5
Have I Told You Lately
WB 6161/promo/silkscreened pic/'93 .... $7
I Don't Want to Talk About It ('89 versions)
WB 3902/promo/'89 .... $5
Lost in You (edit/lp)
WB 3052/promo/silkscreened pic/'88 .... $6
Moment of Glory *WB 4923/promo/'91* $4
My Heart Cant Tell You.. *WB 3261/promo/'88* $5
Rebel Heart *WB 4831/promo/'91* $5
Rhythm of My Heart edit & lp
WB 4742/promo/'91 .... $5
The Motown Song (remix) *WB 4857/promo* $5
The Motown Song single remix 3:55/ power mix 4:46 *WB 5061/promo/'91* $7
The Wild Horse *WB 3145/promo/ps/'88* $6
Your Song *Polydor 669/promo/logo on white/ps/'92* $5

STEWART, ROD & RONALD ISLEY

This Old Heart of Mine ('89 version)
WB 3837/promo/'89 .... $5

STEWART, ROD & RONNIE WOOD

Cut Across Shorty lp/intro edit fade
WB 6213/promo/custom sticker/'93 .... $6

STIGERS, CURTIS

I Wonder Why *Arista 2331/promo/trifold hardcover ps (with poster/ silkscreened pic/'91* $8
Never Saw a Miracle
Arista 2459/promo/rear insert/'92 .... $4
Sleeping With the Lights On *Arista 2430/ promo/ps/logo on black/'92* $4
You're All That Matters To Me new mix & orig
Arista 2391/promo/ps/logo on black $5

STING

All This Time edit & lp *A&M 75021 7486/ promo/gatefold hardcover ps/'91* $5
All This Time/I Miss You ../King of Pain (live)
A&M 75021 2354/stock/ gatefold hardcover ps/'91 .... $6
Be Still My Beating Heart (2 versions)
A&M 17529/promo/ps/'87 .... $10
Englishman in New York/Someone to Watch Over Me/Up From the Skies (10:07)
A&M 31001/stock/3"/ps/'88 .... $7
Englishman in New York/Someone to Watch Over Me/Up From the Skies (10:07)
A&M 75021 2370/promo/ps $6
Fields of Gold *A&M 31458 8111/promo/ silkscreened pic/gatefold hardcvr ps* $5
If I Ever Lose My Faith In You
A&M 31458 8091/promo/silkscreened pic/gatefold hardcover ps/'93 .... $6
Mad About You 3 versions *A&M 75021 7294/ promo/ps/silkscreened/'91* $8
Mad About You 3:52/3:53 *A&M 75021 7499/ promo/logo on white/ps/'91* $5
Nothing 'bout Me 3 versions
A&M 31458 8138/promo/ps $7
The Soul Cages (edit) *A&M 75021 7530/ promo/silkscreened/ps/'91* $5
They Dance Alone *A&M 17613/promo/ps/'87* $8
Why Should I Cry For You extended& lp/ We'll Be Together *A&M 75021 2364/ stock/gatefold hardcover ps/'91* $6
Why Should I Cry For You?
A&M 75021 7535/promo/ps/'91 .... $5
Why Should I Cry For You? (3 versions)
A&M 75021 7547/promo/ps/'91 .... $6

STING & ERIC CLAPTON

It's Probably Me edit & lp *A&M 75021 7391/ promo/"Lethal Weapon" ps/'92* $7

STONE ROSES, THE

Fools Gold 9:53 & 4:15/What the World is Waiting For *Silvertone 1315/promo/ps/'90* $7

I Wanna Be Adored edit & lp/Going Down/ Simone (last 2 non lp) *Silvertone 1301/promo/ps/'89* $7

One Love 3:35 & 7:45/Something's Burning *Silvertone 1399/stock/ gatefold hardcover ps/'90* $7

Standing Here/Elephant Stone 12" mix *Silvertone 42101/promo/silkscreened/ rear insert/'92* $7

STONE TEMPLE PILOTS

Crackerman, Wet My Bed/Crackerman, Plush acoustic take 1 & 2 *Atlantic 4973/ promo/rear insert/'93* $8

Plush 2 vers. *Atlantic 4982/promo/rear insert* $5

Sex Type Thing *Atlantic 4785/promo/ silkscreened/rear insert/'92* $6

STONE, DOUG

Come In Out of the Pain *Epic 74259/promo/rear insert/'92* $4

STONE, STEVE

Faces in the Rain *Epic Associated 73484/ promo/silkscreened/rear insert/'90* $4

Standing on the Edge *Epic 73638/promo/ logo on red/rear insert/'90* $4

STORM, THE

I've Got a Lot to Learn About Love *Interscope 4079/promo/ps/ logo on blue-green/'91* $4

Show Me the Way 3 versions *Interscope 4346/promo/ps/'91* $5

STORY, THE

Grace in Gravity *Elektra 8574/promo/ps/'91* $4

STRADLIN, IZZY

Izzy Stradlin & the Ju Ju Hounds 10 tracks *Geffen 24490/promo silkscreened on stock/ps/'92* $12

Shuffle It all *Geffen 4464/promo/ps/'92* $6

Somebody Knockin' *Geffen 4486/promo/ logo on black/ps/'92* $6

Train Tracks remix & lp *Geffen 4509/promo/ps/'92* $6

STRAIT, GEORGE

Heartland *MCA 54563/promo/rear insert/'92* $5

I've Come to Expect It From You *MCA 53969/promo/rear insert/'90* $5

If I Know Me *MCA 54052/promo/'91* $5

If I Know Me/Unwound both with & without spoken intros *MCA 3026/promo/'91* $6

Love Without End, Amen *MCA 79015/ promo/silkscreened/rear insert/'90* $5

Lovesick Blues *MCA 54318/promo/'91* $5

Overnight Success *MCA 53755/promo/ silkscreened/rear insert/'89* $5

STRAITJACKET FITS

Missing From Melt ep (Missing Presumed Drowned/Bad Note For a Heart single mix/Skin to Wear stripped mix/ In Spite of It all/Cave It) *Arista 2244/stock/ps/'91* $4

Roller Ride/Down in Splendour/Bad Note For a Heart/A.P.S. (last 3 live) *Arista 2356/promo/ silkscreened/rear insert/'91* $8

STRANGLERS, THE

Someone Like You/Motorbike/Something *Epic 2160/promo/silkscreened logo on red/rear insert/'90* $8

Sweet Smell of Success (3 versions)/Instead of This/Poisonality *Epic 2067/promo/ps/'90* $8

STRAW, SYD

Future 40's *Virgin 2788/promo/blue silkscreened/'89/MICHAEL STIPE* $4

Heart of Darkness *Virgin 3139/promo/silkscreened/'89* $4

Think Too Hard *Virgin 2932/promo/ silkscreened logo/'89* $4

STRAY CATS

Bring It Back Again *EMI 04225/promo/ silkscreened cat design/rear insert* $10

Elvis on Velvet lp & edit *Great Pyramid 812/ promo/logo on black/ps/'92* $8

Elvis on Velvet/Let's Go Faster/Lust n Love *Great Pyramid 73333 35884/stock/ gatefold hardcover ps/'92* $6

Gene & Eddie *EMI 4304/promo/rear insert/ silkscreened/'89* $12

Lust in Love 2 versions *Great Pyramid 812/ promo/logo on black/'92* $10

STREISAND, BARBRA

All I Ask of You *Columbia 1258/promo/ps/'88* $8

For All We Know *Columbia 4507/promo/ps/'92* $8

Just For the Record sampler 12 tracks *Columbia 4200/promo/ silkscreened/ps/'91* $20

Places That Belong to You *Columbia 4257/promo/ps/'92* $6

Someone That I Used to Love *Columbia 73099/promo/ps/'89* $8

We're Not Makin' Love Anymore single & lp *Columbia 1816/promo/ps/ silkscreened/'89* $8

STREISAND, BARBRA & DON JOHNSON

Till I Loved You long & short
Columbia 1312/promo/ps/'88 .... $8

STRESS

Beautiful People fade & lp
Reprise 5112/promo/'90 .... $4
Flowers in the Rain lp without intro
Reprise 4722/promo/'91 .... $4
Flowers in the Rain with & without intro
Reprise 4788/promo/'91 .... $4
Rosechild *Reprise 4992/promo/'91* $4
Selftitled 10 tracks *Reprise 26519/*
promo silkscreened/'91 .... $12

STRUMMER, JOE

Shouting Street (2 versions)/Island Hopping
Epic 1770/promo/silkscreened pic/'89 .... $8

STRYPER

Always There For.. *Enigma 086/promo/ps/'88* $6
Always There For You/The Reign/Soldiers
Under Command (live)/R. Sweet
interview pt 1 *Enigma 75509/*
3" CD w/5" ps/stock/'88 .... $6
I Believe In You *Enigma 125/promo/*
custom sticker/'88 .... $6
I Believe In You/Come to the Everlife/Together
Forever (live)/Robert Sweet interview pt 2
Enigma 75028/stock/3" w/5" ps/'88 .... $6
Keep the Fire Burning *Enigma 154/promo/ps* $8
Shining Star edit & lp *Enigma 304/promo/*
silkscreened/ps/'90 .... $5

STUART, MARTY

High on a Mountain Top edit & lp/Me & Hank &
Jumpin' Jack Flash-High on a Mountain..
MCA 54538/promo/'92 .... $4
Honky Tonk Crowd *MCA 54568/promo/'92* $4
Tempted *MCA 54145/promo/rear insert/'91* $4
Till I Found You *MCA 54065/promo/*
silkscreened/ps/'91 .... $4
Western Girls *MCA 79068/promo/*
silkscreened/rear insert/'90 .... $4

STUART, MARTY & TRAVIS TRITT

This One's Gonna Hurt You
MCA 54405/promo/ps/'92 .... $5

STYLISTICS

Always On My Mind
Amherst 11/promo/rear insert/'91 .... $4
Love Talk *Amherst 10/promo/rear insert/'91* $4

STYLZ

Bounce 8 versions *MCA 2703/promo/ps/'93* $5

STYX

Love at First Sight *A&M 75021 7511/*
promo/silkscreened/ps/'90 .... $5
Love is the Ritual *A&M 75021 7428/*
promo/silkscreened/ps/'90 .... $5
Pieces of Eight radio show *In the Studio 134/*
promo/cue sheet/hosted by
Dennis De Young & James Young $25
Radio Made Hits 1975-1991 (13 tracks)
A&M 75021 7465/promo/
logo on blue/ps/'91 .... $25
Show Me the Way (3 versions)
A&M 75021 7438/promo/ps/
silkscreened logo on brown/'90 .... $6

STYX/DENNIS DE YOUNG

Boomchild *MCA 17602/promo/ps/'88* $5

SUBDUDES, THE

Any Cure *Atlantic 2947/promo/rear insert* $3
Need Somebody *Atlantic 2935/promo/ps/'89* $6

SUEDE

Animal Nitrate/To the Birds/My Insatiable One
Columbia 5229/promo/ps/'93 .... $6

SUGAR

A Good Idea/Helpless/Where Diamonds Are
Halos/Slick/Armenia City in the Sky
(last 4 live) *Rykodisc 1030/stock/ps* $4
If I Can't Change Your Mind *Rykodisc 0239/*
promo/silkscreened/ps/'92 .... $4

SUGARCUBES

Birthday 5 versions *Elektra 66366/stock/*
gatefold hardcover ps/custom sticker $5
Birthday lp & icelandic versions
Elektra 8002/promo/ps/'88 .... $8
Coldsweat edit/remix
Elektra 8021/promo/silkscreened/'88 .... $6
Hit *Elektra 8492/promo/logo on black/ps/'92* $4
Motorcrash lp & live/Polo/Blue Eyed Pop
(2nd mix) *Elektra 66726/stock/*
3"/ps/'88 .... $5
Motorcrash lp/live
Elektra 8038/promo/logo on white/'88 .... $7

Planet (3 versions) *Elektra 8141/promo/ silkscreened logo/'89* $6
Regina *Elektra 8109/promo/'89* $5
Vitamin 3:40 & 7:35 & 3:54/Walkabout remix *Elektra 66413/stock/ gatefold hardcover ps/'92* $5
Vitamin edit & E mix *Elektra 8598/promo/logo on blue/ps* $5
Walkabout (remix) *Elektra 8557/promo/ps/ silkscreened/'92* $5

SUGARCUBES/BJORK

Human Behaviour orig./underworld remix 12:05 *Elektra 8784/promo/logo on black/ps/custom sticker/'93* $6

SUICIDAL TENDENCIES

Alone *Epic 2097/promo/logo on black/ rear insert/'90* $5
Asleep At the Wheel 3 versions *Epic 4653/promo/ps/'92* $6
How Will I Laugh Tomorrow (4 versions) *Epic 1555/promo/silkscreened red* $8
I Saw Your Mommy *Epic 5147/promo/ logo on purple/ps/'93* $4
I'll Hate You Better *Epic 4870/promo/ps/silkscreened/'92* $5
Lights . . . Camera. . . Conversation (interview & music) *Epic 2217/promo/ps/'90* $20
Lovely/War Inside My Head *Epic 4011/ promo/silkscreened/rear insert/'91* $6
Monopoly on Sorrow edit & lp *Epic 4736/promo/ps/'92* $5
Send Me Your Money (2 versions)/Lovely/ Don't Give Me Your Nothing/Go'n Breakdown (bleeped versions) *Epic 2278/promo/ silkscreened/rear insert/'90* $8

SUMMER, DONNA

Breakaway *Atlantic 3003/promo/ rear insert/silkscreened logo/'89* $6
Love's About to Change My Heart (5 versions) *Atlantic 2876/promo/rear insert/'89* $8
This Time I Know It's For Real (3 versions) *Atlantic 2718/promo/rear insert/'89* $6
Work That Magic 3:52/5:00/6:20 *Atlantic 4311/promo/rear insert/'91* $8

SUMMER, DONNA/RAY PARKER

Dinner With Gershwin (2 versions)/A Man Should Not Sleep Alone (2 versions) *Geffen 2804/promo/cust.sticker/'87* $8

SUMMER, HENRY LEE

Turn It Up *Epic 4216/promo/logo on brown/ps* $3

SUN 60

Mary Xmess *Epic 4937/promo/ps/'93* $4
Middle of My Life *Epic 4566/promo/gatefold hardcover ps/silkscreened/'92* $5

Out of My Head *Epic 4347/promo/ps/'92* $4
Responsible remix *Epic 4603/promo/ps/'92* $4

SUNDAYS, THE

Can't Be Sure/I Kicked a Boy/Dont Tell Your Mother *Geffen 4168/promo/ hardcover ps/'90* $7
Here's Where the Story Ends *DGC 3998/promo/silkscreened/ps* $4
Love lp & fade *DGC 4460/promo/ps/'92* $4
Love lp & fade *DGC 4465/promo/ gatefold hardcover ps/'92* $5
Wild Horses edit & lp *DGC 4503/promo/ silkscreened/ps/'93* $4

SUNSCREEM

Love U More *Columbia 74769/promo/ps/'92* $4
Pressure Us edit/alt.mix edit *Columbia 5069/promo/ps/'93* $5

SUPER CAT

Dem No Worry We 6 versions *Columbia 44K 74449/stock/ps/'92* $5
Dem No Worry We radio try me mix/12" club/ heavy play mix *Columbia 74720/promo/ps/'92* $6
Dolly My Baby 7 versions *Columbia 44K 74855/stock/ps/'93* $5
Ghetto Red Hot 4 versions *Columbia 74391/promo/ps/'92* $6

SUPER LOVER CEE & CASANOVA RUD

I Gotta Good Thing remix/instrum./ accapella *Elektra 8058/promo/'88* $6

SUPERIORS, THE

Temptation *Columbia 73210/promo/ps/'90* $4

SUPERSNAZZ

Superstupid 12 tracks *Sub Pop 209/promo/ ps/logo on black/'93* $12

SUPERTRAMP

Crime of the Century/In the Studio *dj radio show/promo/hosted by ROGER HODGSON/cue sheet* $25

SUPREME LOVE GODS

Fire *Def American 5946/promo/ps/'93* $4

SURE, AL B.

I Don't Wanna Cry 6 versions *WB 40748/ stock/gatefold hardcover ps/'93* $5
Nite and Day single edit/dusk mix *WB 2976/promo/ps/'88* $7
Off On Your Own (Girl) edit/lp/remix *WB 3202/promo/ps/'88* $7

SURF PUNKS

Party Bomb 14 track *Restless 72321/stock/ps/'88* $15

SURFACE
All I Want is You with & without intro
Columbia 73684/promo/ps/'91 .... $5
Christmas Time is Here
Columbia 74072/promo/ps/'91 .... $4
Never Gonna Let You Down
Columbia 73643/promo/ps/'91 .... $4
The First Time *Columbia 73502/promo/ hardcover mini box cover/'90* $5
You're the One *Columbia 73964/promo/ ps/logo on orange/'91* $4

SURVIVOR
Desperate Dreams *Scotti Bros 73037/ promo/silkscreened logo/'89* $4
Didn't Know It Was Love
Scotti Bros 1292/promo/'88 .... $4

SUSQUEHANNA HAT COMPANY
Too Much Joy rock & real *Giant 4631/promo/ silkscreened/rear insert/'91* $4

Do you have CDs that belong in the next edition of this guide? If so, we'd like to hear from you. See "How You Can Help" on page xiii.

SWALLOW, STEVE
Belles (edit)/Thrills and Spills (edit)/ Playing With Water
ECM SWALLOW 2/promo/logo on red/oversized round package/CARLA BLEY, GARY BURTON, more/'92 .... $6

SWAMP DOGG
She's Built to Kill/Surfin' in Harlem
Volt 34/promo/ps/'91 .... $5

SWAMP TERRORISTS
Nightmare/Truth or Dare/Ostracize/ I Spit on You/Girl the Truth
Noise 3612 44884/stock/ gatefold hardcover ps/'91 .... $6

SWANS
Saved *Uni 17836/promo/custom sticker/'89* $4

SWEAT, KEITH
Dont Stop You Love edit & extended
Elektra 8034/promo/'88 .... $6
Dream Team (Keep It Comin') *Elektra 8617/ promo/silkscreened/ps/'92* $4
I'll Give All My Love to You edit & lp
Elektra 8268/promo/'90 .... $4
Keep It Comin' 5 versions
Elektra 8481/promo/'91 .... $6
Keep It Comin' 5 versions *Elektra 8493/ promo/logo on black/rear insert/'91* $6
Make It Last Forever edit
Elektra 8013/promo/'87 .... $6
Make You Sweat edit/radio/extended
Elektra 8107/promo/silkscreened logo/rear insert/'90 .... $6
Merry Go Round 4 versions
Elektra 8242/promo/rear insert/'90 .... $6
Something Just Aint Right (4 versions)
Elektra 2218/promo/'87 .... $6
Why Me Baby? lp & edit *Elektra 8529/ promo/logo on orange/'91* $4
Why Me Baby? pt 2 k.sweat mix/hip hop mix/ bump dub/lp *Elektra 8569/promo/ silkscreened logo on orange/ custom sticker/'91* $6
Your Love 4 versions *Elektra 8376/promo/ silkscreened/rear insert/'90* $6
Your Love Part 2 (3 versions)
Elektra 8321/promo/rear insert/'90 .... $6
Your Love pt 1 & 2 4 versions
Elektra 8360/promo/logo on brown $6

SWEET F.A.
Liquid Emotion edit/unplugged/live/lp
Charisma 086/promo/ silkscreened/ps/'91 .... $4
Temptation *Charisma 066/promo/ps/'91* $3

SWEET LIZARD ILLTET
Selftitled 11 tracks *WB 5472/promo/ censored edition/ps/'92* $12

SWEET OBSESSION
Elevator (4 vers.) *Epic 73750/promo/ps/'91* $5
Hooked on You edit/version 2/instrumental *Atco 2722/promo/rear insert/'89* $6
If Wishes Came True edit & lp *Atco 3361/promo/rear insert/'90* $4

SWEET SENSATION
Love Child single & extended *Atco 3242/promo/ps/'90* $6
Never Let You Go 5 versions *Atco 2448/promo/rear insert/'88* $6

SWEET WATER
Crawl *Atlantic 5023/promo/silkscreened/ps* $4
Everything Will Be Alright *Atlantic 5024/ promo/silkscreened/ps/'93* $4
Roads Life Goes ep (Everything Will Be Alright/Michelle Was/Head Down) *Atlantic 4790/promo/silkscreened pic/rear insert/'92* $6

SWEET, MATTHEW
Divine Intervention *Zoo 17035/promo/ silkscreened/ps/'91* $4
Evangeline *Zoo 17090/promo/logo on gold/ps* $4
Girlfriend/Superdeformed demo/Teenage Female demo/Good Friend demo *Zoo 72445 14042/stock/ps/'91* $5
Goodfriend ep (Divine Intervention/Girlfriend/ Day For Night/Thought I Knew You/ Looking At the Sun/Does She Talk + 7) *Zoo 17098/promo/lots of acoustic & live stuff/ps/logo on white/'92* $25
I've Been Waiting *Zoo 17070/promo/ silkscreened/ps/'92* $4
Vertigo 2 vers. *A&M 17706/promo/ps/'89* $4
When I Feel Again *A&M 17801/promo/'89* $4

SWEET, RACHEL/BALDWIN & THE WHIFFLES
Please Mr Jailor/Sh Boom *MCA 18288/promo/rear insert/'90* $5

SWEETHEARTS OF THE RODEO
Buffalo Zone (10 songs) *Columbia 45373/ promo/silkscreened/rear insert/'90* $12
Como Se Dice (I Love You) *Columbia 73360/promo/'90* $4
Devil and Your Deep Blue Eyes *Columbia 74064/promo/ silkscreened logo/rear insert/'91* $4
Hard Headed Man *Columbia 73907/ promo/logo on red/rear insert/'91* $4
Hey Doll Baby/Since I Found You/Midnight Girl/Chains of Gold/Gotta Get Away *Columbia 2823/promo/'87* $6

If I Never See Midnight Again (remix) *Columbia 1509/promo/silkscreened heart/rear insert/'89* $4

SWELL
Room to Think ep (At Long Last/Here It Is/ Life's Great/Give/Just Get Well) *Def American 5917/promo/ silkscreened/ps/'93* $5

SWERVEDRIVER
Rave Down/She's Beside Herself/Kill the Superheroes/Juggernaut Rides/ Sandblasted *A&M 75021 7279/ promo/ps/silkscreened/'91* $8
Reel to Real ep (Sandblasted/Scrawl & Scream/Hands/Jesus) *A&M 75021 2402/stock/ps/'91* $5
Son of Mustang Ford/Laze It Up *A&M 75021 7302/promo/ps/'91* $5

SWING OUT SISTER
Breakout/Twilight World (mix)/After Hours/ Blue Mood *Mercury 1/promo/ps/'87* $10
In Store Play Sampler (Notgonnachange/Am I the Same Girl/Understand/Who Let the Love Out/Breakout + 2) *Fontana 530/promo/ps/'92* $15
Waiting Game lp & remix edit *Fontana 61/promo/ps/'89* $6
You On My Mind *Fontana 112/promo/ silkcreened duo pic/'89* $8

SWV
Going For the Gold Interview 43:44/20:16 *RCA 66235/promo/ps/'93* $15
I'm So Into You 6 version *RCA 62450/promo/rear insert/'92* $6
I'm So Into You 8 versions *RCA 62501/ promo/rear insert/custom sticker/'93* $8
Right Here 6 versions *RCA 62354/promo/rear insert/'92* $6
Right Here 7 versions *RCA 07863 62375/stock/ps/'92* $5
Right Here-Human Nature 6 versions *RCA 62615/promo/rear insert/'93* $6
Weak 6 versions *RCA 62521/promo/rear insert/'93* $7

SYBIL
Beyond Your Wildest Dreams 5 versions *Next Plateau 1006/promo/logo on cream/'93* $6
The Love I Lost 6 versions *Next Plateau 911/promo/'93* $6
You're the Love Of My Life 4 versions *Next Plateau 422 857 065/stock/ps* $5

SYKES, JOHN
Don't Say Goodbye *Geffen 4188/promo/ silkscreened/rear insert/'90* $4

SYLVERS, FOSTER
I'll Do It remix edit & lp *A&M 17988/promo/ silkscreened logo/'90* $4

SYMONE, RAVEN
That's What Little Girls Are Made Of 6 vers. *MCA 2636/promo/ps/'93* $5

SYSTEM, THE
Coming to America (4 versions) *Atco 2352/promo/'88* $6
Have Mercy (5 versions) *Atlantic 3108/promo/rear insert/'89* $5
Midnight Special (4 versions) *Atlantic 2712/promo/rear insert/'89* $5

T REX
T. Rex: The Essential Collection sampler (9 tracks) *Relativity 0137/promo/'91* $18

T'PAU
Only a Heartbeat *Charisma 041/promo/ps/'91* $6
Whenever You Need.. *Charisma 057/promo/'91* ..$6

T, TIMMY
Cry a Million Tears 5 versions *Quality 19117/ promo/silkscreened/ps/'92* $4
Over You *Quality 15192/promo/ps/ silkscreened/'92* $4
Too Young to Love You *Quality 15116/promo/ps/'91* $4

T-RIDE
Backdoor Romeo *Hollywood 8553/promo/ silkscreened/rear insert/'92* $4
Hit Squad *Hollywood 10208/promo/ silkscreened/'92* $4
I Hunger *Hollywood 10213/promo/silkscreened/ rear insert/custom sticker/'92* $4
Zombies From Hell *Hollywood 8527/promo/ silkscreened/rear insert/'92* $5

T.N.G.
Sweet Okole 2 vers. *Reprise 5684/promo/'92* $4

T42
Desire single & remix *Columbia 74243/promo/ps/'92* $5
Let Me Go 3 versions *Columbia 74468/promo/ps/'92* $5

T99
Anasthasia 3 versions *Columbia 74486/ promo/ps/custom sticker/'92* $4

TA MARA AND THE SEEN
Blueberry Gossip edit & lp *A&M 17556/ promo/gatefold hardcover ps/'88* $6

TABOR, JUNE & OYSTER BAND
'91 tour sampler (Mississippi/Night Comes In/ All Tomorrow's Parties/New York Girls/ Oxford Girl/I Fought the Law/White Rabbit/All Along the Watchtower - last 2 live) *Ryko 9012/promo/ps/'91* $20

TAD
Salem/Welt/Leper *Sub Pop 182/stock/ps/'92* $5

TAFF, RUSS
Winds of Change/I Cry/Take My Hand/Go On *A&M 17900/promo/ps/'89* $4

TAG
Love and Money 10 vers. *Scotti Bros.75302/ promo/trifold ps/silkscreened pic/'91* $5

TAG TEAM
Whoomp! (There it Is) 2 versions *Life 002/promo/logo on red/'93* $7

TAKE 6
Gold Mine *Reprise 3342/promo/'88* $5
I Believe remix *Reprise 4789/promo/'90* $4
I L-O-V-E U video edit/I *Reprise 4392/promo/'90* $5
Spread Love (edit) *Reprise 3468/promo/'88* $4

TAKE 6 & THE YELLOWJACKETS
God Rest Ye Merry Gentlemen *Reprise 5204/promo/'91* $5

TAKE THAT
It Only Takes a Minute radio & remix *RCA 62485/promo/ps/'93* $6

TALK TALK
Spirit of Eden lp *Manhattan 04144/promo silkscreened edit./ps/oversized box* $15

TALKING HEADS
Blind edit/lp *Sire 3022/promo/ps/'88* $6
Lifetime Piling Up *Sire 5151/promo/'92* $3
Nothing But Flowers (edit/lp) *Sire 2947/promo/ps/'88* $6
Sax and Violins radio versions *WB 5335/promo/'91* $4

TALL TALES AND TRUE
Trust lp & acoustic/Heaven Knows/Going Out of My Head *rooArt 207/promo/ silkscreened/'90* $8

TAM TAM
Do the Tam Tam 4:00 & 3:53 & 6:05 *Island 6679/promo/silkscreened/ps* $5

TAMI SHOW
Did He Do It To You edit & lp *RCA 62171/promo/'91* $4

The Truth RCA 2694/promo/ps $4
The Truth rea'zar radio mix/club mix/lp
RCA 62081/promo/rear insert/'91 .... $6

TANGERINE DREAM
Cat Scan (radio edit)/Ghazai (radio edit)/
Optical Grace Private 2042/promo $15
Desert Train (edit) Private 2078/
promo/logo on white/'90 .... $20
Rockoon (radio edit)/Oriental Haze/Interview
(14:33 with EDGAR FROESE)
Miramar 2803/stock/ps/'92 .... $15

TANGIER
On the Line Atco 2730/promo/
silkscreened logo/rear insert/'89 .... $4
Stranded Atco 3779/promo/ps/'91 .... $4

TARA, T.J.
Feel So Good SBK 05400/promo/ps/
silkscreened/'91 .... $4

TATE, DANNY
How Much edit & lp Charisma 096/promo/
silkscreened/ps/'92 .... $4
Lead Me to the Water
Charisma 075/promo/ps/'91 .... $4

TATE, TERRY
Babies Having Babies 4 version
Atlantic 2938/promo/rear insert/'89 .... $5

TATTOO RODEO
Been Your Fool edit & lp Atlantic 3888/
promo/silkscreened/ps/'91 .... $4
Let Me Be the One edit & lp Atlantic 4234/
promo/silkscreened logo/rear insert $4

TAYLOR, GARY
Tease Me (3 vers.) Virgin 2372/promo/ps/'88 ..... $4

TAYLOR, JAMES
(I've Got to) Stop Thinkin' 'Bout That
Columbia 4338/promo/ps/'91 .... $5
Copperline Columbia 4183/promo/ps/'91 .... $5
Everybody Loves to Cha Cha Cha
Columbia 4499/promo/ps/'92 .... $5
Like Everyone She Knows edit & lp
Columbia 4746/promo/ps/'92 .... $5
Never Die Young Columbia 2906/promo/ps/'88 ... $6

TAYLOR, JAMES (JT)
Sister Rosa (3 vers.) MCA 18011/promo/'89 ...... $5

TAYLOR, JOBETH
If This Isn't Love Interscope 3859/promo/
logo on white/ps/'91 .... $4

TAYLOR, JOHNNY
Crazy Over You Malaco 2178/promo/'92 .... $5

TAYLOR, LISA
Secrets of the Heart Giant 5099/promo/'92 .... $4

TDC
Keep Groovin (6 versions)
Mercury 347/promo/silkscreened/'90 .... $5

TEARS FOR FEARS
Advice For the Young At Heart 1990 vers. & lp
Fontana 206/promo/silkscreened
logo on black/'90 .... $7
Advice For the Young At Heart/Johnny Panic
../Music For Tables
Fontana 875 145/stock/ps/'90 .... $6
Break It Down Again edit/lp
Mercury 953/promo/ps/'93 .... $5
Goodnight Song radio/lp
Mercury 1032/promo/ps $4
Laid So Low Fontana 639/promo/
gatefold hardcover ps/'92 .... $5
Laid So Low + 2 Fontana 866 585/stock/ps $6
Sowing the Seeds of Love 7" version
Fontana 118/promo/ps/
silkscreened red/'89 .... $6
Sowing the Seeds of Love full version &
u.s. radio edit Fontana 119/promo/
ps/silkscreened green/'89 .... $7
Sowing the Seeds of Love/Tears Roll Down/
Shout u.s. remix Fontana 874 711/
stock/ps/silkscreened/'89 .... $6
Woman in Chains lp & instrumental/Always in
the Past/My Life in the Suicide Ranks
Fontana 876 249/promo/
silkscreened logo on white $7
Woman in Chains lp & instrumental/Always in
the Past/My Life in the Suicide Ranks
Fontana 876 249/stock/ps/'89 .... $6
Woman in Chains lp & other Fontana 163/
promo/silkscreened logo/'89 .... $7

TECHNOTRONIC
Get Up! (Before the Night is Over) 4 versions
SBK 19704/stock/ps/'90 .... $6
Get Up! (Before the Night is Over) 4 versions
SBK 05327/promo/ps/'90 .... $6
Pump Up the Jam (4 versions)
SBK 05317/promo/ps/'89 .... $8
Pump Up the Jam (4 versions)
SBK 19701/stock/ps/'89 .... $8
This Beat is Technotronic 4 versions
SBK 05341/promo/ps/
custom sticker/'90 .... $6

TEENAGE FANCLUB
Star Sign edit & lp DGC 4333/promo/ps/'91 .... $5
The Concept status quo edit/denim edit/lp
DGC 4370/promo/
gatefold hardcover ps/'91 .... $8
What You Do to Me DGC 4420/promo/
silkscreened/gatefold hardcover ps $5

What You Do to Me satan versions & lp/ Like a Virgin/Maharishi Dug the Scene/Life's a Gas *DGC 4417/promo/ silkscreened/custom sticker* $10

TEENAGE MUTANT NINJA TURTLES

Count on Us *MCA 1037/promo/rear insert/'90* $4

TEKNOE

(I Wanna) Be Like Mike 3 versions *A&M 75021 7318/promo/ps/'91* $5

TELEVISION

Call Mr. Lee *Capitol 79452/promo/ silksreened/ps* $5
In World *Capitol 79557/promo/ silkscreened/ps/'92* $5

TEMPLE OF THE DOG

Hunger Strike *A&M 75021 7538/promo/ silkscreened/ps/'91* $6
Say Hello 2 Heaven edit & lp *A&M 75021 7230/ promo/silkscreened on green/ps/'91* $6

TEMPO, NINO

Darn That Dream *Atlantic 3979/promo/ rear insert/'90* $4

TEMPTATIONS, THE

Get Ready 1990 (4 versions) *MCA 1050/promo/rear insert/'90* $5
My Girl/Theme From My Girl *Epic 74108/promo/ps/'91* $5
Shake Your Paw *GRP 9953/promo/ps/ silkscreened "Garfield"/'90* $5
The Jones 4 vers. *Motown 1628/promo/ps/'91* $5
The Jones 5 vers. *Motown 1016/promo/'91* $5

TEN INCH MEN

Crazy Daydream *Victory 912/promo/ silkscreened/ps/'93* $4

10,000 MANIACS

Because the Night unplugged *Elektra 8846/promo/ps/'93* $5
Candy Everybody Wants *Elektra 8690/promo/logo on green* $4
Candy Everybody Wants single remix *Elektra 8702/promo/logo on purple/ps/'92* $6
Eat For Two *Elektra 8103/promo/'89* $5
Few and Far Between *Elektra 8787/promo/silkscreened/'92* $5
Few and Far Between/Candy Everybody Wants/ To Sir With Love/Let the Mystery Be *Elektra 66296/stock/ps/'93* $6
Like the Weather *Elektra 2226/promo/'87* $6
MTV Unplugged full length *Elektra 615932/ ltd edition package (hand-printed paper envelope cover* $20
My Mother the War *Elektra 8259/promo/ rear insert/silkscreened orange/'90* $5
Poison in the Well *Elektra 8167/promo/ silkscreened/ps/'89* $6
These Are Days *Elektra 8641/promo/ silkscreened/ps/'92* $6
These Are Days/Trouble Me/Like the Weather/ What's the Matter Here *Elektra 8655/promo/ps/'92* $12
Trouble Me *Elektra 8077/promo/ps/'89* $8
Trouble Me/The Lions Share *Elektra 69298/ps/3"/stock/'89* $8
What's the Matter Here lp/edit *Elektra 8011/promo/ps/'88* $8
What's the Matter Here/Cherry Tre *Elektra 69388/ps/3"/stock/'88* $10
You Happy Puppet *Elektra 8124/promo/'89* $5
You Happy Puppet/Gun Shy (acoustic)/ Wildwood Flower/Hello In There *Elektra 66669/stock/ps/'89* $7

TEN TRAY

I Convey! louie louie remix & orig. mix *Smash 629/promo/ps/logo on yellow* $4

TEN YEARS AFTER

Highway of Love edit & lp *Chrysalis 23447/ promo/rear insert/'89* $4
Lets Shake It Up lp & edit *Chrysalis 23413/ promo/gatefold hardcover ps/'89* $6

TERMINATOR X

Juvenile Delinquent 3 versions *Columbia 73894/promo/ps/'91* $4
Homey Don't Play Dat vocal & instr. *Columbia 73759/promo/ silkscreened/ps/'91* $5

TERRELL

Shoutin' Ground *Giant 4404/promo/rear insert/'90*$4

TERRI & MONICA

Uh Huh vibe 1/vibe 2 *Epic 77110/promo/ps/ silkscreened pic/'93* $5

TERRY, TONY

Everlasting Love edit/lp/easy listening *Epic 74119/promo/ps/'91* $4
Forever Yours (2 versions) *Epic 1136/promo/rear insert/'87* $5
Head Over Heels (3 versions) *Epic 73619/promo/ps/'90* $5

TESH, JOHN

A Thousand Summers live, radio remix & lp edit *Private Music/promo/ps/'88* $6
That Ole Demon Meanness edit, lp & rubble mix *Private Music/promo/ps/'88* $6
You Are Here edit, lp, extended mix (8:06) *Private Music/promo/ps/'88* $6

You Break It *Cypress 17886/promo/ silkscreened pic/'89* $6

TESLA

Call It What You Want *Geffen 4351/promo/ custom sticker/'91* $5
Call It What You Want lp & edit *Geffen 4348/promo/ gatefold hardcover ps/'91* $5
Heavens Trail *Geffen 3406/promo/ps/'89* $6
Love Song CHR edit & Rock edit *Geffen 3648/promo/'89* $6
Paradise (3 vers.) *Geffen 4211/promo/ps/'91* $6
Psychotic Supper 13 tracks *Geffen 24424/ stock/promo silkscreened/'91* $10
Signs (clean versions) *Geffen 4178/promo/ps/'90* $5
Song & Emotion fade/lp/edit/rockline versions *Geffen 4425/promo/ps/'92* $6
Stir It Up 3 versions *Geffen 4450/promo/ silkscreened/ps/'92* $5
The Way It Is (edit) *Geffen 3886/promo/ silkscreened/ps/'90* $4
What You Give edit & lp *Geffen 4380/promo/ gatefold hardcover ps/'91* $5

TESTAMENT

Electric Crown edit & lp/Signs of Chaos *Atlantic 4553/promo/ silkscreened/ps/'92* $6
Greenhouse Effect (live)/The Ballad *Attlantic 3286/promo/rear insert/ silkscreened logo/'89* $5
Return to Serenity 2 vers. *Atlantic 4726/promo* $4

TEXAS

Everyday Now guitar, lp & edit *Mercury 139/promo/silkscreened logo on white/'89* $4
I Don't Want a Lover edit & lp *Mercury 60/promo/ps/'89* $5
In My Heart lp & guitar versions *Mercury 549/promo/gatefold hardcover ps/logo on white/'91* $5
In My Heart/You Gave Me Love/Livin' For the City/I Don't Want a Lover (last 2 live) *Mercury 548/promo/gatefold hardcover ps/logo on white/'91* $8
Why Believe in You aor & lp *Mercury 632/ promo/logo on white/ hardcover gatefold ps/'91* $4
Why Believe in You/Is What I Do Wrong/ Hold Me Lord *Mercury 607/promo/ gatefold hardcover ps/logo on red/'91* $5
Why Believe in You/Is What I Do Wrong/ Hold Me Lord/Livin' For the City (live) *Mercury 866 165/stock/ps/'91* $5

TEXAS TORNADOS

A Man Can Cry (single versions) *Reprise 4527/promo/'90/ DOUG SAHM, more* $6
Did I Tell You/Hey Baby *Reprise 5246/promo* $6
Is Anybody Goin' to San Antone (remix) *Reprise 5029/promo/'91* $6
La Mucura *Reprise 5055/promo/'91* $5
Tus Mentiras *WB 5707/promo/'92* $6
Who Were You Thinkin' Of *Reprise 4309/ promo/'90/DOUG SAHM, more* $6

THAT PETROL EMOTION

Groove Check 7" edit/12" *Virgin 2469/promo/'88* $6
Hey Venus *Virgin 3211/promo/silkscreened* $5
Sensitize *Virgin 3316/promo/silkscreened/'90* $5

THE, THE

Dogs of Lust 3 versions *Epic 4836/promo/silkscreened/ps/'92* $7
Interview & Live Music *Epic 1867/promo/ps* $25
Jealous of Youth 7" & 12"/Beyond Love *Epic 49K 73151/stock/ps/'90* $6
Live in New York 7 tracks live *Epic 002012/promo/ps* $20
Love is Stronger Than ../Infected (live 7/90) *Epic 5108/promo/logo on brown/ps* $8
Slow Emotion Replay + 5 live *Epic 5218/ promo/ps/silkscreened/'93* $10
The The Vs the World (11 tracks including unrel. & extended versions) *Epic 1958/ promo/silkscreened logo/ps/'89* $25

THELONIOUS MONSTER

Blood is Thicker Than Water 2 versions *Capitol 79492/promo/ps/logo on red* $5
Body and Soul? *Capitol 79590/promo/ silkscreened/custom sticker/'92* $4

THERAPY?

Nausea clean versions/Teethgrinder remix *A&M 31458 8086/promo/ps/ silkscreened/'92* $5
Perversonality/Total Random Man/ Neck Freak new versions/Bloody Blue *A&M 31458 8124/promo/gatefold hardcover ps/silkscreened/'93* $6

THEY EAT THEIR OWN

Like a Drug clean & not so clean *Relativity 0115/ promo/silkscreened/ps/'90* $4

THEY MIGHT BE GIANTS

Birdhouse in Your Soul *Elektra 8136/promo/ silkscreened logo/'90* $6
Hey, Mr. DJ *Restless 009/promo/'91* $5
I Palindrome I *Elektra 8573/promo/'92* $4
I Palindrome I/Cabbagetown/Siftin'/Larger Than Life *Elektra 66425/stock/ gatefold hardcover ps/'92* $5

Istanbul (Not Constantinople) *Elektra 8182/ promo/silkscreened/rear insert/'90* $4
Istanbul (Not Constantinople) lp & brownsville mix/J.K Polk/Stormy Pinkness/Ant *Elektra 66631/stock/ps/'90* $5
Purple Toupee *Bar None 190/promo/ps/'89* $6
The Guitar 3versions/Welcome to the Jungle/ I Blame You *Elektra 66394/stock/ gatefold hardcover ps/'92* $5
The Guitar (The Lion Sleeps Tonight) *Elektra 8606/promo/'92* $4
The Statue Got Me High *Elektra 8523/promo/ silkscreened/ps/'92* $4
Theyll Need a Crane/Santas Beard/Purple Toupee + 2 *Restless 138/promo/ custom sticker/'88* $8
Twisting *Elektra 8166/promo/silkscreened/ rear insert/'90* $4

THIN LIZZY
Dedication *Mercury 409/promo/logo on black silkscreened/'91* $6

THINK OUT LOUD
After All This Time *A&M 17534/promo/ps* $4

THINK TREE
Abbreviated *Caroline #2/promo/silkscreened* $4
Rattlesnake *Caroline #3/promo/ silkscreened/rear insert/'92* $4

3RD AVENUE
I've Gotta Have It 5 versions *Solar 74548/promo/ps/'92* $4

3RD BASS
Brooklyn Queens (4 versions) *Def Jam 73328/promo/ps/'90* $6
Gladiator 4 versions/Word to the Third *Columbia 44K 74245/stock/ps/'92* $5
Gladiator main mix/easy mo bee remix/main mix instrumental *Columbia 74235/promo/ logo on brown/ps/'92* $6
Pop Goes the Weasel 3 versions *Def Jam 73728/promo/ps/'91* $6
The Cactus Album sampler (6 songs) *Def Jam 1919/promo/ps/'89* $15
The Gas Face radio mix & instrumental/ Wordz of Wizdom radio mix *Def Jam 73046/ps/'89* $6

3RD EYE & THE GROUP HOME
Ease Up main/instrumental/clean radio *Uptown 2683/promo/rear insert/'93* $5

THIRD WORLD
Committed edit & lp *Mercury 706/ promo/logo on green/ps/'92* $5
Forbidden Love (4 versions) *Mercury 54/ promo/silkscreened/ps/'89* $5
It's the Same Old Song radio, club & lp version *Mercury 97/promo/groovin' silkscreened/'89* $5
Love Will Always Be There (3 versions) *Mercury 157/promo/silkscreened* $5
Mi Legal 3 versions *Mercury 830/promo/ logo on green/'93* $5

38 SPECIAL
Comin' Down Tonight remix & lp *A&M 17759/ promo/ps/silkscreened/'89* $4
Like No Other Night *A&M 17378/promo/ tri fold hardcover ps/'86* $6
Live From Electric Ladyland *Album Network/ promo/live from 8/12/91/'91* $25
Rock & Roll Strategy *A&M 17623/promo/ ps/silkscreened/'88* $5
Second Chance (edit) *A&M 17671/promo/ silkscreened graphics/'88* $4
Signs of Love *Charisma 070/promo/ rear insert/'91* $4
The Sound of Your Voice edit *Charisma 050/promo/'91* $4
The Sound of Your Voice edit & lp *Charisma 046/promo/ gatefold hardcover w/booklet/'91* $5
Wild Eyed Southern Boys/In the Studio *show #156/promo/aired 6/17/91* $20
You Definitely Got.. *Charisma 083/promo/'91* $4

THIS MORTAL COIL

THIS MORTAL COIL
1 CD sampler from 4 CD box set (Song to the Siren/You & Your Sister/Come Here My Love + 9) *4AD 5876/promo/ silkscreened/gatefold hardcover ps* $20

THIS PICTURE
Breathe Deeply Now/The Offering/Death's Sweet Religion (acoustic)/I Can't Help Myself *RCA 62177/promo/ps* $5
Naked Rain edit & remix/With You I Can Never Win/Stronger Than Life Itself (live) *RCA 62052/promo/ps/'91* $5

Naked Rain edit & remix/With You I Can Never Win/Stronger Than Life Itself (live) *RCA 62052/stock/ps/'91* $5
Step Up/Hey Mister Caterpillar/The Great Tree *RCA 62261/promo/ps/logo on purple/'92* .. $5

THOMAS, B.J.
Dont Leave Love (Out There all Alone) (edit) *Reprise 3668/promo/'89* $4
Midnight Minute *Reprise 3883/promo/'89* $4

THOMAS, CHRIS
Wanna Die With a Smile on My Face *Sire 4029/promo/'90* $4

THOMAS, EARL
I Won't Be Around *Bizarre Straight 90112/ promo/logo silkscreened/rear insert* $4

THOMAS, LILLO
Out There Doing Wrong 4 versions *THG Music 865/promo/rear insert* $5

THOMAS, MICKEY
Sing guitar intro & single version *Columbia 1452/promo/'89* $4

THOMPSON TWINS
Bombers in the Sky (4 versions) *WB 3901/promo/custom sticker/'89* $6
Come Inside 5 versions/The Saint 2 versions *WB 40071/stock/gatefold hardcover ps/'91* $5
Come Inside (single edit) *WB 4941/promo/ silkscreened/ps/'91* $5
Get That Love *Arista 9577/promo/ps/'87* $10
Groove On 3 versions *WB 5207/promo/'91* $6
Long Goodbye 7" & extended *Arista 9600/promo/ps/'87* $12
Play With Me (Jane) 8 versions *WB 40607/stock/'92* $5
Queer 12 tracks *WB 26631/promo only silkscreened/ps/'91* $15
Sugar Daddy (4 vers.) *WB 3677/promo/'89* $6
Sugar Daddy 4 versions/Monkey Man *WB 21320/stock/ps/'89* $5

THOMPSON, JEFF
The Greatest Man I Never Knew *Arista 2201/ promo/silkscreened pic/rear insert* $5

THOMPSON, MICHAEL
Can't Miss *Geffen 3473/promo/ps/'89* $4
Give Love a Chance (edit) *Geffen 3601/promo/'89* $4
How Long 10 tracks *Geffen 24225/promo/ silkscreened logo/rear insert/'89* $8

THOMPSON, RICHARD
I Feel So Good *Capitol 79730/promo/ logo on white/rear insert/'91* $5
I Feel So Good/Harry's Theme/Backlash Love Affair *Capitol 15728/stock/ps/'91* $6
Read About Love *Capitol 79885/promo/ silkscreened/cust.sticker/rear insert* $5
Turning Of Tide *Capitol 79388/promo/ps/'88* $7
Watching Dark sampler (A Man in Need/Keep Your Distance/Crash the Party/From Galway../For Shame../Beat the Retreat + 1) *Hannibal 5303/promo/ps/'93* $15

THOROGOOD, GEORGE
Bad to the Bone new edit new mix/new lp mix *EMI 04880/promo/silkscreened/ps* $6
Bone a Fide Badness sampler (If You Don't Start Drinkin'/Bad to the Bone/I Drink Alone/Willie & Hand Jive/Who Do You Love + 3) *EMI 4715/promo/ ps/silkscreened/'91* $18
Boogie People *Capitol 4780/promo/ silkscreened/ps/'91* $6
Hello Little Girl *EMI 04754/promo/ silkscreened logo on purple/ps/'91* $6
If You Don't Start Drinking... *EMI 4697/promo/ silkscreened/rear insert/'91* $6
Oklahoma Sweetheart/Six Days on the Road *EMI 4736/promo/ps/silkscreened/'90* $8
Treat Her Right *EMI 04030/promo/ps/'88* $6
You Talk Too Much *EMI 79235/promo/ps* $6

THOUSAND YARD STARE
Buttermouth 3 versions/Twice Times/ Weatherwatching-Another and On *Polydor 799/promo/silkscreened/ps* $5
Comeuppance 2 versions/Moccapune e.p. uk instr.remix/Wish a Perfect/ Standoffish *Polydor 782/promo/ logo on pink/ps/'92* $5
0-0 a.e.t. (No Score After Extra Time)/ Village End/Wonderment *Polydor 850/promo/logo on cream/ps* $5

THRASHING DOVES
Angel Visit *A&M 17704/promo/ps/'89* $4

THREADGILL, HENRY
Try Some Ammonia/Better Wrapped (both edit & lp versions) *Axiom 6763/promo/ logo on black/rear insert/ custom sticker/'93* $5

3D
You Ain't All That 6 versions/L'Amour 4 vers. *Capitol 79831/promo/silkscreened/ps* $4

311
Do You Right 2 vers. *Capricorn 5975/promo/ ps/custom sticker/'93* $4
My Stoney Baby *Capricorn 6334/promo/ rear insert/'93* $4
Visit *Capricorn 6141/promo/ps/'93* $4

360'S
Free/It *Link 100/promo/silkscreened/ps/'90* $4
Step Outside/G.L.O.B./1000 Wishes *Link 106/promo/silkscreened/rear insert* $5

THRILL KILL KULT
Sex on Wheelz 3 versions *Interscope 4622/promo/ps/'92* $7

THROBS, THE
Come Down Sister *DGC 4196/promo/ps/'91* $5
Sweet Addiction *DGC 4228/promo/'91* $4
Language of Thieves & Vagabonds 11 tracks *DGC 24316/promo silkscreened/ ps/custom sticker/'91* $12

THROWING MUSES
Counting Backwards/Same Sun/Amazing Grace *Sire 21833/stock/gatefold hardcover ps/'91* $6
Dio/Summer St./Manic Depression/Handsome Woman/Jak/City of the Dead/Firepile remix *Sire 5832/promo/ silkscreened/custom sticker/'93* $8
Dizzy remix & too many notes mix *Sire 3618/promo/'89* $5
Firepile *Sire 5653/promo/silkscreened/'92* $5
Not Too Soon/Cry Baby ../Him Dancing (remix)/ Dizzy (remix) *Sire 40135/stock/ gatefold hardcover ps/'91* $6
Red Heaven 13 tracks *Sire 5650/promo/'92* $12
The Real Ramona (12 tracks) *Sire 26489/ promo/silkscreened grapefruit/ps* $15

THUNDER
Backstreet Symphony full lp *Capitol 93614/ with original cover (call-girl, a drunk, etc)/stock/ps/'90* $15
Dirty Love 2 vers. *Geffen 4222/promo/ps/'90* $4
Does It Feel Like Love edit & lp *Geffen 4454/ promo/silkscreened pic/ps/'92* $4
Love Walked In edit & lp *Geffen 4323/promo/ logo on black&blue/custom sticker/'91* $4
Until My Dying Day edit & lp *Geffen 4292/ promo/ps/silkscreened/'91* $4

THUNDER, SHELLY
Break Up *Mango 7830/promo/silkscreened/'89* ... $4

TIFFANY
All This Time *MCA 17597/promo/ps/'89* $6
Feelings of Forever *MCA 17534/promo/ps/'88* ... $6
Here in My Heart lp & edit *MCA 1191/promo/ logo on green/rear insert/'90* $5
Hold An Old Friend's Hand *MCA 17786/ promo/custom sticker/'88* $6
I Always Thought Id See You Again *MCA 18402/promo/rear insert/'90* $5
Its the Lover *MCA 17977/promo/custom sticker/'88* $6
New Inside (4 versions) *MCA 1106/promo/ rear insert/'90* $6
New Inside (4 versions) *MCA 1136/promo/ silkscreened/rear insert/'90* $8
New Inside (4 versions) *MCA 53952/ stock/gatefold hardcover ps/'90* $5
Radio Romance *MCA 17794/promo/ custom sticker/'88* $6

TIGER
Who Planned It 3 versions/Windscreen 2 vers. *Chaos 42K 74944/stock/ps/'93* $4

TIKARAM, TANITA
Cathedral Song *Reprise 3418/promo/ silkscreened/'88* $5
Good Tradition *Reprise 3416/promo/ silkscreened logo/'89* $4
Only the Ones We.. *Reprise 4686/promo/'91* $4
Twist in My Sobriety edit & lp *Reprise 3417/ promo/silkscreened/'88* $6
We Almost Got It Together *Reprise 3888/promo/'90* $4

TIL TUESDAY
(Believed You Were) Lucky *Epic 1298/promo/ps/'88* $6
Rip in Heaven *Epic 1501/promo/yellow silkscreened w/logo/'88* $6

TILLIS, MEL
City Lights *Radio 001/promo* $4

TILLIS, PAM
Blue Rose Is *Arista 2408/promo/ logo on blue/ps/'92* $4
CD sampler (Don't Tell Me What to Do/Put Yourself In My Place/Blue Rose Is/ Maybe It Was Memphis/interview) *Arista 2130/promo/ps/'90* $12
Do You Know Where Your Man Is *Arista 2606/promo/ps/logo on pink* $4
One of Those Things *Arista 2203/promo/ silkscreened logo on red/rear insert* $4

TIMBUK 3
Easy *IRS 17549/promo/ silkscreened pic/rear insert* $4
National Holiday *IRS 014/promo/silkscreened/ps/'89* $4
Sunshine *IRS 67070/promo/ silkscreened/rear insert/'91* $4

TIME GALLERY
Taking the Best faded & new lp versions *Atlantic 2652/promo/rear insert/'89* $4

TIME, THE
Chocolate edit/remix edit/lp *Paisley Park 4500/promo/ custom sticker/rear insert/'90* $6

Chocolate (5 versions)/My Drawers
Paisley Park 21588/stock/ps/ custom sticker/'90 .... $4
Jerk Out edit & lp *Paisley Park 4347/promo/ rear insert/'90* $4
Jerk Out (5 versions)
Paisley Park 21701/stock/ps/'90 .... $5
Pandemonium (15 tracks) *Paisley Park 27490/ promo/silkscreened/gatefold hardcover/ with book & clock (!)/'90* $20
Shake! *WB 4587/promo/ prod & written by PRINCE/'90* $6
Shake! (4 versions) *Paisley Park 4549/promo/ prod by PRINCE/'90* $8
Words & Music Reunion... (songs & interview)
PaisleyPark 4377/promo/rear insert $15

TIMELORDS, THE
Doctorin' the Tardis 3 versions
TVT 4024/stock/3"/ps/'88 .... $10

TIMES 3
Typical Relationship 4 versions
Solar 4578/promo/logo on pink/ps $5

TIMES TWO
Cecilia (3 versions) *Reprise 3131/promo/ silkscreened/rear insert/'88* $4
Strange But True edit/12" remix
Reprise 2940/promo/ps/'88 .... $4

TITANIC LOVE AFFAIR
Planet Strange *Charisma 055/promo/'91* $4

TITIYO
My Body Says Yes radio & club mix
Arista 2224/promo/silkscreened/ps $4

TKA
Crash (3 versions) *WB 4511/promo/ rear insert/custom sticker/'90* $5
I Won't Give Up on You (4 versions)
WB 4369/promo/rear insert/'90 .... $5
You Are the One (3 versions)
WB 3642/promo/'89 .... $5

TLC
Ain't 2 Proud 2 Beg single/lp/instrumental
LaFace 4008/promo/logo on green/ rear insert/'91 .... $7
Ain't 2 Proud 2 Beg 5 versions *LaFace 4009/ promo/silkscreened/ps/'91* $7
Baby Baby Baby remix edit/remix rap/remix instrumental *LaFace 4032/promo/ ps/logo on pink/'92* $5
Baby Baby Baby edit/lp/instrumental
Laface 4028/promo/'92 .... $5
Get It Up 4 versions *Epic 77059/promo/ silkscreened/rear insert/'93* $5
Hat 2 Da Back edit/extendedremix/instrum.
LaFace 24046/stock/ps/'93 .... $5
Hat 2 Da Back edit/lp/instrumental
LaFace 4043/promo/ps/logo on blue $5
What About Your Friends 5 versions
LaFace 4033/promo/silkscreened/ps $6

TNT
Intuition edit & lp *Mercury 72/promo/ps/'89* $4
Tonight I'm Falling *Mercury 37/promo/ps/'89* $4

TOAD THE WET SPROCKET
All I Want *Columbia 4359/promo/ps/'92* $6
All I Want/All She Said
Columbia 38K 74355/stock/ps/'92 .... $6
Come Back Down *Columbia 1960/promo/ silkscreened/ps/'90* $7
Five Live ep (Jam/One Little Girl/Scenes From a Vinyl Recliner/Come Back Down/ Hold Her Down)
Columbia 4509/promo/ps/'92 .... $12
Hold Her Down *Columbia 4262/promo/ps/'91* $6
I Will Not Take These Things For Granted
2 vers. *Columbia 4929/promo/ps/'93* $5
Is It For Me *Columbia 4145/promo/ps/'91* $6
Jam (too Long, Too Late)/Liars Everywhere (acoustic)/Hold Her Down
Columbia 2059/promo/ps/'90 .... $8
Walk on the Ocean single & lp
Columbia 4683/promo/ps/'92 .... $6

TOBIN, KAREN
Carolina Smokey Moon *Atlantic 4003/promo/ silkscreened/ps/'91* $4

TODAY
I Got the Feeling (6 versions)
Motown 1102/promo/'90 .... $5

TOM TOM CLUB
Call of the Wild (4 versions)
Sire 3662/promo/'89 .... $6
Suboceana 7" remix/7" dance edit/dream master remix *Sire 3494/promo/'89* $5
Sunshine and Ecstasy edit & radio remix
Reprise 5438/promo/logo on gold/'92 .... $4
Sunshine and Ecstasy 7 versions *Sire 40444/ stock/gatefold hardcover ps/'92* $5
You Sexy Thing
Sire 5672/promo/silkscreened/'92 .... $4
You Sexy Thing 8 vers. *Sire 40600/stock/'92* $5

TOMLINSON, MICHAEL
Gettin' Gone *Cypress 17815/promo/ silkscreened lettering/'89* $4

TONE DEF
Bushwack 2 versions/So Funky
A Lasting Impression 53401/ promo/ps/custom sticker/'92 .... $5

TONE LOC
All Through the Night 4 versions/Pimp Without a Caddy 2 versions *Delicious Vinyl 422 866 105/stock/ps* $5
All Through the Night radio/bnh remix *Delicious Vinyl 6684/promo/ rear insert/'91* $4
Cool Hand Loc 3 versions *Hollywood 10178/ promo/silkscreened/'92* $5
Funky Cold Medina (7" version) *Delicious Vinyl 104/promo/'89* $7
Hit the Coast edit & dj *Delicious Vinyl 5199/promo* $4
I Got It Goin' On remix *Delicious 106/promo* $5
Posse Love 4 versions *A&M 31458 8177/ promo/silkscreened pic/'93* $5
Wild Thing *Delicious 102/promo/'88* $6

TONIO K
Stay *A&M 17548/promo/ gatefold hardcover ps/'88* $5

TONY! TONI! TONE!
Coolin' at Christmas with 3T (7 track ep) *Wing 359/promo/silkscreened pic/ps* $8
Feels Good (4 versions) *Wing 267/promo/ silkscreened/die cut fold out hardcover ps/'90* $8
For the Love Of You (4 versions) *Wing 96/ promo/silkscreened group pic/'89* $8
House Party II (I Don't Know What You Come to Do) 8 versions *MCA 1563/promo/ps/'91* $6
If I Had No Loot *Wing 926/promo/silkscreen/ trifold hardcover/'93* $5
It Never Rains (4 versions) *Wing 345/promo/silkscreened/ps/'90* $7
It Never Rains (single versions) *Wing 337/promo/silkscreened/ps/'90* $5
The Blues (4 versions) *Wing 204/promo/silkscreened/'90* $6
Whatever You Want edit & lp *Wing 396/ promo/silkscreened/rear insert/'91* $6

TOO MUCH JOY
Besides ep (Nothing on My Mind edit/Soft Core/Drum Machine/Take a Lot of Drugs/ King of Beers acoustic) *WB 5045/promo/rear insert/'91* $8
Crush Story *Giant 4650/promo/rear insert* $4
Donna Everywhere *Giant 5640/promo/rear insert/'92* $4
In Perpetuity *Giant 6021/promo/'92* $4
Long Haired Guys From England clean & lp *Giant 4914/promo/'91* $5
Starry Eyes/No One Can Be That Stupid *Giant 5868/promo/ps/'92* $6
Susquehanna Hat Company rock & real vers. *Giant 4631/promo/ silkscreened/rear insert/'91* $5
That's a Lie (remix)/Seasons in the Sun/If I Was a Mekon *Giant 4352/promo/ silkscreened/rear insert/'90* $8

TOO SHORT
I Want to Be Free 6 versions *Jive 42068/ promo/custom sticker/rear insert/'92* $7
In the Trunk 5 versions *Jive 42072/promo/ custom sticker/'92* $7
Short But Funky (4 vers.) *Jive 1429/promo/ ps/custom sticker/'91* $7
The Ghetto (5 versions) *Jive 1397/promo/rear insert/'90* $7

TOOKES, DARRYL
What About Me?/African Eyes/Rio/Mama *SBK 05320/promo/gatefold hardcover ps/'89* $5

TOOL
Sober *Zoo 17121/promo/silkscreened/ rear insert/'93* $4
Sweat/Hush/Part of Me/Cold and Ugly (live)/ Jerk Off (live)/Opiate *Zoo 72445-11027/stock/ps/ silkscreened/'92* $5

TOP
Easy (Livin' on Cloud Nine) remixed & rerecord/ No. 1 Dominator live *Island 6709/ promo/logo on blue/rear insert/'92* $4

TOP CHOICE CLIQUE
I Think to Myself lp & instrumental *A&M 31458 8136/promo/ps/ silkscreened/'93* $4

TORA TORA
Amnesia/Shattered/Dead Man's Hand/ Faith Healer *A&M 75021 7380/ promo/silkscreened/ps/'92* $4
Dead Man's Hand *A&M 31458 8024/ promo/silkscreened/ps/'92* $4
Faith Healer remix *A&M 75021 7394/ promo/silkscreened/ps/'92* $4
Phantom Rider remix & lp *A&M 17983/promo/silkscreened/'89* $4
Walkin' Shoes *A&M 17756/promo/ps/silkscreened* $4
Wild America ep (Amnesia/Shattered/ Dead Man's Hand/Faith Healer) *A&M 75021 7380/promo/ silkscreened/ps/'92* $5

TORN, DAVID
Voodoo Chile edit & lp *Windham Hill 90-12/promo/ps/'90* $4

TOTAL ECLIPSE
Fire in the Rain radio & lp *Tabu 28965 1816/ promo/silkscreened/ps/'92* $4

Time's a Changin' edit & lp *Tabu 31458 8063/ promo/silkscreened/'92* $4

TOTAL LOOK & THE STYLE

Room 252 4 versions *Columbia 74341/promo/ps/'92* $4

TOTO

Can You Hear What I'm Saying *Columbia 73488/promo/ps/'90* $4

Stay Away *Columbia 1055/promo/'88* $4

TOUPS, WAYNE

Fish Out of Water *Mercury 394/promo/ps/'91* $4

TOWER OF POWER

Mr Toad's Wild Ride/Miss Trouble/You Can't Fall Up/Someone New *Epic 4025/ promo/ps/silkscreened/'91* $8

TOWNER, RALPH & PETER ERSKINE

Magic Pouch/Magnolia Island/Waltz For Debby/ The Sign *ECM TOWN 2/promo/ silkscreened/gatefold hardcover ps* $5

TOWNSELL, LIDELL

Nu Nu 6 vers. *Mercury 645/promo/silkscr/'92* $4

TOWNSELL, LIDELL & M.T.F.

Get With U radio/nu orig./lp 7" edit *Mercury 716/promo/ps/'92* $4

TOWNSHEND, PETE

A Friend is a Friend edit & lp *Atlantic 2781/promo/ps/'89* $5

Don't Try to Make Me .. *Atlantic 5220/promo* $5

English Boy no dialogue/censored dialogue *Atlantic 5102/promo/ silkscreened/rear insert/'93* $5

Fire *Atlantic 2974/promo/ps/'89* $6

TOY MATINEE

Last Plane Out edit & lp *Reprise 4331/promo/rear insert/'90* $4

The Ballad of Jenny Ledge (3 versions) *Reprise 4589/promo/'90* $4

TOYS, THE/EDDIE RAMBEAU

A Lovers Concerto/Concrete and Clay *Collectables 8142/stock/'91* $4

TRACTORS CHRISTMAS

The Santa Claus Boogie/Swingin' Home For Christmas *Arista 2505/promo/ logo on red/ps/'92* $5

TRAFFIC

Traffic Report compilation *Island 2158/promo/ps/'87* $20

TRAGICALLY HIP, THE

At the Hundredth Meridian radio & lp *MCA 2616/promo/silkscreened/ die-cut multi-fold ps/'93* $4

Courage *MCA 2499/promo/multifold cover* $4

Three Pistols *MCA 1270/promo/ps/'91* $4

TRANSVISION VAMP

(I Just Wanna) B With U 6 versions *MCA 1586/promo/ps/'91* $5

(I Just Wanna) B With You lp & 12"/Trash City/Tell That Girl to Shut Up/Sex Kick/I Want Your Love (last 4 live) *MCA 54113/stock/gatefold hardcover ps/'91* $5

(I Just Wanna) Be With U (alt.single mix) *MCA 1673/promo/logo on grey/ps* $5

Baby Don't Care 7" & lp *MCA 17985/ promo/silkscreened pic/'89* $6

I Want Your Love *Uni 17801/promo/ custom sticker/'89* $5

I Want Your Love lp & dont want your money mix *Uni 18003/promo/'89* $5

If Looks Could Kill 4:11 & 6:40 *MCA 2030/promo/ps/'91* $6

Tell That Girl to Shut Up *Uni/promo/silkscreened pic/'88* $7

TRASH CAN SINATRAS

Bloodrush *Go Discs 895/promo/ silkscreened/ps/'93* $5

Obscurity Knocks edit & lp *Go London 392/ promo/silkscreened/ps/'91* $6

TRAVELING WILBURYS

End of the Line *WB 3364/promo* $6

End of the Line/Congratulations *Wilbury 27637/stock/3"/3x6 ps/'88* $10

Handle With Care *WB 3258/promo/ silkscreened/rear insert/'88* $10

Inside Out *Wilbury 4652/promo/'90* $6

Last Night *WB 3337/promo/'88* $8

She's My Baby *WB 4518/promo/silkscreened/ rear insert/'90* $6

Vol. 3 (11 tracks) *WB 26324/promo only silkscreened/ps/'90* $25

Wilbury Twist *WB 4642/promo/'90* $6

TRAVIS, RANDY

Better Class of Losers *WB 5185/promo/'91* $4

Cowboy Boogie single/extended *WB 6346/promo/'93* $5

Heroes and Friends (long edit) *WB 4598/promo/'90* $5

Honky Tonk Moon *WB 3167/promo/ps/'88* $5

Honky Tonk Moon/Young Guns (non lp) *WB 27833/3" CD stock w/ps* $5

How Do I Wrap My Heart Up For Christmas/ Santa Claus is Coming to Town *WB 4605/promo/'88* $5

I Told You So (remix) *WB 3072/promo/ps/'88* $5

I'd Surrender All *WB 5405/promo/'91* $5
It's Just a Matter of Time vocal & instrumental *WB 3660/promo/'89* $5
It's Just a Matter of Time (country remix) *WB 3712/promo/'89* $5
Look Heart, No Hands *WB 5762/promo/'92* $5
Straight Talk With (interview by RALPH EMERY) *WB 6363/promo/'93* $15
Too Gone too Long *WB 2904/promo/ps/'87* $5

TRAVIS, RANDY & GEORGE JONES

A Few Ole Country Boys *WB 4429/promo/rear insert/'90* $5

TREAT HER RIGHT

Junkyard *RCA 9000/promo/ps/'89* $4
Marie *RCA 9040/promo/ps/'89* $4
Picture of the Future *RCA 8928/promo/ps* $4

TRESVANT, RALPH

Do What I Gotta Do 7 versions *MCA 1444/promo/'91* $5
Money Can't Buy You Love edit without rap *Perspective 31458 8021/promo/logo on black/'92* $5
Money Can't Buy You Love edit/lp/instrum. *Perspective 28968 1714/promo/ps/logo on black/'92* $5
Money Can't Buy You Love 3 diggidy diamonds mixes *Perspective 31458 8044/promo/logo on green/'92* $5
Rated R 5 vers. *MCA 54148/stock/ps/'91* $5
Sensitivity (3 versions) *MCA 1097/promo/silkscreened green/'90* $5
Sensitivity (3 versions) *MCA 53933/stock/gatefold hardcover ps/'90* $5
Stone Cold Gentleman (3 versions) *MCA 1340/promo/'91* $5
Stone Cold Gentlemen edit with rap/edit without/lp *MCA 1310/promo/'90* $5
Yo, Baby, Yo 7 vers. *MCA 1561/promo/ps/'91* $6

TREY LEWD

Hoodlums Hoo Ride edit & lp *Reprise 5659/promo/'92* $5

TRIBE

Here at the Home *WB 5370/promo/custom sticker/'91* $4

TRIBE AFTER TRIBE

Ice Below/Childspeak/Sinnerman *Megaforce 961/promo/ps/'93* $4

TRILOBITES, THE

New Head *rooArt 212/promo/silkscreened/ps/'89* $6
Savage Mood Swing 12 tracks *rooArt 842 646/stock/promo stencil on disc/ps/'89* $12

TRILOGY

Good Time 3 versions *Atco 4695/promo/logo on blue/ps/'92* $4
Love Me Forever or Love Me Not 5 versions *Atco 3680/promo/ps/'90* $4

TRINERE

Games lp & house *Luke 3902/promo/rear insert/'91* $5
It's the Music 4:14/dance edit 4:35 *Luke 4215/promo/rear insert/'91* $5

TRIP

Chill Out Jack single & lp *MCA 1583/promo/"Fisher King" ps/'91* $4

TRIP SHAKESPEARE

Across the Universe 11 tracks *A&M 7502 15294/promo/silkscreened/ps/custom sticker/'90* $12
Bachelorette *A&M 75021 7283/promo/silkscreened/ps/'91* $5
Gone Gone Gone remix & lp *A&M 75021 8017/promo/silkscreened green/'90* $4
Pearle lp & remix *A&M 75021 8100/promo/silkscreened/'90* $5
Pearle/Gone Gone Gone (remix)/The Slacks *A&M 887 847/promo/gatefold ps/'90* $5
The Crane/Toolmaster of Brainerd/Reception/Applehead Man (last 3 live) *A&M 18024/promo/silkscreened* $8
Volt ep (Whats So Funny About Peace../Something in the Air/Ballad of El Goodo/Time of the Season + 2) *Black Hole 89248/stock/ps/'92* $5
Your Mouth lp & edit/Susannah *A&M 75021 7311/promo/ps* $5

TRIPLE M

Prisoner of Passion 3 versions *A&M 75021 7287/promo/ps/'91* $4

TRIPLETS, THE
Light a Candle ac mix/soft ac mix/chr mix/ spanglish *Mercury 576/promo/logo on brown&black/custom sticker/'91* $4
Sunrise single & lp *Mercury 460/ promo/silkscreened logo/ps/'91* $4
You Don't Have to Go Home Tonight *Mercury 390/promo/silkscreened/ps* $4

TRIPP, GREGG
I Don't Want to Live Without You 3 versions *Impact 1698/promo/rear insert/'91* $4

TRITT, TRAVIS
Can I Trust You With My Heart *WB 5857/promo/'92* $5
Country Club *WB 3511/promo/'89* $5
Here's a Quarter *WB 4816/promo/ silkscreened/rear insert*...........................$5
Nothing Short of Dying (single versions)/ Bible Belt *WB 5409/promo/'92* $5
Put Some Drive In Your Country remix & lp *WB 4446/promo/'90* $5
Straight Talk with Travis Tritt (interview by CHARLIE DANIELS) *WB 4726/promo/ps/'91* $15
The Whiskey Ain't Workin' *WB 5122/promo/ recycled foldout ps/'91* $5
Winter Wonderland/Santa Looked a Lot Like Daddy/Christmas Just Aint Christmas Without You *WB 5767/promo/'92* $5

TRITT, TRAVIS & FRIENDS
Lord Have Mercy on the Working Man edit & lp *WB 5660/promo/'92* $5

TRIUMPH
Child of the City edit *Victory 834/ promo/logo on purple/'92* $5

TRIXTER
Line of Fire *Mechanic 18244/promo/ silkscreened/ps/'90* $5
One in a Million radio edit/video edit *MCA 1098/promo/ps/silkscreened*............$5
Road of a Thousand Dreams *MCA 2309/promo/ps/'92* $4

TROCCOLI, KATHY
Can't Get You Out of My Heart ac mix & lp *Reunion 4422/promo/silkscreened/ gatefold hardcover ps/'92* $5
Everything Changes 6 versions *Reunion 4371/ promo/silkscreened/gatefold hardcover ps/'92* $6
Everything Changes lp & ac mix *Reunion 4381/ promo/gatefold hardcover ps/'91* $6
Pure Attraction 10 tracks *Reunion 24453/ promo/rear insert/custom sticker* $12
You've Got a Way *Reunion 4336/promo/ps/'91* ...$4
You've Got a Way lp & remix *Geffen 4410/ promo/gatefold hardcover ps/'92* $6

TROOP
Spread My Wings 5 versions *Atlantic 3132/promo/rear insert/'89* $6
Sweet November 2 vers. *Atlantic 4723/promo*.....$5
Whatever It Takes 15 tracks *Atlantic 82393/ promo/gatefold hardcover ps/insert* $12

TROOP/LEVERT
For the Love of Money-Living For the City 4 vers. *Giant 4936/promo/'91* $6

TROOP/LEVERT & QUEEN LATIFAH
For the Love of Money-Living For the City medley downtown/uptown/ext. *Giant 4822/promo/ps/'91* $6

TROUBLE
'Scuse Me *Def American 5792/promo/'92* $4
Manic Frustation 11 tracks *Def American 5599/promo/ps/'92* $12
Memory's Garden *Def American 5538/promo/ps/'92* $4
The Misery Shows (edit)/A Sinners Fame/ Psych. Reaction *Def American 4101/ promo/silkscreened logo/rear insert*..........$5

TROWER, ROBIN
Bridge of Sighs/In the Studio *dj radio show/ promo/hosted by Robin/cue sheet*..........$25
Turn the Volume Up *Atlantic 3172/promo/ silkscreened logo/rear insert/'90* $5

TRUTH BE KNOWN
War 3:59 & 5:40 *Sisapa 76707/ promo/rear insert/'90*.................................$4

TRUTH INC.
Can I Get With You Tonight *Interscope 4571/promo/ps/'92* $4

TRUTH, THE
Throwing It All Away *IRS 17776/promo/ custom sticker/'89* $4

TSOL
Hell on Earth *Enigma 271/promo/silkscreened/ custom sticker/'90* $5

TUCK & PATTI
Castles Made of Sand/Little Wing (edit) *Windham Hill 17934/promo/ps/'89* $4
Love Warriors/Castles Made of ../If Its Magic + 1 *Windham Hill 17818/promo/ps/'89* $4
Time After Time edit & lp/Up & At It *Windham Hill 17633/promo/ps/'88* $4

TUCKER, MAUREEN
Life in Exile After Abdication (9 songs) *50,000,000,000...Watts 007/ps/stock/JAD FAIR, LOU REED, more* $12

TUCKER, TANYA
It's a Little Too Late 2:37/3:37 *Liberty 79600/promo/logo on blue-green/rear insert/'92* $5
Walking Shoes *Capitol 79955/promo/silkscreened logo/'90* $5

TUNG TWISTA
Ratatattat/Back to School *Zoo 17092/promo/logo on black/rear insert/'92* $4

TURNER, TINA
Foreign Affair (full length) *Capitol 93129/silkscreened/passport package (limited)/stock/'89* $15
I Don't Wanna Fight 7 versions *Virgin 12775/promo/rear insert/'93* $6
I Don't Wanna Love You *Capitol 79272/promo/logo on white/rear insert/'89* $8
Look Me in the Heart *Capitol 79918/promo/silkscreened logo on white/'89* $5
Love Thing *Capitol 79947/promo/ps/'91* $6
Love Thing/Foreign Affair/Steamy Windows *Capitol 15786/stock/ps/'91* $6
Steamy Windows *Capitol 79825/promo/silkscreened/ps/'89* $5
Steamy Windows 6 versions *Capitol 79907/promo/silkscreened* $8
Tearing Us Apart/Nutbush/Addicted to Love/Its Only Love (all live) *Capitol 79330/promo/ps/'88* $10
The Best single & lp *Capitol 79709/promo/ps/'89* $6
Undercover Agent For the Blues *Capitol 79770/promo/'89* $6
Way of the World *Capitol 79116/promo/logo on blue/rear insert/'91* $6
Why Must We Wait Until Tonight edit/lp *Virgin 12812/promo/silkscreened logo/rear insert/'93* $6

TURTLE ISLAND STRING QUARTET
Crossroads (edit) *Windham Hill 90-10/promo/ps/'90* $4

TURTLES, THE
Happy Together/You Baby/She'd Rather Be With..+1 *Rhino 73017/stock/3"/ps* $5

TWISTER ALLEY
Dance *Mercury 955/promo/ps/'93* $4

TWITTY, CONWAY
Crazy in Love *MCA 79067/promo/rear insert/'90* $4
Fit to Be Tied Down *MCA 79000/promo/rear insert/'90* $4
One Bridge I Didn't Burn *MCA 54077/promo/rear insert/'90* $4

TWO BIT THIEF
Broken Hearts edit & lp *Combat 0906/promo/silkscreened/ps/'90* $4

2 DEEP
I Didn't Do My Homework edit & long *Cold Chillin' 4021/promo/'90* $4

2 HOUSE
Go Techno 5 versions *Pyrotech 4540/promo/rear insert* $5

2 LIVE CREW
Banned in the USA *Atlantic 3483/promo/rear insert/'90* $5
Banned in the USA (4 versions) *Luke 96440/promo/rear insert/'90* $6
Banned in the USA (4 versions) *Atlantic 3486/promo/rear insert/'90* $6
Do the Bart lp & remix *Atlantic Luke 3692/promo/rear insert/silkscreened yellow/'90* $4
Hangin' With the Homeboys *Luke 3898/promo/rear insert/'91* $4
Mama Juanita (3 versions) *Atlantic 3570/promo/logo on black/rear insert/'90* $5

2 TOO MANY
Where's the Party 4 vers. *Jive 42049/promo/silkscreened/ps/custom sticker/'92* $4

21 GUNS
Knee Deep *RCA 62309/promo/silkscreened/ps/'92* $4
Walking remix *RCA 62479/promo/logo on purple/rear insert/'93* $4

22 UNLIMITED
No Limit 3 versions *Critique 15498/promo/'93* $4
The Magic Friend edit & ext./Eternally Yours *Radikal 15493/promo/'92* $4
Twilight Zone radio & no rap mix *Critique 154892/promo/'92* $4

24-7 SPYZ
Don't Break My Heart edit & lp *In Effect 0613/promo/silkscreened/ps/'90* $4
This is ep (Stuntman radio versions & lp/Tick Tick Tick/My Desire/Peace & Love/Earthquake) *East West 4270/promo/'91* $10

25TH OF MAY, THE
It's All Righ/F.T.R.T.V./Shelter/Things Are Getting Better (all live) *Arista 2450/promo/ps/'92* $6

It's All Right 3 versions *Arista 2438/ promo/silkscreened/ps/'92* $5

29 PALMS

Magic Man *IRS 67047/promo/silkscreened/'90* ... $4

TYKETTO

Forever Young edit & lp *DGC 4207/promo/ps/'91* $4

TYLER, BONNIE

Bitterblue radio mix *RCA 62300/promo/rear insert/'91* $5
Hide Your Heart *Columbia 1279/promo/'88* $5
Save Up All Your Tears *Columbia 1366/promo/ silkscreened blue/'88* $5
Secret Dreams and Forbidden Fire (9 songs) *Columbia 2280/promo/ps/'86* $6

TYNER, MCCOY

The Turning Point ep (Passion Dance/Let It Go/Update - all edits) *Verve 777/ promo/logo on red/rear insert/'92* $6

TYPE O NEGATIVE

Unsuccessfully Coping.. (3 versions)/ Gravitational Constant *Road Racer 038/promo/ps* $6

TYSON, MOSES

Deck of Cards *Curb 050/promo/silkscreened* $4

U 96

Das Boot techno versions/ecstasy on board versions/echo mix/speed versions *Cohiba 22102/promo/ logo on gold/custom sticker/'92* $6

U-KREW

If U Were Mine edit & extended *Enigma 219/promo/silkscreened/ custom sticker/'89* $4
Let Me Be Your Lover CHR edit *Enigma 291/promo/cust.sticker/'90* $4

U.G.K.

Use Me Up 9 versions *Jive 42121/promo/ rear insert/custom sticker/'93* $4

U.N.V.

Something's Goin' On 3 versions *Maverick 6162/promo/silkscreened* $6

U2

All I Want Is You (2 versions)/Unchained Melody/ Everlasting Love *Island 2770/ promo/rear insert/'89* $20
Angel of Harlem *Island 2559/promo/'88* $15
Angel of Harlem/A Room at the Heartbreak Hotel/Love Rescue Me *Island 96590/ stock/3" in 3x12 box package/'88* $10
Desire *Island 2500/promo/ps/'88* $20
Even Better Than the Real Thing *Island 6723/promo/ps/'92* $12
Even Better Than the Real Thing 5 versions *Island 422-864 281/stock/ps/'92* $8
Even Better Than the Real Thing 6 versions *Island 6735/promo/logo on black/ custom sticker/'92* $25
Even Better Than the Real Thing/Salome/ Where Did It All Go Wrong/Lady with the Spinning Head extended *Island 422-866 977/stock/ps/'92* $8
God Part 2 (remix)/Desire (remix) + Rattle & Hum b sides *Island 2677/promo/ custom sticker/'88* $30
Mysterious Ways *Island 6698/promo/ silkscreened/ps/'91* $12
Mysterious Ways ultimatum & perfecto mix *Island 6701/promo/logo on white/'91* $30
Mysterious Ways 5 versions *Island 422 866 189/stock/ps/'91* $8
Numb perfecto mix/4:18 *Island 6795/promo/silkscreened/'93* $12
October (full length) *Island 90092/stock/ orig. gatefold softcover with German made CD* $25
One *Island 6706/promo/ps/'91* $12
One/Lady With the Spinning ../Satellite of Love *Island 422-866 533/stock/ps/'92* $8
The Fly *Island 6680/promo/silkscreened/ps* $10
The Fly/Alex Descends Into Hell../Lounge Fly Mix *Island 422 868 885/stock/ps/'91* $8
Until the End of the World *Island 6704/promo/logo on white/'91* $10
Who's Gonna Ride Your White Horses 2 vers./ Paint It Black/Fortunate Son *Island 422 864 521/stock/ps/'92* $8
With or Without You/In God's Country/ 11 O'clock Tick Tock (live) *Island 422 878 389/stock/ps/'92* $8
Zooropa *Island 6792/promo/silkscreened* $10

U2 & BB KING

When Love Comes to .. *Island 2659/promo/'89* ... $12
When Love Comes to Town single & live/ Dancing Barefoot/God Part II *Island 96570/stock/3"/'89* $8

UB40

Breakfast in Bed *A&M 17595/promo/ps/'88* $5
Breakfast in Bed edit/lp *A&M 17648/ promo/silkscreened pic/'88* $5
Can't Help Falling in Love single & 12" *Virgin 12772/promo/rear insert/'93* $6
Groovin' edit & lp *Virgin 4202/promo/'89* $4
Groovin'/Singer Man/Sweet Cherrie/Stick By .. *Virgin 96241/stock/ gatefold hardcover ps/'91* $5
Here I Am (Come and Get Me) edit & lp *Virgin 3038/promo/silkscreened/'89* $5

Here I Am (Come and Take Me) (3 versions)
Virgin 3671/promo/'89 .... $6
Higher Ground lp/punjabi dub
Virgin 12811/promo/silkscreened/'93 .... $6
Kingston Town *Virgin 3317/promo/ silkscreened logo/'89* $4
Red Red Wine *A&M 17619/promo* $5
The Way You Do the Things You Do
Virgin 3262/promo/silkscreened logo $4
Wear You to the Ball (3 versions)/Sweet Cherrie/Stick By Me *Virgin 3607/ promo/silkscreened logo* $6
Where Did I Go Wrong *Virgin 17703/promo* $4

UFO
Between a Rock and a Hard Place/Lights Out
Metal Blade 157/promo/rear insert $6

UGLY KID JOE
As Ugly As They Wanna Be sampler (Madman/ Whiplash Liquor/Too Bad/Everything About You/Sweet Leaf/Funky Fresh..)
Stardog 868 823/stock/ ps/silkscreened pic/'91 .... $5
Busy Bee edit & lp *Stardog 789/promo/ silkscreened/ps/'93* $5
Cats in the Cradle *Mercury 813/promo/ silkscreened/gatefold ps/'92* $5
Everything About You clean edit
Stardog 584/promo/gatefold hardcover ps/silkscreened logo/'91 .... $5
Goddamn Devil *Mercury 788/promo/logo on black/gatefold hardcover ps/'92* $5
Madman radio remix *Mercury 640/promo/ logo on green/gatefold hardcover ps* $5
So Damn Cool *Mercury 777/promo/logo on white/gatefold hardcover ps/'92* $5
Sweat Leaf/Funky Fresh Country Club
Stardog 566/promo/gatefold hardcover ps/silkscreened/'91 .... $5

UK BASSHEADS
Is There Anybody Out There 3:28 & 9:12/ Non Verbal Communication 4:30
Capitol 15829/stock/ps/'91 .... $5

ULTRA NATE
Deeper Love (Missing You) 8 versions
WB 40140/stock/gatefold hardcover ps/'91 .... $5
Is It Love (3 versions)/Scandal (2 versions)
WB 40007/stock/gatefold hardcover ps/'91 .... $5

ULTRA VIVID SCENE
Blood and Thunder remix edit & remix
Chaos 4826/promo/silkscreened/ps $6
Candida 2 versions/She's a Diamond/Winter Song/This is the Way 2
Chaos 5111/promo/ps/'93 .... $8
Special One/Lightning/Kind of a Drag/ A Smile and a Death Wish
4AD 73534/logo on black/stock/ps $6

ULTRAMAGNETIC M.C.S
Make It Happen edit & instrumental
Mercury 605/promo/logo on red/ps $6

UNCANNY ALLIANCE
I Got My Education 6 versions
A&M 31458 8077/promo/ps/'92 .... $5

UNCLE GREEN
I Know All About You *Atlantic 4495/promo/ silkscreened pic/rear insert/'92* $4

UNDER NEATH WHAT
Firebomb Telecom (7:08)/Le Freak/Animal Blue
Atco 3222/promo/ps/ silkscreened pic/'89 .... $6

UNDERWORLD
Change the Weather *Sire 3823/promo/'89* $4
Glory Glory live edit/full length/lp
Sire 3084/promo/ps/'88 .... $6
Show Some Emotion edit/remix
Sire 3191/promo/ps/'88 .... $5
Stand Up edit, lp, And Dance, Ya House
Sire 3639/promo/'89 .... $4
Underneath the Radar 7"/12"/lp
Sire 2942/promo/ps/'88 .... $7

UNITY 2
Buckwheat the Rebel 4 versions/Brooklyn Story bump godz remix
Reprise 40023/stock/gatefold hardcover ps/'91 .... $5
Shirlee *WB 3818/promo/'89* $4

UNIVERSE & DEXTER WANSEL
Love is Beautiful *Zoo 17050/promo/logo on blue/rear insert/custom sticker/'91* $4

UNTOUCHABLES, THE/THE DRIFTERS
Under the Boardwalk untouchables/drifters
Enigma 095/promo/ps/'88 .... $10

Phil Upchurch

"Poison"

a jazz update of the hit by Bell Biv Devoe

UPCHURCH, PHIL
Poison/All I Want From You/When We Need It..
Ichiban 096/promo/ps $5

URBAN DANCE SQUAD
Bureaucrat of Flaccostreet edit & lp
Arista 2354/promo/logo on green/ps $5
Clashing Perspectives ep (Mr EZway/Wino the Medicineman/Comeback/Son of tha Culture Clash) *Arista 2360/ promo/logo on green/ps/'91* $8
Deeper Shade of Soul edit/dance/live
Arista 2041/promo/ps/'90 .... $5
Hollywood Live (Man on Corner/45 Caliber/ Fastlane + 1) *Arista 2150/promo* $10
Routine 3:53 & 5:01 *Arista 2395/ promo/ps/logo no black/'92* $4

URBAN SOUL
Alright 6 versions *Chrysalis 23712/ promo/rear insert/'91* $5

URE, MIDGE
Cold, Cold Heart lp & ac mix
RCA 62216/promo/rear insert/'92 .... $6
Cold, Cold Heart with fade/lp
RCA 62033/promo/ps/'91 .... $6

URGE OVERKILL
Sister Havana *Geffen 4527/promo/ silkscreened/ps/'93* $5
The Urge Overkill Story ... Stay Tuned 1988-1991 (The Candidate/What's This Generation Coming To + 6) *Touch and Go UOSAMP/promo/ gatefold hardcover ps/'93* $12

UROHAUZ
Nothing Changes (4 versions) *Profile 7272/ promo/silkscreened red logo on blue* $4

UTAH SAINTS
I Want You *London 815/promo/logo on white* $5
Something Good 3 versions *London 736/ promo/silkscreened/'92* $5
What Can You Do For Me 1926 melodic mix/ def mix 7"/7" versions
London 871/promo/ps/silkscreened $5
What Can You Do For Me 1926 melodic mix/ drill mix/hard mix/club/A Trance For
London 857 103/stock/ps/'93 .... $5

VAI, STEVE
For the Love of God *Relativity 0117/promo/ silkscreened/ps/'91* $6
I Would Love To *Relativity 0113/ promo/silkscreened/ps/'90* $6
The Audience is Listening/The Animal/ Erotic Nightmares *Relativity 0110/ promo/silkscreened/ps/'90* $8
The Reaper *Interscope 4271/promo/ silkscreened pic/rear insert/'91* $6
The Reaper Rap *Interscope 4075/ promo/rear insert* $6

VAIN
Beat the Bullet
Island 2793/promo/rear insert/'89 .... $4
Who's Watching You *Island 3111/promo/ gatefold hardcover ps/'89* $4

VALE, LISA
Love Plus Love *Atlantic 4662/promo/ silkscreened pic/ps/'92* $5
Remember edit & lp *Eastwest 4529/promo/ foldout hardcover ps/silkscreened pic* $5
Waiting in the Wings edit & lp
Eastwest 4817/promo $4
Waiting in the Wings edit & lp
Eastwest 4833/promo/ silkscreened pic/rear insert/'92 .... $5

VAMP
Heartbreak, Heartache *Atlantic 3063/promo/ rear insert/silkscreened logo/'89* $4

VAN HALEN
Black & Blue fade/lp version
WB 3085/promo/ps/'88 .... $8
Dreams live edit *WB 6158/promo/'93* $5
Feels So Good *WB 3279/promo/'88* $6
Feels So Good remix edit/lp version
WB 3422/promo/'88 .... $7
Finish What Ya Started (remix)
WB 3240/promo/ps/'88 .... $7
Man on a Mission *WB 5407/promo/'91* $5
Poundcake *WB 4884/promo/logo on blue/ rear insert/'91* $6

Right Now *WB 5030/promo/'91* $6
Right Now single & edit *WB 5150/promo/'91* $6
Runaround *WB 4922/promo/silkscreened pic* ... $10
Top of the World *WB 5027/promo/'91* $5
When It's Love 2 vers. *WB 3142/promo/ps/'88* $6
Won't Get Fooled Again (live lp versions) *WB 5961/promo/silkscreened/'93* $6

VAN SHELTON, RICKY
After the Lights Go Out *Columbia 74104/ promo/rear insert/'91* $5

VAN ZANT, JOHNNY
Brickyard Road edit & lp *Atlantic 3383/ promo/silkscreened logo on blue/ rear insert/'90* $6
Hearts Are Gonna Roll edit & lp *Atlantic 3568/promo/rear insert/'90* $5
Love is Not Enough edit & lp *Atlantic 3714/ promo/logo on red/rear insert/'90* $6

VANDROSS, LUTHER
Any Love edit & lp *Columbia 1290/promo/ silkscreened logo/rear insert/'88* $5
Don't Want to Be a Fool *Epic 4139/promo/ logo on blue/ps/'91* $5
Don't Want to Be a Fool *Epic 73879/promo/ logo on blue/ps/'91* $4
Heart of a Hero *Epic 74738/promo/logo on black/ps/'92* $4
Here and Now 7" edit & lp *Epic 1942/promo/silkscreened/'89* $4
I Really Didn't Mean It (4 versions) *Epic 2740/promo/ps/'87* $6
Little Miracles *Epic 74945/promo/ps/'93* $4
Power of Love - Love Power 4 versions *Epic 73779/promo/ps/'91* $6
Power of Love - Love Power single & instrum. *Epic 73778/promo/silkscreened/ gatefold box type ps/'91* $6
Sometimes It's Only Love edit *Epic 74226/ promo/silkscreened/rear insert/'92* $5
The Rush 4 versions *Epic 74049/promo/ logo on white/ps/'91* $6
Treat You Right (edit) *Epic 73258/ promo/rear insert/'90* $4

VANGELIS
Good to See You edit & lp *Atlantic 3908/ promo/logo on blue/ps/'90* $6

VANILLA ICE
Ice Ice Baby radio edit/radio mix/club mix *SBK 05357/promo/silkscreened/ ps/woc/'90* $8
Rollin' in My 5.0 (4 versions) *SBK 05393/ promo/silkscreened/cust.sticker/'91* $6

VANILLA ICE & NAOMI CAMPBELL
Cool As Ice 5 versions *SBK 05413/promo/ gatefold hardcover ps/'91* $7

VANITY KILLS
Holiday of Passion *Hollywood 8395/ promo/rear insert/logo silksr./'91* $4

VANNELLI, GINO
If I Should Lose This Love *Vie 4300/ promo/logo on black/rear insert* $6

VAUGHAN BROTHERS
Good Texan *Epic 73673/promo/ps/'90* $6
Selftitled (full cd) *Epic 2169/promo/ silkscreened/foldout cover/'90* $20
Telephone Song *Epic 2250/promo/ps/'90* $6
Tick Tock *Epic 2207/promo/ps/'90* $6
Tick Tock (edit) *Epic 73576/promo/ logo on blue/ps/'90* $6

VAUGHAN, STEVIE RAY
Crossfire *Epic 1638/promo/silkscreened/'89* $6
Crossfire edit & lp *Epic 1887/promo/ silkscreened/'89* $6
Crossfire (short versions 3:35) *Epic 1732/promo/silkscreened/'89* $6
In the Beginning 9 tracks *Epic 4822/stock cd with limited edition promo cardboard cover/'92* $15
Interchords music & interview (for The Sky is Crying) *Epic 4418/promo/ silkscreened/ps/'92* $20
Little Wing *Epic 4435/promo/silkscreened/ rear insert/'92* $8
October 3, 1954-August 27, 1990 (14 tracks) *Epic 2221/promo/silkscreened/ rear insert/'90* $20
Shake For Me *Epic 4846/promo/'92* $6
The House is Rockin' *Epic 1931/promo/ silkscreened/rear insert/'89* $6
The Sky is Crying *Epic 4181/promo/ps/'91* $6
Wall of Denial/The House is Rockin'/ Leave My Girl Alone/Crossfire (last 3 live) *Epic 1998/promo/silkscreened light blue/rear insert/'90* $15

VAUGHAN, STEVIE RAY/JEFF BECK
16 track sampler *Epic 1901/promo/ps/'89* $20
Riviera Paradise (edit)/2 Rivers *Epic 1930/ promo/silkscreened/rear insert/'89* $8

VEGA, SUZANNE
99.9 Fº *A&M 31458 8051/promo/gatefold hardcover ps/silkscreened pink/'92* $6
99.9 Fº/In Liverpool live *A&M 31458 8052/ promo/silkscreened orange/ gatefold hardcover ps/'92* $6
Blood Makes Noise *A&M 31458 8018/promo/ silkscreened/gatefold hardcover ps* $5
Book of Dreams *A&M 18015/promo/ silkscreened green/ps/'90* $5
Days of Open Hand (11 tracks) *A&M 75021 3933/promo/trifold hardcover with hologram cvr/booklet* $20

In Liverpool *A&M 31458 8140/promo/ silkscreened/gatefold hardcover ps* $6
Luka/Left of Center/Neighborhood Girls (last 2 live) *A&M 12372/stock/ps/'88* $8
Luka/Left of Center/Neighborhood Girls (last 2 live) *A&M 31003/stock/3"/ps* $8
When Heroes Go Down *A&M 31458 8093/ promo/silkscreened/ps/'92* $5

VEGA, SUZANNE & D.N.A.
Tom's Diner 12" & 7" *A&M 75021 7479/ promo/silkscreened pic/'90* $8

VELDT, THE
CCCP with & without intro/Cradle Will Fall *Stardog 7701/promo/silkscreened/ gatefold hardcover ps/'92* $5

VELOCITY GIRL
Audrey's Eyes radio & lp/Copacetic *Sub Pop 13/promo/rear insert/'93* $5

VENTURES, THE
Walk Don't Run/Hawaii 5-0/Perfidia/Wipe Out *Rhino 73020/3"/ps/stock/'88* $6

VENUS BEADS
Moon is Red/Precious Little *Emergo 037/promo/ps/'91* $4

VERONIQUE
Forget Me Nots 6 versions *Ear Candy 38005/promo/ps/'91* $5

VERTICAL HOLD
A.S.A.P. 3 versions *A&M 31458 8053/promo/ gatefold hardcover ps/silkscreened* $5
Seems You're Much Too Busy 9 versions *A&M 31458 8083/promo/ silkscreened/ps/'93* $5

VERVE
Slide Away *Vernon Yard 12790/promo/ silkscreened pic/rear insert/'93* $5

VESTA
Always edit & lp *A&M 31458 8181/ promo/logo on brown/ps/'93* $4
Congratulations *A&M 17764/promo/ps/'88* $4
Do Ya 7 versions *A&M 75021 7289/promo/ silkscreened/ps/'91* $5
Special edit & lp *A&M 75021 7221/promo/ silkscreened pic/ps/'91* $4

VIENNA
Talking with the Heart *WB 2795/promo/ps* $3

VIERRA, CHRISTINA
You Can Float in My Boat 7"/lp/12" *WB 3225/promo/silkscreened/ rear insert/'88* $5

VINTON, BOBBY
Mr. Lonely/Letter to a Soldier *Curb 033/promo/'90* $4
What Did You Do With Your Old *Curb 76751/promo/'90* $4

VINTON, BOBBY & GEORGE BURNS
I Know What It Is to Be Young *Curb 1014/ promo/logo on brown/ps/'92* $5

VIOLENT FEMMES
American Music *Slash 4770/promo/ silkscreened/rear insert/'91* $6
Nightmares *WB 3444/promo/'89* $5
Why Do Birds Sing (13 tracks) *Slash 26476/ promo/silkscreened/'91* $15

VIOLET HOUR, THE
Falling/Wind Blowin'/The Spell/Better Be Good/Could Have Been *Epic 148/ promo/silkscreened/rear insert/'91* $6

VITAL SIGNS
The Boys & Girls Are Doing It *A&M 17702/promo/ps/'89* $4

VIXEN
Edge of a Broken .. 7" & lp *Manhattan 04099/ promo/ps/silkscreened pic/'88* $10
How Much Love single & lp *EMI 04541/promo/ silkscreened/gatefold hardcover (it flashes)/'90* $10
Love is a Killer *EMI 4657/promo/silkscreened logo on red/rear insert/'90* $5
Love Made Me *EMI 04268/promo/ silkscreened/'89* $5

VOICE FARM
Free Love 4 versions *Morgan Creek 0001/promo/ps/'91* $5
Hey Freethinker 4:09/7:49/4:50 *Morgan Creek 0006/promo/'91* $5
Seeing is Believing *Morgan Creek 0014/ promo/logo on black/ps/'91* $4

VOICE OF THE BEEHIVE
Adonis Blue/Shine On/Sit Down (live) *London 609/promo/logo on white/'91* $6
Monsters and Angels *London 513/promo/ logo on purple/ps/'91* $6
Perfect Place 7" & lp *London 534/promo/ logo on purple/gatefold hardcover ps* $6

VOICE OF THE CITY
Stand and Be Proud 6 versions *Scotti Bros. 72392 75333/promo/ ps/logo on gold/'92* $4

VOICES
My Mama Didn't Raise No Fool 3 versions
Zoo 17097/promo/ silkscreened/rear insert/'92 .... $5
Yeah Yeah Yeah 4 versions *Zoo 17078/ promo/silkscreened/ps/'92* $5

VOICES THAT CARE
Voices That Care 4 vers.
Giant 40054/stock/ps/'91 .... $8

VOIVOD
Angel Rat sampler (Clouds in My House/ The Prow/Angel Rat/Panorama)
Mechanic 2000/promo/silkscreened/ps $6
Astronomy Domine/The Known Knows
MCA 17979/promo/silkscreened/ rear insert/'89 .... $6
Clouds in My House/The Prow/Angel Rat/ Panorama *Mechanic 2000/promo/ silkscreened/'91* $6
Into My Hypercube/Missing Sequences
MCA 18196/promo/silkscreened/ rear insert/'89 .... $6

VOLLENWEIDER, ANDREAS
Dancing With the Lion (edit) *Columbia 1629/ promo/silkscreened/ps/'89* $5
Dancing With the Lion/Pearls and Tears/ See, My Love/Still Life
Columbia 1507/promo/ps/'89 .... $5

VON GROOVE
The Metal Radio ep (Once is Not Enough/ C'mon C'mon/House of Dreams/ Sweet Pain/Smaug)
Chrysalis 05482/promo/silkscreened $5

VOYCE
Here We Are 5 versions
Atco 4735/promo/ps/'92 .... $4
Within My Heart 5 versions *Atco 4020/ promo/silkscreened/rear insert/'91* $4

VOYCEBOXING
Pain radio/extended/jeep mix
GRP 9961/promo/ps/'91 .... $4

WAILERS BAND, THE
Irie *Atlantic 2743/promo/rear insert/'89* $4
My Friend 7 versions *Tabu 28965 1701/ promo/logo on purple/ps/'91* $4

WAILING SOULS
All Over the World edit & radio without rap
Chaos 4647/promo/ps/'92 .... $4
Get Real 2 versions/Smart Attack 3 versions
Chaos 4776/promo/logo on red/ps $4
If I Were You radio/lp/dub *Chaos 74763/promo/ ps/custom sticker/logo on grey/'92* $4
Shark Attack lp & club dub/You Ain't Leaving/ Sweet Black Angel roots rock versions/ You Ain't Leaving club dub
Chaos 4619/promo/ps/'92 .... $4
Sweet Black Angel lp/altern./digital b remix
Chaos 5107/promo/ps/'93 .... $4

WAINWRIGHT, LOUDON III
People in Love *Charisma 12764/promo/'92* $6

WAITE, JOHN
Times Are Hard For Lovers
EMI 79054/promo/ps/'87 .... $5

WAITS, TOM
Bone Machine: Operator's Manual interview
Island 6743/promo/ps/'92 .... $15
Goin' Out West *Island 6727/promo/ logo on black/ps/'92* $5
I Don't Wanna Grow Up *Island 6748/promo/ silkscreened/ps/'92* $5

WAKELING, DAVE
I Want More *IRS 1991/promo/silkscreened/'91* $4

WALDMAN, WENDY
Letters Home ep (Living in Hard Times/ Destined to Be Wild/Easy Way Out/ Cross Roads/Liner Notes + interview)
Cypress 112/promo/ps/'87 .... $10

WALKABOUTS, THE
Dead Man Rise/The Anvil Song/Hangman (last 2 live)/Train to Mercury gospel remix *Sub Pop 150/ stock/ps/silkscreened/'92* $5

WALKER, CHRIS
Giving You All My Love 7" & lp
Pendulum 8427/promo/'91 .... $4
No Place Like Love edit *Pendulum 8576/ promo/silkscreened pic/'92* $4
Take Time edit & 7" *Pendulum 8520/ promo/logo on black/ps/'91* $4

WALKER, JERRY JEFF
Nolan Ryan (He's a Hero to Us All)/Mr Bojangles/ Pickup Truck Song
Ryko 1020/stock/ps/'90 .... $6

WALKING WOUNDED
Raging Winds of Time *Chameleon 67/promo/ ps/silkscreened/'89* $4

WALL, WENDY
Dig That Crazy Beat new remix & lp
SBK 05329/promo/ps/'90 .... $4
Real Love 3:32 & 3:59/A Conversation With Wendy *SBK 05308/promo/ps/'89* $6

WALLFLOWERS, THE
Ashes to Ashes 2 vers. *Virgin 12690/promo/ logo on black/rear insert/'92* $4
Be Your Own Girl edit & lp *Virgin 12763/ promo/logo on pink/'92* $4

WALSH, JOE
All of a Sudden *Epic Associated 4092/ promo/rear insert/'91* $4
Fairbanks Alaska *Epic 4804/promo/logo on black/rear insert/'92* $4
Look At Us Now *Epic 4202/promo/logo on gold/rear insert/'91* $4
Ordinary Average Guy *Epic 3070/promo/silkscreened/ps/'91* $5
The Smoker You Get... radio show *In the Studio #167/promo/broadcast 9/91* $20
Vote For Me *Sony 4680/promo/ ps/silkscreened/'92* $4

WALTER & SCOTTY
I Want to Know Your Name edit & lp *Capitol 79706/promo/ silkscreened/ps/'93* $5
Sticks and Stones edit & lp *Capitol 79785/ promo/silkscreened/'93* $5

WANG CHUNG
Praying to a New God edit & lp *Geffen 2501/promo/ gatefold ps/silkscreened/'89* $8

WAR
Don't Let No One Get You Down radio & ext. *Avenue 90132/promo/ silkscreened/ps/'92* $5

WAR BABIES
Cry Yourself to Sleep 3 versions *Columbia 4654/promo/rear insert/'92* $4
Hang Me Up edit & lp *Columbia 4185/promo/ps/'91* $4

WARD, BILL
Snakes and Ladders *Chameleon 77/promo/silkscreened pic* $6

WARINER, STEVE
Crash Course in the Blues *Arista 2461/ promo/logo on black/ps/'92* $5
Leave Him Out of This *Arista 2349/ promo/ps/silkscreened/'91* $5
MCA Radio Special (8 songs) *MCA 3022/promo/rear insert/'90* $18
The Domino Theory *MCA 53733/promo/ silkscreened/ps/'90* $5
The Tips of My Fingers *Arista 2393/promo/ silkscreened/ps/'92* $5

WARINER, STEVE/SKIP EWING
On Christmas Morning/Christmas Carol *MCA 1164/promo/rear insert/'90* $6

WARNER BROS. SYMPHONY ORCHESTRA
Bugs Bunny on Broadway 12 tracks *WB 26494/promo only silkscreened/ps/'91* $15

WARNES, JENNIFER
First We Take Manhattan/The Time of My Life (w/BILL MEDLEY)/Up Where We Belong (w/JOE COCKER) *Cypress 37581/stock/3"/5" ps/'88* $10

WARRANT
Big Talk 2 vers. *Columbia 1839/promo/ps/'89* ... $5
Blind Faith *Columbia 73598/promo/ silkscreened/ps/'91* $5
Cherry Pie single & lp *Columbia 73510/ promo/silkscreened/ps/'90* $5
Down Boys *Columbia 1430/promo/ silkscreened logo on green/'89* $6
Down Boys *Columbia 1602/promo/ silkscreened logo on green/'89* $6
Heaven 2 vers. *Columbia 1695/promo/ps/'89* $6
I Saw Red *Columbia 73597/promo/ps/'90* $6
Inside Out censored & uncensored *Columbia 4701/promo/ps/'92* $5
Machine Gun *Columbia 4685/promo/ps/'92* $5
Sometimes She Cries 4:11/4:44 *Columbia 73095/promo/ps/'90* $6
The Bitter Pill 3 versions *Columbia 4818/promo/ps/'92* $6
The Hole in My... *Columbia 4829/promo/ps/'92* $5
Uncle Tom's Cabin top 40 & lp *Columbia 73644/promo/ps/'91* $5
We Will Rock You *Columbia 74207/promo/ps* $5

WARRIOR SOUL
Last Decade Dead Century (11 tracks) *DGC 24285/gatefold diecut ps/promo/'90* $12
Love Destruction *DGC 4457/promo/ silkscreened/ps/'92* $4
Superpower Dreamland/Trippin' on Ecstasy/ Interview with Kory Clarke *DGC 4153/promo/custom sticker/'90* $5
The Wasteland censored & lp *DGC 4242/promo/ps/'91* $4

WARWICK, DIONNE
Sunny Weather Lover *Arista 2477/promo/ps* $4
Where My Lips Have Been *Arista 2558/ promo/ps/logo on blue/'93* $5

WARWICK, DIONNE & J. OSBOURNE
Love Power *Arista 9567/promo/ps/'87* $5
Take Good Care of You and Me *Arista 9901/ promo/ps/silkscreened yellow* $5

WARWICK, DIONNE & THE SPINNERS
I Don't Need Another Love single & phil.ext.
Arista 9940/promo/silkscreened/ps $5

WAS (NOT WAS)
Anything Can Happen pop & r&b
Chrysalis 43365/promo/'89 .... $6
Papa Was a Rollin' Stone (3 versions)
Chrysalis 23550/promo/ps/'90 .... $6
Papa Was a Rollin' Stone edit & rapless
Chrysalis 23584/promo/rear insert $6

WASH, MARTHA
Carry On 9 versions *RCA 62367/*
stock/ps/logo on purple/'92 .... $6
Give It To You 4 versions *RCA 62461/*
promo/ps/custom sticker/'92 .... $6
Give It To You edit/edit with piano/lp
RCA 62434/promo/ps/'92 .... $5
Now That You're Gone 7"/lp
RCA 62525/promo/rear insert/'93 .... $4
Runaround 4 versions/Now That You're
Gone 7" *RCA 62542/ps/stock/'93* $5

WASHINGTON SQUARES
Everybody Knows *Gold Castle 79514/promo* $4
Fourth Day of July *Gold Castle 79652/promo* $4

WASHINGTON, GROVER (JR)
Jamaica edit & lp *Columbia 73040/promo/*
silkscreened green/ps/'89 .... $4
Love Like This edit & lp
Columbia 4524/promo/ps/'92 .... $4
Sacred Kind of Love edit & lp
Columbia 73234/promo/ps/'90 .... $4
Take Five *Columbia 4724/promo/ps/'92* $4

WASHINGTON, KEITH
Are You Still in Love With Me edit & lp
Qwest 4877/promo/'91 .... $4
Kissing You 2 vers. *Qwest 4671/promo/ps* $4
Stay in My Corner edit/lp/karaoke
Qwest 6429/promo/'93 .... $5

WASP
Animal (F**k Like a Beast)/Show No Mercy
Restless 72104/stock/gatefold ps $8
Forever Free edit & lp *Capitol 79707/*
promo/silkscreened/'89 .... $5
Live ... Animal ep (Animal (F**k Like a Beast)
& Hellion (both live)/Mississippi
Queen) *Restless 72235/*
gatefold ps/stock/'87 .... $8
The Real Me *Capitol 79507/promo/*
silkscreened/'89 .... $6

WATANABE, SADAO & PATTI AUSTIN
Any Other Fool (edit) *Elektra 8114/*
promo/silkscreened blue/'89 .... $4

WATER WALK, THE
Never Leaving Eden Again (edit) *IRS 67033/*
promo/silkscreened/rear insert/'90 .... $4

WATERBOYS, THE
And a Bang on the Ear edit & lp/The Raggle
Taggle Gypsy (live) *Chrysalis 23377/*
promo/custom sticker/rear insert/'89 .... $8
Dream Harder Interview
Geffen 4522/promo/ps/'93 .... $15
Preparing to Fly *Geffen 4544/promo/ps/'93* $5
The Return of Pan *Geffen 4518/promo/*
ps/embossed jewel box/silkscreened $6
The Whole of the Moon/Killing My Heart/Old
England (live) *Chrysalis 23716/*
promo/silkscreened/rear insert/'91 .... $8

WATERFRONT
Cry 3:52/7:04 *Polydor 38/promo/ps/'89* $4
Move On edit & lp *Polydor 128/silkscreened* $4
Nature of Love 3:55/4:52 *Polydor 94/promo/*
silkscreened duo pic/'88 .... $4

WATERS, CRYSTAL
Gypsy Woman 3 versions *Mercury 449/*
promo/silkscreened/rear insert/'91 .... $5
Makin' Happy 4 versions *Mercury 538/*
promo/silkscreened/rear insert/'91 .... $5

WATERS, KIM
Sweet & Saxy/Soul Serenade
Warlock 7074/promo/silkscreened $5

WATERS, ROGER
Hey You/Another Brick in Wall pt 2
Mercury 349/promo/
silkscreened logo on "wall" $8
Live in Berlin ep (Young Lust/Another Brick pt
2/Run Like Hell/Bring the Boys Back
Home) *Mercury 318/promo/*
silkscreened/rear insert/'90 .... $10

P.Floyd sampler (Another Brick 2/Hey You/ When Tigers Broke Free/Gunners Dream + 2) *Columbia 2126/promo/ps/'90* $20
The Bravery of Being Out of Range *Columbia 4830/promo/ps/'92* $8
The Tide is Turning *Mercury 367/promo/ silkscreened/rear insert/'90* $6
Three Wishes *Columbia 4941/promo/ps/'93* $6
What God Wants, Part 1 lp/video *Columbia 4607/promo/ps/'92* $8

WATERS, ROGER & CYNDI LAUPER

Another Brick in the Wall pt 2 (live) *Mercury 342/promo/silkscreened/ cust. sticker/'90* $7

WATLEY, JODY

Friends 4:09/5:20/8:10 *MCA 17864/ promo/custom sticker/'89* $8
I Want You 5 versions *MCA 2064/promo/rear insert/'91* $6
I Want You 8 versions *MCA 2048/ promo/logo on brown/ps/'91* $6
I Want You single/instrumental/suite *MCA 1634/promo/rear insert/'91* $6
I'm the One You Need *MCA 2049/promo/rear insert/'91* $5
I'm the One You Need 4 versions *MCA 2163/promo/rear insert/'92* $6
I'm the One You Need 5 versions *MCA 2162/promo/rear insert/'92* $6
I'm the One You Need 5 versions *MCA 2236/promo/ps/'92* $6
I'm the One You Need funky chicken vocal & instrum. *MCA 54382/stock/ps/'92* $5
It All Begins With.. *MCA 2226/promo/ps/'91* $5
Most of All remix *MCA 17533/promo/ps/'88* $6
Precious Love 3:50/4:55 *MCA 18114/promo/'89* $5
Precious Love lp edit/remix edit/tongue in groove mix *MCA 18215/promo/'90* $6
Real Love single, radio edit & extended *MCA 17790/promo/ps/'89* $6
The Jody Watley Story *Unistar/promo/ The Weekly Specials 3/27-29/92* $20

WATTS, CHARLIE

Loverman edit & lp *Continuum 12201/ promo/logo on white/rear insert/'92* $10
Practising, Practising, Just Great *ps/promo* $15

WAY MOVES, THE

One More Kiss radio & one more mix *Chameleon 75/promo/tri fold hardcover ps/silkscreened/'90* $5
Revel (In Your Time) *Chameleon 90/promo/ silkscreened logo on red/'90* $4

WAYBILL, FEE

Meeting Half the Way *Sisapa/promo/rear insert/'90* $5

WEAVER, JASON

I Wanna Be Where You Are edit/lp/instrum. *Motown 374631076/promo/ps/'92* $5

WEDNESDAY WEEK

What We Had 13 tracks *Enigma 73215/stock/ps/'86* $12

WEE PAPA GIRLS

The Bump (5 versions) *Jive 1362/promo/rear insert/'90* $5

WEEN

Push th Little Daisies 3 versions/Ode to Rene/ I Smoke Some Grass/Mango Woman *Elektra 8717/promo/gatefold hardcover ps/silkscreened/'92* $5
Push th' Little Daisies censored edit & lp *Elektra 8715/promo/silkscreened/'92* $5

WEISBERG, TIM

Outrageous Temptations/Castaways + 2 *Cypress 17791/promo/ silkscreened pic/'89* $5

WELCH, KEVIN

Stay November/Audio Bio *WB 3347/promo* $4

WELLER, PAUL

Above the Clouds *London 861/promo/'93* $4
Into Tomorrow lp & demo/Feelin' Alright/Ohio/ Don't Let Me Down *London 824/ promo/logo on blue/'92* $8
Uh Huh Oh Yeh *London 764/promo/ logo on green/ps/'92* $4

WELLS, PETER

Between the Saddle and the Ground *Zoo 17007/promo/silkscreened/ rear insert/'91* $4

WENDY AND LISA

Are You My Baby edit/"My Mans" 12"/dub/ bonus beats *Columbia 1459/ promo/silkscreened/'89* $8
Honeymoon Express *Columbia 2914/promo/ps/'88* $6
Strung Out (3 versions) *Virgin 3473/ promo/silkscreened logo/'90* $6
The Closing Of the Year 4:20/5:58 *Geffen 4480/promo/"Toys" ps/'92* $6
Why Wait For Heaven/Mother of Pearl *Virgin 3635/promo/silkscreened/ custom sticker/KD LANG/'90* $6

WENDYS, THE

The Sun's Going to Shine For Me Soon edit/lp/ MTV 120 Minutes segment *Eastwest 4115/promo/ silkscreened/ps/'90* $6

WEST COAST RAP ALL STARS

We're all in the Same Gang (3 versions) *WB 21725/stock/ps/'90/with ICE T, TONE LOC, MC HAMMER, NWA, many more* $5

WESTERBERG, PAUL

Dyslexic Heart *Epic 4479/promo/ps/'92* $5
World Class Fad censored & lp/First Glimmer *Sire 6229/promo/ silkscreened/rear insert/'93* $5

WESTON, RANDY

Discussions on The Spirits of Our Ancestors music & interview (16 tracks in all) *Antilles 002/ promo/silkscreened/'92* $12

WESTWORLD

Lipsyncher 4 versions *MCA 2150/promo/rear insert/'92* $5

WET WET WET

Wishing I Was Lucky *Uni/promo/ps/ silkscreened pic/'88* $5

WHALUM, KIRK

Love is a Losing Game single *Columbia 4964/promo/ps/'93* $5

WHEELER, CARON

Blue (Is the Colour of Pain) (5 versions) *EMI 4695/promo/silkscreened/ rear insert/'91* $6
I Adore You 8 versions *Perspective 31458 8057/ promo/silkscreened/'92* $6
Livin' in the Light edit *EMI 4684/promo/ rear insert/silkscreened/'90* $5
Livin' in the Light (5 versions) *EMI 4519/ promo/silkscreened/ps/'90* $6
Livin' in the Light (radio edit) *EMI 4684/promo/silkscreened/'90* $5
Massive 4:10 & 6:46/Blak History *EMI 4710/promo/silkscreened/ rear insert/'90* $6
UK Blak (3 versions) *EMI 4710/promo/ silkscreened/rear insert/'90* $6

WHEELER, CHERYL

Estate Sale *Capitol 79193/promo/'90* $4

WHEN IN ROME

Heaven Knows *Virgin 2599/promo/'88* $5
Sight of Your Tears 7" & 12" *Virgin 2679/ promo/silkscreened/'88* $6
The Promise *Virgin 2428/promo/ps/ logo on red/'88* $6

WHIRLING DERVISHES

Wish It Would Snow ep (Chill/Winter Kills/ You're a Mean One Mr Grinch/Sinning and Skating) *WM 10734/stock/ ps/silkscreened/'92* $5

WHISPERS, THE

Innocent 8 versions *Capitol 79175/promo/'90* $6
Mind Blowing 6 vers. *Capitol 79449/promo/ silkscreened/custom sticker/'90* $6
My Heart Your Heart (5 versions) *Capitol 79339/promo/silkscreened/ custom sticker/'90* $6

WHISTLE

Bad Habit 4 versions *Select 004/promo/'90* $5
I Am 7 versions *Select 8494/promo/ logo on black/'92* $5

WHITE BOY WORRY

Survive 5 versions *Axis 008/stock/ps/'90* $4

WHITE LION

Cry For Freedom edit & lp *Atlantic 3060/ promo/rear insert/'89* $4
Little Fighter *WB 2778/promo/ps* $4
Love Don't Come Easy *Atlantic 3786/ promo/logo on purple/ps/'91* $4
Radar Love edit & lp *Atlantic 2874/ promo/rear insert/'89* $4
When the Children Cry edit & lp *Atlantic 2461/promo/rear insert/'88* $4

WHITE TRASH

Apple Pie *Elektra 8365/promo/ps/ logo on blue/'91* $4
The Crawl *Elektra 8507/promo/silkscreened/ rear insert/'91* $4

WHITE ZOMBIE

Black Sunshine lp & psycho head mix *Geffen 4443/promo/silkscreened pic* $6
Black Sunshine/Thunder Kiss '65 2 versions *Geffen 4435/promo/ps/'92* $5
Thunder Kiss '65/Welcome to the Planet.. *Geffen 4188/promo/ gatefold hardcover ps/'92* $6

WHITE, BARRY

Good Night My Love 3:10 & 5:08 *A&M 75021 8093/promo/ silkscreened logo on tan/'89* $5
I Wanna Do It Good to Ya 4:19/7:32 *A&M 18009/promo/silkscreened/'89* $6
I Wanna Do It Good to You *A&M 17996/ promo/silkscreened/'89* $4

Put Me in Your Mix edit & lp *A&M 75021 7288/ promo/silkscreened/ps/'91* $4
Put Me in Your Mix 2 vers. *no label or #/promo/ testpressing/custom sticker* $6
Super Lover 5:44/5:47/4:21 *A&M 17879/promo/silkscreened logo* $6
When Will See You Again 4:08 & 7:29 *A&M 75021 8077/promo/ silkscreened/'89* $5

WHITE, BARRY & ISAAC HAYES

Dark and Lovely 10:05 *A&M 75021 7322/promo/ps/'91* $6
Dark and Lovely 4:54/10:09 *A&M 75021 7327/promo/ps/'91* $6

WHITE, JJ

The Crush *Curb 063/promo/ps/'91* $4

WHITE, KARYN

Do Unto Me edit & lp *WB 5250/promo/'91* $5
Do Unto Me 4 versions/Walkin' the Dog 4 vers. *WB 40566/stock/gatefold hardcover ps/'92* $6
Ritual of Love words & music *WB 5131/promo/ silkscreened pic/rear insert/'91* $10
Romantic edit & lp *WB 4800/promo/ silkscreened pic/rear insert/'91* $6
Romantic 7 versions *WB 40069/promo/ gatefold hardcover ps/'91* $6
Romantic edit & lp *WB 4800/promo/ silkscreened pic/bonus video/super custom box (holds both video & cd)* $15
Secret Rendezvous (5 versions) *WB 3436/promo/'88* $8
Slow Down *WB 3402/promo/'89* $4
Superwoman edit & lp *WB 3375/promo/silkscreened pic/'88* $6
The Way I Feel About You 6 versions *WB 40256/stock/ gatefold hardcover ps/'91* $5
The Way I Feel About You edit & lp *WB 5135/promo/'91* $4
The Way You Love Me (3 versions) *WB 3309/promo/'88* $8
Walkin' the Dog *WB 5081/promo/'91* $5

WHITESNAKE

Crying in the Rain *Geffen 2844/promo/ps/'88* $6
Fool For Your Loving (3 vers.)/Judgment Day *Geffen 3817/promo/ps/silkscreened* $8
Fool For Your Loving (CHR mix) *Geffen 3808/promo/ silkscreened red/ps/'89* $6
Fool For Your Loving (CHR mix)/Judgment Day (for Rockers only) *Geffen 3828/ promo/silkscreened/ps/'89* $8
Give Me All Your Love (2 remixes) *Geffen 2932/promo/ps* $8
Now You're Gone remix & lp *Geffen 3917/ promo/silkscreened logo on red/'89* $6
Snakebites (11 song dj only sampler) *Geffen 3846/promo/silkscreened/ps* $20
Still of the Night *Geffen 2669/promo/ gatefold hardcover ps/'87* $12
The Deeper the Love fade & lp *Geffen 3887/promo/silkscreened/'89* $5

WHITLEY, CHRIS

Big Sky Country edit & lp *Columbia 4135/promo/ps/'91* $4
Living With Law *Columbia 4057/promo/ps/'91* ... $4
Poison Girl *Columbia 4340/promo/ps/'91* $4
Poison Girl/Make the Dirt Stick/Kick the Stones/Poison Girl/Living with the Law/A Pint of Lotion (last 5 live) *Columbia 44K 74247/ps/stock/'92* $6

WHO, THE

Join Together/Eminence Front/Rough Boys/ Pinball Wizard/I Can See For Miles *MCA 18258/promo/ps/'90* $15
Saturday Night's Alright *Polydor 586/ promo/red on white silkscreened/ps* $8

WHODINI

Freaks (4 versions) *MCA 1267/promo/'91* $5
Judy inside out party flip 7"/12"/instrumental *MCA 1457/promo/'91* $5
Smilin' Faces Sometimes radio/club/instr./ trunk of funk versions *MCA 1585/promo/'91* $6

WHODINI & MILLIE JACKSON

Be Yourself (3 versions) *Arista 9628/promo/ps/'87* $6

WIDESPREAD PANIC

Makes Sense to Me/Send Your Mind edit/ Walkin' (For Your Love) live *Capricorn 5096/promo/ps/'91* $5
Walkin' (For Your Love) edit & lp *Capricorn 4946/promo/rear insert* $4

WIDOWMAKER
The Widowmaker radio edit *Esquire 74340/ promo/silkscreened pic/rear insert* $4

WIEDLIN, JANE
Fur 10 tracks *Manhattan 48683/stock/ps* $12
Guardian Angel *EMI 4669/promo/silkscreened/ rear insert/'90* $6
Inside a Dream single/12"/12" edit *Manhattan 04113/promo/ps/'88* $8
Rush Hour (2 vers.) EMI 4017/promo/ps/'88 .... $8
World on Fire (5 versions) *EMI 4575/promo/ silkscreened/rear insert/'90* $8
World on Fire 5 versions *EMI 4575/promo/ matchbook like ps/'90* $15

WILCOX, DAVID
(Mostly) Live - Authorized Bootleg ep (Going Somewhere/4 Lane Dance/Sat.They'll All Be Back../Daddy's Money/Johnny's Camaro + 1) *A&M 75021 7241/ promo/ps/'91* $12
Eye of the Hurricane/The Kid/Do I Dare + 2 (last 4 live) *A&M 18007/promo/ps/ silkscreened/'89* $10
She's Just Dancing *A&M 75021 7298/ promo/silkscreened/ps/'91* $4

WILD
Hurricane *Columbia 1176/promo/ps/'88* $4

WILD FLOWERS, THE
This Feeling's Gone edit & lp/Shakedown *Slash 3993/promo/'90* $4

WILD SWANS
Music & Talk from Liverpool *Sire 3062/promo/ps/'88* $10
Young Manhood *Sire 2964/promo/ps* $5

WILDE, DANNY
The Stuff That Dreams Are Made Of *Geffen 3665/promo/ps/'89* $4
Time Runs Wild *Cypress 17806/promo/ silkscreened/'89* $4
Time Runs Wild *Geffen 2891/promo/ps* $4

WILDE, EUGENE
Ain't Nobody's Business (3 versions) *MCA 17944/promo/custom sticker* $4
How About Tonight 5 versions *MCA 2184/promo/rear insert/'92* $4

WILDE, KIM
You Came *MCA 17596/promo/ps/'88* $5

WILDER, WEBB
Cold Front/Rock & Roll is #1 + interview *Island 2835/promo/rear insert/'89* $8
Hittin' Where It Hurts *Island 3162/promo/ rear insert/'90* $5
Human Cannonball gunpowder mix & lp/Burning God of Love/Rock, Rock, Rock/The Story of the Human Cannonball *Island 3023/promo/rear insert/'89* $12
Sittin' Pretty *Praxis 17066/promo/ silkscreened/rear insert/'91* $4
Tough It Out *Zoo 17025/promo/ps/ silkscreened/'91* $4

WILDSIDE
How Many Lies edit & lp *Capitol 79360/promo/ custom sticker/'92* $4

WILL & THE BUSHMEN
Book of Love *SBK 05333/promo/ gatefold hardcover/'90* $4
Suck on This/Dear Alex/Moosehead/Cant Turn Back the Clock/Shake Some Action (all live) *SBK 05328/promo/ silkscreened/ps/'90* $12

WILL TO POWER
Boogie Nights *Epic 73670/promo/ps/'91* $4
i'm Not in Love *Epic 73636/promo/ purple on black silkscreened/'90* $4

WILLIAMS BROTHERS, THE
Can't Cry Hard Enough *WB 4791/promo/'91* $4

WILLIAMS, ALYSON
Can't Have My Man edit/lp/instrumental *OBR 74224/promo/silkscreened pic/ps/'92* $5
Everybody Knew But Me edit/lp/instrumental *OBR 74493/promo/ps/silkscreened* $5
Just My Luck edit/lp/instrumental *Columbia 74171/promo/ps/'92* $5
She's Not Your Fool vocal & instrumental *Def Jam 73725/promo/ps/'91* $5
She's Not Your Fool limited edit.radio edit *Columbia 4189/promo/ps/'91* $5
Sleep Talk 5:25 & 7:56 *Def Jam 1436/promo/ps/'89* $6

WILLIAMS, CHRISTOPHER
Every Little Thing U Do edit/lp/radio/ supermen mix/mr. kent's mix *Uptown 2655/promo/rear insert/'93* $4
Every Little Thing U Do 7 version *Uptown 2600/promo/rear insert/'93* $5
One Girl edit & lp *Geffen 3479/promo/'89* $4
Talk To Myself 7", lp & 12" *Geffen 3674/promo/'89* $4
Talk To Myself edit & lp *Geffen 3544/promo/ps/'89* $4

WILLIAMS, DENIECE
Every Moment 4:24 & 6:16/Do You Hear What I Hear? *MCA 18028/promo/'89* $5

WILLIAMS, FREEDOM

Voice of Freedom 6 versions
Columbia 44K 74943/stock/ps/'93 .... $5

WILLIAMS, GEOFFREY

Blue *Atlantic 3152/promo/silkscreened logo/custom sticker/rear insert/'90* $4
Deliver Me Up 5 versions *Giant 40554/stock/ gatefold hardcover ps/'92* $4
It's Not a Love Thing UK mix/USA mix
Giant 5282/promo/rear insert/'92 .... $5
It's Not a Love Thing 4 versions
Giant 5350/promo/rear insert/'92 .... $5

WILLIAMS, HANK (JR)

Aint Nobodys Business *WB 3909/promo/'90* $5
All My Rowdy Friends (Are Here on Monday Night) *WB 3838/promo/'89* $7
All My Rowdy Friends are Coming Over For Monday Night Football '90 versions
Warner Curb 4484/promo/'90 .... $5
Angels Are Hard to Find *WB 4962/promo/'91* $4
Come On Over to the Country edit & lp
Curb 5434/promo/ps/'92 .... $4
Diamond Mine *Curb/Capricorn 6173/promo* $4
Everything Comes Down to Money and Love
Curb 5895/promo/ps/'93 .... $4
Everything Comes Down to Money and Love/ S.O.B. I'm Tired *Capricorn 5980/ promo/rear insert/'93* $5
Finders Are Keepers (remix)
WB 3574/promo/'89 .... $5
Hotel Whiskey *Capricorn 5296/promo/'92* $5
I Mean I Love You *WB 4606/promo/'90* $4
If It Will It Will edit
Warner Curb 4794/promo/'91 .... $4
Lyin' Jukebox *Capricorn 5613/promo/'92* $4
Man to Man (remix) *WB 4063/promo/'90* $5
Monday Night Football Boogie video version
Curb 5109/promo/ps $6
Pure Hank Radio Special (6 segments - over 45:00) *WB 4825/promo/'91* $20
Theres a Tear in My Beer (duet w/Hank Sr.)
WB 3399/promo/'89 .... $5
You're Gonna Be a Sorry Man (remix)
WB 3179/promo/ps/'88 .... $6

WILLIAMS, HANK (JR)/ CRANK THE HANK!

A Little Less Talk.../Low Down Blues
Capricorn 5426/promo/'92 .... $6

WILLIAMS, JOHN

Born on the Fourth of July 3:25/3:55
MCA 18122/promo/'89 .... $5
Raiders March (edit) *WB 3560/promo/'89* $6
Theme From Jurassic Park
MCA 2738/promo/ps/'93 .... $6

WILLIAMS, LENNY

Givin' Up on Love single & 12"
Crush Music 663/promo/'88 .... $5

WILLIAMS, LUCINDA

Hot Blood edit & lp *Chameleon 8669/ promo/logo on green/rear insert/'92* $4
Six Blocks Away *Chameleon 8630/promo/ps* $4

WILLIAMS, VANESSA

Just ForTonight single edit *Wing 673/promo/ logo on red/gatefold hardcover ps/'91* $6
Running Back to You 7:56/5:09/5:02/7:01
Wing 867 519/stock/ trifold hardcover ps with poster/'91 .... $6
Running Back to You the mix & edit
Wing 434/promo/silkscreened/trifold hardcover ps with popout pic/'91 .... $8
Save the Best For Last *Wing 593/promo/ gatefold hardcover ps/'91* $6
The Comfort Zone 3 vers. *Wing 579/promo/ silkscreened brown/'91* $6
The Comfort Zone 5 vers. *Wing 583/promo/ brown silkscreened/ gatefold hardcover ps/'91* $7
The Quiet Zone ep (Still in Love/What Will I Tell My Heart/You Gotta Go/ Strangers Eyes/Have Yourself a Merry Little..) *Wing 446/promo/ silkscreened/ps/'91* $8
The Right Stuff (4 versions)
Wing 14/promo/ps/'88 .... $8
Work to Do 5 versions *Wing 759//promo silkscreened pic/gatefold hardcover ps* $8

WILLIAMS, VESTA

Sweet Sweet Love 7" edit/lp
A&M 17630/promo/'88 .... $4

WILLIAMS, VICTORIA

Tarbelly and Featherfoot/Boogieman/ I Cant Cry Hard Enough/Summer of Drugs *Rough Trade 10/promo/ silkscreened/'90* $10

WILLIS, BRUCE

Save the Last Dance For Me
Motown 17993/promo/'89 .... $5

WILLSON-PIPER, MARTY

Luscious Ghost 2 versions/In Circles
Ryko 1025/stock/ps/'92 .... $6
Questions Without Answers/New York Buddha
Ryko 0114/promo/silkscreened pic/ rear insert/'89 .... $8
She's King/Listen-Space/Frightened Just Because... (alternate versions)
Ryko 1002/3"/gatefold ps/stock/'88 .... $8

WILSON PHILLIPS
Give It Up 5 versions/Daniel *SBK 19763/ stock/ps/custom sticker/'92* $5
Hold On *SBK 05334/promo/ gatefold hardcover ps/'90* $10
Hold On single fade & lp *SBK 05334/promo/ logo on gold blend background/'90* $6
Impulsive (4 versions) *SBK 05359/promo/ gatefold hardcover ps/silkscreened* $6
Release Me edit & lp/brief interview (1:36) *SBK 05342/promo/silkscreened/ gatefold hardcover ps/'90* $10
The Dream is Still Alive (4 versions) *SBK 19736/stock/gatefold hardcvr* $6
The Dream is Still Alive (4 versions) *SBK 05391/promo/silkscreened/ gatefold hardcover/'91* $8
You Won't See Me Cry *SBK 05449/promo/ gatefold hardcover with foldout poster/'92* $6
You're in Love edit & lp/Hold On/Release Me (last 2 live)/Morning Tea in Tokyo (1:46 interview) *SBK 19729/promo/ silkscreened/trifold hardcover ps/ custom sticker/'91* $15

WILSON, ANN & NANCY
Here is Christmas *Capitol 79870/promo/ silkscreen logo on green/rear insert* $15

WILSON, BRIAN
Interview & music from solo lp *Sire 3248/promo/ps/'88* $20
Love & Mercy *Sire 3168/promo/ps/'88* $6
Melt Away *Sire 3303/promo/'88* $6
Night Time *Sire 3200/promo/ps/'88* $6
Selftitled (entire lp) *Sire 3176/promo only cloth cover, silkscreen & booklet* $25

BRIAN
WILSON
An interview with music from the Sire/Reprise album, cassette and Compact Disc Brian Wilson
PRO-CD-3248

WILSON, CASSANDRA
My Corner of the Sky/Round Midnight/ Desperate Move *Wilson 2/promo/ ps/silkscreened/'92* $4

WILSON, CHARLIE
Sprung on Me lp/beatapella/suite *MCA 2224/promo/rear insert/'92* $4

WILSON, DANNY
If Everything You Said Was True edit & lp *Virgin 2777/promo/silkscreened/'89* $4

WILSON, NANCY (OF HEART)
All For Love *WTG 1511/promo/ silkscreened grey/'89* $8

WILSON, NANCY
Don't Ask My Neighbors edit & lp *Columbia 73353/promo/ps/'90* $5
Heaven's Hands edit & lp/Do You Still Dream About Me *Columbia 1973/promo/ps* $6
I Can't Teach My Old Heart New Tricks *Columbia 4198/promo/prod.& cowrit.by BARRY MANILOW/ps/'91* $5
Quiet Storm ep (I Can't Teach My Old Heart.../ When October Goes/With My Lover Beside Me/Love Is Where You Find It..) *Columbia 4240/promo/ps/ prod.&writ.by BARRY MANILOW/'91* $8

WILSON-JAMES, VICTORIA
Bright Lights 4 versions *Epic 73837/ promo/logo on green/rear insert/'91* $4
One World edit & lp & 12"/Woman of Colours *Epic 73981/promo/logo on blue/ps* $5
Through (4 vers.) *Epic 73707/promo/ps/'91* $4

WINANS, BEBE & CECE
Depend on You 7 versions *Capitol 79228/ promo/silkscreened/'91* $6
Depend on You lp/extended *Capitol 79323/promo/silkscreened* $5
I'll Take You There 10 versions *Capitol 79873/promo/'91* $6
It's OK 5 versions *Capitol 79126/promo/'91* $6
Lost Without You lp & edit *Capitol 79565/promo/custom sticker* $4
Silent Night/Still in Love With You *Capitol 79912/promo/silkscreened* $5
The Blood edit/extended/instrumental/lp *Capitol 79402/promo/'91* $5

WINANS, THE
It's Time edit & lp *WB 3953/promo/'90* $4
Payday 4 versions *Qwest 6249/promo/'93* $5
When You Cry edit & lp *WB 4457/promo/'90* $4

WINANS, VICKIE
Don't Throw Your Life Away lp/instr./suite *MCA 2014/promo/rear insert/'91* $5

WINBUSH, ANGELA
Its the Real Thing long & short *Mercury 121/promo/silkscreened pic* $6

No More Tears vocal & radio
Mercury 181/promo/silkscreened pic $5
Please Bring You Love Back edit & extended
Mercury 305/promo/silkscreened/'90 ....$6

WINBUSH, ANGELA & RONALD ISLEY
Lay Your Troubles Down (3 versions)
Mercury 248/promo/silkscreened pic $5

WINDOWS
New Sneakers *Cypress 17813/promo/ silkscreened/'89* $4

WINGER
Blind Revolution Mad lp & edit
Atlantic 5063/promo/silkscreened/ps/'93 ..$5
Can't Get Enuff edit & lp *Atlantic 3393/promo/ gatefold hardcover die cut ps/ silkscreened blue/'90* $6
Down Incognito
Atlantic 5061/promo/silkscreened/ps/'93 ..$5
Easy Come Easy Go edit remix & remix
Atlantic 3690/promo/ps/'90 ....$5
Headed For a Heartbreak 3:59/5:12
Atlantic 2655/promo/ps/'88 ....$5
Hungry *Atlantic 2803/promo/ps/'89* $5
Miles Away edit & lp *Atlantic 3566/promo/ps/ silkscreened logo on blue/'90* $5
Seventeen edit/lp *Atlantic 2631/promo/ rear insert/'88* $5

WINTER HOURS
Roadside Flowers/Just Like Love/Still (non lp)
Chrysalis 23487/promo/ silkscreened/rear insert/'89 ....$5

WINTER, EDGAR
Cry Out *Rhino 90021/promo/'90* $4
Cry Out *Rhino 90021/promo/silkscreened earth/ rear insert/'89* $7
They Only Come Out at Night/In the Studio
show #170/promo/aired 9/23/91 ....$20

WINTER, JOHNNY
Illustrated Man *Charis. 052/promo/rear insert/'91* .$5
Johnny Guitar *Charis.12722/promo/logo on blue* .$5
Life is Hard edit & lp
Charisma 069/promo/silkscreened/'91 .....$5
Please Come Home For Christmas/Johnny Guitar/ Illustrated Man *Charisma 12630/stock/ps* $6

WINTER, JOY
In Time You'll See (5 versions)
Epic 2115/promo/silkscreened/'90 ....$4
In Time You'll See (2 versions)
Epic 73324/promo/ps/'90 ....$4

WINWOOD, STEVE
Back in the High Life (8 tracks)
Island 25448/stock/ps/'86 ....$15
Don't You Know What the Night ..? remix/lp/ extended *Virgin 2427/promo/ps/'88* $6
Hearts on Fire 4:07/5:25
Virgin 2637/promo/silkscreened/'88 ....$5
Holding On 4:15/6:14
Virgin 2516/promo/silkscreened/'88 ....$8
I Will Be Here (3 versions)
Virgin 3763/promo/silkscreened/'90 ....$6
In the Light of Day lp & edit
Virgin 3868/promo/silkscreened/'90 ....$5
One and Only Man edit & lp
Virgin 3517/promo/silkscreened/'90 ....$5
One and Only Man (4 versions)
Virgin 3670/promo/silkscreened/'90 ....$6
Refugees of the Heart 8 tracks *Virgin/promo/ trifold cover with transparency/ silkscreened/outer cloth sleeve/'90* $20
Roll With It (2 versions) *Virgin 9326/promo/ps/'88* $6
Roll With It (7" versions)/The Morning Side
Virgin 99326/stock/3"/ps/'88 ....$6
Time is Running Out edit & lp
Island 2792/promo/rear insert $6

WIR
So and Slow it Grows 3:59 & 5:13 *Mute 8450/ promo/silkscreened logo on blue/ rear insert/'91* $6

WIRE
Drill: In Every City? 2 vers. *Mute 8351/ promo/silkscreened/rear insert/'91* $7
Eardrum Buzz 7" edit/12" version
Enigma 166/promo/silkscreened white/custom sticker/'89 ....$8
Eardrum Buzz 7" edit/12" vers./Offer/Its a Boy
Enigma 75520/stock/ps/3"/'89 ....$8
Kidney Bingos/Over Theirs live/Drill live/Pieta
Restless 72245/stock/3"/5" ps/'88 ....$8
Life in the Manscape *Enigma 285/promo/ silkscreened/custom sticker/'90* $8
Life in the Manscape *Enigma 301/promo/ silkscreened/custom sticker/'90* $6
Life in the Manscape (3 vers.)/Gravity Workshop/ Who Has Nine? *Enigma 75553/stock/ps* ..$6
Silk Skin Paws/German Shepherds/Ambitious (remix)/Come Back in Two Halves (rerecorded) *Restless 72299/stock/ 3"/5" ps/silkscreened/'88* $8

WIRE TRAIN
Crashing Back to You *MCA 2304/promo/ps/'92* .$5
Should She Cry *MCA 18470/promo/rear insert* ...$5
Spin *MCA 1108/promo/silkscreened/ rear insert/'90* $5
Stone Me *MCA 2202/promo/ps/'92* $5
Stone Me edit & lp *MCA 2244/promo/ps/'92* $5

WISHBONE ASH
Keeper of the Light *IRS 006/promo/ silkscreened/ps/'89* $5

WITNESS
Go Right Ahead *Lection 272/promo/silkscreen/'90* $4
Old Landmark long, short & instrumental
Lection 230/promo/silkscreened/'90 ....$4

WOBBLE, JAH
Visions of You edit & lp *Atlantic 4462/promo/silkscreened/rear insert/'91* $4

WOLF, PETER
99 Worlds *MCA 18188/promo/ps/'90* $4
99 Worlds (repeated 9 times)
Album Network/promo/ps/'90 ....$6
When Women are Lon..*MCA 18383/promo/ps/'90* $4

WOLFGANG PRESS, THE
A Girl Like You
4AD 5415/promo/logo on brown/ps $5
A Girl Like You 4 versions/Mama Told Me Not to Come 7"/Louis XIV *4AD 40547/stock/gatefold hardcover ps/'92* $6
Mama Told Me Not to Come 7"/up all night/go back *4AD 5753/promo/silkscreened logo on orange/rear insert/'92* $8

WOLFSBANE
I Like It Hot *Def American 3583/promo/ps/'89* $4

WOMACK & WOMACK
Teardrops *Island 2286/promo/ps/'88* $6
Passion & Pain edit & lp *WB 6099/promo/'93* $4
Priorities 7" & instrum.l *Solar 74600/promo/silkscreened logo/rear insert/'90* $5

WONDER STUFF, THE
Cartoon Boyfriend/Get Together/Gimme Some Truth/Inside You *Polydor 234/promo/silkscreened/'90* $8
Caught in My Shadow 3:45 & 4:38
Polydor 476/promo/silkscreened/ps/'91 ....$6
Don't Let Me Down, Gently
Polydor 137/promo/silkscreened/'89 ....$5
The Size of a Cow vocal & vers./Maybe elect. & santa fe acoustic/The Takin' is Easy *Polydor 562/promo/silkscreened/'91* $8
Welcome to the Cheap Seats UK remix
Polydor 631/promo/silkscreened logo/'92 .$5

WONDER, STEVIE
Fun Day 3 vers. *Motown 1649/promo/ps/'91* $6
Fun Day 8 vers. *Motown 1692/promo/ps/'91* $6
Gotta Have You (3 versions)
Motown 1145/promo/ps/'91 ....$6
Keep Our Love Alive vocal/instrumental
Motown 18241/promo/ps/'90 ....$6
My Eyes Don't Cry (extended)
Motown 17658/promo/ps/'88 ....$6
Skeletons 7" & 12" versions
Motown 13/promo/3" CD/'87 ....$6
These Three Words 3 versions *Motown 1007/promo/trifold hard cover ps/'91* $6
You Will Know (3 verions)/interview
Motown 27/promo/3"/5" ps/'87 ....$8

WOOD, BRENTON
That's the Deal 4 versions/This Love is For Real
Beckwood 51492/promo/silkscreened pic/rear insert/'92 ....$5

WOOD, D.D.
Louie Cooper lp & string versions
Hollywood 10274/promo/gatefold hardcover ps/silkscreened/'93 ....$4

WOOD, LAUREN
Fallen *EMI 04587/promo/silkscreened pic (from "Pretty Woman")/rear insert/'90* $5

WOOD, RONNIE
Josephine in your face mix & lp
Continuum 13210/promo/logo on gold/ps .$7
Show Me/Breathe On Me
Continuum 12210/promo/trifold hardcover ps/silkscreened pic/'92 ....$7
Slide on Live 13 tracks *Continuum 19309/promo silkscreen/insert/blue plastic ps* ...$20
Slide on This 13 tracks *Continuum 19210/promo/catalogue of art prints/gatefold hardcover ps/'92* $20

WOOD, RONNIE & BO DIDDLEY
Live at the Ritz 10 tracks
Victory 383 480 008/stock/ps/'87 ....$15

WOOD, RONNIE & HOTHOUSE FLOWERS
Like It *Continuum 12211/promo/silkscreened pic/rear insert/'92* $7

WOODS, PHIL
Full House 6 tracks *Milestone 9196/stock with promo silkscreened/ps/'92* $10

WOOTEN BROTHERS
Friendz 7" & extended *A&M 75021 7421/promo/silk. logo on green/'90* $4

WOP BOP TORLEDO
Jungle Fever (radio versions)
Charisma 010/promo/ps/'90 ....$4

WORLD PARTY
Give It All Away 4:23/8:36 *Chrysalis 04526/promo/silkscreened/rear insert/custom sticker/'93* $6
Hollywood *Chrys. 04575/promo/silkscreen pic* ...$5
Is It Like Today? edit/lp *Ensign 04694/promo/ps/custom sticker/silkscreened/'93* $6
Message in the Box *Chrys.23507/promo/ps/'90* ..$5
Way Down Now *Chrysalis 23522/promo/foldout lyric poster ps/'90* $6

WORLD TRADE
The Revolution Song edit & lp
Polydor 92/promo/ps/'89 .... $4

WORRELL, BERNIE
BW Jam (2 versions/Funk a Hall Licks/Poppa Chubby`` *Gramavision 74450/stock/ps/'90* $6
Time Was 3:10/7:00 *Gramavision 7010/promo/ps/BOOTSY COLLINS/'93* $6

WRATCHCHILD AMERICA
3D ep (Surrounded by Idots/Desert Grins/Draintime)
Atlantic 3737/promo/ps/'91 .... $6

WRECKX-N-EFFECT
Knock n Boots 4 versions/Rump Shaker radio remix *MCA 54583/promo/'93* $6
My Cutie *MCA 2680/promo/'93* $5
My Cutie 7 vers. *MCA 2735/promo/rear insert* ... $6
Rump Shaker 6 versions
MCA 2221/promo/rear insert/'92 .... $8
Wreckx Shop 8 versions *MCA 2454/promo/'92* . $6

WRIGHT, GARY
Dream Weaver waynes world versions/orig.
Reprise 5305/promo $6
It Ain't Right (remix) *Cypress 17617/promo/silkscreened pic/'88* $5
Who I Am/Dream Weaver/10:42 interview
Cypress 17584/promo/ps/silkscreened ... $12

WRIGHT, MICHELLE
All You Really Wanna Do *Arista 2208/promo/silkscreened/rear insert/'91* $4
He Would Be Sixteen *Arista 2480/promo/ps/'92* ... $4
One Time Around *Arista 2444/promo/ps/'92* $4
Take It Like a Man *Arista 2406/promo/ps/'92* $4

WYNETTE, TAMMY
I'm Turning You Loose *Epic 73579/promo/rear insert/'90* $5
Let's Call it a Day Today *Epic 73427/promo/'90* .. $5

WYNETTE, TAMMY & RANDY TRAVIS
We're Strangers Again
Epic 73958/promo/rear insert/'91 .... $5

WYNN, STEVE
Carolyn *Rhino 90042/promo/silkscreened/ps/'90* $6
Drag (edit)/Christines Tune (live)/Younger (live)/How's My Little Girl *Rhino 90114/promo/silkscreened/ps/'92* $12
Kerosene Man/Something to Remember Me By/Kool Thing/Boy in the Bubble/Conspiracy of the Heart *RNA 74427/stock/ps/'91* ... $8
Tuesday *Rhino 90125/promo/silkscreened/ps/'92* $6

X
Wild Thing 3:18 & 6:18
Curb 10538/promo/custom sticker $10

X-CLAN
Fire & Earth 3 vers. *Polydor 582/promo/ps/'91* $4
Fire & Earth video versions *Polydor 651/promo/logo on red/'92* $5

XTC
Dear Madam Barnum *Geffen 4447/promo/'92* $5
Extrovert/Heaven is Paved With Broken Glass/Blame the Weather/Respectable Street *Geffen 4251/promo/silkscreened/hardcover ps/'90* $10
King For a Day *Geffen 3522/promo/'89* $5
King For a Day czar mi & versailles mix/Toys/Desert Island *Geffen 21236/stock/silkscreened pic/ps/'89* $8
Mayor Of Simpleton *Virgin 3408/promo/ps/'89* ... $7
NAC Sampler ep (My Bird Performs/Wrapped in Grey/Rook/Books Are Burning) *Geffen 4398/promo/gatefold hardcover ps/'92* $8
Radios in Motion ... A History of XTC (Ballad of Peter Pumpkinhead/Mayor of Simpleton/King For a Day/Dear God/Grass + 3) *Geffen 4397/promo/gatefold hardcover ps/'92* $15
Rag & Bone Buffet 24 tracks *Geffen 24417/promo/ps/custom sticker/'90* $15
The Ballad of Peter Pumpkinhead edit & lp
Geffen 4394/promo/silkscreened/ps/'92 ... $6
The Ballad of Peter Pumpkinhead long edit/short edit/lp *Geffen 4407/promo/silkscreened/ps/'92* $6
The Ballad of Peter Pumpkinhead/The Smartest Monkeys/My Bird Performs/Always Winter Never Christmas (last 2 home demos) *Geffen 21813/stock/ps/'92* $6
This is Not the New Album ep (The Ballad of Peter Pumpkinhead/Books are Burning/Crocodile) *Geffen 4396/promo/gatefold hardcover ps/'92* $8

XTRA LARGE
Hooker (edit)/Lovely Host/Eggsbunk/Hooker
Giant 5681/promo/ps/'92 .... $5

XYMOX
At the End of the Day 2 versions/Dreamhouse/ Dawn to Earth *Wing 867 321/stock/ps* ... $7
Imagination edit & lp
Polygram 123/promo/silkscreened/'89 ...... $6
Phoenix of My Heart-Wild Thing (2 versions)/ Twisted/All Fold Up
Wing 868 133/stock/ps/'91 .... $7
Wonderland/Dancing Barefoot *Mercury 520/ promo/silkscreened/custom sticker/'91* $6

XYZ
Inside Out *Enigma 238/promo/silkscreened/ cust. sticker/prod by DON DOKKEN/'89* ... $4
What Keeps Me Loving You *Enigma 263/promo/ logo on red/custom sticker/'90* $4

Y&T
Don't Stop Runnin'/From Yesterday & Today (live)
Metal Blade 6461/promo/ silkscreened/rear insert/'91 .... $5
Don't Be Afraid of the Dark (3 versions)
Geffen 4106/promo/ps/ silkscreened orange/'90 .... $5
Don't Be Afraid of the Dark (rock edit)/Summertime Girls *Geffen 4134/promo/silkscreened logo on orange/'89* $5

YA KID K
Awesome (You Are My Hero) radio & 12"
SBK 05384/promo/ps/'91 .... $4

YALL SO STUPID
85 South lp & instrumental *Rowdy 5000/ promo/silkscreened/ps/'92* $4

YANKOVIC, WEIRD AL
Isle Thing/The Hot Rocks Polka *Rock n Roll 1776/ promo/silkscreened pink/'89* $6
Money For Nothing/Beverly Hillbillies
Scotti Bros 1723/promo/ silkscreened purple/'89 .... $6
Smells Like Nirvana *Scotti Bros 75314/ promo/silkscreened/ps/'92* $5
Taco Grande *Scotti Brothers 75338/promo/ silkscreened/'92* $5
The White Stuff *Scotti Bros 75346/promo/ silkscreened/'92* $5
UHF *Scotti Brothers 1706/promo/ silkscreened pic/'89* $6
You Don't Love Me Anymore *Scotti Bros 75329/ promo/logo on red/'92* $5

YANNI
Nice to Meet You edit/alternate edit
Private 81002/promo/logo on blue/ps/'92 . $5
Swept Away (remix)/In the Mirror
Private Music 2084/promo/ps/'90 .... $5

YASMIN
Stop This Scene (remix)/Late at Night (2 versions)/ Remember You/Summertime (remix)
Geffen 4231/promo/ps/'91 .... $6

YATES, LORI
Promises, Promises *CBS 1583/promo/ silkscreened pic/rear insert/'89* $4

YAZZ
Stand Up For Your Love .. 4:19/7:16/4:17/7:05
Elektra 8063/promo/'88 .... $5
The Only Way is Up *Elektra 8031/promo/'88* $4
The Only Way is Up (3 versions)
Elektra 66732/stock/3"/ps/'88 .... $5
Treat Me Good 3:35/4:40/6:35
Big Life 293/promo/logo on white/'90 .... $5

YEARWOOD, TRISHA
Like We Never Had a Broken Heart
MCA 54172/promo/rear insert/'91 .... $5

YELLO
The Race (3 versions)
Mercury 113/promo/silkscreened/'89 .... $6

YELLOWJACKETS
Geraldine (edit)/Storytellers (edit)
MCA 17995/promo/'89 .... $4
Local Hero edit & lp *MCA 17659/promo/ps/'88* ... $5

YEN
Talk to Me (5 versions)
IRS 027/promo/silkscreened/rear insert ... $5

YES
90125 In the Studio *Album Network #65/ promo/dj radio show/'89* $30
I Would Have Waited Forever edit & lp
Arista 2344/promo/silkscreened/ps/'91 ..... $8
Lift Me Up edit with acappella intro & without/lp
Arista 2218/promo/ps/silkscreened/'91 ..... $8
Lift Me Up top 40 edit & rock radio edit
Arista 2248/promo/silkscreened/ps/'91 ..... $8
Love Will Find the ..edit/lp *Atco 2088/promo/'87*. $10
Make It Easy 2:47 & 4:02
Atco 4008/promo/logo on black/ps/'91 ...... $8
Rhythm of Love (3 versions) *Atco 2089/promo* .. $12
Saving My Heart
Arista 2263/promo/silkscreened/ps/'91 ..... $8
The Yes Album in the studio *Album Network #116/ promo/dj only radio show/'90* $30
Yesyears sampler (8 tracks) *Atco 4009/ promo/silkscreened/rear insert/'91* $25

YO YO
Home Girl Don't Play Dat remix & lp
Eastwest 4619/promo/silkscreened/ps $4

IBWin' Wit My CREWin' radio *Eastwest 5018/ promo/prod.by ICE CUBE/ silkscreened/ps/'93* $4
The Bonnie & Clyde Theme radio versions *Eastwest 5138/promo* $4
Ain't Nobody Better 3 versions *East West 4038/ promo/silkscreened/ps/'91* $4

YOAKAM, DWIGHT

A Thousand Miles From Nowhere *Reprise 6057/ promo/rear insert/logo on white/'93* $5
A Thousand Miles From ..edit *Reprise 6282/ promo/logo on black/rear insert/'93* $6
Ain't That Lonely Yet *Reprise 6028/promo/silkscreened/ps/'93* .. $6
It Only Hurts When I...*Reprise 5041/promo/'90* $5
Long White Cadillac edit & FM *Reprise 3706/promo/'89* $8
Nothing's Changed Here *Reprise 4885/promo/'90* $5
Suspicious Minds edit *Epic 74753/promo/ps/'92* $6
Takes a Lot to Rock.. *Reprise 5273/promo/'90* $6
Takes a Lot to Rock You/If There Was a Way/ Dangerous Man+1 *Reprise 4623/promo* .. $8
The Heart That You... *Reprise 5377/promo/'90* ... $4
Truckin' edit & lp *Arista 2249/promo/ silkscreened/rear insert/'91* $7
You're the One *Reprise 4684/promo/'90* $4

YOAKAM, DWIGHT & BUCK OWENS

Streets of Bakersfield *Reprise 3163/promo/ps/'88* $6

YOAKAM, DWIGHT & PATTY LOVELESS

Send a Message to My Heart *Reprise 5545/promo/'90* $5

YOTHU YINDI

Djapana 5 vers./Gapu tidal mix *Hollywood 66358/ stock/gatefold hardcover ps/'92* $5
Treaty 4 versions *Hollywood 66451/stock/ gatefold hardcover ps/'92* $5
Treaty lp & filthy lucre radio mix *Hollywood 8508/ promo/silkscreened/rear insert/'92* $5

YOUNG BLACK TEENAGERS

Nobody Knows Kelli/Proud to Be Black (3 vers.) *MCA 18416/promo/rear insert/'90* $6
Roll w/the Flavor 2 vers. *Soul 2634/promo/ps/'93* $4
Tap the Bottle lp & instrumental *Soul 2459/promo/ps/'92* $5
To My Donna *Soul 1292/promo/rear insert/'91* ... $4

YOUNG GODS, THE

Skinflowers 4 versions *Play It Again Sam 206/ stock/ps/'92* $5

YOUNG M.C.

Bust a Move *Delicious Vinyl 105/promo/'89* $6
I Come Off *Delic. Vinyl 3192/promo/rear insert* ... $5
Principal's Office *Delicious 3068/promo/ rear insert/custom sticker/'89* $5
That's The Way Love Goes 5 versions *Capitol 16750/stock/ps/'91* $5
That's The Way Love Goes 5 versions *Capitol 79819/promo/silkscreen/ps/'91* $6

YOUNG, NEIL

Arc, the Single *Reprise 5232/promo/'91* $6
Crime in the City (fade) *Reprise 3952/promo/'89* . $6
Freedom *Reprise 25899/promo/ps/ silkscreened pic (cover)/'89* $20
Harvest Moon short edit/long edit/lp *Reprise 5811/promo/silkscreened/'92* $6
Inca Queen edit & lp *Geffen 2796/promo/ gatefold hardcover ps/'87* $10
Long May You...*Reprise 6292/promo/rear insert* ... $6
Long May You... edit & lp *Reprise 6337/promo* .. $6
Love to Burn edit & lp *Reprise 4669/promo/'90* $6
Mansion on the Hill edit & lp *Reprise 4448/ promo/silkscreened pic/rear insert/'90* $8
Mansion on the Hill edit & lp/Dont Spook the Horse *Reprise 21759/stock/gatefold hardcover* .. $5
No More edit & SNL vers. *Reprise3864/promo/'89* $6
Over and Over edit & lp *Reprise 4576/promo/'90* $6
Rockin' in the Free World (3 versions) *Reprise 3729/promo/'89* $8
Ten Men Workin (2 versions) *Reprise 3073/ promo/logo on purple/'88* $10
This Notes For You lp/live/edit of live *Reprise 3091/promo/ps/'88* $15
Unknown Legend *Reprise 5960/promo/'92* $6
War of Man *Reprise 5864/promo/'92* $6

YOUNG, PAUL

Heaven Can Wait (2 versions) *Columbia 73557/promo/ps/'90* $5
Oh Girl *Columbia 73377/promo/ps/'90* $5
Softly Whispering I Love You edit & lp *Columbia 2282/promo/ps/'91* $5
What Becomes of the Brokenhearted *MCA 2106/ promo/"Fried Green Tomatoes" ps/'91* $5

YOUSSOU N' DOUR
Eyes Open sampler 7 tracks
Columbia 4585/promo/ps/'92..................$10

Z'LOOKE
I Can't Stop Thinkin' 3 versions/Co-Medina 3 vers. .
Orpheus 74125/promo/ silkscreened logo/rear insert/'91..............$4

Z, BOBBY
Lie By Lie david Z mix & rock mix edit
Virgin 3037/promo/'90..............................$5
You Are Everything
Virgin 3273/promo/silkscreened/'90..........$5

ZADORA, PIA
Heartbeat of Love *CBS Association 3075/ promo/ps/'89*..$4
Heartbeat of Love (5 versions)
CBS Association 1928/promo/ps/'89........$6
If You Were Mine *Epic 73392/promo/rear insert*...$5

ZAN
House You 4:13/3:47/6:28 *WB 3684/promo/'89* .$4

ZANDER, ROBIN
I've Always Got ..*Intersc.5012/promo/rear insert*...$7
I've Always Got You *Interscope 5013/promo/ logo on blue/ps/'93*....................................$8

ZAP MAMA
Bottom edit,long/Take Me Coco/Plekete/Mizike
Luaka Bop 6111/promo/ silkscreened pic/rear insert/'93................$4

ZAPP
Fire 7" & lp/Jake E Stanstill
Reprise 3951/promo/'89..........................$5
I Play the Talk Box edit & lp
Reprise 3814/promo/'89..........................$5
Ooh Baby Baby *Reprise 3656/promo/'89*..........$5

ZAPP & ROGER
Mega Medley Radio Edit/Mega Mix Show/ Mega Medley With Bonus Beats
Reprise 6370/promo/'93..........................$6

ZAPPA'S UNIVERSE
Choice Morsels (Sofa/Jazz Discharge Party Hats/ Nite School/Echidna's Arf/Hungry Freaks, Daddy) *Verve 726/promo/silkscreened/ rear insert/DWEEZIL, STEVE VAI, DALE BOZZIO, more/'93*........................$10

ZAPPA, DWEEZIL
Anytime at All/Vanity 2 versions/Return of the son of Shoogagoogagunga/ You Can't Judge A Girl...
Barking Pumpkin 666/promo/ps/'91........$10

ZAPPA, FRANK
Peaches en Regalia/I'm Not Satisfied/ Lucille Has Messed My Mind Up
Rykodisc 1001/stock/3"/ps/'87................$12
Sexual Harassment in Workplace/Watermelon in Easter Hay *Rykodisc 1010/stock/3"/ps* .$10

ZEVON, WARREN
Excitable Boy In the Studio *radio show/promo/ cue sheet 4/23/90*..................................$25
Finishing Touches edit *Giant 5017/promo/'91*.....$5
Reconsider Me (new recording)
Virgin 2216/promo/silkscreened/'87..........$7
Searchin' For a Heart
Giant 5171/promo/custom sticker/'91.......$8
Run Straight Down
Virgin 2987/promo/silkscreened/'89..........$5
Sentimental Hygiene Long/short
Virgin 2033/promo/ps...............................$6
Splendid Isolation edit & lp
Virgin 3157/promo/silkscreened/'89..........$6

ZOE
Sunshine On a Rainy Day 2 versions
Polydor 711/promo/silkscreened/ps/'92....$5

ZOO, THE
How Does It Feel (edit) *Capricorn 5892/ promo/MICK FLEETWOOD/'92*...............$4
Reach Out edit
Capricorn 5620/promo/rear insert.............$4
Shakin' the Cage 10 tracks *Capricorn/promo/ dj only silkscreened/M. FLEETWOOD*....$10
Shakin' the Cage edit *Capricorn 5436/promo/ MICK FLEETWOOD/ps/'92*.....................$4
Shakin' the Cage radio edit *Capricorn 5436/ promo/oversized die cut cover/'92*...........$6

ZORN, JOHN
The John Zorn Radio Hour
no label #8195/promo/ps/'90.................$15

ZUCCHERO & PAUL YOUNG
Senza Una Donna edit & lp
London 527/promo/logo on white/ps/'91...$5

ZYDECO, BUCKWHEAT
Cry to Me *Charisma 094/promo/silkscreened/'92* $5
Hey Good Lookin' *Island 6626/promo/ silkscreen/rear insert/sticker/'90*...............$5
Hey Joe edit & lp *Charisma 079/promo/ trifold hardcover ps/'92*............................$6
My L'il Girl (edit)/On a Night Like This
Island 2146/promo/ps/'87..........................$8

ZZ TOP
Burger Man *WB 4938/promo/'90*......................$6
Concrete and Steel
WB 4494/promo/silkscreened/ps/'90........$6
Decision or Collision *WB 4719/promo/'90*..........$6
Doubleback single & edit *WB 4074/promo/'90*....$6

Give It Up *WB 4584/promo/'90* $6
Give It Up (5 versions) *WB 21840/stock/ hardcover ps/'91* $6
My Head's in Mississippi *WB 4777/promo/'90* $6
Recycler (full lp) *WB 26458/promo only metal outer package/custom sticker/'90* $25
Recycler (world premier broadcast) *Album Network/WB/promo/rear insert* $25
Viva Las Vegas 8:36/5:11 *WB 5483/promo/'92* ..$8
Viva Las Vegas edit & lp *WB 5357/promo/silkscreened/'90* $6

Various Artists Compilations

1993 NARM SAMPLER
w/COVERDALE-PAGE, S.EARLE, MICHAEL NESMITH, ELTON JOHN, SLOAN, CHANTE MOORE..(17 in all)
Uni 2632/promo/ps/'93 .... $8

2001: A POST MODERN ODYSSEY
w/SHAKESPEARS SISTER, BAD, SUGARCUBES, D. HARRY, 13 more
Hits HT006/promo/ps/'89 .... $8

A LITTLE ON THE CD SIDE 1
w/HINDU LOVE GODS, ENO & CALE, EDIE BRICKELL, POSIES, SOUL ASYLUM, WENDY & LISA + 11 *Musician 9101/promo/ silkscreened/gatefold hardcover ps* $8

A LITTLE ON THE CD SIDE 2
w/JUDYBATS, JAN GARBAREK, DARDEN SMITH, MAGGIE'S DREAM, WILLIE NILE, MATERIAL ISSUE, STEVE MORSE... *Musician 9102/ promo/gatefold hardcover ps* $8

A LITTLE ON THE CD SIDE 3
w/ADRIAN BELEW, PETER CASE, SARAH MCLACHLAN, DOWNY MILDEW, BEDLAM, HOLLY COLE, SHAKESPEARS SISTER +11
Musician/promo/gatefold hardcover ps/'92 .... $8

A LITTLE ON THE CD SIDE 4
w/PALE DIVINE, VAN MORRISON, SCHOOL OF FISH, DAVE ALVIN, DAVID BOWIE, TEXAS TORNADOS, AL DIMEOLA, BRUCE COCKBURN (30 in all) *Musician 9104/ promo/gatefold ps/2 cds* $12

A LITTLE ON THE CD SIDE 5
w/ADRIAN BELEW, PETER CASE, SARAH MCLACHLAN, DOWNY MILDEW, BEDLAM, SHAKESPEARS SISTER, A.DIMEOLA + 11 *Musician 9105/promo/ gatefold hardcover ps/'92* $8

A LITTLE ON THE CD SIDE 6
w/PAUL WELLER, ENO, 4 NON BLONDES, JULIAN COPE, 311, TELEVISION, T. MONSTER, MACEO PARKER, JEFF HEALEY...
Musician/promo/gatefold hardcover ps $8

A LITTLE ON THE CD SIDE 7
w/PJ HARVEY, MICHAEL PENN, BLIND MELON, LYLE LOVETT, DIXIE DREGS, TOM WAITS, JUDE COLE, many more (30 in all)
Musician/promo/trifold hardcover/booklet/2 cds/'92 .... $12

A LITTLE ON THE CD SIDE 8
w/PAUL WELLER, ENO, JULIAN COPE, TELEVISION, JEFF HEALEY...
Musician 9018/promo/trifold hardcover ps/'92 .... $8

A LITTLE ON THE CD SIDE 9
w/HOTHOUSE FLOWERS, ROSANNE CASH, BRIAN MAY, MICHAEL PENN, MICHAEL MANTLER & JACK BRUCE, GOO GOO DOLLS+11 *Musician/promo/ trifold hardcover ps* $8

A LITTLE ON THE CD SIDE 10
w/DANIEL LANOIS, MARIA MCKEE, X, PERE UBU, PJ HARVEY, FRANK GAMBALE, DEVLINS, CRAIG CHAQUICO, JOHNNY CLEGG...
Musician 9110/promo/trifold hardcover ps/silkscreened/'93 .... $8

A LITTLE TASTE
w/RY COODER, 54 40 + 2
WB 2866/promo/3" sampler on custom card $6

A LUMP OF COAL
w/CARNIVAL ART, CLOCKHAMMER, HOODOO GURUS, PRIMITIVES, THE WEDDING PRESENT...
First Warning 72705-75702/promo/ silkscreened/cust.sticker/'91 .... $6

A RESTLESS WORLD
w/THE DOUGBOYS, YMO, CIRITH UNGOL, BARBIE BONES, G. SAGE, BAND OF SUSANS, HELLION, BOBBY SHERMAN, FEAR, DOA + 9
Restless 002/promo/ps/'91 .... $8

A SNEAK PEAK
w/ART GARFUNKEL, JIMMY CLIFF, JAMES TAYLOR, MIDNIGHT OIL, DYLAN, N.LOWE, JON ANDERSON, JOE ZAWINUL, much more
Columbia 2890/promo/ps/2 cds/'88 .... $15

A TASTE OF EAR CANDY
w/JIBRE WISE ONE (2), AUDREY WHEELER (If We Try a Little Harder/ Get It White It's Hote) *Ear Candy 1001/ promo/gatefold hardcover with booklet ps/'91* $6

A WAKE-UP CALL FOR THE 90S
w/OZZY, ALICE COOPER, SHARK ISLAND, PRONG, SUICIDAL TENDENCIES, RIOT, KREATOR + 8
Epic 1974/promo/ps/'90 .... $8

A YEAR GO WE HADN'T HEARD OF THEM EITHER
w/DOUBLE, LOVER SPEAKS, DAVID & DAVID, BRICKLIN, ROSIE VELA (2 songs each) *A&M 17413/promo/ tri fold open up hardcover ps/'86* $8

A&M GOSPEL
w/KINGDOM, WILLIAMS BROTHERS, ALBERTINA WALKER, COMMISSIONED, THOMAS WHITFIELD...
A&M 75021 7254/promo/'92 .... $6

A&M GOSPEL SALUTES BLACK HISTORY MONTH
w/GMWA MASS CHOIR, HERMAN HARRIS, TONY MCGILL, DAWKINS & DAWKINS, ALBERTINA WALKER...
A&M 31454 8022/promo/'93 .... $6

A&M NIGHTPLAY CD SAMPLER
w/BREATHE, TUCK & PATTI, SHANICE WILSON, GIANT STEPS, TAMARA & THE SEEN, JEFFREY OSBORNE... *A&M/promo/ps/'88* $6

A&M PRESENTS CD3
w/STING, S. VEGA, SQUEEZE, OMD & CD3 info *A&M 17543/promo/ ps/3"/'88* $6

A&M RECORDS SAMPLER
w/MINT CONDITION, AARON NEVILLE, KEVIN MONTGOMERY, SWERVEDRIVER (2 each)
A&M 31454 8047/promo/ silkscreened/'93 .... $6

ABBEY ROAD DISTRIBUTORS
w/LUIS ENRIQUE, ROBERTO CARLOS, WILLY CHIRINO, LA MAFIA, JOSE LUIS RODRIGUEZ, ANA GABRIEL, RUBEN BLADES...
Sony Discos 10026/promo/ps/'92 .... $6

AC CD - THE NEW POWER SOURCE 12/91
w/AMY GRANT, NATALIE COLE, BARRY MANILOW, (3), STEPHANIE MILLS... (all christmas songs)
Mainly Adult Contemporary/promo/ps $7

AC CD - THE NEW POWER SOURCE 8/89
w/SWING OUT SISTER, ANNE MURRAY, MILLI VANILLI, DOOBIE BROTHERS, ROXETTE... *Mainly Adult Contemporary/promo/back ps/'89* $6

AC CD - THE NEW POWER SOURCE 7/89
w/JACKSON BROWNE, MADONNA, VAN MORRISON, DIANA ROSS, ROBERT PLANT, STEVE WINWOOD, DR JOHN... *Mainly Adult Contemporary/promo/back ps/'89* $6

AC CD - THE NEW POWER SOURCE 6/89
w/BETTE MIDLER, DONNY OSMOND, INDIGO GIRLS, RICHARD MARX...
Mainly Adult Contemporary/promo/ back ps/'89 .... $6

AC CD - THE NEW POWER SOURCE 5/89
w/10,000 MANIACS, DUSTY SPRINGFIELD, DR JOHN, CSNY...
Mainly Adult Contemporary/ promo/back ps/'89 .... $6

AC CD THE NEW POWER SOURCE 4/89
w/CAROLE KING, ROY ORBISON, SOUTHERN PACIFIC, TANITA TIKARAM...
Mainly Adult Contemporary/promo/ps/'89 . $6

ADD TO YOUR FUTURE
w/FOUR TOPS, GAP BAND, JERMAINE STEWART, MILLI VANILLI...
Arista 9791/promo/ps/'88 .... $6

ALBUM NETWORK IN STORE PLAY TUNEUP (4/91)
w/FISHBONE, QUEEN, SCHOOL OF FISH, RORY GALLAGHER, PAT BENATAR, ALICE IN CHAINS, ROD ARGENT...
promo/open up ps w/song by song bios ... $6

ALBUM NETWORK CD TUNEUP #1 (5/1/87)
w/STEVE JONES, DAVID BOWIE, JOHN HIATT, CURE, KD LANG + 12
promo/ps/'87 .... $15

ALBUM NETWORK EXPAND O CD TUNE UP 1 (2/12/9)0)
w/HOUSE OF LOVE, COWBOY JUNKIES, CHURCH, OINGO BOINGO, SINEAD O'CONNOR, DEL AMITRI, FALL, DAVE EDMUNDS... *promo/open up ps w/brief song by song bios* $6

ALBUM NETWORK
TOP 40 TUNEUP #1 (2/15/88)
w/JOE COCKER, THE CHURCH, TIFFANY, AGNETHA FALTSKOG, LOS LOBOS, ICEHOUSE, MIKE OLDFIELD...*promo/ open up ps w/brief song by song bios* $15

ALBUM NETWORK
CD TUNEUP #2 (5/25/87)
w/DAN FOGELBERG, NEIL YOUNG, MARSHALL CRENSHAW, CHRIS ISAAK, T'PAU, GREAT WHITE + 11 *promo/open up ps w/brief song by song bios* $12

ALBUM NETWORK
IN STORE PLAY TUNEUP 2 (6/91)
w/CIRCLE OF SOUL, RICHARD THOMPSON, MARK COHN, CHRIS REA, WARRANT, SARAYA, JAMES BROWN, DREAD ZEPPELIN... *promo/open up ps w/brief song by song bios* $6

ALBUM NETWORK
TOP 40 TUNEUP #2 (3/14/88)
w/JOHNNY HATES JAZZ, MIDNIGHT OIL, THE ALARM, DONALD FAGEN, BUSTER POINDEXTER, + 9 *promo/open up ps w/brief song by song bios* $10

ALBUM NETWORK
CD TUNEUP #3 (6/22/87)
w/FIXX, INXS, LOS LOBOS, PAT METHENY, GARY MOORE, TSOL, SAINTS, KEEL, 9 more *promo/open up ps w/brief song by song bios* $10

ALBUM NETWORK
TOP 40 TUNEUP #3
w/CLAPTON, SMITHEREENS, TONIO K, DEBBIE GIBSON, 11 more *promo/open up ps w/brief song by song bios* $8

ALBUM NETWORK
TOP 40 TUNEUP #4
w/CHICAGO, GRAHAM PARKER, ICE T, FAT BOYS.. *.promo/open up ps w/brief song by song bios* $8

ALBUM NETWORK
CD TUNEUP #4 (7/13/87)
w/TWISTED SISTER, REPLACEMENTS, GUNS N ROSES, DIO, JOE ELY, 10,000 MANIACS, 11 more *promo/ open up ps w/brief song by song bios* $10

ALBUM NETWORK
CD TUNEUP #5 (8/3/87)
w/THE CULT, SLADE, GENE LOVES JEZEBEL, PRETENDERS, RICHARD MARX, CUTTING CREW, 9 more *promo/open up ps w/brief song by song bios* $8

ALBUM NETWORK
EXPAND O CD TUNE UP 5 (7/30/90)
w/PIXIES, STRANGLERS, STEVE WYNN, CAVEDOGS, MOTHER LOVE BONE, CURTIS MAYFIELD & ICE T, HEART THROBS, CONCRETE BLONDE, JANES ADDICTION...*promo/open up ps w/brief song by song bios* $6

ALBUM NETWORK
EXPAND O CD TUNE UP 6 (8/27/90)
w/POSIES, LILAC TIME, COCTEAU TWINS, PREFAB SPROUT, MEGADETH... *promo/open up ps w/song by song bios* ...$6

ALBUM NETWORK
CD TUNEUP #6 (8/24/87)
w/REM, KISS, GUAD. DIARY, DBS, RED HOT CHILI PEPPERS, FAB.T-BIRDS, ITS IMMATERIAL, GENE LOVES JEZEBEL... *promo/open up ps w/brief song by song bios* $8

ALBUM NETWORK
TOP 40 TUNEUP #6 (7/27/88)
w/FLESH FOR LULU, PM, BEACH BOYS, TONI CHILDS, TRANSVISION VAMP, RECKLESS SLEEPERS, ROD STEWART, HOUSE OF SHOCK.. *promo/open up ps w/brief song by song bios* $8

ALBUM NETWORK
TOP 40 TUNEUP #7
W/BON JOVI, BEAT FARMERS, NEIL YOUNG, TOM WAITS, ...*promo/open up ps w/brief song by song bios* $6

ALBUM NETWORK
EXPAND O CD TUNE UP 7 (9/24/90)
w/REDD KROSS, BOOK OF LOVE, KIRSTY MACCOLL, INSPIRAL CARPETS, ENO & CALE + 12 *promo/open up ps w/brief song by song bios* $6

ALBUM NETWORK
CD TUNEUP #7 (9/14/87)
w/BILLY THORPE (2), CRUZADOS (2), NEIL YOUNG, BODEANS, TOM WAITS, MSG, JIMMY CLIFF... *promo/open up ps w/brief song by song bios* $8

ALBUM NETWORK
TOP 40 CD TUNEUP #7 (8/31/88)
w/SIOUXSIE & BANSHEES, AMY GRANT, DEPECHE MODE, ELTON JOHN, ROBERT CRAY, ZIGGY MARLEY, STEVE MILLER, AL STEWART...*promo/ open up ps w/brief song by song bios* $6

ALBUM NETWORK
CD TUNEUP #8 (10/5/87)
w/ROBBIE ROBERTSON, THE ALARM, MARTHA DAVIS, 54-40, LOVE AND ROCKETS, THE TRUTH, AZTEC CAMERA, TESLA, 8 more *promo/open up ps w/brief song by song bios* $8

ALBUM NETWORK
EXPAND O CD TUNE UP 8 (10/22/90)
w/PWEI, SOUP DRAGONS, SISTERS OF MERCY, DANIELLE DAX, ALICE IN CHAINS, SKINNY PUPPY, U2, LIVING COLOUR, ECHO & BUNNYMEN...*promo/open up ps w/brief song by song bios* $6

ALBUM NETWORK
TOP 40 TUNEUP #8 (9/28/88)
w/HALL & OATES, MARC ALMOND, VAN HALEN, KANSAS, 38 SPECIAL, RANDY NEWMAN... *promo/open up ps w/brief song by song bios* $6

ALBUM NETWORK
TOP 40 TUNEUP #9 (10/31/88)
w/TRAV. WILBURYS, ART OF NOISE, EDIE BRICKELL.. *promo/open up ps w/brief song by song bios* $6

ALBUM NETWORK
EXPAND O CD TUNE UP 9 (1/21/91)
w/GODFATHERS, PWEI, TOO MUCH JOY, INSPIRAL CARPETS, KITCHENS OF DISTINCTION, HAVANA 3AM... *promo/open up ps w/song by song bios* ...$6

ALBUM NETWORK
CD TUNEUP #9 (10/26/87)
w/TRIUMPH, U2 (Silver & Gold/Spanish Eyes), ROBBIE ROBERTSON, DEPECHE MODE, REPLACEMENTS... *promo/ open up ps w/brief song by song bios* $12

ALBUM NETWORK
CD TUNEUP #10 (11/16/87)
w/LITTLE FEAT, SQUEEZE, WHITESNAKE, GENE LOVES JEZEBEL, KISS, VAN MORRISON + 12 *promo/open up ps w/brief song by song bios* $8

ALBUM NETWORK
EXPAND O CD TUNE UP 10 (2/18/91)
w/JESUS JONES, HORSE FLIES, SOUP DRAGONS, SISTERS OF MERCY, HAPPY MONDAYS, CAVEDOGS, WAYNE TOUPS... *promo/open up ps w/brief song by song bios* $6

ALBUM NETWORK
TOP 40 TUNEUP #10 (12/12/88)
w/GUNS N ROSES, HOTHOUSE FLOWERS, ROD STEWART, FLEETWOOD MAC, GUY, DURAN DURAN, KEITH SWEAT... *promo/open up ps w/song by song bios* ...$6

ALBUM NETWORK
TOP 40 TUNEUP #11 (2/13/89)
w/TRAV. WILBURYS, VAN HALEN, NEW ORDER, NEVILLE BROS, CSNY... *promo/open up ps w/song by song bios* ...$6

AALBUM NETWORK
EXPAND O CD TUNE UP 11 (3/25/91)
w/HOODOO GURUS, XYMOX, MARSHALL CRENSHAW, ROBIN HOLCOMB, DREAM WARRIORS... *promo/open up ps w/song by song bios* ...$6

LBUM NETWORK
TOP 40 TUNEUP #12 (3/20/89)
w/GUNS N ROSES, ELVIS COSTELLO, WATERFRONT, PHOEBE SNOW... *promo/open up ps w/song by song bios* ...$6

ALBUM NETWORK
CD TUNEUP #13/best new music '88
w/CHURCH, DOKKEN, MEGADETH, ZODIAC MINDWARP, ECHO, LITA FORD, JESUS & MARY CHAIN + 27 *promo/open up ps w/brief song by song bios/2 CDs* $15

ALBUM NETWORK
TOP 40 TUNEUP #13 (4/17/89)
w/MIKE & MECHANICS, CURE, DONNA SUMMER, MELISSA ETHERIDGE, FREDDIE JACKSON... *promo/open up ps w/song by song bios* ...$6

ALBUM NETWORK
TUNEUP IN STORE PLAY #13
w/MATTHEW SWEET (Goodfriend 13 tracks), SONNY LANDRETH (Outward Bound 11 tracks), KEITH RICHARDS, PAUL WELLER, many more *promo/ open up ps w/brief song by song bios/3 cds/multiple booklets* $20

ALBUM NETWORK
TOP 40 TUNEUP #14 (5/22/89)
w/WANG CHUNG, DION, DONNY OSMOND, THE CULT, ROXETTE, BILLY SQUIER.. *promo/open up ps w/song by song bios* ...$6

ALBUM NETWORK
EXPAND O CD TUNE UP 14
w/WONDER STUFF, XYMOX, RAINDOGS, MARY'S DANISH, GANG OF FOUR, MEAT PUPPETS... *promo/open up ps w/brief song by song bios* $6

ALBUM NETWORK
IN STORE PLAY TUNEUP #14
w/GENE LOVES JEZEBEL, BON JOVI, SCREAMING TREES, JOHNNY WINTER, TORI AMOS, BOB MARLEY, CURVE, HELMET, (31 in all) *promo/open up ps w/brief song by song bios/2 cds*..............$12

ALBUM NETWORK
CD TUNEUP #14 (2/22/88)
w/LOS LOBOS, REM, JONI MITCHELL, ROBYN HITCHCOCK, GUNS N ROSES, 13 more *promo/open up ps w/song by song bios* ...$6

ALBUM NETWORK
CD TUNEUP #15 (3/15/88)
w/TALKING HEADS, B. FERRY, LYLE LOVETT, PREFAB SPROUT + 14 *promo/open up ps w/song by song bios* ...$6

ALBUM NETWORK
ROCK 40 #15 (6/19/89)
w/CHER, RED SIREN, THE CALL, CROWDED HOUSE, HOWARD JONES, SPIRIT, JAMES INGRAM *promo/open up ps w/brief song by song bios* $6

ALBUM NETWORK
CD TUNEUP #16 (4/4/88)
w/SCORPIONS, NEIL YOUNG, LIVING COLOR, POISON, TONIO K + 13 *promo/ open up ps w/brief song by song bios* $6

ALBUM NETWORK
IN-STORE PLAY TUNEUP #16 (2/93)
w/MICK JAGGER, LENNY KRAVITZ, BLACK UHURU, K.RICHARDS, D.DREGS, QUICKSAND, BLIND MELON, SOUL ASYLUM (26 tracks in all) *promo/open up ps w/brief song by song bios* $12

ALBUM NETWORK
TUNEUP ROCK 40 #16
w/STARSHIP, BEE GEES, TOM PETTY, JACKSON BROWNE, ICEHOUSE, TODD RUNDGREN, BEACH BOYS, MARSHALL CRENSHAW... *promo/open up ps w/brief song by song bios* $6

ALBUM NETWORK
TUNEUP ROCK 40 #17
w/TINA TURNER, THE CULT, TEXAS, GIANT, REM, JODY WATLEY, B52S, COVER GIRLS... *promo/open up ps w/brief song by song bios* $6

ALBUM NETWORK
CD TUNEUP #17 (4/25/88)
w/JOAN JETT, VINNIE VINCENT, G. PARKER, 13 more *promo/open up ps w/brief song by song bios* $6

ALBUM NETWORK
CD TUNEUP ROCK 40 #17 (8/21/89)
w/TINA TURNER, THE CULT, TEXAS, REM, TEN YEARS AFTER, B52S, RANDY CRAWFORD + 10 *promo/open up ps w/brief song by song bios* $6

ALBUM NETWORK
ROCK 40 #17 (8/21/89)
w/TINA TURNER, THE CULT, TEXAS, REM, B52S, JODY WATLEY, TEN YEARS AFTER... *promo/open up ps w/brief song by song bios* $6

ALBUM NETWORK
ROCK 40 #18 (9/25/89)
w/THE ALARM, EURYTHMICS, ICEHOUSE, DEBORAH HARRY, GIANT, DANNY ELFMAN, KIX... *promo/open up ps w/brief song by song bios* $6

ALBUM NETWORK
IN-STORE PLAY #18 (5/93)
w/PJ HARVEY, ROCKET FROM THE CRYPT, THE FLUID, TAYLOR DAYNE, CRANBERRIES, DIESEL, VINCE NEIL, BOB GELDOF, ANTHRAX... *promo/ open up ps w/brief song by song bios* $6

ALBUM NETWORK
CD TUNEUP ROCK 40 #18 (9/25/89)
w/THE ALARM, EURYTHMICS, THOMPSON TWINS, ICEHOUSE, DANNY ELFMAN, KIX + 12 *promo/open up ps w/brief song by song bios* $6

ALBUM NETWORK
CD TUNEUP #18 (5/16/88)
w/PETER MURPHY, HONEYMOON SUITE, GUNS N ROSES, ERIC BURDON, STEVE FORBERT, WILL & THE KILL + 12 *promo/open up ps w/song by song bios* ...$6

ALBUM NETWORK
ROCK 40 #19 (10/23/89)
w/WHITESNAKE, SMITHEREENS, TOM PETTY, BEE GEES, ANDERSON-BRUFORD-WAKEMAN-HOWE, TINA TURNER... *promo/open up ps w/song by song bios* ...$6

ALBUM NETWORK
CD TUNEUP #19 (6/6/88)
w/IGGY POP, NEIL YOUNG, CHURCH, 10,000 MANIACS, JESUS & MARY CHAIN, CLASH, GEORGIA SATELLITES + 11 *promo/open up ps w/song by song bios* ...$7

ALBUM NETWORK
TOP 40 TUNEUP #20
w/JETHRO TULL, Z.MARLEY, CINDERELLA G.ALLMAN...*promo/open up ps w/brief song by song bios* $6

ALBUM NETWORK
CD TUNEUP ROCK 40 #20 (11/27/89)
w/QUINCY JONES, KATE BUSH, EURYTHMICS, ELTON JOHN, GLORIA ESTEFAN, GREAT WHITE, KINKS + 10 *promo/open up ps w/song by song bios* ...$6

ALBUM NETWORK
EXPAND O CD TUNE UP 20 (1/13/92)
w/SOCIAL DISTORTION, LUSH, JULES SHEAR, SUGARCUBES, JOHN MELLANCAMP, LIGHTN. SEEDS, JUDYBATS...*promo/open up ps w/brief song by song bios* $6

ALBUM NETWORK
CD TUNEUP #20 (6/27/88)
w/GREGG ALLMAN, JETHRO TULL, ZIGGY MARLEY, AZTEC CAMERA, STEVE FORBERT, GARY WRIGHT + 11 *promo/open up ps w/brief song by song bios* $6

ALBUM NETWORK
CD TUNEUP #21 (7/18/88)
w/LITTLE FEAT, BRIAN WILSON, CHRISSIE HYNDE & UB40, LIVING COLOUR, FLESH FOR LULU, ROSSINGTON BAND, HOTHOUSE FLOWERS, IN TUA NUA, JOHN CAFFERTY + 21 *promo/2 discs/open up ps w/brief song by song bios* $15

ALBUM NETWORK
CD TUNEUP #22 (8/8/88)
w/JOAN ARMATRADING, GRAHAM PARKER, LETS ACTIVE, ALL ABOUT EVE, BRYAN FERRY, CLAPTON, SEDUCE... *promo/open up ps w/song by song bios* ...$6

ALBUM NETWORK
EXPAND O CD TUNEUP #22 (3/9/92)
w/JESUS & MARY CHAIN, BEASTIE BOYS, DYLANS, AFGHAN WHIGS, CHRIS MARS, MICHELLE SHOCKED, JOHN PRINE, RECOIL... *promo/open up ps w/brief song by song bios* $6

ALBUM NETWORK
NEXT 40 #22 (2/19/90)
w/AEROSMITH, GAP BAND, SIN.O'CONNOR, LA GUNS, PETER MURPHY, GREAT WHITE... *promo/open up ps w/brief song by song bios* $6

ALBUM NETWORK
CD TUNEUP #23 (8/29/88)
w/HUEY LEWIS, BIG COUNTRY, JIMMY PAGE, GUNS N ROSES, JOHN HIATT, DAVID LINDLEY, LONNIE MACK, AL STEWART + 10 *promo/open up ps w/brief song by song bios* $6

ALBUM NETWORK
CD TUNEUP #24
w/RANDY NEWMAN, MELISSA ETHERIDGE, BUNBURYS, JIMMY BARNES + 13 promo/open up ps w/song by song bios ...$6

ALBUM NETWORK
NEXT 40 #24 (4/23/90)
w/WILSON PHILLIPS, WHITESNAKE, THE CHURCH, BILLY IDOL, YELLO, SUZANNE VEGA... *promo/open up ps w/brief song by song bios* $6

ALBUM NETWORK
NEXT 40 #25 (5/28/90)
w/MIDNIGHT OIL, SOUL II SOUL, ADAM ANT, POINTER SIS., FASTER PUSSYCAT... *promo/open up ps w/song by song bios* ...$6

ALBUM NETWORK
EXPAND O CD TUNE UP 25 (6/8/92)
w/BILLY GOAT, SUGARCUBES, WIRE TRAIN, MISSION UK, CHILLS, CONCRETE BLONDE, CAUSE & EFFECT... + CATHER. WHEEL Ferment (12 tracks) *promo/open up ps w/brief song by song bios/2 cds*..............$12

ALBUM NETWORK
CD TUNEUP #25
w/STEVE EARLE, 38 SPECIAL, JOAN JETT, OZZY OSBOURNE, DREAM SYNDICATE, HOUSE OF LORDS... *promo/open up ps w/song by song bios* ...$6

ALBUM NETWORK
EXPAND O CD TUNEUP #26 (7/6/92)
w/PJ HARVEY, SOUP DRAGONS, MINISTRY, WHITE ZOMBIE, KITCHENS OF DISTINCTION, BEAUTIFUL SOUTH, CARTER... *promo/open up ps w/brief song by song bios* $6

ALBUM NETWORK
CD TUNEUP #26 (10/31/88)
w/REM, QUIET RIOT, SIOUXSIE, STEVE WINWOOD, EVERLY BROS, JOHN HIATT, BILLY BRAGG, SONIC YOUTH, ALICE COOPER + 9 *promo/open up ps w/brief song by song bios* $6

ALBUM NETWORK
CD TUNEUP #27 (11/21/88)
w/K. RICHARDS, ROBERT CRAY (guitar solo mix), SAINTS, 11 more *promo/open up ps w/brief song by song bios* $6

ALBUM NETWORK
NEXT 40 #27 (7/30/90)
w/DEPECHE MODE, TONY TONI TONE, SMITH EREENS, STRYPER... *promo/open up ps w/brief song by song bios* $6

ALBUM NETWORK
NEXT 40 #28 (8/20/90)
w/WARRANT, DURAN, DEVO, JANE CHILD, HOUSE OF LOVE, HOTHOUSE FLOWERS... *`promo/open up ps w/brief song by song bios* $6

ALBUM NETWORK
CD TUNEUP NEXT 40 #28 (8/20/90)
w/WARRANT, WORLD PARTY, DURAN DURAN, HOUSE OF LOVE, DEVO, YAZZ...*promo/ open up ps w/brief song by song bios* $6

ALBUM NETWORK
CD TUNEUP #29 (1/30/89)
w/ELVIS COSTELLO, XTC, MOJO NIXON, 15 more *promo/open up ps w/brief song by song bios* $6

ALBUM NETWORK
CD TUNEUP ROCK 30 (2/20/89)
w/BONNIE RAITT, GARY MOORE, FASTWAY, INDIGO GIRLS, SAINTS, DURAN + 11 *promo/open up ps w/song by song bios* ... $6

ALBUM NETWORK
CD TUNEUP ROCK 31 (3/13/89)
w/RAMONES, TONE LOC, UFO, DICKEY BETTS, 14 more *promo/open up ps w/brief song by song bios* $6

ALBUM NETWORK
CD TUNEUP ROCK 32 (4/3/89)
w/GODFATHERS, REPLACEMENTS, TRAV.WILBURYS, IN TUA NUA, LIVING COLOR, BLACK SABBATH + 12 *promo/open up ps w/song by song bios* ... $6

ALBUM NETWORK
TUNEUP ROCK #35
w/AC-DC, VAN MORRISON, LIVING COLOUR, SOCIAL DISTORTION, REPLACEMENTS, IRON MAIDEN... *promo/open up ps w/brief song by song bios* $6

ALBUM NETWORK
EXPAND O CD TUNEUP #33 (3/9/93)
w/JUDYBATS, SHEEP ON DRUGS, SUNSCREEM, CRUSH, DEVLINS, FUNLAND, RADIOHEAD, SUEDE, WOOL, SWELL... *promo/open up ps w/song by song bios* ... $6

ALBUM NETWORK
CD TUNEUP ROCK 33 (4/24/89)
w/LOVE & ROCKETS, QUEEN, CURE, 10,000 MANIACS, 13 more *promo/open up ps w/brief song by song bios* $6

ALBUM NETWORK
TUNEUP ROCK #35 (6/5/89)
w/VAN MORRISON, PIXIES, CULT, U2, WASP, S.R.VAUGHN, 24 more *promo/ open up ps w/brief song by song bios/ 2 cds/2 booklets* $20

ALBUM NETWORK
CD TUNEUP ROCK 36 (6/26/89)
w/QUEENSRYCHE, STEVE WINWOOD, SONIC YOUTH, LOU REED *promo/open up ps w/brief song by song bios* $6

ALBUM NETWORK
CD TUNEUP ROCK 37 (7/17/89)
w/STEVE STEVENS, ALICE COOPER, PETER GABRIEL, REPLACEMENTS, 14 more *promo/open up ps w/song by song bios* ... $6

ALBUM NETWORK
CD TUNEUP ROCK 38 (8/7/89)
w/ANDERSON-BRUFORD-WAKEMAN-HOWE, MICK JONES, TEN YEARS AFTER, 10,000 MANIACS, GIRLSCHOOL + 13 *promo/open up ps w/song by song bios* ... $6

ALBUM NETWORK
TUNEUP ROCK #38 (8/7/89)
w/ANDERSON-BRUFORD-WAKEMAN-HOWE, MICK JONES, STEVE JONES, TEN YEARS AFTER, 10000 MANIACS, STEVIE RAY VAUGHAN... *promo/ open up ps w/brief song by song bios* $6

ALBUM NETWORK
TUNEUP ROCK #39 (8/28/89)
w/MELISSA ETHERIDGE, THE ALARM, RICKIE LEE JONES, JETHRO TULL, TINA TURNER, TANGIER, WHITE LION + 9 *promo/open up ps w/song by song bios* ... $6

ALBUM NETWORK
TUNEUP ROCK #41 (10/9/89)
w/JOE SATRIANI, XYX, SMITHEREENS, JEFF BECK, KISS, DAVE EDMUNDS, DION, BEAT FARMERS.. *promo/open up ps w/brief song by song bio* $6

ALBUM NETWORK
TUNEUP ROCK #42
w/ERIC CLAPTON, SCORPIONS, KINKS, LAURIE ANDERSON, ALARM, SOUNDGARDEN, DOGS D'AMOUR... *promo/open up ps w/brief song by song bios* $6

ALBUM NETWORK
CD TUNEUP ROCK 42 (10/30/89)
w/CLAPTON, KINKS, SCORPIONS, LAURIE ANDERSON, THE ALARM, SOUNDGARDEN... *promo/open up ps w/brief song by song bios* $6

ALBUM NETWORK
TUNEUP ROCK #43
w/THE ANGELS, TOM PETTY, GIANT, LA GUNS, THE CURE, ALL ABOUT EVE, ALICE COOPER, STEVIE RAY VAUGHN *promo/open up ps w/song by song bios* ...$6

ALBUM NETWORK
CD TUNEUP ROCK 43 (11/20/89)
w/TOM PETTY, JON ANDERSON, LA GUNS, THE CURE, ALICE COOPER, STEVIE RAY VAUGHN, 54-40 + 10 *promo/open up ps w/song by song bios* ...$6

ALBUM NETWORK
CD TUNEUP ROCK 44 (1/15/90)
w/BALAAM & ANGEL, DAVE EDMUNDS, JESUS & MARY CHAIN, THE ALARM, ENUFF Z'NUFF, NEIL NORMAN + 12 *promo/open up ps w/song by song bios* ...$6

ALBUM NETWORK
CD TUNEUP ROCK 47 (3/19/90)
w/RAVE UPS, JOE SATRIANI, MICHELLE SHOCKED, ALICE COOPER + 13 *promo/open up ps w/song by song bios* ...$6

ALBUM NETWORK
CD TUNEUP ROCK 49 (4/30/90)
w/CONCRETE BLONDE, JOHN DOE, WORLD PARTY, Y&T, KISS, SMITHEREENS, SQUEEZE, SILOS, NICK LOWE + 10 *promo/open up ps w/song by song bios* ...$6

ALBUM NETWORK
CD TUNEUP ROCK 50 (5/21/90)
w/PETER MURPHY, STEVE VAI, JOHN HIATT, SLAUGHTER, JESUS & MARY CHAIN, HELIX, 11 more *promo/open up ps w/brief song by song bios* $6

ALBUM NETWORK
CD TUNEUP ROCK 51 (6/11/90)
w/HOTHOUSE FLOWERS, GENE LOVES JEZEBEL, QUEENSRYCHE, MISSION UK, STEVE EARLE + 13 *promo/open up ps w/brief song by song bios* $6

ALBUM NETWORK
CD TUNEUP ROCK 52 (7/2/90)
w/BAD COMPANY, HOUSE OF LOVE, ERIC CLAPTON, ELO, IGGY POP, ERIC JOHNSON, DEVO, SOCIAL DISTORTION, BILLY IDOL, DORO, MICHELLE MALONE, AZTEC CAMERA, many more *promo/ open up ps w/song by song bios/2 cds* ...$15

ALBUM NETWORK
CD TUNEUP ROCK 53 (7/23/90)
w/REO SPEEDWAGON, LA GUNS, SMITHEREENS, MOTLEY CRUE, STYPER, 12 more *promo/open up ps w/brief song by song bios* $6

ALBUM NETWORK
CD TUNEUP ROCK 54 (8/13/90)
w/HOUSE OF LORDS, DON DOKKEN, ANTHRAX, JEFF LYNNE, JANET JACKSON, BLACK SABBATH, 10 more *promo/open up ps w/song by song bios* ...$6

ALBUM NETWORK
TUNEUP ROCK #54 (8/13/90)
w/HOUSE OF LORDS, DON DOKKEN, LITTLE CAESAR, ANTHRAX, LITTLE FEAT, JANET JACKSON, RIVERDOGS, JEFF LYNNE... *promo/open up ps w/brief song by song bios* $6

ALBUM NETWORK
TUNEUP ROCK 55 (9/3/90)
w/NEIL YOUNG, LIVING COLOUR, HOUSE OF LOVE, JOHN HIATT, HOTHOUSE FLOWERS, JOE COCKER.. *promo/ open up ps w/brief song by song bios* $6

ALBUM NETWORK
TUNEUP ROCK #56 (9/24/90)
w/KING SWAMP, SLAUGHTER, THE CALL, DAVE STEWART, MISSION UK, STEVE EARLE, FLEETWOOD MAC, STEVIE RAY VAUGHN (0:30 interview) *promo/ open up ps w/brief song by song bios* $6

ALBUM NETWORK
TUNEUP ROCK #57 (10/15/90)
w/THE ALARM, EDIE BRICKELL, JANES ADDICTION, BLONZ, ENO & CALE, CHARLATANS UK, INDIGO GIRLS (Hammer and a Nail)...*promo/open up ps w/brief song by song bios* $6

ALBUM NETWORK
TUNEUP ROCK #58 (11/5/90)
w/AC-DC, VAN MORRISON, IRON MAIDEN, REPLACEMENTS, SOUL ASYLUM, SOCIAL DISTORTION + 10 *promo/open up ps w/song by song bios* ...$6

ALBUM NETWORK
TUNEUP ROCK 59 (11/26/90)
w/FIREHOUSE, PETER GABRIEL, MOTHER LOVE BONE, STEVE EARLE, ALLMAN BROTHERS, DOUG SAHM, SUICIDAL TEND.... *promo/open up ps w/brief song by song bios* $6

ALBUM NETWORK
TUNEUP #60 (1/7/91)
w/RUNDGREN, LIVING COLOUR, FIREHOUSE, STEVE VAI, VAUGHAN BROTHERS, JUDAS PRIEST... *promo/open up ps w/brief song by song bios* $6

ALBUM NETWORK
TUNEUP ROCK #62 (2/25/91)
w/REM, REPLACEMENTS, VAN MORRISON, NILS LOFGREN & BRUCE SPRINGSTEEN, SISTERS OF MERCY, STEVE MORSE... *promo/open up ps w/brief song by song bios* $6

ALBUM NETWORK
TUNEUP 63 (3/18/91)
w/ENUFF Z'NUFF, PAT BENATAR, THROBS, LENNY KRAVITZ, SCHOOL OF FISH, SUE MEDLEY, THUNDER... *promo/ open up ps w/brief song by song bios* $6

ALBUM NETWORK
TUNEUP ROCK 65 (4/29/91)
w/ALDO NOVA, HOODOO GURUS, STING, DREAD ZEPPELIN, JOE WALSH, TRIXTER... *promo/open up ps w/brief song by song bios* $6

ALBUM NETWORK
TUNEUP ROCK #66 (5/20/91)
w/HOODOO GURUS, MATERIAL ISSUE, MIND FUNK, ERIC GALES, EXTREME, BODEANS, TAJ MAHAL, RAINDOGS... *promo/open up ps w/song by song bios* ...$6

ALBUM NETWORK
CD TUNEUP ROCK 67 (6/10/91)
w/NEVERLAND, STAN RIDGEWAY, ELO 2, SEAL, TAJ MAHAL, FOUR HORSEMEN, MOODY BLUES, RIC OCASEK + SUICIDAL TENDENCIES (Alone) single *promo/open up ps w/brief song by song bios/2 cds* $12

ALBUM NETWORK
TUNEUP ROCK #68 (7/1/91)
w/CONTRABAND, LA GUNS, LIVING COLOUR, ANIMAL LOGIC, ROD STEWART, SQUEEZE + 11 *promo/open up ps w/brief song by song bios* $6

ALBUM NETWORK
TUNEUP 69 (7/22/91)
w/THE SCREAM, KIK TRACEE, SARAYA, ALDO NOVA, DILLINGER, FIREHOUSE, STEVE HOWE... *promo/open up ps w/brief song by song bios* $6

ALBUM NETWORK
TUNEUP 70 (8/12/91)
w/NORTHSIDE, BAD II, TIN MACHINE, RIC OCASEK, SCORPIONS, ROBYN HITCHCOCK, KING OF FOOLS...*promo/ open up ps w/brief song by song bios* $6

ALBUM NETWORK
CD TUNEUP ROCK 71
w/NIRVANA, CONTRABAND, LA GUNS, RIC OCASEK, LLOYD COLE, EUROPE, SHOOTING STAR...*promo/open up ps w/brief song by song bios* $6

ALBUM NETWORK
TUNEUP 73 (10/14/91)
w/THE WHO, SOUNDGARDEN, WARREN ZEVON, PEARL JAM, SCHOOL OF FISH, DRAMARAMA, FIREHOUSE... *promo/open up ps w/song by song bios* ...$6

ALBUM NETWORK
TUNEUP 74
w/TIN MACHINE, JOAN JETT, NEVERLAND, BLUR, THE CULT, PEARL JAM, EUROPE, RICHIE SAMBORA.. *promo/open up ps w/song by song bios* ...$6

ALBUM NETWORK
CD TUNEUP ROCK 75 (11/25/91)
w/PEARL JAM, JOHN MELLENCAMP, TOAD THE WET SPROCKET, LLOYD COLE, BILLY BRAGG, RED HOT CHILI PEPPERS... *promo/open up ps w/song by song bios* ...$6

ALBUM NETWORK
CD TUNEUP ROCK 76 (1/6/92)
w/BODEANS, MIDGE URE, LENNY KRAVITZ, MSG, KIX, UGLY JOE KID, LA GUNS, LILLIAN AXE, GARY MOORE, CARL PERKIN *promo/open up ps w/brief song by song bios* $6

ALBUM NETWORK
TUNEUP ROCK 77
w/BRITNY FOX, TEXAS, SOCIAL DISTORTION, YNGWIE MALMSTEEN, SARAH MCLACHLAN, MATTHEW SWEET, CHIEFTAINS... *promo/open up ps w/brief song by song bios* $6

ALBUM NETWORK
CD TUNEUP ROCK 81 (4/27/92)
w/XTC, CRACKER, SANTANA, SPIN DOCTORS, RINGO STARR, SHOTGUN MESSIAH, HARDLINE... *promo/open up ps w/brief song by song bios* $6

ALBUM NETWORK
CD TUNEUP ROCK 82
w/INDIGO GIRLS (Galileo), DEL AMITRI, M.ETHERIDGE, BLACK SABBATH, PETER MURPHY, SOUP DRAGONS... *promo/open up ps w/song by song bios* ...$6

ALBUM NETWORK
CD TUNEUP ROCK 84 (6/20/92)
w/DIXIE DREGS, TROUBLE, BONHAM, HOUSE OF LORDS, PANTERA.. *promo/open up ps w/song by song bios* ...$6

ALBUM NETWORK
CD TUNEUP ROCK 85 (7/20/92)
w/CLAPTON, GRAHAM PARKER, DELBERT MCCLINTON, GIN BLOSSOMS, MARK CURRY + 7 *promo/open up ps w/brief song by song bios* $6

ALBUM NETWORK
CD TUNEUP ROCK 87 (8/31/92)
w/THE ZOO, MICHAEL PENN, CATHERINE WHEEL, ASIA... + rock the vote psas from M.ETHERIDGE, KISS, L7, MEGADETH, LEMONHEADS, HELMET *promo/open up ps w/brief song by song bios* $6

ALBUM NETWORK
CD TUNEUP ROCK 88 (9/21/92)
w/BAD COMPANY, FAITH NO MORE, SUICIDAL TENDENCIES, SUGAR, TEMPLE OF THE DOG... *promo/open up ps w/brief song by song bios* $6

ALBUM NETWORK
CD TUNEUP #91 (11/23/92)
w/GENE LOVES JEZEBEL, TRIUMPH, T-RIDE, JAYHAWKS, REMBRANDTS, BLIND MELON, DARLENE LOVE, DAN BAIRD, TELEVISION more *promo/open up ps w/brief song by song bios* $6

ALBUM NETWORK
ROCK TUNEUP #93 (1/25/93)
w/SLOAN, PHISH, COPPERHEAD, GIN BLOSSOMS, HEAVY BONES, TROUBLE, 21 GUNS, FLOTSAM AND JETSAM... *promo/open up ps w/song by song bios* ...$6

ALBUM NETWORK
ROCK TUNEUP #95 (3/8/93)
w/SONIC YOUTH, THE THE, PAUL RODGERS, RIC OCASEK, SCHOOL OF FISH, ARCADE, ROCKHEAD, JESUS, JELLYFISH... *promo/open up ps w/brief song by song bios* $6

ALBUM NETWORK
TUNEUP #106 (10/25/93)
w/BUFFALO TOM, GUNS N ROSES, AFGHAN WHIGS, CONCRETE BLONDE, BABY ANIMALS, LILLIAN AXE... *promo/ open up ps w/brief song by song bios* $6

ALBUM NETWORK UNSIGNED BANDS - AUSTRALIAN EDITION (10/31/88)
w/MACHINATIONS, PAINTERS & DOCKERS, WIZARDS OF OZ, 12 more *promo/fold out ps/'88* $6

ALBUM NETWORK UNSIGNED BANDS CD TUNEUP #1 (5/16/88)
w/CASANOVA, HUMAN DRAMA, ETC., NIKITA, VICE, RUNNER-UP, THE PASSENGERS, BRITTON, ONE THOUSAND STEPS, ONE FOUR FIVE...*promo/open up ps w/brief song by song bios* $10

ALIAS WITH A BULLET
w/SMALL, ARCHERS OF LOAF, PICASSO, MATT KEATING, THE LOUD FAMILY, GAME THEORY, TOMMY KEENE, YO LA TENGO.. *Alias/promo/silkscreened/back ps* $5

ALL ROADS LEAD TO BURBANK
w/SQUEEZE, SEAL, ERASURE, ELECTRONIC, THOMPSON TWINS, JANES ADDICTION (Aint No Right - live), RAMONES (Blitzkrieg Bop - live)... *WB 4960/promo/ps/'91* $10

ALMO ST FREE CD
w/JOHN HIATT, NEVILLE BROTHERS, DAVID BAERWALD, JOAN ARMATRADING, STAN GETZ, BLUES TRAVELLER + 2 *A&M 75021 8052/promo/logo on grey/'90* $6

ALTERNATIVE STATES
w/DAVE STEWART, BOXCAR, THE HOLLOW MEN, DREAMS SO REAL, THE CHURCH... (mostly 2 each) *Arista 2111/promo/ps/'90* $6

AMERICAN EXPLORER SERIES
w/JOHNNIE JOHNSON, JIMMIE DALE GILMORE, VERNARD JOHNSON, CHARLIE FEATHERS, BOOZOO CHAVIS (2 each) *Nonesuch 8379/promo/ps/silkscreened*....$8

AMERICAN ORIGINALS SELECTED CUTS VOL. 2
w/MEL TILLIS, LEFTY FRIZZELL, CLAUDE KING, MARTY ROBBINS, GEORGE MORGAN (2 each) *CBS 1831/promo/silkscreened/ps/'90* $6

AMPCRUSHERS
w/BABES IN TOYLAND, BLACK SABBATH, ICE-T, DAMN YANKEES, FAITH NO MORE, MINISTRY, MUDHONEY...
WB 5764/promo/silkscreen/rear insert......$6

AMPLE SAMPLES
w/MICHELLE MALONE, CHURCH, DAVE STEWART, SNAP,DREAMS SO REAL + 8
Arista 2058/promo/silkscreened/ps/'90 .....$6

AND MUSIC FOR ALL
w/DON HENLEY, NELSON, LITTLE CAESAR, CHER, EDIE BRICKELL, PETER GABRIEL, JONI MITCHELL...
Geffen 4199/promo/ps/'91 ....$6

ANGEL FALL/WINTER '91 HIGHLIGHTS
w/MCCARTNEY, KIRI TE KANAWA, PLACIDO DOMINGO & ITZHAK PERLMAN...
Angel 79044/promo/ps/'91 ....$7

ARGH!!! IT'S A LOUD ROCK CD
w/IGGY POP, URBAN DANCE SQUAD, LIMBOMANIACS, MOTHER LOVE BONE, PRIMUS, EXODUS, STEVE VAI, COLD SWEAT, TAD...*Argh 001/promo/ps/'90* ..$10

ARGH!!! IT'S A LOUD ROCK CD
w/MOTORHEAD, PRIMUS, BANG TANGO, MIND FUNK, KING OF KINGS, METAL CHURCH...*Argh 004/promo/ps/'91* $8

ARGH!!! IT'S A LOUD ROCK CD VOL. 2
w/QUEENSRYCHE, MEGADETH, MINISTRY, JETBOY, BLACK SABBATH, CLOCKHAMMER, CARCASS, PANT RA... *Argh 002/promo/ps/'90* $8

ARISTA FROM LA ROOM
w/B. MANILOW, CHURCH, W. HOUSTON
Arista 9635/promo/ps....$6

ARISTA TOP 40
w/HALL & OATES, CHURCH, T TWINS, PATTI SMITH...*Arista 9756/promo/ps/'88* $6

ARISTA'S FALL A/C SAMPLER
w/EXPOSE, EURYTHMICS, TAYLOR DAYNE, BARRY MANILOW + 4
Arista 9910/promo/ps/'89....$6

ARISTA'S NEW MUSIC SAMPLER
w/DAVE STEWART, BOXCAR, HOLLOW MEN, DREAMS SO REAL, CHURCH, MICHELLE MALONE, SAMPLES...
(2 songs each) *Arista 2111/promo/ps/'90* $7

ATCO HITS SPRING '91
w/OUTLAW BLOOD, PLEASURE BOMBS, NOISY MAMA, RAINDOGS, FLIES ON FIRE, REMBRANDTS *Atco 3970/promo/ps/'91* .$5

ATLANTIC'S HITS FOR THE HOLIDAYS
w/PHIL COLLINS, LED ZEPPELIN, DEBBIE GIBSON, INXS, BETTE MIDLER, RATT, WINGER...
Atlantic 3645/promo/2 cds/ps/'90....$15

ATLANTIC'S YEAR IN REVIEW: 1988
w/MIKE & MECHANICS, PHIL COLLINS, INXS, DEBBIE GIBSON...
Atlantic 2566/promo/back ps/'89....$10

ATLANTIC'S YEAR IN REVIEW: 1989
w/MIKE & MECHANICS, DEBBIE GIBSON, STEVIE NICKS, DONNA SUMMER, SKID ROW, PHIL COLLINS...
Atlantic 3129/promo/ps $8

ATLANTIC'S YEAR IN REVIEW: 1990
w/EN VOGUE, DEBBIE GIBSON, BETTE MIDLER, PHIL COLLINS, INXS, WINGER...
Atlantic 3674/promo/ps/'90 ....$8

ATLANTIC'S YEAR IN REVIEW: 1991
w/RUDE BOYS, GENESIS, STEVIE NICKS, INXS, BETTE MIDLER, JULIAN LENNON, ESCAPE CLUB...
Atlantic 4338/promo/ps/'91 ....$8

ATLANTIC'S YEAR IN REVIEW: 1992
w/GENESIS (3), INXS (2), TORI AMOS, SAIGON KICK, MR BIG, LEMONHEADS...
Atlantic 4894/promo/booklet ps/'92....$8

AURAL FIXATIONS
w/JAMES BROWN, WONDER STUFF, GANG OF 4, TIN MACHINE (Shakin' all Over), MEAT PUPPETS (Funnel of Love), ANTHRAX, KATE BUSH... 17 in all
Polygram 419/promo/ps/'91 ....$6

BAD DOG SAMPLER
w/LIGHTNING SEEDS, RICHARD BARONE, CONCRETE BLONDE, OINGO BOINGO, WIRE TRAIN, STEVE EARLE...
MCA 18422/promo/ps/'90 ....$7

BAIT: ALLURRING SOUNDS FROM MCA
w/WRECKX N EFFECT, CHRISTOPHER WILLIAMS, PARENTAL ADVISORY, B.BROWN POSSE, SHAI, MARY J. BLIGE, MARK COLLIE, IGUANAS... *MCA 2619/promo/silkscreened/ps/'93* $7

BANDS YOU'VE NEVER SEEN ON HEE HAW
w/PERE UBU, YELLO, DOGS D'AMOUR, STYLE COUNCIL, 13 more *Polydor 88/ promo/ps/silkscreened/'89* $6

BARCELONA GOLD
w/ROD STEWART, INXS, ERIC CLAPTON, FREDDIE MERCURY, more *WB 26974-2/stock/ps/'92* $12

BBC CLASSIC TRACKS
w/AWB, HENDRIX, ANIMALS, WHO, JOE JACKSON... *Westwood One #90-38/ promo/cue sheets/'90* $12

BBC CLASSIC TRACKS
w/DEEP PURPLE, JIMI HENDRIX (Killing Floor), YARDBIRDS (For Your Love), ELTON JOHN, STONES *Westwood One #90-39 (9/24/90)/promo/extensive cue sheets*....$12

BBC CLASSIC TRACKS
w/QUEEN, WHO, LOS LOBOS, ELO, BEATLES (Money) *Westwood One #90-40/ (10/1/90)/promo/extensive cue sheets*....$12

BEDROCK VS. JELLYSTONE
w/VANESSA PARADIS, SHAKESPEARS SISTER, CATHY DENNIS, HOTHOUSE FLOWERS, LOREZO, PAUL WELLER + 19 *PLG 632/promo/ gatefold hardcover ps/2 cds/'93* $10

BEST OF JAMES BOND
w/P. MCCARTNEY, TOM JONES, DURAN, JOHN BARRY, more *EMI 98560/stock/ps/2 cds/'92* $20

The Best Of San Antonio, Texas
Featuring Sir Doug, Augie, Kevin and The Blacktears, Charlie Beall, Steve Mallet and more

BEST OF SAN ANTONNIO
w/AUGIE MEYERS, KEVIN & BLACKTEARS, STEVE MALLETT, more *Kevin Kat 14/stock/ps/'93*.......................$10

BILLBOARD TOP HITS 1975-1979
w/AMERICA, LINDA RONSTADT, ELTON JOHN, HALL & OATES, QUEEN, ABBA, ERIC CLAPTON, BLONDIE, KNACK... *Rhino 90075/promo/gold silkscreened/ps/'91* $8

BIZARRE/STRAIGHT SAMPLER
w/ALICE COOPER (3), TED NUGENT (2), TOM WAITS, TIM BUCKLEY (5), LENNY BRUCE, GTOS (2), LORD BUCKLEY, CAPT.BEEFHEART (2)... *Rhino 90086/promo/ps/silkscreened/'91* .$12

BLACK LIGHT SPECIAL
w/GOO GOO DOLLS (2), BELLY (2), DINOSAUR JR (2), PURE, BASH & POP, MUDHONEY, SAINT ETIENNE, JUDYBATS *WB 6105/promo/booklet ps* ..$6

BLACK MUSIC MONTH 1991
w/TRACIE SPENCER, FREDDIE JACKSON, PHIL PERRY, DIANNE REEVES, BEBE & CECE WINANS, KING TEE, NAT KING COLE... *Capitol 79731/promo /silkscreened/ps/'91* $8

BLACK MUSIC MONTH 1992
w/ERIC B & RAKIM, DAZZ BAND, PATTI LABELLE, JODECI, JODY WATLEY + 8 *MCA 2281/promo/ps/'92* $8

BLACK MUSIC MONTH 1993
w/TONY TONI TONE, JOE, BUJU BANTON, DAVID MORALES, WILL DOWNING, WALTER BEASLEY, OLETA ADAMS, THIRD WORLD + 8 *Mercury 685/promo/ gatefold hardcover ps/silkscreened/'93* $8

BLINK, AND ITS A HIT
w/SADE, PREFAB SPROUT, BASIA, BROS, TEENA MARIE, 9 more *CBS 1146/promo/ps/'88* $6

BOBBY POE CONVENTION SAMPLER 1991
w/READY FOR WORLD, PATTI LABELLE & MICHAEL MCDONALD, BOSTON, KIM WILDE, TIFFANY, BELINDA CARLISLE... *MCA 1530/promo/'91* $6

BOY HOWDY & SIRE...
w/MY BLOODY VALENTINE, BEATMASTERS, BETTY BOO, RIDE, JOHN WESLEY HARDING, BRADFORD... *Sire 4442/promo/ps/'91* $6

BOYS UNITED
w/BOOK OF LOVE, ERASURE, MARC ALMOND, MORRISSEY, BARNAKED LADIES, DEBORAH HARRY, JUDYBATS... *Sire 6101/promo/ps/'93* $7

BRIDGES - BLACK HISTORY MONTH 1993
w/PATTI LABELLE (Up There With You), BOBBY BROWN, SHAI, BELL BIV DEVOE, WRECKX N EFFECT, MARY J BLIGE, CHANTE MOORE...*MCA 2573/promo/ps* $8

BRILLIANT NEW MUSIC
w/RICHARD THOMPSON, ANIMAL LOGIC, PHIL PERRY, OR N MORE... *Cema Distributors 79939/promo/ps/'91* $7

BURNING LEAVES
w/SONIC YOUTH (2), SUNDAYS (2), NIRVANA, WARRIOR SOUL (2), SLOAN (2), CELL (2)... *DGC 4474/promo/ps/'92* $6

BZZ
w/KATE BUSH, PSYCH. FURS, B.A.D., POI DOG PONDERING.. *Columbia 1926/promo/ps/'89* $7

CAPITOL CHRISTMAS SAMPLER
w/NAT KING COLE, ELLA FITZGERALD, FRANK SINATRA, DEAN MARTIN, BEACH BOYS, ANNE MURRAY... *Capitol 79385/promo/ps/'90* $8

TRADITIONS IN COUNTRY MUSIC DPRO-79249 (79241)
THE R&B LEGACY - THE KING TO THE HAMMER DPRO-79248 (79241)
ROCKIN' THE TOWER! DPRO-79247 (79241)
MEMORIES ARE MADE OF THIS, PART 2: THE 60's AND BEYOND DPRO-79246 (79241)
MEMORIES ARE MADE OF THIS, PART 1: THE 50's & 60's DPRO-79245 (79241)
CLASSIC ROCK ROOTS DPRO-79244 (79241)
WHEN AM WAS KING: 1955-1974 DPRO-79243 (79241)
THE BIRTH OF A DREAM: CAPITOL'S EARLY HITS DPRO-79242 (79241)

CAPITOL'S 50TH ANNIVERSARY
wB.OWENS, 5 KEYS, BEATLES, N. DIAMOND D. MARTIN, DURAN, SEGER, S. MILLER, PEGGY LEE, SINATRA, HEART, more *Capitol 79241/ps/promo/book8 cds* $200

CAPITOL LEANING TOWER PIZZA
w/JOHNNY CLEGG, HEART, LLOYD COLE, DAVE EDMUNDS, ERIC JOHNSON, STANLEY JORDAN... *Capitol 79968/ promo/silkscreened pizza/nifty pizza box container w/"menu" inserts* $12

CBS RECORDS COMPACT DISC DEMONSTRATION
w/BOB DYLAN, MICHAEL JACKSON, JOURNEY, JAMES TAYLOR, MEN AT WORK, DAN FOGELBERG, EWF, ELO + classical selections *CBS 1734/promo/rear insert* ..$8

CBS RECORDS LIMITED EDITION RADIO SAMPLER
w/DOUG STONE, LES TAYLOR, DOLLY PARTON, CHARLIE DANIELS, MARY CHAPIN CARPENTER, WILLIE NELSON RODNEY CROWELL... (2 each) *CBS 1966/promo/ps/'90* $6

CD HITS SAMPLER
w/BELLE STARS, CAROLE KING, ETTA JAMES & DAVE STEWART...
Capitol 79570/promo/'89 ..... $6

CD SAMPLER ONE
w/OZZY OSBOURNE, WALKING WOUNDED, MARYS DANISH, DRAMARAMA, JOHN LEE HOOKER
Chameleon A ORC D1/promo/ps/'90 ..... $6

CD3/ATLANTIC-VIRGIN
w/INXS, AC-DC, MIKE OLDFIELD, WHITE LION
Atlantic Virgin 000029/promo/ps/'88 ..... $6

CD3/ELEKTRA-ASYLUM
w/CURE, 10,000 MANIACS, DOKKEN, K. SWEAT
Elektra-Asylum 000038/promo/ps/3"/'88 .. $8

CD3/WB-GEFFEN
w/D LEE ROTH, KEITH SWEAT, AEROSMITH, DEBBIE GIBSON *WB 000030/promo/3"* $6

CD3/WB-GEFFEN
w/D.LEE ROTH, MADONNA, AEROSMITH, MORRIS DAY
WB Geffen 0000031/promo/ps/3"/'88 ..... $8

CDX VOLUME 20
w/RANDY TRAVIS, GREAT PLAINS, PATTY LOVELESS, RICKY SKAGGS, DESERT ROSE BAND, DAVIS DANIEL, GEORGE FOX, JOHN GORKA...
Compact Disc Xpress/promo/ps 12/91 .... $6

CDX VOLUME 23
w/MARTY STUART, LITTLE TEXAS, HANK WILLIAMS JR, REMINGTONS, LEE GREENWOOD, VINCE GILL, STEVE WARINER...*CDX #23/promo/back ps/'92* . $6

CELEBRATE THE SEASONS
w/ELTON JOHN, VINCE GILL, BOBBY BROWN, PETER GABRIEL, PATTY SMYTH, IZZY STRADLIN, GEORGE STRAIT..
MCA 2497/promo/ps/'92 ..... $7

CENTURY 21 #105
w/STEELY DAN, CYNDI LAUPER, ALAN PARSONS, GLORIA ESTEFAN, SIMPLY RED, BILLY OCEAN, GENESIS, W.HOUSTON, SPRINGSTEEN...
Golddisc/promo $12

CENTURY 21 #171
w/PAULA ABDUL, PAUL MCCARTNEY, DONNA SUMMER, NKOTB, CHICAGO, MICHAEL BOLTON, MADONNA, GLORIA ESTEFAN...*Golddisc #171/promo* $12

CENTURY 21 #231
w/ELTON JOHN (2), MADONNA, CHICAGO, MOTELS, ELVIN BISHOP, L.RONSTADT, O.N.JOHN, MICHAEL BOLTON, TOTO...
Gold Disc/promo $12

CENTURY 21 #309
w/BEATLES (2), CARPENTERS, ELVIS PRESLEY, DIANA ROSS, STEVIE WONDER, D.SPRINGFIELD, JIM CROCE, ROD STEWART, PLAYER...*Gold Disc/promo* $12

CERTAIN DAMAGE VOL. 1
w/INXS, LOUDNESS, PETER TOSH, SKINNY PUPPY, ECHO, WIRE TRAIN, REDD KROSS, BEAT FARMERS + 26
CMJ 0001/promo/ps/2 CDs/booklet/'87 .. $25

CERTAIN DAMAGE VOL. 3
w/ROBBIE ROBERTSON, RED HOT CHILI PEPPERS, CABARET VOLTAIRE, BRYAN FERRY, FIELDS OF NEPHILIM, AZTEC CAMERA...*CMJ 0003/promo/ps* .. $8

CERTAIN DAMAGE VOL. 5
w/TREAT HER RIGHT, RUBEN BLADES, MORRISSEY, RODNEY CROWELL, RAINMAKERS, BEARS, LUXURIA...
CMJ 005/promo/ps $7

CERTAIN DAMAGE VOL. 10
w/TRANSV.VAMP, PSYCH.FURS, FISHBONE, FEELIES, TALK TALK, SUICIDAL TENDENCIES... *CMJ 010/promo/ps* $6

CERTAIN DAMAGE VOL. 12
w/PURSUIT OF HAPPINESS, FEELIES, DE LA SOUL, 16 more *CMJ 012/ps/promo* $6

CERTAIN DAMAGE VOL. 13
w/THE FALL, SANDMEN, SAINTS, TONE LOC, CELTIC FROST, SLICK RICK, TOOLS, BIG LADY K... *CMJ 013/ps/promo* $6

CERTAIN DAMAGE VOL. 16
w/NEVILLE BROS, HOUSE OF FREAKS, SWAMP ZOMBIES, 15 more *CMJ 016/promo/ps* . $6

CERTAIN DAMAGE VOL. 18
w/TIN MACHINE, PIL, PERE UBU, DEAD MILKMEN, FAITH NO MORE, 12 more
CMJ 018/promo/ps $6

CERTAIN DAMAGE VOL. 19
w/FETCHIN BONES, CHRIS ISAAK, SUN RA, SONIC YOUTH +14 *CMJ 019/promo/ps* $6

CERTAIN DAMAGE VOL. 21
w/CAMPER VAN BEETHOVEN, FLIES ON FIRE, ERIC ANDERSEN, LENNY KRAVITZ..
CMJ 021/promo/booklet ps/'89 ..... $6

CERTAIN DAMAGE VOL. 22
w/JONATHAN RICHMAN, EAT, EURYTHMICS, MEKONS, NINE INCH NAILS, LA GUNS, ADULT NET, SOUNDGARDEN...
CMJ 022/ps/promo $6

CERTAIN DAMAGE VOL. 24
w/RAVE UPS, TRANSVISION VAMP, AARON NEVILLE, WHY NOT, VOIVOD...
CMJ 024/promo/ps $6

CERTAIN DAMAGE VOL. 25
w/EVERYTHING BUT GIRL, OINGO BOINGO, CRAMPS, BLUE NILE, THEY MIGHT BE GIANTS, 13 more *CMJ 025/promo/ps* $6

CERTAIN DAMAGE VOL. 26
w/POI DOG PONDERING, CHILLS, CHURCH, DEL AMITRI, THE FALL, LUKA BLOOM, 13 more *CMJ 026/promo/ps* $6

CERTAIN DAMAGE VOL. 30
w/REPLACEMENTS, REDD KROSS, TEXAS TORNADOS, JANES ADDICTION, REM (20 second PSA), HEX + 12
CMJ 030/promo/ps $6

CERTAIN DAMAGE VOL. 31
w/JESUS & MARY CHAIN, GOO GOO DOLLS, SKINNY PUPPY, PIXIES, DARDEN SMITH, DANIELLE DAX, SPOT 1019...
CMJ 031/promo/ps $6

CERTAIN DAMAGE VOL. 32
w/BLUE RODEO, THROWING MUSES, MATERIAL ISSUE, HAVANA 3 AM, COCTEAU TWINS, HORSE, TOO MUCH JOY + 12
CMJ 032/promo/ps/'91 .... $6

CERTAIN DAMAGE VOL. 33
w/XYMOX, MIND FUNK, UNITY 2, PHRANC, HORSE FLIES, GOO GOO DOLLS, LIQUID JESUS, JAN GARBAREK, DEFINITION OF SOUND...
CMJ 033/promo/ps $6

CERTAIN DAMAGE VOL. 35
w/ANTHRAX, SMASHING PUMPKINS, PERE UBU, INDIGO GIRLS (1,2,3 live), HOUSE OF LOVE, JAMES, DANIELLE DAX...
CMJ 035/promo/ps/'91 .... $6

CERTAIN DAMAGE VOL. 38
w/MY BLOODY VALENTINE, HOLE, PIXIES, FLOWERED UP, PRONG, DEAD CAN DANCE, TEXAS, SINEAD O'CONNOR, ENYA, N.EBB. *CMJ 038/promo/ps/'91* $6

CERTAIN DAMAGE VOL. 40
w/CHRIS BELL, BODYCOUNT, MICHELLE SHOCKED (3), JAMES, BLACK CAT BONE, DHARMA BUMS, HAPPYHEAD...
CMJ 040/promo/ps/'92 .... $6

CERTAIN DAMAGE VOL. 41
w/BEASTIE BOYS, PRONG, MICHELLE SHOCKED (3), SOUP DRAGONS, CHRIS MARS, MOTHERS FINEST, PANTERA, TOOL... *CMJ 041/promo/ps/'92* $6

CERTAIN DAMAGE VOL. 43
w/PRAXIS, CATHERINE WHEEL, HOUSE OF LOVE, RAMONES, LULABOX, BLIND MELON, TOOL, BLEACH + 12
CMJ 043/promo/ps/'92 .... $6

CERTAIN DAMAGE VOL. 44
w/SCREAMING TREES, HOUSE OF PAIN, BOO RADLEYS (4), OFRA HAZA, CATHERINE WHEEL, HOUSE OF LOVE, EMF, JAMES + 25 *CMJ 044/promo/ps/2 cds* .. $12

CERTAIN DAMAGE VOL. 45
w/BEST KISSERS, DINOSAUR JR, HENRY ROLLINS (5), BUTTHOLE SURFERS, THE THE, THERAPY?, TEXAS TORNADOS, DIG, BASH & POP...
CMJ 045/promo/ps/'93 .... $6

CERTAIN DAMAGE VOL. 46
w/JELLYFISH, FLUID, AMERICAN MUSIC CLUB, FUNLAND, MIND BOMB, LUNA, RADIOHEAD, REMAINS...
CMJ 046/promo/ps/'93 .... $6

CERTAIN DAMAGE VOL. 48
w/VERVE, MERCURY REV, X, BABES IN TOYLAND, GREG GINN, ONYX, GRETA, CANDLEBOX, ANYTHING BOX, MONA LISA OVERDRIVE (19 in all)
CMJ 048/promo/ps/'93 .... $6

CERTAIN DAMAGE VOL. 50
w/BUFFALO TOM, BARKMARKET, BAD BRAINS, THERAPY?, UNREST, FUDGE TUNNEL, GRETA, MIND BOMB, CLUTCH...
CMJ 050/promo/ps/'93 .... $6

CHAMELEON COLORS
w/WAY MOVES, DRAMARAMA, BONEDADDYS, JOHN LEE HOOKER, CANNED HEAT...
Chameleon A ORC D2/promo/ps/'90 .... $6

CHARISMA
w/BRENT BOURGEOIS (4), K.MACCOLL (2), SOMETHING HAPPENS (2), PROPAGANDA (3), MAXI PRIEST (2), AGE OF CHANCE (2) *Charisma 002/ promo/box package/'90* $8

CHARTBREAKERS MUSIC SERVICE
w/REM, MARIAH CAREY, THE KNACK, BOB SEGER, COLOR ME BADD, MARTIKA, QUEEN, LUTHER VANDROSS, RICK ASTLEY, NEIL DIAMOND...
TrueSource/promo/ps/'91 ....$6

CHECK IT OUT!
w/BOOK OF LOVE, MARC COHN, RUDE BOYS, JELLYFISH, A-HA, KINGS X, GARY MOORE... *WEA C10 1/promo/ps/'91* $6

CHICAGO NINETEEN 92
w/LYN JACKSON, OPERATION DOPE, SULLY MICHAELS, I SPEAK JIVE, CRAC'D ACTOR, DARTARNIA PRINCE, JJ EVANS... *Savant 1003/promo/ps/'92* $6

CHR SAMPLER CD
w/BELL BIV DEVOE, ADAM ANT, ALISHA, PETER WOLF, OINGO BOINGO...
MCA 18469/promo/'90 ....$7

CHR SAMPLER VOL.1
w/ADAM ANT, OINGO BOINGO, BEL BIV DEVOE, ELTON JOHN, TOM PETTY, BELINDA CARLISLE... *MCA 18338/promo/ps/'90* ..$6

CHRISTMAS BONUS
w/EDIE BRICKELL, CHRIS REA, ENYA, DON HENLEY, MARIA MCKEE, P.GABRIEL, R.L. JONES, PAT METHENY, ON JOHN
Geffen 3876/promo/silkscreened/'89 ....$6

CHRYSALIS ...
LISTEN TO THE NINETIES
w/SINEAD O'CONNOR, WORLD PARTY, PAUL CARRACK, ELISA FIORILLO, SLAUGHTER, PURSUIT OF HAPPINESS..
Chrysalis 23512/promo/cassette and CD in special die cut box type package ..$12

CLASSIC ROCK BOX
w/BOWIE, SPRINGSTEEN, DYLAN, ELTON JOHN, more
WNEW-FM/4 cds/promo/foldout box $40

CLASS OF '93
w/CLAPTON, DR JOHN, SIR MIX A LOT, CHAKA KHAN, more
Reprise 6155/promo/rear insert/'93 ....$10

CMJ NEW MUSIC JULY
w/MATTHEW SWEET, FRONT 242, PAUL WESTERBERG, VERVE, CATHERINE WHEEL, SHEEP ON DRUGS, PHARCYDE, BLIND MELON...
Certain Damage/promo/ps/'93 ....$6

CMJ NEW MUSIC OCTOBER
w/STEREOLAB, UNCLE TUPELO, BIG STAR, POGUES, IGGY POP, MY LIFE WITH THRILL KILL KULT, JAMIROQUAI, COCTEAU TWINS... (19 in all)
Certain Damage 93/promo/ps/'93 ....$6

CMJ PRESENTS THE DIGITAL DOPE: BEATBOX CD VOL. 2
w/DEF JEF, MC 900FT JESUS, FU-SCHNICKENS, KMD, JIBRI, THREE TIMES DOPE, POPS COOL LOVE, UNDERGROUND MAFIA...``` *CMJ 002/promo/ps* $6

COCA COLA VOLUME 1
w/FREDDIE MERCURY & M.CABALLE, EN VOGUE, ERIC CLAPTON, NATALIE COLE, LUIS MIGUEL, TRAVIS TRITT
WB 5508/promo/silkscreened/ps/'92 ....$6

COLUMBIA STREET SOUNDS
w/BOOTSY, FISHBONE (1 remix), PUBLIC ENEMY, SLICK RICK...
Def Jam 1360/promo/ps/'88 ....$8

COMPACT DISCOVERY
w/DAVID LEE ROTH, AEROSMITH, DEBBIE GIBSON + 1 *Sony/promo/ps/'88* $8

COMPILATION DISC #28
w/ROXY MUSIC, show tunes galore, MICHAEL JACKSON... (88 tracks in all - all brief edits) *WB 28/promo/ps* $12

CONFESSIONS OF AN IRS GROUPIE
w/HUNTERS & COLLECTORS, LETS ACTIVE, TIMBUK 3, many more *IRS/promo/ps/'88* $6

COW COW BOOGIE VII
w/RESTLESS HEART, JUDDS, JUICE NEWTON, JOEL SONNIER & DON WILLIAMS *RCA 9701/promo/'89* $6

CRUZ FALL '93 SAMPLER
w/ALL (2), GREG GINN (4), SKIN YARD (2) *Cruz/promo/ps/'93* $6

CURB COUNTRY '91 - MARCH
w/SAWYER BROWN, JUDDS, JOHN ANDREW PARKS, HAL KETCHUM, CEE CEE CHAPMAN, TIM MCGRAW *Curb 051/promo/ps/'91* $6

DANCEHALL SUPERHITS
w/FOXY BROWN, TONY REBEL, SHABBA RANKS, YELLOWMAN, PINCHERS, BERES HAMMOND & CUTTY RANKS... *Pow Wow 7425/promo/silkscreened/'92* ...$6

DECADENT MUSIC
w/THEY MIGHT BE GIANTS, FASTER PUSSYCAT, GIPSY KINGS, GEORGIA SATELLITES, SUGARCUBES, 6 more *Elektra 8149/promo/ps/'90* $6

DEDICATED - AN INTRODUCTION
w/CHAPTERHOUSE, SPIRITUALIZED, CRANES, THIS PICTURE, SPACEMEN 3 (at least 2 ea.) *RCA 2460/promo/ps/'90* ..$6

DE 793
w/RAGING SLAB, SWELL, JAYHAWKS, ART OF ORIGIN, MESSIAH, SUPREME LOVE GODS, FLIPPER, MEDICINE, JESUS & MARY CHAIN... *Def American/promo/ps/'93* $6

D.I.Y.
w/SEX PISTOLS, GENERATION X, RAMONES, CARS, more *Phino 90134/promo/ps/'92* $12

DICK TRACY GOES COUNTRY
w/KD LANG, JERRY LEE LEWIS (It Was the Whiskey Talkin' - 2 vers.), BRENDA LEE *Sire 4078/promo/ps/'90* $8

DISCOVER HITS POST MODERN
w/RAVE UPS, SUGARCUBES, ERASURE, PETER MURPHY... *Hits 001/promo/ps* ..$8

DISCOVERY
w/JEAN LUC PONTY, TOWER OF POWER, DAN SIEGEL, JOHN BARRY, PHIL KEAGGY, TONY TERRY, PETER HIMMELMAN... *Sony 4137/promo/ps/'91* $6

DO YOURSELF A FAVOR
w/MARTI JONES, JESSE JOHNSON, R. VELA more *A&M 831 468/promo/ps/'87* $6

DODGY BOILERS
w/DIVINYLS, UB40, STEVE WINWOOD, IGGY POP, BASSOMATIC, BOY GEORGE, AFTERSHOCK, KID FROST, HARMONY... *Virgin PRCD BOILER/promo/ silkscreened/back ps/'91* $8

DREAMLAND
Dreamland - w/MARY CHAPIN CARPENTER, ROSANNE CASH, GLORIA ESTEFAN, EMMYLOU HARRIS, CAROLE KING... *Columbia 4897/promo/ps/'92* $6

E/P/A'S NEW YEAR'S SOLUTION
w/TEENA MARIE, GLORIA ESTEFAN, SADE, 11 more *Columbia 2920/promo/ps/'88* $6

EAR THIS
w/CINDERELLA, KISS, MISSION UK, SCORPIONS, MICHAEL MONROE, LA GUNS, MORTAL SIN, 8 more *Polydor 161/promo/ps/silkscreened/'90* $6

EAR THIS/ALTERNATIVE SAMPLER VOL. 1
w//CHICKSAW MUDD PUPPIES, EAT, THE FALL, HOUSE OF LOVE, MISSION UK, MICHELLE SHOCKED, WONDER STUFF, XYMOX, TRILOBITES... *Polygram 162/ promo/silkscreened logo/ps/'90* $6

EARNOG
w/U2, VAN MORRISON, PM DAWN, LA GUNS, TIN MACHINE, THE WHO, VOICE OF BEEHIVE, KATE BUSH, TONE LOC... *Polygram 448/promo/ps/'91* $6

EARPHORIA
w/NIRVANA, NORTHSIDE, SIOUXSIE & BANSHEES, CANDY SKINS, XTC, NITZER EBB... 16 more *Geffen 4335/ promo/gatefold hardcover ps/'91* $6

EAST COAST FAMILY
1 - 4 - All - 4 - 1 (4 vers.) w/ANOTHER BAD CREATION, BOYZ II MEN, MC BRAINS... *Motown 3746310732/promo/'92* $5

ELEKTRA ENTERTAINMENT - THE 90'S
w/TREVOR RABIN, MOTLEY CRUE, 10,000 MANIACS, CURE (Love Song remix), JACKSON BROWNE, SUGARCUBES... *Elektra 8110/promo/booklet ps/'89* $8

ELEKTRA: MUSIC OF CHAMPIONS
w/BILLY BRAGG, LISA FISCHER, THE DOVES, JOHN CAMPBELL, DESMOND CHILD, SHIRLEY MURDOCK... *Elektra 8445/promo/silkscreened/ps/'91* ...$6

EMI - ENERGY MILESTONES IMAGINATION
w/NATALIE COLE, ROBERT PALMER, DAVID BOWIE, RED HOT CHILI PEPPERS, GO WEST, O'JAYS, DIANE REEVES, + 9 *EMI 04528/promo/tri fold cover/'90* $6

EMI LATIN
w/PANDORA, ALVARO TORRES, SELENA *EMI Latin 79857/promo/silkscreened/ back ps/'93*..$6

EMI LEGENDS OF ROCK N ROLL...
w/HOLLIES, YARDBIRDS, DON MCLEAN (3 songs each - from boxed sets) *EMI 04888/promo/silkscreened/ps/'92*......$8

EMI NEW VISIONS
w/ALEX BUGNON, DIANNE REEVES, NAJEE, (4 tracks each) *EMI 04611/promo/ silkscreened/back ps/'90*..........................$6

ENIGMA SUMMER GRAND SLAM
w/DUSTY SPRINGFIELD, WIRE, BARDEUX, GIRLSCHOOL, MOJO NIXON, SANDRA BERNHARD, + 3 *Enigma 202/promo/silkscreened/ps/'89* $6

EVEN BETTER THAN THE REAL THING
w/U2, SHAKESPEARS SISTER, SANTANA, M. ETHERIDGE, HOUSE OF LORDS, ELP, LA GUNS, PM DAWN... *Polygram 518/ promo/silkscreened/ps/'92* $6

F*CK DANCE, THIS IS ART
w/MARC RIBOT, EVAN LURIE, ALLEN GINSBERG, WILLIAM BURROUGHS (2 each) + bonus Burroughs interview excerpts *Island 6638/promo/ps/'90* $10

FALL RADIO COMPILATION
w/SIR MIX A LOT, SIDE F-X, HIGH PERFORM ANCE, CRIMINAL NATION *Nastymix PRO 1/promo/ps/'90* $8

FIT TO BE TIED
w/JEFF HEALEY, BUNBURYS, PATTI SMITH, CHURCH... *Arista 9755/promo/ps/'88* $7

FIVE
w/DAN SIEGEL, ROY HARGROVE, JEAN LUC PONTY, TOM SCOTT, EARL KLUGH + 3 *Pioneer/promo/ps/insert*...........................$6

FIVE EASY PIECES
w/HANK WILLIAMS JR, SAWYER BROWN, JOHNNY LEE, CEE CEE CHAPMAN, VEGA BROS. *Curb 023/promo/back ps/'90*.....................$6

FLASH FORWARD
w/GLORIA ESTEFAN, GODFATHERS, STRANGLERS, R. SAKAMOTO, 8 more *CBS 1033/promo/ps/'88*............................$7

FOLLOW OUR TRACKS
w/ELVIS COSTELLO, NEW ORDER, RAMONES, VIOLENT FEMMES, REM... *WB 3503/ promo/ps/rear insert w/tour dates* $10

FOLLOW OUR TRAX VOL. 2
w/KD LANG, DANIELLE DAX, ELVIS COSTELLO, LOU REED + 7 *WB 3650/promo/ps/'89*..$8

FOLLOW OUR TRAX VOL. 3
w/ELECTRONIC, JESUS & MARY CHAIN, THE CHILLS, MINISTRY, RICHARD HELL, DANIEL LANOIS...
WB 4018/promo/ps/'90 ....$6

FOLLOW OUR TRAX VOL. 3
w/IAN MCCULLOCH, 54 40, MIGHTY LEMON DROPS, ERASURE, DEBORAH HARRY, B52S, TOM TOM CLUB, POWERMAD, FAITH NO MORE
Reprise 3831/promo/ps/'89......................$6

FOLLOW OUR TRAX VOL. 3
w/JESUS & MARY CHAIN, LAURIE ANDERSON, DAVID BYRNE, GEORGE CLINTON, OFRA HAZA + 14
WB 3821/promo/ps/'89 ....$7

FOLLOW OUR TRAX VOL. 4
w/DEBBIE HARRY, DEPECHE MODE, ERASURE IAN MCCULLOCH, BRYAN FERRY, NICK LOWE, TANITA TIKARIM...
Reprise 4019/promo/ps/'90......................$6

FOLLOW OUR TRAX VOL. 5
w/DEPECHE MODE, LUSH, REPLACEMENTS, MORRISSEY, HINDU LOVE GODS, SINATRA, TEXAS TORNADOS...
Reprise 4557/promo/ps/'90......................$6

FOLLOW OUR TRAX VOL. 5
w/ECHO, JANES ADDICTION, GANG OF 4, DEVO, LOS LOBOS, ENO & CALE, DANIELLE DAX...*WB 4555/promo/ps/ silkscreened/'90* $6

FOLLOW OUR TRAX VOL. 6
w/ELVIS COSTELLO, REM, DANIELLE DAX, ELECTRONIC, JANES ADDICTION (No One's Leaving - live), JUDYBATS, BOOK OF LOVE...
WB 4634/promo/ps/'91 ....$6

FOLLOW OUR TRAX VOL. 6
w/MORRISSEY, VIOLENT FEMMES, BOMB THE BASS, LUSH, RIDE, CHRIS ISAAK, BODEANS, many more
Reprise 4635/promo/ps/'91......................$6

FOLLOW OUR TRAX VOL. 7
w/ERASURE, MARC ALMOND, THE FARM, SQUEEZE, OCEAN BLUE, MORRISSEY, LUSH, THE CULT, TEXAS TORNADOS, HOUSE OF FREAKS...
Reprise 5067/promo/silkscreened/ps/'91..$6

FOLLOW OUR TRAX VOL. 7
w/MINISTRY, RED HOT CHILI PEPPERS, ELECTRONIC, SEAL, REM, TOO MUCH JOY, PRINCE, THOMPSON TWINS, DINOSAUR JR (19 in all)
WB 5066/promo/silkscreened/ps/'91 ....$6

FOLLOW OUR TRAX VOL. 8 "ANOTHER DISC, ANOTHER PLANET"
w/RIDE, T. TIKARAM, PALE SAINTS, BIG CAR, BARKMARKET, LUSH, SIR MIX A LOT, LITTLE VILLAGE, IAN MCCULLOCH...
Reprise 5349/promo/silkscreened/ps/'92..$6

FOLLOW OUR TRAX VOL. 8 "CUE IT UP"
w/JESUS & MARY CHAIN, RED HOT CHILI PEPPERS, DAVID BYRNE, KD LANG, SEAL, LOU REED, BODY COUNT... (18 in all) *WB 5348/promo/ps/ "8 ball" silkscreened/'92* $6

FOUNDATIONS FORUM '88
w/KEITH RICHARDS, HELLOWEEN, QUEENSRYCHE, 20 more
Concrete 8801/promo/ps/2 discs $15

FROM HENDRIX TO REPLACEMENTS
w/4 ECHO & BUNNYMEN songs, + 5 more bands
WB 2776/promo/ps $8

FROM THE HIP VOL. 1
w/DESERT ROSE BAND, KELLY WILLIS, JOE ELY, GEORGE STRAIT, MARTY STUART... *MCA 3026/promo/ps/'90*.......$6

FROM THE HIP VOL. 2
w/MARK COLLIE, MARTY BROWN, DESERT ROSE BAND, TRISHA YEARWOOD, JERRY JEFF WALKER...
MCA 3028/promo/ps/'91 ....$6

FULL HOUSE
w/EARL KLUGH, JOE SAMPLE, BELA FLECK, ERIC LEEDS, MARK WHITFIELD (2 each) *WB 4883/promo/ps/'91* $6

FULLY AMPED
w/RAMONES, SPREAD EAGLE, FLOTSAM & JETSAM, STEELHEART, LIQUID JESUS, HARDLINE, TRIXTER
MCA 2397/promo/ps/'92 ....$6

GIVE PEACE A CHANCE
title song featuring ADAM ANT, PETER GABRIEL, OFRA HAZA, BRUCE HORNSBY, C.LAUPER, IGGY POP, TOM PETTY + *Virgin PRCD PEACE/promo/ custom sticker (with new lyrics)/'91* $8

GIVE US LIBERTY AND DARN GOOD MUSIC
w/ARMORED SAINT, JOE JACKSON, THE FARM, CHRIS REA, ELECTRONIC, STRESS, SEAL, PRIMUS, HAVANA BLACK, many more (36 in all) *WEA DGM91/promo/ps* .$12

GLOBAL VOYAGE
w/PAUL HORN, PAUL GREAVER... *Global Voyage 331/promo* $5

GNU MUSIC?
w/TRANSVISION VAMP, HORSE FLIES, RICHARD BARONE, MARSHALL CRENSHAW, ENERGY ORCHARD... *MCA 1547/promo/ps/'91* $6

GOLDMINE 1992 MUSIC SAMPLER
w/NRBQ, CLOCKHAMMER, CUB KODA, JONATHAN RICHMAN, MARTY BALIN, KATIE WEBSTER, SPANIC BOYS... *Major Flash 107/promo/t rifold hardcover ps/'92* $6

GOOD RECORDS DONT KNOW etc
w/CHRIS STAMEY, ITS IMMATERIAL, W.DEVILLE + more *A&M 17524/promo* .$6

GOSPEL MUSIC/ IT'S GOOD FOR THE SOUL
w/DARYL COLEY, SANDRA CCROUCH, NEW LIFE, MARVIN WINANS, TRAMAINE HAWKINS, MOM & POP WINANS, RON WINANS...*Sparrow 70804/promo/ trifold envelope ps/'93* $6

GUITAR PLAYER MAG. PRESENTS LEGENDS OF GUITAR
w/ELMORE JAMES, FREDDIE KING, CARL PERKINS, CHUCK BERY, LINK WRAY, GENE VINCENT, JIMI HENDRIX, YARDBIRDS...*Rhino 90047/promo/ silkscreened/ps/'90* $8

GYROSCOPE LABEL SAMPLER 1993
w/ROGER ENO & KATE ST.JOHN (3), HAROLD BUDD (2), LARAAJI (3), BRIAN ENO (1), DJIVAN GASPARYAN (3)*Gyroscope 001/ promo/ps/logo on black/'93* $6

HANDEL'S MESSIAH A SOULFUL CELEBRATION
Comfort Ye My People/Hallelujah/Lift Up Your Heads O Ye Gates/But Who May Abide the Day of His Coming
Reprise 5769/promo/'92 ....$6

HAPPY 5TH ANNIV. 91X
w/SEX PISTOLS, T.HEADS, JESUS & MARY CHAIN, SMITHS, DEPECHE MODE, JOY DIVISION...*WB 3300/promo/ps/'88* ..$8

HAPPY HOLIDAYS FROM MCA
w/BING CROSBY, LEROY ANDERSON, MEL TORME *MCA 18100/promo/ silkscreed purple/Christmas card ps/'89* .$12

HAPPY NEW YEAR FROM BMG
w/MARTHA WASH, BUDDY GUY, ANGELA OFILL, BILLY OCEAN, BROOKS & DUNN, ROLLINS BAND, AIMEE MANN... (20 in all) *BMG 66154/ promo/logo on red/'92* $8

HARD ATTACK COMPACT DISC SAMPLER
w/CRUZADOS, INXS, MARILLION, THE CALL, ROBIN TROWER, X, GREAT WHITE, LONG RYDERS, TONIO K... *The Hard Report Vol. 1/promo/ps/'87* $10

HARD GROOVES 1
w/THE BLESSING, BANG TANGO, CONTRABAND, GLENN FREY, THE FIXX, MARSHALL CRENSHAW... *MCA 1509/promo/ps/'91* $6

HARD HITTERS VOLUME 3
w/METALLICA, SUICIDAL TEND., OZZY, ANTHRAX, RAGE, SCREAMER, EXCITER + 8 *The Hard Report/promo/ps/fall '88* $8

HECK ON WHEELS
w/MINISTRY (2), FAITH NO MORE (3), FLAMING LIPS, L7, BABES IN TOYLAND, JESUS & MARY CHAIN, BOMB, DANZIG... *WB 5787/promo/rear insert/'92* $6

HERD THIS!/1991 NARM SAMPLER
w/HORSE, PHIL PERRY, RICHARD THOMPSON, DAVE KOS, MANTRONIX, TRACIE SPENCER, THE BOX, SUAVE, CAVEDOGS... *Capitol 79692/promo/ps* ...$6

HERE IT IS, THE MUSIC
w/J. GARCIA, F. ZAPPA, MCLAUGHLIN, RESIDENTS, HENDRIX, 13 more *Ryko 00099/promo/booklet ps/'88* $10

HIGHWAYMAN 2
American Remains w/WAYLON, WILLIE, JOHNNY CASH, KRIS *Columbia 73572/promo/back ps/'90* $6

HIGHWAYMAN 2
selftitled (10 tracks) w/WAYLON, WILLIE, JOHNNY CASH, KRIS *Columbia 45240/ promo/silkscreened pic/back ps/'90* $15

HITCHHIKER RADIO SAGA 3
w/DARDEN SMITH, MARY CHAPIN CARPENTER, INDIGO GIRLS, RODNEY CROWELL, ROSANNE CASH... (all interview & music) *Columbia 3033/promo/ps/'91* $15

HITCHHIKER SAMPLER - VOLUME 1
w/LORI YATES (3), ROSANNE CASH, O'KANES, MARY CHAPIN CARPENTER (2), DARDEN SMITH, RODNEY CROWELL *Columbia 1560/promo/ps/'89* $8

HITDISC 900
w/JESUS JONES, FISHBONE, PAT BENATAR, MARTIKA, TG SHEPPARD, HANK WILLIAMS, JR., MARTY STUART, TAMMY WYNETTE...*TM Century 900/ promo/rear insert/(7/26/91)* $6

HITDISC 903B
w/JETHRO TULL, CROWDED HOUSE, TIN MACHINE, BAD ENGLISH, SCORPIONS, DILLINGER...*TM Century 903/promo/ rear insert/(8/16/91)* $6

HITDISC 910B
w/T.TURNER, BONNIE RAITT, CHEAP TRICK, HEART, EXTREME, LA GUNS, KIX, QUEEN.. *TM Century 910/promo/ rear insert/(10/4/91)* $6

HITMAKERS TOP 40
CD SAMPLER VOL. 5 5/6/88
w/ROD STEWART, INXS, DOKKEN, CLIFF RICHARD, 14 more *promo/rear insert* $6

HITMAKERS TOP 40
CD SAMPLER VOL. 7 6/24/88
w/BASIA, JOAN JETT, SCORPIONS, 10,000 MANIACS, 12 more *promo/rear insert* $6

HITMAKERS TOP 40
CD SAMPLER VOL. 9 7/29/88
w/DEBBIE HARRY, DIVINYLS, CLIFF RICHARD, SMITHEREENS + 10 *promo/rear insert* .$6

HITMAKERS TOP 40
CD SAMPLER VOL. 10 8/26/88
w/WAS NOT WAS, JIMMY PAGE, DEP. MODE, 11 more *promo/rear insert* $6

HITMAKERS TOP 40
CDSAMPLERVOL.11 9/23/88
w/HALL & OATES, JOHN LENNON (Jealous Guy), DURAN, HUEY LEWIS, 14 more *promo/rear insert* $6

HITMAKERS TOP 40
CD SAMPLER VOL. 12 10/21/88
w/NEW KIDS ON BLOCK, SOUTHSIDE JOHNNY, MICHAEL JACKSON, CHEAP TRICK, 14 more *promo/rear insert* $6

HITMAKERS TOP 40
CD SAMPLER VOL. 13 11/11/88
w/MARC ALMOND, VINNIE VINCENT, ALICE COOPER, 14 more *promo/rear insert*.....$6

HITMAKERS TOP 40
CD SAMPLER VOL. 14 12/9/88
w/GUNS N ROSES, PAT BENATAR, U2, DURAN, ANN WILSON & R ZANDER, 10 more *promo/rear insert* $6

HITMAKERS TOP 40
CD SAMPLER VOL. 15 1/20/89
w/DOKKEN, T. WILBURYS, STRYPER, OZZY, 14 more *promo/rear insert* $6

HITMAKERS TOP 40
CD SAMPLER VOL. 16 (2/10/89)
w/XTC, TANITA TIKARIM, E.COSTELLO, LIVING COLOUR, 14 more *promo/rear insert*....$6

HITMAKERS TOP 40
CD SAMPLER VOL. 17 3/3/89
w/CHER & PETER CETERA, SINEAD O'CONNOR, CARLY SIMON, 14 more *promo/rear insert* $6

HITMAKERS TOP 40
CD SAMPLER VOL. 18 3/24/89
w/GUNS N ROSES, REPLACEMENTS, SIGUE SIGUE SPUTNIK, 14 more *promo/rear insert* $6

HITMAKERS TOP
40 CD SAMPLER VOL. 20 5/5/89
w/REM, LOVE & ROCKETS, THE CULT, BILLY SQUIRE, 9 more *promo/rear insert* $6

HITMAKERS TOP 40
CD SAMPLER VOL. 21 5/26/89
w/TOMMY PAGE, INDIGO GIRLS, WIRE, DUSTY SPRINGFIELD, BILLY SQUIER, THE FIXX, BANANARAMA... *promo/ps* $6

HITMAKERS TOP 40
CD SAMPLER VOL. 25 8/18/89
w/MOTLEY CRUE, DE LA SOUL, PAUL McCARTNEY, TREVOR RABIN, GARY NUMAN, ICEHOUSE, 13 more
promo/rear insert $6

HITMAKERS TOP 40
CD SAMPLER VOL. 26 9/8/89
w/THE ALARM, GIRLSCHOOL, FASTER PUSSYCAT, THOMPSON TWINS, CULT, HOODOO GURUS, DONNY OSMOND +12 *promo/rear insert* $6

HITMAKERS TOP 40
CD SAMPLER VOL. 30 12/1/89
w/KATE BUSH, MADONNA, PAUL CARRACK, DEPECHE MODE, QUINCY JONES, 11 more *promo/rear insert* $6

HITMAKERS TOP 40
CD SAMPLER VOL. 31 1/19/90
w/THE ALARM, UB40, BIG DADDY KANE, LEVEL 42, 10 more *promo/rear insert* $6

HITMAKERS TOP 40
CD SAMPLER VOL. 35 4/20/90
w/BILLY IDOL, SQUEEZE, NINE INCH NAILS, CHURCH, DEBORAH HARRY, SOUL II SOUL, HOUSE OF LOVE...
promo/rear insert $6

HITMAKERS TOP 40
CD SAMPLER VOL. 36 5/11/90
w/JOE COCKER, JANE CHILD, FAITH NO MORE, MOTLEY CRUE, PRETENDERS, TECHNOTRONIC, 12 more
promo/rear insert $6

HITMAKERS TOP 40
CD SAMPLER VOL. 37 6/1/90
w/INDIA, SUNDAYS, ERASURE, BAD COMPANY, WILSON PHILLIPS, MICHAEL PENN, THE MISSION + 11 *promo/rear insert* $6

HITMAKERS TOP 40
CD SAMPLER VOL. 38 6/22/90
w/FLEETWOOD MAC, POISON, QUINCY JONES, STEVIE B, CONCRETE BLONDE...
promo/rear insert $6

HITMAKERS TOP 40
CD SAMPLER VOL. 39 7/13/90
w/GENE LOVES JEZEBEL, WAS NOT WAS, DEVO, LAURIE ANDERSON, BEACH BOYS, LLOYD COLE, DON DIXON..
promo/rear insert $6

HITMAKERS TOP 40
CD SAMPLER VOL. 40 8/3/90
w/LITA FORD, DEPECHE MODE, PRETENDERS, BILLY IDOL, SMITHEREENS, STRYPER, 11 more *promo/rear insert* $6

HITMAKERS TOP 40
CD SAMPLER VOL. 41 8/24/90
w/HOUSE OF LOVE, MARIA MCKEE, RAILWAY CHILDREN, 15 more *promo/rear insert* .. $6

HITMAKERS TOP 40
CD SAMPLER VOL. 42 Sept. 14, 1990
w/INFO.SOCIETY, WENDY & LISA, THE CURE, DREAD ZEPPELIN, SOUP DRAGONS, HOTHOUSE FLOWERS...
promo/rear insert $6

HITMAKERS TOP 40
CD SAMPLER VOL. 43 10/5/90
w/BAD CO., DON HENLEY, FAITH NO MORE, THE TIME, IGGY POP, GLORIA ESTEFAN, SINEAD O'CONNOR, DONNY OSMOND... *promo/rear insert* $6

HITMAKERS TOP 40
CD SAMPLER VOL. 44 10/26/90
w/LL COOL J, PAUL SIMON, NOTORIOUS, JUDE COLE, CYNDI LAUPER, DURAN, MAGGIES DREAM + 11
promo/rear insert $6

HITMAKERS TOP 40
CD SAMPLER VOL. 45 (11/16/90)
w/BILLY IDOL, TRAV.WILBURYS, CHRIS ISAAK, HINDU LOVE GODS, IGGY POP, CINDERELLA... *promo/rear insert* $6

HITMAKERS TOP 40
CD VOL. 47 (1/25/91)
w/WILSON PHILLIPS, LITTLE CAESAR, BOOK OF LOVE, UB40, RICK ASTLEY, FAST EDDIE... *promo/rear insert* $6

HITMAKERS TOP 40
CD SAMPLER VOL. 48 2/15/91
w/INFO.SOCIETY, MICHAEL MCDONALD, JASMINE GUY, SCORPIONS, CATHY DENNIS, ROBERT CRAY, SOUP DRAGONS... *promo/rear insert* $6

HITMAKERS TOP 40
CD SAMPLER VOL. 49 3/8/91
w/REPLACEMENTS, SHEILA E, REM, TOY MATINEE, DAMN YANKEES, DANIEL ASH, THE FIXX, DEEE LITE, TONY ORLANDO... *promo/rear insert* $6

HITMAKERS TOP 40 CD SAMPLER VOL. 50 3/29/91
w/JANES ADDICTION, QUINCY JONES, BOY GEORGE, DAVID LEE ROTH, SCORPIONS, NILS LOFGREN & BRUCE SPRINGSTEEN, LISA FISCHER...
promo/rear insert $6

HITMAKERS TOP 40 CD SAMPLER VOL. 51 4/19/91
w/GERARDO, HEART TO HEART, JUDE COLE, SAMANTHA FOX, TEDDY PENDERGRASS, GARDNER COLE, BETH NIELSEN CHAPMAN...
promo/rear insert $6

HITMAKERS TOP 40 CD SAMPLER VOL. 52 5/10/91
w/SEAL, ENUFF Z'NUFF, ELECTRONIC, SHEILA E, ELVIS COSTELLO, BETTY BOO, TRIPLETS, LENNY KRAVITZ, FULL MOON + 10 *promo/rear insert* $6

HITMAKERS TOP 40 CD SAMPLER VOL. 53 5/31/91
w/BLACK CROWES, BOOKER T, DESMOND CHILD, CATHY DENNIS, MATERIAL ISSUE, DREAM WARRIORS...
promo/rear insert $6

HITMAKERS TOP 40 CD SAMPLER VOL. 54 6/21/91
w/PAT BENATAR, RIC OCASEK, VELVET, JASMINE GUY, CONTRABAND, OMD, FREDDIE JACKSON, DECADANCE + 11
promo/rear insert $6

HITMAKERS TOP 40 CD SAMPLER VOL. 55 7/12/91
w/VAN HALEN, KIX, ERASURE, TEVIN CAMPBELL, STRESS, ENUFF Z'NUFF, MUSTO & BONES, REMBRANDTS + 10
promo/rear insert $6

HITMAKERS TOP 40 CD SAMPLER VOL. 55 8/23/91
w/ANIMAL LOGIC, THE FARM, ZIGGY MARLEY, JAMES INGRAM, BODEANS, REMBRANDTS, THOMPSON TWINS + 11
promo/rear insert $6

HITMAKERS TOP 40 CD SAMPLER VOL. 58 9/13/91
w/DIRE STRAITS, SCORPIONS, HEART, CANDYLAND, ANGELICA, TYKETTO + 10 *promo/rear insert* $6

HITMAKERS TOP 40 CD SAMPLER VOL. 62 11/15/91
w/SOUTHSIDE JOHNNY, ENYA, JERMAINE JACKSON, ARTHUR BAKER, SQUEEZE, CATHY DENNIS, LITTLE FEAT, AARON NEVILLE... *promo/rear insert* $6

HITMAKERS TOP 40 CD SAMPLER VOL. 63 12/13/91
w/SIOUXSIE & BANSHEES, THE FARM, SIMPLY RED, RYTHM SYNDICATE, MASSIVE ATTACK, ERIN CRUISE...
promo/rear insert $6

HITMAKERS TOP 40 CD SAMPLER VOL. 69 5/8/92
w/PM DAWN, KATHY TROCCOLI, CHARLATANS UK, ENYA, KD LANG (Constant Craving), ODECI, CRACKER, RINGO STARR, V.WILLIAMS... *promo/rear insert* $6

HITMAKERS TOP 40 CD SAMPLER VOL. 75
w/CLAPTON, GABRIEL, ROXETTE, NEVILLE BROTHERS, MICHAEL PENN, KISS, RICHARD MARX + 11 *promo/rear insert*.. $6

HITMAKERS TOP 40 CD SAMPLER VOL. 85
w/TINA TURNER, RU PAUL, LOUIE LOUIE, CATHY DENNIS, JEFFREY GAINES, TAKE THAT, SHAI, DINA CARROLL, PAUL PARKER... *promo/rear insert* $6

HITS AIN'T NUTHIN' BUT A NARM THING
w/JUICEMASTER, D-INFLUENCE, INNER CIRCLE, RUN DMC, STEREO MCS, PARIS, LAURA ENYA, VOX..
Hits 5017900/promo/ps $6

HITS NIGHT OF THE LIVING POST MODERN
w/DEPECHE MODE, PERE UBU, GODFATERS, LOVE & ROCKETS, TOM TOM CLUB, INDIO... *Hits 005/promo/ps* $8

HITS POST MODERN SYNDROME/ JUST ANOTHER HOLIDAY
w/DINOSAUR JR, JESUS JONES, SONIC YOUTH, THE THE, DURAN DURAN, GREEN JELLO, EUGENIUS, MICHAEL PENN...
Hits 011/promo/foldout ps $8

HITS YOU MIGHT HAVE MISSED
w/KENNY LOGGINS, SPRINGSTEEN (If I Should Fall Behind), RODNEY CROWELL
Columbia 5221/promo/rear insert/'93 .... $6

HOLIDAY GREETINGS FROM GEFFEN RECORDS
w/ROBBIE ROBERTSON, SLASH, AXL, XTC, THUNDER, JOHN KILZER, DON DOKKEN, JUNKYARD, ROXY BLUE (all brief holiday messages) *Geffen 4363/ promo/silkscreened/rear insert/'91* $12

HOLLYWOOD
w/GHOST OF AN AMERICAN AIRMAN, THE FLUID, YOTHU YINDI, BOO YAA TRIBE, T-RIDE, RAW FUSION...
Hollywood 10239/promo/ps/silkscreened .$6

HOLLYWOOD ALTERNATIVE SAMPLER
w/PLEASURE THIEVES, GHOST OF AN AMERICAN AIRMAN, T-RIDE, DEAD MILKMEN, YOTHU YINDI, 360S (2 each except for 360s) *Hollywood 10138/ promo/silkscreened/back ps/'92* $6

HOLLYWOOD AND VINYL
w/THE REIVERS (2), FETCHIN BONES (2), FLESH FOR LULU (2), MARTHA DAVIS, BELOUIS SOME, JOHNNY CLEGG...
Capitol 79215/promo/'87..........................$8

HOT STOCKING STUFFERS '92
w/EXTREME, ELTON JOHN, BOYZ II MEN, SHAKESPEARS SISTER, JULIE ANDREWS & BEN KINGSLEY, SOUP DRAGONS, BOB MARLEY...*PGD 589/ promo/silkscreened wreath/ps/'92* $6

HOT WAX - INVICTUS - GREATEST HITS
w/LAURA LEE, FREDA PAYNE, HONEY CONE, CHAIRMAN OF BOARD, 100 PROOF (4 tracks each) *HDH/promo/ps/'90* $10

HOUSE PARTY II QUIET STORM SAMPLER
w/LONDON JONES, THE FLEX vocal & acapella
MCA 2045/promo/ps/'91 ....$6

HOUSE PARTY II RAP SAMPLER
w/WRECKS N EFFECT, ERIC B & RAKIM, BELL BIV DEVOE, RALPH TRESVANT...
MCA 2043/promo/ps/'91 ....$6

HOW MUCH WOULD YOU PAY?
w/FEELIES/R. HITCHCOK/NEVILLE BROS/ M.SWEET/more (18 cuts)
A&M no #/promo/back ps/silkscreened $6

HOW OUR WORLD FLOATS
w/PIXIES, DEEE-LITE, BEAUTIFUL SOUTH, 10000 MANIACS, INSPIRAL CARPETS, THEY MIGHT BE GIANTS...*Elektra 8282/ promo/gatefold hardcover ps/'90* $6

I WAS A TEENAGE POST MODERN
w/SINEAD O'CONNOR, CHURCH, STONE ROSES, FALL, BLUE NILE, DEBORAH HARRY, HAPPY MONDAYS, 10 more
Hits 008/promo/ps....................................$7

IF THIS WERE A RADIO...
w/MELISSA ETHERIDGE, PHRANC, BLACK UHURU, U2, many more (32 tracks in all)
Island NMS '89/promo/2 CDs/ps/'89.......$15

IN PLAY
w/DION, REMBRANDTS, STRYPER, REVENGE, DURAN, DEEE LITE, 8 more
In Play #6/promo/fold out die cut ps $6

IN PLAY
w/NELSON, LISA STANSFIELD, STEVE WYNN, DEVO, JANET JACKSON, many more
In Play #3/promo/fold out die cut cover/'90 ....$7

IN PLAY
w/STYX, WHITNEY HOUSTON, MARSHALL TUCKER, MAGGIES DREAM, COCTEAU TWINS, RUN DMC...
In Play #10/promo/silkscreened/f oldout cover/'91 ....$6

IN YOUR EAR
w/GODFATHERS, ROACHFORD, EASTERHOUSE, CRUEL STORY OF YOUTH *CBS 1543/promo/3"/ps/'89*........$6

IN YOUR EAR/CBS CD3" SAMPLER
w/LIVING COLOR, PASADENAS, INDIGO GIRLS, OUTFIELD *CBS 1503/promo/ps/3"/'89*...$6

INSIDE TRACKS 1
w/SWING OUT SISTER, RICHARD MARX, ALICE IN CHAINS, PATTY SMYTH, TOAD THE WET SPROCKET, MICHAEL PENN + 1 *Universal One Stop 1/promo/ps/'92*..$6

INTERSCOPE 1991 NATIONAL SALES MEETING SAMPLER
w/KISS, GERARDO, PRIMUS, NEVERLAND, WINGER..*Interscope 8-91/promo/ps/'91* .$6

IRS NO SPEAK - INSTRUMENTAL HITS FOR THE 90S
w/STEVE HUNTER, HANK MARVIN, ALVIN LEE, S.HOWE.. *IRS MILES/promo/ps/'88*.......$8

IT'S AN ALTERNATIVE THING, YOU WOULDN'T UNDERSTAND
w/CHRIS MARS, CATHERINE WHEEL, TOM WAITS, SOUP DRAGONS, MATERIAL ISSUE, GIN BLOSSOMS, U2...
PGD 536/promo/gatefold hardcover ps/silkscreened/'92 ....$6

IT'S KOZMIK
w/ZIGGY MARLEY, PAULA ABDUL, UB40, DIVINYLS, OMD, JOE JACKSON, PATTI LABELLE, RAIN TREE CROW...
Virgin 3950/promo/silkscreened/back ps $12

IT'S A BEAUTIFUL TIME
w/CAMEO, PARLIAMENT, JAMES BROWN, D MOB, KOOL & GANG, many mor
Polydor 186/promo/2 cds/oversized die cut, 3 part flower shaped package $12

IT'S POST MODERN
w/COCTEAU TWINS, REPLACEMENTS, PREFAB SPROUT, 808 STATE, POGUES, JANES ADDICTION...
Hits 010/promo/booklet ps/'90 ....$8

JANUARY 1991 MERCURY NEW RELEASEES
w/DANIELE ALEXANDER, JOHNNY CASH (3 songs each)
Mercury 217/promo/names on purple silkscreened/'91 ....$6

JANUARY BLIZZARD BLITZ OF HITS
w/WAR BABIES, JAMES TAYLOR, BRUCE COCKBURN, MANIC STREET PREACHERS, CHRIS WHITLEY
Columbia 4419/promo/ps/'92 ....$6

JAZZIZ ON DISC
w/PAT METHENY, HERB ALPERT, SPYRO GYRA, TOOTS THIELEMANS...
Pioneer/promo/ps/insert/silkscreened.......$6

JAZZPIZAZZ
w/ROY HARGROVE, MARCUS ROBERTS, CARMEN MCRAE, JOHNPIZZARELLI, DUKE ELLINGTON, LOUIS ARMSTRONG, BENNY GOODMAN...
Novus 61083/promo/ps/'91 ....$6

JUBILATION
w/BRANFORD MARSALIS, KIRK WHALUM, MILTON NASCIMENTO...
Columbia 45294/promo/ps/'89 ....$6

JUDGMENT NIGHT
w/CYPRESS HILL & SONIC YOUTH, ONYX & BIOHAZARD, DE LA SOUL & TEENAGE FANCLUB, RUN DMC & LIVING COLOUR, SIR MIX A LOT & MUDHONEY
Immortal 5455/promo/silkscreened/ cust.sticker/'93 ....$8

JUDGMENT NIGHT STREET LEGAL VERSION
w/HELMET & HOUSE OF PAIN, PEARL JAM & CYPRESS HILL, TEENAGE FANCLUB & DE LA SOUL, SLAYER & ICE T, SONIC YOUTH & CYPRESS HILL...
Immortal 5472/promo/ps/'93 ....$12

JUST IN TIME FOR CHRISTMAS
w/RECKLESS SLEEPERS, DBS, WALL OF VODOO, TIMBUK 3..
IRS XMAS/promo/gatefold ps/'87 ....$8

JUST LISTEN
w/BOB MARLEY, PRAXIS, U2, PAUL WELLER, TOM WAITS, JULIAN COPE + 11
PLG 566/promo/logo on white/ps/'92........$6

JUST LISTEN
w/TRAMAINE HAWKINS, PASTOR DONALD ALFORD, WEST ANGELES COGIC MASS CHOIR, OUT OF THE GREY, JIMMY A... *Sparrow/promo/back ps/'91* .$6

KDGC
w/TERRI NUNN, ARC ANGELS (2), TEENAGE FANCLUB, NYMPHS, GALACTIC COWBOYS, LITTLE CAESAR, NIRVANA (2) *DGC 4401/promo/ gatefold hardcover ps/silkscreened/'92* $6

KEY NOTES
w/MILLTOWN BROTHERS (3), FEELIES (2), TEMPLE OF THE DOG (2), WITNESS (2), EXTREME (2), HEARTLAND (2)
A&M 849 347/promo/ multifold hardcover ps/'91 ....$6

KGEF
w/GUNS N ROSES, ROXY BLUE, SPENT POETS, FIONA, PETER CASE, ROBBIE ROBERTSON, NITZER EBB, WHITE ZOMBIE, TESLA *Geffen 4400/promo/ gatefold hardcover ps/silkscreened/'92* $6

MASTER KING SERIES
SAMPLER

KING SAMPLER
w/LITTLE WILLIE JOHN, WYNONIE HARRIS, 5 ROALES, ROY BROWN, more
Rhino 7040/promo/ps/'94 .... $10

LADIES & GENTLEMEN, ELVIS HAS LEFT THE BUILDING
w/HOTHOUSE FLOWERS, ART OF NOISE, YELLO...*Polygram 34/promo/ps/'88* $6

LET GO OF MY EARS
w/ROLLINS BAND, THE SEXTANTS, SUZANNE RHATIGAN, NIKOLAJ STEEN, BABY ANIMALS, DOCTOR RAIN...
Imago/promo/silkscreened/ps $6

LIFE WITHOUT POST MODERN
w/HOTHOUSE FLOWERS, JANE WIEDLIN, LUXURIA, REVENGE, AZTEC CAMERA, BLUE AEROPLANES..
Hit 009/promo/ps/'90 .... $8

LINDBERGH'S BABY
w/TEXAS, RICHIE SAMBURA, JAMES, ALDO NOVA, RATCAT... *Mercury 439/promo/ gatefold hardcover ps/'91* $6

LISTEN TO YOUR HISTORY
w/CLIVILLES & COLE, AL GREEN, SHABBA RANKS, SUPER CAT, MARSALIS (3), PUBLIC ENEMY, KRIS KROSS, LUTHER VANDROSS, many more *Columbia 4460/ promo/silkscreened/ps/'92* $6

LISTEN UP!
w/DONNY OSMOND, ERIC JOHNSON, REVENGE, RIVER CITY PEOPLE, COCTEAU TWINS, MAGGIES DREAM...
Capitol 79373/promo/ps/'90 .... $7

LOLLAPALOOZA
w/JANES ADDICTION, SIOUXSIE, LIVING COLOUR, BUTTHOLE SURFERS, ROLLINS BAND, NINE INCH NAILS..
WB 4926/promo/ps/'91 .... $8

LOLLAPALOOZA '92
w/RED HOT CHILI PEPPERS, MINISTRY, ICE CUBE, SOUNDGARDEN, JESUS & MARY CHAIN, PEARL JAM, LUSH
WB 5500/promo/ps/'92 .... $7

LOLLAPALOOZA '93
w/PRIMUS, ALICE IN CHAINS, DINOSAUR JR, FISHBONE, FRONT 242, TOOL, BABES IN TOYLAND, CELL, MERCURY REV...
Columbia 5256/promo/ps/'93 .... $7

LOUD & PROUD
w/SCORPIONS, EXTREME, WINGER, WARRANT, PRETTY MAIDS, DREAM POLICE, ZED YAGO
Music & Media 50/90/promo/'90 .... $6

LOVE IS LIKE A POKE IN THE EYE WITH A SHARP STICK
w/AMERICAN MUSIC CLUB, CEREBRAL CORPS GODS LITTLE MONKEYS, THE MAGNOLIAS, YO LA TENGO, X-TAL.
(2 each) *Alias/promo/ps* $6

MAC POWER SOURCE
w/G.ESTEFAN, LIVING IN A BOX, LEON REDBONE, DONNY OSMOND, TOMMY PAGE, JOE COCKER, STREISAND, DR JOHN, ANNIE HASLAM + 23
Mainly Adult Contemporary 12-89/ promo/2 cds/ps/'89 .... $15

MAD FLAVOR VOLUME ONE
w/SIR MIX A LOT, KID N PLAY, COOKIE CREW, LEVEL III, JODECI, DEF JEF, CHILL DEAL BOYZ...
The Source SOCD1/promo/ps $6

MAGNETIC ATTRACTION
w/JELLYFISH, MAXI PRIEST, GARY MOORE, KNACK, CORO, RIK EMMET...
Charisma GAVI/promo/silkscreen/ps/'91 .. $6

MALACO SAMPLER
w/THE ROSE BROTHERS, BOBBY BLAND, LITTLE MILTON...
Malaco 1144/promo/ps/'88 .... $6

MARCH MADNESS
w/SOPHIE B HAWKINS, EDDIE MONEY, NEDS ATOMIC DUSTBIN, POI DOG PONDERING, LOVE/HATE, MANIC STREET PREACHERS
Columbia 4489/promo/ps/'92 .... $6

MAXI MEGA MOBILE MASTER MASSIVE...
w/HANOVER FIST, SKINNY PUPPY, NEW MODEL ARMY, DURAN DURAN (Meet El Presidente presid.suite mix/Meet El Beat/ Skintrade parisian mix & sos dub), FREDDIE MERCURY (The Great Pretender ext.)..
Capitol 79023/promo/ps/'87 .... $40

MAY ALL YOUR WISHES BE SALE PRICED
w/BRYAN ADAMS, RICHIE SAMBORA, ROXETTE, VOICE OF BEEHIVE, VAN MORRISON, MOTLEY CRUE, MARIAH CAREY, AMY GRANT...
Navarre/promo/ps/'91 .... $6

MCA BLACK/URBAN CD SAMPLER
w/SHEENA EASTON, BB KING, BOBBY BROWN, NEW EDITION, GUY + 6
MCA 17691/promo/ps/'88 ....$8

MCA CHR CD SAMPLER
w/ELTON JOHN, OLIVIA NEWTON JOHN, KANSAS, DENNIS DEYOUNG, NIGHT RANGER, GLENN FREY, KIM WILDE, OINGO BOINGO. *MCA 17690/promo/ps* .$7

MCA CHR CD SAMPLER
w/JODY WATLEY, BOBBY BROWN, PATTI LABELLE (If You Asked Me To), BELINDA CARLISLE, ELTON JOHN, H.JOHNSON...*MCA 18053/promo/ps/'89* .$6

MCA INSTORE PLAY SAMPLER
w/LYNYRD SKYNYRD, JODY WATLEY, BELINDA CARLISLE & more *MCA 17529/promo* ...$6

MCA NEW MUSIC AOR-ALTERNATIVE
w/TRANSVISION VAMP, STEVE JONES, THE CALL, BEAT FARMERS, SWANS, OINGO BOINGO, 11 more
MCA 17949/promo/ps/'89 ....$8

MCA NEW MUSIC BLACK/URBAN
w/BOBBY BROWN, JODY WATLEY, SHEENA EASTON, PATTI LABELLE, 8 more
MCA/promo/ps/'89 ....$8

MCA PRESENTS A PORTRAIT OF SOUL
w/JODY WATLEY, AARON HALL, DAZZ BAND, JODECI, PATTI LABELLE, GLADYS KNIGHT, ERIC B & RAKIM + 6
MCA 2137/promo/ps/'92 ....$6

MCA RADIO GOLDEN OLDIES VOL. 1
w/CONWAY TWITTY, OAK RIDGE BOYS, GEORGE STRAIT (2), REBA MCENTIRE (2), STEVE WARINER, PATSY CLINE (2), MERLE HAGGARD...
MCA 17296/promo/'92 ....$7

MCA RADIO GOLDEN OLDIES VOL. 2
w/LEE GREENWOOD (2), STEVE WARINER, GEORGE STRAIT (3), DON WILLIAMS (2), JIMMY BUFFETT, PATSY CLINE, MERLE HAGGARD..
MCA 17405/promo/'92 ....$8

MEGAFORCE ENTERTAINMENT CHRISTMAS SAMPLER
w/NUDESWIRL, TRIBE AFTER TRIBE, WARREN HAYNES, M.O.D., S.O.D., SKATENIGS...
Megaforce G14/promo/gatefold hardcover ps/'92 ....$6

MERCURY MENU
w/BON JOVI "Runaway" (live), CINDERELLA "Jumping Jack Flash (live), TEXAS "Livin' For the City" (live) + more
Mercury 133/promo/gatefold hardcover ps/silkscreened/'89 ....$12

METAL DETECTOR
w/DANZIG, SUICIDAL TEND., MEGADETH, BLACK SABBATH, IAN GILLAN + 10
Friday Morning Q'back/promo/late summer '90/ps $7

METAL DETECTOR
w/FISHBONE, MOTORHEAD, MR BIG, ENUF Z'NUFF, MORDRED, DESPAIR, SEPUTLURA, BANG TANGO...
FMQB/promo/ps/silkscreened/spring '91 ..$7

METAL DETECTOR
w/GARY MOORE, KISS, DOGS D'AMOUR, SKID ROW, GIRLSCHOOL, 14 more
Friday Morning Q'back/promo/'89/ps $7

METROMIX
w/C&C MUSIC FACTORY, JASMINE GUY, KLF, MANTRONIX, WHODINI, SLY & FAMILY STONE, BELL BIV DEVOE more (all dj remixes) *Metromix 10/promo/ps*...$15

METROMIX
w/LISA LISA, DE LA SOUL, LL COOL J, ZIGGY MARLEY, COLOR ME BADD... (all dj remixes) *Metromix GT 11/promo/ps* $15

METROMIX
w/MADONNA, LL COOL J, JANET JACKSON, DIANA ROSS... (all dj remixes)
Metromix GT 09/promo/ps $15

METROMIX
w/MC SWAY, LISA STANSFIELD, MC HAMMER, C&C MUSIC FACTORY, PUBLIC ENEMY, LL COOL J... (all dj remixes)
Metromix GT 02/promo/ps $15

MIRACLE ON 57TH STREET
w/HALL & OATES, PATT SMITH, WHITNEY HOUSTON... *Arista 9775/promo/ps/'88* ...$8

MIXED UP - THE WORLD DOMINATION TOUR
w/SKY CRIES MARY (Elephant Song - 2 vers.), LOW POP SUICIDE, CONTAGION, SHRIEKBACK *Capitol 79487/promo/ silkscreened/cust.sticker/'92* $6

MONDO SUPREMO
w/SLOAN, SONIC YOUTH, CELL, NIRVANA, WHITE ZOMBIE, THE SUNDAYS... *Geffen DGC 4501/promo /silkscreened/ps/'93* $6

MOOD INDIGO/ART N SOUL FROM CAPITOL
w/MELI'SA MORGAN (2), STANLEY JORDAN, MC HAMMER, GAP BAND (2), MELBA MOORE (2), ADEVA, DEXTER GORDON, OAKTOWNS 357... *Capitol 79166/promo/ps/'90* $6

MOTOWN SAMPLER
w/DIANA ROSS (This House), EL DEBARGE (Somebody Loves You), THE BOYS (Happy) *Motown 17966/promo/'89* $7

MOTOWN SAMPLER, WHERE THE FUTURE SOUNDS BETTER THAN EVER pt 2
w/STEVIE WONDER, STACY LATTISAW, ADA DYER, GEORGIO, WILSON PICKETT, THE BOYS... *Motown 17724/promo/'88* . $7

MOTOWN SPRING 1990 R&R CONVENTION
w/JOHNNY GILL, POINTER SISTERS, SMOKEY ROBINSON, GOOD GIRLS... (2 tracks each) *Motown 90004/promo/'90* $6

MOTOWN SUMMER HEAT
w/DIANA ROSS, PUBLIC ENEMY, EL DEBARGE... *Motown 17888/promo/'89* $7

MUSIC FOR THE REST OF US
w/EVERYTHING BUT GIRL, CLANNAD, TORI AMOS, ENYA, M. BRENNAN (2 each) *Atlantic 4763/promo/silkscreened/ps/'92* .. $6

MUSIC FOR THE STARVING MILLIONS
w/AZTEC CAMERA, DEPECHE MODE, ERASURE, ICE T, KD LANG, MADONNA, THE SMITHS.. *Sire 2831/promo/booklet ps/'87* $12

MUSIC FROM A QUIET PERSPECTIVE
w/MINT CONDITION (3), SOUNDS OF BLACKNESS (3), LO KEY (2), LISA KEITH (2) *Perspective 75021 7247/promo/ silkscreened/ps/'91* $6

MUSIC MATTERS
w/GOLDEN PALOMINOS, PERE UBU, J ELLYFISH, PETER HOLSAPPLE & CHRIS STAMEY, WONDER STUFF, STRESS... *Details 691/promo/ trifold hardcover ps/'91* $6

MUSIC MATTERS
w/TIN MACHINE, PIXIES, TOAD THE WET SPROCKET, BLACK SHEEP, LLOYD COLE, CURVE, ERASURE, VAN MORRISON... *Details 1191/promo /trifold hardcover ps/holiday '91* $6

MUSIC MONITOR IV
w/THE CROSS (New Dark Ages), ROBYN HITCHCOCK (So You Think You're in Love)... *Music & Media #41/promo/ silkscreened/'91* $6

MUSIC MOST PEOPLE WOULDN'T TOUCH
w/BIRDLAND, LIVE, FATIMA MANSIONS, LONDONBEAT, GOODBYE MR MCKENZIE (2 songs each) *Radioactive 1575/promo/ps/ cust.sticker/silkscreened/'91* $6

MUSIC SPEAKS LOUDER THAN WORDS
w/PHOEBE SNOW, PATTI LABELLE, CYNDI LAUPER, EWF, ANNE MURRAY, ATLANTIC STARR... *Epic 45380/promo/ps/'90* $6

MUSIC THAT'S LARGER THAN LIFE
w/BLEACH, SONIA DADA, ETHYL MEATPLOW, ULTRAMARINE, LUCINDA WILLIAMS, BEL CANTO... *Chameleon-Dali 8668/ promo/silkscreened/ps/'92* $6

MUSIC TO KEEP YOU UP ALL NIGHT
w/DON DIXON, WIRE, TSOL, DEAL MILKMEN, MOJO NIXON, PLAN 9, SMITHEREENS, NECROS, CAT HEADS, PETER HAMMILL... *Enigma 035/promo/gatefold ps/'87* $8

NARADA CONTEMPORARY CHRISTMAS CLASSICS
w/various tunes from Narada holiday releases *Narada 1686/promo/rear insert/'91* $6

NASHVILLE NEW RELEASE
w/TOM WOPAT, DAN SEALS, DAVID SLATER, DEAN DILLON, TANYA TUCKER, SUZY BOGGUSS, DANA MCVICKER *Capitol 79359/promo/custom sticker* $6

NATIONAL PUBLIC RADIO
w/LITTLE RICHARD, DUSTIN HOFFMAN, COKIE ROBERTS, SCOTT SIMON, mostly spoken word *2 CDs/promo/booklet/nice oversized outer package/'91* $15

NEW ARTISTS, THE NEW YEAR
w/SIREN, STATUS QUO, ROBERT CRAY, WAYNE TOUPS.. *Mercury 39/promo/ps* .. $7

NEW EDGE MUZIK
w/FISHBONE, BOB DYLAN, POI DOG PONDERING, BAD, BYRDS, T BONE BURNETTE, ALICE IN CHAINS... *Columbia 2230/promo/ps/'90* $6

NEW STUFF
w/TT D'ARBY, P SURS, DYLAN, M. OIL, JON ANDERSON...*Columbia 1209/promo/ps* .. $6

NFL GOES MOTOWN
w/TEMPTATIONS, 4 TOPS, MIRACLES, SUPREMES, more
Motown 822/promo/ps/'92 .... $8

NIGHT OF THE GUITAR - LIVE!
w/STEVE HOWE, ALVIN LEE, ROBBIE KRIEGER, LESLIE WEST... *IRS 0001/promo/ps/ silkscreened/'89* $10

NO FLIES HERE!
w/LOUD SUGAR, ENGINES, JESUS JONES (2 songs each) *SBK 05397/promo/ps/ silkscreened/'91* $8

NO SPEAK
w/WISHBONE ASH, STEWART COPELAND, WILLIAM ORBIT, PETE HAYCOCK (2 each) *IRS/promo/'87* $10

NOW HOW MUCH WOULD YOU PAY?
w/M SWEET, FEELIES, R. HITCHCOCK, NEVILLE BROS...
A&M 17715/promo/ps/'89 .... $6

ON THE NINETIES TIP..
w/BAD BRAINS, PRIMUS, PUSSY GALORE, MIND OVER FOUR, WHITE ZOMBIE..
Caroline #1/promo/rear insert/'90 .... $6

ON-USOUND VOL. 1
w/ERASURE (Indian rubber mix), SOFT CELL (low voltage mix 13:50), THE CURE (antidote megamix 14:36), U2 (Atomic mix 15:56), SIMPLE MINDS *On USound 2393/ promo/promo remixes/ps* $20

ONE SMALL STEP FOR MANKIND...
w/STAGE DOLLS, U2, DRIVIN'N CRYIN, THE WONDER STUFF, THE MEN, LA GUNS, VOICE OF BEEHIVE, FUNGO MUNGO...
Polygram 467/promo/silkscreened/ps/'92 . $6

OPAL ASSEMBLY 1
w/BRIAN ENO, R. ENO, HAROLD BUDD, HUGO LARGO *Opal 3175/promo/ps/'88* $7

OPERATION ROCK & ROLL
w/JUDAS PRIEST, ALICE COOPER, MOTORHEAD, METAL CHURCH, DANGEROUS TOYS (2 songs each)
Columbia 4097/promo/silkscreen/ps/'91 ... $7

OTHER SIDES
w/NATALIE COLE, ROBBIE NEVIL (total of 3 songs) *EMI 04236/promo/silkscreened* ... $5

OUCH
w/THE SEERS, LIMBOMANIACS, GODFLESH, MOCK TURTLES, MORBID ANGEL, NAPALM DEATH, MIGHTY FORCE...
Relativity 0127/promo/silkscreen/ps/'91 ... $6

PARLIAMENT PLATINUM COLLECTION II
w/BUSTER POINDEXTER, MOODY BLUES, PAUL YOUNG, ERIC CARMEN, MICHAEL BOLTON, ARETHA FRANKLIN
RCA 0912/promo/die cut ps/'90 .... $6

PAVE THE EARTH
w/SOUL ASYLUM, SOUNDGARDEN, SUZANNE VEGA, JOHN HIATT, SUN RA, ROBYN HITCHCOCK, DEL AMITRI, 10 more
A&M 18047/promo/silkscreened/ps/'90 .... $8

PGD PRESENTS GREAT SOUNDS
w/STEVIE WONDER, SQUEEZE, ROBERT PALMER, TEN CC, CLAPTON, BOB MARLEY, MARVIN GAYE, DONNA SUMMER, JOE COCKER, TRAFFIC...
PGD 437/promo/silkscreened/ps/'91 .... $6

PGD PRESENTS GREAT SOUNDS VOL. 2
w/BILLY PRESTON, CLAPTON, STEVIE WONDER, LENNON & ONO, FREE, RAINBOW, ABC, ROD STEWART...
Polygram 517/promo/ps/'92 .... $6

PGD PRESENTS SOUND SAVERS
w/BRYAN ADAMS, BON JOVI, TEMPTATIONS, MARVIN GAYE, MOODY BLUES, U2, THE POLICE, JOE JACKSON, ERIC CLAPTON, SQUEEZE, D. ROSS, 4 TOPS... *PGD 435/promo/ps/'91* $6

PGD SALUTES BLACK HISTORY MONTH TOMORROW
w/X CLAN, PM DAWN, TONE LOC, BARRY WHITE, MINT CONDITION, CHERRELLE, SHANICE, BOYZ II MEN, TEMPTATIONS, VANESSA WILLIAMS + 2 *PGD 466/promo/ps/'92* $7

PGD SALUTES BLACK HISTORY MONTH YESTERDAY
w/JAMES BROWN (3), STEVIE WONDER, DIANA ROSS, BOB MARLEY (2), PARLIAMENT-FUNKADELIC, OHIO PLAYERS... *Polydor 469/promo/ps/'92* $7

PHI BETA CAPITOL
w/BOB SEGER, OAKTOWNS 357, HEART, XYZ, LLOYD COLE, SMITHEREENS, SCHOOLLY D, YOUNG MC, NAT KING COLE...*Capitol 79891/promo/silkscreened/ps/'91* $6

PHI BETA RESTLESS
w/TIME ZONE, REPLACEMENTS, SOCIAL DISTORTION, TMBG, SUBURBS, VANDALS, WIRE, WALL OF VOODOO, SLF, SOUL ASYLUM... *Restless 029/promo/ps/silkscr/'93* $6

PICK THIS
w/SOUL ASYLUM, SCREAMING TREES, TBONE BURNETT, THE SHAMEN, PUBLIC ENEMY, PEARL JAM, INDIGO GIRLS... (20 in all) *Epic 4788/promo/silkscreened/ps/'92* $8

PICKED TO CLICK
w/KEEDY, YES, ALAN JACKSON, LOS LOBOS, ARETHA FRANKLIN, JENNIFER HOLIDAY, THE KLF, STRAITJACKET FITS, EXILE...*Arista 2234/promo/ps/'91* ...$6

PITTSBURGH'S GREATEST HITS
w/ROMANCERS, DEL-RIOS, JEWELS, BLUE SONNETS, more *Itzy 15832stock/ps/'92* $8

PIMPS PLAYERS & PRIVATE EYES
w/BOBBY WOMACK, IMPRESSIONS, 4 TOPS, MARVIN GAYE, ISAAC HAYES, WILLIE HUTCH, CURTIS MAYFIELD... *Sire 26624/promo/silkscreened/ps/'91* $15

itzy records presents
Pittsburgh's Greatest Hits
ELEPHANT WALK
LET'S BE LOVERS
HEY SAH-LO-NEY
"69"
I WANNA CHANCE
FRIED ONIONS
IT'S NEVER TOO LATE
WISDOM OF A FOOL
PLEASE BE MY LOVE TONIGHT
BULLFIGHT
MONKEY MAN
A PENNY FOR YOUR THOUGHTS
SUCH A GOOD NIGHT FOR DREAMIN'
JIMMY LEE
GIVE MY YOUR LOVE
SWINGIN' LITTLE CHICKY
THIS 25TH ANNIVERSARY EDITION HAS 28 OF THE ORIGINAL 32 HITS
plus 12 others
itzy 101

PLAY
w/MISSION UK, HOTHOUSE FLOWERS, HOUSE OF LOVE, FETCHIN BONES, THE FALL, WONDER STUFF, TRILOBITES... *Polygram 185/promo/silkscreened/gatefold hardcover/'90* $6

PLAY THIS
w/CURE,10,000 MANIACS, SISTERS OF MERCY more *Elektra 2213/promo/sticker* $10

PLAY THIS
w/PEABO BRYSON & REGINA BELLE, THE CARS, DOKKEN, SCREAMING BLUE MESSIAHS, KEITH SWEAT *Elektra 2193/promo/'88* $7

PLAY THIS NOW
w/BIG DIPPER, STRANGLERS, RAVE UPS, SOCIAL DISTORTION, O POSITIVE, PREFAB SPROUT.. *Epic 2142/promo/ps/'90* $6

PolyGram Label Group, 825 Eighth Avenue, New York, N.Y. 10019

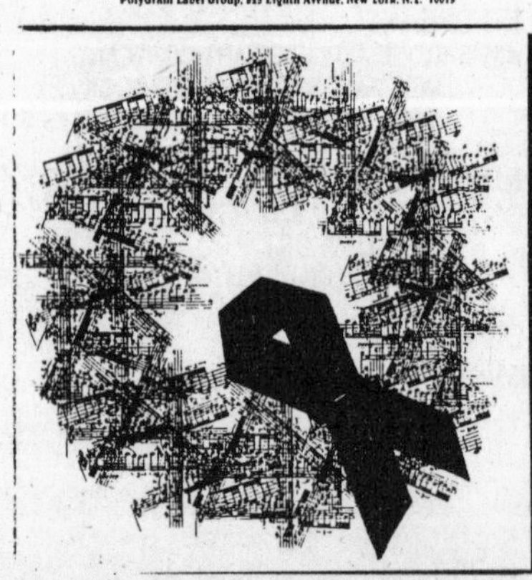

PLG HOLIDAY SAMPLER
w/U2, ELTON JOHN, JAMES BROWN, EMERSON LAKE & PALMER, more
Poly. 771/gatefold hardcover/promo $8

POINTBLANK
w/THE KINSEY REPORT, ALBERT COLLINS, LARRY MCCRAY (2 songs each)
Charisma 026/promo/trifold hardcover ps/silkscreened/'91 ....$6

POINTBLANK EXCLUSIVE PREVIEW
w/POPS STAPLES (2), JOHN HAMMOND (2)
Pointblank 091/promo/ps/'92 ....$5

POLYGRAM COMPACT DISCOVERER - MAY 1987
w/TOM KIMMEL (2), REFUGEE (2), SWING OUT SISTER, JEFF PARIS (2), MISSION UK...
Polygram 062/promo/ps/'87......................$6

POLYGRAM'S WINTER SLAMMIN' CD JAMMIN' SAMPLER
w/BAR KAYS, KURTIS BLOW, JUNIOR, NIA PEEPLES, ANGELA WINBUSH..
Polygram 065/promo/ps/'88......................$6

POLYGRAMS 1988 ALL STAR LINEUP
w/MOODY BLUES, SCORPIONS, CINDERELLA..
Polygram 20/promo/ps/'88........................$8

POP GROOVES 1
w/SHEENA EASTON, GLENN FREY, TRIXTER, GUY, DEL SHANNON, THE FIXX, STEEL PULSE...*MCA 1510/promo/ps/'91* $6

POST GROUNDHOG'S DAY SPECTACULAR
w/NILS LOFGREN, JUNE TABOR, MARTIN SWAN, BARKING TRIBE, JERRY JEFF WALKER, COUNTRY JOE MCDONALD...
Ryko February '91/promo/ps $8

POWER MOVE: SYNDICATE SAMPLER 2
w/HIJACK, DONALD D, DIVINE STYLER, DOMINATION, NILE KINGS, RHAMEL
Epic 1963/promo/ps/'90 ....$6

POWER SURGE 2
w/AEROSMITH, GUNS N ROSES, WHITESNAKE, JIMMY PAGE, TESLA, HANOI ROCKS... (2-3 songs each)
Geffen 3866/promo/2 CDs/ps/'89 ....$15

PROXIMA SAMPLER
w/THE RISE, MIGUEL KERTSMAN, ZIG: CHROME, GUIRE WEBB (2+ each)
Proxima/promo/logo on black $6

PULSE SAMPLER
w/ANNIE LENNOX, B.HORNSBY, BOWIE, W.HOUSTON, KENNY G, AIMEE MANN, JAMES BROWN, KOOL & GANG + 11
BMG 93/promo/ps/'93 ....$6

QUIET CUTS ADULT SAMPLER
w/TONY TONI TONE, OLETA ADAMS, JON LUCIEN, SHIRLEY HORN (2 each)
Mercury 362/promo/ps/'91 ....$6

RADIOACTIVE DO NOT TOUCH
w/BIRDLAND, GOODBYE MR MACKENZIE, FATIMA MANSIONS, LIVE, LONDBEAT (2 each) *Radioactive 1574/promo/ silkscreened/ps/cust.sticker/'91* $6

RADIOACTIVE MIX OF ART
w/B.A.D., JANET JACKSON, DEPECHE MODE (Nothing), TINA TURNER (Steamy Windows), U2 (God Pt 2), REAL LIFE, AHA...*DADC 001/promo/ps/ contains mixing instructions*....................$25

RADIOACTIVE NO SAFE HAVEN
w/LULABOX, RAMONES, A HOUSE, DIG, FATIMA MANSIONS (Angel's Delight - live), LIVE, COOLER THAN JESUS
Radioactive 2382/promo/silkscreened/ps .$6

RADIUM HITS THE STREET
w/PSYCHOTIC YOUTH, SONIC WALTHERS, WANNA-BEES, MAJOR N.A., UNION CARBIDE PRODUCTIONS, STILLBOR
Radium 055/promo/gatefold hardcvr ps....$6

RAZOR & TIE'S ETC.
w/SCOTT KEMPNER, DAVID JOHANSEN, GARY US BONDS, TINA TURNER, more
Razor & Tie/promo....................................$8

RED COLLAGE
w/YELLO, SHEEP ON DRUGS, CAPTAIN HOLLYWOOD PROJECT, PARIS (2), DJ MAGIC MIKE, RONNY JORDAN, BLACK MADDNESS (20 in all)
silkscreened/promo/ps/'93 .... $6

REGGAE SUNSPLASH LIVE
w/MYSTIC REVEALERS (Got to Be a Better Way 4 vers.), WAYNE WONDER (Bonafide Love 5 vers.)
MCA 2472/promo/back ps/'92 .... $6

REINDEER ROCK
w/NIGHTS OF IGUANA, STONE, HEARTHILL, L'AMOURDER, 22 PISTEPIRKKO, JIVETONES, MELROSE, DETHRONE, many more *Promoporo 1/promo/ps/'90* .. $6

RELATIVITY, IN-EFFECT, COMBAT
w/THEL.MONSTER, SHOTGUN MESSIAH, 24-7 SPYZ, FAITH OR FEAR, + many more (2 cuts each) *Relativity/promo/ps/ 3 CDs/fold out ps* $12

RESTLESS RECORDS 1993 NEW ARTIST SAMPLER
w/HANG-UPS, ZUZU'S PETALS, PIGPEN, GIANT SAND, BAND OF SUSANS, BUCK PETS...
Restless 027/promo/ps/silkscreened/'93 .. $6

RETAIL COMPILATION
w/KID SENSATION, CRIMINAL NATION, SIDE F X, SIR MIX A LOT...
Nastymix 2/promo/'90 .... $6

RETURN OF POST MODERN
w/XTC, POGUES, DICKIES, ERASURE, WONDER STUFF, VOICE OF BEEHIVE + 10 *Hits 004/promo/ps* $8

REVENGE OF POST MODERN
w/RAVE UPS, DEL AMITRI, UB40, PETER MURPHY, CRAMPS, PSYCH. FURS, THE ALARM, LAURIE ANDERSON, 10 more *Hits 007/promo/ps* $8

RHYTHM STICK
w/BLACK BOX (Ride on Time), PAULA ABDUL (Cold Hearted), NENEH CHERRY, DEBBIE HARRY (Rapture '88), ABC, LIVING IN A BOX, EXPOSE...
promo only remixes/ps/'89 .... $20

ROAD KILL
w/SONIC YOUTH, CANDY SKINS, SUNDAYS, SLOAN, WHITE ZOMBIE, XTC, CELL, SPENT POETS, SIOUXSIE...
Geffen 4476/promo/custom sticker/'92 ..... $6

ROADRUNNER RECORDS
w/STAR STAR, GRUNTRUCK, OBITUARY, FEAR FACTORY, TYPE O NEGATIVE, WILLARD, ATROCITY, IN THE NURSERY... *Roadrunner 063/promo/ silkscreened/gatefold hardcover ps/'92* $6

ROCK OVER LONDON
w/STING, HAPPY MONDAY, ALAN PARSONS, DEEP PURPLE, SISTERS OF MERCY, ANDY TAYLOR, QUIREBOYS, OUTFIELD.. *radio show/promo/ #91-01 (1/4/91)/cue sheet* $15

ROCK OVER LONDON
w/ROBIN TROWER, BLUE AEROPLANES interview, MISSION, SUPERTRAMP...
radio show/promo/#90-08 (2/23/90)/cue sheet $15

ROCK OVER LONDON
w/PETER GABRIEL (Here Comes Flood -new vers.), PHIL COLLINS (Dont Lose My Number live), ANDREW ELDRITCH interview, CURE (A Forest - tree mix)...
radio show/promo/#90-47/cue sheet $25

ROCK OVER LONDON
w/CLAPTON (Badge - live), PAUL MCCARTNEY, ALARM, BOWIE, SINEAD O'CONNOR.
radio show/promo/#90-05 (2/2/90)/cue sheet $15

ROCK OVER LONDON
w/ALARM, CLAPTON (I Shot Shefiff (live), XTC, SINEAD O'CONNOR, STRANGLERS...
radio show/promo/#90-07 (2/16/90)/cue sheet $15

ROCK OVER LONDON
w/THE WHO (Join Together - live), TANITA TIKARAM, CRAIG ADAMS of THE MISSION (interview), SINEAD O'CONNOR, ROXY MUSIC...*radio show/ promo/#90-10 (3/9/90)/cue sheet* $20

ROCK OVER LONDON
w/GARY MOORE, SQUEEZE (Hourglass - live), NOTTING HILLBILLIES (interview), WHO (I Can See For Miles - live)...*radio show/ promo/#90-11 (3/16/90)/cue sheet* $18

ROCK OVER LONDON
w/THE CURE, STRANGLERS (interview), THE MISSION, LLOYD COLE...*radio show/ promo/#90-12 (3/23/90)/cue sheet* $18

ROCK OVER LONDON
w/ROBERT PLANT, NICK LOWE (excl. ROL session), DEPECHE MODE, GARY MOORE, GEORGE HARRISON...*radio show/promo/#90-18 (5/4/90)/cue sheet* .. $15

ROCK OVER LONDON
w/CHRIS REA (Working on It - live), NICK LOWE (All Men are Liars - live acoustic), NICK LOWE interview, JESUS & MARY CHAIN...*radio show/promo/#90-19* $20

ROCK OVER LONDON
w/PRETENDERS (3), JOE COCKER, FLEETWOOD MAC (Everywhere live), JESUS & MARY CHAIN...*radio show/promo/#90-20 (5/18/90)/cue sheet* $20

ROCK OVER LONDON
w/JOE COCKER, BRUCE DICKINSON, JOE COCKER interview, TALK TALK, PRETENDERS, FLEETWOOD MAC (I Loved Another Woman live)...*radio show/promo/#90-21 (5/25/90)/cue sheet* $20

ROCK OVER LONDON
w/AZTEC CAMERA, WHITESNAKE, SQUEEZE (Is That Love live), ELVIS COSTELLO, DEPECHE MODE... *radio show/promo/#90-22 (6/1/90)/cue sheet* $15

ROCK OVER LONDON
w/BOB GELDOF, CHARLATANS, INSPIRAL CARPETS interview, BOWIE, WORLD PARTY...*radio show/promo/#90-24 (6/15/90)/cue sheet* $20

ROCK OVER LONDON
w/STONE ROSES, HOTSHOUSE FLOWERS, BAD CO., WORLD PARTY interview, JOE COCKER, STEVE WINWOOD...*radio show/promo/#90-26 (6/90)/cue sheet* $15

ROCK OVER LONDON
w/JEFF LYNNE, ERIC CLAPTON, STEVE EARLE interview, BILLY IDOL, DEL AMITRI... *radio show/promo/#90-25 (6/22/90)/cue sheet* $15

ROCK OVER LONDON
w/ADRIAN BELEW & BOWIE, HOTHOUSE FLOWERS, TRAFFIC, STONE ROSES (One Love - 12"), CURT SMITH interview *radio show/promo/#90-30 (6/27/90)/cue sheet* $15

ROCK OVER LONDON
w/PAUL CARRACK & ROGER WATERS (Hey You live), XTC, COCTEAU TWINS, NEIL MURRAY interview, BLIND FAITH, BLUE NILE... *radio show/promo/#90-38 (9/21/90)/cue sheet* $20

ROCK OVER LONDON
w/CURE, TALK TALK (Life's What You Make (live), MOODY BLUES (Its Up to You), AZTEC CAMERA interview...*radio show/promo/#90-36 (9/3/90)/cue sheet* $20

ROCK OVER LONDON
w/DEPECHE MODE, CHINA CRISIS, GARY MOORE (Still Got the Blues live), ROGER WATERS & VAN MORRISON, XTC, CHARLATONS...*radio show/promo/#90-39 (9/28/90)/cue sheet* $18

ROCK OVER LONDON
w/PAUL MCCARTNEY (Birthday live), DEEP PURPLE, U2, RUNRIG interview, MORRISSEY, SIMPLE MINDS (Kick it In live)...*radio show/promo/#90-42 (10/20/90)/cue sheet* $22

ROCK OVER LONDON
w/PAUL MCCARTNEY (Jet - live), POGUES, CURE, ALARM, ROXY MUSIC (Both Ends Burning - live), U2, MORRISSEY...*radio show/promo/#90-43 (10/90)/cue sheet* ... $25

ROCK OVER LONDON
w/TRAV.WILBURYS, DEEP PURPLE, VAN MORRISON, BRIAN ENO & JOHN CALE, PETER GABRIEL, ROD STEWART & TINA TURNER... *radio show/promo/#90-48 (11/6/90)/cue sheet* $15

ROCK OVER LONDON
w/TRAV.WILBURYS, ROBERT PALMER, STEVE WINWOOD, SINEAD O'CONNOR, ANDY TAYLOR, HAPPY MONDAYS... *radio show/promo/#90-44 (11/2/90)/cue sheet* $15

ROCK OVER LONDON
w/LED ZEP, NOTTING HILLBILLIES, GARY MOORE, STONES, F.MAC, CLAPTON, CHRIS REA, ELTON JOHN... *radio show/promo/#90-51/cue sheet* $15

ROCK OVER LONDON
w/QUEEN, PAUL BRADY, STING, THIN LIZZY, NAZARETH, ROBERT PALMER, CROWDED HOUSE, TANITA TIKARIM... *radio show/promo/#91-04 (1/25/91)/cue sheet* $15

ROCK OVER LONDON
w/THE ALARM, CY CURNIN interview, SIMPLE MINDS, CLASH, HAVANA 3AM...*radio show/promo/#91-16 (4/91)/cue sheet*.....$15

ROCK OVER LONDON
w/TRAV.WILBURYS, STEVE WINWOOD, JOHN WESLEY HARDING interview & 50-50 (ROL session), BAD COMPANY, STRANGLERS... *radio show/promo/ #91-02 (1/22/91)/cue sheet*....................$15

ROCK OVER LONDON
w/VAN MORRISON & CHIEFTAINS, WONDER STUFF, SIOUXSIE & BANSHEES, REM (Losing My Religion - acoustic)... *radio show/promo/#91-21 (5/24/91)/cue sheet*...............................$20

ROCK THE VOTE
psas from LENNY KRAVITZ, IGGY POP, LITA FORD, L7, LL COOL J, OZZY, DAVE MUSTAINE, MICHAEL BOLTON, SONIC YOUTH, many more (51 in all) *WB 5721/promo/rear insert/'92*..............$18

ROCK TIL YOU DROP
w/SCORPIONS, KISS, THE MISSION, ERIC CLAPTON, ZODIAC MINDWARP, LA GUNS, WARLOCK, YNGWIE MALMSTEEN...*Polygram 076/promo/ps*..$8

ROCKERS AGAINST DRUNK DRIVING
w/50 dif. PSAs delivered by HEART, REM, MOODYS, OZZY, ELTON JOHN, ACE FREHLEY, many more *R.A.D.D./promo/ fold out ps with mucho info./'87*.............$25

ROOART PRESENTS
w/TALL TALES AND TRUE, HUMMINGBIRDS, TRILOBITES, MARTHAS VINEYARD + 2 *RooArt 145/promo/ps/'90*.......................$6

ROOTS, RAP & REGGAE
w/POSITIVE K, SHOWBIZ & A.G., BOB MARLEY (Jammin' 12" mix), X CLAN, MATERIAL, SALT N PEPA *Polgram 563/promo/ps/'92*.......................$6

ROUNDER CD 45
NRBQ, JONATHAN RICHMAN + 2 *Rounder 1/promo/ps*................................$6

ROUTE 91
w/MAGGIES DREAM, RICHARD THOMPSON, KYM MAZELLE, THE BOX, RIVER CITY PEOPLE...*Capitol 79416/promo/ps/ incredible thick Capitol book on its artists*.......................$20

RUBAIYAT PLUNDERPHONICS
w/DOORS (O Hell), METALLICA (2 Net), TIM BUCKLEY (Anon), CARLY SIMON & FASTER PUSSYCAT (Vane), MC5 (Mother) *Elektra 8247/promo/ silkscreened Jim Morrison/ps (Jim Morrison & Carly Simon mix)/'91*...........$12

RYKODISC REGGAE SAMPLER
w/MIKEY DREAD, KILLER BEES, TIGER, AUGUSTUS PABLO, FOXY BROWN, BUNNIE BRISSETT, SANCHEZ... *Ryko/promo/ps/'91*..................................$6

SAMPLER #1 - ISLAND
w/JULIAN COPE, TRAFFIC, SHRIEKBACK, ROBERT PALMER + 4 *Island 987/promo/ps/'87*..........................$8

SBK THE ARTISTS. THE SONGS. THE PASSION. THE DIFFERENCE.
w/KATRINA & WAVES, WENDY WALL, HERBERT GRONEMEYER, SHINE, WILL AND THE BUSHMEN...*SBK 05310/promo/snazzy gatefold hardcover w/cool rice paper booklet/silkscreened/'89*........................$15

SCHWEPPES PRESENTS THE BRITISH INVASION PT 2
w/THE FIXX, ROD STEWART, THIN LIZZY, SUPERTRAMP, ELVIS COSTELLO, SIMPLE MINDS, PRETENDERS, TRAFFIC, QUEEN, JETHRO TULL, THE POLICE, U2, STONES, GENESIS, MOODY BLUES...*Westwood One #91-27/ promo/cue sheets/6 cds/ aired: week of 7/1/91*..............................$50

SELECTIONS FROM RUBAIYAT
w/CURE, SUGARCUBES, PIXIES, BILLY BRAGG, 10,000 MANIACS + 9 *Elektra 8216/promo/ps/'90*.........................$8

SEPTEMBER SONGS
w/JUNE TABOR, DAVID BOWIE, MICKEY HART, BADFINGER, DEVO, MCGEAR, RINGO STARR...*Rykodisc/promo/rear insert/'90*.$6

SHECKY & JACKIE'S GREATEST HITS
w/SAFIRE, ALDO NOVA, TRIPLETS, MATERIAL ISSUE, XYMOX, KATHY MATTEA, THIN LIZZY, JON LUCIEN... *Mercury 337/ promo/silkscreened/ps/'91*.......................$6

SHECKY & JACKIE'S GREATEST HITS VOL. 2
w/VANESSA WILLIAMS, JAMES, MICHELLE SHOCKED, UGLY JOE KID, RICHIE SAMBORA, TEARS FOR FEARS, GUTTERBOY...*Mercury 478/promo /logo on red/ps/'92* $6

SHECKY & JACKIE'S GREATEST HITS VOL. 3
w/BON JOVI, NOEL, UGLY KID JOE, DEF LEPPARD, ANIMAL BAG, COPPERHEAD, GRETA, PURSUIT OF HAPPINESS... *Mercury 659/promo/silkscreened/ps/'93* ...$6

SHELTER PEOPLE
w/PHOEBE SNOW, LEON RUSSELL, DWIGHT TWILLEY, FREDDIE KING, GAP BAND, DON PRESTON... *Shelter PROMO 1/ promo/ps/'89* $10

SHOCKER
w/MEGADETH, BONFIRE, DANGEROUS TOYS, IGGY POP, DUDES OF WRATH *SBK 05316/promo/ps/'89* $6

SINGLES SCENE
w/GARY MOORE, T'PAU + 3 *Virgin 2018/promo/ps* $6

SMART MUSIC FOR SMART PEOPLE VOL. 1
w/IMMACULATE FOOLS, TWISTED WORLD VIEW, MAXIMUM AMERICA, THE RED HOUSE, ORIGINAL SINS,SELVES + 9 *Best New Music 1001/promo/ps/'88* $6

SOFT SOUL
w/ALEXANDER O'NEAL, MICHAEL JACKSON, LUTHER VANDROSS, BASIA, MIAMI SOUND MACHINE, DAN SIEGEL (2 each except Michael) *EPA 2848/promo/ps/'87* $10

SOLID GOLD COUNTRY
w/LINDA RONSTADT birthday salute (hour of music & interview), RICKY SKAGGS birthday salute (as before), TG SHEPPARD b'day salute.. *Unistar/promo/radio show designed to air 7/15-19/91 /5 cds/box container/cue sheets* $45

SOLID GOLD SCRAPBOOK
w/PAUL ANKA b'day salute (hr of interview & music), PAUL MCCARTNEY & WINGS (hr of interview & music), 3 more discs of interviews & music *Unistar/promo/ 5 cds/cue sheets 7/29-8/2/91* $60

SON OF CD HITS SAMPLER
w/BONNIE RAITT, GREAT WHITE, TIM FINN, MARC ALMOND, 13 more *Capitol 79584/promo/'89* $6

SON OF POST MODERN
w/SUGARCUBES, SIOUXSIE, B.A.D., G. PARKER, many more *Hits 002/promo/ps/silkscreened* $8

SON OF SINGLES SCENE
w/BOY GEORGE, WARREN ZEVON, PRETTY POISON, HUE & CRY... *Virgin 2019/promo/ps/'87* $7

SONGS FROM THE SACRED NAPKIN'
w/BOWIE, KEITH LEVENE, ROBERT HUNTER, ZAPPA, HENRY KAISER + 15 more *Ryko 9001/promo/ps/'90* $8

SONY/BILLBOARD DECADE OF MUSIC VOL. 3
w/AL JARREAU, BOBBY MCFERRIN, HARRY CONNICK JR, LINDA RONSTADT, BANGLES, WHITNEY HOUSTON... *Sony/promo/ps/'92* $6

SOUL HITS OF THE '70S
w/BEN E KING, LABELLE, GEORGE MCCRAE, O'JAYS, BARRY WHITE, SPINNERS, CHI LITES + 1 *Rhino 90080/promo/ gatefold hardcover (with booklet)/ silkscreened/'91* $15

SOUL OF THE SIXTIES VOL. 1
w/RAY CHARLES, HANK BALLARD, JERRY BUTLER, BEN E KING, SHIRLEY ALSTON (SHIRELLES)... (interview & music all) *Unistar/promo/radio show/ 90 min. in 2 cds/cue sheets/box cover 5/25-27/91* $25

SOUL OF THE SIXTIES VOL. 10
w/JIMMY RUFFIN, MARVELETTES, MARY WILSON, GENE CORNISH (YOUNG RASCALS), BRIAN HOLLAND... (interview & music all) *Unistar/promo/ radio show/90 min. in 2 cds/box cover/ cue sheets 7/26-28/91* $25

SOUL OF THE SIXTIES VOL. 2
w/GLADYS KNIGHT, HERB COX (CLEFTONES), GLADYS HARTON (MARVELETTES), CURTIS MAYFIELD... (interviews & music all) *Unistar/promo/radio show/ 90 min. in 2 cds/box cover/ cue sheets 5/31-6/2/91* $25

SOUL OF THE SIXTIES VOL. 3
w/MARVELETTES, JERRY BUTLER, BOOKER T JONES, MARY WELLS, BROOK BENTON... (all interviews & music) *Unistar/promo/radio show/90 min. in 2 cds/box cover/cue sheets 6/8-9/91* $25

SOUL OF THE SIXTIES VOL. 4
w/MARVIN GAYE, STEVIE WONDER, MARTHA REEVES, SMOKEY ROBINSON, FREDDIE SCOTT (music & interviews, all) *Unistar/promo/radio show/90 min. in 2 cds/cue sheets/box cover 6/15-16/91* .$25

SOUL OF THE SIXTIES VOL. 7
w/MARY WILSON & LEVI STUBBS (interviews), 4 TOPS, B. MASON, SMOKEY ROBINSON, SUPREMES... (music) *Unistar/promo/radio show/90 min. on 2 cds/cue sheets/box cover 7/5-7/91* $25

SOUL OF THE SIXTIES VOL. 9
w/CARLA THOMAS, BRIAN HOLLAND, LEVI STUBBS, OTIS WILLIAMS, MARY WELLS... (interview & music all) *Unistar/promo/radio show/90 min.in 2 cds/box cover/cue sheets 7/19-21/91* .$25

SOUND AND VISION VOL. 1
w/DEVO, BARDEUX, THE U-KREW, RED FLAG, WIRE, UNTOUCHABLES *Enigma 216/promo/ps/'89* $6

SOUND AND VISION VOL. 2
w/XYZ, DON DIXON, DEL LORDS, SHOOTING STAR, TSOP, CRAMPS... *Enigma 244/promo/ps/'89* $6

SOUND SAVERS
w/BRYAN ADAMS, BON JOVI, TEMPTATIONS, MARVIN GAYE, MODDY BLUES, CLAPTON, POLICE, U2, SQUEEZE, 4 TOPS, DIANA ROSS. *PGD 435/promo/ps/'91* $6

SOUND SAVERS 3
w/MARVIN GAYE, J.C.MELLENCAMP, SQUEEZE U2, BRYAN ADAMS, KATHY MATTEA, BOB MARLEY, CLAPTON, BON JOVI, RUSH... *PGD 640/promo/ps/'93* $6

SOUNDS BY LIGHT
w/GEORGE CLINTON, D. HARRY, LOU REED (Busload of Faith - live acoustic vers.)... *WEA 3623/promo/ps/'89* $6

SPAWN
w/SONIC YOUTH, SUNDAYS, SLOAN, WHITE ZOMBIE, XTC, SIOUXSIE & BANSHEES... *Geffen/DGC 4476/promo/ps/'92* $6

SPECIAL GRAMMY CD SAMPLER
w/MARIAH CAREY, KRIS KROSS, PUBLIC ENEMY, SPRINGSTEEN, ALICE IN CHAINS, ROGER WATERS, TONY BENNETT + 10 *Columbia 5034/ promo/cust.sticker/'93* $6

SPECIALTY SAMPLER
w/ROY MILTON, JOE LIGGINS, PERCY MAYFIELD, LLOYD PRICE, PEE WEE CRAYTON, FLOYD DIXON, JOE HOUSTON, CLIFTON CHENIER, JESSE BELVIN, GUITAR SLIM, PROFESSOR LONGHAIR, SAM COOKE, 12 more *Specialty 1990/promo/ps* $10

SPIN FONTANA TOUR
w/CATHERINE WHEEL, HOUSE OF LOVE, OCEAN COLOUR SCENE (3 each) *Fontana 556/promo/gatefold hardcover ps/'92* $6

SPIN THIS
w/LEVITATION, DOWNY MILDEW, JESUS & MARY CHAIN, SARAH MCLACHLAN, TORI AMOS, DEL AMITRI, EVERYTHING BUT THE GIRL... *Spin/promo/ps* $6

SPIRAL SCRATCH
w/PIXIES (Tame - demo), MIGHTY LEMON DROPS (Inside Out - live), DRUG FREE AMERICA, CHELSEA (Valium Mother - scratch mix) *Spiral Scratch no #/promo/ from magazine/'89* $15

SPIRIT OF THE FOREST
2 versions w/XTC, KATE BUSH, F. MAC, MR MISTER, DAVE GILMOUR, BRIAN WILSON, JONI MITCHELL, RINGO STARR, JON ANDERSON, OLIVIA NEWTON JOHN, DONNA SUMMER, RAMONES, THOMAS DOLBY, many more *Virgin 2795/promo/'89* $12

SPIRIT OF THE MUSIC
w/CARON WHEELER, IKE & TINA, O'JAYS (3), FATS DOMINO, BOBBY MCFERRIN, ISLEY BROTHERS, DIANNE REEVES... *EMI 04728/promo/silkscreened/ps/'91* $6

SPLUNGE
w/SONIC YOUTH, SLOAN, URGE OVERKILL, MY LITTLE FUNHOUSE, CANDY SKINS, IZZY STRADLIN, POSIES, CELL, NIRVANA... *Geffen 4507/promo/ps/ silkscreened/'93* $6

SPRING BREAK
w/JEAN BEAUVOIR, WOODENTOPS... *Columbia 1090/promo/ps/'88* $6

SPRING BREAK '89
w/BAR KAYS, SHARON BRYANT, CAMEO, SHAKATAK, THIRD WORLD, TONY TONI TONE... *Polygram 099/promo/silkscreened/ps/'89* $6

SPRING BREAKERS '93 - THE ATLANTIC GROUP
w/STONE TEMPLE PILOTS, SNOW, LYNYRD SKYNYRD, INXS, T.RUNDGREN, THE BELOVED, BLACK UHURU + 25 *Atlantic 5021/promo/2 cds/ps/'93* $15

SST GODHEAD STOREDUDE/DUDESS IN-STORE PLAY DEVICE #10
w/MEAT PUPPETS, HR, THE LAST, ALTER NATIVES, ZOOGZ RIFT/SACCHARINE TRUST *SST/promo/silkscreened/'89* $6

SST GODHEAD STOREDUDE/DUDESS IN-STORE PLAY DEVICE #8
w/SCREAMING TREES, ROGER MILLER, SWA, BL'AST, MOFUNGO *SST #8/promo/3"/'89* $8

SST GODHEAD STOREDUDE/DUDESS IN-STORE PLAY DEVICE #9
w/BUFFALO TOM, DC3, TROTSKY ICEPICK, CHRIS D, TAR BABIES *SST #9/promo/silkscreened/with promo info/'89* $8

STEAL THIS DISC
w/ZAPPA, JOHN MCLAUGHLIN, GEORGE THOROGOOD, RESIDENTS, DEVO, JIMI HENDRIX (21 tracks in all) *Rykodisc 00056/promo/booklet ps/'87* $15

STICK IT IN
w/DAVID SYLVIAN, CROSS, BOY GEORGE... *Virgin 2228/promo/2 CDs/ps* $15

SUBMERGE YOURSELF IN SOUND
w/APOLLO SMILE, STAN RIDGWAY, SIOUXSIE, NORTHSIDE, SONIC YOUTH, I LOVE YOU, THE POSIES, WARRIOR SOUL... *Geffen 4250/promo/gatefold hardcover ps/'90* $6

SUBMERGE YOURSELF IN SOUND
w/TERRI NUNN, TEENAGE FANCLUB, GUNS N ROSES, NIRVANA... *Geffen DGC 4399/promo/ps/'92* $6

SUMMER MADNESS
w/DAS EFX, K SOLO, YO YO, KWAME, DA YOUNGSTERS, BLACK UHURU... *Atlantic 4689/promo/back ps* $6

SUMMER MADNESS '93
w/THE PHARCYDE (Otha Fish), TONE LOC (Hit the Coast), BORN JAMERICANS, MASTA ACE, INC.*Delicious Vinyl 5228/promo/rear insert/'93* $6

SUMMER PARTY FACTOR '90
w/BAD COMPANY, MICHEL'LE, SOHO, MS ADVENTURES... *Atco 3504/promo/ps/'90* $6

SUMMER SPECTACULAR 1990
w/LACY J DALTON, PIRATES OF MISSISSIPPI, TRACIE SPENCER, DONNY OSMOND, TIMES 2 at least 2 each *Capitol 79328/promo/ps/'90* $6

SUPER STARS SUPER CD
w/JACKSON BROWNE, STEVIE NICKS, ROY ORBISON, REM, 10,000 MANIACS... *Pioneer WEA PSCD 1/promo/ps/'89* $8

SUPERFLY SAMPLER
w/UZI BROS, TONE LOC, EAZY E (each remix & lp vers.) *Capitol 79203/promo/rear insert/'90* $8

TAKE A HIT
w/CHEAP TRICK, JOAN JETT, TIL TUESDAY, EUROPE + 13 *EPA 1468/promo/ps/'89* $8

TASTY TOWER TREATS
w/TRACIE SPENCER, LONDON QUIREBOYS, ADEVA, MAGGIES DREAM, COCTEAU TWINS, ...*Capitol 79464/promo/unusual pie box container/"menu" insert*.$12

TAYLOR/THE ALBUM SOME PEOPLE CALL "TIME OUT II"
w/NIRVANA (2), GUNS N ROSES (2), TEENAGE FANCLUB (2), TERRI NUNN, NYMPHS, SIOUXSIE & BANSHEES, XTC, RICKIE LEE JONES...*DGC-Geffen 4404/promo/silkscreened (baseball)/ps/'92* $6

TDK MAILROCK
w/ROBYN HITCHCOCK, PM DAWN, VOICE OF BEEHIVE, JAMES, MARYS DANISH 2 each *PGD 428/promo/ps/'91* $6

TDK MAILROCK
w/THE DROP NINETEENS, JESUS LIZARD, THE SKELTONS, DIG, FUDGE, LYRES, LOUD FAMILY... *Caroline CARTDK01/promo/silkscreened/ps* $6

THE BAT IS BACK - AN ALTERNATIVE TENTACLES SAMPLER
w/NOMEANSNO, LARD, NEUROSIS, LES THUGS, ALICE DONUT, TUMOR CIRCUS, VICTIMS FAMILY, JELLO BIAFRA + 2 *Alternative Tentacles 112/ promo/silkscreened pic/ps/'92* $8

THE BEST OF COMIC RELIEF '90 SAMPLER
w/PAULA POUNDSTONE, DANA CARVEY, STEVEN WRIGHT, RITA RUDNER, ROBERT KLEIN *Rhino 90050/promo/ silkscreened/ps/'90* $8

THE BEST OF SUMMER '90
w/BLACK UHURU, BERNIE WORRELL, CHET BAKER, GRANT GEISSMAN... (16 tracks) *Mesa Blue Moon 79001/promo/ps/'90* $6

THE BRENEMAN REVIEW
w/CROWDED HOUSE, MOODY BLUES, JACK MACK, SQUEEZE *promo/rear insert/July '91* $6

THE BRENEMAN REVIEW
w/MIDNIGHT OIL, JIVE BUNNY, ADAM ANT, WILSON PHILLIPS, SMITHEREENS... *promo/#3 - June '90* $6

THE BRIDE OF POST MODERN
w/FEELIES, COCTEAU TWINS, REM, P. FURS, JULIAN COPE...*Hits 003/promo/ps/'88* ... $8

THE CHRYSALIS "NO SH*T HARD ROCK" SAMPLER
w/STAGE DOLLS, TEN YEARS AFTER, SEX HAGS, THE ANGELS *Chrysalis 21738/promo/ps/'89* $6

THE CLASS OF '93
w/CLAPTON (2), KD LANG, CHAKA KHAN, MILES DAVIS, R.HOT CHILI PEPPERS, DR JOHN.. *WB 6155/promo/'92* $6

THE CMJ PRISONER
w/IGGY POP, BOB MOULD (1 live), LENNY KRAVITZ, NRBQ, PIL (1 live), ZIGGY MARLEY, UB40... *Virgin 3073/promo/ silkscreened/custom sticker/'89* $10

THE COLUMBIA RECORD VOLUME 2
w/OMAR & HOWLERS, B. STREISAND, JOURNEY... *Columbia 2716/promo/ps* .. $6

THE DISC OF REVELATIONS
w/THE ALMIGHTY, ATOM SEED, KINGDOM COME, LA GUNS, ANTHRAX... *Polydor 417/promo/silkscreened/ps/'91* $6

THE FACTS ABOUT R.N.A.
w/EXENE CERVENKA, STEVE WYNN, BUDDY BLUE, LENE LOVICH & NINA HAGEN... *Rhino/RNA 90057/promo/ foldout hardcover ps/'90* $6

THE FALL OF DGC
w/NYMPHS, NIRVANA, GALACTIC COWBOYS, TERRI NUNN, WARRIOR SOUL... *DGC 4344/promo/ps/logo on green/'91* $6

THE FUTURE BEGINS
w/POINTER SISTERS, SMOKEY ROBINSON, FLAVOR FLAV, BASIC BLACK more *Motown 1064/promo/'90* $6

THE HITCHHIKER COLLEGE RADIO HOUR
w/ROSANNE CASH, DARDEN SMITH, RODNEY CROWELL...*CBS 1598/promo/ps/'89/ with dialogue - hosted by R. CASH* $15

THE JOHN PEEL SESSIONS
w/INSPIRAL CARPETS, JOY DIVISON, GANG OF FOUR, HAPPY MONDAYS, SMITHS, CHAMELEONS, WIRE, SIOUXSIE, DAMNED, CURE...*D.East India 8601/ promo/gatefold die cut ps/booklet/'91* $12

THE LEGENDS OF GUITAR 2
w/BILLY MURE, YARDBIRDS, LOU REED, TOM PETTY, VENTURES, DICK DALE, CHET ATKINS, STANLEY JORDAN, BOBBY FULLER...*Rhino 90069/promo/ trifold diecut cover/4 "guitar" cards/'91* $15

THE LIVE SHOW
w/BILLY JOEL, SKYNYRD, VAN MORRISON, KINKS, CSN, BOWIE, CREAM, DYLAN... *Radio Today #117/promo/cue sheet /(air date 10/1/90)* $20

THE LIVE SHOW
w/CLAPTON (Badge & Roll It Over), S UPERTRAMP, STING, ROBERT PLANT (Hurting Kind, Dimples), ZEP (Song Remains Same).. *Radio Today #132/ promo/cue sheet/(air date 1/14/91)* $20

THE LIVE SHOW
w/DOOBIE BROTHERS, BONNIE RAITT, CSN, SPRINGSTEEN, STING, WINGS, SEGER, PETTY...*Radio Today #113/ promo/cue sheet/(air date 9/3/90)* $20

THE LIVE SHOW
w/GRATEFUL DEAD, NEIL YOUNG (Mother Earth), JIMMY BUFFETT, BADFINGER (Day After Day), JIMI HENDRIX (I'm a Man)...*Radio Today #130/promo/ cue sheet/(air date 12/31/90)* $20

THE LIVE SHOW
w/HENDRIX (Purple Haze, Wild Thing), JANIS JOPLIN (Down on Me), CREAM (Crossroads), CHEAP TRICK (Hello There, Surrender, Day Tripper)... *Radio Today #131/promo/cue sheet/ (air date 1/7/91)* $20

THE LIVE SHOW
w/RINGO STARR, LEVON HELM, JOE WALSH (last 3 w/All Starr Band), NEIL YOUNG, SIMON & GARFUNKEL, JONI MITCHELL...*Radio Today #119/promo/ cue sheet/(air date 10/15/90)* $20

THE LIVE SHOW
w/ROGER WATERS, TRAFFIC, WHO (Magic Bus), THIN LIZZY, TULL (Fat Man), SPRINGSTEEN (Born to Run), CLAPTON.. *Radio Today #123/promo/cue sheet/ (air date 11/12/90)* $20

THE LIVE SHOW
w/SPRINGTEEN (Trapped), STYX, CHEAP TRICK, BECK, STONES, SUPERTRAMP, DYLAN, HALL&OATES, *Radio Today #125/promo/cue sheet/ (air date 11/26/90)* $20

THE LIVE SHOW
w/STONES, EAGLES, SKYNYRD, FREE (Fire & Water, All Right Now), FRAMPTON (3), DONOVAN... *Radio Today #133/promo/ cue sheet/(air date 1/21/91)* $20

THE NETWORK 40
TUNE UP NEXT 40 #22 (2/19/90)
w/AEROSMITH, GAP BAND, SINEAD O'CONNOR, GIANT, PETER MURPHY, DAVID BYRNE, GREAT WHITE + 9 *promo/booklet ps* $6

THE NETWORK 40
TUNE UP NEXT 40 #25 (5/28/90)
w/MIDNIGHT OIL, FASTER PUSSYCAT, SOUL II SOUL, ADAM ANT, POINTER SISTERS + 8 *promo/booklet ps* $6

THE NETWORK 40
TUNE UP NEXT 40 #26 (6/25/90)
w/POISON, FLEETWOOD MAC, JOHNNY GILL, JUDE COLE, CONCRETE BLONDE, MISSION UK, PAUL YOUNG, MARTI JONES + 7 *promo/booklet ps* $6

THE NETWORK 40
TUNE UP NEXT 40 #28 (8/20/90)
w/WARRANT, TOMMY PAGE, WORLD PARTY, DURAN, HOUSE OF LOVE, SOHO, JANE CHILD, DEVO, MELLOW MAN ACE, HOTHOUSE FLOWERS... *promo/booklet ps* $6

THE NETWORK 40
TUNE UP NEXT 40 #30 (10/22/90)
w/PAUL SIMON, BAD COMPANY, ROBERT CRAZY, CYNDI LAUPER & ROGER WATERS, DURAN, JUDE COLE, JANES ADDICTION... *promo/booklet ps* $6

THE NETWORK 40
TUNE UP NEXT 40 #31 (11/19/90)
w/AC-DC/INXS, CHRIS ISAAK, CINDERELLA, STEVIE WINWOOD, ZZ TOP, BILLY IDOL, CONCRETE BLONDE... *promo/booklet ps* $6

THE NETWORK 40
TUNEUP 32 (1/7/91)
w/REMBRANDTS, DONNY OSMOND, AHA, THE OUTFIELD, NEW KIDS ON BLOCK, HEART, VAN MORRISON... *promo/booklet ps* $6

THE NETWORK 40
TUNEUP 33 (2/11/91)
w/THE TRIPLETS, SOUP DRAGONS, HAPPY MONDAYS, GREAT WHITE, SCORPIONS, ROBERT CRAY + 9 *promo/booklet ps* $6

THE NETWORK 40 TUNEUP 34
w/FIXX, DAMN YANKEES, REBEL PEBBLES, GLENN FREY, TONY TONI TONE, TANGIER, SHEENA EASTON, SCORPIONS... *promo/booklet ps* $6

THE NETWORK 40 TUNEUP 35
w/AC-DC, OLETA ADAMS, SCORPIONS, POISON, BOYZ II MEN, KANE ROBERTS... *promo/booklet ps* $6

THE NETWORK 40
TUNE UP NEXT 40 #36
w/REMBRANDTS, SHEILA E, T'PAU, SEAL, TRIXTER, ERIC JOHNSON, SAFIRE, ELVIS COSTELLO, ELECTRONIC.. *promo/booklet ps* $6

THE NETWORK 40
TUNE UP #40
w/BLUE TRAIN, ANIMAL LOGIC, DIRE STRAITS, CONTRABAND, SCORPIONS, HEART, REMBRANDTS, TRANSVISION VAMP + 5 *promo/booklet ps* $6

THE NETWORK 40 TUNEUP 54 (1/4/93)
w/STEELHEART, STARCLUB, REDMAN, REM, UGLY KID JOE, JUDE COLE, SOPHIA SHINAS, POISON, KURT HOWELL, INXS, F.MAC + 1 *promo/booklet ps*........$6

THE NETWORK 40 TUNE UP #55 (2/8/93)
w/VANESSA PARADIS, K.D. LANG, NOEL, DINA CARROLL, TISHA, SANDY B., RAY CHARLES, THE HEIGHTS... *promo/booklet ps*..........$6

THE NETWORK 40 TUNE UP #59
w/COVERDALE PAGE, STEVE MILLER, WYNONNA, JACKYL, T.T. D'ARBY, DINO, DEACON BLUE...*promo/booklet ps*.........$6

THE NETWORK 40 TUNE UP #60 (7/93)
w/DARDEN SMITH, BELL BIV DEVOE, STEREO MCS, JODECI, BJORK, LATOUR, NICK SCOTTI... *promo/booklet ps*..........$6

THE NEW POWER SOURCE - 10/90
w/BETH NIELSEN CHAPMAN, LOU RAWLS, SHAKATAK, BOBBY CALDWELL, TANIA MARIA, INDIGO GIRLS (You & Me of the 10,000 Wars)...*promo/rear insert/'90*........$6

THE NEW POWER SOURCE - 2/90
w/SINEAD O'CONNOR, NRBQ, DAVID PEASTON, BONNIE RAITT, DANNY O'KEEFE, BOBBY VINTON, CLEO LAINE... *Mac/promo/ps/'90*..........$6

THE NEW POWER SOURCE - 3/90
w/RICHARD MARX, HEART, KISS, ROBERT PLANT, WILSON PHILLIPS, NEVILLE BROS. + 9 *MAC/promo/rear insert/'90*....$6

THE NEW POWER SOURCE - 6/90
w/ANITA BAKER, PAUL YOUNG, SINEAD O'CONNOR, DION, CHRIS REA, MICHAEL FRANKS, SOUTHERN PACIFIC, SLYCE, MAXI PRIEST... *MAC/promo/ps/'90*..........$6

THE NEW POWER SOURCE - 7/89
w/JACKSON BROWNE, MADONNA, VAN MORRISON, DIANA ROSS, BEBE & CECE WINANS, MICA PARIS, DR JOHN... *promo/rear insert/'89*..........$6

THE NEW POWER SOURCE - 9/90
w/JUDY COLLINS, HEART, PETER ALLEN, JULIA FORDHAM, JANE WIEDLIN, JOHN DENVER, SHOES, DAVID LASLEY + 10 *MAC/promo/ps/'90*.........$6

THE POWER OF POSITIVE LISTENING
w/XTC, ARC ANGELS, PAT METHENY, STEVE FORBERT, PETER CASE, KITARO, SPENT POETS *Geffen 4427/promo/ silkscreened/ps/'92*..........$6

THE RETURN OF ... TWISTING YOUR KNOBS...
w/IRON MAIDEN, LIVING COLOUR, PRONG, SUIC.TEND., RIVERDOGS, DANGER DANGER... *Epic 2228/promo/ps/'90*......$6

THE ROCK AND ROLL HALL OF FAME
w/BEATLES, THE WHO, KINKS, FOUR TOPS, ISLEY BROS, CAROLE KING, PLATTERS, LITTLE EVA, many more *no label or #/promo/fold out ps/for 5th annual induction dinner 1/17/90*..........$45

THE SCEPTER RECORDS STORY SAMPLER
w/SHIRELLES (3), MAXINE BROWN, ISLEY BROTHERS, CHUCK JACKSON, BJ HOMAS, DIONNE WARWICK, KING CURTIS, (22 in all) *Capricorn 5422/promo/ps/'92*..........$12

THE SOUND OF SUCCESS
w/RICHARD ELLIOT, RED FLAG, DEVO, MOJO NIXON, DEAD MILKMEN, WIRE, BARDEUX, SANDRA BERNHARD, FASTWAY, UFO... *Enigma 192/promo/ silkscreened/ps/'89*..........$7

THE THREE WORLDS OF TRILOKA
w/JACKIE MCLEAN, RICHIE BEIRACH, JAI UTTAL, ALI AKBAR KHAN, ANDY LAVERNE... *Triloka/promo/ps/'91*..........$6

THE TOWER TRIP
w/SMITHEREENS, FETCHIN BONES, AFRIKA BAMBAATA... *Capitol 79364/promo/ps*..$6

THE UPTOWN SOUND SAMPLER
w/CHRISTOPHER WILLIAMS, HEAVY D, UPTOWN FAMILY, MARY J. BLIGE, FATHER MC, JODECI + 1 *Uptown 2695/promo/ps/'93*..........$8

THE WANNA BE INDIE BUT WE GOT TOO MUCH $ SAMPLER
w/MEDICINE, SUPREME LOVE GODS, RED DEVILS, JAYHAWKS, DANZIG, FLIPPER (2 each) *Def American/promo/'92*..........$6

THE WHITE CHRISTMAS ALBUM
w/JOYRIDE, SWAMP ZOMBIES, TINY LIGHTS, CADILLAC TRAMPS, THE BLACK WATCH, WALKING WOUNDED... *Doctor Dream 9158/promo/ silkscreened/rubber stamp ps/'91*..........$8

THEN
w/STRAW. ALARM CLOCK, NEIL DIAMOND, ELTON JOHN, FEVER TREE, DESMOND DEKKER + 6 *Uni/promo/'88* .$8

THIS IS NOT THE AGE OF AQUARIUS
w/THE MEKONS, SOUNDGARDEN, DEL AMITRI, THE BLUE NILE... *A&M 17946/promo/open-up ps/'89* $6

THIS MUSIC KNOWS WHAT MONTH IT IS
w/ALEXANDER O'NEAL, VERTICAL HOLD, LO-KEY, BOBBY ROSS AVILA, SOUNDS OF BLACKNESS, II CLOSE, VESTA, INTELLIGENT HOODLUM... *A&M 31454 8033/promo/ gatefold hardcover ps/'93* $6

TIME OUT
w/NELSON, SONIC YOUTH, LITTLE CAESAR, THE THROBS, TYKETTO... *DGC 4230/promo/ps/'91* $6

TOUCHING
w/WHISPERS, ADEVA, FREDDIE JACKSON, NATALIE COLE, MELI'SA MORGAN, PEABO BRYSON, GAP BAND, KYM MAZELLE...*Capitol 79465/promo/ gatefold hardcover ps/silkscreened/'90* $6

TRADEMARK OF QUALITY
w/MUDHONEY, REM (Half a World Away - live), BABES IN TOYLAND, BRIAN ENO, JANES ADDICTION, DANIEL LANOIS + 14 (all are rare and unreleased) *WB 5798/promo/ps/'92* $20

TRIPLE X RECORDS #4
w/CELEBRITY SKIN, LAPD, JANES ADDICTION, ANTIETAM, DI, RIKK AGNEW, ANGRY SAMOANS, SKID ROPER, BO DIDDLEY + 10 *Triple X 4/promo/ps/'90* $6

TUNEMASTER
w/CAVEDOGS, DEAD MILKMEN, CRAMPS, DEVO, WIRE, MOJO NIXON, TSOL... *Enigma 300/promo/viewmaster like package/'90* $12

TUNES FROM THE MISSING CHANNEL
w/PM DAWN, STEREO MCS, DREAM WARRORS, DISPOSABLE HEROES OF HIPHOPRISY ANTHRAX (2 each) *Island 6683/promo/ps/'91* $6

ULTRA HOT RAZOR DISC 4
w/PETER GABRIEL, TEARS FOR FEARS, U2, JESUS JONES, ERASURE, T.TWINS, PREFAB SPROUT, ROMEO VOID, THE CURE... *Ultra Hot Razor 04/promo on ly remixes/ps/'92* $25

UNDER CONSTRUCTION
w/DAVID RICE, THRILLCAT, KERMIT RUFFINS, TAB BENDIT (2 tracks each) *Justice 0004/promo/ps/silkscreened/'92* ...$6

UNI/MOTOWN CD SAMPLER
w/TRANSVISION VAMP, STEVE EARL, WET WET WET, BIG BAM BOO, BOYS, STEVIE WONDER, STACY LATTISAW, TODAY...*MCA 17692/promo/ps/'88*..........$8

UNTAMED AND TRUE
w/MARTY STUART, JOE ELY, WYNONNA JUDD, MARK CHESNUTT... (2 each) *MCA Nashville 2291/promo/ps/'92* $6

UNWAXED - AN ESD SAMPLER
w/RESIDENTS, FRED FRITH (2), SPEED THE PLOUGH, JANE SIBERRY, HENRY COW, HAPPY THE MAN, NATIONAL HEALTH, GLENN PHILLIPS (19 tracks in all) *ESD/promo/booklet ps/silkscreened* $12

URBAN NETWORK #2
w/KEITH SWEAT, FORCE MDS, H. HEWITT & more *no label or number/promo/ps*........$6

URBAN NETWORK CD RAP-OLOGY #1
w/PUBLIC ENEMY, ROXANNE SHANTE, HARMONY, LL COOL J, GANGSTARR, CRIMINAL NATION + 16 *2 discs/promo/ps/'90*.............................$15

URBAN NETWORK FUTURE JAMS #29
w/MIKI HOWARD, D.A.T., JOE PUBLIC, CE CE PENISTON, TREY LORENZ, SPECIAL GENERATION, LADY IRENE & MC TROUBLE... *promo/ps (8/28/92)* $6

URBAN NETWORK FUTURE JAMS #30
w/PRINCE, LORENZO, JADE, POSITIVE K, K.SLEDGE, MAXI PRIEST, NYLONS, SHOMARI... *promo/booklet ps/(10/2/92)* .$6

VIRGIN GOES BUCK WILD
w/ROY ORBISON, STEVE WINWOOD, GARY MOORE, KEITH RICHARDS, 13 more *Virgin 2634/promo/ps/'89*..........................$8

VIRGIN MUSIC AROUND THE WORLD
w/BLACK BRITAIN, BOY GEORGE, DEJA, WARREN ZEVON... *Virgin 2086/promo/ps/'87*........................$10

VIRGIN NINETEEN NINETY
w/UB40, SOUL II SOUL, WARREN ZEVON, LENNY KRAVITZ, NRBQ, MIKE OLDFIELD, NENEH CHERRY... *Virgin 3114/promo/ps/'90*..........................$6

VIRGIN SINGLES SAMPLER
w/KEITH RICHARDS, PAULA ABDUL, IN TUA NUA, JOHNNY HATES JAZZ, 3 more *Virgin 2546/promo/'88* $7

VIRGIN SUMMER SAMPLER
w/WARREN ZEVON, BOY GEORGE, ROY ORBISON, CUTTING CREW, PETE WYLIE... (13 in all)
Virgin/promo/envelope ps/'87 ....$15

VIRGIN VERSIONS
w/BOY GEORGE, JOE STRUMMER, ZIGGY MARLEY, JOHNNY HATES JAZZ, PRETTY POISON, SCARLETT & BLACK, AGE OF CHANCE... (all 12" remixes)
Virgin 1288/promo/ps/'88 ....$15

VOLUME HEAD
w/SOUNDGARDEN, DAISY CHAINSAW (2), SWERVEDRIVER (2), KITCHENS OF DISTINCTION, GIN BLOSSOMS (2), DEL AMITRI (2)...*A&M 75021 7358/ promo/silkscreened/ gatefold hardcover ps/'92* $6

WARNER ARCHIVES SAMPLER
w/EVERLY BROS, TONY JOE WHITE, NICO, FACES, more
WB 6532/rear insert/'93 ....$8

WARNER REPRISE HITS OF '90
w/HANK WILLIAMS JR (3), RANDY TRAVIS (3), HIGHWAY 101 (3), TRAVIS TRITT (2), SOUTHERN PACIFIC, CARLENE CARTER, TEXAS TORNADOS...
WB 4675/promo/back ps/'91....................$8

WARNER REPRISE HITS OF '91
w/HOLLY DUNN, RANDY TRAVIS (3), TRAVIS TRITT (4), DWIGHT YOAKAM (3), CARLENE CARTER, LITTLE TEXAS, KENNY ROGERS...
WB 5341/promo/back ps/'92....................$8

WARNER REPRISE LOST IN THE '80s
w/JERRY LEE LEWIS, RODNEY CROWELL, EMMYLOU HARRIS, NITTY GRITTY DIRT BAND, GUY CLARK, BANDANA...
WB 3979/promo/back ps/'90....................$6

WATCH OUR MOVES
w/DANIELLE ALEXANDER, BUTCH BAKER, GRAYGHOST, SHANE BARMBY, KENTUCKY HEADHUNTERS, DONNA MEADE (2 songs each
Mercury 103/promo/silkscreened/'89 ....$6

WATCH OUR MOVES
w/JOHNNY CASH, LARRY BOONE, DAVID LYNN JONES, RONNA REEVES, RICH GRISSOM (2 songs each) *Mercury 132/ promo/silkscreened/back ps/'89* $6

WAVE
w/BIG BRICK BUILDING, CEREAL KILLERS, HARDSOUL POETS, SECOND SKIN,...
Buzz 106/stock/ps/'92 ....$8

WB JAZZ FALL CLASSICS
w/AL JARREAU, JOE SAMPLE, RANDY CRAWFORD, EARL KLUGH, PAT METHENY...*WB 3764/promo/back ps/'89* $6

WE'RE READY
w/THE WONDER STUFF, GANG OF 4, JULES SHEAR, JAMES BROWN, ANTHRAX, EEK A MOUSE, BLUERUNNERS, LATOUR...*Polydor 377/promo/ silkscreened/ps/'91* $6

WE'RE TWO PLANETS OVER
w/ROBIN HARRIS, THE ORB, MATERIAL ISSUE, RATCAT, PERE UBU, DAN REED, XYMOX, HOUSE OF LOVE...
Mercury 375/promo/silkscreened/ps/'91 ...$6

WEA/NARM 1993 NEW & BREAKING ARTISTS
w/BIG DADDY KANE, LEVERT, BRIAN MAY, THE FLUID, RIC OCASEK, JAYHAWKS, CARLENE CARTER, BRYAN FERRY MICK JAGGER + 48 (!) *WEA/promo/ 2 cds/booklet ps/silkscreened/'93* $20

WEIRD NIGHTMARE: SPECIAL SAMPLER
w/CHUCK D, ELVIS COSTELLO, HENRY ROLLINS, DR JOHN, LEONARD COHEN, CHARLIE WATTS...
Columbia 4697/promo/ps/'92 ....$8

WELCOME TO OUR WORLD
w/DIGA RHYTHM BAND, MICKEY HART, RHYTHM DEVILS, BABATUNDE OLATUNJI, (13 tracks in all)
Ryko 9002/promo/ps/'90 ....$8

WHIT RADIO
w/BAD, B.O.C., P. FURS, BOOTSY, DARLENE LOVE...*Columbia 1214/promo/ps/'88* $7

WHITE HOT WINTER
w/DENIECE WILLIAMS, STEVE CAMP, BEBE & CECE WINANS, STEVEN CURTIS CHAPMAN + 12 *Sparrow WNTR 90/ promo/silkscreened/back ps/'90* $6

WHITE MEN CAN'T JUMP EP
w/QUEEN LATIFAH, GO WEST, BEBE & CECE WINANS *EMI 04883/promo/ custom sticker/'92* $6

WING CHRISTMAS
w/VANESSA WILLIAMS, TONY TONE TONI, BRIAN MCKNIGHT, SHARON BRYANT
Wing 357/promo/silkscreened green on white/'90 ....$6

WINTER HEAT
w/MIDNIGHT OIL, T BONE BURNETT, 2 more
Columbia 2921/promo/ps/'88 ....$6

WINTER HITS
w/KIX, BRITNY FOX, REBEL TRAIN, PALE DIVINE, PLEASURE BOMBS
Eastwest 4391/promo/ps/'92 ....$6

WITH OUR COMPLIMENTS
w/MICHAEL JACKSON (2), REO SPEEDWAGON, MIAMI SOUND MACHINE (2), EUROPE (2), SADE, ALEXANDER O'NEAL...
CBS 2861/promo/ps/'87............................$8

WORLD
w/ANOUAR BRAHEM, SHANKAR, EGBERTO GISMONTI (5 tracks total)
ECM WM 2/promo/silkscreened/ps/'91 .....$6

WOULD U LIKE 2 TOUCH MY SAMPLER
w/P. FURS, SHAMEN, CHRIS WHITLEY, SHABBA RANKS, ALISON MOYET, PRONG, POI DOG PONDERING, BAD...
Columbia 4171/promo/ gatefold hardcover ps/'91 ....$8

WOULD YOU LIKE TO TOUCH MY SAMPLER
w/PSYCHEDLIC FURS, SHAMEN, CHRIS WHITLEY, SHABBA RANKS, PEARL JAM, ALISON MOYET, PRONG, many more *CBS 4171/promo/ gatefold hardcover/blue cd/'91* $6

X YEARS OF THE X - 1983-1993
w/NEW ORDER, D. MODE, SMITHS, THE CULT ECHO (Lips Like Sugar 12"), JANES ADDICTION, REM (Losing My Religion live)...*WB 5963/promo/silkscreened/ps* ..$10

YOUNG VIRGINS
w/CUTTING CREW, HEAVEN 17, THE MISSION, KILLING JOKE, many more
Virgin 1016/promo/gatefold ps/'87 ....$8

YULE STRUTTIN'-A BLUE NOTE CHRISTMAS
w/LOU RAWLS, STANLEY JORDAN, DIANNE REEVES, E.ELIAS, BENNY GREEN
Blue Note 79345/promo/back ps/'90 ....$6

ZOOLOGY 101
w/RHYTHM TRIBE (3), LAZET MICHAELS (2), M.GERMINO (2), PETER WELLS (2)
Zoo Entertainment 17009/promo/ps/'91 ...$6

DIRECTORY of BUYERS and SELLERS

After learning the current value of their CDs and old records, some collectors will decide it's time to offer them for sale. Others may choose to purchase additional discs and continue building their collection. Still others will simply want to keep track of some of the latest products, supplies and services available to music collectors.

Regardless of whether you are moving in or out of the hobby, or just curious as to what's going on, let our Buyers and Sellers Directory point you in the right direction. There's something for everyone here — from dealers who want to buy as well as sell CDs and records, to sources for disc care and storage products, to publications vital to the music marketplace.

For infomation about advertising in the Buyers and Sellers Directory section of future record and CD guides, contact: Osborne Enterprises, Box 255, Port Townsend, WA 98368.

OFFICIAL
PRICE GUIDE TO
RECORDS
TENTH EDITION
LISTINGS FOR OVER 10,000 ARTISTS!
BRENDA LEE
RRY OSBORNE

ABOUT THE AUTHORS

Aside from being an avid collector of records for over thirty-five years, and compact discs since 1984, Jerry Osborne has been producing record price guides and reference books since 1975. His published works on music now number about fifty, as he continues turning out several titles each year.

Jerry also writes the popular, syndicated weekly newspaper column, "Mr. Music." He founded two internationally distributed magazines for record collectors: *Record Digest* and *DISCoveries*. Among Jerry's other House of Collectibles titles are: *The Official Price Guide to Records; The Official Price Guide to Memorabilia of Elvis Presley and the Beatles; The Official Price Guide to Movie/TV Soundtracks and Original Cast Albums;* and *The Official Price Guide to Elvis Presley Records and Memorabilia* (scheduled for fall 1994 release.)

In seeking a co-author for this guide, Jerry's first choice was Paul Bergquist, a Los Angeles-based retailer of records and CDs, for over 10 years. Before relocating to the west coast, Paul lived in Alabama and then attended the University of Georgia. After arriving in California, Bergquist became a music buyer for Tower Records. A few years later, Paul realized his dream to have his own mail order record and CD operation. A significant percentage of Paul's sales now are collectible compact discs, and his sales lists and catalogs of collectible CDs formed the foundation of this guide.